# ROUTLEDGE LIBRARY EDITIONS: THE MEDIEVAL WORLD

Volume 29

# MODALITIES IN MEDIEVAL PHILOSOPHY

# MODALITIES IN MEDIEVAL PHILOSOPHY

SIMO KNUUTTILA

LONDON AND NEW YORK

First published in 1993 by Routledge

This edition first published in 2020
by Routledge
2 Park Square, Milton Park, Abingdon, Oxon OX14 4RN

and by Routledge
52 Vanderbilt Avenue, New York, NY 10017

*Routledge is an imprint of the Taylor & Francis Group, an informa business*

© 1993 Simo Knuuttila

All rights reserved. No part of this book may be reprinted or reproduced or utilised in any form or by any electronic, mechanical, or other means, now known or hereafter invented, including photocopying and recording, or in any information storage or retrieval system, without permission in writing from the publishers.

*Trademark notice*: Product or corporate names may be trademarks or registered trademarks, and are used only for identification and explanation without intent to infringe.

*British Library Cataloguing in Publication Data*
A catalogue record for this book is available from the British Library

ISBN: 978-0-367-22090-7 (Set)
ISBN: 978-0-429-27322-3 (Set) (ebk)
ISBN: 978-0-367-15186-7 (Volume 29) (hbk)
ISBN: 978-0-367-15190-4 (Volume 29) (pbk)
ISBN: 978-0-429-05557-7 (Volume 29) (ebk)

**Publisher's Note**
The publisher has gone to great lengths to ensure the quality of this reprint but points out that some imperfections in the original copies may be apparent.

**Disclaimer**
The publisher has made every effort to trace copyright holders and would welcome correspondence from those they have been unable to trace.

# Modalities in Medieval Philosophy

Simo Knuuttila

London and New York

First published 1993
by Routledge
11 New Fetter Lane, London EC4P 4EE

Simultaneously published in the USA and Canada
by Routledge Inc.
29 West 35th Street, New York, NY 10001

© 1993 Simo Knuuttila

Typeset in 10/12 pt Times by
Florencetype Ltd, Weston-Super-Mare
Printed in Great Britain by
TJ Press (Padstow) Ltd, Padstow, Cornwall

All rights reserved. No part of this book may be reprinted or reproduced or utilized in any form or by any electronic, mechanical, or other means, now known or hereafter invented, including photocopying and recording, or in any information storage or retrieval system, without permission in writing from the publishers.

*British Library Cataloguing in Publication Data*
Knuuttila, Simo
  Modalities in Medieval Philosophy. –
  (Topics in Medieval Philosophy Series)
  I. Title II. Series
  189

*Library of Congress Cataloging in Publication Data*
Knuuttila, Simo
  Modalities in medieval philosophy / Simo Knuuttila.
    p. cm. – (Topics in medieval philosophy)
  Includes bibliographical references and index.
  1. Modality (Logic)–History. 2. Philosophy, Medieval.
I. Title. II. Series.
BC199.M6K58 1992
160′.9′02–dc20         92-5203

ISBN 0–415–05052–9

# Contents

|   |   |   |
|---|---|---|
| | *Preface* | vii |
| 1 | **Modalities in Aristotle and other ancient authors** | 1 |
| | *Statistical interpretation of modality* | 1 |
| | *Possibility as a potency* | 19 |
| | *Other ancient modal paradigms* | 31 |
| | *Modal logic and modal syllogistic* | 38 |
| 2 | **Philosophical and theological modalities in early medieval thought** | 45 |
| | *Boethius' modal conceptions* | 45 |
| | *New theological modalities: from Augustine to Anselm of Canterbury* | 62 |
| | *Gilbert of Poitiers, Peter Abelard and Thierry of Chartres* | 75 |
| 3 | **Varieties of necessity and possibility in the thirteenth century** | 99 |
| | *Natural and divine possibilities* | 100 |
| | *Models for modalities in logical treatises* | 106 |
| | *Necessity and possibility in Parisian Aristotelianism: Siger of Brabant and Thomas Aquinas* | 129 |
| 4 | **Fourteenth-century approaches to modality** | 138 |
| | *Duns Scotus' theory of modality* | 139 |
| | *Fourteenth-century discussions of obligational rules* | 149 |
| | *New theories of natural necessity* | 155 |
| | *Modal logic and modal syllogistic* | 162 |
| 5 | **Medieval discussions of applied modal logic** | 176 |
| | *Elements of epistemic logic* | 176 |
| | *Logic of norms and logic of the will* | 182 |

*Roger Roseth and the principles of deontic logic*   190

*Bibliography*   197
*Index of names*   224
*Index of subjects*   231

# Preface

In this work I study the history and development of modal logic and modal conceptions in ancient and medieval thought. The main thesis of the book is as follows. One can find in ancient philosophy three basic modal paradigms: the statistical or temporal-frequency interpretation of modality, the model of possibility as a potency, and the model of diachronic modalities. None of these conceptions, which were well known to early medieval thinkers, included the idea of modality as referential multiplicity with respect to synchronic alternatives. This model was introduced into Western thought in early-twelfth-century discussions which were influenced by Augustine's theological conception of God as acting by choice between alternative histories. Ancient habits of thinking continued to play an important role in scholasticism, however, and the theoretical significance of the new conception was not fully realized before the works of John Duns Scotus and some other early-fourteenth-century thinkers.

In the new modal theory, modal notions were treated in a way which shows similarities to what has been done in the possible worlds semantics of the present century. Duns Scotus and William Ockham gave up the ontological foundation of modality; they tended to regard the non-existent domain of logical possibilities and its modal structures as transcendental conditions of all thinking and being. On the basis of the new modal semantics, it was possible to rethink traditional doctrines of natural necessity and to improve modal logic in a remarkable way. Aristotle's modal syllogistic was regarded as a not very happy fragment of the new detailed theory of modal consequences. This theory also gave rise to discussions of certain questions of epistemic logic and deontic logic.

I have sometimes borrowed passages and material from papers written while this work was in progress: 'The Foundation of Modality and Conceivability in Descartes and His Predecessors' (together with

Lilli Alanen), 'Trinitarian Sophisms in Robert Holcot's Theology', 'Natural Necessity in Buridan' (for these papers, see the Bibliography) and 'Buridan and Aristotle's Modal Syllogistic', in B. Mojsisch and O. Pluta (eds) *Historia Philosophiae Medii Aevi. Studien zur Geschichte der Philosophie des Mittelalters*, Festschrift für Kurt Flasch, Amsterdam: Grüner, 1991, 477–88. I have also borrowed passages from some earlier papers, for example 'Possibility and Necessity in Gilbert of Poitiers', in J. Jolivet and A. de Libera (eds) *Gilbert de Poitiers et ses contemporains: Aux origines de la logica modernorum*, Naples: Bibliopolis, 1987, 199–218, and 'The Emergence of Deontic Logic in the Fourteenth Century', in R. Hilpinen (ed.) *New Studies in Deontic Logic*, Dordrecht: Reidel, 1981, 225–48. I am grateful to Jaakko Hintikka, David Jenkins, Guyla Klima, Douglas Langston, John Marenbon and Gino Roncaglia for comments or discussion.

# 1 Modalities in Aristotle and other ancient authors

## STATISTICAL INTERPRETATION OF MODALITY

Aristotle believed that, even though most singular beings are subjected to the rule of coming to be and passing away, the great chain of being also includes eternal and unchanging substances which represent grades of existence much higher and more perfect than are found in the sublunar world. The central role of the distinction between the domains of mutability and immutability in Aristotle has sometimes been connected with the allegedly Greek experience of the present which, on the one hand, was considered as a non-temporal presence of reality and, on the other hand, seemed continuously to vanish into the flux of time (see the works mentioned in Hintikka (1973: ch. IV) and Gadamer (1965: 117–18)). Referring to 'the pursuit of the eternal', 'living in the present' or 'the vivid sense of the temporal' may be elucidating, but they were not distinctive features of Greek culture alone. The experience described by T.S. Eliot (1943: 5; quoted in Meyerhoff 1968: 76) may occur in many different forms of life:

> Time past and time future
> Allow but a little consciousness.
> To be conscious is not to be in time.
> But only in time can the moment in the rosegarden
> The moment in the draughty church at smokefall
> Be remembered, involved with past and future.
> Only through time time is conquered.

One could perhaps find existential aspects in Aristotle's theory of time and eternity. As for my present purpose, however, it is sufficient to note that in some contexts Aristotle considered the distinction between changing and unchanging beings as overlapping with the

## 2 Modalities in Medieval Philosophy

classification of beings into necessary and contingent ones (see, for example, *Metaphysics* IX.8, 1050b6–34).

According to Aristotle, there is in all transient beings something which can be called the potency of being and which simultaneously is the potency of not being. This factor is matter, the receptor of substantial forms. In an actually existing being, say A, it is the substrate which before the actualization of A was the passive potency of A's existence and which, when A is actual, is similarly ready to receive a form excluding A and hence can be called the potency of not being A belonging to the actual A (*Metaphysics* VII.7, 1032a12–22; *De generatione et corruptione* II.9, 335a33–4).

When discussing eternal things from the point of view of his theory of natural potencies, Aristotle thinks that the omnitemporal actuality of a being is incompatible with its having matter as the potency of being and not being (*Metaphysics* XII.6, 1071b20–2). Even though there can be some kind of matter in eternal things (e.g. matter for change of place, *Metaphysics* VIII.1, 1042b5–6; 4, 1044b7–8; XII.2, 1069b24–6), it is not matter in the sense of potency of being and not being, Aristotle says, because such a potentiality would not remain eternally unrealized and its presence in an allegedly eternal being would lead to its destruction (*Metaphysics* IX.8, 1050b6–20; 10, 1051b28–30; XII.6, 1071b18–20; XIV.2, 1088b14–25). Many scholars have analysed the conceptual and metaphysical presuppositions behind the view that potencies of not being belonging to eternal beings could not remain eternally unfulfilled. Before entering into the details of this question, we can provisorily state that, according to Aristotle, eternal beings are possible because they are actual, and they are necessary and cannot cease to exist because as eternal beings they lack the potency of not being (*De interpretatione* 13, 23a6–26).

Aristotle's most extensive discussion of the modal aspects of omnitemporal beings is found in *De caelo* I.12 where it is argued that everything that exists forever is ungenerated and indestructible. The argument runs, roughly, as follows. Suppose that an eternal being has a potentiality for not being. According to Aristotle's general characterization of possibility in *Prior Analytics* I.13, 32a18–20, a possibility, when assumed realized, results in nothing impossible. But when the possibility of not being is assumed in this case, an impossibility results, because that which always is at some time is not. The crucial part of the argument runs as follows:

> A man has at the same time the capacity of sitting and of standing, because when he has the one, he also has the other, but not in such

a way that he can be standing at the same time as sitting, but only at another time. But if a thing has for infinite time more than one capacity, there is no other time of realization and the times must coincide. Thus if anything which exists for infinite time is destructible, it will have the capacity of not being. Now if it exists for infinite time, let this capacity be actualized, and it will be in actuality at once existent and non-existent.

(*De caelo* I.12, 281b15–23)

This amounts to the claim that while speaking about eternal things or their unchanging properties, including uniform circular motions, we cannot even think without contradiction that they could be non-actual or undergo changes.

The link between necessity and omnitemporal actuality is often assumed without discussion in Aristotle's works. In *De generatione et corruptione* II.9, 335a33–b4, beings are divided into three exclusive groups: some things, namely the eternal ones, exist of necessity, some things of necessity do not exist, and some things can both be and not be. The group of necessary beings is later delineated as follows: 'If a thing is of necessity, it is eternal, and, if it is eternal, it is of necessity' (*De generatione et corruptione* II.11, 338a1–3; cf. *Metaphysics* IX.8, 1050b6–34). Similarly Aristotle says in *Nicomachean Ethics* VI.3, 1139b22–4, that things known cannot be otherwise; they are necessary and eternal, because things that are necessary without qualification are eternal and eternal things are ungenerated and imperishable.

In *Metaphysics* IX.10, 1051b9–17, a related classification is applied to states of affairs and to sentences. This is one of the passages in which Aristotle explicitly refers to his habit of considering temporally indeterminate sentences as paradigms of informative statements in general. Such sentences contain an implicit or explicit reference to the moment of their utterance, e.g. 'Socrates is sitting (now)', and the same sentence may be sometimes true and sometimes false, depending on how things are at the moment of their utterance. (See also *Categories* 5, 4a23–b2. For the prevalence of temporally indeterminate sentences in Aristotle, see Hintikka (1973: ch. IV).) In order to offer a modal classification of temporally indeterminate sentences, Aristotle, in *Metaphysics* IX.10, 1051b9–11, delineates the things they may be about as follows: 'Some things are always combined and it is impossible for them to be separated, and some things are always separated and it is impossible for them to be combined, whereas others can admit of both contraries.' As for the things that can admit of the contraries, Aristotle says (ibid. 13–15) that 'the same opinion and the same statement comes to be false and true, and it can be at one time true and at another time false'. Regarding the things that are incapable of holding otherwise, it is said that the statements do not come to be at one time true and at another time false, but they are always true or always false. An interesting part of this formulation is the claim that sentences pertaining to things which can admit of contraries are sometimes true and sometimes false and that these sentences having changing truth are the sentences which can be true and false. Correspondingly, sentences about unchanging matters are always true or always false and, it seems, as such necessarily true or necessarily false.

Although in the texts mentioned above the modal terms are not defined with the help of the notions of time or frequency, certain connections between the modal and temporal terms are taken for granted. One of these links is the assumption which in the contemporary discussion is somewhat misleadingly called the principle of plenitude and which can be formulated as follows:

(P) no genuine possibility remains eternally unrealized.

The term 'the principle of plenitude' was coined by Arthur O. Lovejoy in his book *The Great Chain of Being* (1936), where he studied the history of three 'unit ideas' from the time of Plato to the nineteenth century. According to Lovejoy, there are some basic ideas which, in various combinations, go on through centuries. The task of a historian of ideas, Lovejoy says, is to analyse the more or less explicit presuppositions of past forms of thought, to isolate 'unit ideas' and to trace their occurrences. The three unit ideas studied in *The Great Chain of Being* are characterized as the ingredients of the complex idea to which the title of the book refers. The first one Lovejoy found fully expressed in Plato's doctrine of the Demiurge, who could not be envious and who therefore translated all possibilities of being into actuality. Lovejoy called this ontological assumption the 'principle of plenitude'. The other two unit ideas constituting the great chain of being Lovejoy found in Aristotle. The 'principle of continuity' states that all possible intermediates between two given natural species are realized, and the 'principle of unilinear gradation' is the thesis that all beings belong to a *scala naturae* (scale of nature) where their status is determined by their degree of perfection. Lovejoy's influential book has stimulated further studies in many areas, some of them critical towards Lovejoy's method and details of his historical interpretations. Many scholars have criticized the methodological concept of unit ideas. As for the principle of plenitude, it has been remarked that, instead of taking it as an autonomous item, one should study the conceptual presuppositions behind the equation between possibilities and their realization, which may be quite different for different authors (see Hintikka 1981).

Recent discussion of the role of the principle of plenitude in Aristotle has received much incentive from Jaakko Hintikka's studies on Aristotle's modal theories. In his paper 'Necessity, Universality and Time in Aristotle', first published in 1957, Hintikka paid attention to certain systematic relations between time and modality in Aristotle and formulated the main variants of the principle of plenitude to be found in Aristotle's works. In addition to (P), quoted above, he mentioned the following principles:

(P)' that which never is, is impossible,
(P)" what always is, is by necessity,
(P)''' nothing eternal is contingent.

In this paper Hintikka restricted (P) and its variants in Aristotle to discussions of everlasting beings, kinds of individuals and types of events. In later works he has called this group of assumptions, with certain further specifications, a statistical model of modality in Aristotle. That something is possible must be shown by its sometimes happening, and what is always is by necessity. Applications of modal notions understood in this way reduce to comparisons of frequencies of what happens at different moments of time. According to Hintikka, this model codifies some of the more or less conscious conceptual presuppositions on which Aristotle based his modal thought. It was not the only one of Aristotle's modal paradigms, however, and hence did not yield to him definitions of the different modal terms (Hintikka 1973: ch. V; Hintikka et al. 1977: 21-2, 31-2, 43-50).

After Hintikka, many scholars have accepted the view that the statistical or temporal-frequency model occurs in some form among the conceptual paradigms of Aristotle's modal thinking. The opinions differ on the question of its importance and the limits of the area of its application (see, for example, Wolf 1979: 77-123; Sorabji 1980: 128-37; Seel 1982: 218-56; Williams 1982: 140; White 1985: 8-69). The idea of an extensional interpretation of modal terms as such has not been strange to post-Kantian philosophers. On the contrary, a number of them have suggested that modal notions could be understood as tools for describing or classifying types of individuals or events from the point of view of their frequencies. Influenced by Kant's philosophy and the empiricist tradition, many nineteenth-century thinkers believed that modal terms should be given a psychological interpretation as referring to the modes of judgements. As for the objective modalities, attempts were made to identify necessity with universality, possibility with existence and contingency with particularity (e.g. A. Comte), or to relegate them to probability as J. Venn did in his theory of probability as a long-run frequency. (For the nineteenth-century French, German and British discussions, see the papers by Engel, Haaparanta and Niiniluoto in Knuuttila (1988).)

In 1918 Bertrand Russell wrote in his article 'The Philosophy of Logical Atomism': 'One may call a propositional function necessary when it is always true; possible, when it is sometimes true; impossible, when it is never true.' This definition amounts to the temporal version of the statistical theory, which entails (P) (Russell 1956: 236; for Russell's modal views, see von Wright 1979a: 231–45). In his book *Untersuchungen über den Modalkalkül* (1952: 16–36) Oscar Becker presented an interpretation of modal calculus which he called statistical and which had a temporal variant similar to what was sketched by Russell. One historical example of what Becker called statistical modalities is Diodorus Cronus's modal theory, on which Nicolai Hartmann based his view of real possibilities (Hartmann 1938: 257; Hartmann 1957; Seel 1982: 22–110) and which A.N. Prior discussed in his book *Time and Modality* (1957: 12–17). Prior wanted to show that the Diodorean modalities, i.e. 'possibly' defined as 'it either is or will be the case that' and 'necessarily' defined as 'it is and always will be the case that', have all the formal properties of the M and L of the Lewis system S4 of modal logic. Prior revised this view, as explained in *Past, Present and Future* (1967: 20–31), where he also said that 'Diodorus seems to have been an ancient Greek W.V. Quine, who regarded the Aristotelian logic of possibility and necessity with some skepticism, but offered nevertheless some "harmless" senses that might be attached to modal words' (ibid.: 16; for a positive evaluation of the Diodorean modalities, see also Denyer 1981). It seems that the interest in the Diodorean modalities in the 1950s was at least partially motivated by the thesis of extensionality or translatability of logical positivism (cf. Poser 1988: 301–27). However, there were not too many people claiming, like Russell, that 'Normally when you say of a proposition that it is possible, you mean something like this: first of all it is implied that you do not know whether it is true or false; and I think it is implied, secondly, that it is one of a set of propositions some of which are known to be true' (Russell 1956: 254). A similar formulation occurred in Peirce's description of 'scholastic account of modality', according to which

> the necessary (or impossible proposition) is a sort of universal proposition; the possible (or contingent, in the sense of not necessary) proposition, a sort of particular proposition. That is to assert 'A must be true' is to assert not only that A is true but that all propositions analogous to A are true; and to assert 'A may be true' is to assert only that some proposition analogous to A is true.
> (Peirce 1901)

This was not the theory Peirce himself considered correct (see also Morgan 1979).

It was commonly thought in medieval times that what has been called the statistical or temporal-frequency model of modality was in some form included in Aristotle's philosophy (see Knuuttila 1981; Alanen and Knuuttila 1988; Chapters 2 and 3 below). I think that this medieval view is correct and I believe, like Hintikka, that the statistical model can be used as one interpretative tool in describing some of the thinking habits which determined Aristotle's use of modal terms.

In *Metaphysics* VI.2, 1026b27–1027a15, *Metaphysics* XI.8, 1064b32–1065a6, and *Physics* II.5, 196b10–21, things are divided into those which, with respect to some conditions, are actual always, for the most part, or accidentally . In *Metaphysics* IX.10, 1051b9–11, another 'statistical' distinction is drawn between things which are combined always, which are never combined and which can be combined and not combined. In all places the first group is characterized by the terms 'always' and 'of necessity' or 'impossibly'. What is meant may be seen from *Prior Analytics* where Aristotle tells in which ways 'to be possible' is used:

> In one way it is applied to that which happens for the most part and falls short of necessity, e.g. a man's turning grey or growing or decaying, or generally to that which naturally belongs to a thing, for it does not have a continuous necessity because a man does not exist forever, but so long as a man exists, it obtains either of necessity or for the most part. In another way it means the indefinite . . . or generally what happens by chance.
> (I.13, 32b4–13)

Modal terms are here used to express relative frequencies of generic states of affairs. The state of affairs that there are separate substances is always actual, that men who exist now have a heartbeat is actual so long as they exist, and that their children have five fingers on each hand is actual in most cases, but they may accidentally have six fingers. The interchangeability of 'always' and 'of necessity' in this context can be seen, for example, by comparing *Metaphysics* VI.2, 1026b31-3, with *Metaphysics* V.30, 1025a20-1; the coincidence is in the former text separated from what is always or for the most part and in the latter text from what is necessarily or for the most part.

Although the classifications just mentioned are abstract and the structures of the things they are applied to are left unexplained, it is possible to describe one of Aristotle's ways of using modal terms with the help of the following equations:

(1) $Lp/q \leftrightarrow (t)(p_t/q_t)$

(2) $Mp/q \leftrightarrow (Et)(p_t/q_t)$

where $Lp/q$ stands for '$p$ is necessary when $q$ is true or actual' and $Mp/q$ for '$p$ is possible when $q$ is true or actual'. The letter $t$ refers to moments of time, and the letters $p$ and $q$ stand for temporally indeterminate sentences or states of affairs. Corresponding non-relative forms are

(3) $Lp \leftrightarrow (t)(p_t)$

and

(4) $Mp \leftrightarrow (Et)(p_t)$.

(In addition to the texts mentioned above, see *Metaphysics* V.5, 1015b11-15, *De part. an.* I.1, 639b24, *De caelo* I.12, 281b15-283a28, *De generatione et corruptione* I.9, 327a11-13, *Physics* III.4, 203b30. *Metaphysics* IX.4, 1047b3-14, is controversial.) It may be in order to notice here that the statistical model sometimes occurs in Aristotle without an explicit mention of the temporal aspect; see, for example, *Topics* II.6, 112b1-20. If no restrictions are explicitly mentioned, Aristotle usually supposes that generalizations are made with respect to time as well as with respect to the species. It is stated in *Posterior Analytics* I.4, 73a28-9, that 'something holds of every case if it does not hold in some cases and not in others, nor at some times and not at others'.

In places where 'always' and 'by necessity' are used interchangeably Aristotle is often speaking about everlasting separate substances or invariant cyclical processes. In fact he believed that the core of the world consists of invariant and everlasting separate substances, regular motions, primary bodies, members of natural species and their properties. The scholars who think that a part of Aristotle's modal thought can be described as a statistical modal theory have often restricted it to this unchanging and self-repeating part of reality. It has been thought that Aristotle's belief in the existence of eternal unchanging entities and motions made the restricted acceptance of (1)–(4) natural for him (see, for example, Wolf 1979: 117–19; Sorabji 1980: 128–37, Dancy 1981: 105–6; Williams 1982: 140, 181–2; Seel 1982: 251–4). This may be true, but it is interesting to ask, of course, why Aristotle was inclined to make use of (P) at all.

One of the dilemmas presented in *Metaphysics* III is the question whether the principles of things are potential or actual. The difficulty, as Aristotle formulates it, is that if they are potential it is possible that none of the things that are should be, because it seems that potentialities need not be actual, at least not as soon as they exist as potentialities. And if they are actual, they are not principles, because potentiality is prior to actuality (*Metaphysics* III.6, 1002b32–1003a5). In *Metaphysics* XII.6, 1071b3–1072a4, Aristotle argues that because potentialities can fail, the eternal first principles must exist and act in a way which is not actualization of a potentiality. Dancy has used the notions of hyper-actuality and hyper-activity when describing things which are what they are and do what they do without any potentiality for being and doing it (Dancy 1981: 74–6). Hyper-actualities or hyper-activities cannot be actualizations of potentialities, Aristotle thinks, because then they would be actualizations of what also could not be, and there cannot be such a potentiality in their cases, because the potentiality of not being should be sometimes actualized. In *De caelo* I.12, Aristotle explains this by supposing that a thing has contrary potencies of which one is always actualized. Unactualized potencies are then not real, because one cannot assume them to be realized at any time without contradiction. The philosophically interesting feature of this reasoning is the fact that, when Aristotle assumes a possibility as realized, he thinks that it should be realized in the one and only history of ours (see also *Physics* VIII.5, 256b3–13). I think that Hintikka was right when he argued that Aristotle's inclination to use modal terms as statistically interpreted was connected with a lack of a systematic conception of synchronic alternative states of affairs (Hintikka 1973: 107–10).

Dancy (1981: 80) and Judson (1983: 228–31) have argued that Aristotle's reasoning in *De caelo* I.12, 281b20–5, involves a crude error. He seems to think that when one supposes a candidate for possibility actualized, by way of checking on its possibility, it is assumed in the history of the actual world without regard to whether the supposition requires changes in what else can be taken to be true or actual. A related remark was made earlier by Williams (1965: 98–9). According to him, Aristotle mistakenly equates the modal distinction between a compound and divided reading of sentences like 'A sitting man can stand' with a temporal distinction between simultaneous and non-simultaneous actualization of contrary capacities. Perhaps Aristotle is not as confused as his critics have taken him to be, however. The passage from *De caelo* I.12 includes an application of the above semantic distinction between the compound and divided readings, presented in *Sophistici elenchi* 166a22–30 and applied in *Metaphysics* IX.3, 1047a16–24. As Aristotle's modal semantics did not contain the idea of synchronic alternative possibilities, possibilities are assumed as realized in the history of the actual world. If Socrates is sitting now, it is not possible that he is standing now, and if he is always sitting, it is not possible that he is standing. This aspect of Aristotle's theory of the genuineness of possibilities seems to exclude all eternally unrealized possibilities. But as will be seen, Aristotle tried to qualify this view with respect to singular future events.

If the temporal-frequency conception of modality is not the only one of Aristotle's modal paradigms and if it is limited to eternal substances and types of events and statements, it is clear that the statistical principles do not yield definitions of Aristotelian modal concepts. Some authors, particularly Sarah Waterlow (1982a) and Jeroen van Rijen (1989), have stressed that, even though principles like (1)–(4) played a role in Aristotle's philosophy, it would be better to call them something else than modal principles; they are not derived from the meaning of modal terms and their acceptance is based on some special metaphysical or ontological views. This remark is connected with an attempt to show that Aristotle's basic modal intuitions build a coherent whole and that, with various additional premises, they may yield seemingly different criteria for classifying things or events into necessary and contingent ones.

According to van Rijen, Aristotle's remarks on the interrelations between modal terms, the basic modal inference rules mentioned in *Prior Analytics* I.15, the related operational definitions of modal concepts (cf. *Prior Analytics* I.13, 32a18–20), the rule of necessitation and the systematic distinction between absolute and qualified modalities build a core of what could be called Aristotle's general theory of necessity and possibility. Van Rijen's formulations of absolute and relative modalities are based on the view that Aristotle considered all modally qualified sentences, apart from the members of the set $S$ of non-logical axioms and definitions, as sentences about the consistency of what we can hold to be the case. This consistency is judged against the total corpus of knowledge which is the set of all logical consequences of S or against a maximal consistent subset of this corpus and some contravening assumptions containing the contravening assumptions (van Rijen 1989: 30–55). This model-theoretic construction of the core of Aristotle's pure modal theory is a systematic philosophical theory rather than a historical reconstruction of Aristotle's intentions. According to Waterlow, Aristotle had a distinctive conception of possibility which Waterlow calls relative temporalized possibility and which she claims to be Aristotle's only conception of possibility (Waterlow 1982a: 25–6, 31–5, 159). Referring to McCall's paper 'Time and the Physical Modalities' (1969), Waterlow characterizes relative temporalized possibilities as follows:

> '$p$' even if false at $t$, is nonetheless possible then if and only if: the actual state of things at $t$ is such that from a description of this, together with the supposition that '$p$' will be true at some later time, there follows no impossible consequence.

Critics have remarked that there is hardly textual evidence for the claim that relative temporalized conception of possibility would be Aristotle's only modal conception (Judson 1983: 243–7; van Rijen 1989: 83).

The idea of drawing a sharp distinction between modal notions and metaphysical principles which influence their application shows similarities to certain contemporary attempts to argue for universal moral principles by claiming that differences in moral judgements are caused by different interpretations of the facts rather than by different moral principles. I shall not enter into the philosophical problems connected with this distinction, whether moral or modal. The fact is that, while speaking about possibilities, necessities and impossibilities, Aristotle did not himself try to solve philosophical problems containing modalities by referring to the idea that actual necessities or impossibilities are based on some extra-modal principles and that they could be other than they are. Aristotle did not draw any systematic distinction between what we call logical or conceptual necessity or possibility on the one hand and physical or natural necessity or possibility on the other.

Contrary to the thesis of Waterlow and van Rijen, I believe that Aristotle's modal thought was based on different paradigms of speaking about necessities and possibilities and that they involve various intuitions which are not reducible to one clear-cut basic theory. A statistical or temporal-frequency interpretation of modality is one level or one strand of Aristotle's modal thinking. Perhaps relative temporalized modalities or diachronic modalities could be called another strand; there are, in addition to these, discussions of possibilities as potencies and attempts to analyse modes of necessity in nature and in syllogistic arguments. Even though it is true that the uses of modal notions in different contexts have formal similarities and that Aristotle to some extent was conscious of the philosophical problems connected with the various uses, it may be, as Jaakko Hintikka has argued, that Aristotle's insights here were not as clear as some commentators have wanted to believe.

The most discussed part of Hintikka's studies on Aristotle's modal theory is his interpretation of *De interpretatione* 9. In the paper 'The Once and Future Sea Fight' (1964), reprinted in *Time and Necessity* (1973), Hintikka wanted to show that Aristotle's main problem in *De interpretatione* 9 was created by his habit of tacitly equating possibility with sometime truth and necessity with omnitemporal truth. The problems of this statistical model broke to the surface when Aristotle tried to define the modal status of temporally definite sentences referring to individual historical events. According to Hintikka, Aristotle probably had temporally definite statements in mind when he said that 'it was always true to say of anything that has happened that it will be so'. His strong reliance on the statistical model is seen from his moving from the infinite past truth of a statement to its necessity: 'But if it was always true to say that it is or will be so, it could not be not so, or not be going not to be so' (18b10–13). On this interpretation, Aristotle's real problem is that temporally definite statements, if they are true, are unchangingly and always true and as such necessarily true. The problem is not really solved. All that Aristotle could do, Hintikka argues, was to transpose the question to a level at which it could be discussed in terms of temporally indefinite sentences; this happens in passage 19a23–7. Aristotle says that what is, necessarily is, when it is, and the meaning of this remark is that what is, immutably is what it is, when it is. When something is necessary in this sense, it does not follow that it would be necessary 'without qualification', i.e. actual at all times. In the same way a true temporally determinate sentence, which as such seems to be necessarily true, may become contingent when the temporal specification is removed.

It is assumed in Hintikka's interpretation that Aristotle did not qualify the truth or falsity of temporally definite future sentences in any way. The problems created by them are left untouched by transferring the scope of interest from temporally determinate events or sentences to corresponding types of events or sentences. Most commentators have thought, however, that Aristotle in some way tried to point out that future contingent sentences differ from other sentences with respect to their truth and falsity. The chapter is very vague in this regard and there is no more consensus among the commentators nowadays than there was in ancient times. The main alternatives of interpretation have been that either Aristotle wanted to restrict the validity of the law of the excluded middle (or the principle of bivalence) or that he wanted to qualify the mode of truth and falsity of future contingent sentences. The latter alternative was common among the medieval commentators from Boethius to Thomas Aquinas; some fourteenth-century thinkers and many modern interpreters have tried to argue for the former alternative (for different views, see Sorabji 1980: 91–103; Normore 1982).

According to the earlier medieval interpretation, if future contingent sentences are true or false, they are true or false in an indeterminate way, because the conditions which make them true or false are not yet settled. This approach was based on the remark in 19a36–9 (see pp. 55–60 and 128 below). If Aristotle had something like this in his mind, it could explain why he perhaps thought that the eternal truth of temporally definite future contingent sentences does not make their truth necessary in the same way in which everlasting beings, essential properties of natural kinds, or self-repeating events are said to be necessary. This is a speculative interpretation only, but it is of some interest that in *Posterior Analytics* I.6 Aristotle seems to imply that certain predicates may belong to their subjects in every instance and at all times without belonging to them necessarily (75a31–4). According to van Rijen, Aristotle considered necessary connections essential and he thought that different invariant features of things can be considered essential, depending on which way, for example in which science, they are attended to. Predicates belonging essentially to a subject when it is treated as something in one way may be non-essential when it is treated as something in another way. They always belong to it – even in the latter case – but this invariant predication is in a sense accidental. Something like this may be included in *Posterior Analytics* I.6 (van Rijen 1989: 132–84). If this is applied to future contingent sentences, they could have been always true or false without being essentially true or false. Van Rijen's interpretation is hypothetical, however, and, as Sorabji has remarked, Aristotle's requirements for necessity are stricter in *Posterior Analytics* I.6 than elsewhere (Sorabji 1980: 132). Anyway, it seems that even though Aristotle often tends to equate necessities with natural invariances, there are places where this equation is questioned without a detailed account of how it is qualified.

Referring to *De interpretatione* 9, 19a18–22, M.J. White has suggested that Aristotle's argumentation in *De interpretatione* 9 is partially based on a temporal-frequency conception of conditional necessity. If sea battles always occur the day after days relevantly similar to today, then it is today definitely true and conditionally necessary that a sea battle occurs tomorrow. If it sometimes occurs but sometimes fails to occur after days relevantly similar to today, then it is today neither definitely true nor definitely false that it occurs tomorrow. According to White, the temporal-frequency model could be appropriate in making modal assessments about kinds of future events and states of affairs. It could also explain why singular future contingent sentences should be treated as lacking truth value. He admits, however, that this interpretation should be taken as a philosophical rather than a historical suggestion (White 1985: 42–54). A number of scholars have recently argued that, instead of the temporal-frequency model, Aristotle had in mind in *De interpretatione* 9 the model of diachronic modalities (see the last section of this chapter).

The question of truth and falsity of future contingent sentences was one of the themes occurring in ancient discussions of Diodorus Cronus' famous argument for determinism. This Master Argument, as it was called, is incompletely known to us through Epictetus' description (*Dissertationes* II, 19, 1–5). It is historically interesting that it has as premises principles which also occurred in Aristotle's modal philosophy (cf. Hintikka 1973: 179–213). According to Epictetus, the point of the argument was to demonstrate that the conjunction of (a) everything past and true is necessary and (b) the impossible does not follow from the possible, which is accepted as evidently true, is incompatible with (c) what neither is nor will be is possible.

In his reconstruction of the argument, Arthur Prior takes (a) and (b) as the premises which, together with two further premises, yield a denial of (c). The additional premises are as follows: (d) from a thing's being the case it necessarily follows that it has always been going to be the case, and (e) of whatever is and always will be false, it has already been the case that it will always be false. Premise (a) is read as, whatever has been the case cannot now not have been the case, and (b) as, if $p$ necessarily implies $q$, then if $q$ is not possible, $p$ is not possible (see Prior 1955; 1957: 86–8; 1967: 32–4). According to this interpretation, no future events can be other than they will be, because this would imply that the past truth or falsity of statements about them is not necessary. Richard Sorabji (1980: 109–11) refers to some ancient texts which suggest that there were thinkers who probably understood Diodorus' argument in a way not very different from Prior's interpretation. Another well-known reconstruction is offered by Jaakko Hintikka. According to him, Diodorus Cronus thought that what is now future will be past and hence necessary. Therefore, to say that a future event can be other than what it in fact will be is to say something from which an impossibility follows, i.e. it follows that it could be true to say that such a thing has not happened of which it will be necessarily true to say that it has happened (Hintikka 1973: 191–3). Although these interpretations are based on different views about the nature of some background assumptions of the argument, both Prior and Hintikka see the basic problem in the fact that possibilities are taken to refer to the actual history of our universe considered as a definite whole. The argument is in this sense based on determinism. (For some other historical or rational reconstructions of the argument, see Schuhl 1960; Rescher 1966b and the revised version in Rescher and Urquhart 1971; Purtill 1973; Michael 1976; Sedley 1977: 97–101; von Wright 1979b; Denyer 1981; Vuillemin 1979, 1984: 15–57; White 1985: 72–91.)

According to Boethius, Diodorus Cronus defined modal terms as follows: (a) the possible is that which either is or will be; (b) the impossible is that which, when it is false, will not be true; (c) the necessary is that which, when it is true, will not be false; and (d) the non-necessary is that which either is already or will be false (Boethius, *In Periherm*. II, 234.22–6). These definitions are based on the assumption that truth-values may be changed. 'Socrates will be sitting at $t_1$' is possible, if true, and it will be impossible after $t_1$. 'Socrates has been sitting at $t_1$' is false before $t_1$, but when it is true after $t_1$, it is necessary. If the definitions are applied to such temporally determinate sentences, which are either always true or always false, modal distinctions become redundant (cf. Kneale and Kneale 1962: 117–21).

Diodorus Cronus was an atomist and he did not care about Aristotle's critical remark that the atoms cannot be in motion. He thought that it is natural to use the perfect tense and to say 'It has moved' without being able to use the present tense sentence 'It is moving' (see Döring 1972: 121–3; Sorabji 1983: 369–71). Against this background, a straightforward version of the Master Argument, applied to allegedly contingent future motions, runs as follows. Counterfactual possibilities are expressed by sentences such as: '$x$ which was not $F$ at $t_1$ has become $F$ at $t_2$'. To assume that this sentence is true is to assume that it is necessarily true at a moment at which it is necessarily true that $x$ has not become $F$ at $t_2$. The second premise of the Master Argument is interpreted here as a version of the Aristotelian principle: if a possibility is assumed to be realized, no impossible conclusion follows. Jaakko Hintikka has argued that in fact the whole argument is a variant of Aristotle's argument in *De caelo* I.12 which Hintikka calls 'Aristotle's own Master Argument'. The difference between Aristotle and Diodorus is that Diodorus wanted to argue for a deterministic view, while for Aristotle it was a cumbersome consequence of his conceptual framework which he tried to qualify in different ways (see the last section in this chapter).

It has been argued that there were certain frequency elements in the Stoic modal theory as well, although they were not used to define modal notions in the Diodorean manner. On the basis of Michael Frede's attempt to reconstruct Stoic modal definitions from secondary sources (mainly Diogenes Laertius VII, 75, and Boethius, *In Periherm.* II, 234.27–235.4; Frede 1974a: 107–17), Susanne Bobzien has presented a detailed picture of the Stoic theory of modality where, it seems, (a) the possible is that which admits of truth and is not externally prevented from being true, (b) the necessary is that which does not admit of falsity or which while admitting of falsity is externally prevented from being false, (c) the impossible is that which does not admit of truth or which while admitting of truth is externally prevented from being true, and (d) the non-necessary is that which admits of falsity and is not externally prevented from being false (Bobzien 1986: 40–9). Frede's reconstruction is an essentially revised version of the interpretation of Martha Kneale (Kneale and Kneale 1962: 123–8). Ancient sources do not include these accounts word for word, formulated with a view to saving the standard relations between modal notions. A different reconstruction without this condition is offered by Mario Mignucci (1978: 325–30) and Jules Vuillemin (1983: 235–47).

According to Bobzien, the first parts of the definitions of necessity and impossibility pertain to temporally indefinite assertions (the Stoic axioms), the truth or falsity of which are independent of changes in the world. Axioms of this type are said to refer to essential predications or logical contradictions (Bobzien 1986: 34–5, 63–7). As for the modal status of the axioms, the truth and falsity of which may be affected by changing things, the Stoic modalities can be understood so that necessity, possibility and impossibility differ from each other on the basis of statistical differences in the occurrences of the external hindrances. An axiom susceptible of falseness is necessarily true now and in the future, when it is externally prevented from being false now and always in the future. An axiom susceptible of truth is impossible now and in the future, when it is prevented from being true now and always in the future. An axiom is contingently true when it can be true and there will be times at which it is not prevented from being false and there will be times at which it is not prevented from being true. A similar classification is applied to past tense and future tense axioms as well. According to Bobzien, modal axioms are assertions about the modal status of the corresponding non-modal axioms at the moment of utterance of the modal axioms. Contingent axioms can begin to be necessary or impossible. What is said about the modality of axioms can be applied to the modality of states of affairs as well (Bobzien 1986: 50–105).

In their reconstructions of the Stoic definitions of modal axioms, Kneale, Frede and Bobzien delete from Diogenes Laertius' account the remark that the non-necessary requires that it be true. It may be, however, that Diogenes' description refers to Stoic usage: 'The necessary is that which is true and does not admit of being false or, admitting of being false, external conditions oppose its being false . . . and the non-necessary is that which is true and may be false when external conditions do not oppose its being false.' If 'admits/does not admit truth/falsity' refers to truth values different from the actual ones, then true axioms are divided into necessary and non-necessary and false axioms into impossible and possible. Some medieval logicians considered it natural to think that, as for the two-edged possibility, 'contingent' refers to what is true but can be false and 'possible' to what is false but can be true (see p. 107). This use of the term 'contingent' corresponds to what Diogenes Laertius says about the Stoic notion of non-necessary.

If it is true that the first parts of the definitions of necessary and impossible axioms refer to some kind of simple modalities, it is significant that the definitions of the possible and the non-necessary are not formed in a similar way. Perhaps one should not call the absolute necessities and impossibilities logical modalities as Bobzien does (ibid.: 63–4). The absence of an unqualified possibility suggests that all modalities are real rather than logical, i.e. the truth of modal axioms is evaluated from the point of view of the actual world and its history. I think that this is taken for granted in Boethius' description:

> The Stoics have postulated as possible that which is susceptible of true affirmation, when things that are external to it but happen

together with it do not in any way prevent it. The impossible is that which never admits of truth, other external things preventing it.
(*In Periherm.* II, 234.27-235.1)

Boethius seems to think that the absence of the obstacles refers to the moment of time at which an allegedly possible axiom is assumed to be true or a state of affairs actual. If Socrates is always sitting, the axiom 'Socrates is standing' is apparently impossible. And if fate antecedently necessitates the events at all future moments of time, then only that which will take place seems to be possible. For this kind of reason Boethius, like Cicero (*De fato* 6.12-8.16) and Plutarch (*De stoicorum repugnantiis* 1055d-e), maintained that the Stoics were committed to Diodorus' view of possibility whether they liked it or not (Boethius, *In Periherm.* II, 235.4-17; cf. Sharples 1983: 12). The authors mention, however, that the Stoics wished to allow for possibilities that will never be actualized (see also Alexander of Aphrodisias, *De fato*, 1983: 53, 176.15-16). It was also commonly known that the Stoics did not accept the conclusion of the Master Argument. They criticized it: Cleanthes by denying the first premise and Chrysippus by denying the second premise (see Epictetus, *Dissertationes* II, 19, 1-5). We do not know, however, what Cleanthes meant, and although a little more is known about Chrysippus' argument, it is far from being clear. Chrysippus defended his view by the example 'If Dion is dead, this is dead' which spoken in the presence of Dion is a sound conditional with a possible antecedent. The consequent cannot be truly uttered at any moment, however (Alexander of Aphrodisias, *In Aristotelis An. pr. comm.* (CAG 2.1), 177.28-178.1; for some discussions, see White 1985: 108-15; Bobzien 1986: 105-13).

According to ancient witnesses, Chrysippus thought that all events are necessitated by earlier states of affairs and the whole is dominated by the cosmic reason which does not act by choices. The critics found it difficult to understand how there could be unrealized possibilities in Chrysippus' cosmos. It is not clear what the Stoics meant when speaking about external obstacles, but they might have thought that possibilities which respect the moment $t_1$ were not externally prevented from being actualized before the relevant constituents of the states of affairs to be actual at $t_1$ were actualized (cf. Reesor 1965: 292-3, 296; Rist 1969: 121-7). All kinds of states of affairs could then be in some sense possible with respect to the future moment $t_1$; at $t_1$ that which is realized is necessary and that which is not realized is impossible. I shall return to Stoic modalities at the end of the next section.

## POSSIBILITY AS A POTENCY

In the third book of *Physics* Aristotle presented his famous definition of motion (*kinēsis*) about which John Locke said that it could hardly be more absurd (Locke, *An Essay concerning Human Understanding* III.4, 8). The definition of motion as the actuality of the potentiality *qua* potentiality and the theory of change in general are connected in an interesting way with Aristotle's modal conceptions. I shall first sketch Aristotle's theory of determining the temporal limits of processes and actualities, because it gave rise to some modal controversies in the Middle Ages and because it is relevant to Aristotle's view of possibility as a potency.

In *Physics* III.1 Aristotle discusses the same basic types of changes as those already listed in Chapter 14 of the *Categories*: the changes of substance – i.e. the generation and corruption – the changes of qualities, the changes of quantities and the changes of place. These are all called *kinēseis* and are treated as time-taking processes between a *terminus a quo* and *terminus ad quem*. It seems that while writing this part of *Physics* Aristotle believed that the changes relevant in natural philosophy take place in the four categories mentioned and that all these changes can be treated as temporal processes.

Another detailed discussion of kinds of changes can be found in *Physics* V.1-2, and it differs in a significant way from that of the third book of *Physics*. Substantial changes are now separated from the class of *kinēseis*. Aristotle states in *Physics* V.1, 224b28-35, that a change may be between terms mutually exclusive and jointly exhaustive or it may be between terms which are mutually exclusive but not jointly exhaustive. A change between contradictory terms cannot be a *kinēsis*, i.e. an actuality of the potentiality of the end *qua* potentiality, different from the beginning state and the end state. Aristotle did not want to qualify the first principles of logic in his natural philosophy.

It is typical of Aristotle's approach in the fifth book of *Physics* that he presents the generation and corruption of a substance as the standard type of instantaneous non-kinetic changes between contradictory terms. *Kinēseis* are characterized as changes between contrary terms in the categories of quantity, quality and place (*Physics* V.1-2, 225a34-226b10). It seems that Aristotle tried to classify kinds of changes in a way which would match his philosophical doctrine of substance, according to which substances are not reducible to other categories and there are no degrees in being a substance. If a thing either is or is not a certain substance, substantial changes must take place between contradictory terms without taking time. It may be that in the discussions of change in the third book of *Physics*, a stage of Aristotle's thought is reflected during which he did not consider individual substantial forms as ontological constituents of reality (see also *Physics* I.7, 190a31–190b9; cf. Morrow 1966: 154–67). But it is also possible that he thought that substantial changes are embedded in processes and did not consider it necessary to draw the finer distinctions presented in *Physics* V.1–2.

The main lines of Aristotle's final theory of changes can be summarized as follows. Let us consider the sentence '$x$ which is $S$ is $F$', where '$S$' stands for a name of substance and '$F$' for a name of quality, quantity or place. Aristotle thought that quantities and places are infinitely divisible and that there are no indivisible changes of $x$ with respect to $F$ of this type. Changes in these categories are necessarily temporal processes between contrary terms having intermediates (*Physics* VI.4, 235a13–37). (For Aristotle's theory of the continuous structure of time, place, quantity and motion, see Furley 1967: 79–103; Miller 1974: 132–55; 1982: 87–111.) It is possible to ask, of course, whether a thing is, say, of a certain size or not; the question is formulated in terms of contradictory alternatives. But according to Aristotle's view, quantitative or local changes between terms conceptualized in this way are in fact embedded in processes. In some places Aristotle says that there are qualitative changes in which the subject does not successively occupy positions in a continuous series between the contrary terms. Even these kinds of changes are infinitely divisible *per accidens*, however, because they are always connected with quantitative or local changes (*Physics* VI.5, 236b2–18; cf. 4, 235a35–6). As for the first part of the sentence, '$x$ is $S$', the coming-to-be and passing-away of $x$'s being $S$ is an indivisible instantaneous change. According to Aristotle, natural changes are of two different logical types, and he tried to connect this distinction with his metaphysical doctrine of the structure of being in the way just delineated.

Aristotle uses the notions of generation and corruption so that they denote pairs of mutually exclusive and jointly exhaustive successive states on one occasion. The instant of time dividing the periods of the initial state and the end state is the point of reference, if it is asked when a certain generation or corruption takes place. In Aristotle's theory this instant is always the first instant of the new state (*Physics* VI.5, 235b6–32). It is implied that the generations and corruptions of substances should not be understood as unique instantaneous events taking place at or before the instant of change. This remark becomes more interesting when it is realized that some philosophers considered changes between contradictory terms as positive events taking place between the periods during which the *terminus a quo* and the *terminus ad quem* of the change obtain. Such a view is mentioned in Plato's *Parmenides* (156C–157A), where it is stated that in generations and corruptions of substances there is a moment of change at which the changing thing has a special status between being and not being. The Law of Excluded Middle is dismissed here, and we can find the same Platonic approach to the limit decision problem later, for example, in Plotinus (*Enn.* VI.1, 16, 35–7) and in Augustine (*De civitate Dei* XII.2). These authors postulated an instantaneous third state between two consecutive contradictory states, because they thought that the change between contradictory terms should be understood as an indivisible positive event. The terms 'generation' and 'corruption' are taken to refer to junctions between successive contradictory states of affairs and these junctions are presumed to have an autonomous ontological status. In Aristotle's theory, the coming-to-be or passing-away of a substance does not exist, and correspondingly there are no instants at which substantial changes as such would be actual.

As for the limits of *kinēseis*, Aristotle's main point is that continuous changes are not actual in an instant and therefore it is not possible to postulate any first or last intrinsic instant of their actuality. Their temporal limits must be external, i.e. there is the first instant of actuality of the *terminus ad quem* as well as the last instant of actuality of the *terminus a quo* (see *Physics* VI.3, 234a24–b9; 5, 235b6–236a27; VIII.8, 263b9–264a6). With changes taking place along a continuous series of positions, there is no first position a changing thing could occupy after the *terminus a quo* and no last position it could occupy before the *terminus ad quem*. Aristotle does not explicitly formulate this argument, but is it clear that Aristotle's view of the extrinsic limits of *kinēseis* follows from his theory of the continuous structure of kinetic changes (cf. Sorabji 1976: 85).

According to Aristotle, rest is another temporal thing which cannot be actual in an instant. The state of rest is characterized as a state of a subject which, without being moved, is capable of being moved (*Physics* III.2, 202a4–5; IV.12, 221b7–14; V.2, 226b13–16; 6, 229b23–231a4; VI.3, 234a31–4; 8, 239a13–14, 26–239b3; VIII.8, 264a22–8). Aristotle seems to suppose that both rest and motion have extrinsic temporal limits. If this is true, how can one avoid the inconsistency that the extrinsic limits of a period of rest are the intrinsic limits of the surrounding periods of motion and the extrinsic limits of a period of motion are the intrinsic limits of the surrounding periods of rest? (For some discussions of the problem, see, for example, Sorabji 1976; Kretzmann 1976.) Modern commentators have not attended to the fact that, while speaking about rest, Aristotle uses expressions like 'rest in health', 'rest in disease' or 'rest in whiteness' (*Physics* V.6, 229b30–1, 230a2, 6–7; VIII.7, 261b2–3, 10–11). So when a thing rests, it is possible to refer to a definite unchanging condition in respect of which it rests as long as it is at rest. The duration of this static state, although not its theoretical limit decision structure, coincides with that of rest. There is no rest in an instant and hence no intrinsic limits of the period of rest. But the actuality of the condition in which an object rests has intrinsic limits. The first instant of actuality of the terminal state of a change is the first instant of actuality of the condition in which the changed thing can rest. This unique instant is the extrinsic limit of both the period of motion and the period of rest. The same idea could be applied to the end of rest and the corresponding beginning of motion. (In *Physics* VI.8, 239a10–b3, it is argued that there is no first instant (or period) of rest. In VI.5, 236a17–20, Aristotle seems to suppose that there is an intrinsic (end) limit of rest. This may be a slip.)

What has been sketched above is a prima facie clear and natural theory of limit assignment in a physical theory operating with the doctrine of categories and with the theory of the continuous structure of time, space and motion. The generations and corruptions of substances take place through instantaneous changes. Qualities, quantities and places, in respect of which there can be kinetic changes, are concomitants of the actualities of essences. They are not ontologically independent. Aristotle says that an individual *kinēsis* is always a change from one state of a substance to another state of that substance. In substantial changes it is the substance itself which changes (*Physics* V.1, 225a35–b3). Even though this kind of theory can be found in Aristotle, there are many passages where all changes are considered as *kinēseis* because, as mentioned above, Aristotle probably thought like this at some stage and because even later he could not wholly free himself from this habit of thought (see, for example, *Physics* VI.4, 234b10–20). This inconsistency created problems for medieval interpreters. Another source of trouble was Aristotle's view according to which it is a kind of empirical fact that all generations and corruptions of substances are connected with preceding changes in other categories. It proved to be a very cumbersome task to explain how this matches the limit decision

Modalities in ancient authors 23

rules for substantial changes and *kinēseis* (see Knuuttila 1986b: 249–51).

Let us now turn to the theory of potentiality and actuality which Aristotle considered an essential part of his natural philosophy and which also played an important role in the first philosophy, as is seen from Book IX of the *Metaphysics* which concentrates on this theme.

In the beginning of the book, Aristotle refers to his doctrine of the categories and to the view that the term 'being' refers primarily to the actuality of a substantial form; a reference to this mode of being is always implied when other things are called beings, and they are said to be in as many ways as there are categories. Other general distinctions are, on the one hand, the distinction between being essentially something and being accidentally something, and, on the other hand, between being potentially something and being actually something. (There is an interesting discussion of Aristotle's theory of substance and related themes in Frede and Patzig (1988). For a more traditional view, see Owens (1963) and Irwin (1988).)

Modern philosophical discussion of being has often been dominated by what could be called Frege's and Russell's thesis that words for being, such as 'is', are genuinely ambiguous, expressing either identity, predication, existence or class-inclusion. Recent historical studies on the works of Plato and Aristotle have made it clear that they handled the concept of being in a way essentially different from what the Frege–Russell thesis leads us to expect, and that, contrary to what has been claimed, this was not necessarily caused by any deep philosophical confusion. The ancient view that 'is' is not genuinely ambiguous did not preclude the recognition of its grammatically different uses, such as the veridical, copulative or existential ones, or of their different nuances. And, as is shown by Aristotle's theory of the categories, one could think that the number of philosophically relevant different uses of 'is' is much larger than what is supposed in the Frege–Russell distinction and, furthermore, that the different senses for 'is' do not constitute a full ambiguity (or homonymy, in Aristotle's terminology) but can be understood as related to each other as cases of *pros hen* multiplicity of uses (see, for example, Frede 1967, Kahn 1973 and the papers of C. Kahn, B. Mates, R. Dancy and J. Hintikka in Knuuttila and Hintikka 1986).

Even though Aristotle characterizes Book IX of the *Metaphysics* as a continuation of the discussion of the problems of substantial being in Books VII and VIII, it is not quite clear how it is related to them.

Anyway, the general theme is potentiality and actuality which are regarded as forming a distinction applicable to beings in all categories. Aristotle says that the basic meaning of 'potency' is connected with the notions of motion and change and that he will first discuss it in this sense, although 'it is not most useful for what we are after now'. Almost half of the book treats this kinetic potency. The main theme of the other part is actuality and its priority over potentiality.

In *Metaphysics* IX.1 Aristotle repeats the main points of his list of the various uses of the term 'potency' (*dynamis*) presented in *Metaphysics* V.12. Potency is primarily the principle of motion or change in something other than the thing moved or changed or in it *qua* other and, furthermore, the principle of being moved or changed by another or by itself *qua* other. Correspondingly, things which primarily are called 'potent' or 'capable' are principles of motion or change in other things or in themselves *qua* other or they are things over which something else possesses such a capacity (cf. *Metaphysics* V.12, 1019a15–20, 33–b1).

In the Middle Ages the active and passive aspects of potentiality were called the *potentia activa* and the *potentia passiva* respectively. Their relationship is described in *Metaphysics* as follows:

> It is plain, then, that in one way there is one potency of acting and being acted on, for something is capable both by itself having the potency of being acted upon and by another thing having the potency of being acted upon by the agency of it, but in another way they are different. For one is in that which is acted upon . . . and the other is in that which acts.
>
> (IX.1, 1046a19–26)

The explanation of the unity of an active and passive potency is sketchy, but Aristotle clearly wants to say that when a thing has an active potency of acting or a passive potency of being acted on, its having an active potency implies that there is a corresponding passive potency, and its having a passive potency implies that there is a corresponding active potency.

In the second chapter the potencies are divided into rational and non-rational potencies, and the distinction is specified by labelling the non-rational potencies as potencies of one result only and the rational potencies as potencies of contrary results. Specific types of non-rational potencies, i.e. certain pairs of active and passive potencies, are the sources of the types of specific natural events (cf. *Physics* I.5). In the case of non-rational potencies, componential active and passive potencies are both directed to one and the same end. As for the rational potencies, people can use the same capacities to contrary ends. For example, medical skill is an intellectual ability of initiating and controlling processes either towards health or sickness, depending on the choice of the person who has the ability.

When Aristotle returns to the question of the detailed structure of potencies in Chapter 5, non-rational potencies are delineated as follows: 'when the agent and the patient come together as being capable, the one must act and the other must be acted on' (1048a5–7). The phrase 'as being capable' (*hōs dynantai*) suggests that one could speak about active and passive potencies as not being capable of acting or being acted on. Aristotle seems to think that this may happen in at least two ways. Potencies are sometimes treated as second-order potencies, i.e. as some kind of material for first-order active and passive potencies which together form a genuine source of motion or change (see Hintikka *et al.* 1977: 50–6). Another way to speak about potencies as unable to be realized is to speak about active or passive first-order potencies as partial potencies.

The idea of a lower-order potency occurs, for example, in *Physics*:

> One who is learning potentially knows in a different way from one who while already possessing the knowledge is not actually exercising it. Whenever that which can act and that which can be acted upon are in contact, what is potential becomes actual: e.g., the learner becomes from one potential something another potential something. For one who possesses knowledge, but is not actually exercising it, knows potentially in a sense, though not in the same sense as before he learnt it. . . . In regard to natural bodies the case is similar. Thus what is cold is potentially hot, and when it has been changed and it is fire, it burns, unless something prevents and hinders it.
>
> (VIII.4, 255a33–b7)

(Some manuscripts have 'what is potential sometimes becomes actual' on line a35; Ross, in Aristotle, *Physics* 696; Waterlow 1982b: 194. See also Aristotle, *De anima* II.5, 417a2–418a6; cf. *Nicomachean Ethics* VII.3, 1147a10–24; *Topics* V.2, 130a19–24.) Although in the texts mentioned Aristotle claims that one can in a sense describe the lower-level potencies as potencies of the effects of first-order potencies, he states in other places that they should be called potencies of their immediate effects only (see, for example, *Metaphysics* VIII.5, 1044b29–1045a6; IX.7, 1049a14–18).

Active and passive first-order potencies, taken separately, are partial potencies in the sense that neither of them is able to initiate a motion or change alone. They can do it only when they have come together and there is no hindrance. When these conditions are fulfilled and a total or full potency exists, it is necessarily realized immediately. A passive non-rational potency is actualized in one way only. A passive rational capacity is a capacity for contrary effects and therefore the activating principle must be selective. But when the process of deliberation has taken place and the agent is ready to act in accordance with it, then even here the action necessarily follows immediately (*Metaphysics* IX.5, 1048a5–7, 13–21; 7, 1048b37–1049a14; *Nicomachean Ethics* VII.3, 1147a25–31).

Aristotle tried to create a philosophical concept of natural power or potency by separating the general constituents of changes taking place in nature. This analysis resulted in three factors: the first-order active component, the first-order passive component and the meeting of these components in such a way that nothing in the things capable or things outside them prevents the interaction. Aristotle could make use of this model in identifying invariant features of various change-initiating situations and thus extend the scope of theoretical knowledge to changing parts of reality, considered as structured by the pairs of goal-directed natural potencies (Gotthelf 1987: 209–11; for agent and patient in Aristotle's natural philosophy in general, see Waterlow 1982b: 159–203). Generic active and passive potencies belonging to natural species are recognized only by their having been realized. That all types of natural potentialities are realized is also implied in the doctrine, according to which the efficient cause which actualizes a passive potency must be of the same kind as the resulting actuality (*Metaphysics* VII.7, 1032a22–5).

When Aristotle describes the various uses of the terms 'potency' and 'possibility' in *Metaphysics* V.12, he says that some senses of 'possible' involve a reference to 'potency' and others do not. What is said to be possible may be a change or a state in a certain subject having a potency of a certain kind or it may be a type of event for which there is a corresponding generic potency pair in nature or rational potency in man. Such things may be discussed as possibilities without particularly attending to the fact that they are the ends of certain potencies. When they are explicitly treated as possibilities *kata dynamin*, however, the notion of possibility refers to the potencies themselves as the bearers of the special potential modes of existence of the ends. It is this notion of possibility as an ontological category in which Aristotle is interested in *Metaphysics* IX; it corresponds to the concept of actuality which Aristotle principally tried to elucidate. As already mentioned, in his proof of the priority of actuality Aristotle introduces a class of actualities which are possible without being actualizations of any potentiality.

The potency-based possibilities of individual states of affairs involve various problems. When does such a possibility begin to exist? As far as it is the potentiality of a definite state of affairs, it seems to exist as an identifiable potentiality of the end only when there is nothing which should be added into it before it becomes the actuality of the end of which it is the potentiality. If this means that an unqualified potentiality of an end only exists when the active and passive potencies are in interaction, one might claim that there is no place for full individual potency-based possibilities in Aristotle's ontology. That Aristotle himself was concerned about this kind of question is seen from Chapter 3 of *Metaphysics* IX. The chapter contains a discussion of the view of some Megarians who argued that a thing is capable of acting when it is acting and that it is not capable of acting when it is not acting. Aristotle does not try to deny this by maintaining that a thing not acting now could, instead of being not acting now, be acting now. He claims that the Megarian view does away with movement and coming-to-be. In order to avoid this, one should notice that there is a real distinction between potencies and actualities and that the potency of some act represents its possibility even when the result is not actualized.

Aristotle seems to believe that the position criticized is based on a fallacious step from an impossibility in the compound sense to an impossibility in the divided sense (see also p. 10 above). Even though something which does not move now cannot move now when it is not moving, it may be possible for it to move later. But how can such a possibility exist as a full potency without having been realized? On the basis of his limit decision theory, Aristotle could have stated that, for the beginning of a motion, there is a last moment of its having not yet begun and there is no first moment of its having already begun. The full possibility of motion exists and is actual *qua* possibility in the last moment in which the motion has not yet begun. As for the instantaneous coming-to-be's of substances or the end states of processes, the situation is more problematic, because in these cases there is a first moment of the new state but no last moment of the preceding state. Anyway, Aristotle had in his theory of the beginning of *kinēseis* an example of a full unrealized potentiality which as a potentiality is actual before actualization.

When speaking about the ends of processes, Aristotle could offer a more elaborate theory of the potentialities of individual states of affairs. According to him, all kinetic changes in the sublunar world are singular processes towards a goal. These goals are potentially existent before they are actualized through time-taking motions or changes. When a *kinēsis* has begun, it is, as a *kinēsis*, the actuality of which the preceding motion-initiating potency was the potentiality. It is an actualization of the possibility of the process it is (*Metaphysics* IX.6, 1048b8–9). But as a goal-directed process, a singular *kinēsis* not only actualizes a preceding possibility of motion or change; it is a gradual actualization of its goal and in this sense it is the actuality of the potentiality of the end *qua* potentiality. It is clear from the Aristotelian definition of *kinēsis* that he regarded *kinēseis* as empirical examples of full potentialities and possibilities as temporally unrealized. The possibilities of the ends of the processes, which are actual *qua* possibilities in the processes, are not realized as soon as they occur as possibilities, although the genuine possibilities of these possibilities are immediately actualized. (For Aristotle's theory of possibility as a *kinēsis*, see Hintikka *et al*. 1977.)

As far as Aristotle considered it important to find a place for unrealized identifiable possibilities representing a non-actualized level of being, he succeeded in doing so to his satisfaction by means of his interpretation of the incipient instant of change and the nature of *kinēsis*. Even though in this way Aristotle could avoid the actualistic determinism of the Megarians, he could not free himself from the problems created by the fact that an actualization still remained a kind of criterion for the genuineness of a full possibility. An instantaneous full possibility of a process is there only when a process follows, and the actuality of the possibility of the end of a process is not identical with any part of a *kinēsis* but with the whole temporal process ending in the goal.

Potency-based possibilities did not create any special problems when treated as generic dispositions, but Aristotle wanted to speak about ontological possibilities of individual states of affairs, too, and then he encountered a conflict of motives. When trying to show that there are identifiable potencies of certain ends, Aristotle was obliged to locate the potencies as near to actualities as possible, because otherwise they would not have been definite potencies of individual ends. On the other hand, in order to maintain the difference between actuality and potentiality, Aristotle had to see to it that there is a sufficient distance between them. The idea of calling the end-directed processes actualities of the potentialities of the ends *qua* potentialities was a clever theoretical effort to speak about full potentialities or possibilities, but it leaves the status of other singular potentialities vague. Aristotle could regard them as partial possibilities, although, as already mentioned, his intuitions here were not very clear. He sometimes refers to levels of potentialities, but in other places he denies that they could be employed. As for the first-level active and passive potencies, he sometimes seems to think that they must both exist with respect to a certain end, when one or another of them is referred to as its possibility; but in other places this is not considered necessary. This hesitation is also reflected in Aristotle's use of dispositional modal terms.

Many authors have attended to ambiguities in Aristotle's treatment of terms like heatable, separable, countable, thinkable or perceptible. In addition to the philological fact that such verbal adjectives may be used in a modal or non-modal way (which causes trouble to translators, e.g. *to khōriston*, 'separate' or 'separable', in the *Metaphysics*), Aristotle's comments on their modal uses seem to be inconsistent. In *Metaphysics* V.15, things able to act and affectible (active and passive potencies) are discussed as examples of relatives. It is said there that something's being thinkable means that there is a thought of it (1021a31). Similarly, in *Physics* IV.14, 223a22–3, Aristotle states that if there cannot exist someone to do the counting, there cannot be anything countable. In *Topics* V.9, 138b27–37, it is stated that air is not respirable if no animal exists of such a kind as to respire it. Quite a different view can be read in *Categories* 7, 7b31–8a6, where it is said that there still would be knowables and perceptibles if there were no animals. In *De anima* III.2, 426a15–26, Aristotle states that perceptibles are perceptible as long as perception is actually occurring and that they are in another way perceptible when they are not perceived (see Kirwan 1971: 165–6; Sorabji 1983: 90–1; Williams 1982: 67, 75; Welsch 1987: 95–8; and p. 25 above).

Analogous attempts to distinguish between various levels of possibilities or potentialities were not unusual in later ancient philosophy. One source for these debates was the theory of modality developed by Philo the dialectician, a pupil of Diodorus Cronus and a friend of Zeno who founded the Stoic school around 300 BC. Philo's definitions of modal concepts are described by Boethius as follows: (a) the possible is that which by the intrinsic nature of the sentence admits of truth; (b) the necessary is that which, when it is true, considered in itself, can never admit of falsity; (c) the non-necessary is that which, considered in itself, can admit of falsity; and (d) the impossible is that which by its intrinsic nature can never admit of truth (*In Periherm.* II, 234.10–21). According to Philo, it is possible for a piece of wood at the bottom of a sea to be burnt, in virtue of the fitness of the subject

(Simplicius, *In Aristotelis Cat. comm.* (CAG 8), 196.1; Alexander of Aphrodisias, *In Aristotelis An. pr. comm.* (CAG 2.1), 184.6–12; Philoponus, *In Aristotelis An. pr. comm.* (CAG 13.2), 169.19–20). The fitness of the subject seems to be a partial potency which can be claimed to exist in a subject even though it were only a second-level potency or a prevented first-level potency. Boethius' example of a Philonian possibility is 'I shall read the *Bucolics* of Theocritus again today'. He says that this, considered in itself, is possibly true, if no external circumstances prevent it (*In Periherm.* II, 234.13–15). If this remark is authentic, it seems that, according to Philo, one could say that things which are prevented from being actualized are possible, although they are not possible in another sense which requires that they are not prevented.

Some Stoics may have accepted Philo's theory of possibility, but according to the ancient sources, the more usual Stoic definition of possibility qualified Philo's definition by adding to the mere fitness the absence of external obstacles as a further prerequisite for something's being possible. The Stoics found it strange to say that something which is prevented from being realized is possible; they thought that such things are impossible. Their own theory, according to which determinism is compatible with possibilities which will not be realized, could be understood so that fate necessitates everything as a kind of active potency, but the number of passive potencies with respect to definite instants of time is greater than what will be realized. As long as they are not prevented by other things which will be actual at the moment with respect to which they are thought to be passive potencies, they in some sense represent open possibilities. It seems that the Stoics were interested in diachronic modalities (see the next section) and that the latter parts of the definitions of the necessary and the impossible refer, either inclusively or exclusively, to axioms or states of affairs which have begun to be necessary or impossible (see also Bobzien 1986: 68–71, 103–5). The picture is more problematic, however, because of the Stoic doctrine that of all possibilities only those which are determined to be realized can be realized, i.e. which are included in the cosmic program which repeats itself in eternally recurring cycles (cf. White 1985: 173–81). Other possibilities seem to be only partial possibilities which cannot be realized. And as already mentioned (p. 18), the critics claimed that the Stoic alternatives to what will take place were fictitious, because they were in fact always excluded from actualization, even though perhaps not prevented in some technical sense.

Referring to the constructed dispute between Diodorus Cronus and Chrysippus in Cicero's *De fato* 6.12–8.16, some authors have suggested that Chrysippus did not regard causal connections as logically necessary and that it is in a logical sense possible that future events are other than what they will be (White 1985: 102–6; for related views, see Sambursky 1971: 78–80; Frede 1974a: 88–9). The main problem in this view is the fact that the Stoic definitions of modalities do not contain synchronically alternative possibilities. Prospective alternative possibilities seem to be based on natural capacities which are not yet prevented by other things; such partial possibilities are not, however, contingent with respect to realization. (Engberg-Pedersen (1990: 207–34) has argued that the Stoics operated with two conceptions of the world and that one of them, 'God's conception', is deterministic and the other, 'the middle size conception', is not.)

Alexander of Aphrodisias claimed that the Stoic possibilities are merely subjective and epistemic: the Stoics thought that the opposites of the things which will take place by necessity are called possible when the causes are not known to us (*De fato* 176.14–24). Boethius describes the Stoic view of chance events in this way (*In Periherm.* II, 194.23–195.1), and he characterizes the Stoic conception of possibility as subjective in the sense that it refers only to general human abilities (ibid. 197.10–23). Many modern commentators have accepted the view that the Stoic notion of possibility is epistemic (see, for example, Faust 1931–2: 271; Long 1970; Sambursky 1971: 75–6; Talanga 1986: 116). This view is based on Alexander's remark and Boethius' description of the Stoic conception of chance. Some scholars have considered the evidence narrow (see Sharples 1983: 135).

## OTHER ANCIENT MODAL PARADIGMS

Many scholars have argued that, independently of what he thought about necessities and possibilities in connection with eternal things or types of powers, beings and events, Aristotle had a further model for discussing necessity and contingency of singular things, and that in this context he made use of what have been called diachronic modalities. In *Truth, Knowledge, and Modality* (1984: 96–103) von Wright delineates the distinction between diachronic and synchronic modalities as follows. The contingent truth $p$ at $t$ presupposes the antecedent possibility of $p$ at $t$ and its contradictory $-p$ at $t$: some time $t'$ before $t$ it was diachronically possible that $p$ at $t$ and it was possible that $-p$ at $t$. At $t$ both alternatives are synchronically possible, although only one of them can be actual at $t$. If a proposition $p$ at $t$ is true but not contingently so, its truth may be antecedently necessary 'sempiternally' or 'from the beginning of the world' (strong necessity) or from a certain time $t'$ before $t$ (weak necessity). Antecedent possibilities may get lost. If the proposition that $p$ at $t$ was antecedently possible and never lost its antecedent possibility, then it will be said to be, at $t$, in the strong sense possible. If the proposition that $p$ at $t$ has lost its antecedent possibility, it is at $t$ possible in the weak sense. Referring to the above model, von Wright has suggested that Aristotle's distinction between simple and qualified necessity in *De interpretatione* 19a23–7 could be understood as follows. The statement 'What is, necessarily is, when it is' seems to say something like

(5) $p_t \to L_t p_t$

or that, if $p$ at $t$, then it is necessary at $t$ that $p$ at $t$. That it is *simpliciter* necessary that $p$ at $t$ is symbolized by

(6) $Lp_t$.

According to von Wright, what Aristotle probably wanted to show was that the truth $p$ at $t$ does not imply (6), i.e. even if the truth $p$ at $t$ is necessary at $t$ owing to lack of the diachronic possibility that $-p$ at $t$, it does not need to be necessary in the sense that it would have been antecedently necessary (von Wright 1984: 72–8; 1979a; 1979c).

The idea of a prospective singular possibility is not explicitly mentioned in *De interpretatione* 19a23–7, but there are some other places where Aristotle seems to speak about genuine possibilities with respect to definite future moments which may remain unrealized or vanish (see *De interpretatione* 19a12–18; *Nicomachean Ethics* III.5, 1114a17–19). In *Metaphysics* VI.3 Aristotle tries to show that, even though the outcome of a particular causal chain is determined before it takes place, the causal chain does not necessarily go backwards infinitely. It may be broken by accidental connections not included in other causal chains. Although Aristotle usually treats the coincidental and the chance-like in statistical terms, without thereby excluding necessary causation (see *Metaphysics* V.30, VI.2; *Physics* II.5), here he seems to argue that an allegedly deterministic causal nexus can be interrupted by undetermined events and that some total individual possibilities may remain unrealized in particular cases. (*Metaphysics* VI.3 is discussed, for example, in Sharples (1975: 259–66), Hintikka *et al.* (1977: 107–17), Sorabji (1980: 3–25), Weidemann (1986a). For temporal prospective possibilities in Aristotle, see also Dancy (1981:

105–6), Seel (1982: 233–50), Vuillemin (1984: 27–57), Weidemann (1986b).)

The commentators have usually considered the role of diachronic modalities in Aristotle rather limited. An exception in this respect is Sarah Waterlow who, in her book *Passage and Possibility: A Study of Aristotle's Modal Concepts* (1982a), claims that Aristotle had a distinctive conception of possibility, which she calls relative temporalized possibility, and that this diachronic model was Aristotle's only conception of possibility (ibid.: 159). The main point in Waterlow's book is that in so far as Aristotle maintained principles like 'If it is possible that *p*, then at some time it is true that *p*' or 'If it is always the case that *p*, then it is necessary that *p*', this was not because of any special interpretation of modal concepts as such, but because of a combination of relative temporalized modalities with some non-modal metaphysical assumptions governing change and becoming in a universe of Aristotelian substances. The metaphysical postulates refer to generic features of the order of substances and regularly recurring states and fundamental processes of nature (ibid.: 65). The validity of the principle of plenitude and the corresponding principle of necessity is restricted to these spheres of reality.

I believe that in the passages mentioned above Aristotle had in mind the idea of diachronic possibilities in the sense of genuine individual possibilities which may remain unrealized. As Aristotle also thought that what is, necessarily is, when it is, he probably assumed that those prospective possibilities which remain unrealized cease to be possibilities, i.e. he made use of the model of diachronic possibilities without the idea of synchronic alternatives. Although this line of thought is not very central in Aristotle's works and although its philosophical details remain unarticulated, as Aristotle himself remarks in *Metaphysics* VI.3, 1027b14–16, it was considered important in the later Peripatetic tradition. When discussing the Stoic determinism, Alexander of Aphrodisias states that things in nature do not happen by necessity, because causes may be prevented from bringing about their effects in a few cases. This was the standard frequency approach to the coincident, but he also realized that something else is needed in meeting the thesis that individual events are embedded in a deterministic causal nexus. Alexander thought that *Metaphysics* VI.3 contained a theory that genuinely indeterminate occurrences may interrupt causal chains (see *De fato* VI, 169.28–170.12; VIII, 174.1–9, 25–8; IX, 175.7–13; *De anima mantissa*, in Sharples 1983: 94–7, 169.34–172.15; for Alexander's partially confused attempts to specify the nature of accidental events and uncaused motions, see Sharples 1983: 22, 132–6; White 1985: 140–68). The Stoics were also interested in diachronic possibilities and related temporal modalities; Alexander thought that it was misleading to speak in their manner about prospective alternatives which in fact cannot be realized.

Alexander of Aphrodisias' indeterministic theory of efficient causality, which took shape in the debate about Stoic views, is similar to what Boethius regarded as the Peripatetic view, and through Boethius' works this conception influenced the medieval picture of Aristotelian physics (see pp. 51 and 135 below). Questions of causal necessity play a more central role there than in Aristotle's writings, although they are not absent from the latter. In his natural philosophy, Aristotle accepted the received view that there are necessary mechanical interactions of the Democritean kind between the basic pairs of active and passive potencies, but he considered it more important to stress that one can see purposive and teleological structures in nature and that the more interesting and relevant notion of necessity in these contexts is that of teleological hypothetical necessity, i.e. the necessity of certain conditions, if a certain end is to be achieved.

What happens by necessity may be compulsory or in accordance with a thing's natural tendency, says Aristotle in *Posterior Analytics* II.11, 94b36–95a2; therefore one can say that 'by necessity a stone is borne both upwards and downwards, but not by the same necessity'. It may be this passage that Aristotle refers to in *De partibus* where the hypothetical necessity, understood as a third mode, is explained as follows:

> It may, however, be asked, which mode of necessity is meant by those who say 'of necessity'. For neither of those two modes which are set forth in our philosophical treatises can be present. There is, however, the third mode, in such things that have coming to be. For instance, we say that food is necessary in neither of the two modes, but because an animal cannot possibly do without it. This is as it were by hypothesis. For just as here is a necessity that the axe be hard, since one must cut with it, and, if hard, that it be of bronze or iron, so too since the body is an instrument – for both the body as a whole and its several parts are for the sake of something – if the end is to be, it must of necessity be of such and such a character, and made of such and such materials.
> (I.1, 642a3–13)

When Aristotle claims in some places that sublunar natural events are dominated by hypothetical necessity (see *Parts of Animals* I.1, 639b21–

640a10, 31–b4; *Physics* II.9; *De generatione et corruptione* II.11, 337b9–338a3), he seems to mean that Democritean necessities are embedded in an unchanging and everlasting order which itself is not a simple sum of necessitated actualizations of element-potentials (see the papers by J.M. Cooper, A. Gotthelf and D.M. Balme in Gotthelf and Lennox 1987: 204–85).

Plato equated the notions of chance and necessity while speaking about the movements of the pre-existing sensible stuff in the *Timaeus*. Its states, not regulated by any plan or design, occur only by necessity and chance. The domain of bare necessity was in Plato's opinion by no means able to provide any ordered universe. This was his criticism of the atomists' doctrine, according to which all events are reducible to the movements of indivisible particles and the necessary patterns of their interaction (*Timaeus* 46d–e, 47e–48b; *Laws* X, 888e–890b). There are some reminiscences of Plato's views in *Physics* II, 8–9, where Aristotle argues that it is incredible that the mechanically necessary movements of elements would yield the ordered universe of ours. It would be what it is only by chance and coincidence. One might ask why Aristotle says that things taking place by necessity and without teleology would take place by chance and spontaneity (198b12–29), as in the same context he also says that such things are unusual exceptions from the common course of events. The answer is that chance-like events are considered as exceptions from what is regulated by teleological patterns which in fact are responsible for the complicated developments in the world. It would not exist at all if basic necessities were without guidance (cf. Gotthelf 1987: 251–3; Cooper 1987: 251–3, 269–74).

Aristotle did not operate with a distinction between conceptual and natural modalities. He shared the general Platonist presupposition similar to the Parmenidean principle that what can be and what is intelligible are the same. It is reflected in Aristotle's methodological device that the order of learning is from the less intelligible by nature and more intelligible to us to what is more intelligible by nature (*Metaphysics* VII.2, 1029b1–12; *Topics* VI.4, 141b3–14; *Posterior Analytics* I.2, 71b33–72a5; *Physics* I.1, 184a16–26; *Nicomachean Ethics* I.4, 1095a30–b13). What is there to be found is an order of simple necessities, necessary properties of transient beings divided into species, teleological hypothetical necessities, mechanical necessities and probabilities in the sense of relative frequency. Plato and Aristotle thought that one can imagine a world less perfect and less intelligible, but not a better one, because all elements of optimal order are exemplified in the universe.

In the *The Great Chain of Being* Lovejoy (1936) presented Plato's metaphysics as an illustration of an approach in which the principle of plenitude is adopted without qualification. This thesis gave rise to a debate about whether there are empty forms in Plato or not. After a critical survey of recent studies, Michael Rohr argues in his paper 'Empty Forms in Plato' (1981) that there are no Platonic forms which have only forms as their instances and that some forms may be temporarily empty, but there are no forms which are never instantiated by any particulars. Aristotle gave up the theory of ideas, but, contrary to what Lovejoy claimed, his metaphysical view of the basic possibilities of being is not very different from that of Plato. In *Metaphysics* VII Aristotle stresses that substances are individual forms. Some commentators have claimed that Aristotle did not any longer use the idea of species forms or secondary substances at all in this treatise (Frede and Patzig 1988), while others have argued that they are considered real but not separate (see, for example, Irwin 1988). Aristotle seems to think that the form of a species could be characterized as a metaphysical possibility which, without being actual *qua* possibility, is actual as a plurality of singular forms of combined substances. These always actualized possibilities can be known, *qua* possibilities of being, through abstraction from the domain of beings and in this way they can also be actual in intellect (see *Metaphysics* VII.17, XIII.10, 1087a15–25).

Most of the ancient metaphysical thinkers entertained the thesis about the universe as a *plenum formarum* in which all possible kinds of things are exhaustively exemplified. It seems that no sharp distinction was drawn between the possible and the conceivable at this level. Some scholars have argued that perhaps Epicurus, as distinct from Lucretius, did not accept the principle of plenitude with respect to types of being (White 1985: 3–4), but neither atomists nor sceptics developed any remarkable theory of unrealized generic possibilities. Lovejoy considered Plotinus' neoplatonic theory of cosmic emanation as the most explicit formulation of the metaphysical form of the principle of plenitude. According to Plotinus, the first principle of being is the One, which as a superentity is beyond the bounds of being. The most perfect principle cannot remain shut up in itself, for it is the unjealous potency of all things (*dynamis pantōn*). 'It is flowing over and its plenitude gives birth to an Other' (*Enn.* V, 2.1.7–9, 4.1.34–6). Plotinus states that everywhere only actualization reveals a power which otherwise would stay hidden and, to be sure, turn out to be unreal. Therefore, the One as the potency of all things actualizes through an emanation all possibilities at different levels of being – it proceeds until it has realized everything that can be (*Enn.* IV, 8.5.33–5; 8.6.12–13; for Plotinus' modal views, see also Buchner 1970).

In so far as ancient authors, while speaking about the metaphysical structure of the universe, equated possibility and intelligibility with actuality, it was natural for them to think that the types of things which never occur are excluded from the domain of what can be. Natural invariances are then necessary and generic possibilities must prove their mettle through sometime actualization. Modal terms are here used in accordance with the statistical or temporal-frequency model, and Aristotle did so in the contexts in which he discussed eternal beings, the natures of things, the types of events, or generic sentences about these kinds of things. Modal terms refer in this approach to what takes place in the one and only world and its history. Correspondingly Aristotle was inclined to think that actualization is the criterion of the genuineness of all possibilities, although the deterministic implications of this view compelled him to search after ways of speaking about unrealized singular possibilities. Diodorus Cronus was a determinist and he did not find problems in giving modal terms an unqualified temporal-frequency interpretation.

Another Aristotelian modal paradigm was that of possibility as a potency. Even though the types of potency-based possibilities belonging to a species are recognized as possibilities because of their sometime actualization and the invariant patterns of interaction between basic potency pairs as natural necessities because of their invariance, the model allowed speaking about all kinds of singular unrealized possibilities by referring to second-order potentialities or to active or passive first-order potentialities. According to Aristotle, a dynamic possibility can be actualized only when the active and passive potency are in contact; the possibility is then necessarily realized, if there is no external hindrance. If partial possibilities cannot be realized without having first become full possibilities, only immediately realized possibilities seem to be genuine possibilities. Aristotle tried to find place for unrealized full possibilities *qua* possibilities through his theory of *kinēsis* as the actuality of the potentiality *qua* potentiality, but it did not help him more than offering place for instantaneous or durational full possibilities of what will be.

The difficulties of the potency model were connected with the fact that it was planned to explain how and why a change takes place. When a component of a full potency is lacking, the same model could be employed to explain why the change cannot take place, i.e. the existence of a merely partial potency is simultaneously the foundation of the possibility and impossibility of the same thing. In Philo's definition of possibility, the existence of a passive potency is considered as a sufficient ground for speaking about a possibility. When the Stoics revised this definition by adding the condition of the absence of external hindrance, thinking that otherwise the alleged possibility cannot be realized, they did not add that an activator is needed as well, because then the difference between potentiality and actuality would disappear. Many ancient writers remarked that it is strange to call such things possible which necessarily remain outside the causal nexus and cannot become actual.

When possibilities are treated as inherent active or passive capabilities which together can form full possibilities, they seem to be constitutionally conditional to the extent that the realization of relevant specifiable circumstances also bring about the realization of possibilities. The Stoics thought that although future events are necessitated, one can speak about alternative prospective possibilities as epistemic possibilities or as possibilities of states of affairs the immediate conditions of which are not yet fixed. This easily led to an intuitive model of diachronic temporal modalities; it is based on the idea that instead of constructing singular possibilities from their existing ingredients one can first assume them as alternative future options and then look at their ontological foundations. Alexander of Aphrodisias claimed that the Stoic doctrine implied that all future events have always been fixed and that the Stoics, as distinct from the Aristotelians, could not admit that there are real future alternatives. According to him, the Peripatetics think that there are genuine prospective alternatives which remain open options until the moment of time to which they refer. I think that in some places Aristotle referred to diachronic modalities of this kind. Neither he nor his followers developed the conception of synchronic alternatives, however. They thought that what is, necessarily is, when it is, and that the rest of alternative possibilities disappear at the moment at which one of them is realized. The Peripatetic theory of alternative prospective possibilities could be called the model of diachronic modalities without synchronic alternatives.

## MODAL LOGIC AND MODAL SYLLOGISTIC

Aristotle's syllogistic theory, as it is presented in the *Prior Analytics*, can be understood as an end result of the project described in the first lines of the *Topics* as follows: 'Our treatise proposes to find a method by which we shall be able to argue from reputable opinions about any subject presented to us, and shall ourselves, when putting forward an argument, avoid saying anything contrary to it.' Against this disputational background, it is natural to think that the new theory was created by identifying types or forms of arguments which, independently of the content of the premises, guaranteed that if the premises were granted, the conclusion could not be denied. Arguments fulfilling this requirement were called syllogisms. (This kind of interpretation is sketched in Kapp 1931; a partial English translation appears in Barnes *et al.* 1975: 35–49; see also Kapp 1943.)

Syllogisms discussed in the theory consist of two subject-predicate premises having one term (the middle) in common, and a conclusion conjoining the other two terms (the major and the minor). The premises and conclusions are either universal or particular: $A$ belongs to all $B$ ($AaB$), $A$ belongs to some $B$ ($AiB$), $A$ does not belong to any $B$ ($AeB$), or $A$ does not belong to some $B$ ($AoB$). The premises of assertoric syllogistic are non-modalized statements; in modal syllogisms at least one of the premises is either necessary or contingent. Three arrangements of the premise pairs are treated: in the first figure the middle term is the subject of the first premise and the predicate of the second premise, in the second figure it is the predicate of both premises and in the third figure the subject of both premises.

Aristotle thought that we immediately see which kinds of arguments are syllogisms in the first figure. He called these moods perfect, and the main part of the theory consisted in showing how the syllogistic moods of the second and the third figure can be reduced to the perfect first figure moods through conversions of the premises ($AiB \leftrightarrow BiA, AeB \leftrightarrow BeA$, and the so-called accidental conversion $AaB \rightarrow BiA$). The *reductio ad impossibile* and *ecthesis* are other inference schemes used in demonstrating that certain types of arguments in the second and third figure are syllogisms (for Aristotle's syllogistic in general, see Patzig 1968).

After the assertoric syllogistic, Aristotle discusses in Chapters 8–22 of the *Prior Analytics* the syllogistic moods with premises modalized as follows: $LL$, $LA$, $AL$, $CC$, $CA$, $AC$, $CL$ and $LC$ ($L$ stands for a necessary premise, $C$ for a contingent premise, and $A$ for an assertoric premise). The notion of contingency is defined so that what is contingent is neither necessary nor impossible (*Prior Analytics* I.13, 32a18–20). In some cases the conclusion is said to be possible ($M$) in the sense that it is not impossible (see, for example, *Prior Analytics*

I.15, 33b28–33, 34b27–31), but the syllogistic logic of this possibility proper is not discussed.

The purpose of the modal syllogistic seems to be to show how the modal status of the conclusion is determined by the modalized premises in arguments the assertoric counterparts of which are syllogisms. The general structure of the theory is analogous to the assertoric syllogistic. According to Aristotle, the conversion of necessary statements is similar to the conversion of assertoric statements, and the same holds true of the conversion of affirmative contingent statements. Negative contingent statements are convertible in the same way as affirmative contingent statements (*Prior Analytics* I.3).

It has been suggested that Aristotle, while discussing the perfect assertoric moods, refers to a figure or diagram not included in the text (see, for example, *Prior Analytics* I.4, 25b35–7). The figure could have been as follows:

A  ─────────────
B  ──────────
C  ───────  .

(See Einarson 1936; Ross, in Aristotle, *Prior and Posterior Analytics* 301–2.) The lines express the generality of the terms (major, middle, minor). In *Prior Analytics* I.1, 24b26–8, it is said that for one term to be in another as in a whole is the same as for the other to be predicated of all of the first. Taking this as a partial interpretation of the diagram, it can be regarded as an illustration of the transitivity of class-inclusion, which makes the validity of the first figure moods, say *Barbara*, obvious: 'If $A$ is predicated of every $B$ and $B$ of every $C$, $A$ must be predicated of every $C$.' In *Celarent* and *Ferio* the first line represents a lack of $A$.

If the statement '$A$ belongs necessarily to all $B$' is read as 'the class of those things which are necessarily $A$ includes the class of those things which are $B$', the lines in the above diagram could be interpreted as standing for necessary terms. 'Necessarily $B$' is a part of the line $B$, and 'necessarily $C$' is a part of the line $C$. It is directly seen that the following combinations of the premises yield perfect moods corresponding to the first figure assertoric moods: *LLL, LAL, ALA*. The same holds, *mutatis mutandis*, of two mixed contingent cases: *CAC* and *CLC*. The three remaining cases with a contingent minor premise are more problematic because of the different possibilities of locating the lines '$B$' and 'contingently $B$' in the same diagram. In *Prior Analytics* I.14, 32b25–32, Aristotle says that the contingent premises could be read like this: '$A$ contingently belongs to all to which *B* contingently belongs.' If this is applied to the first premises of the first figure *CCC* moods, the diagram matches them. The remaining first figure mixed moods with contingent minor premises Aristotle himself treated as imperfect.

The main interpretational problems of Aristotle's syllogistic concern the general purpose of the theory, the sense of the word 'necessarily' attached to the conclusions of assertoric syllogisms, the readings of modalized premises and conclusions, and some apparent inconsistencies in modal syllogistic. The first and the second problem are connected with the question, much debated since Jan Łukasiewicz's *Aristotle's Syllogistic* (1951), whether Aristotle's syllogisms or syllogistic moods are inference rules or conditionals. Although there is a flavour of anachronism in the opposite theses of this controversy, the discussion has enlarged consciousness of the problems connected with historical reconstructions of Aristotle's logic. (For discussions of the controversy, see Frede 1974b: 15–20; Corcoran 1974: 85–132; Lear 1980; Seel 1982: 215–18; van Rijen 1989: 36–50.)

Instead of entering into the details of this topic here, I shall refer to an often commented passage which may shed some light on syllogistic necessity. In *Prior Analytics* I.10, 30b31–40, Aristotle tries to show that a *Camestres* type of argument with an apodeictic major premise, an assertoric minor premise and an apodeictic conclusion is not a syllogism. Referring to an example, Aristotle says that its assertoric conclusion is necessary *toutōn ontōn*, although the conclusion is not necessary *haplōs*. The *toutōn ontōn* necessity of a conclusion can be understood as the necessity by which anybody is bound to concede the conclusion after having conceded the premises (cf. *Posterior Analytics* I.6, 75a18–27). If a syllogistic argument contains modalized premises in virtue of which the conclusion is determined to be necessary or contingent, it is necessary relative to the premises that the conclusion is necessary or contingent. Aristotle probably connected the obviousness of the argumentative necessity of syllogistic conclusions with the transitivity of the class-inclusion mentioned above. When the relative necessity of the conclusion is thus based on an essential feature of the class model, arguments with terms arranged in accordance with it are necessarily syllogisms (*Prior Analytics* I.4, 25b32–5).

In the *Prior Analytics* only some scanty and vague remarks are made about the structure of modalized premises. The variety of the possible readings of a necessary premise can be illustrated in terms of modern symbolic logic as follows:

(7) $L(x)(Ax \to Bx)$
(8) $(x)L(Ax \to Bx)$
(9) $(x)(Ax \to LBx)$
(10) $(x)(MAx \to LBx)$
(11) $(x)(LAx \to LBx)$.

The problem that faces interpreters is that none of the forms of the list which could be continued are uniformly applicable to Aristotle's theory. The situation is further complicated by the fact that in Aristotle's other works one can find various suggestions about the meanings of modal notions (cf. Hintikka 1973: 135-46).

Since Becker's study of Aristotle's modal syllogistic, first published in 1933, there have been many similar attempts at rational reconstructions through choosing some syntactic or semantic principles as the presuppositions on which the theory is built (see Becker 1933; McCall 1963; Rescher 1964; Wieland 1966, 1972, 1975; Schmidt 1989; van Rijen 1989: 185-218; Patterson 1989). As for the coherence of the theory, the results have not been very satisfactory. It has been argued that the reason for this failure is the fact that Aristotle's modal syllogistic is based on different kinds of insights which are not compatible, even though as such they may embody valid ideas (Hintikka 1973: 135-46, 1978: 48-65; see also Smith 1989: 121-2). This was the result of Becker's study as well. According to him, the premises of modal syllogisms are read *de re* (9) and the modal conversion rules are read *de dicto* (7). Becker thought that Aristotle failed to draw a systematic distinction between these types of modal sentences. The above model with lines may explain why it was natural for Aristotle to treat first figure modal syllogisms in a way akin to *de re* reading, but it is clear that the same model cannot be extended to modal conversion rules. (For the question of the use of diagrams in this context, see also Kneale and Kneale 1962: 102.)

On the basis of what Alexander of Aphrodisias and some other ancient writers tell about the views of Aristotle's pupils, it seems that Theophrastus and Eudemus attempted to modify modal syllogistic as follows: modal premises should be read *de dicto* rather than *de re* and the conclusion has the same character as the weaker of the premises. It has been claimed that, according to them, the notion of possibility should be that of possibility proper, but this is less clear (see Becker 1933: 65-7; Bocheński 1956: 116-18; Kneale and Kneale 1962: 101-5; Graeser 1973: 47, 72-8, 87-8).

While discussing the imperfect first figure modal syllogisms with an assertoric major premise and a problematic minor premise, Aristotle formulated the principle: 'If when *A* is, *B* must be, then when *A* is possible, *B* must be possible' (*Prior Analytics* I.15, 34a5–7). On the basis of this, he describes syllogisms as follows: 'If someone were to put the premises as *A* and the conclusion as *B*, it would not only follow that *B* is necessary, if *A* is necessary, but also that *B* is possible, if *A* is possible' (34a22–4). These rules, together with the definitions of interrelations between modal notions presented in various places, embody a virtually exhaustive insight into the basic modal propositional logic. Without entering into the details of Aristotle's partially confused discussions of the structure, conversion and negation of modal sentences and his remarks on the interrelations between the necessary, the impossible and the possible (*De interpretatione* 12–13, *Metaphysics* V.5, 12; *Prior Analytics* I.3, 13, 15; Hintikka 1973: 27–61), I formulate some of the basic modal connections Aristotle takes for granted in the places just mentioned (see also van Rijen 1989: 17–27).

(12) $Lp \leftrightarrow -M-p$
(13) $-Mp \leftrightarrow L-p$
(14) $Mp \leftrightarrow -L-p$
(15) $Cp \leftrightarrow (Mp \ \& \ M-p)$
(16) $Cp \leftrightarrow C-p$.

In addition to these, Aristotle mentions in *De interpretatione* 13 the modal principles

(17) $Lp \to p$
(18) $p \to Mp$
(19) $Lp \to Mp$.

Modal rules from *Prior Analytics* I.15 are similar to the important rules of inference

(20) $\dfrac{L(p \to q)}{Lp \to Lq}$

and

(21) $\dfrac{L(p \to q)}{Mp \to Mq}$.

In *Metaphysics* IX.4, 1047b14–30, Aristotle connects (21) with the characterization of potentiality in *Metaphysics* IX.3, 1047a24–6, which is an application of the definition in *Prior Analytics* I.13, 32a18–20. If the definition of possibility proper is formulated as

(22) $Mp \rightarrow -[L(p \rightarrow q) \& (-Mq)]$,

it is equivalent to

(23) $L(p \rightarrow q) \rightarrow (Mp \rightarrow Mq)$.

Aristotle did not develop his general remarks on modal logic. Some later discussions of (12)–(19) are summarized by Boethius (*In Periherm.* II, 384–394). Principles like (23) and the corresponding principles for necessity and impossibility

(24) $L(p \rightarrow q) \rightarrow (Lp \rightarrow Lq)$
(25) $L(p \rightarrow q) \rightarrow (-Mq \rightarrow -Mp)$

were well known and often used in ancient times, partly because something like (23) or (25) occurred as the second premise of the Master Argument. Some discussions of the nature of necessity also occurred in connection with the controversies about conditionals. Sextus Empiricus refers in several places to a debate between Diodorus Cronus and Philo; Philo seems to have treated conditionals as material implications while Diodorus demanded that sound conditionals should be necessary in the sense of his frequency interpretation of necessity, i.e. never false. Of the different theories described by Sextus Empiricus M. Kneale associates the Stoics with the one according to which 'a conditional is sound when the contradictory of its consequent is incompatible with its antecedent' (Kneale and Kneale 1962: 128–38, 159).

# 2 Philosophical and theological modalities in early medieval thought

In the first section of this chapter I shall discuss the role of ancient modal paradigms in Boethius' works which greatly influenced early medieval thought. I then analyse the confrontation between philosophical and theological modalities in the eleventh century and its connections to Augustine's interpretation of God's freedom and power. Augustine's theology was the main source for the reflected view that Catholic doctrine demands some new ways of thinking about necessity and possibility. Anselm of Canterbury tried to develop a modal semantics which could be applied to theological matters as well, but his project remained unfinished. In the third section I shall show how Gilbert of Poitiers and Peter Abelard, two very different twelfth-century thinkers, made efforts to add the idea of possibilities as synchronic alternatives to traditional modal conceptions, thus bringing a new theoretical element to Western modal thought. I end the section with a short remark on the use of modal terms in twelfth-century Platonic thought.

## BOETHIUS' MODAL CONCEPTIONS

Anicius Manlius Severinus Boethius (480–524), who has been called 'the last of the Romans' or 'the first of the scholastics', intended to translate all the works of Plato and of Aristotle into Latin. Only part of the task was accomplished, namely the translations of Aristotle's logical works. It was mainly through Boethius' translations of Aristotle's *Categories* and *De interpretatione* and through his translation of Porphyry's introduction (*Isagoge*) to *Categories*, that people became acquainted with ancient logical texts until the early twelfth century. Boethius wrote commentaries on Aristotle's *Categories*, *De interpretatione* and *Topics* (lost since antiquity), on Porphyry's *Isagoge*, on Cicero's *Topica*, and possibly glosses to the

*Prior Analytics*. In addition, he wrote logical treatises, *Introductio ad syllogismos categoricos*, *De syllogismis categoricis*, *De hypotheticis syllogismis*, *De topicis differentiis* and *De divisione*. Boethius' works also include books on arithmetic and music, five short theological treatises and the *Philosophiae consolatio*, one of the most well-known classics of philosophy.

Boethius' two commentaries on Aristotle's *De interpretatione*, and his *Philosophiae consolatio*, contain detailed discussions of possibility and necessity. His remarks on modal notions are based mainly on traditional paradigms, which in this way became familiar in early medieval thought. Although Boethius did not introduce any really new modal ideas, he formulated some questions and conceptions in a way which strongly influenced later medieval discussions. Boethius' commentaries on Aristotle's works are based partially on the same patterns, now for the most part lost, as Greek commentaries written at the same time. They are not simply translations of marginalia as suggested by Shiel (1958). Boethius seems to have made extensive use of Porphyry's works, and it is probable that he also used Porphyrian treatises as models for his own logical works. (For Boethius' works and their sources, see Chadwick 1981; Obertello 1981; Gibson 1981b; Ebbesen 1987; and the introductory chapters in Stump 1978, 1988.)

One of the Aristotelian modal paradigms occurring in Boethius is that of possibility as a potency (*potestas*, *potentia*, *cognatio*). According to Boethius, when the term 'possibility' (*possibilitas*) is applied in the sense of a 'potency', it refers to real powers or tendencies, the ends of which are either actual or non-actual at the moment of utterance. Some potencies are never unrealized; their nature is such that they are always actual, and, as such, they are necessarily actual. When potencies are not actualized, their ends are said to exist potentially (*potestate*) (see *In Periherm.* II, 453.8–455.19). Necessarily actual potencies do not leave any room for potencies of their contraries. There are no contrary potencies in these cases, Boethius says, because they would remain unrealized forever and the constitution of nature cannot include elements which would be in vain ('novimus nihil proprium natum frustra naturam solere perficere') (ibid. II, 236.11–18; cf. 243.13–15). It is clearly implied here that all natural types of potencies must prove their mettle through actualization.

The potencies of non-necessary features of being do not exclude contrary potencies. They are not always and universally actualized in the things to which they belong, but as potency-types even these

Early medieval modalities 47

potencies are taken to fulfil the above-mentioned criterion of genuineness:

> Things which neither always are nor always are not, but sometimes are and sometimes are not, have a certain cognation to contraries just because they at some time are and at some time are not. These are between necessary and impossible things.
> (*In Periherm.* II, 237.1–5; cf. I, 120.24–121.16)

Although Boethius thought that all the potencies of species and all the species of potencies are sometimes actualized, he also stressed that, when speaking about individuals, we can refer to potencies which remain unrealized. This is shown by Aristotelian examples such as 'This cloth can be cut up, but it can also wear out', 'This stick can be broken, but it can also remain unbroken', or by referring to alternative possible deeds (see, for example, ibid. I, 106.11–14, 120.9–16, 201.7–8; II, 190.24–191.2, 197.20–3, 207.18–25, 236.22–4, 237.21–238.1, 240.8–14). Even if natural species are not provided with capacities or dispositions which would remain unrealized and hence be of no use in the common course of nature, the individual members of a species do not necessarily embody actualizations of all the possibilities belonging to their species. The idea of unrealized natural possibilities was important to Boethius because he thought that it could be employed in refuting the Stoic doctrine of universal determinism. (Boethius says in many places that the domain of causal necessity is restricted by free choice, chance and possibility. See Kretzmann (1985: 28–9).) Let us have a more careful look at Boethius' attempts to delineate potencies and possibilities which remain unrealized.

In the longer commentary on *De interpretatione*, Boethius sketches in one passage the metaphysical background of the conception of possibility as a potency. According to him, prime matter can be understood as a universal receptacle. The invariant system of nature, consisting of substances and their necessary and contingent characteristics, is built upon prime matter. In this sense, all composed things are actualizations of an ultimate passive potency. The general receptivity of prime matter is structured into the fixed patterns of passive natural potencies (*In Periherm.* II, 238.9–239.12). Passive potencies which are not always actualized cannot actualize themselves; they need an activating principle (ibid. 238.25–6). And because generic natural potencies cannot exist in vain, we are obliged to think that there are corresponding efficient causes or active potencies which at least sometimes turn them into actuality.

As far as Boethius speaks about natural possibilities as generic passive capacities, one easily understands that they may in singular instances remain unactualized. (One could ask, to be sure, why this does not prove that they exist in vain in those individuals.) These unrealized possibilities cannot be played off against causal determinism, however, because they remain unactualized owing to the lack of an activating cause; i.e. when they are unactualized, they cannot be actualized. This was a traditional problem contained in the potency model in which possibilities are identified with various constituents of generic states of affairs (see pp. 26–9 above). All kinds of partial potentialities (affinities, active or passive potencies, abilities, capacities) can remain unrealized, but their status as possibilities is vague, because they cannot be realized without something extra being added to them. Total potencies, which are the only ones that can be actualized, seem to be realized immediately, and so the difference between possibility and actuality tends to disappear.

It is clear from what has been said that Boethius speaks mainly about potencies as generic tendencies or dispositions. Dispositions which are not actualized represent the potential existence of their ends. They are, so to say, actualities minus certain circumstances. Boethius did not pay much attention to Aristotle's attempts to spell out the interactive structure of active and passive potencies in singular cases nor to the idea of finding a place for unrealized full potentialities in processes understood as actualities of potentialities *qua* potentialities. He was inclined to treat potencies as unanalysed generic possibilities of being and action, and in this sense he could also speak about eternally and necessarily actualized potencies. Aristotle did not call these eternal states of affairs actualizations of potencies or potentialities.

Following his sources, Boethius also connected the discussion of potencies to the themes of Stoic physics. While writing the commentaries on Aristotle's *De interpretatione*, he considered himself an Aristotelian indeterminist and criticized the Stoic view that fate as a causal nexus totally determines the future. When Boethius said that Stoic determinism did away with possibility (e.g. *In Periherm.* II, 218.21–3), he did not mean that it did away with partial potencies or possibilities. He seems to have thought that the Philonian definition of possibility as an internal natural disposition, as well as its Stoic revision to the effect that the disposition should not be prevented by external conditions from being realized, were misleading partial definitions or definitions of only partial potencies. Unlike the Diodorean ones, these definitions did not equate possibility with what is or what will be, but they were compatible with a theory of causal chains which necessitate all natural events (ibid. II, 234.10–235.22). Boethius was not satisfied with this kind of compatibilism, and he tried to develop the potency model of possibility in an indeterministic direction.

What did Boethius mean by 'free choice', 'chance' and 'possibility' when discussing Stoic philosophy? Boethius was himself quite ready to believe that the passive and active conditions of a great number of events determine the events by chains of causes which go back in time beyond these changes (see, for example, ibid. II, 193.6–21, 202. 25–203.2, 223.15–23; *Phil. cons.* IV, 6.13; V, 1.19). In such cases the causal chains force the events to take place (*violentia necessitatis*; *In Periherm.* II, 221.30, 223.17). This causal necessity is restricted, however, by acts of free choice, Boethius says, because our decisions and their consequences are not determined by external forces (ibid. II, 195.4–10, 231.5–11). Free choice is an actualizing agency outside the causal chains in nature, and its acts cannot be characterized by the notion of a necessity which refers to the chain of causal necessity (*catena necessitatis*; ibid. II, 246.5–19).

Freedom from external determination does not *eo ipso* mean that the acts of will are connected with genuine alternative possibilities. Perhaps the acts of free choice are internally determined. Indeed, the idea of freedom as mere absence of external constraints was not unusual in ancient thought. Augustine, for example, says that even though people cannot determinate the theologically relevant direction of their will, the *liberum arbitrium* is, nevertheless, in operation when those chosen to be saved love God and those determined to the fires of hell act in a way which deserves punishment (see, for example, *De spiritu et littera* 3.5, 5.7, 8.13; *Epistulae* 217 *ad Vit.*, *CSEL* 57, 416; *Contra duas epistolas pelagianorum* I, 2, 5; cf. Wolfson 1961: 158–76 and, for a more detailed discussion of Augustine's view of the freedom of will, Kirwan 1989: 82–128). A related view can be found in Boethius' *Philosophiae consolatio*. In Book IV he asserts that within God's mind there is a detailed plan of the world and its history. As a divine thought, it is called providence. The providential plan is unfolded in the course of time and this dynamic aspect of providence is called fate (*Phil. cons.* IV, 6.7–10). Fate imposes an order of necessity on things which otherwise would fluctuate at random (ibid. IV, 6.18–21, 54–6). It works through causal chains, and Boethius thought that freedom of the will is preserved by claiming that the souls of good men can ascend to higher spheres where their choices are not determined by fate (ibid. V, 2.1–11).

Although their acts of will are not causally necessitated, they cannot be other than what is included in providence (ibid. V, 6.25–36). Boethius thought that this 'conditional' necessity did not violate freedom of the will, apparently because it did not externally constrain the will. This as such is not very far from the Stoic concept of freedom as voluntariness (cf. *In Periherm.* II, 196.3–5). But Boethius includes something more in his notion of freedom. As will be seen, he tried to develop in connection with the concept of contingency the idea of alternative possible courses of action as temporary prospective options, i.e. options which cease to exist as possibilities after a time. Some formulations of this diachronic model are connected with discussions of free choice (see, for example, ibid. II, 207.18–23; *Phil. cons.* V, 6.32).

Boethius treated chance events mainly as unintended outcomes of action arising from free choice. Chance events were relevant in this context because of the Stoic claim that, contrary to what people believe, they are embedded in the totality of the previous chains of necessitated states (*In Periherm.* II, 194.2–195.2). Boethius could exercise his concept of free choice here and maintain that actions preceding a chance event could have remained undone and that chance coincidences of causal chains were not determined before the choices (ibid. II, 224.2–9). A. A. Cournot, a well known nineteenth-century probability theorist, referred to Boethius and Thomas Aquinas as historical predecessors when presenting his view of randomness as the intersection of independent series of causes. (For the philosophical background of Cournot's theory of chance and probability, see Engel 1988: 196–202, 226–7.) Boethius seems to consider it essential, however, that there are new beginnings in the area of causal chains. Even though chance events may in a sense be meetings of independent causal chains, Boethius stressed that at least one of these chains must lead back to an initiating member which has no causal relation to anything previous to it. This is an indeterminate act of will. With respect to any chance event there was a time at which the event was not yet potentially included in reality through its causes. (For Boethius' concept of chance events see, for example, *In Ciceronis Topica*, PL 64, 1150–5, translated in Stump 1988: 160–6; and Kretzmann 1985.) Boethius probably changed his view on chance later; he maintains in *Phil. cons.* V, 1.11–19, that chance events are unexpected occurrences included in an inevitable causal order.

In addition to chance and free choice, Boethius considered possibility as a third mode of the Aristotelian *ad utrumlibet* contingency given up in Stoic determinism:

Now according to the Aristotelian doctrine, that is contingent which chance brings, or which comes from anyone's free choice and his own will, or which in virtue of a readiness of nature it is possible to bring into both parts – viz., that it happen and that it not happen.
(*In Periherm.* II, 190.1–6, translated in Kretzmann 1985: 29)

Norman Kretzmann has argued that free choice is the only real source for contingency in Boethius (ibid.: 39). Even though free choice certainly was the source of contingency in which Boethius was mainly interested, he preserved the notion of possibility in the list of the modes of *ad utrumlibet* contingency, probably thinking that, according to the Peripatetic doctrine, there is a real factor of indeterminacy in the causal nexus of nature due to which natural events are not causally necessary without qualification. In a few cases the causes may be prevented from their effects by accidental hindrances, and these cases do not have antecedent necessitating causes in the causal chains of events (see *In Periherm.* II, 197.18–198.3). Boethius refers to the Stoic view that chance events are postulated only because we do not always know the causal network well enough (ibid. II, 194.23–195.2). In the same way as when treating this charge he tried to argue against the Stoic notion of possibility, which he describes as a subjective capacity, by referring to the objective indeterminacy of some singular natural events (ibid. II, 197.10–23). Boethius seems to be conscious of some Peripatetic attempts to develop Aristotle's remarks about the bounds of causal chains (in *Metaphysics* VI.3) into a theory of genuinely indeterminate natural possibilities. His descriptions of these possibilities remain vague, however, as did those of Alexander of Aphrodisias (see pp. 33–4).

Another Boethian conception of necessity and possibility, sometimes intertwined with the potency model, is the Aristotelian statistical interpretation of modality. It is based on the view that modal notions can be regarded as tools for expressing temporal or generic frequencies. According to the temporal version of this model, what always is, is by necessity, and what never is, is impossible. Possibility is interpreted as expressing what is at least sometimes actual (*In Periherm.* I, 200.27–201.3; II, 237.1–5, 239.3–6). Correspondingly, a property which belongs to all members of a group is a necessary property. If it is not actual at all in that group, it is impossible; and if it is exemplified at least in one member, it is possible (ibid. I, 120.27–121.16). In connection with the temporal version, Boethius made a distinction between simple and conditional necessity: the former notion signifies uniform actuality without any temporal limits, and the latter refers to permanence during a given period (ibid. I, 121.25–122.4; II, 241.1–242.3; *De hypotheticis syllogismis* 236–8, *PL* 64, 840).

The statistical model occurs in Boethius' theory of the truth of sentences as follows. Like Aristotle, Boethius often treated statement-making utterances as temporally indeterminate sentences having an implicit or explicit reference to the moment of utterance (now) as a part of their meaning. The same sentence can be uttered at different times, and many of these temporally indeterminate sentences may be sometimes true and sometimes false, depending on the circumstances at the moment of utterance. If the state of affairs, the actuality of which makes the sentence true, is omnitemporally actual, the sentence is true whenever it is uttered. In this case, it is necessarily true. If the state of affairs of an assertoric sentence is always non-actual, the sentence is always false and therefore impossible. A sentence is possible only if what is asserted is not always non-actual. This line of thought is included in the following passage from Boethius' shorter commentary on Aristotle's *De interpretatione*:

> Things which are not always existent and which are not always non-existent are the only things for which it is contingent to be and not to be. If they namely were always existent, their state could not change and, therefore, they would be necessarily existent; on the other hand, if they were always non-existent, they would be necessarily non-existent. For as the nature of things which happen varies, so one or the other part of a pair of contradictory propositions has a variable truth. One of them is always true or false, but not in such a definite way that this or that is determinately true, but one or the other. As the state of the things is changeable, so the truth or falsity of propositions is doubtful and it may be that in some cases one part is more frequently true but not always true and the other part is less frequently true but it is not necessarily false.
>
> (*In Periherm.* I, 124.30–125.14)

When Boethius applies the distinction between simple and conditional necessity to sentences, he classes sentences about simple necessities as 'immutably necessary sentences' (ibid. II, 187.8–24), and these are distinct from sentences about conditionally necessary states of affairs, delineated as follows:

> There are other propositions which, without signifying eternal

Early medieval modalities 53

matters, are necessary as long as the things exist about which the proposition asserts or denies something, e.g., when I say 'Man is mortal', as long as man exists, it is necessary that man is mortal. If namely one says: 'Fire is hot', the proposition is necessarily true as long as fire exists.

(*In Periherm.* II, 187.24–188.2)

The idea of determining the modal status of a type sentence by referring to its behaviour at different moments of time, i.e. to its changing or unchanging truth or falsity, yields one form of the statistical model of modality. If it is applied to sentences with a temporally definite index or to type sentences at the moment of their utterance, those sentences will be necessarily true if true and necessarily false if false. Jaakko Hintikka (1973) has suggested that the real background of Aristotle's troubles in his discussion of the future sea fight (*De interpretatione* 9) was precisely this corollary of the statistical model. According to Hintikka, one of the ways in which Aristotle tried to avoid this sort of determinism was to shift the scope of attention from temporally determinate events or sentences to their temporally indeterminate counterparts, which may be contingent. Whatever Aristotle meant by his thesis 'What is, necessarily is, when it is, but not without qualification', Hintikka's interpretation codifies at least one of the ways in which it was read in ancient philosophy. Boethius's comment on *De interpretatione* 19a23–7, in the shorter version of his commentary, runs as follows:

> If a thing necessarily is, when it is, it is not therefore necessarily *simpliciter* and without reference to the present moment. For example, when I am sitting, it cannot be the case that I am not sitting, and it is necessary that I am sitting when I am sitting. However, to be sitting does not apply to me by necessity; I can also stand up.
> 
> (*In Periherm.* I, 121.25–122.4)

The necessity by which a sitting Socrates sits when he sits is called temporal necessity (ibid. I, 121.20) or, as in the longer commentary, conditional necessity (ibid. II, 241.7–243.27). Boethius' example of simple necessity is the motion of sun, of which he says that 'it is not because the sun is moved now, but because it will always be moved, that there is necessity in its motion'. A conditional necessity, like Socrates' sitting, is similarly necessary as long as its condition is actual. 'It is not possible that somebody could be sitting and not sitting at the same time, and therefore nobody who is sitting can be not sitting at the time when he is sitting' (ibid. II, 241.1-13). It is thought here that because

(1) $M(p_t \ \& \ -p_t)$

is not acceptable, one should also deny

(2) $p_t \ \& \ M_t \ -p_t$.

The denial of (2) is equivalent to

(3) $p_t \rightarrow L_t p_t$.

This line of thought is natural only when possibilities are treated without an idea of synchronic alternatives. As has been seen above, (2) was generally denied in ancient philosophy. Even though Boethius in some places made use of the model of diachronic prospective possibilities, he did not develop the idea of simultaneous synchronic alternatives. The comments on temporal or conditional necessity in the commentaries on *De interpretatione* 9 seem to be based, however, on the temporal-frequency model of modality.

The main point in Boethius' discussion of the distinction between simple and temporal or conditional necessity is that the latter does not imply the former (*In Periherm.* II, 241.20-2). It is true to say about a sitting marble Socrates that it is sitting by necessity without qualification; as for the living Socrates, he is sitting necessarily at the times when he sits, but not without qualification (ibid. 242.24-243.4). If the temporal condition (*condicio temporis*) is separated from the sentence pertaining to living Socrates, it becomes false (ibid. 242.1-3). The whole distinction seems to be reduced to one between what is invariant *simpliciter* and what is invariant in a definite period of time.

The conception of temporal necessity, as Boethius describes it in the texts quoted, can be understood as a special case of the statistically interpreted simple necessity. A predicate may sometimes be inherent in a subject and sometimes not, although at any definite moment of time it unchangeably belongs to it or does not belong to it. From the point of view of a temporally indeterminate approach, the temporal necessity or impossibility of momentary instantiations is a relatively harmless incident which does not affect the generic contingency. But the philosophical question which vexed Boethius concerned whether everything happens by necessity, so that the temporal necessity of what is, when it is, is no more an innocent side-effect of the statistical approach. As an indeterminist, Boethius was committed to maintaining that some events are not necessary; referring to what happens at other times or in other circumstances is then irrelevant *vis-à-vis* the alleged necessity of present and future singular events. Furthermore, it may be reasonable to suppose that the sentences about future contingent events are true or false omnitemporally. When all true sentences about contingent singular events then are also true whenever uttered, they seem, according to Boethius' statistical necessity, to be necessarily true. Let us see whether Boethius had anything more to offer here than what seems to be included in the texts quoted above: a philosophically unsatisfactory habit of changing the focus from problematic temporally determinate events and sentences to their temporally indeterminate counterparts.

When discussing the truth and falsity of future contingent sentences, Boethius formulated some distinctions which he considered relevant. Let us have a look at the following passage from the longer commentary on *De interpretatione*:

> Some people, the Stoics among them, believed that Aristotle said that contingent propositions about future events are neither true nor false. When he said that they are no more related to being than to not being, they took him to mean that there is no point in considering them true or false, for they thought that they are neither true nor false. But this is false, for Aristotle does not say that both [of the members of contradiction] are neither true nor false, but that each one of them is either true or false, yet not in a definite way like propositions about past or present matters. Rather, statement-making utterances [in contradictory pairs] are somehow of a twofold nature; some are not only true and false, but such that one of them is definitely true and the other is definitely false; others are such that one is true and the other is false, but in an indefinite way and changeably, due to their own nature and not to our ignorance or knowledge.
> (*In Periherm*. II, 208.1–18)

The interesting thing here is that Boethius wants to include all sentences about future contingencies in the last group which is described in a very similar way in the shorter commentary:

> For as the nature of things which happen varies, so one or the other part of a pair of contradictory propositions has a variable truth. One of them is always true or false, but not in such a definite way that this or that is determinately true, but one or the other. As the state of things is changeable, so the truth or falsity of propositions is doubtful.
> (*In Periherm*. I, 125.5–11)

What is said here could be summarized as follows. Although it holds for each moment of time that the members of a contradiction divide between themselves the two truth-values, the division is not always made in the same way in a pair of contingent sentences. How does this statistical idea elucidate the nature of a pair of contradictory sentences referring to a singular future event? When explicitly discussing one such case, Boethius gives the following answer:

> As that which is, necessarily is, when it is, but not *simpliciter* without a temporal qualification, so in a pair of contradictory contingent propositions the affirmation or the negation is necessarily true, but neither the affirmation *simpliciter* and in a definite way nor the negation, but whichever of them is made certainly true through the event.
>
> (*In Periherm.* I, 123.29–124.7)

One gets the impression, right or wrong, that temporally determinate sentences about future events are first translated into temporally indeterminate sentences which can be labelled as contingent in a straightforward way. Statistical contingency is then considered as a qualification of the manner in which temporally determinate sentences are true. Temporally determinate sentences which are once true are always true, and it is their mode of being always true which Boethius tries to qualify, thus attempting to avoid the conclusion that they would be necessarily true *simpliciter*. The mutability with respect to truth and falsity, belonging to temporally indeterminate sentences about contingent events or states of affairs, is proved by real changes of truth-values. Nothing of this sort happens to temporally determinate sentences. Does Boethius call their truth or falsity mutable only because of some sort of systematic confusion? (Cf. Knuuttila 1981a: 177–8; as for the problematic term '*commutabiliter*', see also Mignucci 1989: 69–70.)

Boethius thought that the Diodorean definition of possibility as that which is or will be does not have deterministic implications if applied to types of events and to corresponding temporally indeterminate sentences. This line of thought figures in Boethius' discussion of the truth of future contingent sentences, but this is not the whole story. Boethius' main concern was the Stoic theory of causal determinism, and this doctrine led him to attend to diachronic possibilities. Some of the *prima facie* strange phrases in Boethius' remarks on the truth of future contingent sentences can be explained against this background.

When Boethius refers to chance, free choice and possibility in connection with individual contingent events, his examples often include temporalized modal notions which refer to prospective possibilities at a given moment of time (see, for example, *In Periherm.* I, 106.11–14, 120.9–16; II, 190.14–191.2, 197.20–198.3, 203.2–11, 207.18–25). A temporally determinate prospective possibility is unrealized before the time to which it refers, and it may remain unrealized even when the time is present. This means, however, that the possibility does not exist any longer. It ceases to exist when its opposite is actualized. It is interesting that Boethius did not develop in this context the idea of simultaneous synchronic possibilities which would remain intact even when diachronic possibilities have vanished. On the contrary, he insisted that, at any present moment of time, only what is actual at that time is at that time possible at that time. The following quotation may serve as a typical example of Boethian diachronic modalities:

> Suppose that when leaving my house yesterday, I met a friend I had wanted to meet, although not at that time. Before I met him it was possible that I would not meet him, but when I met him or after I had met him, it is not possible that I did not meet him. Or suppose that I voluntarily left for the countryside last night. Before it happened, it was possible that I would not leave, but after I left or when I left, it was not possible that what happened would not happen or what has happened would not have happened. Further, this tunic I wear can be cut. Suppose that it has been cut yesterday. When it was cut or after it was cut, it was not possible that it would not be cut or have not been cut, but before it was cut it was possible that it would not be cut.
> (*In Periherm.* II, 190.14–191.2)

The examples are given in the past tense because Boethius wants to point out a difference between applying the diachronic modal structure to past or present things and applying it to future things. With respect to past and present events, the realization of the antecedent possibilities is already definite and certain, but this is not the case with future contingencies. On the contrary, for them 'either this or that will be and, in fact, will be by necessity, but it is not possible that one thing or event would already now be definite and certain' (ibid. II, 191.19–22). Because there are objective individual *ad utrumlibet* contingencies, the result of some prospective possibilities is indefinite and uncertain (*indefinitus et incertus*), 'not only to us who are ignorant, but to nature' (ibid. II, 192.4–5).

The statistical interpretation of modality offers the following imaginary relativization of the necessity of the present:

(4) $(Ep)(t)(p_t \rightarrow L_t p_t \,\&\, M_t - p_{t'>t})$

or

(5) $(Ep)(t)(p_t \rightarrow L_t p_t \,\&\, M - p_{t'\neq t})$.

The possibility to be otherwise is here disconnected from what is said to be necessary. The diachronic model is more satisfactory in this respect. With its help Boethius could maintain at least that what is now might have been previously precluded from being:

(6) $(Ep)(t)(p_t \rightarrow L_t p_t \,\&\, M_{t'<t} - p_t)$.

On the basis of the insight included in (6), Boethius was able to state that contradictory sentences are possible with respect to a future moment of time, although this cannot be said to hold when that moment has become present. As long as alternative possibilities exist, the conditions of the truth or falsity of the corresponding temporally definite sentences are not yet established. Even though the sentence which will prove to be true has been always true, it has been always true in an uncertain and indefinite way only, because its truth conditions are of this sort. This interpretation has been presented by Mario Mignucci (1989); he refers to the systematic discussion of determinism and knowledge of the future by von Wright (1984: 52–67).

I believe that when Boethius characterized the truth and falsity of sentences about future contingent events as *mutable*, he had in mind the statistical type of possibility. This is a surmise based on the fact that in the context in which this phrase occurs Boethius refers to statistical ideas. When he said that future contingent sentences are true or false in an *indefinite* way, the term 'indefinite' was derived from a diachronic model of modality. According to Boethius, sentences are definitely true or definitely false depending on whether what they signify is definite and settled. Concerning two prospectively possible alternative events, either can happen. The results are not definitely settled beforehand. In this sense, sentences about future contingent events, if they are true or false, are true or false in an indefinite way (*In Periherm.* II, 189.5–192.22, 200.18–201.2).

Boethius did not develop the idea of synchronic unrealized possibilities in connection with his intuitive model of diachronic possibilities. He supposed that whatever will be at a future moment is the only thing which can be when all alternative possibilities are dropped.

This supposition probably led Boethius to confused attempts to modify the truth of temporally determinate true sentences, either by referring to the behaviour of corresponding temporally indeterminate sentences or by postulating changes in the mode of their truth, depending on when they are uttered. We can observe that if temporally determinate true sentences are divided into definitely true and indefinitely true sentences, all indefinitely true sentences about future contingent events will begin to be definitely true. As definitely true singular sentences are necessarily true when they refer to what is already actualized and is temporally necessary, and as indefinitely true sentences lack this feature, Boethius could think that this circumstance in some way relativizes the statistical necessity belonging to temporally definite sentences as sentences which are true whenever uttered.

It is assumed above that Boethius considered all future contingent propositions either true or false, although they are true or false in a mutable and indeterminate way. Some authors have claimed that these qualifications mean that Boethius in fact wanted to express that the so-called Principle of Bivalence (PB),

(PB)  $T(p) \vee F(p)$,

is not valid with respect to future contingent sentences, although the Law of Excluded Middle (LEM),

(LEM)  $T(p) \vee - T(p)$,

could remain intact. If $p$ has a neutral truth value, it could be characterized as being not true (see, for example, Rescher 1968: 186; Frede 1970: 25; 1985: 43–5; Craig 1988: 85–7). As is seen, for example, from *In Periherm.* II, 208.1–11, there are problems with this truth-value gap interpretation, criticized in many recent works (see, for example, Bosley 1978; Sharples 1978: 263–4; Sorabji 1980: 93–4; Mignucci 1989: 50–2).

According to Norman Kretzmann (1987), Boethius' view was that, for each contingent proposition about the future, one of the two truth-values is going to achieve definiteness and, furthermore, whenever a proposition does not yet have a definite truth-value it has the disjunctive property of being either true or false. Boethius' examples are usually ambiguous and the idea of 'broad bivalence' is compatible with many of them. I believe, however, that Boethius thought that future contingent sentences are subjected not only to LEM but also to PB. The most explicit evidence is *Phil. cons.* V, 4.19: 'I do not think that any man would say that those things which are happening now were not going to happen before they happened.' The same view is probably included in *In Periherm.* II, 226.9–12: 'God knows future events as happening contingently and not necessarily so that he does not ignore that a different event could take place' (see Mignucci 1989: 75).

If the truth and falsity of sentences is thought to be known through the existing conditions which make them true or false, the possibilities of foreknowledge are very limited in an indeterministic world. Much of what is going to take place is not included in the chains of causes. To know the truth or falsity of indefinitely true sentences about future contingent events does not belong to human epistemic possibilities; therefore, to speak of them as true or false without qualification is to speak falsely (cf. *In Periherm.* II, 211.26–213.18, translated in Kretzmann 1987: 79–80). Boethius seems to have thought that such sentences can be known to be true or false only through some kind of immediate vision. This probably was the reason for Boethius' view that God knows everything in a non-standard timeless way; God has the infinity of changing time present to him (*Phil. cons.* V, 6.25–31; for the discussions of Boethius' conceptions of time and eternity, see Stump and Kretzmann 1981; Sorabji 1983: 253–67; Craig 1988: 91–7). The conception of timeless knowledge would be needed to explain how there can be knowledge at all about future contingent events. It has been claimed that, on Boethius' view, God does not know future contingents in advance, because foreknowledge would imply theological fatalism (see, for example, Craig 1988: 90–1). This, however, is denied in *Phil. cons.* V, 4.4–8.

Some medieval authors interpreted Boethius' distinction between simple and conditional necessity in *Phil. cons.* V, 6.26–30, as a distinction between *necessitas consequentiae* and *necessitas consequentis* (see, for example, Thomas Aquinas, *Summa contra gentiles* I, 67). Standard scholastic examples of ambiguous sentences analysed with the help of the distinction mentioned were of the type 'If God knows that $p$, then necessarily $p$'. According to scholastics, from the true *necessitas consequentiae* reading

(7) $L(K_G p \to p)$

the false and deterministic *necessitas consequentis* reading does not follow:

(8) $K_G p \to Lp$.

Patch (1935: 402), Henry (1967: 178) and many others have claimed that this is what Boethius wanted to demonstrate when he wrote:

For there are two kinds of necessity, one simple, as for example that it is necessary that all men are mortal, and one conditional, as for example, if you know that someone is walking, he must be walking. . . . things when considered with reference to God's sight of them are necessary as a result of the condition of divine knowledge, but when considered in themselves they do not lose the absolute freedom of their nature.

(*Phil. cons.* V, 6.27–30)

According to Boethius, the necessity belonging to events as objects of divine knowledge is relativized by the fact that before the occurrence of some of them it was possible that they would not happen (*Phil. cons.* V, 6.32). This remark shows that the conditional necessity he is speaking about is in fact related to the discussion of temporal necessity in the commentaries on *De interpretatione* 9 and to the form (3). Temporal necessity is here relativized with the help of the conception of diachronic possibilities.

Although it is not clear whether the conception of the necessity of consequence played a role in *Phil. cons.* V, 6, it is often discussed in Boethius' logical treatises. In his theory of the logic of conditionals, Boethius states that the purpose of a conditional statement is to assert that there is a necessary consequence between the things signified by the antecedent and the consequent respectively. The necessity of consequences or corresponding conditional statements consists in the immutability of consequential relations. According to Boethius, genuine conditional statements refer to consequences of nature (*consequentia naturae*), but there are accidental (*secundum accidens*) conditionals, too. He does not explain this distinction, but the examples offered suggest that necessary consequences referred to by accidental conditionals are merely omnitemporal simultaneous actualities of the antecedent and the consequent. Accidental conditionals would then be necessary in the statistical sense that the truth of the antecedent is never separated from the truth of the consequent (*De hypotheticis syllogismis* 218, 250, *PL* 64, 835, 843).

In his treatises on topics, Boethius attempted in some places to present a complete classification of the types of simple necessary conditionals on the basis of the relations between the terms of antecedents and the terms of consequents (see, for example, *De topicis differentiis*, *PL* 64, 1178d–1180a, 1204a, translated in Stump 1978; *In Ciceronis Topica*, *PL* 64, 1124b–1130c, translated in Stump 1988; the discussion in Stump 1978: 105–9; Green-Pedersen 1984: 78–81). Boethius' distinction between natural and accidental conditionals and his theory of natural simple conditionals as being based on the relationships between topical concepts, such as whole–part, genus–species or cause–effect, influenced medieval discussions of conditionals (see, for example, Peter Abelard, *Dialectica* 283.37–284.17, 472.1–36).

## NEW THEOLOGICAL MODALITIES: FROM AUGUSTINE TO ANSELM OF CANTERBURY

One Boethian theme, already discussed by some patristic thinkers, was the question about the relation between the philosophical theories of possibility and necessity and the theological doctrine of divine omnipotence and providence. According to Boethius, all causally determined natural events, as well as free choices outside the causal chains, are included in providence and cannot escape this ultimate metaphysical necessity (*Phil. cons.* IV, 6; V, 6). Boethius tried to avoid the deterministic implications of this supernatural necessity by claiming that things which are necessary in the vertical, atemporal order of providence can be contingent in the horizontal, historical order (ibid. V, 6.26–30). This dualistic idea is problematic in many ways and not just because of Boethius' somewhat confused methods of saving the contingency of individual events in the historical order. Boethius did not discuss the question of the relationship between omnipotence and philosophical modalities, which later became a topic of keen interest in early medieval philosophy.

The emergence of some new ideas pertaining to modal theory took place in theological contexts. Philosophical modal paradigms proved problematic when applied without qualification to theological questions. In the eleventh century, some of these problems were formulated in a manner which stimulated Western thought for centuries. One of the basic questions was whether the necessary or the impossible put limits on divine power.

Gerbert of Aurillac, Abbo of Fleury and Garland the Computist, among other tenth- and eleventh-century logicians, were acquainted with the *Categories* and *De interpretatione* of Aristotle, the *Topica* of Cicero, the *Isagoge* of Porphyry, Boethius' commentaries on these works and Boethius' own logical monographs. Garland's *Dialectica* summarizes the main doctrines of the sources in six books (see Lewry 1981: 94–100). At the same time, many people were interested in such philosophical works as the *Timaeus* of Plato, available in a partial translation by Calcidius (c.400) and read with Calcidius' commentary on it, Boethius' *Philosophiae consolatio*, and Macro-

Early medieval modalities 63

bius' neoplatonic commentary on Cicero's *Somnium Scipionis*. (For the sources and historical background of early medieval philosophy and logic, see Marenbon 1981, 1983; Pinborg 1972; Ebbesen 1982.) Some of these authors began to discuss the question of how Christian doctrine stands with the ancient philosophical heritage and how each should take the other into account. As attested by the well-known controversy between Berengar of Tours (d. 1088) and Lanfranc (1010–89) over the Eucharist, which concentrated partly on the question of the application of logic to the Christian mysteries, the matter was not merely of theoretical interest. Boethius' theological treatises, the *Opuscula sacra*, were discussed in the schools alongside elementary logic (Gibson 1981a: 220), and it seems to have been this coexistence of theology and dialectic which led to the quarrels of the eleventh century.

Lanfranc, who died as Archbishop of Canterbury, was an Italian, and so was Peter Damian (1007–72), an influential monastic writer and counsellor to many popes. Peter Damian's book *De divina omnipotentia* is a good source of eleventh-century controversies about the relationship between theology and philosophy. According to Damian, many teachers of his day were applying logic to theology in a way which threatened orthodoxy. While generally condemning the misuse of logic in theology, i.e. logic as a mere verbal art teaches nothing but how to make statements and consequences of words (*De div. omnipot.* 604a–b, 615a), Peter Damian was particularly concerned about the view, in his opinion quite common among the dialecticians, that divine omnipotence cannot violate natural necessities.

The first group of Peter's examples of philosophical necessities, not acceptable without qualification in theology, comprises traditional examples of invariant causal relations between active and passive potencies of nature. According to Peter, such invariances are not necessarily in force, since they remain in control of their creator (see, for example, *De div. omnipot.* 610d–615b). It has been assumed that Berengar of Tours was one of the dialectical theologians Peter Damian is attacking (see A. Cantin's introduction to *De div. omnipot.* 38), and this may be true, though Berengar's position was more sophisticated than the idea criticized by Peter Damian. Berengar discussed the doctrine of transubstantiation in his works and he regarded it as an impossibility (*Rescriptum contra Lanfrannum* 158–9). Because the alleged transubstantiation does not fulfil the philosophical criteria for natural changes, the presence of Christ in the sacrament of Holy Communion should be understood in another way. Berengar did not deny that some kind of change takes place in the Eucharist (ibid. 84, 114–15); he apparently thought that this change, and miracles in general, are added to the natural course of events in a manner which does not violate its natural regularities.

According to Damian, God can change the invariant patterns called natural necessities. These necessities, which express the natural *consuetudo* (*De div. omnipot.* 611b, 614a), are not necessarily operative and they are not autonomous:

> Is it a wonder when he, who gave the law and order to nature, exercises the power of his will to the same nature so that the necessity of nature does not rebel against him, but acts submitted to the laws, like a servant? The nature of things itself has a nature, namely the will of God, so that as what is created obeys the laws of nature, so, when ordered, it reverently obeys God's will, giving up its rights.
>
> (*De div. omnipot.* 612c–d)

From the point of view of the history of philosophy, this controversy proved to be very fruitful. Thinkers who in principle accepted Damian's view of the contingency of natural necessities had to consider which of the traditional necessities are necessary only *secundum consuetudinem* and which are necessary independent of present actualities. Peter Damian was not himself interested in the philosophical implications of his remarks, but others were.

Another philosophical notion of necessity discussed by Damian is the necessity connected with dialectical consequences or consequences of discourse (*consequentia disserendi*). It is delineated as follows:

> According to the consequence of discourse, if it is going to rain, then it is entirely necessary that it will rain and thus entirely impossible that it will not rain. Thus, what is said about past things, can be concluded no less with respect to present and future things, for as what has been, necessarily has been, so what is, as long as it is, necessarily is, and what will be, it necessarily will be. ... Who would not patently see that if these arguments, having the order of the words they have, are applied to the faith, the divine power is shown to be impotent in all moments of time.
>
> (*De div. omnipot.* 603a–b, d)

Damian here describes what Boethius called temporal necessity and he attends to the fact that, if it is applied to all moments of time, everything is necessary. Even God cannot do anything but what he in fact does. He also mentions that the dialecticians have introduced the *ad utrumlibet* contingency in order to show that something can be otherwise than it is. This solution, Damian says, is based on the variable nature of things and therefore does not solve the problem contained in the claim that what is, necessarily is, when it is (ibid. 602d–603a). Neither is referring to states of affairs at different times a proper way of discussing God's possibilities, because the created course of nature would then be the criterion for determining what is possible for God (ibid. 619b–c). Peter Damian's short descriptions of what he considered the standard philosophical modalities evidently drew, directly or indirectly, on the *De interpretatione* 9 and Boethius' commentaries on it (cf. Isaac 1953: 45–7). Peter Damian has at times been characterized as a simple monk who did not understand much about the logic which he criticized the use of in theology. Perhaps this picture is not quite justified. He correctly identified the weak points in the Boethian approach to the necessity of what is, whether in terms of the statistical model or in terms of the diachronic model of possibility.

The starting point of Peter Damian's treatise is the following statement by Jerome: 'I will speak boldly; although God can do all things, he cannot raise up a virgin, after she has fallen' (Jerome, *Epistulae* I, 150; see also Oakley 1984: 41–4). The idea that what is past is necessary was commonly entertained by ancient philosophers; it was also included in the first thesis of the Master Argument of Diodorus Cronus. Jerome accepted the view that changing past things is a genuine impossibility and that God cannot undo past events. But Peter Damian did not like the expression that there is something God cannot do. He asserted that, even if it sounds natural to say that, after the foundation of Rome, it is no longer possible that Rome does not exist, yet divine omnipotence is outside time, and there can be no changes in God's possibilities to do things. Therefore, the historical beginning of the existence of Rome does not have any influence on the fact that God can see to it that Rome never exists (*De div. omnipot.* 619a).

Many authors have thought that Damian's views imply that God can change the past and that the Law of Contradiction does not put limits on divine power (see, for example, Endres 1910: 23–4; Copleston 1972: 67; Oakley 1984: 44). This kind of argument seems to be found in the following passage:

> That something has been made and that something has not been made cannot be the case with respect to one and the same thing.

These are contraries to the extent that if the one is, the other cannot be: of what has been, it cannot be truly said that it has not been, and of what has not been, it cannot be truly said that it has been. Contraries cannot belong to one and the same thing together. This is correctly called an impossibility with respect to the limited power of nature, but it cannot be applied to the divine majesty.

*(De div. omnipot.* 612a–b).

The text is in many ways ambiguous, however. For one thing, it may be that the impossibility spoken of in the last sentence refers to a physical restoration which is discussed in the treatise before the quoted passage. And even if it refers to a real contradiction, the remark could be understood as forbidding one to use the notion of impossibility when speaking about God (cf. *De div. omnipot.* 597b–c). In this case it does not imply that God can bring about contradictory states of affairs. Peter Damian takes it for granted that, when the conception of God's power is found problematic, something is wrong in the manner in which the problem is formulated. If it is asked whether God can do bad or harmful things, it is wrongly assumed that such states of affairs are brought about by a power. According to Damian, they belong to the domain of nothingness in the sense that they are shortcomings rather than any positive things. Following the neoplatonic view of Augustine and Boethius, he states that to bring about things into the domain of nothingness is not a sign of ability but of inability (*Phil. cons.* III, 12.27–9; IV, 2.44; Augustine, *De civitate Dei* XII, 6–8). According to Damian, this view can be applied to the question of whether God can realize contradictory states of affairs (*De div. omnipot.* 610b–d). They would be bad and harmful, and, as such, they are not objects of a power. Furthermore, if it is claimed that when an individual event has taken place, God cannot prevent it any longer, God's power is treated with the help of temporal terms which are inadequate. There is no temporal order in the non-temporal eternity where God makes his decisions (*De div. omnipot.* 619a–620c).

There are passages in which Damian refers to the idea of alternative providential programmes, but he does not elaborate upon this thought while discussing the question of God's having power over the past (ibid. 599b–600b, 614d). It seems that, while defending the absolute nature of God's power, Damian had in his mind various vague ideas pertaining to modality, tense, temporality and non-temporal eternity. He was led in his thought by the Augustinian conception of God acting by choice, which implies a theory of alternative possible states of affairs, but he did not manage to create a coherent whole of the pieces. Even though many authors have recently criticized the received view according to which Peter Damian thought that the Law of Contradiction does not put limits to divine omnipotence (see Kenny 1979: 100–5; Moonan 1980; Marenbon 1983: 82–3; Holopainen forthcoming), the traditional view is not wholly without justification. I think that Peter Damian was conscious of some problems in his approach and that, instead of solving them, he insisted that they should not be discussed at all. According to Damian, God's choice is eternal and God has a power of realizing the content of the actual choice as well as the contents of all possible alternative choices. It is clear that the temporal results of the actual choice exclude a choice with incompatible temporal results and that God's possibilities (opportunities) to use his power to realize another choice are restricted by the actual choice. If this is denied and if it is claimed that one should not conclude that God can make contradictory things, the concept of divine power becomes mysterious and incomprehensible. It cannot be discussed with the help of standard modal notions, because then one should either restrict God's power or accept contradictions in theology.

Jerome's view of divine omnipotence was not exceptional in ancient theology. Many patristic theologians presumed more or less explicitly that through his power God can actualize only things which are possible as such. But there were also writers relying in theological contexts upon the philosophically problematic assumption of an unqualified divine omnipotence (see Grant 1952; Wiles 1965: 221–34). The starting point of these discussions was the fact that there were some places in the Bible (e.g. Mark 10:27; Matthew 19:26; 26:53; Luke 1:37; 18:27) where the actual history was not taken as an exhaustive manifestation of God's omnipotence. To treat omnipotence as an executive power within the scope of what is possible was natural for theologians who interpreted the Platonic doctrine of an intelligible world as ideas in the mind of God. (For the theory of ideas in early Christian thought, see Wolfson 1956: 257–86.) In this approach it would be strange to think that God could will or do something which he knows to be unintelligible or contradictory. Some examples from the works of Augustine may illustrate this line of thought.

In *De spiritu et littera* Augustine gives an answer to a theological question by Tribune Marcellinus. Part of Marcellinus' query concerned how Augustine could say that something is possible even though there is no example of it in the world. In Marcellinus' opinion, to call such things possible was not comprehensible (*De spiritu et littera* 1–2). The question was raised in accord with the statistical interpretation of possibility discussed above as one of the ancient modal paradigms. In *De civitate Dei* Augustine mentions other objections to Christian doctrines based on the view that the ordinary course of nature defines what is possible or impossible (*De civitate Dei* XXI, 5–8; XXII, 4, 11). Augustine's answer in each case is that things which seem impossible may otherwise be possible, because God can do them. He also mentions the idea, repeated later by Peter Damian and many others, that miraculous events are not unnatural. Our concept of nature is based on observational regularities, but total nature is God's will or providential design, which itself provides natural history with all kinds of exceptional events. They are incomprehensible to men and function to demonstrate God's sovereignty to believers (*De civitate Dei* XXI, 8).

Although Augustine stresses that a great part of God's power is not comprehensible to man, he says that God's works are not irrational (*De civitate Dei* XXI, 5). Augustine asserts an eternal system of mathematical, dialectical and metaphysical principles based on 'the archetypal forms or stable and unchangeable reasons of things, which are not themselves formed but are contained in the divine mind eternally and are always the same' (*De diversis quaestionibus q.* 46). A rational will cannot wish anything unrealizable – e.g. to change unchangeable truths – and it is clear that the power of realization, conceptually distinct from the will, is real only as far as the will to which it is attached is rational. When Augustine defined omnipotence as a power to do what one wills (see, for example, *Enchiridion* 96; *De civitate Dei* XXI, 7), he took it for granted that God's will cannot be directed to anything which is irrational, for such volitions would prove that God is not omnipotent.

Following the Platonic tradition, Augustine thought that the generic forms of being belong to a perfect scale and that God does not leave any part of it unrealized. In this sense he asserted an equation between possibilities and their realizations, i.e. he accepted in one form the idea dubbed by Lovejoy 'the principle of plenitude' (*De civitate Dei* XI, 22; XII, 27; *Confessiones* XIII, 2; Lovejoy 1936: 67). Yet he also claimed that some divine possibilities are never realized. Although this view remains in the periphery of Augustine's thought, it is historically significant, because it motivated later theologians to rethink the meaning of modal notions. An interesting example of an unrealized possibility is mentioned in Chapter 19 of Book XII of *De civitate Dei*. Augustine criticizes the ancient doctrines which claimed that the only permissible notion of infinity is the infinite *in potentia*. According to him, an infinite series of numbers exist actually in God's thought, and God could create an infinite number of individuals of a species and know each of them simultaneously. Although Augustine thought that the number of species is finite and that they are all realized, he also had in mind the speculative idea of a divine choice among infinite alternatives, an idea which later became common in medieval modal metaphysics.

Augustine qualified the notion of God's power by relating it to other divine attributes, for example, 'God could according to his power, but not according to his justice' (*Contra Gaudentium* I.30; cf. Origen, *In Matthaeum commentariorum series* 95, *PG* 13, 1746; see also Courtenay 1985: 244–5; Funkenstein 1986: 126). In his voluntaristic theory of providence, Augustine referred to unrealized divine possibilities by the slogan '*Potuit sed noluit*' ('He could, but he did not want to'; see, for example, *Contra Faustum* 29.4; *De natura et gratia* 7). The phrase became well known in early medieval times. It was not introduced by Augustine but was used by other theologians before him (see, for example, Tertullian, *De cultu feminarum* I, 8). When Augustine used this conception in his analysis of the freedom of will, he had in mind an intuitive model of diachronic possibilities. Before a choice is made, it is possible that the act of choice will be this or that. According to Augustine, divine foreknowledge about free choices does not influence them, and God's knowledge about them could be other than what it is. 'He does not sin, if he wills not to sin and if he had willed not to sin, then God would have foreseen that refusal' (*De civitate Dei* V, 10).

The view that real alternative possibilities are open to the will before it makes a choice qualifies the concept of freedom of will. Freedom is not mere absence of external constraint. But this freedom is complicated by Augustine's view that men are unable to choose love and obedience to God. So the alternatives open to the will are real concrete possibilities only as alternatives compatible with the basic direction of will. Although people are said to sin freely, they do not sin freely in the sense that they act against some natural option open to them without grace to love God. Interpreters have differed about whether Augustine's account of foreknowledge and freedom of will is deterministic or not (for different views, see Craig 1988: 60–78). The theological doctrine of man's inability to choose love and obedience to God without the help of grace may explain why both views can find support in Augustine's works (for Augustine's concept of will, see also Kirwan 1989: 82–128; Holmström-Hintikka 1991: 154–77).

Augustine's method of justifying faith in omnipotence consisted of an attempt to undermine trust in natural necessities as inviolable invariances. Peter Damian did the same, but he was less sure about the status of the principles of logic. The differences notwithstanding, both authors were convinced that the Catholic doctrine of God is incompatible with the 'philosophical' doctrines of necessity and possibility. The conception of necessities as autonomous natural regularities of cosmic activity restricted God's freedom and sovereignty, and the theory of possibilities as potentialities or probabilities, which prove their reality through actualization, set heterodox limits to God's power and will. This problem was much discussed in twelfth-century philosophical theology, and it is remarkable that no important proponents of an unqualified omnipotence arose, although fideistic views, openly hostile to philosophy, were not absent (see, for example, William of Conches' anticlerical response in the *Dragmaticon* 68–9, and in the *Philosophia* 39). Reflected solutions were sought in the direction anticipated by Christian Platonists of the patristic period. The Augustinian approach, in which God's power is regarded as an executive power between alternatives and correspondingly limited by God's actual choice and God's other attributes, was widely accepted and applied, e.g. in glosses on the Scripture.

Anselm of Canterbury's (1033–1109) discussion of modal notions was an early attempt to explicate theological modalities at a more theoretical level. As distinct from Peter Damian, he was interested in modal conceptions themselves and tried to codify some aspects of the semantics implied in the Christian use of the notions of necessity and possibility. Anselm's endeavour to develop a modal theory remained sketchy, but some thinkers of the next generation, such as Gilbert of Poitiers and Peter Abelard, continued the attempt to revise traditional modal paradigms. Gilbert of Poitiers (*c*.1085–1154), who taught theology at Chartres and in Paris before being made Bishop of Poitiers, was one of the most original theologians in the twelfth century. Starting from the Augustinian idea of alternative providential designs from which God chooses the actual history, Gilbert formulated some basic features of the intensional interpretation of modality developed later by Duns Scotus and other fourteenth-century thinkers. I think that Gilbert's work shows how the idea of modality as multiplicity of reference with respect to synchronic alternative domains owes its origin to Christian theology. While Gilbert presented his ideas as succinct remarks without detailed

*Early medieval modalities* 71

analysis, Peter Abelard (1079–1142) tried to examine the foundations of philosophical modal theories in a more systematic manner. The result is an interesting combination of traditional and new views including the idea of synchronic alternatives. I shall discuss the modal conceptions of Gilbert and Abelard in the next section.

Anselm of Canterbury, born in Aosta in 1033, was a pupil of Lanfranc at Bec and succeeded him as Archbishop of Canterbury in 1093. The debate about the relationship between faith and reason, sharpened by the works of authors like Berengar of Tours, Lanfranc and Peter Damian, strongly influenced Anselm's thought. Anselm became an original representative of rational systematic theology which comprised investigations concerning the meaning of the modal notions in Catholic doctrine. In the late incomplete work, the *Lambeth Fragments* (in *The Memorials of St Anselm*), Anselm tried to present a general analysis of predication and, as a part of it, a general account of the uses of modal terms. Although the project remained unfulfilled, some main features of Anselm's modal theory can be formulated on the basis of the *Lambeth Fragments* and his other works.

Anselm seems to have thought that a general theory of predication could be built on an analysis of the possible bases for the ascription of 'facere' (to do, to make, to bring about). This combination of agency and predication was based on the view that in some sense a subject can always be considered a cause of its predicate (*The Memorials of St Anselm* 343.9–12). Eileen Serene (1981) has summarized Anselm's analysis of direct and indirect modes of agency in the *Lambeth Fragments* as follows. A subject ($A$) may be said to bring about a state of affairs ($s$) directly or through other states of affairs ($m, n, o, r$) causally related to $s$ only if at least one of these six conditions is satisfied:

(i) $A$ directly brings about $s$;
(ii) $A$ directly fails to prevent $s$ from occurring;
(iii) $A$ brings about $m$, and $m$ causally contributes to the occurrence of $s$;
(iv) $A$ fails to bring about $n$, and $n$'s not occurring causally contributes to the occurrence of $s$;
(v) $A$ prevents $o$ from occurring, and $o$'s not occurring causally contributes to the occurrence of $s$;
(vi) $A$ fails to prevent $r$ from occurring, and $r$'s occurring causally contributes to the occurrence of $s$.

Anselm holds that a predicate is properly ascribed if and only if the subject directly does what is ascribed to it. In all other cases, an ascription of a predicate is improper (*The Memorials of St Anselm* 347.15–28). Anselm assumes that there are various connections between improper and proper ascriptions of nouns or predicates, as can be seen from the conceptual structures connected with such notions as, for example, similitude, cause, effect, genus, species, whole and part, but he did not manage to bring them into a systematic theory (ibid. 347.5–8; for Anselm's semantic programme, see Serene 1981: 121–30; Henry 1967: 17–21; 1975). Some contemporary thinkers have found Anselm's analysis of 'facere' interesting because it shows certain similarities to modern theories of the logic of action (Danto 1973: 7–8; Walton 1976; Dazeley and Gombocz 1979: 72–85; Segerberg 1989: 222–4).

I shall not enter into the complicated details of Anselm's unfinished agency theory of predication. It is interesting, however, that he did not consider the verb 'to be' as the basic one in his semantic theory. Abelard later tried to develop a theory of predication in which a two-part form of proposition was preferred to the three-part form consisting of a subject term, a predicate term and an interposed copula. He was inclined to interpret the copula as an auxiliary verb, which in conjunction with a predicate noun does duty for verbs which may not yet be invented (see Jacobi 1986).

According to Anselm, the predicate 'is necessarily $F$' properly ascribes constraint to its subject, and the predicate 'is possibly $F$' properly ascribes a capacity to its subject. If modal terms are used in any another way, they are used improperly (see Serene 1981: 129). The *Lambeth Fragments* do not contain a theory of how these improper uses should be analysed. Clearly, however, Anselm was interested in improper modalities because of their importance for certain theological doctrines. One should be able to speak theologically about possibilities which belong to unrealized objects and about modes of necessity which do not include constraint. In the treatise the student presents the following problem: If something which can $F$ can do it only by virtue of its capacity to $F$ and if something which does not exist has no capacities, i.e. no capacity for being and no capacity for not being, it seems to be both necessary and impossible for something which does not exist to be and not to be (*The Memorials of St Anselm* 341.7–39). In Chapter 12 of his dialogue *De casu diaboli*, Anselm discusses the question concerning how it was possible for the world to exist prior to its creation. He first says that it could have existed because of God's ability to create it, but the answer remains ambiguous, because Anselm also says that the world in itself did not

Early medieval modalities 73

have the capacity of being (*Opera omnia* I, 253.4–254.9). Eileen Serene has argued that, when Anselm in the *Lambeth Fragments* distinguishes between various modes in which a subject can count as 'something', he attended to the improper uses without the requirement that the subject exists, because he wanted to find a way of speaking about the capacities of non-existent objects (Serene 1981: 125–7). If this is true, Anselm probably thought that one cannot speak about the possibility of unrealized things by referring only to God's power, for what God can do must in some sense be also possible in itself. Although we do not have Anselm's final answer to the opening question of the treatise, it seems that he was interested in the philosophical question of the nature of possibilities *qua* possibilities, considered apart from their ontological foundation. This problem naturally suggested itself when divine omnipotence was considered as an executive power with respect to possible states of affairs.

In discussing his potency model of possibility, Anselm thought, as did Aristotle, that full potencies or possibilities are combinations of various partial potencies. In Chapter 3 of the *De libertate arbitrii* (*Opera omnia* I, 213.5–25), Anselm analyses a person's ability to see a mountain; its components are said to be (a) the power of seeing, (b) the power in the thing to be seen, (c) the power which helps the sight (e.g. light) and (d) the power consisting in the fact that nothing obstructs the view. It is then stated that, if one of these four powers is missing, the other three are not able to accomplish the result. A person can see the mountain in the full sense of the word only when the four powers are present. We meet here the same problem which was found in Aristotle's theory of potency-based possibilities: it is difficult to keep full potency, or possibility, and actuality separate. In *De casu diaboli* (*Opera omnia* I, 275.25–33, 276.14–15) Anselm states that what particularly is needed for an act of will, in addition to the ability to will, is the act of using the ability.

Anselm's difficulties with partial and full potencies become clear in his discussion of sin and grace. He supposes that men have an ability to keep uprightness of will for its own sake, although they cannot use this ability because of Adam's fall. When Anselm says that men can exist without sin and that they are free not to sin, his assertion reflects a partial possibility founded on the presence of a particular power in person, and when he says that they cannot be without sin, this impossibility is based on an absence of one or another component power of upright life. Anselm connects the notion of freedom with a particular partial potency of action; consequently, he does not hesitate to call free an act which in fact is impossible. Because of his confused views about the relationship between partial and full potencies, Anselm could consider the presence of a partial potency as sufficient ground for calling something possible and to claim, at the same time, that the absence of another partial potency is sufficient ground for calling the same thing impossible (see *De libertate arbitrii* 12; *De concordia praescientiae et praedestinationis et gratiae Dei cum libero arbitrio* III, 3, in *Opera omnia* II, 265.26–267.5; for Anselm's theory of will, freedom and grace, see also Hopkins 1972: 141–85).

In addition to the question of unrealized possibilities, the student of the *Lambeth Fragments* raises concern about expressions claiming either that something is impossible for God or that God is something by necessity (*The Memorials of St Anselm* 342.1–9). Anselm thought that God's inability to lie, God's being necessarily just and similar theological predications are examples of improper necessity, because they are consequences of the correctness of God's unchangeable will and do not imply a constraint on God (see, for example, *Cur Deus homo* II, 5, 10, 17, in *Opera omnia* II, 100.20–8, 108.6–9, 122.25–124.2; *De concordia* I, 2, in *Opera omnia* II, 247.8–11). This kind of necessity occurs in Anselm's distinction between 'antecedent' necessity (*necessitas antecedens, necessitas praecedens*) and 'subsequent' necessity (*necessitas subsequens, necessitas sequens*), to which he refers when discussing questions pertaining to future contingents, foreknowledge and freedom (*Cur Deus homo* II, 17, in *Opera omnia* II, 125.8–126.2; *De concordia* I, 3, in *Opera omnia* II, 248.5–249.9). Necessary by antecedent necessity are events or states of affairs compelled or constrained by external causes. When something is called necessary in the sense of subsequent necessity, however, there is no reference to such constraint but only to the fact that nothing can affect its being the case. Anselm says that this is the Aristotelian necessity by which all that has been necessarily has been, all that is necessarily is and necessarily is going to have been, and all that is going to be necessarily is going to be. Even God cannot change the past or make something that is the case not the case, but this inability is 'improper', because God is not externally compelled to accept the order or course of events in the world.

Anselm does not offer a detailed analysis of the modes of improper necessity. We can reasonably consider subsequent necessities as relative necessities of some kind, although Anselm does not explicitly discuss their foundation, except for the short remark that they are states of affairs which nothing can bring about to be not the case (*Cur Deus homo* II, 17, in *Opera omnia* II, 125.12). Similarly, Anselm often speaks about necessary arguments without explaining why they are necessary. As for future contingent events, he thought that propositions about them are either true or false. True propositions are necessarily true by subsequent necessity, but this does not cause any constraint on future events some of which are brought about by uncaused acts of will (*Cur Deus homo*, in *Opera omnia* II, 125.24–8; *De concordia* I, 3, in *Opera omnia* II, 250.25–251.2).

## GILBERT OF POITIERS, PETER ABELARD AND THIERRY OF CHARTRES

Abelard, Gilbert and Thierry of Chartres lived during the period which many scholars, following the great American medievalist Haskins (1927), have called the renaissance of the twelfth century. One significant feature of this intellectual movement was its wide interest in cosmology and natural philosophy, which was inspired by Plato's *Timaeus* and the late-ancient Platonic tradition. In the first half of the twelfth century, authors like Thierry of Chartres, William of Conches and their fellow Platonists created a world view in which 'scientific' cosmological studies were seen as legitimate and important ways of explaining the Christian doctrines of creation and the Trinity (see the literature in Courtenay 1984; Wetherbee 1988). Some quotations from the works of Thierry of Chartres will exemplify the role that modal concepts played in this philosophical approach. I shall mainly concentrate on the discussions of Gilbert of Poitiers and Peter Abelard, however, because they are more significant from the point of view of the development of modal thought. I describe first Gilbert's modal views as a reflected version of the new theologically motivated approaches to modality which started to emerge in various forms in the first half of the twelfth century. Then I treat the interplay of old and new modal ideas in Peter Abelard (1079–1142) who, from a less theological starting point, tried to formulate a satisfactory theory of the meaning and logical properties of modal terms.

According to Gilbert, 'the wisdom of this world' (*sapientia huius mundi*) makes use of a notion of necessity which is derived from unchangeable customary regularities (*necessitas consuetudini accommodata*). Like Peter Damian, Gilbert stressed that these natural necessities are not absolute. In his unedited commentary on the Pauline epistles, for instance, Gilbert wrote as follows:

It says that philosophy is knowledge about natural things and that it is deduced from rational principles, but the necessity which belongs to them is the customary one. One divine power is the source of the motion and substance of all things and of the connection of the causes of those things which are said to belong to them. Some people, who don't understand what is said, when hearing that some things are called necessary, not considering the reasons for saying so, deprive them of God's power, thinking that what is called necessary on the basis of the custom of nature cannot be not the case absolutely. This is why they deny that a virgin could have given birth to a child and other similar things called impossible in the sense just mentioned.

(The Latin text is quoted in Nielsen 1982a: 136)

Natural regularities are in force only if God wills to keep them in force. Thus, traditional natural necessities, when treated as necessities without qualification, are wrongly defined. Gilbert thought that the ancient philosophical heritage included errors and that it could not therefore be taught as an intact whole. Gilbert did not want to reduce philosophy to theology, but he insisted that the shortcomings of philosophical definitions, as pointed out by theology, should be corrected. He did not argue that revealed truths as such had to play a role in philosophy, but he thought that they can show which ideas natural reason mistakenly regards as absolute truths or necessities. It is worth adding that no piece of philosophy, as opposed to theology, by Gilbert survives (for this theme, see Nielsen 1982a: 136–42).

One example of Gilbert's correction of traditional thinking is his new formulation of the view that states of affairs which are always (*simpliciter* or under given conditions) actual are, for that reason, necessary. One can accept this idea, Gilbert argues, when the prevalence of the invariances in question is viewed as conditioned. They are conditioned, of course, by divine will. This kind of necessities are regularities included in the actualized divine plan. They are theologically contingent, first, because it is not necessary that anything is created and, second, because the regularities of the actual world are not necessarily contained in those other providential programmes God could have realized instead of the actual one. The following quotations may serve as examples of Gilbert's terminology:

> Because no temporal things are free from mutability, the whole customary necessity belonging to them is shaky. Whatever namely is said to be or not to be by necessity with respect to them, in a certain way it neither necessarily is nor necessarily is not so. For that to which the notion of necessity applies due to custom only is not absolutely necessary.
>
> (*De Trin.*, in *The Commentaries on Boethius* 164.36–41)

Early medieval modalities 77

When it is said that man cannot be dissolved or that man cannot be not dissolved, it is not because God could not do it, but because divine will ordained that the condition of man is such before the fall or after the fall or after the resurrection. In the same way it is said that the sun cannot be not moving, although divine power could stop it from moving. There is an infinitude of similar cases.
(*Contra Eut.*, in *The Commentaries on Boethius* 322.43–9)

According to Gilbert, God has chosen the actual world and its history from among alternative providential programmes. If God had so willed, he could have realized a world with totally different individuals (*De Trin.* 129.25–8), or with different natural invariances (*Contra Eut.* 322.43–9), or he could have realized in our actual world histories different from those which have taken place (see Nielsen 1982a: 139 n.95). However, Gilbert did not claim that divine omnipotence has no limitations. Although all natural necessities are contingent in the sense that it depends upon God's will whether there are any actual states of affairs or whether they are regulated by those customs they now obey, there are a number of necessities which are not relative (see, for example, *Contra Eut.* 272.27–44, 310.56–63, 318.34–6, 337.95–338.2). Gilbert seems to think, like Augustine, that the validity of these necessary principles, some of which are traditional topical rules, is independent of divine will.

Gilbert did not discuss the meaning of modal notions in a systematic way, but his scattered remarks on the subject are interesting, especially as they pertain to the theory of alternative providential programmes. One could say that his theological criticism of philosophical modalities and his attempts to develop more adequate conceptions are based on the intuitive idea that the meaning of modal notions is spelled out by considering alternative states of affairs at the same time. Augustine's *potuit sed noluit* principle is given a more elaborate meaning by treating divine possibilities as embedded in providential models of which only one is actual. Natural laws, which are chosen to be in force in the actual world, are not inevitably included in all providential programmes, and they are therefore not absolutely necessary. Gilbert assumes that an unlimited number of *possibilia* are unrealized in the actual world (see, for example, *Contra Eut.* 273.68–70).

Many scholars, following a medieval tradition (see, for example, Bonaventure, *In Sent.* I, *d.* 42, *a.* 3, *concl.*; de la Torre 1987: 334), have claimed that, according to Gilbert, God can undo the past (see

Nielsen 1982a: 139; Schmidt 1956: 126–7; van Elswijk 1966: 307–10; Courtenay 1973: 148). One text thought to be relevant here is from the commentary on *De Trinitate*:

> All things are similarly subjected to his power, so that as those, which have not been existent can have been existent, and those which do not exist or will not exist, can exist, in the same way those, which have been existent, can have been non-existent, and those which are or will be, can be non-existent.
> (*The Commentaries on Boethius* 129.25–8)

In the commentary on *Contra Eutychen* Gilbert writes:

> It holds of everything that when it did not exist, it could exist through divine power, and when it exists, by the same power it can be non-existent. For divine power would not be immutable, if a thing which has begun to exist, could not be non-existent, because it could be non-existent when it did not exist.
> (*The Commentaries on Boethius* 267.94–268.98)

No paradoxical formulations are put forward here. Gilbert thought that all thinkable states of affairs and historical sequences belong to the scope of God's power. He did not want to claim that they could be simultaneously actualized or that what has taken place can be undone in one and the same history. Gilbert's idea of alternative total histories as objects of God's non-historical choice is seen from the commentary on *Contra Eutychen*:

> As for human beings . . . it is so ordained by divine power and will that one can correctly say as follows: they first can and then cannot be dissolved or be not dissolved. This does not mean that God in some sense would begin or cease to have power – his power is eternal – but that of all things subjected to his power he, because of his will only, ordained that some things are to be changed and others are not to be changed. . . . God never ceased to have the power he had, but divine will ordained that it would be so if human beings did not sin.
> (*The Commentaries on Boethius* 358.28–359.62)

God's power and God's will are not the same. Gilbert saw, more clearly than Peter Damian did, that although divine executive power is immutable, divine choice determines which of the alternative possibilities can be realized in one and the same history. In his *Regulae caelestis iuris*, which is influenced by Gilbert's ideas, Alan of Lille expresses the same view by referring to a distinction between what God can do and what God can do *in actu* (pp. 168–9). This was later called the distinction between *potentia Dei absoluta* and *potentia Dei ordinata* (see pp. 100–2 below). It is also relevant here that Gilbert seems to regard a number of natural invariances as non-absolute necessities because of their having been chosen rather than because of their being susceptible of changes as Peter Damian thought. (For the view of the relative autonomy of secondary causes, see also William of Conches, *Dragmaticon* 39; Newell 1990: 284.)

It is evident that Gilbert did not accept the traditional theory of the necessity of the present which was based on the lack of the idea of synchronic alternatives. If Socrates is presently sitting but could at the same time be standing, we could think that his standing now belongs to a possible history. This line of thought presupposes that we can speak about the same being occurring simultaneously in alternative states of affairs. Nothing like that can be found in the Aristotelian tradition, in which a thing is individuated by its actual history, i.e. by being 'this' actualization of a substantial form. On this view, Socrates' alleged possibility of standing at the moment when in reality he is sitting is suspicious, because the subject of the possible standing should be a person different from the one who is now sitting. Against this background it is interesting that Gilbert tried to develop a theory of individuals in which the possible properties of singular things played an important role.

In his study on Gilbert's thought, Lauge Nielsen has extensively discussed Gilbert's notions of unity, singularity and individuality which create some order in the prima facie confused ontology built on the distinction between the concepts *quod est*, what it is, and *quo est*, that which makes it so (Nielsen 1982a: 58–69; see also Marenbon 1988a). One of Nielsen's points is that Gilbert introduced a new theory of personality which included modal considerations. This is a historically important and interesting part of Gilbert's modal theology. Nielsen states that the modal element in the concept of personality distinguishes it from the concept of individuality (1982a: 62–4, 180, 184), but in fact it is the concept of the individual which primarily contains the modal element:

> The property of something, which is naturally dissimilar to everything else that actually or potentially was or is or will be, is truly called and truly is, not only singular or particular, but individual. . . . For this reason Plato's whole form, which is neither in act nor by nature similar to anything else, is truly individual.
> (*Contra Eut.*, in *The Commentaries on Boethius* 274.81–90)

Gilbert distinguishes between words like 'man' or 'sun', which are called appellative names by grammarians and divided names by dialecticians, and words like 'Plato', which are called proper names in grammar and individual names in dialectic. According to Gilbert, the referents of appellative names are divided (*diuidua*), and those corresponding to proper names are individual (*indiuidua*). The concept (*quo est*) of man, for example, is divided in act and by nature, because it refers to several actually existing beings, similar to each other by nature. The concept of sun is also divided, but only by nature. Only one sun exists in the actual world, but the concept can also be applied to infinitely many possible suns that are similar to each other by nature (*Contra Eut*. 273.50–74). An individual concept cannot be applied to many, whether actual or possible. The requirements for individuality are not met by generic forms nor by their singular instantiations *qua* instantiations of generic forms. Gilbert remarks that no part of an individual is an individual, although the word is often used in a way that suggests this. Parts of an individual are singular but not individual (*Contra Eut*. 274.77–80; see also Marenbon 1988a).

The individual form by which Plato is Plato is described by Gilbert as 'Platoness collected from all things which, in act and by nature, have been, are, or will be Plato's' (*De Trin*. 144.77–8). It is 'neither in act nor by nature similar to anything else' (*Contra Eut*. 274.75–6). As 'by nature' is here used to refer to what could be, Plato's Platoness can be delineated as comprising everything which Plato was, is and will be plus what he could be without ever being it.

As Gilbert himself indicates, many masters were in his time interested in exploring notions like identity, difference, singularity or individuality which, through Boethius' *Opuscula Sacra*, became central theoretical concepts of theology. Peter Abelard often refers to different modes of identity (see, for instance, *Theologia 'Scholarium'* I.19–20, II.95–6; cf. also the *Sententiae*, tentatively ascribed to Abelard and edited by Minio-Paluello 1958: 116.11–25; and van der Lecq 1987: 49–50). One of his distinctions is the same, which in the contemporary discussion has been called a distinction between numerical sameness (or numerical identity) and qualitative sameness (or qualitative identity). Two suitcases, for example, may be identical in the sense of being exactly alike without being numerically the same. Through his notion of the individual Gilbert refers to numerically identical things which, on a certain ontological level, lack qualitative identity or sameness with respect to all other actual or potential beings. Individuals are both actually and metaphysically

Early medieval modalities 81

unique. Nothing like this is included in Abelard's discussions of individuals. Boethius proposed the term 'Platonitas' for the incommunicable quality which makes Plato unique, while 'humanitas' signifies a universal quality which is found also in other beings. Boethius did not refer to merely possible objects in this context. (See *In Periherm.* II, 136.17–137.26; cf. de Rijk 1988: 16–17. For the distinction between particularity and individuality in Boethius, see also his commentary on Aristotle's *Categories*, PL 64, 169 and Gracia 1984: 83–7.)

It is probable that Gilbert's idea of alternative possible histories made the modal definition of individuality natural for him. One could think, like Leibniz, that it would be sufficient that the complete notion of an actualized individual comprises all predicates referring to any moments of its history (*Discours de Métaphysique*, in *Die philosophischen Schriften* IV, sect. 8–9, 13). This would mean, however, that the same individual could not occur in alternative providential programmes, which is contrary to Gilbert's basic theological view. He says, for example, that there are many different ways in which the second person of the Trinity could have fulfilled the purpose of incarnation (see Nielsen 1982a: 139). Gilbert seems to think that beings that are included in the providential programme of actual history could have different properties in alternative histories and that their individual concepts must distinguish the same individual from the actual world as well as from the alternative worlds and histories which could have been actualized by divine will and omnipotence. Although this idea of cross-world identity (cf. Hintikka 1969: 99–103, 139–41) is not explicitly mentioned in Gilbert, his modal definition of Plato's Platoness is probably based on an intuitive view similar to that which has made modern logicians speak about trans-world lines of cross-identity between the embodiments of the same individual in different 'possible worlds'. This way of thinking easily suggested itself in connection with the Augustinian model of God acting by choice among alternative histories.

One could characterize Gilbert's idea of the concept of an individual as similar to Leibniz's *inesse* principle, with the important difference that, according to Gilbert, the concept of an individual also comprises possible predicates. In a more detailed comparison, we should note Gilbert's doctrine of categories and his idea that the accidents grouped under the last seven Aristotelian categories are, as Nielsen says, 'the circumstances in which each thing finds itself, the thing's status, and therefore cannot be said to contribute to the thing's being' (1982a: 56). Perhaps it is only an academic question, however, whether these kinds of qualifications belong to the individual form and concept or whether they belong to the '*status*' part of the actual and possible histories of an individual.

The interesting thing in the remarks of Gilbert of Poitiers on modality is the fact that they can be understood as a more or less conscious attempt to develop a new modal semantics in which the Augustinian doctrine of God as choosing among possibilities is interpreted in terms of alternative domains. He uses theologically reinterpreted modal terms in accordance with what could be called an elementary theory of modality as referential multiplicity. Necessities and possibilities are not considered primarily as types of events or individuals, instantiated in various degrees in actual history. Modal terms basically refer to things and structures in various conceivable states of affairs which, as the intensional correlates of divine choice and power, are in principle realizable. For example, 'it is possible that $p$' is true if there is a conceivable history in which $p$ is true. There is no demand that the conceivable history in which $p$ is true should at some time become part of actual history.

I think that Gilbert's discussion of the concept of the individual shows that his insight into modal matters was deeper than what one could prima facie assume when reading his idiosyncratic theological treatises. Gilbert of Poitiers had several followers in the later twelfth century (see Marenbon 1988b). Gilbert's influence on logic is visible from the anonymous *Compendium Logicae Porretanum* (Ebbesen *et al.* 1983).

Peter Abelard was a contemporary of Gilbert and, as John of Salisbury mentions in the report of his studies in Paris, a leading logician of his time. He was called the Peripatetic from Le Pallet (*Peripateticus Palatinus*) after his birthplace (John of Salisbury, *Metalogicon* II.10, 77.31–78.7). The greater part of Abelard's partially surviving logical works consists of a series of commentaries on ancient textbooks of logic. His early works include short commentaries on the *Isagoge* of Porphyry, the *Categories* and *De interpretatione* of Aristotle and the *De divisione* of Boethius. These works were edited by Dal Pra in 1954. In 1919–27 Geyer edited a series of more extensive commentaries on the *Isagoge*, the *Categories* and the *De interpretatione*. He considered these texts as parts of a single work which, in accordance with the opening word, he called *Logica 'Ingredientibus'*. In 1954 Dal Pra edited a commentary on *De topicis differentiis* of Boethius which he regarded as a part of *Logica 'Ingredientibus'*. The manuscript on which Geyer based his edition contained, instead of Abelard's own ending for his commentary on *De interpretatione*, the work of a different author (497.20–503.28). In 1958 Minio-Paluello edited the authentic version of the final sections of Abelard's *De interpretatione* commentary from another manuscript. A third commentary on the *Isagoge* was edited by Geyer in 1933. He thought that this work was the first part of a new series of commentaries which he called, in accordance with the opening phrase, *Logica 'Nostrorum petitioni sociorum'*. It is possible that Abelard wrote other commentaries, for instance on Boethius' textbooks on categorical and hypothetical syllogisms, but it is not certain. Abelard also wrote a logical compendium, the *Dialectica*, which has been edited by de Rijk (1956). In addition to logical treatises, Abelard's works include books on theology and moral philosophy. (For Abelard's works and thought, see Beonio-Brocchieri Fumagalli 1969; Luscombe 1970; Tweedale 1976; Jolivet 1982; Luscombe 1988.)

Abelard's way of discussing modal concepts was largely shaped by the doctrines in the traditional texts which he analysed and discussed in his works. As with many other traditional topics, Abelard was not very satisfied with the received views, and this led him to develop some new systematic insights into modal matters as well. The basic conceptions of Abelard's modal theory are to be found in a survey serving as an introduction to Chapters XII–XIII of his long commentary on *De interpretatione* (*Super Periermenias*, edited by L. Minio-Paluello, 3–47). A rather different and possibly earlier account occurs in the section on modality in the *Dialectica* (191.1–210.19).

According to Abelard, modal terms in the most proper sense of the word are adverbs expressing the way in which the determinant predicated of a subject inheres in it. Terms like 'necessarily', 'well' or 'rapidly' are used in this manner; some other adverbs like 'possibly' and 'falsely' are also called modals, but this is due to their position in sentences rather than to their meaning; their task does not consist in modifying actual inherences. When nominal modes (*casuales*), for example, 'it is necessary that' or 'it is possible that', are understood in an adverbial manner, they are in the same way divided into proper and improper modes. Abelard thinks that the reason why Aristotle treated mainly nominal modes in *De interpretatione* 12–13 was that they involve more problems than simple adverbial modes. According to him, this is patently seen from the fact that nominal modes occur in sentences such as 'Necesse est Socratem currere', which can be understood in two ways: either modal terms qualify the predicate part of the corresponding non-modal sentence or, as suggested by the grammatical construction, they are predicates in sentences the subjects of which are accusative and infinitive phrases (*Super Periermenias* 3.7–9.11). The ambiguities of sentences including nominal modes demand that the relations between various readings of modal sentences be investigated. Furthermore, questions pertaining to the quantity (universal, particular, indefinite, singular), quality (affirmative, negative) and conversion of modal sentences as well as to the equipollences and other relations between them have to be discussed separately with respect to different readings of them. This is what Abelard does in the first part of the modal tractate in *Super Periermenias* (9.12–34.8). The rest is devoted to a discussion of modal sentences with determinations. Abelard thought that the difference between the grammatical constructions of modal sentences with adverbial modes and those with nominal modes is linked to a systematic distinction which, referring to Aristotle's *Sophistici elenchi* 4, 166a23–30, he calls the distinction between readings *de re* and *de sensu* or *per divisionem* and *per conpositionem* (13.15–14.13). Although Abelard often employs these pairs interchangeably, he also mentions in a somewhat ambiguous way that the compound reading could be regarded as a subcase of the *de sensu* reading. Furthermore, he says that a modal sentence may be read *personaliter* or *inpersonaliter*, i.e. an impersonal construction such as '*necesse est* . . .' or '*possibile est* . . .' may be understood in a personal way as stating something about the subject of the corresponding categorical sentence, or it may be understood as a merely impersonal modal expression. I shall return to these questions.

Abelard was one of the first medieval authors to discuss Aristotle's distinction between reading modal sentences in a compound sense and reading them in a divided sense. It is historically significant that he considered the elucidation of this topic as one of the main tasks of his modal analysis. As will be seen, a similar interest in modalities *de dicto* and *de re* much dominated the subsequent discussions in logical treatises. Abelard also applied this tool of analysis to theological questions and formulated certain solutions which became common in medieval scholasticism (see p. 94 below).

Abelard's description of what he considered the Aristotelian distinction in modal sentences between the readings *per conpositionem* and *per divisionem* runs as follows:

> It seems that there are two possible expositions of expressions such as 'It is possible that he who is standing is sitting'. As Aristotle teaches in the *Sophistic Refutations*, the meaning is different when what is said is taken to be divided or compound. It is compound if

standing and sitting are combined with the same subject simultaneously, as if we were to say: 'It is possible that he who is standing is sitting while he remains standing', i.e., 'to sit and to stand at the same time' (as if we were to say: 'It is possible that it should happen as this proposition says: "A standing man is sitting" '), which is quite false, because then two opposites could belong to the same subject at the same time. In this case the term 'possible' is applied, as it were, to the whole meaning of the proposition, as if we were to say: 'It is possible that it should happen as this proposition says: "A standing man is sitting" '. But if it is taken to mean that he who is standing can be sitting at some time, we don't combine opposites, and through the term 'possible' we don't refer to the proposition, but instead to the thing itself when we say: 'He who is standing can be sitting at some time' and 'It is not possible that it should happen as this proposition says: "A standing man is sitting." '

(*Super Periermenias* 13.15–14.4)

It may be noticed that while Abelard here speaks about the Aristotelian distinction between expositions *per conpositionem* and *per divisionem*, he later (30.29, 31.7, 32.9–11, 14–15, 20) refers to it as the distinction between *per coniunctionem* and *per divisionem*.

The distinction just mentioned was connected with many philosophical problems. Some of these difficulties can be discerned from Abelard's discussion of the question whether modal sentences *de sensu* imply modal sentences *de re*. He says first that *prima facie* one can always infer from an affirmative possibility sentence read *de sensu* an affirmative reading *de re*. This thesis is then discussed in the light of two counterexamples:

It is argued, to the contrary, that if it is possible that all substances are spirits (i.e. it is possible that things are as this proposition says: 'Every substance is a spirit', because it could happen that there are only spirits, and then this proposition would be true: 'Every substance is a spirit'), it is not therefore true *de rebus* that every substance could be a spirit. And now, while I don't have a son, the proposition *de sensu* saying that 'It is possible that my son is living' seems to be true, i.e. it is possible that it happens as this proposition says: 'My son is living', because perhaps it will be so, but the proposition *de rebus* saying that 'My son can be living' is not true, because through the subject term 'my son' I suppose that my son exists and I connect 'can be living' with the subject as if he were existent.

(*Super Periermenias* 30.3–16)

Admitting that the inference from *de sensu* to *de re* is not valid in these cases, Abelard remarks that he is using the terms *de sensu* and *de re* in the same way as Aristotle used the terms *per coniunctionem* and *per divisionem* and that the distinction, understood in this way, maintains the inference from an affirmative possibility sentence *de sensu* to a corresponding possibility sentence *de re*. It seems that both readings are then in fact '*de rebus*', and the difference between them is as follows: the former asserts that the various qualifications mentioned in a non-modal sentence can belong simultaneously to an existing subject, and the latter asserts that they can belong to the subject without claiming that they can belong to it at the same time (*Super Periermenias* 30.25–31.10). What is meant is the difference between

(9) $x$ which is or can be $F$ can be $G$ while remaining $F$

and

(10) $x$ which is or can be $F$ can be $G$.

Abelard does not explain in any depth the nature of those unrealized possibilities which, in the above quotation, exemplify *de sensu* possibilities without *de re* counterparts. He thought that they did not belong to an Aristotelian modal theory. When he seems to exclude merely possible things from his own major distinction in modal theory as well, one could assume that he did not consider them systematically interesting in the way Gilbert of Poitiers did. One might also ask whether Abelard was compelled to delete such possibilities because of his well-known theological view that God can do only what he does (*Theologia christiana* V.29–32, pp. 358–9; *Theologia 'Scholarium'* III.27–38, pp. 511–16), sometimes called 'the theological version of the Master Argument of Diodorus' (Faust 1931–2: 193). But these guesses are premature.

As for the theological question, Abelard was unwilling to treat God's wisdom, power and benevolence separately in the manner suggested by, for example, Augustine (*Contra Gaudentium* I.30) or Origen (*In Matthaeum commentariorum series* 95, *PG* 13, 1746). The created order is the best one which can be and the only one God can create, although it is not the only possible world (see *Logica 'Ingredientibus'* 430.23–6). As for the surmise that Abelard excluded unrealized beings from his modal theory, it is important to notice that in the passage just mentioned Abelard does not claim that there are no *de sensu* possibilities without corresponding *de re* possibilities

Early medieval modalities 87

belonging to actual beings. When Abelard calls the Aristotelian *de sensu* reading a reading *de sensu per coniunctionem* (31.7, 32.7–21), he probably wanted to assert that this is one *de sensu* reading. As already seen, it is a *de sensu* reading with existential import. In addition there are possibility sentences *de sensu* which have a merely impersonal exposition, in which case they do not have existential import. Abelard found it ontologically problematic to speak about possibilities *qua* possibilities that are not reducible to active or passive potencies in existing things. Instead of dropping them, however, he thought that they should be treated like universals, *dicta* of propositions, and other abstract matters which are objective and real without being existing entities. Modal terms as parts of impersonally understood constructions do not name things any more than the clauses in their scope, but they still express some aspects of the domain of what can be conceived (20.13–21.3). (For impersonal modal constructions in Abelard, see Tweedale 1976: 255–72; Jacobi 1985: 30–40.)

Abelard deals extensively with the distinction between different readings of modal expressions also in the *Dialectica* where he claims that William of Champeaux, one of his teachers, held the view that all modal sentences should be understood *de dicto*. Abelard considers this opinion absurd, and he tries to show that *de dicto* readings are always wrong if they are taken to mean, as William allegedly did, that some kind of modal property belongs to the *dictum* of an assertoric sentence (*Dialectica* 195.11–198.11). Without developing the details of the theory of impersonal modalities, he remarks that one should understand expressions in which a modal property is seemingly predicated of a *dictum* as expressions referring to abstract modal states of affairs, such as what 'nature' permits or demands (*Dialectica* 205.20–206.2).

As for the principles of modal logic, Abelard refers to the rules that, if the antecedent is possible or necessary, the consequent is possible or necessary, and if the consequent is impossible, the antecedent is impossible (*Dialectica* 202.6–8). While discussing the conversions of modal sentences, Abelard remarks that if modal sentences *de dicto* are read in an impersonal manner, they are without quantity and cannot be converted. The equipollences and conversions of categorical sentences can be applied to their non-modal parts, however (*Super Periermenias* 14.14–17.8). Modal sentences *de re* are not convertible in such a manner that the resulting sentence would be a modal sentence, but they can be converted so that the subject term of the converted sentence is modalized (*Super*

*Periermenias* 11.17–12.20). Abelard also discusses the rules of equipollences between various modes in combination with negations and shows how the relations of the assertoric square of opposition apply to the groups of equivalent singular modal sentences *de re*; the same relations were later often illustrated by the square of opposition for modal sentences (see p. 108). Furthermore, Abelard formulates four groups of equivalent affirmative or negative universal modal formulae with different modes and similarly four groups of particular formulae. According to him, one can easily see which groups are contradictories, contraries and subcontraries in the lists of universal and particular formulae respectively. He seems to think that these relationships are the same as those between singular modal sentences *de re*, which is totally wrong (*Super Periermenias* 21.22–26.5; see also Jacobi 1980: 402).

As Abelard regarded the Aristotelian composition–division distinction as the historical starting point of his modal theory and as he noticed that in Aristotle it is intertwined with a temporal distinction of some sort, he tried to explore this matter as carefully as possible. Part of this attempt consisted of specifying the relationship between simple modal sentences *de sensu* or *de re* and modal sentences with determinations.

Abelard divided modal sentences with temporal determinations into two groups, depending on whether the determination is intrinsic or extrinsic. An intrinsic determination of a modal sentence is a *dum* clause constructed from the elements of the non-modal roots of the modal sentence ('It is possible that Socrates runs when he runs'); an extrinsic determination has an alien part ('It is possible that Socrates runs when he lives'). Sentences with determinations can be understood in two ways. They may be considered as complex temporal sentences (*hypotheticae temporales*) having as their parts a modal sentence and a non-modal sentence which specifies the moment of time in which the modal sentence is true. In this interpretation, the sentence 'It is possible that he who stands sits while he stands' is analysed as follows: a man is standing and during the time in which he is standing it is true that he can be sitting. If the sentence is considered as expressing a possible conjunction of predicates with respect to the subject at the moment of temporal determination, it is called a proper modal sentence. The above example would then claim that a man who is standing can be sitting while remaining standing (*Super Periermenias* 34.9–37.24; *Dialectica* 206.16–33).

When comparing simple modal sentences with modal sentences

possessing temporal determinations, Abelard says that the latter are not true if the *dum* phrase is not true. The function of the temporal 'dum' is to express that now, while the categorical sentence in the determination is true, the modal part is true as well. Categorical sentences are treated as temporally indeterminate statements which can be true or false, depending on the facts at the moment at which they are uttered (*Super Periermenias* 31.16–24; cf. 36.28–30, 39.8–13, 40.5–9; for Abelard's view of the changing truth of assertions, see, for example, *Logica 'Ingredientibus'* 367.13–26, *Dialectica* 219.32–220.7 and Nuchelmans 1973: 150–62). Although Abelard regards the 'now while' reading of the *dum* phrase as the basic one, he sometimes takes it to mean 'at those times when' (*Super Periermenias* 38.6–26). If Abelard tried to express that something is true at a determinate moment of time, it is worth noticing how difficult this was for him. The sentence 'Socrates can sit while he is standing', read as a complex temporal sentence, can be regarded as an instance of the form

(11) $(Ex)(Fx \ \& \ M-Fx)$

where '$x$' refers to individuals of a species which actually exist now. When the sentence is considered as a determinate modal sentence it still has reference to the present moment of utterance, but it also asserts that the subject, while remaining as it is, can receive another qualification (see *Super Periermenias* 37.6–11). Its form is then

(12) $(Ex)(Fx \ \& \ M(Fx \ \& \ -Fx))$.

The alleged difference between determinate 'modal' (12) and 'temporal' (11) possibility sentences on the one hand and simple possibility sentences *de sensu* or *de re* on the other hand (31.11–24) becomes clear when the latter are written as follows:

(13) $(Ex)M(Fx \ \& \ -Fx)$

and

(14) $(Ex)(M(Fx) \ \& \ M(-Fx))$.

Abelard seems to think that temporally indefinite sentences expressing simple *de sensu* possibilities (read *per coniunctionem*) or *de re* possibilities do not necessarily assert anything about actual states of affairs except the actuality of the subjects of which the possibilities are maintained. These are possibilities only as long as the things of which they are attributed exist. I have not used temporal indices in the forms (11)–(14); the question how they should be written is intertwined with difficult problems of interpretation.

Simple *de sensu* possibilities (*per coniunctionem*) and *de re* possibilities are possible qualifications of things or combinations of such qualifications. They are expressed in temporally indeterminate modal sentences which are true if uttered as long as their subjects exist. Possibilities are then regarded as generic capacities which belong to all members of a certain species and which as such belong immutably to individuals. Abelard describes possibilities of this kind as follows:

> We believe that what we see to occur in one member of a species can occur in all the individuals of the same species, because we comprehend potencies and impotencies in accordance with nature so that a thing is susceptible only of what is permitted by its nature and it cannot receive anything excluded by its nature. As all members of a species are of the same nature – this is why the species is said to be the whole substance of the individuals – they all are capable and incapable of the same things.
>
> (*Dialectica* 385.1–8)

One example of an unrealized generic possibility belonging to Socrates is his possibility of being a bishop:

> his nature is not repugnant to being a bishop, as we can realize from other members of the same species which we see already participating in the property of being a bishop. For we judge that when something occurs in one individual of a species, it can occur in all the individuals of the same species, because they are entirely of the same nature.
>
> (*Dialectica* 193.36–194.3)

Possibilities of this kind are immune to change. Thus, Abelard can say that a man whose leg is cut off can be a biped or walk *simpliciter*, or that a person, after having been blinded, can see (*Logica 'Ingredientibus'* 229.34–6, 274.10–12, 429.21–5; *Dialectica* 385.11–14; *Super Periermenias* 41.21–2).

Abelard often characterizes modalities such as those referred to above in terms of possibility as equated with what nature allows or what is not repugnant to it. Impossibility is equated with what is repugnant to nature, and necessity with what nature demands. Other nominal definitions of 'necessary' are 'unchangeable', 'inevitable' and, in a certain sense, 'determinate' (*Dialectica* 98.16–18, 193.31–194.9, 196.29–197.31, 200.25–35, 204.11–12, 205.28–30, 391.36–392.1; *Super Periermenias* 21.2–3, 27.22–6, 41.29–30, 43.4–6; *Editio super Aristotelem De interpretatione*, in *Scritti di Logica* 99.32–44, 111.18–24; see also Jolivet 1966). According to Abelard, we obtain our knowledge of the nature of things through inductive abstraction and our knowledge about what nature in general allows is derived from what in fact has been exemplified in some individuals. Abelard's view concerning types of natural possibilities could be called an epistemically motivated frequency interpretation.

Even though people who have lost their legs or sight can walk or see *simpliciter*, they cannot in another sense see or walk after such misfortunes (see, for example, *Logica 'Ingredientibus'* 429.21–45; *Super Periermenias* 41.21–2; *Dialectica* 385.11–14). While discussing the traditional theory of temporal necessity in connection with determinate modal sentences, Abelard says that the temporal determination in sentences like 'This necessarily stands when he stands' belongs to the mode (*Super Periermenias* 42.1–6). As one of the nominal definitions of 'necessarily' is 'unchangeably' (41.29–30), a temporally determinate necessity sentence, analysed in this way, maintains that something unchangeably is as it is during the time described in the determination. This temporally restricted necessity, which Abelard called determinate necessity as distinct from simple necessity, belongs to all actual things, because they are what they are in a determinate way; in so far as they are not unchangeable without qualification, they are non-necessary *simpliciter* (*Editio super De int.* 111.18–112.6; *Theologia 'Scholarium'* III, 101, p. 541). This notion of necessity could be formulated in terms of Boethian temporal necessity:

(3) $p_t \rightarrow L_t p_t$.

What does Abelard mean when he stresses, like Aristotle and Boethius, that things, which necessarily are as they are, when they are, can be otherwise *simpliciter*? The possibilities of interpretations proliferate here, and unfortunately Abelard did not formulate any systematic answer to the question. One group of examples contains sentences stating that, for example, it is impossible that this man has two legs after having lost them, but it is not therefore true *simpliciter* that it is impossible that this man has two legs. In the light of Abelard's view of natural possibilities as generic capacities belonging to all members of species, simple possibilities may be such common capacities. When such a possibility of Socrates is not now actualized, it cannot be now actualized, although it remains a generic possibility belonging to Socrates *qua* member of the human race. Correspondingly, the truth of a temporally indefinite sentence cannot change now when it is true, although it remains capable of change. If simple possibilities are interpreted in this way, they are not alternatives for things which are necessary by determinate necessary. A shifting of the scope of attention from definite and individual cases to their indefinite and generic counterparts occurs in Boethius' discussion of Chapter 9 of *De interpretatione*. In *Dialectica* 221.3–13 Abelard says that sentences which are false at a particular moment, and therefore necessarily false at that moment, are not for this reason necessarily false *simpliciter*, since this would mean that sentences which are false could not become true.

In some places Abelard qualifies the necessity of the present by referring to the antecedent alternative possibilities of which the unrealized ones vanish at the moment of the actualization of the present (see, for example, *Logica 'Ingredientibus'* 273.29–274.4). This is another Boethian model of which Abelard made use; as we have seen, Boethius did not connect it with alternative synchronic possibilities. So it did not qualify the temporal necessity of what is actual at the moment at which it is actual. In the light of these examples, it seems that forms (11)–(14), applicable to personal possibilities, should be provided with indices showing that, at any point of time, mutually exclusive states of affairs are not both actualizable with respect to that point of time.

Even though Abelard probably considered this way of speaking natural, he might have had some other ideas in his mind as well. In *Super Periermenias* 37.26–7 Abelard puts forward the following formulation pertaining to the possibilities of sitting and standing: 'It is possible that this man is sitting now, and it is possible that this man is standing now'. This looks like

(15) $M_t p_t$ & $M_t - p_t$.

In the subsequent discussion, Abelard asserts that the sentence: 'It is possible that Socrates, who is standing now, is sitting at all times of his life' is true, which also seems to imply that (15) is considered as a valid form. Weidemann (1981) has argued that what we find here is a theory of contrafactually interpreted alternative individual possibilities. According to him, this is Abelard's basic conception of temporally defined possibilities. It may be that something like (15) is what Abelard intended in the lines 37.26–7 of *Super*

*Periermenias.* What is found on the next page, however, shows that his views on the matter were not very clear:

> It must be also noticed that when we say: 'If it is possible that he [Socrates] is sitting at all times of his life, it is possible that he is sitting when he is not sitting', this is acceptable only if 'when' serves as a conjunctive in its temporal sense, as if we were to say: 'It is possible that he is sitting at a time at which he is not sitting, like tomorrow or at another time at which he does not actually sit, because the time has not yet come'.
> (*Super Periermenias* 38.27–39.2)

This means that, according to Abelard, when it is true that Socrates is not sitting, it is possible that he can sit, but sitting can occur only at a moment of time different from the one at which he is not sitting. The purpose of the explanatory sentence is to indicate the time to which the possibility of sitting refers, i.e. to those times at which Socrates is not yet sitting. This becomes clear when Abelard continues as follows:

> If 'dum' does not have only a temporal sense, but also that of a conjunction (as if we were to say: 'It is possible to sit while not sitting, i.e., the time already existing at which he is not sitting'), then what is said by the following proposition is possible: 'Socrates is sitting and not sitting'.
> (ibid. 39.4–8)

The 'modal' reading of the sentence 'It is possible that he is sitting when he is not sitting' was formulated earlier in (12), without indices, in a way corresponding to

(16) $-Fa \mathbin{\&} M(-Fa \mathbin{\&} Fa)$.

It is here elliptically exemplified by a sentence of the form

(17) $-Fa \mathbin{\&} M(Fa)$

probably because

(18) $(-Fa)_t \mathbin{\&} M_t(Fa)_t$

and

(19) $(-Fa)_t \mathbin{\&} M_t(-Fa \mathbin{\&} Fa)_t$

are considered as equivalent.

Weidemann correctly criticizes in his paper some parts of my earlier interpretation of the passage 38.6–39.11 in Knuuttila (1981a:

184). However, his own attempt to show that Abelard's thought is based on the idea of counterfactual possibilities demands some spurious changes of the text. Thus, he deletes sentence 39.1-2, where it is said that he who is not sitting can sit at another time, and he changes the example in passage 39.4-8, quoted above, into 'It is possible to sit and not to sit while not sitting'. These are just the sentences which make one wonder whether (15) is applicable here (see also Marenbon 1991).

Even though one cannot claim that Abelard's modal thinking was systematically based on a model of counterfactual synchronic alternatives, it probably played some role in his thought. It seems, however, that Abelard did not see very clearly the relationships between the various modal paradigms which shaped his thinking. As already mentioned, Abelard seems to propose a non-Aristotelian reading of possibility sentences *de sensu* without existential import; therefore, he invokes at times the distinction between *de sensu* and *de re* modalities in a way which involves (15). One example is his discussion of the question whether the possibility of events having happened otherwise implies the possibility of error in God. The starting point was Cicero's argument against the omniscience of God which was also mentioned in Augustine's *De civitate Dei* V, 9. Abelard considered it a sophism to be solved as follows. The sentence 'A thing can be otherwise than it is' can be read as a modal statement *de sensu*, in which case it is false, and the possibility of God's error does not follow from it. But does it follow if the antecedent is read *de re* and is true? Abelard does not say that the *de re* possibility of being otherwise refers to a time other than the time at which the event takes place and that God, therefore, cannot err. Here the *de re* possibility seems to be a purely modal alternative. From the possibility that things are otherwise the possibility of God's error does not follow, for if things were otherwise, God would possess a different knowledge of them (*Logica 'Ingredientibus'* 430.2-27; *Dialectica* 217.27-219.24). While analysing the sentence 'Things cannot be other than as God foreknows them', Peter Lombard said, following Abelard, that the quoted sentence is true in the compound sense and false in the divided sense. The truth of the compound sense saves God's infallibility and the falsity of the divided sense, exposed with help of the idea of divine alternatives, expresses God's freedom and the metaphysical contingency of the future (*Sententiae* I, d. 38).

On the basis of what has been said above, it seems that there were different strands in Abelard's modal thought and that he only partly managed to construct a complete theory. He sometimes applies to things the concept of possibility as that which nature allows and the concept of necessity as that which is inevitable and unchangeable or which nature does not allow to be otherwise. Some formulations show similarities to Boethian diachronic modalities without synchronic alternatives and with the axiom of temporal necessity of the present (3). In some places Abelard makes use of the traditional habit of qualifying the necessary through a generalization with respect to time or species. Like Anselm, Abelard was interested in the modalities pertaining to non-existent entities such as unborn children or chimeras (*Super Periermenias* 30.3–24; *Dialectica* 201.32–3). This led him to considerations of the ontological status of possibilities *qua* possibilities. Abelard thought that one could speak about possibilities and necessities as items of the domain of non-things, consisting of the natures of things, assertoric contents of propositions and other intelligible matters which in some way determine the order of existing things without being part of it. To read modal propositions in an impersonal manner is to treat them as expressions about this non-existing a priori structure of reality. Abelard did not develop the intuitive model of alternative possible worlds that Gilbert of Poitiers did, but he was more conscious than Gilbert of the philosophical questions connected with the nature of modalities.

Abelard was aware that some new insights were embedded in his theory of impersonal modalities, which had as their intensional correlate a 'nature' that deontologically divided thinkable matters into necessary and contingent ones. From the point of view of what nature demands or permits, all actual states of affairs are contingent in the sense that their existence is not demanded by nature (see *Logica 'Ingredientibus'* 430.23–6; *Super Periermenias* 75.18–76.5). Actually existing things which necessarily are what they are by temporal necessity are not metaphysically necessary.

Abelard's difficulties with specifying the relationship between various types of modalities without the model of synchronic alternatives can be seen from his discussion of wholes, parts and their changes (see *Dialectica* 546.21–555.19). According to D.P. Henry, Abelard's position could be characterized as asserting that proper names of objects extended in time are common nouns covering many successive time-slices of what would ordinarily be regarded as the objects in question (Henry 1985: 65–92). If an individual concept consists of a series of actual states, using it in a model of synchronic alternatives is problematic. Gilbert of Poitiers seems to have realized this (see pp. 79–82 above).

A great part of Abelard's *Dialectica* consists of discussions of topics, consequences and conditionals. Like Boethius, Abelard thought that true conditionals express necessary connections between the antecedents and the consequents (*Dialectica* 271.22–34). Necessary consecutions expressed by true conditionals are, according to Abelard, embedded in the a priori structure of reality. They are eternal and immutable laws of nature (*Dialectica* 279.12–14, 280.12–18). It seems that Abelard's metaphysical attitude towards logic made him think that, even though it is impossible that the antecedent of a true conditional is true when the consequent is false, this fact should not be considered as a sufficient condition for the truth of a genuine conditional. According to him, the real meaning of conditionals depends on a stricter kind of necessity in which the antecedent of itself requires (*ex se exigit*) the consequent (*Dialectica* 253.28–30, 283.37–284.17). Boethius made an analogous distinction in *De hypotheticus syllogismis* (218, *PL* 64, 835). According to him, a conditional is accidental when the antecedent and the consequent are independent, but the truth of the antecedent is never separated from the truth of the consequent. Non-accidental conditionals refer to consequences of nature (see pp. 61–2 above). Martin (1987: 388–97) has shown how Abelard came to his position by excluding forms later called paradoxes of strict implication as well as some of the maximal propositions of topics implying similar problems. There was, after Abelard, a living debate in the twelfth century about the conditions for the validity of conditionals. The followers of Adam of Balsham, the *Parvipontani*, began to regard the inseparability requirement as a sufficient condition for the truth of a conditional. This involved an explicit acceptance of the apparently paradoxical principles 'From the impossible anything follows' and 'The necessary follows from anything' (see Martin 1987: 398–400; for medieval theories of consequences, see also Boh 1982).

Thierry of Chartres, probably the younger brother of the famous master Bernard of Chartres, taught at Chartres and possibly in Paris as well. He died after 1156. Thierry was one of the most influential teachers of his generation. Theologians, philosophers, grammarians or cosmologists like Clarembald of Arras, John of Salisbury, Peter Helias and Hermann of Carinthia were Thierry's disciples. The known works of Thierry include a commentary on Cicero's *De inventione*, a commentary on the pseudo-Ciceronian *Ad Herennium*, various works on Boethius' theological treatises, a cosmological commentary on the opening of the *Genesis* (*Tractatus de sex diebus operibus*) and an introduction and comments on a collection of texts on the seven liberal arts called the *Heptateuchon*. (For the life and works of Thierry of Chartres, see Dronke 1988a.)

When discussing the nature of the universe in his treatises on Boethius' *De Trinitate*, Thierry made use of a modalized cosmological scheme composed of several traditional themes. It did not have much influence on later medieval thought, but Nicholas of Cusa quoted and developed it further in his own works (see, for example, *Trialogus de Possest*). In the lections on Boethius' *De Trinitate*, Thierry writes as follows:

> One and the same universe exists in absolute necessity (*necessitas absoluta*), in necessity of complexion (*necessitas conplexionis*), in absolute possibility (*possibilitas absoluta*) and in determinate possibility (*possibilitas determinata*). These are the four modes of existence of the universe. . . . The universe exists in absolute necessity in a certain simplicity and union of all things, which is God. It exists in necessity of complexion in a certain order and progression, but immutably. It exists in absolute possibility, in possibility without any actuality. And it exists in determinate possibility – both possibly and actually. Absolute necessity is the enfolding (*conplicatio*) of all things in simplicity. Necessity of complexion is the unfolding (*explicatio*) of those things in a certain order. This order the physicists call fate. Absolute possibility is the enfolding of that same universe in the pure possibility from which all things come to actuality. This possibility the physicists call primordial matter and chaos. Determinate possibility is the unfolding of absolute possibility in actuality with possibility.
> (*Lectio super Boethii librum De Trinitate* in *Commentaries on Boethius* 157.88–158.14; the translation is taken, with some changes, from Dronke 1988a: 369; cf. *Glosa super Boethii librum De Trinitate*, in *Commentaries on Boethius* 273.26–53)

It has been thought that all four modal expressions used here are of Thierry's own devising (Dronke 1988a: 369). It may be more correct to say that Thierry created a certain kind of whole from traditional themes. *Necessitas conplexionis* is used as a technical term by Boethius who applies it to hypothetical syllogisms (*De hypotheticis syllogismis* 308.16, 314.33–4). Boethius says in the same work that something can be necessary (or possible) either *absolute, nulla conditio determinationis apposita*, or with such determinations (236.67–238.77). The work was included in the *Heptateuchon* of Thierry of

Chartres. The idea of Providence as a detailed model or plan in the mind of God, unfolded through an inevitable process called fate, was discussed in the Books IV and V of Boethius' *Philosophiae consolatio*, to which Thierry refers as a source of his distinctions (*Glosa* 273.48–53; *Lect.* 165.81–8). In order to save freedom of the will, Boethius said that a part of Providence is realized through voluntary acts which are not determined by the causal chains of fate, although they cannot be otherwise with respect to providential necessity (see above, pp. 49–50). When Thierry says that the universe exists immutably in the necessity of complexion, he may have in mind invariant dynamic patterns which do not pertain to acts of will. The matter as the basic passive potency of being and as a universal receptacle of whatever is going to occur in the world was extensively discussed in Calcidius' commentary on Plato's *Timaeus* (273.7–346.13; cf. Boethius, *Commentarii in librum Aristotelis Perihermeneias* II, 238–9). In addition to Boethius' *Philosophiae consolatio*, Calcidius' commentary was a commonly used source book for discussions of providence and fate (see 181.13–215.10).

# 3 Varieties of necessity and possibility in the thirteenth century

In this chapter I shall first sketch the nature of the distinction between divine and natural modalities in twelfth- and thirteenth-century Western theology, in Moses Maimonides and in Islamic theology. It seems that although new twelfth-century modal ideas were included in the standard conceptions of divine possibilities, only a few thinkers realized their theoretical significance. A temporal-frequency model was considered, partly for epistemic reasons, as adequate in natural philosophy.

The discussions of the structure and meaning of modal sentences in logical treatises are investigated in the second section. Many logicians presented the equipollences of different modes in combination with negations and the basic relations between modals with the help of a square of opposition. As for the meaning of modal terms, some writers had in mind the idea of synchronic alternatives, but it was more usual to treat modal sentences in accordance with traditional paradigms. The conception of diachronic modalities was developed further as part of the theory of accidental necessities and impossibilities which was also employed in the new obligations logic. It is remarkable that the application of the distinction between the readings *de dicto* and *de re* of modal sentences to various problems was usually connected with diachronic or temporal-frequency paradigms without synchronic alternatives. The intuitions of the meaning of the distinction just mentioned were not always clear, as can be seen from some confused attempts to explain the conversions of modal sentences *de re*. Theoretical uncertainty is also reflected in Albert the Great's commentary on Aristotle's modal syllogistic.

In the third section I shall treat the Aristotelian theories of Thomas Aquinas and Siger of Brabant which to some extent were influenced by the works of Avicenna and Averroes. The rise of Aristotelianism strengthened traditional habits of thinking about modal matters;

much of the mid-thirteenth-century modal thought can be described as a systematization of the themes which were familiar to medieval thinkers since Boethius' works. When Thomas Aquinas, Bonaventure or Henry of Ghent operated with the notion of God's absolute possibilities, these possibilities were thought to have an ontological foundation. God's act of thinking consists of understanding the infinite ways in which his essence could be imitated by finite beings – all possibilities conceived by God's eternal cognitive act are derived from divine being. In the Parisian condemnations of 219 articles in theology and natural philosophy, God's freedom and power were stressed in a way which could motivate interest in studying the meaning of modal terms in general. This document had certain influence on early fourteenth-century discussions of the foundations of modality and intelligibility.

## NATURAL AND DIVINE POSSIBILITIES

In the first half of the thirteenth century the distinction between God's power to act and his exercised power, which was implied in the Augustinian formula '*potuit sed noluit*', was developed and baptized *potentia Dei absoluta/potentia Dei ordinata*. The terms occur, for example, in Hugh of St Cher who commented on the *Sentences* between 1230 and 1238. God's ordained power was commonly equated with the power through which the chosen providential plan is carried out. So the generic necessities and possibilities of nature could be regarded as ontological categories of the actual world kept in force by the ordained power of God. But theologians lacked unanimity about how absolute power should be delineated. Thomas Aquinas defined it as the capacity to realize what is absolutely possible, i.e. what can be described in compatible terms (*Summa theologiae* I, *q*. 25, *a*. 3, *a*. 5; for the development of the doctrine, see Courtenay 1985: 246–51; Oakley 1984: 47–59; Funkenstein 1986: 124–52).

As we have seen, some early twelfth-century thinkers were conscious of the theoretical significance of the originally theological idea of linking the meaning of modal terms with alternative states of affairs. Although the masters of later generations were acquainted with this way of understanding modalities, only a few of them tried to explicate its systematic import with respect to modal thought in general. They tended to consider the doctrine of divine possibilities, formulated in terms of the distinction between *potentia absoluta* and *potentia ordinata*, as a theological matter which did not affect the use of traditional modal paradigms in other disciplines. This attitude was strengthened in the thirteenth century by the wide reception of Aristotle's philosophy and its modal conceptions. (For some exceptions, see the end of the next section.)

Gilbert of Poitiers accepted the traditional notions of necessity and possibility as tools for speaking about nature in a secular sense. He seems to have thought that the statistical model corresponds to our natural epistemic capacities. We know that something is realizable or possible if we have observed an instance of it, and we believe that what is the case cannot be otherwise if we have never observed anything contrary to it. Miracles, however, are included in the actual providential design, which is the real nature; therefore, natural modalities do not determine what can take place in the world (see, for example, *Contra Eut.*, in *The Commentaries on Boethius* 323.59–67). This way of separating statistically interpreted natural possibilities and necessities from intensionally interpreted divine modalities was quite common in the twelfth and thirteenth centuries. Possibilities *secundum inferiorem causam* were said to be possibilities *secundum cursum naturae* and possibilities *secundum superiorem causam* were God's possibilities *simpliciter* or possibilities included in nature understood as the providential plan of God. (For some twelfth-century examples see, for example, Simon of Tournai, *Expositio super simbolum*, 1st edn 36–43, 2nd edn 48–54; Simon of Tournai, *Disputationes* XXXV, 2; Peter of Poitiers, *Sententiae* I, 67.498–68.502; Robert of Melun, *Oeuvres* II, 80.1–7; Alan of Lille, *Regulae caelestis iuris* 164–5; cf. Courtenay 1984: III.8–12.)

Alan of Lille wrote that things called possible according to lower causes are called so according to the common course of events, which also can be characterized as consuetude, the proverbial second nature of things. General kinds of natural possibilities are thus possibilities which are already exemplified in the course of time and based on the nature of things. *Cursus naturae* and *consuetudo* show which are the kinds of possibilities *secundum inferiorem causam*. Correspondingly, God's possibilities can be impossibilities according to nature, which fixes the simple notion of possibility:

> We call those things possible according to a higher cause which can be realized by a higher cause, namely God, although they cannot take place according to nature, for example that the donkey of Balaam could speak, a virgin could give birth to a child and so on. What is possible according to nature is called possible *simpliciter*,

and what is called impossible according to lower causes, is not called possible *simpliciter*, but possible for God.

(*Regulae caelestis iuris* 165)

As Alan of Lille thought that all types of natural possibilities had to show their genuineness through actualization, he found no difficulty in asserting the possibility of picturing impossible things. People drawing or painting chimeras and other fancy objects actually illustrate such things (*Anticlaudianus* I.122–4, *PL* 210, 491). In his book on architecture written in the first century before Christ, Vitruvius had condemned the use of pictures of things which cannot be (*De architectura* VII, 5; cf. De Bruyne 1969: 41). In the twelfth century, strange figures were not unusual in the decoration of church buildings. It is not always easy to say whether they were meant to be pictures of real or of non-existent animals, but in both cases they were intended probably to demonstrate God's power by showing the actual or possible plurality of what divine power could bring about. Beside the descriptions of animals in encyclopaedias and bestiaries, relevant biblical sources were Chapter 4 of the *Revelation of John*, which tells about strange heavenly creatures praising the omnipotence of God, and Chapter 11 of the *Wisdom of Solomon*, which describes uncreated possible animals. Bernard of Clairvaux thought that fictitious pictures disturbed religious meditation (*Apologia ad Guillelmum*, *PL* 182, 914–16).

One might ask why the authors who, in connection with certain theological questions, strongly criticized the principle of plenitude were inclined to accept it when speaking about necessities and possibilities in natural philosophy. As for such significant figures as Moses Maimonides and Thomas Aquinas, it seems that they considered divine possibilities as a theme about which men should not speculate, for their content remains beyond the limits of human epistemic possibilities. They are a matter of faith only, and the role left to reason was to derive from the common course of nature the necessities and possibilities of the created order.

According to Thomas Aquinas, the human intellect can grasp intelligible structures in extramental reality, because it can abstract the intelligible essence or form from matter (*Summa theologiae* I, *q*. 54, *a*. 4c, *q*. 79, *a*. 4, *q*. 85, *a*. 1). From empirical data called phantasms the agent intellect abstracts the likeness of the quiddity of sensible things. This intelligible species actualizes the potential intellect, and it forms the corresponding concept or, as Aquinas also calls it, the mental word (*Summa theologiae* I, *q*. 14, *a*. 12c, *q*. 85, *a*. 1, *ad*

4; *Quaestiones quodlibetales* V, *q.* 5, *a.* 2*c*; VIII, *q.* 2, *a.* 2*c*). In some places Aquinas says that we can know the generic essences of things through the properties of their singular actualizations (*Summa theologiae* I, *q.* 13, *a.* 8, *ad* 2; III, *q.* 25, *a.* 5, *ad* 4). But there are many other passages which state that all or almost all essences remain unknown to us (*Summa theologiae* I, *q.* 29, *a.* 1, *ad* 3, *q.* 77, *a.* 1, *ad* 7; *In Post. an.* II, *lc.* 13, *n.* 533; *De spiritualibus creaturis,* a. 11, *ad* 3, *Summa contra gentiles* IV, *c.* 1; *De veritate q.* 10, *a.* 1). (For further examples, see Kane 1957: 90–2; Kenny 1969: 90.) The discrepancy between these statements may be explained by the fact that, according to Aquinas, the human knowledge of essences is always imperfect and partial. The human intellect does not fully comprehend the intelligibility of essences which are conceptualized in the intellect. Aquinas believes that in heaven the human intellect will be improved in this respect so that it will fully understand the intelligible nature of the essences it now knows only partially. In addition, the intellect will come to know, in so far as it is possible for men, those actualized essences it has not known earlier as well as essences which remained unactualized (*Summa theologiae* I, *q.* 12, *a.* 8*c*, *ad* 4).

The epistemic motivation for the statistical interpretation of natural modalities can be derived from the above sketch of Aquinas' metaphysics of knowledge. As the human intellect does not fully comprehend the intelligibility of the essences which it conceptualizes, people cannot be sure whether predicating an unexemplified quality to members of a species yields a contradiction or a possibility. And as for imagined but unrealized essences, we cannot know whether or not they are possible. God knows it because he knows everything. This way of thinking is connected with the view that the absolute possibilities are, after all, ontologically real. They are included in God's eternal thought, which is identical with his essence. Although God's power is defined by means of the notion of absolute possibilities, these possibilities are not autonomous but are embedded in God's thinking, which thus defines the scope of conceivability. Much of God's thought-content is beyond the boundary of human knowledge which operates with concepts derived from the existing order of reality. This order of things does not inform us about unrealized absolute possibilities which, though unrealized, have a certain kind of existence in God's essence. This is a Christian variant of the ancient metaphysical doctrine that modality and intelligibility are real moments of being. It can also be found in Bonaventure and Henry of Ghent. (For the thirteenth-century views of the ontological foundation of absolute possibilities in God, see Wippel (1981) where the following texts are commented on: Thomas Aquinas, *Summa theologiae* I, *q.* 15, *a.* 1-3, *q.* 25, *a.* 3; *De veritate q.* 2, *a.* 3, *q.* 3, *a.* 2; Henry of Ghent, *Quodlibeta* 9, *q.* 1-2. In addition to these, see also Bonaventure, *Sent.* I, *d.* 35, *a. un., q.* 1-2, 5 in *Opera omnia.*) I shall return to Aquinas' views on modality in the third section of this chapter and to the question of the foundation of modality and intelligibility in Chapter 4.

There were similar discussions about theological and philosophical modalities among Jewish and Muslim writers. In *The Guide of the Perplexed* (I, 73, the tenth premise) Moses Maimonides (1135-1204) refers to some Islamic theologians (the Mutakallimun) as maintaining that 'everything that may be imagined is an admissible notion for the intellect'. And, Maimonides continues, 'they say of the existent things – provided with known forms and determinate sizes and necessarily accompanying modes that are inchangeable and immutable – that their being as they are is merely in virtue of the continuance of a habit.' (For some problems of translation of the passage (Pines 1974), see Ivry 1982: 67-9.)

The views which Maimonides criticizes were part of an argument offering a rationale for the creation of the world. Certain Islamic theologians argued that, because the world could be constructed in many imaginably different ways, there must be an agent who is the cause of its being as it is. Some adherents of radical occasionalism ascribed all effects in the world to God, who was thought to create all things from nothing at every moment of time and who was supposed to be capable of producing combinations of effects without any limits other than the necessity of his unity (see Wolfson 1976: 434-44, 578-89; Sorabji 1983: 297-302). Al-Ghazālī (1058-1111), a leading Ashʿarite theologian, stressed that natural invariances are due to the prior decree of God, who creates things side by side, and not to any inherent necessity in things created. We can have scientific demonstrations concerning natural matters, because God disrupts the order of habitual causes and effects only on the rare occasions when miracles are required (Marmura 1990: 98-103; for God's power in Islamic theology, see also van Ess 1985; Frank 1985).

Maimonides' main critical point is the claim that the Mutakallimun conceive possibilities on the basis of imagination rather than intellect. Maimonides himself appears uncertain, however, about the criterion by which one can distinguish whether something is said to be possible only by imagination or by intellect, especially as far as God's possibilities are concerned. In his third philosophical argument for God's existence, Maimonides makes use of the principle that, if something can be destroyed, it will at some time be destroyed (*The Guide of the Perplexed* II, 247, 249). The same argument, derived from Aristotle's *Metaphysics* XII, 6, occurs in the well-known third way of Thomas Aquinas (see *Summa theologiae* I, *q*. 2, *a*. 3). It seems that Maimonides considered this form of the principle of plenitude as a philosophical criterion of what is possible. In a letter to his Hebrew translator Samuel ibn Tibbon he explains how the principle is in his opinion correct:

> For example when we say that writing is possible with respect to the species man, it is absolutely impossible that there will never be a time at which some man is writing . . . but if you say that no man at any time will write, then writing will be impossible with respect to that species. But this is not the case of the possibility with respect to an individual, for this particular little boy may or may not write, and certainly this possibility does not determine that he will write. But as for the possibility of writing with respect to the species, it is absolutely impossible that there will never be a time at which some man is writing.
> (Quoted from Manekin 1988: 187)

Even though Maimonides accepted the principle of plenitude with respect to general kinds of beings and events, he thought that it was not directly applicable to divine possibilities. Maimonides writes:

> For if the philosopher says, as he does: That which exists is my witness and by means of it we discern the necessary, the possible and the impossible; the adherent of the law says to him: The dispute between us is with regard this point. For we claim that that which exists was made in virtue of will and was not a necessary consequence. Now if it was made in this fashion, it is admissible that it should be made in a different way, unless intellectual representation decides, as you think it decides, that something different from what exists at present is not admissible.
> (*The Guide of the Perplexed* I, 73)

We cannot know unrealized divine possibilities and we should not speculate about them, because we cannot decide whether they are truly attributed to God or attributed only by false imagination (ibid. III, 15). (For Maimonides' modal views, see also Ivry 1982, 1985; Funkenstein 1986: 128–9, 227–31; Manekin 1988.) Although Christian thinkers also called natural necessities habitual, many of them were inclined to think, like Maimonides, that such invariances are necessary due to the nature of things. It seems that the idea of relatively autonomous consuetudinary necessities, which was later systematically developed by Thomas Aquinas, did not gain any popularity among Islamic theologians.

## MODELS FOR MODALITIES IN LOGICAL TREATISES

One can find in late twelfth- and early thirteenth-century logical treatises various discussions of the structure and meaning of modal sentences influenced, first, by the newly discovered translations of the *Prior Analytics*, the *Topics* and the *Sophistici elenchi* of Aristotle and, second, by the interaction between logical and grammatical approaches, promoted particularly by the wide interest in sophisms and fallacies. The new terminist logic, distinguished for its contextually oriented approach to the properties of terms, was developed in somewhat different ways in Oxford and Paris, and even these two main traditions were not without internal disputes. Instead of tracing the views of various schools separately, however, I shall in this section delineate the main features of the treatment of modal sentences and modal terms in the late twelfth and early thirteenth centuries up to the time of the compendia by William of Sherwood, Peter of Spain, Roger Bacon and Lambert of Auxerre. In his *Logica Modernorum* (1962–67) de Rijk edited twenty treatises from this period; since then other previously unknown logical texts have been published, and this new material has given rise to remarkable revisions of the traditional view of the history of medieval logic. Much paleographical and historical work is still needed before a complete systematic analysis of the discussions of the period is possible (for texts and studies, see Pinborg 1972, 1979; de Rijk 1982; de Libera 1982; Tweedale 1988; Jacobi 1988). Let us begin with some terminological remarks.

As already stated, Aristotle had two notions of possibility. According to him, the possible and the impossible can be taken as contradictories, so that all that is not impossible is possible (e.g. *De interpretatione* 12, 22a11–13; 13, 22a22–37). But he also formulated the concept of a two-edged possibility which is contrasted not only to impossibility but also to necessity (e.g. *Prior Analytics* I, 13, 32a18–20). Aristotle had two words for 'possible'; one of them was '*dynaton*' and the other was '*endechomenon*', but he did not systematically employ them to mark the distinction just mentioned (see Hintikka 1973: 27–40).

In the Latin translation of *De interpretatione* by Marius Victorinus, which was known to Boethius, Aristotle's two words for 'possible' were rendered by the Latin terms '*possibile*' and '*contingens*' respectively (Becker-Freyseng 1938: 20–4). In his commentaries on *De interpretatione*, Boethius somewhat confusingly states that these words can be considered as synonyms or can be treated as having different meanings (*In Periherm.* II, 382.17–22, 384.6–7, 392.17–393.12). The words were later often used synonymously (see, for example, Peter Abelard, *Dialectica* 193.31), and this usage can still be seen from the squares of opposition for modalities in William of Sherwood and Peter of Spain in the middle of the thirteenth century (William of Sherwood, *Introductiones in logicam* 45; Peter of Spain, *Tractatus* 16). John of Salisbury, however, did mention in his *Metalogicon* (III, 4) that absence of impossibility did not warrant calling something contingent according to the usage of his time, i.e. the mid-twelfth century. The anonymous author of the treatise called *Dialectica Monacensis* (c.1200) described the terminological situation by saying that the term 'possible' can be used for both what is necessary and what is contingent, constituting something like a genus of two species of modality, namely the necessary and the contingent (de Rijk 1967: II-2, 481.9–13, 20–1). The purpose of this not quite happy formulation was to fix terminologically the difference between possibility proper and contingency, and this became the dominant way of using the words in later medieval logic. It was supported by the need for different terms for possibility and contingency in dealing with Aristotle's modal syllogistic (cf. Albert the Great, *Liber I Priorum analyticorum, tract.* IV, c. 4, 546). Some authors stated that '*contingens*' is used of what is true or actual but can be false or non-actual, while '*possibile*' refers to what is false or non-actual but can be true or actual (see de Rijk 1967: II-1, 467; II-2, 391.18–19; Roger Bacon, *Summulae dialectices*, 2.1.6., 247, 395–6, 408–10). Although it was considered in some contexts natural to use the terms in this way, the distinction did not become a systematic part of modal language.

Modifying Boethius' systematization of Aristotle's remarks in *De interpretatione* 12 and 13, some logicians presented the equipollences and other relations between modals with the help of a square of opposition the basic form of which was as follows on p. 108 (de Rijk 1967: II-1, 469–70, II-2, 393.6–394.5, 431.19–26, 483.1–484.5; William of Sherwood, *Introductiones in logicam* 45.11; Peter of Spain, *Tractatus* I.25, 16.12–13; Thomas Aquinas, *De modalibus* 62–74). Others, like Abelard, explained the relations without a diagram (*Super Periermenias* 22.4–25.4). The square could be taken to refer to modals *de dicto* or to singular modals *de re*. Peter Abelard tried, without success, to determine the relations between quantified

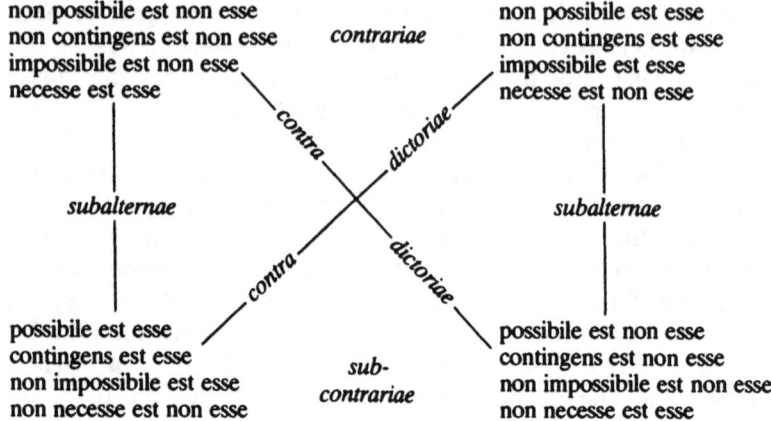

*de re* modals as well (p. 88 above). It seems that this question was not discussed much before its solution in the early fourteenth century (see pp. 168–9).

The sections about modal sentences often begin, as in Abelard, with remarks on adverbial modes. The author of the *Dialectica Monacensis* states, for example, that the modal adverb qualifies the composition between the subject and the predicate, and the structure of the sentence can be described as follows:

(1) quantity/subject/mode, copula/predicate.

One problem of interpretation here is connected with the quality (affirmative, negative) of sentences; the sign of negation can be located in two different places as follows:

(2) quantity/subject/quality, mode, copula/predicate

or

(3) quantity/subject/mode, quality, copula/predicate.

If negative sentences are read in accordance with (2), then the mode is denied in them; if they are read in accordance with (3), the modal adverbial qualifies a negated predication (de Rijk 1967: II-2, 479.35–480.3).

As for the modal sentences with nominal modes, the author of the *Dialectica Monacensis* says that they can be read in two different ways. One can apply to them an adverbial type of reading, and this is said to be how Aristotle treats modal sentences in the *Prior Analytics*. In this approach the quality and quantity of a modal sentence is determined by the corresponding non-modal sentence, although Aristotle seems to have thought, the writer remarks, that modal sentences are affirmative or negative depending on whether the mode is affirmed or denied. It is stated that, in addition to this interpretation of modal sentences with nominal modes, they can be read in a manner in which that which is asserted in a non-modal sentence is considered as the subject about which the mode is predicated. The subject term of the construction is the accusative and infinitive element of sentences like *Omnem hominem esse animal est necessarium*. These sentences, the author says, are always singular and their form is as follows:

(4) subject/copula/mode.

This reading is said to be the one which Aristotle presented in *De interpretatione* (ibid. 480.3–26).

Despite the common usage of this distinction pertaining to sentences with nominal modes, various opinions proliferated concerning what it meant. I shall not enter here into the details of the discussions concerning the differences between grammatical and logical analyses of propositions nor into the complicated questions pertaining to the nature of propositions and their *dicta*. It is enough to note that many logicians connected the grammatical analysis with what was considered a logical distinction between *de dicto* (*sensu composito*) and *de re* (*sensu diviso*) expositions of sentences with modal qualifiers. The account of the *Dialectica Monacensis* is typical in its main lines, but the views about the details varied (see Jacobi 1980: ch. 4; cf. Maierù 1972: ch. 5). In the twelfth century some logicians began to make use of the grammatical distinction between categorematic and syncategorematic words, i.e. the distinction which originally was drawn between words that can be used as subject terms or predicate terms and other words. This doctrine was applied to modal terms which, according to William of Sherwood, determine the predicate when used categorematically and the composition of the verb with the subject when used syncategorematically (William of Sherwood, *Syncategoremata* 72–4; translation by Kretzmann: 100–6; for an early example, see *Sincategoremata Monacensia*, in Braakhuis 1979: 99–100; translated in Kretzmann and Stump 1988: 168–9).

Klaus Jacobi (1980: 86–7) describes the syntactic background of the basic distinction, which was often called that between Aristotle's views in *Prior Analytics* and his views in *De interpretatione*, as follows:

(5) Mod. (Distr. ($S$ is [not] $P$))

and

(6) Distr. ($S$ is Mod. [not] $P$).

As Jacobi himself remarks, this rational reconstruction of the scope of the debates is somewhat problematic. Some authors considered *de dicto* reading non-modal (e.g. Peter Abelard, *Dialectica* 206.2–3; Lambert of Auxerre, *Logica* 30.17–31.18), while others claimed the same about *de re* reading (de Rijk 1967: II-1, 332), apparently because *de re* modalities were taken to connote the properties of things in a manner which distinguished them from modal predicates. Different views of the significance of this not merely syntactically understood difference are reflected in the controversy about the nature of modal sentences. But it is probably true, as Jacobi argues, that some logicians, William of Sherwood among them, came near to the idea of treating syncategorematic modal terms as operators which qualify the composition in different ways, depending on how they are placed (see William of Sherwood, *Syncategoremata* 72–4; *Introductiones in logicam* 90.11–24; translation by Kretzmann: 141–2; Jacobi 1980: 207–9, 339–41).

Referring to a standard theory of the early medieval period, the author of the *Dialectica Monacensis* says that the matter of an assertoric sentence may be natural, remote or contingent. True affirmative sentences of a natural matter maintain the existence of natural compounds which cannot be otherwise; these sentences, as well as the natural compounds, are called necessary. False affirmative sentences of a remote matter maintain the existence of compounds which are necessarily non-existent; they are called impossible. Sentences of a contingent matter are about compounds which can be actual and which can be non-actual (de Rijk 1967: II-2, 472.9–473.22; cf. 81.24–30, 115.5–12, 156.9–27, 188.5–11, 361.27–31, 384.26–385.3, 425.14–20; William of Sherwood, *Introductiones in logicam* 36.15–37.2; Peter of Spain, *Tractatus* I.13–14, 7.3–31). In the discussion of this doctrine, an explicitly statistical notion of contingency is employed in the twelfth century *Excerpta Norimbergensia* (de Rijk 1967: II-2, 115.5–12); it is stated there that the matter is natural when the predicate belongs to all instances of the subject term, it is remote when the predicate never belongs to the subject term, and it is contingent when it belongs to some instances of the subject term. (See also 138.24–6, where the author remarks that universal propositions are false and particular propositions are true in contingent matter – a view later repeated by Thomas Aquinas in *In Periherm.* I, *lect.* 13, *n.* 168.) Albert the Great similarly said that things in the contingent matter are neither always actual nor always non-actual; they are sometimes actual and sometimes non-actual (*Liber I Perihermeneias*, tract. 5, c. 6, 422).

When Western writers became acquainted with Aristotle's modal syllogistic, they thought that modal premises of syllogisms should be considered modal sentences *in sensu diviso* or *de re* (see Peter Abelard, *Super Periermenias* 10.22–11.16; Ebbesen *et al.* 1983: II, 10; *Summe Metenses*, in de Rijk 1967: II-1, 468; *Dialectica Monacensis*, in de Rijk 1967: II-2, 480.10–16; Albert the Great, *Liber I Priorum analyticorum*, tract. 4, c. 2, 540–3; Lambert of Auxerre, *Logica*, 30.17–23). Lambert of Auxerre, who did not treat the details of modal syllogisms, dealt extensively with the Aristotelian rules of conversion for modal sentences which he thought to be meant for modals *in sensu diviso*. Lambert found problems in the conversion of affirmative divided sentences *de necessario*, because the original subject term should become a necessarily affirmed predicate term of the converted sentence. The subject term of a sentence *de necessario*, Lambert says, can be taken to refer to beings having the form which is named by the term, and, according to him, the term should be understood in the same way in the converted sentence (*Logica* 39.1–41). Even though the author believes that he in this way avoids making a non-modalized characterization a necessary property, one could ask why 'A thing which is $S$ is necessarily $F$' should be equivalent to 'A thing which is $F$ is necessarily a thing which is $S$'. Lambert seems to confuse different types of necessity. Another possibility is that what he says is in some way based on the Aristotelian thesis of the necessity of the present. It was later explicitly mentioned and used in this context by Richard of Campsall in his questions on Aristotle's *Prior Analytics* (edited by Synan, 1968). The work was probably written in the first decade of the fourteenth century (see ibid. 19; cf. Tachau 1988: 158–66). Campsall thought, like Lambert of Auxerre, that divided sentences *de necessario* about actually existing things are convertible in the same way as assertoric sentences. In his proofs Campsall operates with the principle that that which is now possible with respect to the present moment of time must be actual (ibid. 5.40, 6.22–4; see also p. 164 below.)

Lambert states that sentences *de possibili* (in the sense of possibility proper) are converted in the same way as sentences *de necessario*. This would be in accordance with Campsall's theory of strictly present tense modalities, but Lambert probably had something else in his mind. He remarks that if that which is said to belong possibly is a non-regressive form, the resulting sentence must be provided with a reference to the future, for example, 'This boy can be an old man' is converted into 'A future old man can be this present boy' (*Logica* 37.36–38.25). When Lambert discusses the doctrine of the ampliative force of 'can' or 'potentially' in his logic, he states that they extend the supposition of the subject term to include non-existent things as well (ibid. 213.34–215.22, 228.26–229.14). In Lambert's examples non-existent possible beings are future things. Peter of Spain similarly says that when 'potest' ampliates the subject term to stand for things which can be, they are those which will be (*Tractatus* IX.5, 196.1–10). Lambert thinks that 'This boy can be an old man' should be read: 'This which is a boy can in future be an old man', and his conversion rule seems to imply the Diodorean conception of possibility, i.e. if a boy can be an old man, he will be an old man. Or perhaps Lambert simply confused *de dicto* and *de re* readings?

Albert the Great was probably acquainted with Lambert's treatise on logic, and he gives the same conversion rules for modal sentences, apparently thinking that they are applied to modal sentences *de re*. Albert did not find them problematic, because he accepted the axiom of the necessity of the present and, as already mentioned, some form of the temporal-frequency interpretation of possibility. While arguing for the validity of the conversion rules for sentences *de necessario*, Albert assumed that when something is true its denial is not contingent then, for if it is assumed to be true, something impossible follows (*Liber I Priorum analyticorum*, tract. 1, c. 11, 476). And in his proof of the rule that if the antecedent is possible, the consequent must be possible, Albert states that when a possibility can be realized, it at some time will be realized (*id quod est possibile, est hoc quod cum possibile sit fieri, aliquando fiet*), while that which is impossible will never be realized. If the consequent were impossible, it would never be actual, and at some time the possible antecedent would be true and the consequent false (ibid. tract. 4, c. 6, 550).

As for modal sentences *de contingenti*, Lambert of Auxerre concentrates on descriptions of the different uses of the notion of contingency and on distinctions pertaining to the narrow contingency (neither necessary nor impossible), paying special attention to the difference between indifferent contingency (*contingens infinitum*) and contingency in which things have a natural tendency to possess a certain attribute and to possess it more often than not (*contingens natum*) (*Logica* 39.42–9.43; for similar discussions, see Albert the Great, *Liber I Priorum analyticorum*, tract. 1, c. 12–15, 476–85). Lambert of Auxerre, like Albert the Great, the author of the *Dialectica Monacensis*, and some others, called the narrow contingency *contingens ad utrumlibet*. But the indifferent contingency was also called *ad utrumlibet*, and this usage later became more common (see Jacobi 1980: 92–4). According to Lambert, universal and particular divided sentences *de contingenti* imply sentences *de contingenti* of the opposite quality. They are converted by the conversion of terms into particular sentences. He does not tell how the subject terms of the sentences should be read, but he remarks that the conversions of *de contingenti nato* sentences, whether with respect to quality or terms, result in sentences which do not express the same type of contingency. Albert the Great presents the same rules and similar remarks. It seems that Lambert of Auxerre and Albert the Great were only partly conscious of the problems connected with the conversion of sentences *de contingenti*. The views of their predecessors were rather confused as well (cf. Jacobi 1980: 83–4, 382).

Albert's extensive work on the *Prior Analytics* was one of the first Latin treatises on it and the oldest of those which are edited. His remarks on modal syllogistic are sometimes obscure, partly because they are based on various intuitions which are not necessarily compatible. Albert's inclination to apply the statistical interpretation of modalities to universal and particular sentences sheds some light on his confused theory of the distinction between simple assertoric statements (*de inesse simpliciter*) and assertoric statements as of now (*de inesse ut nunc*). According to Albert, assertoric premises in valid mixed necessary and assertoric syllogisms are *de inesse simpliciter* and not *de inesse ut nunc*. Simple assertoric premises, Albert says, refer to necessary matter and hence can be taken to be necessarily true (*Liber I Priorum analyticorum*, tract. 3, c. 3–4, 523, 525). Treating temporally unrestricted premises in this way is natural only when necessary truth is equated with omnitemporal truth. Albert defines *de inesse simpliciter* differently while discussing mixed contingent and assertoric syllogisms (ibid. tract. 4, c. 10, 558–9; cf. Mignucci 1969: 907–9). He tried to elucidate these distinctions by referring to the categorical structure of reality repeated in the syllogisms.

The temporal-frequency interpretation of modal sentences was formulated in a very explicit manner in Averroes' (1126–98) treatise on assertoric sentences which is included in the group of questions on logic in *Aristotelis Opera cum Averrois Commentariis* (I.2b and 3, 78r–80r). The Arabic text is published by Dunlop (1962) and translated by Rescher (1963: 94–105). According to Averroes, the $S$'s are necessarily $P$'s when all $S$'s are always $P$'s and the $S$'s are contingently $P$'s when some $S$ at least sometimes is $P$. While discussing mixed necessary and assertoric syllogisms, Averroes tries to solve some problems by distinguishing between essentially necessary premises in which both the terms are necessary (*semper ens*) and incidentally necessary and essentially assertonic premises having only a necessary predicate term which always applies to the thing referred to by the subject term (ibid. 84ff.; see also Manekin 1992: 300–9). The statistical model of modality is often employed in Averroes' other works as well and they probably influenced Albert's modal thinking (see, for example, *Questions in Physics* 33–6, 144–5; Jalbert 1961: 37–40; Rescher 1963: 93–4; Leaman 1988: 29–44). Gersonides' (1288–1344) treatment of modal logic and modal syllogistic, based on a temporal-frequency interpretation of modality, owes a great deal to Averroes' views (see Manekin 1992).

Discussions of the relationship between temporal and modal conceptions were not uncommon in earlier Arabic logic, as can be seen from Averroes' critical description of Avicenna's (980–1037) views in the treatise on assertoric propositions just mentioned. In the part on logic of the *al-Ishārāt wat-Tanbīhāt* Avicenna distinguishes between the types of attribution which are called necessary as follows: (a) the $S$'s exist always and have $P$ at all times of their existence; (b) the $S$'s without being eternal have $P$ at all times of their existence; (c) the $S$'s have $P$ as long as they are qualified in a certain way; (d) the $S$'s have $P$ as long as they have $P$; and (e) the $S$'s have $P$ at some non-determined times (*Remarks and Admonitions* 92–3). Possible attributions are divided into those which are (a) not necessarily non-existent, (b) neither necessarily non-existent nor necessarily existent, (c) not necessary in any sense and (d) not necessary in the future (ibid. 95–7). After some remarks on the different types of modes, Avicenna discusses the equipollences and conversions between modal sentences. Similar classifications can be found in other works of Avicenna and in earlier Arabic treatises, for example, al-Fārābī's (c.870–950) short treatise on Aristotle's *De interpretatione*. According to al-Farabi, 'possible' is most properly applied to what is non-existent at present but is apt to exist, and apt not to exist, at any moment in the future (*Commentary and Short Treatise* 247). (For temporal and modal concepts in Arabic logic, see also Rescher 1966a.) It is in order to remark here that although Avicenna did not discuss the question of the actualization of possibilities in his logic, his metaphysics was necessitarian. (Some relevant texts are translated in Hourani 1972; see also Marmura 1984.)

It is maintained in a number of twelfth- and thirteenth-century logical treatises that modes may belong to what they signify either *per se* or *per accidens*. In his *Introductiones in logicam* William of Sherwood formulated the distinction as follows:

> Notice, however, that 'impossible' is used in two ways. It is used in one way of whatever cannot be true now or in the future or in the

past, and this is 'impossible *per se*' – e.g., 'A man is an ass'. It is used in the other way of whatever cannot be true now or in the future although it could have been true in the past, as if I were to say, 'I have not walked', and this is 'impossible *per accidens*'. Similarly, in the case something cannot be false now or in the future or in the past it is said to be 'necessary *per se*' – e.g., 'God is'. But it is 'necessary *per accidens*' in case something cannot be false now or in the future although it could have been [false] in the past – e.g., 'I have walked'.
(*Introductiones in logicam* 41.8–16; translated by Kretzmann 1966: 41)

A similar classification, often in almost identical terms, can be found in many twelfth- and thirteenth-century logical works (de Rijk 1967: II-1, 371; II-2, 390.18–31, 429.1–10, 481.22–482.14; Roger Bacon, *Summulae dialectices* 2.1.6, 366–72). (For an application of accidental modalities outside logic, see, for example, Raoul of Longchamps, *In Anticlaudianum Alani commentum* 72.) One typical feature here is that the difference between modalities *per se* and modalities *per accidens* is spelled out with respect to sentences, of which some have a changing truth-value. Correspondingly, both temporal and modal words are used in the explications. This combination of terms was commonly used in the twelfth- and thirteenth-century discussions of the assertoric square of opposition. William of Sherwood, for example, describes it as follows:

The law of contraries, it should be noted, is that they can never be true at the same time but they can be false at the same time. . . . The law of subcontraries, on the other hand, is that they can never be false at the same time but they can be true at the same time. . . . The law of contradictories is that they can be neither true at the same time nor false at the same time, as is clear enough.
(*Introductiones in logicam* 35.35–36.15; translated by Kretzmann 1966: 32–3)

Why did William use both the verb 'can' and the temporal word 'never' in the rules of contraries and subcontraries? The first answer could be that these words traditionally occurred in discussions of the logical square. In *Peri Hermeneias* of Apuleius of Madaura, in which the traditional logical square first explicitly appears, we read that contrary propositions 'never become true at the same time; yet they sometimes falsely pretend at the same time' (*Opera* III, 180.3–5; cf. Sullivan 1967: 64–8). The source of the idea of the square is, of course, Aristotle's *De interpretatione* (17b22–4), where the corresponding rule runs as follows: 'They cannot be true at the same time, but their opposites can both be true at the same time.' A combination in which temporal or quasi-temporal and modal words occur together can be found in Boethius and, commonly, in early medieval texts (see, for example, Boethius, *De syllogismis categoricis PL* 64, 802; Garland the Computist, *Dialectica* 53.1–6; de Rijk 1967: II-2, 137.27–9, 361.16–18, 384.15–17, 473.24–7).

Early medieval logicians often taught, following Boethius, that typical statement-making utterances are temporally indeterminate sentences (*enuntiatio, propositio*) having an implicit reference to the time of utterance (now) as a part of their meaning; thus, the same sentence can be sometimes true and sometimes false when asserted at different times. Some writers preferred speaking about the assertoric contents (*dicta*) of propositions, but they were commonly understood as temporally indeterminate types as well (see Nuchelmans 1973: 133–76). If sentences are treated in this way, it is natural to speak about their properties by means of both temporal and modal qualifiers. William of Sherwood's first rule 'Contraries can never be true at the same time' would then be read as follows: 'Contraries can never be uttered in a way that makes them both true at the same time.' If this is applied to the discussion of modalities *per se* and *per accidens*, the sentences which are either necessary or impossible *per se* and those which are either necessary or impossible *per accidens* would differ from each other in the sense that the clause 'cannot be falsely/truly uttered' belongs to the former at all times and to the latter before or after a real change in the actual world. This link to actual history would reduce the distinction between necessity *per se* and *per accidens* to a difference between generic sentences which are always true if uttered and those which during certain periods are always true if uttered. *Mutatis mutandis*, the same would hold of the different kinds of impossibility.

Some treatises state that necessities and impossibilities *per se* and *per accidens* are said absolutely, as distinct from respective or comparative necessities or impossibilities; e.g. 'That you are sitting, when you are sitting, is necessary' or 'That you are not sitting, when you are sitting, is impossible' both have some kind of condition or determination included in the sentence (de Rijk 1967: II-2, 390.18–19, 25–6, 429.1–2). According to the early thirteenth-century *Logica 'Ut dicit'*, true future tense singular assertions, such as 'The Antichrist will be existent', are necessary *per accidens*, for though they cannot have been false in the past nor false now, they can be false in the future (de Rijk 1967: II-2, 390.21–2). The point is apparently that true future tense sentences referring to singular events cease to be true when those events take place. Other authors usually connected accidental necessities and impossibilities with past tense singular sentences or *dicta*, such as 'That Caesar has been'. The approach in the *Logica 'Ut dicit'* seems to be based on the temporal-frequency interpretation of modality – in fact it is explicitly stated in one place in the treatise that *necessario* means the same as *in omni tempore* (411.8–9). If the statistical interpretation of necessity is applied to past or future tense type sentences about singular states of affairs, they are either always true or false (necessary or impossible *per se*) or always true or false *a parte ante* or *a parte post* (necessary or impossible *per accidens*). The truth-value of all *per se* contingent sentences of this kind changes once.

This interpretation is compatible with the characterization of the distinction between necessity *per se* and *per accidens* in the *Dialectica Monacensis* as that between 'infallible truth' with respect to all times and with respect to a period with a beginning in time (481.25–30). But as the author of this treatise, like some others, was mainly interested in the accidental necessity and impossibility of past tense singular sentences, he probably connected them with the diachronic model of alternative possibilities. If it was possible before William goes to Paris both that William will be in Paris and that he will not be in Paris, and if the possibility of his not having been in Paris ceased to exist when he came to Paris, then 'William has been in Paris' began to be necessarily true when it lost its prospective contingency. This is probably what is meant in the passage 481.22–482.14 of the *Dialectica Monacensis*. (One should read *preterito* instead of *presenti* in 481.30, 32.)

Certain interest in singular prospective potency-based possibilities is visible from a threefold classification also mentioned in *Logica 'Ut dicit'*. According to it, 'possibility' may refer to the potency which can bring about a being which does not yet exist (*potentia ante rem et ante actum*), to an unactualized potency belonging to an existent thing (*potentia cum re et ante actum*) or to an already actualized potency (*potentia cum re et cum actu*) (de Rijk 1967: II-2, 391.8–11, 728.31–729.3)

The authors of the period do not usually specify in their examples of accidental necessities and impossibilities whether it is simply thought that the possibility of uttering truly certain type sentences varies or whether it is assumed that a prospective possibility of being either true or false disappears. The former alternative occurs in Peter of Spain's discussion of the sentence 'What is impossible can be true'.

According to him, the sentence 'Antichrist has not been' will be accidentally impossible, but it can be true, because it is true now (*Tractatus* IX.4, 195.4–24; cf. the slightly different discussion of the example in de Rijk 1967: II-2, 729.8–18). The coming Antichrist was a rather popular figure in thirteenth-century logical treatises. William of Sherwood presents another sophism which runs as follows:

> The soul of Antichrist will be necessarily. Proof: The soul of Antichrist will have necessary being because at some time it will have unceasing, incorruptible being. On the contrary, [the soul of Antichrist] will be contingently because it is possible that it will not be. It is clear that it is proved in case ['necessarily'] is categorematic and disproved in case it is syncategorematic and [there is] a determination of the predicate in respect of the composition, for in that case 'the soul of Antichrist contingently will be' is true, but in the other case false.
>
> (*Syncategoremata*, ed. O'Donnell: 73; translated by Kretzmann 1968: 101)

In the *Logica 'Ut dicit'* 'that Antichrist will be' is an example of an accidentally necessary *dictum* which cannot have been false in the past and cannot be false now, although it can be false in the future (de Rijk 1967: II-2, 390.21–2). The syncategorematic reading of 'The soul of Antichrist will be' with a modal term would then be necessary *per accidens* and contingent *per se*, because when the soul of Antichrist is born, it is no longer true that it will be born. If William of Sherwood consistently thought that all possibilities will be realized, as he assumes in *Introductiones in logicam* 90.11, he could have understood the contingency of the *dictum* in the same way. According to Alexander of Aphrodisias, some Stoics maintained that if 'There will be a sea battle tomorrow' is true today, it is not necessarily true, because it does not remain true after the sea battle has taken place (*De fato* 177.7–9; cf. Frede 1974a: 47).

Analogous discussions were connected with the treatment of sophisms or fallacies based on the ambiguity of sentences like 'He who is standing can be sitting'. In his explanation of *Sophistici elenchi* 166a22–30 Abelard said that the possibility of sitting, belonging to a person who is now standing, refers to an indefinite time in the true *per divisionem* reading of the sentence 'He who is standing can be sitting'. Abelard's own view, as discussed earlier in Chapter 2, is not quite clear. In any case, when Aristotle's *Sophistici elenchi* began to be better known and the distinction between the readings of modal sentences in the composite sense (*de dicto*) and in the divided sense

*Necessity and possibility in the 1200s* 119

(*de re*) became a standard part of the doctrine of modal sentences, almost every logician wanted to express his view of Socrates' possibilities for sitting and standing. In the twelfth- and thirteenth-century treatises the usual composite reading of 'A standing man can sit' was 'It is possible that a man sits and stands at the same time' and the corresponding divided reading was 'A man who is standing can sit at another time'. (Examples of this kind of analysis are extant in many anonymous logical treatises. These and those of William of Sherwood, Peter of Spain and Lambert of Auxerre are discussed in Knuuttila 1981a: 187–98. See also Ebbesen 1981: II, 457–8.) Typically, 'at another time' or something similar was almost always added to the true divided reading. Aristotle's original example simply asserted that a man can simultaneously have potencies the realizations of which are mutually exclusive.

In some texts the reason for referring to another time is that possibilities are linked to their actualizations. The true divided reading is taken to express that there is a time at which the person who is now sitting is standing. William of Sherwood, for example, begins his discussion of the sample example 'That a white thing is black is possible' with the premise: 'Whatever is possible will be true.' In the divided reading 'white' does not belong to the subject at the moment to which the possibility refers, i.e. at the moment when the thing which is white now is black (*Introductiones in logicam* 90.11–24). It was more usual, however, to think that there are potency-based possibilities referring to future or diachronical alternative possibilities. The alternative *sensu composito* and *sensu diviso* readings can be symbolized as follows:

(7) $-M_t(p_t \ \& \ -p_t)$

or

(7') $-M(p_t \ \& \ -p_t)$

and

(8) $p_t \ \& \ M_t -p_{t'>t}$.

This distinction can be based on a theory of diachronic alternatives, but it is natural also for those who believe in a Diodorean manner that all possibilities will be realized. Another temporal frequency approach alternative to (7) is

(9) $p_t \ \& \ M-p_{t' \neq t}$

When Albert the Great wants to explain how actualized things, which are determinately what they are, can be called contingent, he simply refers to the doctrine of contingent matter in which things neither always are nor always are not (*Liber I Perihermeneias*, tract. 5, c. 7, 422; cf. Thomas Aquinas, *De veritate* q. 2, a. 12, ad 4 in *Quaestiones disputatae*).

One could remark, referring to prospective diachronic possibilities, that it was possible at $t'$ for Socrates not to stand at the present moment $t$, although he is standing at $t$, i.e.

(10) $p_t$ & $M_{t'<t}-p_t$.

This form is not an answer to the *stans potest sedere* problem, but because of the Augustinian *potuit sed noluit* principle, it was well known to theologians. In spite of the problems in applying temporal distinctions to God's power, (10) was employed in the discussions of such theological questions as whether God can do things which are impossible *per accidens* (see, for example, Albert the Great, *Sent.* I, d. 42, 6, ad q. 1, ad 1, ad 2 in *Opera omnia*, and other texts mentioned in de la Torre 1987: 331-4).

Different conceptions of possibility could motivate the view that the true reading of 'A man who is standing can be sitting' demands a reference to another time. They did not include the idea of synchronic alternatives and the authors making use of them did not therefore consider the form

(11) $p_t$ & $M_t-p_t$

the denial of which is equivalent to

(12) $p_t \rightarrow L_t p_t$

which was the reading many thirteenth-century writers gave to the Aristotelian principle: 'What is necessarily is when it is.' In his commentary on *De interpretatione*, Thomas Aquinas says that, even though true present tense singular statements are determinately true and in this sense necessarily true, some of them were not beforehand determinately going to be true (*In Periherm.* I, lect. 15, n. 201; see also Siger of Brabant, *De necessitate et contingentia causarum*, in Duin 1954: 32.4-18; Albert the Great, *Liber I Perihermeneias*, tract. 5, c. 6, 421).

According to Thomas Aquinas, the necessary truth of 'If God knows that $p$, then $p$' (*necessitas consequentiae*) does not imply the truth of 'If God knows that $p$, then $p$ is necessary' (*necessitas consequentis*) (see, for example, *Summa contra gentiles* I.67; *De veritate* q. 2, a. 12, ad 4, and *De malo* q. 16, a. 7, ad 15, in *Quaestiones disputatae*). In the passage from the *De veritate* (*ad* 2, *ad* 4) Aquinas thinks that the divided reading (*necessitas consequentis*) is true in the sense that things are objects of God's knowledge as present, i.e. as temporally definite. If they are not always actual, they can be called contingent as well. This is the traditional attempt to qualify the necessity of the present which is implied in the temporal-frequency interpretation of modality (see also pp. 133–4 below).

When discussing the *ambulans potest sedere* sophism, the author of the *Dialectica Monacensis* says that in the *de re* reading of modal sentences the original *dictum* is divided: the predicate term is applied to beings classed under the subject term, not as qualified by what is expressed by the subject term, but as such, and the nominal mode is applied to this part (de Rijk 1967: II-2, 570.18–571.9). This description does not exclude the possibility of reading the sentence 'He who is standing can be sitting' as follows: 'He who is now standing could, instead of being now standing, be now sitting.' In the *Dialectica Monacensis* and some other treatises of the same period, it was stated that the verb 'can' ampliates the subject term so that it can stand, not only in relation to actual beings, but also in relation to merely possible beings (de Rijk 1967: II-2, 623.33–624.26; see also 1967: II-1, 459, II-2, 345.14–34). The basic form of a possibility sentence *de re* is then taken to be as follows: 'Something which is or can be *A*, can be *B*.' The corresponding *de dicto* reading is: 'Something which is *A* is *B*' is true of some actual or merely possible beings.

The new twelfth-century theory of modality as referential multiplicity is reflected in the logical texts in which the domain of merely possible beings is mentioned in connection with the theories of supposition and ampliation and in which mutually exclusive singular possibilities are treated as alternative synchronic possibilities. It seems, however, that the theory of synchronic alternatives was not much developed in thirteenth-century logic. It was usual to analyse the divided possible sentences without any mention of (11), although form (11) as such was not unknown. It may be true, as Klaus Jacobi (1983) has claimed, that (11) was defended as consistent by the scholastics. The reason for this generalization could be that it was in some sense heretical to deny it. The conspicuous absence of (11) from many thirteenth-century discussions of modalities *de dicto* and *de re* or modalities *per se* and *per accidens* could be understood as a preference for leaving the idea of alternative states of affairs as the basis of modality in the background as specifically theological matter.

As already mentioned, some twelfth-century theological formulations, based on the idea of synchronic alternative possibilities, became an established part of scholastic theology. In addition to the distinction between what is possible according to higher or lower causes (see pp. 100–2) or Peter Lombard's originally Abelardian analysis of the sentence 'Things cannot be other than as God foreknows them' (see p. 94), the same conception also occurred in answers to the question of whether God could have made something better or in another and better way. (For the discussion of this question by Roland Bandinelli and Peter Lombard, see Boh 1985; see also Hugh of St-Victor, *De sacramentis christianae fidei*, PL 176, 215.) This did not mean, however, that theologians in general would have been eager to study modal questions. One exception is Peter of Poitiers who, in his *Sententiae* (c.1170), shows theoretical interest in some aspects of the new modal semantics. According to him, although a true sentence can be false, it cannot begin to be false (*Sententiae* I, 12.212–15). If Socrates is sitting at the moment $t_1$, it is possible that he is not sitting at $t_1$. The true temporally definite sentence 'Socrates is sitting at $t_1$' can be false, even if it were an object of God's knowledge (*Sententiae* I, 12.172–3, 13.138–45). It is thought here that the basic form of declarative sentences is temporally definite. (For the medieval debate about this question, see Nuchelmans 1973: 177–89. For the term *nominales* in this context, see also Normore 1987.) The role of the idea of synchronic alternative states of affairs is seen from Peter's discussion of some modal fallacies:

> This is a fallacy: It is possible that somebody who is not predestined can be predestined, *ergo* he can begin to be predestined, or, somebody who is predestined can be not predestined, *ergo* he can cease to be predestined, or, a soul which is not to be saved can be such that it is to be saved, *ergo* it can begin to be such that it is to be saved.
>
> (*Sententiae* I, 12.202–7)

Similar themes were developed more systematically in Robert Grosseteste's *De libero arbitrio* (c.1230). Grosseteste was not satisfied with the custom of considering the present states of affairs as necessary. He described the background of this way of thinking as follows:

> If Socrates is white at this moment of time, it is not possible that he is not white at this moment of time, because if there is such a possibility, it can or cannot be realized. If it can be realized, let us suppose that it is realized. It follows that something is and is not

white at the same indivisible moment of time. This is impossible. But if it cannot be realized, the possibility is in vain. However, no possibility is in vain.

(*De libero arbitrio* 173.15–174.2)

According to Grosseteste, it is true that unrealized possibilities can begin to be realized only in the future, if ever, but he did not accept the view that things cannot be other than they are when they are. Genuine possibilities may remain unrealized and still be possibilities, although they are no longer realizable possibilities, because actual history is an explication of only one of the eternal alternatives with respect to which things are primarily called necessary, possible or impossible. Modalities at this basic level are called modalities 'from eternity and without beginning'. Mathematical truths are necessary in this strong sense of necessity. In addition to them, there are necessities and impossibilities which have a beginning and which are eternal contingencies (ibid. 168.26–170.33; for Grosseteste's views, see also Normore 1982: 364–6).

A new type of logical writings later classed as treatises on obligations (*De obligationibus*) emerged in the thirteenth century. They were probably connected with disputations practised as part of the logic courses of the time. Obligations treatises contain norms (obligations) for certain kinds of dialectical disputations as well as investigations of the questions which arise in such exercises. The increasing interest in this branch of logic in the fourteenth century shows that some obligational problems proved to be of great philosophical and logical interest. In the basic type of disputation, called *positio*, the opponent puts forward an initial proposition (*positum*) which is usually contingent and false. During the disputation the respondent is obliged to treat the *positum* as he treats propositions which he knows to be true. After the *positum* the opponent puts forward other propositions, and the respondent must react by saying 'I grant it' (*concedo*), 'I deny it' (*nego*) or 'I doubt it' (*dubito*). The opponent tries to trap the respondent into conceding something contrary to the *positum*, to propositions which are correctly granted or opposites of propositions correctly denied, or to propositions which follow from these ones. In other words, the respondent's task is to answer in a logically consistent way, and the opponent attempts to invalidate this consistency. (For general discussions of the obligations literature, see Ashworth

1981; Stump 1982; Spade 1982a, 1982c; Spade and Stump 1983; Knuuttila and Yrjönsuuri 1988; Stump 1989: 177–269.)

In the second part of his unpublished dissertation Romuald Green (forthcoming) has edited two obligations treatises. The first is putatively attributed to William of Sherwood and the other to Walter Burley; the latter was written around 1302. It may be that William of Sherwood is not the author of the first treatise (see Stump and Spade 1983); however, both of the tracts can be considered as representative of the thirteenth-century tradition of obligational tractates. Parts of Burley's treatise are translated by Kretzmann and Stump (1988: 370–412). de Rijk has edited (1974–6) three short treatises on obligations from the thirteenth century called *Tractatus Emmeranus de falsi positione*, *Tractatus Emmeranus de impossibili positione* and *Obligationes parisienses*. The *Tractatus Sorbonnensis de petitionibus contrariorum*, edited in the same series of texts, is not directly about obligations. All these tracts are less systematic than the putative Sherwood treatise.

In the 1270s Boethius of Dacia discussed obligational disputations in the eighth book of his *Quaestiones super librum Topicorum*. It is historically interesting that Boethius connected them with Aristotle's theory of dialectical games which is presented in the eighth book of the *Topica*. Aristotle's work probably had some influence on the development of the rules of obligations, although it was not their only basis.

Aristotle classified dialectical disputations into different kinds according to whether the participants are engaged in competition, in teaching and learning or in inquiry (*Topics* VIII, 5, 159a25–8). A disputation always takes place in such a way that a questioner tries to refute a thesis held by a respondent by asking yes-or-no questions. The questioner tries to force the answerer to deny the thesis or to answer questions in an implausible way. In Chapters 1–4 of the *Topics* VIII, various rules are given for the questioner. In Chapters 4–10 Aristotle discusses the strategies of the answerer. After dividing the theses into reputable, implausible and neutral ones, Aristotle formulates the basic rules for the respondent in Chapter 5. If the thesis is implausible without qualification and the intended end or conclusion of the opponent's argument is correspondingly reputable without qualification, the respondent 'ought not to grant either what does not seem to be the case without qualification, or what seems to be the case, but to a less degree than the conclusion'. If the thesis is reputable without qualification, 'the respondent should admit all views that seem to be the case and, of those that do not, all that are less implausible than the conclusion'. If the thesis is neutral, 'anything that appears to be true should be granted, and, of views that do not seem true, any that are more reputable than the conclusion'.

One could follow these rules in eristic disputations, thinking that the opponent cannot develop arguments for implausible or neutral conclusions from statements which are more plausible or more familiar, just because the intended end of the opponent is implausible or neutral. If the opponent is arguing for a conclusion which is reputable without qualification, the respondent can make the task difficult by being selective in the way described. It is clear, however, that when formulating the above rules, Aristotle had in mind a respondent who is co-operative and wants to investigate, together with the opponent, whether and how one can develop arguments for views generally held to be obviously true, obviously false or neither obviously true nor obviously false (*Topics* VIII.5, 159a32-7). The rules can be understood as rules for finding arguments, strong or weak, with respect to various dialectical questions. A respondent who masters this method should, of course, be able to find straightforward strategies for winning the case in actual competitive disputations.

Although the task of the opponent in obligations disputations and the role of the questioner in Aristotelian dialectical disputations have something in common, the differences between these games are obvious. Aristotle is interested in real eristic argumentation and in methodological rules for dialogues the purpose of which is to investigate what kind of arguments one can find for views classified into reputable, implausible or neutral. Obligations treatises concentrate only on the questions pertaining to the consistency of the set of the respondent's answers. They develop a theory about certain formal aspects of disputation which were not in the same way attended by Aristotle.

The first rule for *positio* in the tracts edited by Green runs as follows: 'Everything which is *positum* and put forward during the disputation, must be granted.' This can be formulated as follows:

(13) $(p)(P_a p \rightarrow OC_a p)$

(For any proposition $p$ put forward in a disputation, if the person $a$ has admitted as the *positum* that $p$, it is obligatory that $a$ concedes that $p$.) The obligation can be understood in the sense of a technical norm of consistency, but it is interesting that some authors located obligational disputations in a wider context of what may be called the ethics of disputation in general. It was thought that the participants of any disputation should grant or deny assertions in accordance with what they know, if they for special reasons are not freed from these disputational prima facie duties (Green forthcoming: II, 2.4–6, 53.18–19, 84.27–9; de Rijk 1974: 103.20–3; de Rijk 1975a: 27.6–21). The normative side of the games influenced fourteenth-century discussions of the logic of norms (see pp. 189–90, 195–6).

Further *positio* rules are based on a distinction between pertinent and impertinent propositions. A pertinent or relevant proposition either (a) necessarily follows from the *positum* and/or what has been granted and/or the opposite(s) of what has been correctly denied or (b) is incompatible with them. The rules for propositions the pertinence of which is related to the *positum* are as follows ('$K_a p$' stands for '*a* knows that *p*', '$N_a p$' stands for '*a* denies that *p*' and '$G_a q$' stands for '*a* has earlier conceded that *q* or correctly denied that $-q$'):

(14) $(p)(q)(P_a p \;\&\; K_a L(p \rightarrow q) \rightarrow OC_a q)$

(15) $(p)(q)(r)(P_a p \;\&\; G_a q \;\&\; K_a L(p \;\&\; q \rightarrow r) \rightarrow OC_a r)$

(16) $(p)(q)(P_a p \;\&\; K_a L(p \rightarrow -q) \rightarrow ON_a q)$

(17) $(p)(q)(r)(P_a p \;\&\; G_a q \;\&\; K_a L(p \;\&\; q \rightarrow -r) \rightarrow ON_a r)$.

Propositions are impertinent if none of the pertinence rules apply to them. When impertinent propositions are put forward, they must be granted, denied or doubted according to their own quality, i.e. they are treated on the basis of the general honesty rules. These rules as applied to impertinent propositions run as follows:

(18) $(p)(Ip \;\&\; K_a p \rightarrow OC_a p)$

(19) $(p)(Ip \;\&\; K_a -p \rightarrow ON_a p)$

(20) $(p)(Ip \;\&\; -K_a p \;\&\; -K_a -p \rightarrow OD_a p)$.

('$I$' stands for 'impertinent' and '$D_a p$' for '*a* expresses his doubt or uncertainty whether *p*'.) (For the rules (13)–(20), see Green forthcoming: II, 2–3, 46–8; de Rijk 1974: 106–7, 1975a: 29.)

Although the basic rules of the game of obligation are simple, they provided a fruitful setting for discussing various semantic and inferential questions. Special attention was paid to the fact that, depending on the order in which propositions are discussed, the same proposition may be granted in one game and denied in another game. I shall not enter into the details of obligational problems here; instead I shall make some comments on the contingency of the *positum* and how different modal ideas affected the obligational rules.

As already mentioned, the *positum* was usually an assertoric statement which was false but possible. How some authors understood the notion of possibility in this context can be seen from their comments on the common thirteenth-century rule which says that, if the *positum* is a contingent sentence that is false at the present instant of time $A$, it must be denied as repugnant that now is the instant $A$ (Green forthcoming: II, 8.32-3, 59.20-1; de Rijk 1974: 112.18-19; 1975a: 32.3-4). The background of the rule is described in the putative Sherwood treatise as follows:

> When a false contingent sentence concerning the present instant has been posited, one must deny that it is the present instant. This is proved as follows. Let $A$ be the name of the present instant; it is a discrete name and not a common name. When it is false that you are in Rome, it is impossible that it is true then or in $A$. It can become true only through a motion (*motus*) or through a change (*mutatio*). It cannot become true through a motion in $A$, because there is no motion in an instant. And it cannot become true through a change, since if there were a change into truth in $A$, the truth would be in $A$; for whenever there is a change, there is the term of that change. So it is impossible that this false sentence becomes true in $A$. Therefore, if it is true, $A$ is not present.
> (Green forthcoming: II, 8.32-9.8)

The sentence 'You are in Rome' is here treated as a temporally indefinite statement which can be true or false when uttered. The author thinks that it cannot be true at the instant when it is false, because the possibility to be otherwise refers to a real change. I have just quoted a passage from Robert Grosseteste's *De libero arbitrio* containing a related argument which was presented by people who did not believe that things at a certain instant could be otherwise then. Possibilities are in both places taken to refer to an actualization in the future of the actual world.

The author of the putative Sherwood treatise elucidates his view of the contingency of a false *positum* by referring to the distinction between compound and divided readings of sentences like 'A white thing can be black'. In the true *sensu diviso* reading the term 'possible' ampliates the predicate to a future time while the subject term refers to a thing which is now white (Green forthcoming: II, 5.7-27). The notion of contingency is in this tract used mainly in accordance with the model of prospective diachronic possibilities without synchronic alternatives. So the author states that when 'You are in Rome' is a false contingent *positum* and $A$ is the present instant, '$A$ was going to be' must be granted as impertinent and true and similarly '$A$ has been' is to be granted if it is proposed next (Green forthcoming:

II, 10.5–9). According to the *Obligationes parisienses*, the time of the *positum* can also be a past moment (de Rijk 1975a: 32.8–21). Walter Burley does not tell definitely what he thinks about this matter, but he stresses that the instant of the *positum* cannot be identified with any definite instant (Green forthcoming: II, 62.19–21). Interestingly enough, the author of the *Obligationes parisienses* mentions the possibility that one could deny all affirmative propositions about temporal relationships between the actual instant *A* and the *positum* instant, provided that '*A* has been' and '*A* will be' are put before '*A* was going to be'. (I have read '*A* fuit futurum' instead of '*A* fit futurum' and '*A* non fuit' instead of '*A* non fit' on lines 12, 18, 21.) In this case, the instant of the *positum* is thought to be outside the history (ibid. 32.22–35; cf. Yrjönsuuri 1992).

It may be noticed that all these authors represent the view that, if something is the case, it was earlier true that it is going to be the case. Abelard accepted the Boethian view that future contingent propositions are true or false, although they are not true or false in a determinate way before their occurrence (see Peter Abelard, *Logica 'Ingredientibus'* 422.26–36; *Dialectica* 212.13–21). Boethius and Abelard retained the principle of bivalence for all assertoric sentences, but they rejected universal application of the stronger principle that every statement is determinately true or determinately false (see also Lewis 1987). It was the standard view in the thirteenth century as well that singular future contingent sentences are true or false, although their truth is not naturally knowable (see Thomas Aquinas, *In Periherm.* I, lect. 13, n. 169, 175; *De veritate* q. 1, a. 5.; *Summa theologiae* II.2, q. 171, a. 3; Bonaventure, *Sent.* I, d. 40, a. 2, q. 1).

When a *positum* or another proposition is repeated in a disputation, the assumed or real truth-value of the proposition may have been changed as a result of the answers already given. According to obligations rules, what has been granted must be granted when it is proposed again. Consequently one has to grant propositions which have become impossible *per accidens* or to deny propositions which are necessary *per accidens*, but it was thought that this did not affect the consistency which is evaluated with respect only to the instant of the *positum*. The time rule just mentioned also demanded that certain accidental necessities are denied or accidental impossibilities are granted (Green forthcoming: II, 7.31–8.31, 57.3–12, 61.1–2; de Rijk 1975a: 32.24–35). In the treatises edited by Green, the impossibility *per accidens* is connected with temporally indeterminate singular sentences which, after having been true, have begun to be unchangingly false. In the *Obligationes parisienses* the accidental impossibility of 'A will be', when the instant A is present or has been present, is understood in the same way. 'A will be' becomes false when A is actual. The accidental necessity of 'A was going to be' is explicated by stating that it is impossibly false now and in the future although it could be false in the past (ibid.: 32.24–35). This may imply the idea of prospective alternative possibilities.

Early obligations treatises include special rules for games called *positio impossibilis*. It was stated that the *positum* must not be contradictory so that the same predicate is affirmed and denied of a subject. This would destroy the game. It was also noticed that the rule *Ex impossibili sequitur quodlibet* cannot be applied in a disputation of this type, i.e. the respondent may grant that the *positum* is impossible, but he should not think that all answers are then acceptable. An acceptable impossible *positum* must be thinkable (*opinabile*) (Green forthcoming: II, 24.17–27.14, 83.10–84.23; de Rijk 1974: 117.23–123.6). The authors do not explain how the borderline is drawn between false contingent propositions and impossible ones. Probably they thought that impossibilities are generic states of affairs not exemplified in the world. The background of this view could be a statistical conception of contingency applied to generic states of affairs.

The thirteenth-century rule for treating the time of the *positum* had some strange influences on the game. The respondent is obligated to react to the *positum* and to the relevant propositions from the point of view of an imaginary instant of time and to the impertinent propositions in accordance with the status of knowledge at the time of disputation, although originally impertinent propositions are then treated as relevant propositions that are true or false at the imagined instant. Even if the list of answers consisting of temporally indefinite now-statements can be consistent, the asymmetry between pertinent and impertinent propositions shows that the list is a piece of coherent nonsense. This certainly was one of the factors which led to a radical reconsideration of the time rule in fourteenth-century discussions (see Chapter 4).

## NECESSITY AND POSSIBILITY IN PARISIAN ARISTOTELIANISM: SIGER OF BRABANT AND THOMAS AQUINAS

When classifying sentences on the basis of the traditional doctrine of necessary and contingent matter, Thomas Aquinas delineates them as follows:

In necessary matter all affirmative enunciations are determinately true; this holds for enunciations in future time as well as in past and present time; and negative enunciations are determinately false. In impossible matter the contrary is the case. In contingent matter, however, universal enunciations are false and particular enunciations are true. This is the case in enunciations about the future as well as those of the past and present. In indefinite enunciations, both are at once true in the future enunciations as well as in those of the present or the past.

(*In Periherm.* I, *lect.* 13, *n.* 168, translation by Oesterle 1962)

This account includes a statistical interpretation of necessity and contingency with respect to types of events and states of affairs. It belongs to the introductory remarks of Aquinas' discussion of the future sea-battle problem, in which one of his tasks was to locate singular propositions about future contingents in the above scheme. In an interesting remark on Diodorus' definitions of modal notions, Thomas Aquinas says that they can be criticized for being formulated a posteriori. In his opinion, the statistical interpretation of modality is secondary and should be understood in the light of the basic necessities and possibilities included in the nature of things:

Some who distinguished them according to result – for example Diodorus – said that the impossible is that which never will be, the necessary, that which always will be, and the possible, that which sometimes will be, sometimes not. . . . The first distinctions are a posteriori, for something is not necessary, because it always will be, but rather, it always will be because it is necessary; this holds for the possible as well as the impossible. . . . Others distinguished these better by basing their distinction on the nature of things. They said that the necessary is that which in its nature is determined only to being, the impossible, that which is determined only to nonbeing, and the possible, that which is not altogether determined to either. . . .

(*In Periherm.* I, *lect.* 14, *n.* 183, translation by Oesterle 1962)

If the Diodorean formulations are turned in the way Thomas Aquinas thinks they should be turned, something will be at some time and not be at other times, because it is possible and neither necessary nor impossible. So the actuality at some moment of time remains the indicator of the genuineness of an alleged possibility and the statistical use of modalities is legitimate, although it is not primary. What is more close to 'the nature of things' is another Aristotelian modal paradigm, namely that which is connected with the concept of potency. An elaborate version of this model played a significant role in Aquinas' theory of the principles of natural philosophy (for some discussions of the topic, see Jacobi 1977; Aertsen 1987: chs 6–8).

Thomas Aquinas divides the necessities pertaining to the structure and behaviour of things into those founded on intrinsic principles, i.e. the form or the matter of things, and those founded on extrinsic principles, i.e. the efficient and final causes (*Summa theologiae* I, *q*. 82, *a*. 1c; III, *q*. 14, *a*. 2c; *In Metaphys.* V, *lect*. 6, *n*. 832–4). Generic natural potencies are, *qua* potentialities, intrinsically necessary features of things. They consist of passive potencies, determined by the nature of the subjects in which they occur, and of the corresponding activators, called active potencies, which are similarly determined by the intrinsic principles of their subjects (see, for example, *Summa theologiae* III, *q*. 13, *a*. 1c; *In Metaphys.* IX, *lect*. 1, *n*. 1782). Thus the generic partial potentialities, divided into passive propensities and related activating principles, belong as such to the necessary order which is based on the nature of things.

In his description of active and passive partial possibilities, Thomas Aquinas refers to the dynamic necessity by which the active potency acts and the passive potency is acted on, when the agent and the patient meet in a way appropriate to the potency in question (*In Metaphys.* IX, *lect*. 4, *n*. 1818). From the point of view of passive potencies, this is an extrinsic necessity of actualization and it is based on the metaphysical principle, according to which intrinsically necessary potentialities, divided into active and passive components, necessarily co-operate, when they can do so. As for the heavenly bodies, the meeting of the active and passive potencies is continuous and exhaustive in the sense that no partial potentialities remain unrealized. In the sublunar world this concourse is neither continuous nor complete with respect to passive potencies, owing to the circularity of the influence of the higher active potencies and various complexities in the system of lower motions (see, for example, *In Metaphys.* VI, *lect*. 3, *n*. 1210–12; XII, *lect*. 6; *In Phys.* II, *lect*. 14; VIII, *lect*. 8; *In Periherm.* I, *lect*. 14, *n*. 184; *Summa theologiae* I, *q*. 115, *a*. 3; *Summa contra gentiles* III, *c*. 82–6).

All natural invariances, whether static or dynamic, are essential in Thomas Aquinas. This becomes more apparent when we attend to what he says about absolute modalities. According to Aquinas, absolute possibilities and those referring to potencies are different, because the former ones are defined independently with the help of the notions of coherence or compatibility between the subject and the predicate (see, for example, *In Metaphys.* IX, *lect.* 1, *n.* 1775). For Aquinas this means that one can speak about things as absolute possibilities without reference to existence outside the divine essence. As already mentioned in the first section of this chapter, Aquinas thought that what is coherent or incoherent between a subject and its attributes is determined by the metaphysical forms which are the possible modes of imitating the divine being. So absolute possibilities are not metaphysically prior with respect to being. They are models for finite being as deduced from divine being (see, for example, *Summa theologiae* I, *q.* 15, *a.* 1–3, *q.* 25, *a.* 3).

Those metaphysical forms which are instantiated in the world bring with them the necessities and possibilities that are attached to them. Therefore, the intrinsic necessities based on the metaphysical structure of beings are called absolute natural necessities (*Summa theologiae* I, *q.* 82, *a.* 1c). The extrinsic necessity connected with the efficient causation is a conditional necessity of actualization. It refers to what happens in a metaphysically necessary way when things provided with the necessary properties they have are actualized in a dynamic order, kept in motion by the first mover. There are, of course, unrealized divine possibilities, and the world as such is contingent, because it is created (see *Quaestiones disputatae de potentia q.* 1, *a.* 5, *q.* 3, *a.* 15). But contrary to what might be expected in view of the twelfth-century background, these theological modalities were not very relevant in Aquinas' natural philosophy. Their main import is that the states of affairs, the structures of which are metaphysically necessary, are contingent with respect to actuality. In this sense the natural necessities are hypothetical metaphysical necessities.

These remarks shed light on Aquinas' notions of miracles and divine omnipotence. According to him, God cannot violate absolute necessities. This means that the miraculous events, taking place against the common course of nature, must always occur through a separate supernatural causation. They do not qualify natural necessities. There are things which are impossible for inferior causes to perform, though they are possible to the divine cause. Miraculous acts do not change the nature of things; through them is actualized something which otherwise lacks a cause in nature (see *De potentia q.* 6, *a.* 1–2). Thomas Aquinas explains this by postulating a special *potentia oboedientialis* by which things receive exceptional influences from the divine cause (*De potentia q.* 1, *a.* 3, *ad* 1, *q.* 6, *a.* 1, *ad* 18; *Quaestio disputata de virtutibus in communi q. un.*, *a.* 10, *ad* 13).

Discussions of causality among the mid-thirteenth-century Aristotelians were strongly influenced by the theories of Avicenna and Averroes. A general starting-point was Avicenna's definition of the relationship between *causa* and *effectus* according to which every effect is necessary in relation to its cause. A usually accepted specification, put forward by Averroes, was that the effect necessarily follows when the cause is not impeded from producing the effect. In the Averroistic approach, attention was directed towards a classification of causes with regard to their possible hindrance. As Averroes considered the frequency interpretation as the basic model of modality, it is understandable that he treated causal modalities in a statistic-temporal way in his natural philosophy. (For a detailed discussion of the theme, see Maier 1949: 219–50.)

Following the Averroistic analysis of causes, Siger of Brabant and Thomas Aquinas defined necessary causes as causes which *in statu causae* always bring about their effects. The causes *ut in pluribus* are contingent, because they are hindered in a few cases (*ut in paucioribus*) from working by accidental impediments. In addition there are causes *ad utrumlibet* which represent the special case of a 50 per cent incidence rate. Although every effect is necessary with respect either to its proximate or to its remote cause, the causal necessity of an event is qualified in terms of the nature of its proximate cause. If the proximate cause is generically contingent, its actual effect can be called contingent as well (Siger of Brabant, *Quaestiones in Metaphysicam* (Vienna) 369.51–370.81, 378.58–380.26; *De necessitate et contingentia causarum*, in Duin 1954: 28.10–30.49, 32.1–34.34; Thomas Aquinas, *In Periherm*. I, lect. 13, n. 172, lect. 14, n. 197; *In Phys*. II, lect. 8, n. 210). A particular cause is here considered necessary or contingent, depending on how the causes of the same type usually behave. Similarly an actually necessitated effect can be called contingent by referring to what happens in other similar cases.

In his attempts to reconcile divine foreknowledge and contingency, Thomas Aquinas is often content with an application of this model. God can apprehend the whole of history, because it is eternally present to him. Things seen as actual are necessary by supposition (i.e. with respect to God's knowledge) and they are also necessarily realized in the sense that no thing can prevent the actual providential plan from being carried out. Historical states of affairs, however, can be called contingent if their proximate causes are not necessary in the statistical sense (*causa ut semper*) (see, for example, *Scriptum super sententiis* I, d. 38, q. 1, a. 5; *Summa contra gentiles* I, c. 67; *Summa theologiae* I, q. 14, a. 13). In the more elaborated versions of the argument, Aquinas says that God disposes necessary or contingent causes for the effects, depending on whether he wills them to be necessary or contingent. 'And according to the condition of these causes, effects are called either necessary or contingent, although all depend on the divine will as on a first cause, which transcends the order of necessity and contingency' (*In Periherm.* I, lect. 14, n. 197, translation by Oesterle). The ultimate source of contingency is God's eternal will, which does not realize everything that is possible. It may be that Thomas Aquinas began to stress the importance of the concepts of God's will and absolute possibility in this context in order to keep his distance from some of his contemporaries who argued for physical determinism or metaphysical necessitarianism. Aquinas's treatment of this question remains unsatisfactory, however. He though that God's actual knowledge is necessary in the sense in which everything that is necessarily is, when it is, and that the objects of God's knowledge are necessary by this temporal necessity with respect to their actuality (*Summa theologiae* I, q. 14, a. 13, ad 2). This means that things known to God as present cannot be other than they will be; 'that which already is cannot, with respect to that moment of time, not be' (*Summa contra gentiles* I.67). (For some problems in Aquinas' theory of omniscience and contingency, see also Prior 1968: 26–44; Craig 1988: 99–126.)

Siger of Brabant tells that there were masters who thought that, even if effects can be called statistically contingent with respect to their proximate causes, they are necessitated by the totality of past causes. Causes necessarily bring about their effects if not impeded, and if a cause is impeded, it is necessarily impeded by preceding causes. When commenting on this view, Siger says that a full analysis of the co-operation of inferior causes between two given points of time demands the human impossibility of attending to potentially infinite aspects. According to this idea, later used by Leibniz and many others, a physical reality may be causally necessary while appearing contingent to man, because the proof of necessary connections among all causal factors would be infinitely long (*De necessitate et contingentia causarum*, in Duin 1954: 26.67–79; *Quaestiones in Metaphysicam* (Cambridge), in Duin 1954: 97.16–98.32; *Quaestiones in Metaphysicam* (Vienna) 372.56–74). In her studies on thirteenth-century physics, Anneliese Maier characterizes the medieval statistical approach to the causes and effects as an application of epistemic probability to physics (Maier 1949: 226; 1964–7: 452). She could have used Siger's remark just mentioned as evidence for the view that some Parisian masters thought that alternative possibilities

*Necessity and possibility in the 1200s* 135

with respect to singular events are subjective and compatible with determinism. But this was not the common view; Thomas Aquinas did not accept it and even Siger of Brabant refuted it, at least in some places.

As shown in Chapter 2, Boethius strongly criticized the Stoic interpretation of chance as a merely epistemic notion. Correspondingly, he tried to sketch a physical theory of objectively accidental events, and similar ideas are to be found in Siger of Brabant and Thomas Aquinas. They thought that there are individual indeterminate possibilities in the causal matrix. Accidental impediments of causes may occur without having essential previous causes. The fortuitous indeterminacy factor itself is treated as if it were an essential feature of the material substrate of the actual world (*De necessitate et contingentia causarum*, in Duin 1954: 29.33–30.49, 31.78–32.00; see also Siger of Brabant, *Quaestiones in Physicam* 162.1–167.77; Thomas Aquinas, *Summa theologiae* I, q. 115, a. 6; *In Periherm.* I, lect. 14, n. 185–9; for Siger's views, see also Ryan 1983).

When discussing the first principles, Siger uses the notions *necessarium, impossibile aliter se habere, immobile* and *sempiternum* as convertible (*Quaestiones in Metaphysicam* (Vienna) 376.1–377.7). This statistical notion of necessity is applied to the first cause *simpliciter*, because it is wholly outside the region of change. Celestial bodies exemplify necessity through their uniform motions, and in the lower spheres necessity is found in the natural causes that always produce their effects or, in so far as they are contingent causes, always produce their effects when not impeded by accidental coincidences (ibid. 377.8–378.48). According to Siger, the creative act of the first cause is, philosophically speaking, eternal and necessary. It necessarily produces the system of secondary causes (*De necessitate et contingentia causarum*, in Duin 1954: 19.29–24.34). Because Siger does not make any sharp distinction between logical and natural modalities, the structure of reality described in the theory is something which cannot be conceived to be other than what it is. The first cause is considered a remote cause of accidental and chance events in the sense that, when it eternally produces the system of secondary causes, it leaves room for coincidences. The first cause does not directly bring about individual chance events; it is the necessary cause of the class of such events (ibid. 26.80–28.9, 31.78–32.00, 42.10–25). Siger seems to have thought that this rather strange combination of global determinism and local indeterminism implies a partial denial of divine foreknowledge (ibid. 42.10–18). When accused of heresy, he became more cautious when speaking about indeterminate events in nature (see *Quaestiones in Metaphysicam* (Vienna) 370.1–387.89; Hissette 1977: 42–3).

Siger of Brabant, Boethius of Dacia and other proponents of the Parisian Aristotelianism left the absolute divine possibilities to faith and theology. According to them, to know that something is possible is to know that it can be produced by natural causes. The indeterminacy prevents one from claiming that whatever can be, will be; however, it was thought that there are no eternally frustrated types of possibilities and that a complete natural philosophy would include an account of all of them. Things philosophically impossible were said to be possible according to Catholic faith, but the emphasis was put on the incomprehensibility of the mysteries of the faith (see the anonymous commentary on Aristotle's *Physics*, in Zimmermann 1968: 1.3–18, 25.3–11; Boethius of Dacia, *De aeternitate mundi* 352; Ebbesen 1986: 132–4).

Certain conceptions of natural necessity and possibility were among the teachings of the arts masters which led to the condemnation of 219 articles in theology and philosophy by the Bishop of Paris in 1277. Etienne Tempier and his advisors thought that philosophers were unduly constraining God's power (see Hissette 1977; Wippel 1977; Grant 1986). They rejected as heretical the view according to which God could not do things that where naturally impossible in the prevailing scientific world view, thus emphasizing God's absolute power defined through absolute possibilities (see the articles 17, 20–3, 27, 33, 66–70, 72, 184, 196–9). Modern scholars have wondered whether this attack upon arts masters was justified because they only seem to have taught, like Thomas Aquinas, that to know unrealized divine possibilities does not belong to the epistemic possibilities of men (see, for example, Hissette 1977: 43–9, 275–6, 287–9). Theologians apparently believed that it was the notion of absolute divine power as such which was claimed to be philosophically unintelligible. In the anonymous commentary on Aristotle's *Physics* (in Zimmermann 1968) it is said that Christians must believe that God can bring about contradictory states of affairs (25.3–11), but this view seems to have been exceptional.

It has been argued that the strong assertion of God's absolute power in the Paris Condemnation had the effect that imaginary examples and hypothetical possibilities became increasingly used in natural philosophy. The widening of the realm of possibilities served to push the examination of things beyond the physical possibilities licit within Aristotelian natural philosophy (Murdoch 1974; Grant

1979, 1986). One could also say that the Condemnation contributed to a critical reconsideration of the traditional modal paradigms themselves. The question of the nature of natural modalities was one of the starting points of the extensive discussion of modality in the early fourteenth century.

# 4 Fourteenth-century approaches to modality

In the first part of this chapter I shall describe the modal theory of John Duns Scotus which can be regarded as a systematization of the theory of modality as referential multiplicity, some elements of which were put forward in the twelfth century. The starting point of Scotus' theory is the conception of synchronic alternatives and the refutation of the Aristotelian thesis of the necessity of the present. According to Scotus, that is logically possible the formulation of which does not contain a contradiction, and possibilities are partitioned into groups of possible states of affairs on the basis of the relations of compossibility.

A historically important part of Scotus' theory is the view that the domain of possibility is an a priori area of what is intelligible and as such does not have any kind of existence. It is objective, however, in the sense that it would be comprehended in the same way by all omniscient intellects thinking about all thinkable things. I argue that this transcendental theory of modality and conceivability also occurs in William of Ockham.

The Scotist style modal theory, to some extent similar to contemporary possible worlds semantics, influenced fourteenth-century obligations logic, as will be shown in the second section of this chapter. In the third section I shall discuss the concept of natural nomic necessity in John Duns Scotus, William of Ockham and John Buridan which, in accordance with the new modal semantics, was distinguished from the conception of logical necessity. I also refer to an early fourteenth-century controversy about the status of the first principles in natural philosophy – some authors thought that there are real contradictions in nature. The development of modal logic will be treated in the last section. On the basis of the new modal semantics, fourteenth-century authors could formulate the traditional equipollences and other relations between modal sentences in a manner much more complete and satisfactory than is found in the works of their predecessors. Questions of modal logic were discussed separately with respect to modal sentences *de dicto* and *de re*; modal sentences *de re* were further divided into two groups depending on whether the subject terms refer to actual or possible beings. It was thought that logicians should also analyse the relationships between these readings and, furthermore, the consequences having various types of modal sentences as their parts. Aristotle's modal syllogistic was regarded as a fragmentary theory in which the distinctions between different types of fine structures were not explicated. Ockham, Buridan and Pseudo-Scotus did not try to reconstruct it in its historical form as a uniform system; they believed, like some modern commentators, that such a reconstruction is not possible.

I shall discuss only the emergence of new modal conceptions in this chapter; I shall not trace their later development nor the role of the traditional modal paradigms in late medieval thought.

## DUNS SCOTUS' THEORY OF MODALITY

Henry of Ghent was a member of the group whose task was to compose the articles of the Parisian condemnation in 1277. He treated questions concerning divine power in his own writings as well, and these texts influenced later developments of modal theory; e.g. John Duns Scotus and William of Ockham formulated some of their ideas while criticizing Henry's views. Henry of Ghent presented at least two different theories of the relations between modality and divine power. According to the first, something is possible because God can do it, and God cannot do something because it is impossible. According to the second theory, both possibilities and impossibilities are defined by referring to divine power. The content of God's power is determined by the divine essence as imitable; this imitability consists of essences which have a special kind of being (*esse essentiae*) as eternal aspects of God's being. Actual existence can be communicated to these essences by God's power (Henry of Ghent, *Quodlibeta* 6, *q*. 3; 8, *q*. 3). (The relevant passages are quoted in the Vatican edition of Scotus' works, *Ord*. I, *d*. 43, 352–5. See also Wolter 1950: 70–6; Wippel 1981: 740–51.)

As part of his criticism of Henry's theory of theological modalities, Duns Scotus developed the famous and sometimes misunderstood model of divine psychology in which certain relations between theological, metaphysical and modal notions are defined. Scotus makes use of the traditional doctrine of instants of nature which also mark the stages of conceptual priority. According to him, we can suppose that in the first instant of nature everything receives intelligible being (*esse intelligibile*) in the intellect of God. Because the intelligible being comprises the individual concept of each thing that can be known, every thinkable thing receives possible being (*esse possibile*) in the second instant of nature, in which they are understood as the intentional correlates of divine power and choice. Scotus states that things in this area of possible being have properties which are mutually exclusive. Although such properties can belong to the subjects separately, they are not compossible. Possibilities must therefore be thought of as partitioned into classes on the basis of relations of compossibility. Impossibility is nothing but incompossibility between possible properties or states of affairs. One of the compossible sets into which the possibilities are partitioned is then chosen by divine will to be actualized through divine power (*Ord.* I, *d.* 43, *q. un. n.* 14, *Lect.* I, *d.* 39, *q.* 1–5, *n.* 62–3; *Ord.* I, *d.* 35, *q. un. n.* 32, 49–51, *d.* 38, *q. un. n.* 10; for Scotus' modal metaphysics, see also Knuuttila 1981a: 217–34; 1986a: 207–13).

Although this theological model includes a summary of some aspects of Scotus' modal theory, it is an answer to Henry of Ghent's views and should be understood against this background. Scotus wants to make it clear that, contrary to Henry of Ghent, one should not think that the domain of possibility is, theologically speaking, posterior to God's active power. An infinite power can realize what is realizable, and what is realizable can be decided without any reference to the power. Furthermore, the questions of possibility and impossibility cannot be separated from each other, because impossibility is defined by using the notion of compossibility. Scotus uses the terms 'intelligible being' and 'possible being' in this connection, because they were used by Henry of Ghent, but his point is simply that, when the term 'possible being' is applied to what God can do, the content of this intentional correlate of divine omnipotence is determined neither by the executive power nor by any ontologically given realm of *esse intelligibile*. If the possibilities are to have some actuality or *esse* of the kind Henry attributes to them, they must be thought of as produced in intelligible being and possible being, because they do not have any ontological status or foundation by themselves. But what is possible is, as such, intelligible and possible without having intelligible or possible being. Possibilities would be possibilities (although not actualizable or thinkable in the sense of being related to a power or intellect) even if there were no God or no active power or intellect:

Nothing is impossible without qualification except when to be is repugnant to it without qualification. When to be is repugnant to something, it is primarily repugnant to it because of it itself and not because of its affirmative or negative relation to something else. . . . Therefore that is impossible without qualification to which to be is primarily repugnant as such and which is such that it is repugnant to it to be primarily by itself and not because of some relation to God, either affirmative or negative. It would be repugnant to it to be even when God, *per impossibile*, would not exist. . . . What is possible as a term or an object of omnipotence is something to which to be is not repugnant and which necessarily cannot be by itself. A stone, produced into intelligible being by divine intellect, is such formally by itself and principally by intellect; hence, it is formally possible by itself and, so to say, principally by divine intellect.
(*Ord*. I, *d*. 43, *q. un. n*. 5–7; see also *Ord*. I, *d*. 36, *q. un. n*. 60–1)

Duns Scotus' metaphysics is based on the insight that 'being' is a univocal notion. He criticized the Aristotelian view, accepted by Thomas Aquinas and many others, that 'being' is an analogous term the meaning of which is a disjunction of several components related to one focal meaning. In this theory, the basic meaning is the conception of essence having individuated existence; other meanings are the conceptions of the actuality of substance as being qualified by the modifications listed in Aristotle's doctrine of categories. Scotus tries to point out that in all alleged analogous meanings of 'being' there is a univocal element which conceptually precedes all other meanings attached to the word. This univocal concept of being is expressed by the formulation 'that to which to be is not repugnant' (*cui non repugnat esse*). In the metaphysical sense *ens* is a univocal word which can be truly applied to anything which can be and which therefore is something positive and distinct from the absolute nothingness of impossible things. Because the univocal notion of being signifies nothing but compatibility with existence, real or mental existence is not a part of its meaning. When something is compatible with existence, it is also intelligible. We do not have an idea of a possible thing which could not be identified as something if realized (Knuuttila 1986a: 207–10; cf. Honnefelder 1972, 1979).

When Scotus says that God produces things in intelligible being, he means that they are given an ontological status, weaker than existence, as intentional correlates of divine thought. Although God's intellect in this sense eternally produces its objects, it does not create them by choice. God's infinite intellect comprehends all that can be thought without contradiction (*Ord.* I, d. 43, q. un. n. 5, 14). This view implies that the infinite content of intelligible being would be the same for any omniscient intellect. Any such intellect would recognize the same domain of possibility with its relations of compossibility and its necessary and contingent states of affairs. Intelligible being in God's intellect could be characterized as an actualization of what is potentially an object of thought. This intentional actuality is caused, but possibilities and impossibilities stand as such in themselves and present themselves as possible or impossible to any intellect which contemplates them, as well as to any power which might actualize them. While speaking about the difference between eternally unactualized possible and impossible things, Scotus formulates this view as follows:

> 'Not to be something' belongs eternally to a man and 'not to be something' belongs to a chimera. The affirmation 'to be something' is not repugnant to the man – the negation prevails only because a power does not actualize it, but it is repugnant to the chimera, because no cause could make it to be something. Why it is not repugnant to the man and why it is repugnant to the chimera is only because this is this and that is that, and this holds good for any intellect thinking about the matter, because, as stated earlier, what is formally repugnant to something by itself is repugnant to it, and what is not formally repugnant to something by itself is not repugnant to it. It should not be imagined that this is not repugnant to the man, because the man is a being *in potentia*, and that this is repugnant to the chimera, because the chimera is not a being *in potentia*. On the contrary, the man is a possible being by logical potency, because it is not repugnant, and the chimera is an impossible being by opposite impossibility, because it is repugnant. From this possibility the objective possibility follows, provided that there is divine omnipotence to which all possibilities are objects, although it by itself is something else. This logical possibility could remain separately in power by its own nature (*absolute ratione sui posset stare*) even if there were, *per impossibile*, no omnipotence to which it would be an object.
>
> (*Ord.* I, d, 36, q. un. n. 60–1)

Some scholars have argued that, according to Scotus, God in some sense creates possibilities, i.e. they are dependent on God (see, for example, Wolter 1950: 263; Normore 1986: 232; de Muralt 1986: 345–61). I think that the passages quoted above clearly show that possibilities *qua* possibilities are independent of God in Scotus' view. Possibilities in *esse intelligibile* as recognized objects of divine power are, as such, possibilities in themselves without having any kind of being.

Scotus heavily criticized extensional modal theories in which the actualization at some moment of time was explicitly or implicitly used as the criterion of the genuineness of possibility. So he redefined a contingent event as follows:

> I do not call something contingent because it is not always or necessarily the case, but because its opposite could be actual at the very moment when it occurs.
> (*Ord.* I, d. 2, p. 1, q. 1-2, n. 86; *De primo principio* IV, 4)

The criterion of what is possible is that we without contradiction can think that it takes place in at least one of a set of alternative states of affairs. This is what 'logical possibility' means. (The term 'logical possibility' was introduced by Scotus. See, for example, *Ord.* I, d. 2, p. 2, q. 1-4, n. 262; I, d. 7, q. 1, n. 27, *Lect.* I, d. 7, q. un. n. 32-3, d. 39, q. 1-5, n. 49-51, 54.) An important feature of Scotus' reformulation of contingency is the insistence that synchronic alternatives should be considered as the starting point of modal definitions. (For the historical development of Scotus' views about possibility and contingency, see Vos 1985: 211-14.) The above definition of synchronic contingency is part of an argument that the first cause does not act necessarily. According to Scotus, one cannot hold this view without giving up the Aristotelian thesis of the necessity of the present. So the eternal act of divine will is free only if it is a choice between genuine alternatives and in a real sense could be other than it is. In the same way, if there is an angel who exists for a single instant and that angel wills freely, then while the angel wills something it is still possible for it to will something else (*Lect.* I, d. 39, n. 52; cf. Knuuttila 1981a: 218-25; Normore 1985: 6-7).

Scotus considered the domain of intelligible being, which is actualized in God's intellect, as consisting of all thinkable individuals, their properties and their mutual relations. Because many possibilities are mutually exclusive, the domain of possible states of affairs must be structured into 'possible worlds' on the basis of compossibility relations. (It should be noted here that although Scotus' theory of modality can be characterized as an intuitive predecessor of possible worlds sematics, he did not himself use the notion of a possible world in a technical sense.) Now, one of the pairs of disjunctive attributes, which in Scotus' metaphysics are said to be in disjunction coextensive with being, is the pair 'potential–actual' (*Ord.* I, *d.* 7, *q.* 1, *n.* 72; cf. Wolter 1947: 145–8). Does this mean that we cannot speak about the same individual as actual and as non-actual? Although Scotus does not explicitly discuss this question exactly, he gives examples in his writings which suggest a negative answer. Possible individuals should then be understood as divided into two groups, depending on whether existence in the actual world is or is not an element of their individual concept. (For the view that individuals can be members of alternative possible worlds, see *Ord.* I, *d.* 40, *q. un. n.* 7, *d.* 44, *q. un. n.* 11.) It is important to attend to Scotus' remarks that the same individual can occur in alternative states of affairs, because there have been possible worlds theories in which this is denied. Leibniz thought that every substance has a complete notion which refers to everything included in its history. This is true of actual as well as of merely possible substances, and in each case the complete notion contains predicates referring to one world only. (See, for example, *Discours de Métaphysique* 9–11; translated by Loemker in Leibniz 1975: 308–9. For Leibniz's modal theory, see Schepers 1965; Mates 1968; Poser 1969; Hintikka 1981; Estermann 1990.) It is implied in Scotus' approach that the concepts of individuals contain contingent attributes, and so his notion of the individual shows similarities to Gilbert Poitiers' theory (see pp. 79–82 above), according to which the complete notion of Plato contains not only his historical predicates but also his unactualized possibilities.

On the basis of his conception of possibility, Scotus revised the traditional rules of obligations logic in a significant way. If the individuals in Scotus' model were world-bound, as recently suggested by Douglas Langston (1990), they would not have synchronic *de re* alternatives. This is not compatible with the Scotist obligational principle that one can grant the false and contingent sentence 'You are standing' and then, with respect to the same actual instant of time, grant as impertinent and true sentences which happen to be true (see p. 149 below). That individuals are not world-bound is also implied in Scotus' doctrine of human free will which is formulated with the help of the conception of synchronic contingency. Scotus explicitly denies that the traditional model of diachronic possibilities without synchronic alternatives is a sufficient conceptual tool for discussing the freedom of will. An act is free only when real possibilities to act in another way are not lost before it takes place. The link between the will and the act of will at the moment of the act of will must be non-necessary. It must be true in the divided sense that with respect to the very moment when the will is willing it could be willing otherwise (*Sent.* I, *d.* 39, *n.* 50–1). The idea of the contingent relation between will and its acts at the moment of the act can be understood so that the acts of will belong to the concept of an individual will or person as choices between genuine alternatives, i.e. the person chooses itself through its acts from among real alternatives.

Douglas Langston has argued that Scotus' notion of freedom does not entail the view that persons could be different from what they are in the world chosen by God. Alternative possibilities are only logical possibilities which are open to God and his choice (Langston 1986, 25–52). Scotus stresses, however, that synchronic alternatives relevant in the analysis of the freedom of will are not only logical. They are based on potencies which are explicitly called logical and real (*Sent.* I, *d.* 39, *n.* 49, 51).

Scotus' followers had difficulties in understanding the doctrine that singular acts of will are genuinely contingent while there is a full and true description of the actual world in God's intellect (see Schwamm 1934). Scotus apparently thought that divine knowledge includes knowledge of all individual acts of will as free choices between real alternatives, but he did not explain how this kind of knowledge is possible. Scotus and Ockham did not qualify the view that sentences about future contingent events are true or false, but they did not accept the Boethian-Thomist theory that future contingent sentences are known to God because the flux of time is simultaneously present to divine eternity. Although they did not present any positive theory of the divine foreknowledge, their way of formulating the question was the background for Luis de Molina's (1535–1600) famous doctrine of 'middle knowledge'. (For Molina's view on God's knowledge of future contingents, see Freddoso 1988 and Langston 1986: 55–74; for late medieval discussions of the theme, see also Normore 1985; de la Torre 1987; Hoenen 1989; Baudry 1989.)

The view that God in Scotus' theory creates possibilities *qua* possibilities had already been put forward by William of Ockham, who criticized Scotus' conception of God's intellect, will and power as separated by the instants of nature. Ockham remarks that one cannot say that possibilities are produced into intelligible being because, as far as possibilities are treated as such, it does not make any difference whether they occur in the scope of an intentional attitude or not (*Ord.* I, *d.* 43; *Opera theologica* (*OT*) IV, 646.8–17). Ockham also states that if that which is possible is not possible before it is produced into intelligible being, it is incompatible with existence (ibid. 647.8–13). Even if Scotus had thought that modalities are created, it would not follow that things which are possible would have been impossible beforehand. He did not think in this way, however. Ockham's criticism is based on a wrong interpretation of Scotus' theory where the instants of nature are introduced to distinguish between the acts of God's intellect, will and power. According to Scotus, all the things which are produced by divine intellect into intelligible being or possible being are possible in themselves. He did not think that the intellect by thinking about an object creates its logical possibility.

A further element in Scotus' model criticized by Ockham is the remark that possibilities and impossibilities in the second instant of nature are possibilities and impossibilities due to the formal nature of things, although they depend upon God's intellect as upon a principle. In saying this, Scotus meant that the objects of will and power are presented to them by the intellect which primarily gives some kind of being to things which are thinkable. Ockham criticized this as if the meaning were that possible beings receive a special nature of possibility by which they are made possible:

> whatever inheres in a creature as something real, the creature has from God as from a principle. But it does not have everything that can be predicated of it from God as from a principle, except in the way that God can be said to have such predicates as may be affirmed of Him from God, because such predicates, when they are actual and in reality, are from God. And hence possible being is something a creature has of itself, but not really as something inhering in it, but it is truly possible of itself, just as a man of himself is not a donkey. Therefore, arguments like the above do not hold except for those things that in reality have something like the whole has its parts and accidents. Nor is it a proper way of speaking to say that a creature has possible existence, but rather one should say properly that a creature is possible, not because it has something, but because it can exist in reality.
> (*Ord.* I, *d.* 43, *q.* 2; *OT* IV, 649.18–650.6)

While speaking about possible beings, Ockham also stresses in other places that there are no entities like 'possible being' or 'intelligible being' distinct from the thing itself. Possible beings are possible in and by themselves, but as such they do not have any kind of actuality (see, for example, *Summa logicae* I, *c.* 38, 108.54–66, *c.* 72, 216.58–217.85; *Ord.* I, *d.* 36; *OT* IV, 545.7–561.21; *Quodlibeta* II, *q.* 9; *OT* IX, 153.76–9).

Ockham says in *Ord.* I, d. 36 (*OT* IV, 538–40) that one of the meanings of the term 'being' is 'that to which existence in the world is not repugnant' (*cui non repugnat esse in rerum natura*). Possible beings are beings which though they do not exist can, however, exist. Ockham's purely modal understanding of *possibilia* is in fact very similar to what Duns Scotus said about logical possibilities. Both writers denied the view that merely possible existence would be a species of existence. (For merely possible entities in Ockham's thought, see also Karger 1980: 244–64; McGrade 1985; Adams 1987: 415–16, 1056–61.) It may be that in his criticism of Scotus' view Ockham wanted to demonstrate how one might read Scotus' theory without believing himself that it was what Scotus meant.

The most important feature of Scotus' modal theory is that, historically speaking, it systematically developed the conception of modality as referential multiplicity with respect to synchronic alternative models. In this form the Scotist theory, directly or indirectly, very much influenced late medieval and early modern modal theories until Descartes and Leibniz (see, for example, Alanen and Knuuttila 1988; Dekker 1989; Coombs 1990). A significant aspect of Scotus' theory was its new conception of the foundation of modalities. As mentioned above, a Christian variant of the ancient doctrine of modality and intelligibility as moments of being was developed by such thirteenth-century Parisian scholars as Thomas Aquinas, Bonaventura and Henry of Ghent, who thought that God's eternal intellectual act as the primary conceptualization of what can be thought includes all the ways in which his essence could be imitated by finite beings. This view is also reflected in Walter Burley's *De puritate artis logicae* where he wrote:

> The term 'being' (*ens*) can be taken in three ways. In one way it is taken as the most transcendent term common to all intelligible things, and in this sense being is the adequate object of intellect. . . . In the second way it is taken to mean a being whose existence is not prohibited and in this sense all possible beings are beings. . . . In the third way it is taken to mean an actually existing being. . . . When something is called a being in the first way, it is a being in intellect, because it is an object of an intellect. So it is objectively a being in intellect. A being called a being in the second way is a being in its causes or a being which exists in its cause.
> (*De puritate artis logicae, tractatus longior* 59.3–14)

'An intelligible being' is equated here with 'a being in intellect' and 'a possible being' with 'a being in its causes'. We have seen that Scotus often used these notions, but he also introduced an important reevaluation of their meaning. In Duns Scotus' modal theory, the ontological foundation of thinkability and logical possibility is given up. The domain of logical possibility, structured by logical necessities and divided into different classes of compossible states of affairs, is taken as the a priori area of conceivability. Scotus and Ockham thought that necessary and possible truths are prior to any intellect and being, whether divine or earthly, although as such they are not actual in any sense. Any predication which does not contain a contradiction is logically possible. According to this view, necessary truths are neither realistic nor constructivistic, but are some kinds of absolute preconditions of thinking. This was stressed by the slogans that possibilities as such do not have any actuality and that they are what they are, even if, *per impossibile*, there were no divine intellect or power.

This theory of the domain of possibility as a non-existent transcendental and objective precondition of all being and thinking became one of the alternative approaches in the late medieval discussion of the foundation of thinking and being. Through Suárez's works it was also well known in the seventeenth century. In his discussion of eternal truths, Descartes criticized the classical view of the ontological foundation of modality as well as the 'transcendental' theory of modality and conceivability. His doctrine of eternal truths created *ex nihilo* is a constructivistic doctrine of rationality and intelligibility. Scotus, Ockham and Suárez thought that necessary truths cannot be other than they are, independently of who is thinking about them. This was what Descartes wanted to deny:

> As for the eternal truths, I say once more that they are true or possible only because God knows them as true or possible. They are not known as true by God in any way which would imply that they are true independently of him. . . . In God willing and knowing are one single thing, in such a way that by the very fact of willing something He knows it, and it is for this reason that such a thing is true.
>
> (To Mersenne, 6 May 1630, in *Philosophical Letters* 13)

Descartes claims that the domain of conceivability is freely set by God and that it could therefore have been different from what it is. (To Mersenne, 15 April 1630, in *Philosophical Letters* 11). Contrary to what has often been maintained, this does not imply any contradiction, because according to Descartes' view, notions or propositions chosen to be necessary or possible are in themselves modally indifferent (see Alanen 1985; Alanen and Knuuttila 1988: 11–17).

Like Duns Scotus, Ockham discussed Henry of Ghent's view that things are possible because God can make them and impossible because God cannot make them (*Ord.* I, *d.* 43; *OT* IV, 641.14–645.7). As shown by Wolter (1950), some neo-scholastic textbooks have erroneously attributed this view to Ockham, which again has been taken as evidence that Ockham anticipated the view, wrongly imputed to Descartes, that God could arbitrarily make the possible impossible and vice versa. Ockham, however, held no such view and in fact argued against Henry's opinions. Although Ockham's views about modality are different from those of Descartes, some similarities can be found between Descartes' theory of modality and Ockham's theory of the foundations of ethics. According to many scholars, Ockham would be committed to a form of moral voluntarism in claiming that the only foundation for moral law is God's will which poses its objects freely without any previous determination (see Holopainen 1991). In so far as one accepts this interpretation of Ockham's views, one could also regard Descartes' theory of the creation of eternal truths as an extension of moral voluntarism to the laws of logic and hence to the principles of reason. Ockham took a step towards voluntarist constructivism, but he restricted the idea only to moral truths.

## FOURTEENTH-CENTURY DISCUSSIONS OF OBLIGATIONAL RULES

Duns Scotus' new modal semantics led him to reject the thirteenth-century obligational *positio* rule, according to which the respondent must deny that the actual 'now' of disputation is the instant in which the false and possible *positum* is treated as true. He said that this rule can be deleted from the *positio* disputation without making any other changes (*Lect.* I, *d.* 39, *q.* 1–5, *n.* 56, 59). This became the standard approach in the fourteenth century, i.e. it was commonly entertained that the *positum*, which is false and contingent, is a synchronic alternative of the actual world.

Scotus' revision makes intelligible the list of obligational answers, which previously had been nonsensical, though coherent. It can be understood as a partial description of a possible world as follows. The actual world has a special status in the sense that propositions which are true about it are treated as truths which prima facie must be conceded; they are denied only if necessary. During the disputation we are ready to change our picture of the actual world, i.e. we are ready to move to other worlds partially described by the same propositions which are true about the actual world. Accepting the *positum* is the first step in this direction. The *positum* specifies a subset of the worlds in which we might exist. The next steps bring about further specifications the nature of which may depend on the order of the propositions put forward by the opponent. (For discussions on the order of propositions in the obligations treatises, see Ashworth 1981: 183–6; Knuuttila and Yrjönsuuri 1988: 195–7.)

Scotus did not change the traditional principle that one should grant the propositions describing the actual world whenever it is possible, which is understandable against the background of the honesty rules mentioned earlier (see pp. 125–6 above). The number of false propositions introduced into the list of answers remains in this way as small as possible. However, the disadvantage of this strictness is that we easily get very far from the actual world. It is of philosophical interest that in some cases the matrix of the answers remains nearer to the actual world when it contains more falsehoods, i.e. when counterfactual conditionals are accepted as tools of reasoning. The *positum* is then regarded as fixing a possible world as close as possible to the actual world and obligational propositions are evaluated from the point of view of that possible world. Late medieval discussions of these kinds of problems have been studied to some extent. Eleonore Stump and Paul Vincent Spade have shown that in his *Sophismata* Richard Kilvington suggested the idea that impertinent propositions should be given the responses which would be appropriate if the *positum* were true, and this world would otherwise differ as little as possible from the actual world (*Sophism* 47). (Richard Kilvington's *Sophismata*, written in Oxford in the early 1320s, was edited and translated by Barbara and Norman Kretzmann in 1990). Although there are various historical and philosophical problems in Kilvington's remarks on obligational disputations, it seems that in a remarkable way he formulated some properties of counterfactual conditionals in this context (Spade 1982c: 19–28; Stump 1982: 329–32; 1989: 222–35). Kilvington's attempt to qualify obligational rules with the help of counterfactual conditionals did not find many adherents. Most authors accepted the traditional rules with the Scotist correction and dropped the *positio impossibilis* which became spurious in the light of new modal semantics (see Ashworth 1985).

Another revision of the rules was offered by Roger Swyneshed in the early 1330s. His basic idea was that a proposition is pertinent or inpertinent in virtue of its relation solely to the *positum*. The rules

## Fourteenth-century approaches to modality 151

(15) and (17) of the standard approach are dropped (see p. 126 above). Two much-debated corollaries were formulated by Swyneshed as follows: (a) one need not grant a conjunction in virtue of having granted all its conjuncts, and (b) one need not grant any part of a disjunction in virtue of having granted the disjunction (*Obligationes* 257). It is easily realized that, instead of operating with one matrix of answers, Swyneshed thinks that there are two of them, one for the *positum* and relevant propositions and one for irrelevant propositions. Both columns are treated separately except that an irrelevant proposition already discussed during the disputation can be presented again as a second *positum* and added into the *positum* matrix. Irrelevant propositions are treated in accordance with the standard honesty rules (ibid. 273–5). Swyneshed's approach was not very influential, but it contains interesting philosophical insights. The rules can be understood as rules for a discourse in which two independent possible domains are treated simultaneously. The remarks pertaining to the additional *positum* involve the idea that a domain may be changed during the disputation. (For other interpretations of Swyneshed's rules, see Spade 1982a: 335–41; 1982c, 28–31; Stump 1989: 215–22, 241–5.)

There was an interesting partial analogy to Swyneshed's obligations rules in Robert Holcot's contemporaneous fideistic conception of theology. Holcot's views were influenced by William of Ockham's theory of how certain Trinitarian sentences may be believed to be possible and intelligible without being understood. Logical problems of the Trinity, as they were conceived in the Middle Ages, can be illustrated by the much debated expository syllogism:

haec essentia divina est pater
haec essentia divina est filius
ergo pater est filius.

Some features of Ockham's position become clear from his discussion of the *positio impossibilis* rules of obligations (*Summa logicae* III. 3.42, 739–41).

Ockham stresses that in a *positio impossibilis* disputation the proposition presented as a *positum* cannot be logically impossible, and that only those propositions which follow from the *positum* and/or the correctly granted propositions by natural and simple consequences which are evident and *per se notae* must be granted as relevant. Ockham seems to think that an impossible *positum* should be a natural or doctrinal impossibility. (For a conception of weak necessity and impossibility in Ockham, see pp. 155–6 below.) The only examples discussed are Trinitarian propositions and their purpose is to show that theologically indirect proofs are often as much matters of faith as the articles which are proved. Suppose that the *positum* is as follows: the Holy Spirit does not proceed from the Son. It is then proposed: the Holy Spirit does not differ from the Son. This, Ockham says, is irrelevant and false and must be denied. However, if the opponent has earlier put forward the conditional: if the Holy Spirit does not proceed from the Son, the Holy Spirit does not differ from the Son, a Catholic believer grants this as irrelevant and true. And after this, the respondent should accept the proposition: the Holy Spirit does not differ from the Son. Ockham remarks that games of this kind do not go in this way, if the respondent is an *infidelis*.

In the beginning of part III of his *Summa logicae* (360.29–32), Ockham states that the articles of faith are not probable and appear false to natural reason. We could think that the Trinitarian forms are presented as *posita* to a respondent who is using only natural reason. Which kinds of conclusions should be granted? According to Ockham, the *distinctio non-identitatis formalis* between the essence and the persons should be granted when it evidently follows from the Scriptures or the determinations of the church (*Ord.* 1, *d*, 2, *q*. 1, *q*. 11; *OT* II, 17–18, 364–78). Referring to this distinction one could deny the conclusion of the above expository syllogism. So it seems that if someone has accepted the conjunction of the premises as a *positum*, the formal distinction should also be regarded as a valid principle, but this is only because the naturally impossible *positum* has been accepted as possible. Ockham says that it is not any easier to accept the formal distinction than to accept the notion of Trinity of persons with the unity of essence. The formal distinction does not explain anything; it is exercised only by those who believe that the Trinity is possible.

Ockham seems to think that the respondent may grant that the Trinitarian entity is possible without being able to explain its nature in any understandable way. It is thinkable that the world could be such that we would not understand it at all by those conceptual tools we think we understand the actual world with. (For such worlds, see Lewis 1986: 91; Kusch 1989: 93–102.) Although Ockham thought that certain articles of faith are incomprehensible and the entities they refer to are like beings in an alien world, he did not want to argue for the view that no natural theology is possible. This seems to be how Robert Holcot thought, however. According to him, a Catholic must

## Fourteenth-century approaches to modality 153

believe that the articles of faith concerning the Trinity are true. The propositions must be accepted separately, one by one, and the believer is permitted to draw, with respect to them, only those consequences which are similarly included in holy doctrine. In the question *Utrum haec est concedenda, Deus est Pater et Filius et Spiritus Sanctus* Holcot says:

> Catholicus nulla logica debet uti in concedendo et negando sive propositiones sive consequentias nisi determinatione ecclesiae.
> (*Exploring the Boundaries of Reason* 35)

Although the views of Ockham and Holcot differ to some extent, both of them thought that if one starts from the notion of the possibility of strange entities, then, instead of trying to construct the laws of possible alien worlds, one should say that we could possibly understand them if we learned a new system of symbolic representation. Ockham applied this idea only to some Trinitarian forms, while Holcot considered those examples as paradigm cases for theology in general. Holcot's positivist attitude towards revelation is an exaggerated version of Ockham's theory, according to which our insufficient knowledge of the properties of the terms of the Holy Trinity prevents us from using them as replacements of variables in logical forms. Ockham was inclined to think that semantic relations of mental language are inaccessible. If something which cannot be conceptualized in it is claimed to be possible, it must be treated as an element of a world which is totally different from the one connected with our mental language. In so far as Ockham and Holcot assumed that alien possible objects cannot be understood, because understanding them would demand us to leave human language as the universal medium of human understanding, a critic could remark that it is not necessary to leap in one bound to another world which we do not understand. We could also proceed step by step and construct new modes of understanding, thinking that semantic relations, instead of being inaccessible, are inexhaustible (see Knuuttila, forthcoming; cf. Kusch, 1989). It is in order to notice that in his *Questions on the Sentences* Holcot denied the validity of traditional logic with respect to supernatural matters, but he changed his mind later and accepted, like Ockham, the universal validity of the principles of logic (see Gelber in *Exploring the Boundaries of Reason* 26–7; for medieval approaches to the logic and semantics of theological language, see also Gelber 1974; Maierù 1986, 1988; Shank 1988).

In Swyneshed's approach one simultaneously treats two possible worlds whilst keeping them separate. Similarly, Holcot thinks that a Catholic has in his mind a column for the answers of natural reason and a column of faith, and that there are no connections between them, except that something may be added to the column of faith as a new *positum*. The philosophical similarity between Holcot's treatment of propositions of faith and Swineshed's obligational rules is based on the view that one may in argumentative contexts have in mind two unconnected domains of discourse.

In Holcot's time people were acquainted with a further version of obligations rules which has not been considered in modern discussion and which may shed new light on the habits of thought reflected in Swyneshed's obligations rules and in Holcot's theological method. In his questions on Aristotle's *Prior Analytics*, Richard of Campsall sketches rules for games in which there are two opponents and correspondingly two different *posita*. As the answers given to one opponent become pertinent only with respect to the answers given to that opponent, the Swyneshed type conjunction and disjunction rules are considered natural (15.11–18, 15.47, 227–9, 237–8). Swyneshed's rules were interpreted in this way by Stanislaus of Znaim who taught in Prague during 1388–1413 (see his *De vero et falso* 209.12–211.13).

Holcot may have been familiar with these rules, although he does not refer to them. When formulating the rules of what a Catholic should concede or deny, Holcot remarks that the answer to the question of whether something is contradictory or not is different, depending on whether it is given in the light of natural reason or in accordance with Catholic doctrine (*Exploring the Boundaries of Reason* 39.177–87). One traditional theological doctrine was also connected with the theme of different domains. In his book *De genesi ad litteram*, Augustine said that God is the author of two books, the book of Scriptures (*liber scripturae*) and the book of Nature (*liber naturae*). This idea was commonly employed in medieval theology in connection with the question of faith and reason. The divine authorship of the book of nature gave certain legitimation to natural philosophy and theology which, in the Augustinian tradition, was thought to be improved by divine revelation, which included truths available only through faith. In the thirteenth century, the two-books model was sometimes modified to the effect that the divine intellect itself was called a book containing everything that can be known. The books of Nature and Scriptures could then be regarded as two partial editions of the original book (see Köpf 1974: 233–4, 238, 249–50). In Holcot's fideistic approach, reading one book is quite a different activity from reading the other.

## NEW THEORIES OF NATURAL NECESSITY

Duns Scotus called those actual predications and states of affairs contingent which could be otherwise with respect to the point of time in which we attend to them. Necessary attributes and relations should apparently be attached to things in all those sets of compossibilities in which they occur. Against this background one could ask which of the natural invariances treated as necessities in earlier approaches were necessary in this strong sense of necessity, and which of them were merely empirical generalizations without being logically or metaphysically necessary. Since the twelfth-century discussions, a common remark in this context was that the existence of the world is contingent and, in this sense, its structures are only contingently actual even if they were conditionally necessary as such. It was also commonly thought that something which is necessary with respect to inferior causes may be contingent with respect to superior causes. Thomas Aquinas referred in this connection to a special *potentia oboedientialis* by which things can receive direct influence from the divine first cause. This was needed when natural necessities were regarded as hypothetical metaphysical necessities (see *De potentia q. 1, a. 3, ad 1, q. 6, a. 1, ad 18; De virtutibus in communi q. un., a. 10, ad 13* in *Quaestiones disputatae*). Scotus' point was that nomic invariances, even though often considered conditional metaphysical necessities, do not necessarily have anything in common with conceptual necessities. He and his followers thought that the structures of natural invariances may be metaphysically and logically contingent. Miraculous events could then be interpreted as voluntary suspensions of the laws of nature themselves.

In an often quoted passage (*Ord.* I, *d.* 3, *p.* 1, *q.* 4, *n.* 237) Duns Scotus says that scientific knowledge of the lowest degree is about invariances which cannot be reduced to self-evident principles. Such invariances are in power in the actual world and they cannot be changed by natural agents, although they could be changed by divine omnipotence. According to Scotus, none of the causal connections of the actual world fulfils the criteria of the strong necessity (cf. *Ord.* I, *d.* 8, *p.* 2, *q. un.*, *n.* 306). It seems that Duns Scotus' notion of natural necessity, not reducible to logical necessity, is a little stronger than the merely temporal-frequency conception of necessity.

We can find a similar distinction in William of Ockham who, in spite of his continuous criticism of Scotus' views, often based his thought on the philosophical insights of the latter. While commenting on the distinction between the notions of separable and inseparable accidents, Ockham writes as follows:

> A separable accident is one which can be removed from its subject by nature without the destruction of that subject; whereas, an inseparable accident is one that cannot be removed by nature without the destruction of the subject. It could, however, be so removed by divine power.
> (*Summa logicae* I.25, 83.50–3)

In his book on Ockham's physics, Goddu states that Ockham tried to find a way of expressing physical necessities such that they are not reducible to logical ones, but he, like Aquinas and Duns Scotus, did not succeed in expressing less than logically necessary events as not logically necessary (Goddu 1984: 72–3). Goddu does not discuss the texts just mentioned where the idea of natural necessities as not logical or metaphysical is formulated. (For Ockham's conception of natural necessity, see also Kusch 1990.)

While discussing the question concerning whether we can have certain knowledge about nature, John Buridan says that such a certainty demands firmness of truth and firmness of assent. The firmness of truth is divided into two types: there are sentences whose truth is firm in the sense that they cannot be falsified in any case (*casus*), and there are sentences which are firm on the supposition of the common course of nature. An example of the latter type of firmness is the assertion that fire is hot. It is not falsified on the supposition of the common course of nature, although God could make fire cold and so the sentence 'Every fire is hot' would be falsified. This is the same example that Scotus and Ockham used. As for the firmness of assent, conditionally firm general truths are firmly accepted as expressing natural necessities when their instances have been observed to be true in many cases and to be false in none, and it is supposed that nature functions in a regular manner (*In Metaphysicen Aristotelis quaestiones* II, q. 1, f. 8v; see also *Quaestiones super libris quattuor De caelo et mundo* I, q. 1, 6.22–3).

Buridan's account of the firmness of truth is based on the same distinction between conceptual and merely natural necessities that we found in Duns Scotus and Ockham. There are sentences which cannot be falsified by any thinkable cases or states of affairs, and in addition to these strong necessities there are sentences expressing natural necessities, i.e. sentences which can be falsified, although not by the natural things of the actual world. Buridan remarks that the doctrine of creation qualifies traditional necessities about nature so that they cannot be treated simply as eternal truths (see, for example, *Tractatus de consequentiis* 112–13). Furthermore, like Scotus and Ockham, Buridan also took it for granted that many of the traditional natural necessities, however they are formulated, do not fulfil the criteria of strong firmness or necessity.

Moody was the first to pay attention to this feature in Buridan's thought. In his paper 'Ockham, Buridan, and Nicholas of Autrecourt', Moody describes the medieval development culminating in Buridan's thought as follows:

> Because the laws of nature are metaphysically contingent, they are scientifically necessary only by a hypothetical necessity – *ex suppositione naturae*. Thus an ineradicable element of *hypothesis* is introduced into the science of nature, and, as its counterpart, the principle that all scientific hypotheses require empirical verification, and retain an element of probability which cannot be completely eliminated.
> (Moody 1975: 156; the paper was first published in 1947)

Anneliese Maier heavily criticized Moody's thesis of the origin of hypothetico-deductive reasoning in Buridan (Maier 1964–7: 403; for an evaluation of Maier's views about the conceptions of natural necessity in the Middle Ages, see Knuuttila 1989). It is true that Moody exaggerated the role of hypothetico-deductive reasoning in Buridan and that there are some terminological problems in Moody's early paper. But what was correctly noticed there, and what Maier did not realize, was Buridan's acceptance of the idea of equivocity of 'necessity' and his insistence that nomic necessities are unchangeable *ex suppositione communis cursus naturae*. Like Scotus and Ockham, Buridan thought that unqualified modal truths are what they are independently of whether there is a world or not. God does not create logical possibilities, but they are not realizable without God's power as the ultimate activator. Propositions about natural invariances are called necessary in the sense that they are never falsified by the common course of nature. (For Buridan's view of modalities as independent of God, see *In Metaphys.* II, *q*. 1; for merely possible beings without any kind of existence, see, for example, *Quaestiones super octo Physicorum libros Aristotelis* I, *q*. 15; *Tractatus de consequentiis* 27.31–28.52; for divine power, see also *Quaest. super Phys.* I, *q*. 22.)

William Wallace has also criticized Moody's views, starting from his studies on Aquinas' ideas about demonstration *ex suppositione*. Thomas Aquinas states that in natural philosophy we can study contingent processes by noting how they terminate in the majority of cases. Formulating this end as an ideal *suppositio*, we can reason back to the causes that are required for its production. This *ex suppositione* procedure yields *propter quid* demonstrations that are proper to natural science. According to Wallace, Buridan's use of the notion *ex suppositione* comes close to that of Thomas Aquinas (Wallace 1972: 76–80; 1981: 132–3, 344–6). I think, however, that these conceptions are connected with very different views on necessity in natural philosophy. Buridan thought that the common course of nature is the supposition which guarantees the firmness of truth to propositions of natural philosophy. They can constitute scientific knowledge only because no stronger firmness is demanded, as Buridan often repeats, and in this sense there is a hypothetical element in his conception of science (see, for example, *In Metaphys.* II, q. 1, f. 9r; *Quaest. super Phys.* I, q. 4, f. 5v; cf. Federici Vescovini 1983: 294). Moody mistakenly attributed this view to Thomas Aquinas; as Wallace has pointed out, his *ex suppositione* approach did not contain any attempt to qualify the concept of apodeictic scientific knowledge. According to Wallace, while Aquinas believed that one may demonstrate on the basis of a *suppositio* that abstracts from chance impediments, Buridan applied this view by claiming that one must abstract from God's suspension of the laws of nature so as to perform a miracle (Wallace 1981: 152). This alleged analogy is not very useful for Wallace's thesis, because chance events in Aquinas are occurrences which do not violate causal structures as such. But God's power, according to Buridan, may change these structures themselves. Abstracting from accidental impediments is, for Aquinas, a methodological device with the help of which one can concentrate on what is assumed to be metaphysically necessary. Abstracting from divine power is in Buridan a theoretical postulate about the meaning of necessity in science.

In his treatises on Aristotle's works, Buridan makes use of the Aristotelian modal paradigms called above the potency model and the statistical or temporal-frequency interpretation of modal notions. Buridan delineates the first model as follows. There is a certain number of types of potencies in nature. All natural possibilities as generic tendencies are realized. Potencies cannot be eternally frustrated, because nothing is in vain in nature. Individual possibilities in the sense of partial potencies may remain unrealized (*Quaest. super De caelo et mundo* I, q. 23–6, 112–28). Buridan also reminds his readers that, according to Aristotle, what always is, is by necessity, from which it follows that what never is, is impossible, and that genuine possibilities cannot remain unrealized (see, for example, *Quaestiones longe super librum Perihermeneias* 52.9–11; *Tractatus de consequentiis* 112.48–59; *In Metaphys.* VI, *q.* 5, *f.* 37r). As Buridan was conscious of the philosophical problems related to this way of thought, he claimed that, while speaking about future contingents and freedom of the will, Aristotle did not operate with partial possibilities only, but also applied the idea of diachronic possibilities, i.e. the idea of alternative prospective possibilities of which one is realized and the others fade away (*Quaest. super Periherm.* 54.4.–57.10; *In Metaphys.* VI, *q.* 5, *f.* 36v; *Quaestiones super decem libros Ethicorum Aristotelis* III, *q.* 1, *ff.* 36r–37v).

Another more elaborate version of the statistical model in Buridan is connected with his view that the terms of sentences used in natural philosophy have natural supposition. They supposit for everything (past, present, future) they signify. So 'Thunder is a sound in the clouds' is read 'Any thunder, whenever it was or is or will be, is or was or will be a sound in the clouds' (*Quaest. super Eth.* VI, *q.* 6, *ff.* 122v–123r*;* for natural supposition, see also Scott 1965: 662–71, de Rijk 1973; King 1985: 43–5). According to Buridan, in natural philosophy the necessity of sentences means that they are true universal affirmative sentences of this type. If universal negative sentences are true, they are impossible. Sentences having empty terms belong to the last-mentioned category (*Quaest. super Eth.* VI, *q.* 6, *f.* 123r; *Quaestiones in duos libros Analyticorum priorum Aristotelis* I, *q.* 25 (I have used the forthcoming edition by Hubien)).

Buridan says once that necessary sentences of natural philosophy are also hypothetically necessary and that they cannot be falsified by any case (*Quaest. in An. pr.* I, *q.* 25). This remark should not be read as meaning that all natural necessities are reducible to logical or metaphysical necessities, because it is thinkable, for example, that fire would be cold. Buridan was inclined to accept the statistical interpretation of modality in natural philosophy, but perhaps a vague reference to the idea of counterfactual support of natural laws is included in the remark that they are qualified hypothetical necessities. According to Buridan, the Aristotelian principle that all generable things will be generated does not apply to individuals. But if the unrealized members of species were realized in the actual world, they would obey its natural laws. This means that even though the structures of nature are not conceptually necessary, there is in nature no power which could change them. Buridan also states that there are some principles of natural philosophy that can be formulated as hypothetical conceptual necessities *simpliciter* (*Quaest. super Eth.*

VI, q. 6, f. 123r). But like Scotus and Ockham, he presents the statement 'Every fire is hot' as a typical example of natural necessities, thus endorsing the new fourteenth-century view of nomic necessities as logically contingent.

A different discussion of natural necessities was involved in the early fourteenth-century limit decision controversy roused by the thesis of Landulph Caraccioli, John Baconthorpe, Hugh of Newcastle and some others, stating that there are real contradictions in nature. Aristotle's theory of limit decision (see pp. 20–3 above) was treated in the thirteenth century both in physics and in the theory of logical analysis of sentences with syncategorematic terms, in this case sentences with the words 'begins' and 'ceases'. (There are many recent works on medieval analysis of *incipit/desinit* sentences; see the bibliographical notes in Nielsen 1982b; Knuuttila 1986b; Tabarroni 1989.) The general background of the contradiction theory of change and the relevant, mostly unedited texts are discussed in Knuuttila and Lehtinen (1979) and in Knuuttila (1986b) (see also Kretzmann 1982a, Spade 1982b; Trifogli forthcoming). Without entering into the details here, it is sufficient to state that the proponents of the contradiction theory assumed it an Aristotelian doctrine that contradictory terms of an instantaneous change are simultaneously actual at the moment of change. This view was totally wrong, of course, but as mentioned in Chapter 1, Aristotle's various remarks on the limit decision problem do not build a coherent whole. If all of what Aristotle says about the matter is accepted, some kind of contradiction theory easily suggests itself.

One of the philosophical arguments used by Landulph Caraccioli and John Baconthorpe runs as follows: if the terms of instantaneous change are both in the same instant of time and if these terms are contradictory, it follows that contradictory statements are true in the same instant of time. The minor premise, according to which the terms are contradictory, is commonly accepted. The major premise can be proved as follows. The terms are in the same instant or they are in different instants. In the first case, a contradiction follows. In the second case, there will be some intermediate time and the change is not instantaneous. Landulph goes on by stating that one could respond that the terms are not in the same nor in different instants, because the whole preceding time corresponds to the *terminus a quo* and the ultimate instant of time corresponds to the *terminus ad quem*. This Aristotelian reply was in fact the most common argument against Landulph, presented for example by John of Jandun, John the Canon, Francis of Meyronnes, Francis of Marcia and Michael of

Massa. Landulph's answer was as follows: as for instantaneous changes, durational measurement is accidental. If we remove from an object its accidental properties, nothing essential is changed. Let us take away the preceding time from a generation. Then we have in the ultimate instant the generation, and if we have the generation, we have the *terminus a quo* and the *terminus ad quem*. A variant of this argument runs as follows: if the whole preceding time corresponds to the *terminus a quo* and the ultimate instant of it to the *terminus ad quem*, we can ask which is the measure of the change as such. This measure cannot be the preceding time, because then the change is not instantaneous. If the measurement is the last instant, contradictory sentences are true at the same time. This is proved as follows. The change is not a term but an acquisition of a term. Therefore in the same instant of time a thing is not in so far as it is coming to be and it is in so far as it is produced.

Aristotle's notion of change between contradictory terms refers to the succession of contradictory states on an occasion. The first instant of the latter state is called the instant of change, but in fact it is the instant of having been changed. The question Baconthorpe and Caraccioli presented to the adherents of the orthodox Aristotelian view was the same as we have found in Plato and Augustine (see p. 21): how is it possible that something has been changed without being in change. Aristotle's physical model, based on the idea of continuity, does not include an element which would function as a transformer between not being and being. In the Platonic tradition it was thought that generations and corruptions themselves are something which take place at the instant at which neither of the contradictories describing the terms of change are true. Instead of accepting the Platonic doctrine of truth-value gaps, which contains the problem that a change into the intermediate state seems to demand another intermediate state and so on, our fourteenth-century writers presented the theory of actual contradictions in nature. They thought it philosophically satisfactory, because it explained the intuitive idea that in a change between contradictory terms the change as such is a kind of link between not being and being.

According to Landulph, contradictory terms of change, which can be present in the same instant of time, belong to different instants of nature. With the help of this distinction he wanted to say that real contradictions should be considered as instantaneous overlappings of states of affairs, which in the conceptual order are mutually exclusive and jointly exhaustive. The purpose of his theory is to show that nature does not obey the Law of Contradiction, although it obeys the

Law of Identity and the Law of Excluded Middle. In Landulph's theory, the principles of logic are valid with respect to the Trinity and other non-temporal theological matters. It is only the changing part of reality which does not fully obey logic. Petrus Rogerii, later Pope Clement the Sixth, denied the Law of Contradiction in certain theological connections, and the same holds of Holcot's early non-standard logic of faith, which he gave up later, and of the anonymous author of the early fourteenth-century work *Centiloquium* (see Maier 1967: 257–85; Boehner 1958: 351–72; Gelber in Robert Holcot, *Exploring the Boundaries of Reason* 45–6).

## MODAL LOGIC AND MODAL SYLLOGISTIC

The new modal semantics influenced early fourteenth-century modal logic which can be regarded as a remarkable revision and systematization of precedent approaches. This medieval theory of modal sentences and consequences served, more or less directly, as the basis for modal logic until the eighteenth century. I shall sketch its main lines by concentrating on three works. The first is an anonymous treatise on Aristotle's *Prior Analytics*. Its author is called Pseudo-Scotus since the work is included in the seventeenth-century edition of John Duns Scotus' works (*Opera omnia* I, 273–341; I refer to this work as *PS*). The second is William of Ockham's *Summa logicae* (*OSL*). With respect to the variety of combinations of different types of premises in modal syllogisms, it includes the most extensive fourteenth-century discussion of the topic. The third work is John Buridan's *Tractatus de consequentiis* (*BC*) which was edited by Hubien in 1976 and translated (in some places freely) by King in 1985. According to the editors, Ockham's *Summa logicae* was written in 1323 and Buridan's *Tractatus de consequentiis* in 1335. Buridan discussed modal logic and modal syllogistic also in his *Summulae de dialectica* and in *Quaestiones* on Aristotle's *Prior Analytics*. Some modal questions are treated in his *Quaestiones* on Aristotle's *De interpretatione*. I refer mainly to the *Tractatus de consequentiis* because it contains a concise summary of Buridan's modal theory. If John of Cornwall is the author of the treatise of Pseudo-Scotus, as many scholars have assumed, it is later than the works of Ockham and Buridan. Many of the questions are very similar to those in Buridan's *Quaestiones* on the *Prior Analytics*. (For late medieval modal logic, see also McDermott 1972; Normore 1975; Freddoso 1980; King 1985: 51–6, 79–82; Hughes 1989.)

Buridan presents modal logic in the *Tractatus de consequentiis* as a part of his general theory of consequences. It includes sections on the equipollences between various modes in combination with negations and on the relations of the standard square of opposition between them, on the nature and conversions of composite and divided (*de dicto* and *de re*) modal sentences, on the mutual relationship between these two types of modal sentences and their relations to assertoric sentences, on further modal consequences and on modal syllogisms. The same themes occur in all works mentioned. Fourteenth-century modal logic strived for generality, and this had effects on the attitudes towards Aristotle's modal syllogistic. For one thing, it was thought that the notion of possibility proper ($Mp = -L-p$) must be added into modal syllogistic as the basic notion. Furthermore, it was considered imperative to distinguish between different types of modal sentences and to discuss their syllogistic behaviour separately. When Aristotle's modal syllogistic was viewed from the point of view of this systematic approach, it appeared as a not very well organized fragment of a larger theory which remained beyond Aristotle's purview.

I have already referred to Richard of Campsall's *Quaestiones super librum Priorum Analeticorum* (c.1308) which in some respects anticipated the new fourteenth-century modal logic, although it simultaneously operated with certain traditional assumptions refuted in the works of the next generation. Fourteen of Campsall's twenty questions are about modal sentences and two are about past and future tense sentences. Differing from the habits of his predecessors, Campsall almost always begins the discussions of various modal questions by referring to the distinction between composite and divided readings. He apparently thought that modal logic should deal with both of them, although he tried to show that Aristotelian modal moods are often valid only when the premises are divided modals. Campsall was also conscious of the fact that the number of problems in Aristotle's theory is much larger than was recognized by his predecessors, but instead of interpreting or evaluating Aristotle's modal syllogistic from the point of view of a reflected general theory, he tried to save it with different *ad hoc* distinctions. (If the edition of the text by Synan is correct, there must be many writing mistakes in the manuscript on which it is based.)

Campsall treats the conversions of composite sentences *de necessario* or *de contingenti* as conversions of the modified assertoric part of composite modals. When discussing the conversion of the universal negative sentence *de necessario*, he refers to the rule: 'The antecedent is necessary; therefore the consequent is necessary' (ibid. 5.39). The conversion of particular affirmative sentences is said to be based on the rule: 'If one of the convertibles is necessary, the other is necessary as well.' The third rule mentioned is: 'The universal *de inesse* is necessary and affirmative; therefore the converted indefinite is necessary' (ibid. 6.21). The conversion of composite particular affirmative sentences *de contingenti* is based on the rule: 'One of the convertibles is contingent; therefore the other is contingent as well' (ibid. 7.32). Campsall remarks that the accidental conversion of universal affirmative sentences *de contingenti* does not always result in the same kind of contingency.

According to Campsall, divided modal sentences *de necessario* are converted in the same way as assertoric sentences (ibid. 5.40, 6.22–4), and the same holds true of affirmative sentences *de contingenti*, which are equivalent to sentences *de contingenti* with opposite quality (ibid. 7.33–47). While arguing for the conversion of universal negative divided sentences *de necessario*, Campsall refers to what he calls a necessary consequence: 'C can be one of those which are now under B; therefore it is one of those which are now under B' (ibid. 5.40). This principle is an example of Campsall's different formulations of the doctrine of the necessity of the present. He also claims, for example, that it is true to say of any sentence, when it is true, that it is necessarily true in the divided sense (ibid. 5.43, 6.36). Whatever is actual or true, when it is, is necessarily actual or true in the divided sense, but it does not follow that what is necessarily true or actual in this way is itself an instance of *sensu diviso* necessary predication:

> A divided affirmative sentence *de necessario* is true only if what is under the predicate term is invariable with respect to what is under the subject term when it exists. This holds true when the terms are common. As for singular terms, that which is signified by one should not be variable with respect to that which is signified by the other when it exists.
>
> (ibid. 6.25)

Invariable attributes either follow from the essence of the subject or they are other unchanging characteristics (ibid. 5.43, 45). It is easily seen that Campsall does not manage very well in his attempt to defend the conversion rules for divided sentences *de necessario*. 'Every grammarian is necessarily man' is true, but 'Some men are necessarily grammarians' does not fulfil the truth conditions for divided sentences *de necessario*. While discussing the conversion rules for divided sentences *de necessario*, Campsall has in mind sentences the terms of which refer to things 'now'. He thinks that what is signified by the predicate term cannot change now with respect to what is signified by the subject term, and that all true sentences include this restricted necessity which does not differ from the Boethian temporal necessity of the present. Campsall does not care about the fact that this necessity, which he seems to consider as sufficient for converted sentences, is not the defined *sensu diviso* necessity which apparently is taken to characterize those divided necessity sentences which should be converted. A further complication is that Campsall did not consider the necessity of the present as sufficient to save mixed necessary and assertoric moods. According to him, the assertoric premise must be either necessarily true without qualification or necessarily true as long as the things exist to which its subject term refers (ibid. 12.30–2). It may be noticed that Campsall's treatment of composite modal sentences is straightforwardly statistical: a temporally indeterminate sentence is necessarily true *simpliciter*, if it is true at all times, and it is contingent if it is sometimes true and sometimes false (for the necessity of the sentences *de inesse simpliciter*, see ibid. 12.31, 18.36). Campsall once states that 'in the composite sense . . . it does not follow: "that A is B" is contingent or possible; therefore "that A is B" is true' (ibid. 19.21). If a sentence is contingent, it does not follow that it is true now or *simpliciter*, although it apparently is true at some time.

Affirmative divided sentences *de contingenti* with terms referring to actual things imply the corresponding assertoric sentences, but the rule is not applied to sentences with terms referring to things which contingently are under the terms (ibid. 19.21). The doctrine of the conversion of divided universal and particular sentences is said to hold of all kinds of *de contingenti* sentences. According to Campsall, this is evident when the terms are understood in the same way in both parts of a conversion.

Campsall believes that Aristotle's modal syllogistic includes principles like 'possibility implies actuality' and 'actuality implies necessity'. Much of his work consists in a somewhat confused attempt to qualify these principles by separating, for example, between strictly present tense modalities, relative temporal modalities and contingent predications with actual and non-actual subjects (see ibid. *q.* 18 and 19). Did Campsall himself accept the extensional modal principles or did he consider them only as historical constructions demanded, in his opinion, by Aristotle's theory of modal conversions and proofs of some modal moods, particularly those of mixed contingent and assertoric premises? The assumption that Campsall aimed at a merely historical reconstruction is perhaps not warranted, but it easily suggests itself, because some of Campsall's allegedly Aristotelian principles were just those which were regarded as mistaken by the logicians of the next generation. Let us now return to these more advanced theories.

Using the tools of traditional formal logic, the four types of categorical sentences with common terms can be expressed as follows: $AaB$ (Every $A$ is $B$), $AeB$ (Every $A$ is-not $B$ or, alternatively, No $A$ is $B$), $AiB$ (Some $A$ is $B$) and $AoB$ (Some $A$ is-not $B$). Their truth conditions were often given in terms of supposition theory as follows: provided that no semantic paradoxes are involved in the sentences, a universal affirmative sentence ($AaB$) is true iff $A$ stands or supposits for something and $B$ supposits for everything for which $A$ supposits. A particular affirmative sentence ($AiB$) is true iff $A$ stands for something and $B$ also stands for it. Negative sentences did not have existential import, and negatives with empty subject terms were considered automatically true. Aristotelian conversion rules, namely the simple conversions $AeB$ iff $BeA$ and $AiB$ iff $BiA$, and the so-called accidental conversion, if $AaB$ then $BiA$, are valid in this interpretation (*OSL* II.2–4, 249–66; 21, 318–21; *BC* I.5, 25–6; 8, 44–5; *PS* I.12–15, 290–6).

As far as the authors treated sentences as tensed, the above remarks were taken to pertain to sentences the copulas of which are understood as present tense verbs. Since the twelfth century, there have been various attempts to define the truth conditions of past and future tense sentences which were considered as complete sentences not to be replaced by tenseless constructions. This topic, connected with the theory of ampliation, was an essential part of early fourteenth-century logic as well. According to Buridan, the supposition of the subject term of the past tense sentence '$A$ was $B$' is ampliated so that it stands for past and present $A$'s while the predicate term stands for past $B$'s, i.e. '$A$ was $B$' is read: 'What was or is $A$ was $B$'. Similarly, in '$A$ will be $B$' the supposition of the subject term is ampliated so that it stands for present and future $A$'s. It is read: 'What is or will be $A$ will be $B$'. Temporal ampliation was also caused by terms which imply or determine a different time, even though the copula is in the present tense. When the restrictive phrase 'which is' (*quod est*) was added to the subject term, it prevented ampliation (see *BC* I.6, 26–30; 8, 45–7; cf. *OSL* II.7, 269–72; 22, 321–5; *PS* I.17, 297–9; Walter Burley, *De puritate artis logicae* I.2, 47–53). In question 11 of his *Quaestiones super librum Priorum Analeticorum*, Richard of Campsall discussed syllogisms with tensed premises, and this syllogistic tense logic was developed further in Ockham's *Summa logicae* (III.1.17–19, 406–11). (For medieval tense logic, see also Normore 1975, 1985; Broadie 1987: 124–37.)

As already mentioned, some early thirteenth-century logicians applied the theory of ampliation to sentences *de possibili* so that the relevant domain was taken to include actual and merely possible beings. This step was natural for those thinkers who adopted the idea of modality as multiplicity of reference with respect to alternative domains. This is how the subjects in unqualified sentences *de possibili* were understood by Ockham (I.72, 216; II.25, 331–2), Buridan (I.6, 27) and Pseudo-Scotus (I.3, 277; 26, 311)

Following the traditional doctrine of the matter of sentences, fourteenth-century logicians stated that assertoric sentences are necessary, possible or impossible depending on whether they can or cannot be true or false. Only those sentences were counted as modal, however, which included modal terms connected to the copula (divided or *de re* modals) or connected by the copula to sentences or to *dicta* (composite or *de dicto* modals) (*BC* II.1, 56; *PS* I.25, 309; William of Ockham, *Expositio in librum Perihermeneias Aristotelis* 459–66).

According to Buridan, who thought that composite modal sentences can be quantified, universal composite modals with the mode necessity or possibility as a subject and the *dictum* as a predicate are simply convertible. Affirmative particular sentences are simply converted, too; only negative particular sentences are not converted. If the *dictum* is the subject, all sentences are simply convertible with the exception that universal affirmative sentences are converted accidentally (*BC* II.7, 71–2). Ockham did not discuss these conversions in *Summa logicae*; Pseudo-Scotus said that they are the same as the conversions of standard assertoric sentences (*PS* I.25, 310). It is not clear why he thought so. The deviations Buridan mentions are rather obvious: 'Every possible (necessary) *dictum* is that $A$ is $B$' is converted into 'Anything which is that $A$ is $B$ is possible (necessary)' and 'Something which is that $A$ is $B$ is not possible (necessary)' is converted into 'Some possible (necessary) *dictum* is not that $A$ is $B$'.

The conversions of composite sentences *de necessario* and *de possibili* with respect to the *dictum* were the same as those of the *dictum*, and they were said to hold by the rules that if the antecedent is possible then the consequent is possible, and if the antecedent is of necessity then the consequent is of necessity, or, as with simple conversions, if one of the convertibles is possible (necessary) then the other is possible (necessary) as well. Of composite sentences *de contingenti* only those with simply convertible *dicta* are converted;

168  *Modalities in Medieval Philosophy*

the rule that if the antecedent is contingent then the consequent is contingent is not valid (*PS* I.25, 310; 30, 319; *OSL* II.24–5, 27, 327–8, 330–1, 334; *BC* II.7, 72–3). The whole logic of composite modal sentences was in fact based on the Aristotelian principles which, as noticed above, were commonly known in early medieval logic as well:

(1) $L(p \to q) \to (Lp \to Lq)$

and

(2) $L(p \to q) \to (Mp \to Mq)$.

(In the fourteenth century there were extensive discussions of the nature of consequences; see, for example, Adams 1973; Boh 1982; King 1985: 59–69; Stump 1989: 251–69.) When modal syllogisms were regarded as syllogisms with respect to the *dictum*, connecting the mode 'necessary' with the premises and conclusions of valid assertoric syllogisms yielded valid modal syllogisms. This was based on (1) and the rule

(3) $(Lp \;\&\; Lq) \to L(p \;\&\; q)$.

Uniform syllogisms consisting of composite modals *de contingenti* or *de possibili* were not considered valid, because the compossibility of two possible premises was not assured. Ockham and Pseudo-Scotus remarked that, because *de dicto* necessities are compossible with any *de dicto* possibilities or contingencies, mixed composite necessary and possible or contingent syllogisms with possible or contingent conclusions are valid. Buridan did not mention this (*PS* I.27, 313; 33, 323; *OSL* III.1.20, 412–13; 1.23, 419; 1.44, 474; 1.47, 479; *BC* IV.1, 113). Although alethic propositional modal logic was considered relatively simple and not very interesting, it was used as a starting point for philosophically more stimulating applied modal logic (see Chapter 5).

The main object of the fourteenth-century modal logic was the theory of divided modals. Some treatises include discussions in which the logical relations between various divided modal sentences are codified in the same way as the relations between the types of assertoric sentences in the square of opposition. Buridan paid much attention to this topic. He thought that there are two types of copulas, the affirmative 'is' and the negative 'is-not', and that modality is part of the copula in divided modal sentences. Combining the equivalences between quantifiers with negations (e.g. *omne – nullum non – non quoddam non*) and equivalent modalilities, Buridan arranged divided modals into eight groups of nine equivalent formulae. In the *Summulae* these groups are presented in a diagram showing the relations of contradiction, contrariety, subcontrariety and subalternation between them (for this octagon of opposition in Buridan, see Hughes 1989: 99, 109–10). I quote from Buridan's diagram two groups of equivalent forms:

Omne B necesse est esse A
Omne B impossibile est non esse A
Omne B non possibile est non esse A
Nullum B non necesse est esse A
Nullum B non impossibile est non esse A
Nullum B possibile est non esse A
Non quoddam B non necesse est esse A
Non quoddam B non impossibile est non esse A
Non quoddam B possibile est non esse A

Quoddam B possibile est non esse A
Quoddam B non necesse est esse A
Quoddam B non impossibile est non esse A
Non omne B non possibile est non esse A
Non omne B necesse est esse A
Non omne B impossibile est non esse A
Non nullum B possibile est non esse A
Non nullum B non necesse est esse A
Non nullum B non impossibile est non esse A

(cf. *OSL* III.3.13–16, 642–9; *PS* I.26, 312). Fourteenth-century logicians were interested in the problems connected with the analysis of negative sentences and they linked the question of the classification of modal sentences into affirmative and negative ones to this theme.

According to Buridan and Pseudo-Scotus, the subject terms of all divided modals are ampliated to stand for actual and possible beings which fall under those terms. The phrase 'what is' (*quod est*) attached to the subject terms restricts them to stand for actual beings only (*BC* II.4, 58; 6, 61, 63; *PS* I.26, 312–13). Divided modals *de necessario* with restricted subject terms are not converted simply or accidentally, and the same holds true of the conversions of divided sentences *de necessario* with non-restricted subject terms, with the exception that universal negative sentences are simply convertible (*BC* II.6, 67; *PS* I.26, 312–13). Unlike Buridan and Pseudo-Scotus, Ockham did not accept any conversions of terms of divided necessity sentences. In the chapter about these conversions, Ockham starts with the example

'No man is necessarily a donkey; therefore, no donkey is necessarily a man'. This consequence, Ockham says, is not founded on any valid conversion rule. The example is about sentences with a negated necessity mode rather than about negative sentences *de necessario*. Anyway, it becomes clear later that Ockham denies all conversions of divided necessity sentences (*OSL* II.24, 329–30; III.1.21, 416). Ockham's position is connected with the fact that he did not treat divided necessity sentences with unrestricted subject terms at all in his modal logic.

About unrestricted divided possibility sentences, Ockham, Buridan and Pseudo-Scotus state that affirmative modals are converted in the same way as assertoric sentences. Those with restricted subject terms are not convertible (*OSL* II.25, 331–2; III.1.24, 423–4; *BC* II.6, 66–7; *PS* I.26, 312). According to Buridan and Pseudo-Scotus, an unrestricted divided sentence *de contingenti ad utrumlibet* can be converted into one of the opposite quality, but no conversions of the terms are valid (*BC* II.6, 68; *PS* I.30, 320). Ockham states that the subject term of '*A* is contingently *B*' may refer to things which are *A*, which are *A* or are contingently *A*, or which are contingently *A*. Unrestricted universal contingency sentences are accidentally convertible and particular sentences are simply convertible (*OSL* II.27, 338; III.1.27–8, 430, 433).

While discussing the logical properties of the unrestricted divided modal sentences, Buridan and Pseudo-Scotus made some comments on the question whether such sentences should be treated as categorical sentences having a disjunctive subject (what is or can be . . .), as they did, or whether they should be taken as complex sentences (*BC* II.4, 58–60; *PS* I.26, 310–11). According to Pseudo-Scotus they could be read as conjunctions or disjunctions as follows: 'Every *A* is-necessarily/possibly(-not) *B*' is a conjunction of 'Everything which is *A* is-necessarily/possibly(-not) *B*' and 'Everything which can be *A* etc.' and 'Some *A* is-necessarily/possibly(-not) *B*' is the disjunction: 'Something which is *A* is-necessarily/possibly(-not) *B*' or 'Something which can be *A* etc.'. Pseudo-Scotus states that if divided sentences are read in this way, there is no conversion of necessity sentences except if they are simply necessary. He does not mention that there is always an accidental conversion from universal negative to particular negative necessity sentences. Divided possibility sentences are, in his opinion, converted in the same way as assertoric sentences. As for affirmative possibility sentences, they are converted into particular affirmatives, because unrestricted divided possibility sentences are so converted. Of negative divided sentences *de possibili*, neither the restricted ones nor the non-restricted ones are converted. I do not see why Pseudo-Scotus claimed that a universal negative possibility sentence read in the way just explained is simply convertible.

According to Hughes (1989: 108), one could give a Kripke-style possible worlds semantics for Buridan's modal system and then an axiomatic basis for it. I think that the general ideas of Buridan and Pseudo-Scotus can be described with the help of some conceptions similar to those on which the possible worlds semantics is based, although many basic theoretical questions of modern formal semantics were beyond the purview of medieval authors. Constructing the details of the intuitive model which the authors possibly had in mind is a cumbersome task. They usually discuss particular questions by producing examples and counterexamples without much explanation. As Buridan and Pseudo-Scotus start with the thesis that the subject terms of divided modal sentences refer to what is or can be, some aspects of their theory of the truth conditions of divided modal sentences can be illustrated as follows. Things picked up by the subject terms are possible beings with possible histories. These individual collections of possible and necessary properties can be described with finite lines. 'An $A$ is possibly $B$' is a line including at least one point which is $A$ and one point which is $B$; 'An $A$ is not possibly $B$' is described with a line including a point $A$ and lacking a point $B$; 'An $A$ is necessarily $B$' is a line including a point $A$ among the points any one of which is $B$.

Ockham and Buridan state that the truth of 'A white thing can be black' demands the truth of 'This can be black' and that 'This can be black' and ' "This is black" is possible' mean the same (*OSL* II.10, 276–9; III.1.32, 448; 3.10, 633–4; *BC* II.7, 75–6). It is reasonable to suppose that the possible truth of 'This is black' means that it is true in at least one of the possible states of affairs in which the possible being referred to by 'this' occurs, and that the necessary truth of 'This is black' means that it is true in all worlds in which the thing referred to by 'this' occurs. Quantifiers range over possible beings signified by the subject terms, and the truth of divided quantified sentences demands the truth of all or some of relevant singular sentences of the type just mentioned. Universal and particular affirmative composite sentences maintain that their *dicta* are true in all possible states of affairs (necessity sentences) or in some possible states of affairs (possibility sentences).

One might wonder why Ockham, instead of regarding the reading with actual or possible subjects as basic for all modals, discussed the necessity sentences with the restricted subject terms and the contingency sentences either with restricted or with ampliated contingent subject terms. This makes his modal syllogistic less systematic than the systems of Buridan and Pseudo-Scotus. It seems that the differences are connected with the fact that the authors did not make use of the same notion of necessity while discussing divided modals. If the distinction between divided necessity sentences with restricted and unrestricted subject terms is not nugatory, one should admit that possible beings may have necessary properties without occurring in every possible world. This condition is fulfilled by relative or conditional *de re* necessity as Buridan and Pseudo-Scotus understood it. That which can be *A* is of necessity *B* in this sense iff it, when thought to be actual, is in any case *B* independently of what else it might be. This notion of necessity is weaker than that of simple necessity by which a thing is necessarily something without qualification, i.e. always and in all thinkable states of affairs, and it is stronger than that of temporal necessity by which an actual thing is invariably something in the actual world (for these types of necessity, see *BC* IV.1, 112; *PS* I.26, 311). Some of Ockham's examples also refer to this type of necessity (see, for example, *OSL* III.1.32, 448.117–22), but his syllogistic theory of divided necessity sentences is based on the view that only actual beings have necessary properties. Ockham seems to be inclined to think that the singular sentences ('This is/is-not *B*') in which true divided necessity sentences are analysed are to be treated in logic as necessary without qualification, i.e. true in all possible worlds. This would mean that true affirmative divided necessity sentences must be about necessarily existing beings, i.e. God or Gods (*OSL* III.2.5, 512–13). Although there were later authors thinking in the same way (see, for example, Jeronimo Pardo's *Medulla dyalectices* (1505), *f*. 107v, quoted in Coombs 1990: 92), Buridan and Pseudo-Scotus did not accept this view. Divine beings often occur in their examples as well, but they held that necessity sentences with unrestricted subject terms are not reducible to those with restricted subject terms. Buridan remarks, for example, that mixed first figure moods with an assertoric major premise, a minor premise *de necessario* and an assertoric conclusion are valid when the subject term of the minor premise is restricted (*BC* IV.2, 124). This restriction is not necessary if *de re* necessity means simple necessity.

Buridan states that the relations between divided modal sentences and the corresponding non-modal sentences are governed by the following principles. There are no valid consequences from divided possibility sentences to corresponding assertoric sentences or from assertoric sentences to corresponding divided necessity sentences.

From universal and particular affirmative assertoric sentences the corresponding divided possibility sentences follow by a valid consequence, and there is a valid consequence from an unrestricted universal negative necessity sentence to a universal negative assertoric sentence (*BC* II.6, 64–6). For reasons already mentioned Ockham's position with respect to these relationships is different: composite and divided necessity sentences imply corresponding assertoric sentences (*OSL* III.3.11, 637–8). As for the relationships between modal sentences *in sensu composito* and *in sensu diviso*, Buridan states that from composite universal and particular affirmative possibility sentences corresponding particular divided possibility sentences follow, and from an unrestricted universal negative divided necessity sentence a universal negative composite necessity sentence follows (*BC* II.7, 76–8). According to Ockham, composite and divided readings of all singular modal sentences are equivalent, provided that the subject terms are demonstrative pronouns or proper names. Divided necessity sentences which are universal, particular, or have as their subject a common term with a demonstrative pronoun do not imply corresponding composite modals, and the same holds *e converso* with the exception that affirmative composite sentences having as their subject a common term with a demonstrative pronoun imply a corresponding divided necessity sentence. Ockham's rules for universal and particular possibility sentences are the same as those of Buridan (*OSL* III.3.10, 632–4).

In Buridan's divided modal syllogistic, all four first figure moods corresponding to the direct assertoric ones are valid when they are modalized as follows: *MMM, LLL, CCC, MLM, LML, MCM, CMC, LCL, CLC*. (When the conclusion is necessary or contingent, it is also possible.) In addition, *LAL, MAM* and *CAC* are similarly valid except that the conclusion is always particular (*BC* IV.2–3, 115, 118–19, 124, 130–1). The first group can be delineated as follows: if that which is or can be *P* is necessarily, possibly or contingently (not) *Q*, and if that which is or can be *S* is necessarily, possibly or contingently *P*, then that which is or can be *S* is necessarily, possibly or contingently (not) *Q*. It does not matter by which modality the minor term is connected to the middle term – the modality of predication in the conclusion is always that of the first premise. The same principle holds true of the cases where the major premise is modalized and the minor premise is assertoric, but the conclusions are then always particular. Buridan regarded these moods as perfect and clear through the *dictum de omni et nullo*.

Peter King has remarked that when divided modal syllogisms are read, starting from the second premise, like 'Some $S$ is necessarily something which is possibly $Q$' and this is abbreviated by 'Some $S$ is necessarily possibly $Q$', we have here iterated modalities. Part of Buridan's modal syllogistic could then be taken as specifying how iterated modal terms are to be treated, i.e. what single modal term corresponds to an iterated pair of modal terms. Referring to the reduction laws which occur as theorems of the system S5, King says that Buridan's modal logic is roughly S5 (King 1985: 80–2). Although the analogy is interesting, Buridan did not attend to the questions of iteration in modal syllogistic. All that he says is based on the fact that the distribution of the ampliated subject term of the major premise for everything that is or can be $P$ includes everything that necessarily, possibly or contingently is $P$.

Among the valid moods mentioned above, one can find only twenty of the thirty-two Aristotelian first figure modal moods. Buridan also accepted the universal negative of $ALA$, and so we have twenty-one of the Aristotelian moods in Buridan's list of unqualified and direct first figure divided modal moods. Buridan also discusses the moods in which the subject terms or some of them are non-ampliated ($L'$, $M'$, $C'$). According to him, all four first figure moods are valid in $L'L'L'$, $M'L'M'$, $AL'A$, and also in $MAM'$ when the assertoric premise is a purely affirmative categorical present tense sentence. Buridan does not explicitly accept $LAL'$ and $CAC'$, but he mentions that $LAL$ and $CAC$ must be qualified in the same way as $MAM$. When $LAL'$ and $CAC'$ are added to the list, the number of accepted Aristotelian moods is twenty-eight. The third type of modal syllogisms, dealt with in the *Tractatus de consequentiis*, are mixed modal and assertoric moods where the assertoric premise is hypothetically treated as a composite necessary premise. This is the only way of accepting the Aristotelian $ACM$ case (*BC* IV.2–3, 117, 119, 123–5, 131).

Buridan made some historical comments on Aristotle's theory: he said, for example, that Aristotle meant by 'simply assertoric sentences' assertoric sentences which are necessary; that Aristotle considered sentences like 'A horse is an animal' simply necessary because of his view of the eternity and unchangeability of natural species; and that Aristotle understood mixed modal syllogisms as divided modal syllogisms (*BC* IV.1, 111–12, *Quaest. in An. pr.* I, q. 30). However, he did not make any attempt to reconstruct Aristotle's modal syllogistic as a uniform system; in the light of his modal principles, such a construction was impossible. Some Aristotelian moods are valid only as mixed composite and divided modal syllogisms, some are valid in this way and as divided modal syllogisms with non-ampliated subject terms, and some are valid only with ampliated subject terms. Buridan thought that Aristotle's modal syllogistic is a partial theory of valid modal deductions where the different types of fine structures made use of in dealing with modal premises are not distinguished (see also *OSL* III.1, 31, 443).

Some moods which are accepted as valid in the *Tractatus de consequentiis* are not mentioned in the *Quaestiones* on the *Prior Analytics* (I.31–9) or in the *Summulae* (V.6–7), and some valid moods which are discussed in the *Summulae* are omitted in the *Tractatus de consequentiis*. (Accounts in the two last-mentioned works are compared in Hughes 1989: 111.) Buridan's treatment of modal moods in all works is restricted to those the unmodalized counterparts of which are valid direct moods of three syllogistic figures. He does not treat valid indirect moods nor moods with singular terms.

Ockham's divided modal syllogistic also concentrates on the moods which have valid assertoric counterparts, but his discussion is more thorough than that of Buridan. Ockham considers the indirect moods as well, and he treats the combinations in which one of the premises is a composite modal and the other a divided modal. He mentions some moods with restricted premises which are valid in Buridan's system also although Buridan does not mention them, e.g. all first figure moods $MM'M'$, $CC'C'$, $M'AM'$, $C'AC'$ and the third figure moods $MM'M$ and $M'MM$. (As mentioned above, Ockham's reading of divided sentences *de contingenti* differs from that of Buridan.) As Ockham considered the subject terms of divided necessity sentences as restricted, he did not accept any first figure $LML$ moods with divided premises nor any second figure moods with divided necessity sentences as premises the proofs of which in Buridan are based on the mentioned $LML$ moods. In the same way Ockham did not accept divided first figure $LCL$ moods (*OSL* III.1.21, 44, 416–17, 476). Pseudo-Scotus' discussion of divided modal moods is of the same type as that of Buridan, but it is less detailed.

# 5 Medieval discussions of applied modal logic

The rise of the new modal logic in the fourteenth century was accompanied by an increasing interest in the question of whether there were other concepts having properties similar to those of basic modal notions. Many logicians thought that the logic of pure modal terms could be used as a model for studying the logical behaviour of related concepts, and it became a kind of standard method of applied modal logic to consider, for example, whether the basic rules for modal sentences *de dicto*, namely

(1) $\dfrac{L(p \to q)}{Lp \to Lq}$

and

(2) $\dfrac{L(p \to q)}{Mp \to Mq}$

held as well for other concepts showing prima facie similarities to the notions of necessity and possibility. In his *Questions on Aristotle's Prior Analytics*, the anonymous fourteenth-century writer called Pseudo-Scotus gives the following list of words which are interesting in this respect: *verum, falsum, per se, scitum, dubitum, opinatum, creditum, apparens, notum, volitum* and *dilectum* (John Duns Scotus, *Opera omnia* I, q. 25, 310, q. 36, 328–9; for a more comprehensive catalogue, see de Rijk 1975b: 216). As will be seen, other authors added normative notions, such as *obligatum, licitum* and *illicitum*, to the list.

## ELEMENTS OF EPISTEMIC LOGIC

Knowledge and belief were widely considered as partially analogous to necessity and possibility respectively. Although the inference rules of modal logic *de dicto* just mentioned were usually not accepted as rules for knowledge and belief, there was a vivid discussion of some other important questions pertaining to epistemic logic. The standard Aristotelian reason for not accepting (1) or (2) with respect to knowledge and belief is stated by John Buridan as follows:

> From composite sentences *de scito*, *de opinato*, *de dubitato*, and other similar modals, there is no valid syllogism. It does not follow: 'That every B is A is known by Socrates, and that every C is B is known by Socrates, therefore that every C is A is known by Socrates', because although the two premises are known by Socrates, he nevertheless may perhaps fail to order them in a syllogism, or fail to see that the third follows from them.
> (*Tractatus de consequentiis* IV, cap. 1, concl. 3, 114.107–12)

Medieval authors generally did not operate with the conception of logical omniscience that is included in some modern theories (see the discussions in Hintikka 1962: 29–39; 1970, 32–47; Lenzen 1978: 53–68). They treated the logic of epistemic notions from the point of view of factual attitudes. The opinions were not wholly unanimous here, however. Peter of Poitiers mentions that, according to some twelfth-century thinkers, knowing the antecedent implies knowing the consequent (*Sententiae* I, c. 9, 82.139–83.154). Another example of this line of thought is Ralph Strode's (fl. *c*.1370) influential tractate on consequences where the author formulated twenty-four general rules of consequences. According to him, if the antecedent is known, the consequent is also known (*Consequentiae Strodi*, Venetiis 1484, fol. 2A, quoted in Boh 1986b: 536). Most of the other epistemic rules are also without reference to a person in Strode, who possibly formulated them from the point of view of an ideal reasoner. The logicians who commented on Strode's rules usually considered the reference to a person essential in epistemic contexts and added the condition that the consequences must not only be valid, but must be known to be valid as well. (For these comments in Paul of Venice, Paul of Pergula, Peter of Mantua and Anthony of Frachantian, see Boh 1986a, 1986b, 1990.)

In the prologue to his *Commentary on the Sentences*, William of Ockham states that some acts of the intellect are apprehensive and others are judicative. An apprehensive act can be directed to anything which may occur as an object of a cognitive power. It is an act of entertaining the content of a possible judgement. A judicative act is an act by which the intellect assents to or dissents from the complex objects of apprehension. We assent to what we regard as true and we dissent from what we regard as false (*Ord., prol., q.* 1, 16.3–18). I shall not enter into the details of Ockham's view; it is sufficient to realize that a distinction between apprehensive and judicative acts or notions was commonly drawn in the late medieval and early modern periods (see Broadie 1989: 125–48; Tachau 1988: 116–17; for the question of whether the propositional object of an emotion is assented to, see Adam Wodeham, *Lectura secunda in librum primum Sententiarum d.* 1, *q.* 5, *a.* 5).

In one of his various lists of the uses of the term '*scire*', Ockham states that the term is used to express (a) firm cognition of a truth, (b) evident cognition of a truth, (c) evident cognition of a necessary truth or (d) evident cognition of a truth through evident cognition of other truths disposed so that they produce the evident knowledge of the conclusion (*Expositio in libros Physicorum Aristotelis prol.* 5.29–6.50). It is assumed that a firm or evident cognition includes assent or dissent. If the assent (or dissent) is considered an act of judicative belief, Ockham's remarks on the concept of knowledge could be regarded as implying the principle

(3) $K_a p \rightarrow B_a p$

which is sometimes called the corner stone of epistemic logic. Robert Holcot explicitly treated assent as a belief. According to him, the most common sense of believing (*credere*) is to assent to what is stated by a proposition. 'A proposition is believed when it is assented to, and in this way we believe what we know as well as what we opine' (*Sent.* I, *q.* 1, *a.* 1).

Ockham remarks that the first use of the term 'to know' does not differ from that of true belief, and he considered it less proper than those which include a reference to evidence as some kind of justification. Instead of the definition

Df$_1$   $K_a p = B_a p \,\&\, p$

he prefers

Df$_2$   $K_a p = B_a p \,\&\, p \,\&\, J_a p$

($J_a p$ stands for 'the person $a$ is justified in believing that $p$'). As shown by Ivan Boh, some later authors were reluctant to accept at all the first use of '*scire*'. Their reasons were similar to those which have been presented in the contemporary discussion of the Gettier problem (Boh 1986a: 94–7). Boh refers to a passage from Peter of Mantua's *Logica* which shows that a person could be said to know (in the first sense of '*scire*') that *p* even when the assent is based on a mistake:

> Let it be assumed that Plato is the person in front of you and you know him to be running, but you believe that he is Socrates, so that you firmly believe that Socrates is running. However, let it be so that Socrates is in fact running in Rome and you don't know this. Given this, you both know that Socrates is running and also do not know that Socrates is running, and thus, by the same evidences what is known is doubtful to you.

Many fourteenth-century authors engaged in the controversy over the objects of knowledge and belief and the nature of what is complexly signifiable, i.e. what can be signified only by a proposition (see Tachau 1987: 161–87; 1988: 303–9, 353–6, 365–8). In addition to this, they were also interested in the more traditional question of the role of the will in assenting to a proposition. It was usually thought that evident assent was caused naturally and that there were types of inevident assent which were in some way freely caused, such as the religious assent of faith or the opinionative assent based on probabilistic arguments. Robert Holcot argued that all genuine beliefs were caused naturally, but this view was considered exaggerated. (See *Sent.* I, *q.* 1, *a.* 1; Holcot's view is criticized in, for example, Peter of Ailly, *Sent.*, *princ.* III, *q.* 1 D, *quaest. q.* 1, *a.* 2 BB. For the discussion of this question in Paris between 1500 and 1530, see Broadie 1989: 149–78.)

The theory of free assent was sometimes connected with the question of making moral decisions in uncertain cases, which anticipated the later controversy over probabilism and probabiliorism. (For probabilism in general, see Deman 1936.) I have already referred to the fact that Aristotelian *ut in pluribus* contingencies were interpreted as quasi-statistical objective probabilities in the thirteenth century. Thomas Aquinas, Boethius of Dacia and some other Parisian masters applied this view to the Aristotelian dialectical probabilities by stating that what is probable in the sense that most experts accept it is probably true because it is not probable that the majority of well-informed experts would be mistaken in the same way (see Thomas Aquinas, *Summa theologiae* II.1, *q.* 105, *a.* 2, ad 8; 2, *q.* 70, *a.* 2c; Boethius of Dacia, *Quaestiones super librum Topicorum* III, *q.* 14, 187; for this notion of probability and its role in later medieval thought, see Kantola forthcoming). These examples show that, contrary to what has been sometimes maintained (see Hacking 1975: 34), an intuitive conception of objective frequency probability, different from epistemic probability, was developed in the Middle Ages (cf. the discussions in Byrne 1968 and Goddu 1989).

The question of the relationship between epistemic statements *de dicto* and *de re* belonged to standard fourteenth-century topics of epistemology. The nature of the themes which were found interesting can be exemplified by examining why the substitutivity of identity does not hold within the scope of a cognitive verb according to Buridan, and why he, in spite of this, admits the existential generalization with respect to a term occurring within the scope of a verb expressing knowledge. It was commonly thought that knowledge statements *de re*, understood in a certain way, did not follow from knowledge statements *de dicto*. (See, for example, the extensive discussion of the question in the second chapter of William of Heytesbury's *Rules for Solving Sophismata*, Venice 1494, translated in Kretzmann and Stump 1988: 436–72.) Buridan says, however, that when Socrates knows that some $A$ is $B$, then of something which is $A$ he knows that it is $B$. The reason for denying this could be that Socrates does not know which $A$ is $B$. Buridan would agree that in this sense the *de re* reading does not follow from the *de dicto* reading. His point is, however, that there is another kind of *de re* reading (or which might be called so) which does follow from the *de dicto* reading. It is a kind of intermediate reading between pure *de dicto* and *de re* readings. The idea can be formulated as follows. According to Buridan, statements of the type

(4) $K_s(Ex)(Fx)$

imply that there are individuals which have the property $F$, although $s$ does not necessarily know which they are. But in principle they are identifiable, and if we suppose that one of them is $z$, we can write:

(5) $K_s(Ex)(Fx) \rightarrow (Ex)((x = z) \mathbin{\&} K_s(Fx))$.

From the *de dicto* statement 'Socrates, who is sitting in a cellar, knows that a star is above', the *de re* reading understood as 'There is a star which Socrates knows as the star which is above' does not follow, but the following *de re* reading does follow: 'There is a star of which Socrates knows that it is above, although Socrates does not know which star it is' (John Buridan, *Sophismata* IV, 13–14; translation by Scott 1966: 128–33; see also Moody 1975: 353–70).

Buridan was not the first to employ this reading. In his *De obligationibus*, Walter Burley discussed the following case:

'You know that Marcus is running. But Marcus is Tullius.

Therefore, you know that Tullius is running.' And furthermore, 'Therefore, you know who is called Tullius'. But it was posited that you don't know this. Solution. This is multiplex: 'You know that Tullius is running.' It may signify that you know the dictum: 'That Tullius is running', and this is false and the consequence is not valid. Or it may signify that of that person who is Tullius you know that he is running, and this can be true, although you don't know who is signified by this term 'Tullius'.

(Green forthcoming: II-39.29–40.7)

As (1) was not accepted for knowledge, the inference

s knows that Marcus is running, and Marcus is Tullius; therefore, s knows that Tullius is running

would not be valid on the *de dicto* reading of the first premise and the conclusion even when s knew that Marcus is Tullius. And it is not valid on the genuine *de re* readings of them, because the substitutivity of identity breaks down within the scope of the cognitive verb. But if the intermediate reading mentioned above is applied to the conclusion, then the inference is valid on any reading of the first premise (for Burley's example, see also Weidemann 1980: 33).

The same analysis can be found in many fourteenth-century writers. In the sophism 45 of Richard Kilvington's *Sophismata*, the statement 'You know this to be everything that is this' is discussed as an obligational proposition in a game where it is assumed that the respondent sees Socrates from a distance without knowing that it is Socrates. After having granted as the *positum* the conjunction of 'You know this to be everything that is this' and 'Socrates is known by you to be this', one should grant: 'You know this to be that which is Socrates' or 'Socrates is known by you to be this', but it does not follow further that one should grant: 'Therefore, this is known by you to be Socrates.' The idea is that *de re* readings can vary, depending on what is included in the scope of the knowledge operator. (For a discussion of the sophism, see Kretzmann 1988a. William of Heytesbury probably had this analysis in mind in *De sensu composito et diviso*, Venice 1494, f. 4ra, translated in Kretzmann and Stump 1988: 432. For the intermediate reading, see also Richard Billingham, *Speculum puerorum* 374; Albert of Saxony, *Sophismata* III, 32–3.)

Many themes of medieval epistemic logic are still unexplored, and the same holds true for the other areas of late medieval intensional logic as well. Epistemic logic was only one branch of applied modal logic. It is historically interesting that we find in the fourteenth century a counterpart to what has been going on in intensional logic during the present century, when theories of epistemic logic and deontic logic have been developed on the basis of the rediscovered modal logic.

## LOGIC OF NORMS AND LOGIC OF THE WILL

In the fourteenth-century deontic theory the following equivalences analogous to those between modal concepts were used:

(6) $-O-p \equiv Pp$

(7) $-P-p \equiv Op$

(8) $-Op \equiv P-p$

(9) $-Pp \equiv O-p$

(10) $Op \equiv F-p$

(11) $Fp \equiv O-p$.

$O$ stands here for obligation (*obligatum*), $P$ for permission (*licitum*) and $F$ for prohibition (*illicitum*). I have not found any explicit table of these equivalences, but they were supposed to be generally known and often used, for example, in the works of William of Ockham. It is true, but perhaps only a trivial point, that some of the equivalences just mentioned were used already in early medieval thought. More interesting is the fact that there were some twelfth-century writers who in a certain way anticipated the later habit of treating deontic concepts as a kind of modal concepts. According to one definition of modal terms, often repeated by Peter Abelard, necessity is identified with what nature demands, possibility with what nature allows and impossibility with what nature forbids (see pp. 90–1 above).

In the beginning of his ethics (*Scito teipsum*), Abelard discusses the question whether it is possible that the antecedent is permitted or obligatory while the consequent is forbidden. He says that such obligations or permissions are irrational (*Ethics (Scito teipsum)* 20.1–11). Later Abelard presents an argument in which he seems to accept a principle analogous to (1) as a legal principle. Abelard discusses the following case. A judge knows that an innocent is accused by his enemies. The judge cannot rebut false witnesses by convincing reasons. If the man is punished on the basis of the testimony of the witnesses, an innocent man is punished. Abelard says that because the judge is obligated to do as the antecedent says, i.e. to punish on the basis of the testimony of the witnesses, 'thus he ought to punish him who ought not to be punished'. 'Through the compulsion of the law' the judge must behave against his conscience (ibid. 38.22–40.5, 40.15–16).

Abelard's argument, which was later often criticized, is interesting from the point of view of deontic logic. It is one of the first discussions of deontic consequences. On the basis of what has been said above about the method of discussing questions of applied modal logic in general, it is not surprising that one can find in the fourteenth-century treatises more explicit discussions of the following rules of inference:

(12) $\dfrac{L(p \to q)}{Op \to Oq}$

and

(13) $\dfrac{L(p \to q)}{Pp \to Pq}.$

In his *Quodlibet* I, question 8, Robert Holcot first argues for (12) (Ms. London, British Library, Royal 10 C VI, *f*. 152ra–152rb). Unfortunately, his discussion of the rule remained unfinished and it is not quite clear whether Holcot thought that (12) and (13) hold without qualification. Gregory of Rimini seems to accept (12) for simple inferences and thinks that the consequence in alleged counterexamples is a consequence 'as of now' and not simple. In fact he explicitly says only that (12) does not hold for consequences 'as of now', i.e. for the cases when $p$ implies $q$ in the sense that the conjunction $p \ \& \ -q$ is false now, while $M(p \ \& \ -q)$ is true (*Sent.* II, *d*. 38–41, 304.29–305.6). A more systematic discussion of the principles of deontic logic is found in the opening question of the *Commentary on the Sentences* by Roger Roseth, an English Franciscan who lectured on the *Sentences c*.1335. A detailed explanation of why (12) and (13) cannot be accepted in deontic logic without qualification is a part of Roseth's attempt to treat the basic questions of ethics in a systematic manner from the point of view of the logic of norms. (The first question of Roseth's *Commentary on the Sentences* was partly published as the first question of the *Determinationes magistri Roberti Holkot* at Lyon in 1518. The printed version is very unreliable. I refer to Ms. *Oxford*, Oriel College 15, *f*. 235r–279v. For other manuscripts, see Doucet 1953: 89–93; Courtenay 1978: 120–1.) Roseth's approach sheds light on the late medieval discussion of the foundations of ethics. His tractate on the logic of norms was associated with a deontological conception which, for various reasons, was approved by many fourteenth-century thinkers. One of the background ideas responsible for this was the voluntaristic theory of choice, which made problematic the teleological construction of the binding strength of morality. Roger Roseth's conception of ethics was particularly influenced by William of Ockham's theory which could be understood to provide a detailed model for a deontological divine command ethics.

According to Ockham, the moral term 'virtuous' is a connotative term which signifies primarily an act of will and which connotes that the act has been freely and consciously elected in accordance with right reason or in order to fulfil divine law (*Quaestiones variae* q. 8, a. 1, 417.189–418.210; *Sent.* III, q. 12, 422.14–21, *Quodlibeta septem* III, q. 14). Ockham thought that willing to fulfil divine law *qua* moral law is intrinsically virtuous (*Quaestiones variae* q. 7, a. 1, 327.99–328.128; *Quodlibeta septem* III, a. 14). The content of such an act is conjunctive. It includes both the will to fulfil any particular precept of moral law and the will to behave in a certain manner so that the law is fulfilled in prevailing circumstances (*Quaestiones variae* q. 7, a. 4, 395.459–69; *Sent.* III, q. 7, 211.1–20, q. 11, 385.10–386.11). One could say that an intrinsically virtuous act consists of a second-order act of willing to fulfil moral law through voluntary acts and a first-order act of willing which is in the scope of the second-order act and which has as its object a state of affairs other than an act of will. First-order acts of will, actual deeds, habits and persons can be called virtuous through extrinsic denomination (*Sent.* III, q. 11, 359.5–361.7, 383.19–387.7). The complex virtuous act of will as a whole is intrinsically virtuous in the sense that it is necessarily virtuous when the divine moral law is in force. (For Ockham's theory of the foundations of ethics, see Holopainen 1991.)

As already mentioned in the preceding chapter, William of Ockham did not consider moral truths necessary; that something is obligatory or permitted is true relative to the actual moral law which, as distinct from the the conceptual truths, does not prevail by necessity. The new interest in the foundation of normative systems is also reflected in Duns Scotus' discussion of the thirteenth-century doctrine of God's absolute power and his ordained power. According to Scotus, a juridical distinction is drawn between *potentia de facto* (what a person can do without qualification in a certain situation) and *potentia de iure* (what a person can do in a situation without violating the laws). The first potency is called an absolute power and the second an ordained power. When an agent does not have the power of changing laws, he or she cannot exceed the limits of ordained potency without violating actual norms. When an agent has the power of changing laws, exceeding the actual order may be legitimate. An agent who has an absolute power to change laws is sovereign (*Ord.* I, d. 44; see also Courtenay 1985: 253–4; Randi 1986). Duns Scotus apparently thought that God is sovereign with respect to all nomic necessities of the actual world (see p. 155 above).

While discussing the difference between theoretical and practical knowledge, William of Ockham formulated some important principles pertaining to the theory of ethics and norms in general. He heavily criticized authors who, like Henry of Ghent, argued that theoretical knowledge and practical knowledge differ from each other by having different ends. According to Ockham, it is true that the end of theoretical knowledge ought to be that of achieving truth and that the aim of practical knowledge ought to be right conduct; it does not follow from how things ought to be, however, that they are so or that being so is part of their nature (*Ord., prol., q.* 11, 304.15–21, 308.19–26, 309.11–16).

Ockham thought that the distinction between theoretical and practical sciences is based on a difference between the contents of conclusions drawn in various branches of knowledge (ibid. 315.3–13). He classified as practical sciences ethics, grammar, logic, rhetoric and the mechanical arts. They are practical, because they concern human action in so far as they direct it. Theoretical knowledge does not pertain to human action in this way (ibid. 316.7–9, q. 12, 338.2–8; *Summulae philosophiae naturalis* 149.298–314). According to Ockham, ethics, as distinct from logic, grammar and other forms of practical knowledge, is not just ostensively directive, but also dictative. Ostensive practical knowledge consists of instructions that lead action to a desired goal. These instructions can be characterized as technical norms which indicate the means that are necessary for obtaining the goal. The question of the normative status of goals is not relevant in ostensively directive knowledge. Dictatively directive knowledge, however, does formulate norms which are not just technical instructions. They tell what should be done and what should be avoided (*Ord., prol., q.* 11, 316.8–25; *Sent.* III, q. 12, 420.3–10; *Summulae philosophiae naturalis* 149.298–314; see also Holopainen 1991: 50–61; Freppert 1988: 21–4; Panaccio 1990).

Ockham's distinction between ostensive and dictative practical knowledge is obviously similar to Immanuel Kant's distinction between hypothetical and categorical imperatives. Kant's remarks on the hypothetical imperatives were connected with what he regarded as an analytical truth about the will. According to this theory, whoever wills a particular end, wills also the means which are indispensably necessary and in his power, as far as reason has decisive influence on his action (*Grundlegung zur Metaphysik der Sitten* 46). The same principle occurs in nearly the same form in the first distinction of Ockham's commentary on the *Sentences*: 'Whoever efficaciously wills something, wills also everything without which, in his opinion, the intended end cannot be obtained at all' (*Ord*. I, d. 1, q. 6, 505.5–6). There has been some question of whether the hypothetical imperatives are prescriptions (for different views, see, for example, Niiniluoto 1986). According to Alan Donagan, they can be regarded as prescriptions when understood as disjunctive norms; we must choose the means or give up the goal (Donagan 1977: 212–13). This seems to be how Ockham understood the normative structure of ostensive principles. He said that when a person has chosen a goal, the result of the ostensive reasoning is binding (*necessitatur voluntas ad volendum*), although it can liberate itself from this necessity by ceasing to will the goal (*cessante volitione efficaci*) (*Quaestiones variae* 6, *a*. 9, 259.168–73).

Medieval views on the will were much influenced by Augustine's analysis, through which a conception similar to Ockham's notion of the efficacious will was well known. It is useful to look at this topic, because some ideas developed in the discussions of the concept of will were later employed in deontic logic. In medieval Augustinian approach, the human mind is considered as a centre of powers tending in opposite directions. The strongest of competing desires is realized and it is identified as the actual will. Although the will is said to be often divided, inclinations which remain unrealized are considered as movements of the will in an improper sense only, if they do not influence the behaviour in free circumstances. The voluntaristic peculiarities of this view became clearly visible when in the thirteenth century it met the Aristotelian theory of choice, which concerns the means only; acts contrary to the ends or deliberated means were considered acts of akrasia unchosen by the will (see Saarinen forthcoming).

In the beginning of the third book of the *Nicomachean Ethics*, Aristotle refers to mixed acts which no one prefers without qualification, although they can be chosen as means in certain circumstances. Aristotle mentions as an example the act of throwing goods from a threatened ship into sea in a storm. Peter Abelard and his pupils stressed that acts reluctantly committed as necessary conditions for achieving an end are not willed, although they as concomitants of the acts of will are in some sense voluntary (Peter Abelard, *Ethics* 16.30–2; *Commentarius Cantabrigiensis in Epistolas Pauli* II,

289; III, 453; *Sententiae Petri Abelardi (Sententiae Hermanni)* 110–12). In his influential *Summa aurea* (*c*.1225), William of Auxerre said that the means in this case are willed together with the end (*coniunctim*), but they are not willed separately (*divisim*). The alternative which is reluctantly given up is an object of conditional will (*velleitas* or *voluntas conditionalis*). The conditional will is, generally, a readiness to will something only when certain specific conditions are fulfilled (*promptitudo volendi sub conditione*) (*Summa aurea* I, tract. 12, *c*. 4, *q*. 4; III, tract. 17, *c*. 5). Similar analyses, without a fixed terminology, can be found in many twelfth-century authors. They are often connected with biblical quotations from *Matthew* 26:39 and *Philippians* 1:23 (see Saarinen, forthcoming). William of Auxerre did not discuss the various types of conditional will, but Peter of Poitiers, who did not use the term, mentioned some alternatives in his *Sententiae*. A person may be reluctantly ready to will something, if it is the only way of securing the necessities of life, very useful, or demanded by earlier agreements or promises (*Sent.* II, 98–9; IV, *c*. 17, *PL* 211, 1203).

William of Auxerre illustrates the doctrine that what is not willed *divisim* can be willed *coniunctim* with an example of a man who wants to get 100 marks although he then will become dirty (*esse in luto et habere centum marchas*) – a result which he does not will *divisim* (*Summa aurea* III, tract. 17, cap. 2, 5). He does not tell whether it is being in the mud that earns the money or whether it is a side effect of doing a dirty work. In the first case, it is voluntarily chosen as a means to an end, but in the second case it could be said to be willed *coniunctim* as a foreseen unavoidable consequent. Thomas Aquinas applies this idea in his distinctions between acts that are directly voluntary and those that are indirectly voluntary and between states of affairs willed *per se* and those willed *per accidens*. A foreseen side effect which is included in the scope of an act of will only accidentally is not directly voluntary, although it is indirectly voluntary in the sense that one could prevent its occurrence by giving up the direct act of will (*Summa theologiae* II.1, *q*. 6, *a*. 3; 2, *q*. 64, *a*. 7–8). This discussion has been one of the starting points of the doctrine of double effect, which still plays an important role in Roman Catholic moral theology.

The basic distinctions of the medieval logic of will so far attended to are those between willing something *simpliciter*, willing something as a means, willing something indirectly as a side effect and willing something conditionally. Conditional will was considered as a potential act of will which is actualized when the conditions are fulfilled.

Since Abelard, authors stressed that the necessary conditions of what is willed are sometimes tolerated rather than willed in any active manner. In spite of this, many of them thought that it is true, at least in the weak sense of voluntary acceptance, that willing the antecedent implies willing the consequent. Some writers, however, denied this, and their reasons for doing so seem to be similar to those which led Roger Roseth to deny (12) and (13) in deontic logic.

Many fourteenth-century authors discussed the example of the man who wills to be in the mud with 100 marks and yet does not will to be in the mud. William of Ockham and Robert Holcot understood it so that the man of the example wills to be in the mud on the condition that he receives 100 marks (William of Ockham, *Expositio super libros Elenchorum* 54.18–55.3; *Summa logicae* III.4, c. 13, 836.157–63; Robert Holcot, *Utrum cum unitate essentiae*, in *Exploring the Boundaries of Reason* 84.525–86.563). Referring to the example, Holcot remarks that if the propositional object of the will is taken to be a conjunction, it follows that the conjuncts are willed and the man wills to be in the mud. Walter Burley, however, denied this when using the same example to claim that willing the antecedent does not imply willing the consequent. He wrote:

> This consequence is valid: I am in the mud with 100 florentines; therefore I am in the mud. It does not follow, however: I want to be in the mud with 100 pounds; therefore I want to be in the mud. It is not necessarily so that he who wants the antecedent wants the consequent.
> (*De puritate artis logicae* 206.34–207.2; cf. 87.25–31)

Some twelfth-century authors had already answered negatively the question of whether willing the antecedent implies willing the consequent. Peter of Poitiers writes:

> If it is argued: 'Abraham willed to obey God and he knew that he could not obey God without killing his son; therefore he willed to kill his son', some people solve the problem by stating that if something follows from something, it does not follow, as with knowing, that he who wills or can do the antecedent wills or can do also the consequent. They want to show this with logical and theological examples. . . . 'If this person is in some way in Rome, he is in Rome; this person wills to be in some way in Rome, but he does not will to be in Rome'.
> (*Sent.* I, c. 9, 82.139–83.154)

The authors do not explain the background of their denial of the principle that willing the antecedent implies willing the consequent, but they seem to have thought as follows. One could suppose that a person, contrary to his or her will, is becoming dirty in any case and that he or she is choosing a certain mode of becoming dirty which is that of being dirty with 100 florentines. Willing the antecedent does not then imply willing the consequent, and the consequent is neither a *divisim* unwilled means nor a side effect. In so far as one is willing something with respect to a state of affairs which will be realized contrary to one's will, as some people might will that they survive nuclear war, the case is analogous to the logic of contrary-to-duty imperatives. This idea was not popular, but it is presented by Peter of Poitiers who in the fourth book of his *Sententiae* discusses again the example of willing to be in Rome in some way without willing to be in Rome. He explains it by referring to the fact that a person can will to repent of sins without willing to be guilty of a sin (*Sent.* IV, *cap.* 16, *PL* 211, 1199). This example of conditional will is the same which Roger Roseth later used in his discussion of conditional norms.

Before turning to Roseth's theory of conditional norms, let us have a look at some earlier discussions of conditional obligations. The treatise on natural law in William of Auxerre's *Summa aurea* shows how the theme could occur in theology. William asks whether norms which seem to be relevant after the Fall only were included in natural moral law in its original form. It seems, for example, that 'You shall not steal' is without point if there is no property. William says that norms of these kinds were included in original natural law potentially with respect to possible states of affairs. Although William does not mention it, the duty of restitution would then probably begin to be in force only when stealing is possible and its prohibition has been violated (*Summa aurea* III, *tract.* 18, *c.* 3, 377–8).

Conditional norms were also discussed in treatises *De obligationibus* which as such had nothing especially to do with morality or ethics. However, some authors explicitly located obligational disputations into a wider context of what may be called the ethics of disputation in general. It was said that, in a disputation where one part puts forward assertions, the other part must grant, deny or doubt them, according to whether he knows or does not know them to be true or false. These rules formulate certain duties of honesty; they can be called prima facie duties of the respondent in a disputation or, *mutatis mutandis*, duties of a person answering yes/no questions. In a *positio* type of disputation, the respondent is partially freed from the honesty rules; they are overridden by the obligational consistency rule (see pp. 125–6 above). An interest in the logic of norms is seen in the discussion of cases where the expression 'must be granted' (*concedendum*) occurs as a part of the *positum*. It was noticed that a *positum* of the type 'That you are in Rome must be granted' can be read prescriptively as a norm or descriptively as a norm proposition expressing the existence of a norm (Green forthcoming: II, 38–40, 49–50). The initial proposition including '*concedendum*' is read descriptively in a *positio* disputation, but it is read normatively in the species of disputations called *petitio* (ibid. II, 41). In the game called *positio dependens* a proposition becomes the *positum* on some condition (ibid. II, 23, 76–9). While discussing the question of how the conditional *positum* should be understood, Walter Burley emphasized that the disputational act by which the condition is fulfilled cannot be an act which fulfils or violates the obligation introduced by it. Neglecting this creates confusion. The same point was one of the background ideas of Roger Roseth's theory of how conditional obligations should be formulated.

## ROGER ROSETH AND THE PRINCIPLES OF DEONTIC LOGIC

The increased interest in the theory of norms in the fourteenth century is clearly visible in Roger Roseth's commentary on the *Sentences* where the whole opening question is at least formally dedicated to the problem of whether somebody can be obligated to something against his or her conscience. The first article contains a detailed discussion of the terms *maximum* and *minimum*. Tractates *De maximo et minimo* belonged to the fourteenth-century trend to apply the rules of logical analysis to questions of natural philosophy and to create 'conceptual algorithms' for basic theoretical terms. As John Murdoch has shown, these analytical languages were interdisciplinary – for example, there was a tendency to apply physical analytical languages into theological questions (Murdoch 1975). The first article of the question, which was later also copied as a separate tract *De maximo et minimo*, is an example of this practice. Although it concentrates on the properties of the terms *maximum* and *minimum* in natural philosophy, it is also meant to shed light on the ethical problem of whether, as regards intensity, there is a maximal or minimal performance of the act prescribed. I will forgo comment on this discussion and be content to make some remarks on the second article, the title of which is 'Whether anything can be rationally obligated to somebody, if it is permitted and not against the

## Medieval discussions of applied modal logic    191

salvation of the soul' (Roger Roseth, *Lectura super Sententias* 249rb–256rb).

Roseth assumes that the actual divine law (*lex statuta Dei*) is rational and that God is a sovereign moral authority who can introduce new precepts or change the old ones. He first formulates five general principles or rules which define the rationality of new norms, given by a legitimate authority, and the rest of the article consists of a discussion of various objections to the rules of rationality. The rules are as follows:

(i) Every precept by which I am obligated to something permitted which is in my power and which I am allowed to will according to the divine law without any precept is a rational precept according to the divine law.

(ii) No such precept is rational according to the divine law, by which I am obligated to something permitted which I cannot will in a permitted way according to the divine law except when I am so obligated.

By these rules Roseth defines the formal rationality of a system of norms: describing behaviour in accordance with the norms must not yield contradictions, i.e. a person should not violate a norm in a system by fulfilling a norm in the system (cf. ibid. 251va). In so far as obligations pertain to the acts of will, they should be permitted. Roseth states that there are omissions or commissions which are permitted, although it is not permitted to will them; as they cannot be licitly willed, they cannot as such be prescribed in a rational system of norms. Roseth's conception of the rationality of norms is not merely formal, however. He adds to the first rule that what is prescribed must be in the power of the agent in such a way that fulfilling the obligation does not result in a great disaster, for example, death. Roseth refers here to the dictates of natural right reason, apparently thinking that any rational system of norms should in some understandable way serve human good. Rules (iii) and (iv) are connected with the catholic doctrine of the salvation of the soul:

(iii) Not everything which is not against the salvation of the soul can be prescribed according to the divine law. (The second 'not' is mistakenly missing from the manuscript I have used.)

(iv) Not everything which is for the salvation of the soul can be prescribed according to the divine law.

The fifth rule refers to the doctrine of God's absolute power through which an act which is licit *de se* but cannot be licitly willed can be changed into an act which can be willed in a licit way:

(v) Whatever is permitted in the second way can, by the absolute power of God (*de potentia Dei absoluta*), become something which can be willed in a permitted way (ibid. 249rb–249va).

The rest of the article discusses various possible objections to these rules. I shall not comment on every objection and every answer given by Roseth. I shall only mention some general ideas pertaining to deontic logic. The first monastic objection to the first rule runs as follows. If you are at your devotions (in a supererogatory manner) and your prelate orders you to do something which is permitted but not supererogatory, then the precept is irrational, for your supererogatory action is meritorious with respect to your eternal life, and the new norm would prevent you from acting in such a highly meritorious way (ibid. 249va). The basic idea in Roseth's answer is that the value of supererogatory acts, which are not obligatory but meritorious if committed, must not be thought to be greater than that of fulfilling obligations. Then the merit one earns from works of supererogation can never compensate the demerit ascribed by an eventual omission of an obligation because of acting in a supererogatory way. Otherwise one could avoid fulfilling his or her duties by acts of supererogation (ibid. 250ra–251ra).

Another objection based on the idea of supererogation easily suggests itself. One could ask whether works of supererogation are counterexamples to the claim that if something is permitted and it is permitted to will it, God can obligate one to do it. Roseth did not discuss this question, but Uthred of Boldon, another Englishman from the mid-fourteenth century, argued that God can command men to perform supererogatory actions, but it must be understood that obligations of this kind refer to two different states of affairs. Acts which are supererogatory, when they are prescribed, cannot any more be supererogatory (Uthred of Boldon, *Quaestiones seu determinationes* q. 5, a. 1–2).

A further objection to the first rule is based on an acceptance of (13) as a rule of deontic inference. The opponent says that if you sleep, you omit to act in a meritorious way. If the antecedent is permitted in the first way, the consequent is so permitted also. The consequent cannot be obligated, however, because such an obligation would be violated only by meritorious acts (ibid. 249vb).

The example is tricky in many ways, as Roseth remarks in his answer. As for the question of whether there might be norms which cannot be fulfilled without violating other norms, Roseth thinks in the same way as William of Ockham. In *Quodlibeta septem* III, question 14, Ockham tries to show that loving God (in the sense of willing to fulfil divine law) is necessarily virtuous *stante praecepto divino*, i.e. that it is necessarily virtuous, provided that divine law remains in force. According to Ockham, God can add into the divine law an obligation to the effect that all obligations must be violated. Such a rule, if it is given at the same level as the others, makes the system of norms irrational, because then no rule can be fulfilled without violating the others. God can make it impossible for man to act meritoriously by making the divine law irrational. Roseth later treats this question in the same way (ibid. 255va–256rb); here he only mentions certain difficulties, which arise when one tries to defend the rationality of the command in question. The discussion is somewhat half-hearted, however, because Roseth thinks that there is a formal mistake in the counterargument. The possibility of the problematic norm is introduced incorrectly in the example, because (13) has been accepted without qualification (ibid. 251rb). The same point is repeated in the discussion of the third counterexample, which is a variant of the second one (see ibid. 251va).

Roseth formulates some examples by which he wants to show that rules (12) and (13) cannot be accepted in deontic theory. The examples present cases in which it is permitted or obligatory to will to behave as the antecedent indicates as well as forbidden to will to behave as the consequent indicates. Much use is made of the sentence: 'If one repents of his sin, he is guilty of a sin'. According to the divine law, it is obligatory to will to repent of one's sins, but it is forbidden to will to be guilty of a sin. Examples of this kind show that there are obligations which can be rationally fulfilled only in cases in which some norms have been already violated. Roseth makes use of the same concept of efficacious will which Ockham formulated in his works (see ibid. 255rb). Because being guilty of a sin is a necessary condition for repenting one's sins, the latter cannot be efficaciously willed without willing the former except when one is already in a state of sin. This shows that (12) and (13) can be defended only if there are no conditional norms, by which, for example, one's conduct, after having violated certain norms, is regulated. After Roderick Chisholm's (1963) paper 'Contrary-to-duty Imperatives and Deontic Logic', this class of norms is called contrary-to-duty imperatives. Roger Roseth noticed that this type of obligation prevents one from accepting the rules of inference of modal logic in deontic logic without qualification. As shown above, similar remarks were made earlier in connection with the notion of will.

According to Roseth, these are not, however, the only problematic cases. As already seen, he thought that sometimes the antecedent is permitted and it is permitted to will it while the consequent is permitted in such a way that it is not permitted to will it. This means that under certain circumstances it is permitted to behave as the consequent indicates, although it is not permitted to will to behave in that way. If one is in such a situation, then he or she can will to behave in accordance with the antecedent, so that willing it efficaciously does not imply that something forbidden is also willed. So there is a second class of conditional obligations and permissions, and they regulate conduct in situations in which the moral agent has not violated any rules but in which he or she cannot will to be without violating some rules. This group of obligations and permissions could serve, *mutatis mutandis*, as Roseth's answer to the so-called paradox of the Good Samaritan.

Some of the examples discussed by Roger Roseth had already been known for generations. In his century, however, a deeper interest developed in the logical properties of deontic concepts used in problematic cases. For example, Thomas Aquinas mentions in several places that a man can be *perplexus ex suppositione*, i.e. he can be in a situation in which it is forbidden to do something as well as to omit doing it. But instead of considering the general principles of deontic thought, Aquinas is satisfied with giving practical advice. Many of his examples of being perplexed are of the same type. A man has committed a forbidden act, and he has to do something next. Doing it in a sinful state, however, is forbidden. The solution is that the man should repent of his sin (see, for example, *Summa theologiae* II.1, *q.* 19, *a.* 6, *ad* 3; III, *q.* 64, *a.* 6, *ad* 3, *q.* 82, *a.* 10, *ad* 2; *Quaestiones disputatae de veritate q.* 17, *a.* 4, *ad* 8; *Sent.* II, *d.* 39, *q.* 3, *a.* 3, *ad* 5; IV, *d.* 24, *q.* 1, *a.* 3, *q.* 5, *ad* 1).

One could suppose that the general formula of Roseth's conditional obligation would be something like

(14) $L(p \rightarrow Oq)$

where $p$ is forbidden or something permitted in such a way that it is not permitted to will it. It is historically interesting that (14) is not the candidate Roseth accepted as the formula of conditional obligation. The reason for this appears when we look at his discussion of the fourth argument against the first rule. This counterargument runs as follows. Suppose that it is obligatory to will to repent if one is guilty of a sin. Otherwise it is forbidden. Socrates is not guilty of any sin and, in spite of that, he wills to repent. One could ask whether he should repent or not. If he should, he is doing what he ought to do, but then he should not repent. If he should not, he violates a rule and he ought to see that he repents. So if he should not repent, he should repent and vice versa (Roger Roseth, *Lectura super Sententias* 249vb).

According to Roseth, the intention of the rulegiver is that Socrates ought to will to repent of his sins only when he is guilty of a sin which is different from the sin that he wills to repent when he has not sinned before his repenting. So Socrates, while willing to repent in this way, violates the intention of the rulegiver, although he *secundum formam verborum* seems to fulfil his obligation (ibid. 251vb). In order to avoid difficulties of this kind, one apparently should add to the formula (14) a qualification to the effect that the condition must be fulfilled in such a way that the conditional obligation is not fulfilled *ipso facto*. It seems that Rosetus would have been happier with the following formula:

(15) $L(p \to Oq)$ & $-L(p \to q)$.

This happens to be almost the same as the definition of the deontic operator $Q$ introduced by von Wright in order to solve difficulties of other attempts to define conditional obligation. According to von Wright, $Q(q/p)$ can be read as follows: 'Assuming that it is in the agent's power to produce "$p$", then by producing this he becomes 'obligated' to produce also "$q$", unless "$q$" is something which is of necessity there as soon as "$p$" is there' (von Wright 1971: 169).

Roseth is not satisfied, however, with (15). Something is still needed. In order to show this, he discusses a variant of a well-known medieval sophism. According to it, Socrates is obligated to cross a bridge if and only if he says something true. Socrates says: 'I shall not cross the bridge.' If this is true, then the condition is fulfilled but the obligation cannot be fulfilled. Roseth says that in this case the obligation is rational only if it is restricted in such a way that Socrates' saying the truth does not make it impossible that Socrates will cross the bridge (*Lectura super Sententias* 252ra). When this restriction is added to (15), the final formula of conditional obligation runs as follows:

(16) $L(p \to Oq)$ & $-L(p \to q)$ & $M(p \& q)$.

Roseth's discussion of the correct form of conditional norms was probably influenced by the treatment of *positio dependens* in obligations logic. According to Walter Burley, the conditional obligation to grant the *positum* begins to be in force only when the condition is first fulfilled by a disputational act, which is different from an act of granting the *positum*. He also mentions that the condition should not make granting the *positum* impossible (Green forthcoming: II, 76–9). (For an attempt to apply limit decision rules to the periods of actuality of norms, see Uthred of Boldon, *Quaestiones seu determinationes q. 5, a. 1–2*.)

The last example occurs in variant forms in medieval discussions of semantic paradoxes. Roger Roseth presents other similar problems among the arguments against the second rule. One of them runs as follows. Suppose that Socrates is guilty of a sin *a*. He then goes to the priest and says against his conscience that he is guilty of a sin different from *a*. According to the divine law it is forbidden to lie. It seems, however, that Socrates can *bona conscientia* say so. Thus it seems that something forbidden can be rationally prescribed without referring to the absolute power of God, i.e. without changing the actual permissions (*Lectura super Sententias* 252ra). While discussing this and other related cases, Roseth introduces several rules by means of which certain types of paradoxes can be solved. The basic idea is that a part cannot stand for the whole of which it is a part (*pars non potest supponere pro toto cuius est pars*). If Socrates says 'This sentence is false', referring to the sentence he utters, he lies because 'false' in that sentence cannot stand for that sentence. And if Socrates while guilty of one sin only says 'I am guilty of two sins', he lies because 'sin' in that sentence cannot refer to that sentence (ibid. 253r). (For the medieval discussions of semantic paradoxes, see Roure 1970; Ashworth 1976; Spade 1980, 1982d.)

# Bibliography

Abbreviations: CSEL, Corpus Scriptorum Ecclesiasticorum Latinorum; CCSL, Corpus Christianorum, Series Latina; CCCM, Corpus Christianorum, Continuatio Mediaevalis; *PL*, J.P. Migne, *Patrologiae Cursus Completus, Series Latina*; *PG*, J.P. Migne, *Patrologiae Cursus Completus, Series Graeca*.

Abelard, Peter, *Dialectica*, ed. L.M. de Rijk (Wijsgerige teksten en studies 1), Assen: Van Gorcum, 1956 (2nd edn, 1970).
―― *Peter Abaelards Philosophische Schriften I. Die Logica 'Ingredientibus'*, ed. B. Geyer (Beiträge zur Geschichte der Philosophie und Theologie des Mittelalters XXI, 1-3), Münster: Aschendorff, 1919-27.
―― *Peter Abelard's Ethics*, with introduction, English translation and notes by D.E. Luscombe, Oxford: Clarendon Press, 1971.
―― *Scritti di Logica (Editio super Porphyrium, Glossae in Categorias, Editio super Aristotelem De interpretatione, De divisionibus, Super Topica glossae)*, ed. M. Dal Pra, Florence: La Nuova Italia Editrice, 1969 (1st edn, 1954).
―― *Super Periermenias XII-XIV*, ed. L. Minio-Paluello, in *Twelfth Century Logic. Texts and Studies II. Abaelardiana inedita*, Rome: Edizioni di Storia e Letteratura, 1958.
―― *Theologia Christiana*, ed. E.M. Buytaert (CCCM 12), Turnholt: Brebols, 1969.
―― *Theologia 'Scholarium'*, ed. E.M. Buytaert and C.J. Mews (CCCM 13), Turnholt: Brebols, 1987.
Adams, M. (1973) 'Did Ockham Know of Material and Strict Implication? A Reconsideration', *Franciscan Studies* 33: 5-37.
―― (1987) *William Ockham*, 2 vols, Notre Dame, IN: Notre Dame University Press.
Aertsen, J. (1987) *Nature and Creature. Thomas Aquinas's Way of Thought*, Leiden: Brill.
Alan of Lille, *Anticlaudianus*, ed. R. Bossuat, Paris: Vrin, 1955 (*PL* 210, 485-576).
―― *Regulae caelestis iuris*, ed. N.M. Häring (1981), *Archives d'histoire doctrinale et littéraire du moyen âge* 78: 97-226.
Alanen, L. (1985) 'Descartes, Duns Scotus and Ockham on Omnipotence

and Possibility', *Franciscan Studies* 45: 157–88.
Alanen, L. and Knuuttila, S. (1988) 'The Foundations of Modality and Conceivability in Descartes and His Predecessors', in S. Knuuttila (ed.) *Modern Modalities. Studies of the History of Modal Theories from Medieval Nominalism to Logical Positivism* (Synthese Historical Library 33), Dordrecht: Kluwer, 1–69.
Albert the Great, *Liber I Priorum analyticorum*, in *Opera omnia*, ed. A. Borgnet, vol. I, Paris: Vivès, 1890–9.
—— *Liber Perihermeneias*, in *Opera omnia*, ed. A. Borgnet, vol. I, Paris: Vivès, 1890.
Albert of Saxony, *Sophismata*, Paris, 1502 (reprinted, Hildesheim: Olms, 1975).
Alexander of Aphrodisias, *In Aristotelis Analyticorum priorum librum I commentarium*, ed. M. Wallies (Commentaria in Aristotelem Graeca 2.1), Berlin: Reimer, 1883.
—— *De fato (On Fate)*, text, translation and commentary by R.W. Sharples, London: Duckworth, 1983.
Ammonius, *In Aristotelis De interpretatione commentarius*, ed. A. Busse (Commentaria in Aristotelem Graeca 4.5), Berlin: Reimer, 1897.
Anselm of Canterbury, *Memorials of St Anselm*, ed. R.W. Southern and F.S. Schmitt (Auctores Britannici Medii Aevi 1), London: Oxford University Press, 1969.
—— *Opera omnia*, ed. F.S. Schmitt, Edinburgh: Nelson, 1946–51.
Apuleius, *Opera III*, ed. P. Thomas, Leibzig: Teubner, 1908.
Aquinas, Thomas, *Aristotle: On Interpretation. A Commentary by St Thomas and Cajetan*, translated by J.T. Oesterle, Milwaukee, WI: Marquette University Press, 1962.
—— *De modalibus*, ed. I.M. Bocheński (1940), *Angelicum* 17: 180–218.
—— *In duodecim libros Metaphysicorum Aristotelis expositio*, ed. M.R. Cathala and R.M. Spiazzi, Turin: Marietti, 1971.
—— *In libros Aristotelis Peri hermeneias et Posteriorum analyticorum expositio*, ed. R.M. Spiazzi, Turin: Marietti, 1964.
—— *In octos libros Physicorum Aristotelis expositio*, ed. M. Maggiòlo, Turin: Marietti, 1954.
—— *Questiones disputatae*, vol. I, ed. R.M. Spiazzi, Turin: Marietti, 1964. (This volume contains *Quaestiones disputatae de veritate*.)
—— *Quaestiones disputatae*, vol. II, ed. P. Bazzi, M. Calcaterra, T.S. Centi, E. Odetto and P.M. Pession, Turin: Marietti, 1965. (This volume contains, among others, *Quaestiones disputatae de potentia, de spiritualibus creaturis, de virtutibus in communi, de malo*.)
—— *Quaestiones quodlibetales*, ed. R.M. Spiazzi, Turin: Marietti, 1956.
—— *Scriptum super Sententiis*, ed. P. Mandonnet and M.F. Moos, Paris: Lethielleux, 1929–56.
—— *Summa contra gentiles*, 3 vols, ed. C. Pera, P. Marc and P. Caramello, Turin: Marietti, 1961–7.
—— *Summa theologiae*, 3 vols, ed. P. Caramello, Turin: Marietti, 1948–50.
Aristotle, *Categoriae et Liber de Interpretatione (Categories)*, ed. L. Minio-Paluello (Scriptorum Classicorum Bibliotheca Oxoniensis), Oxford: Clarendon, 1949.
—— *De anima*, ed. W.D. Ross (Scriptorum Classicorum Bibliotheca Oxoniensis), Oxford: Clarendon, 1989.

—— *De caelo*, ed. D.J. Allan (Scriptorum Classicorum Bibliotheca Oxoniensis), Exford: Clarendon, 1936.
—— *Metaphysics*, a revised text with introduction and commentary by W.D. Ross, 2 vols, Oxford: Clarendon, 1924.
—— *Nicomachean Ethics*, ed. I. Bywater (Scriptorum Classicorum Bibliotheca Oxoniensis), Oxford: Clarendon, 1970.
—— *On Coming-to-be and Passing-away* (*De generatione et corruptione*), a revised text with introduction and commentary by H.H. Joachim, Oxford: Clarendon, 1922.
—— *Parts of Animals* (*De partibus animalium*), ed. A.L. Peck (Loeb Classical Library), London: Heinemann, and Cambridge, MA: Harvard University Press, 1937.
—— *Physics*, a revised text with introduction and commentary by W.D. Ross, Oxford: Clarendon, 1936.
—— *Prior and Posterior Analytics*, a revised text with introduction and commentary by W.D. Ross, Oxford: Clarendon, 1949.
—— *Topica et Sophistici elenchi*, ed. W.D. Ross (Scriptorum Classicorum Bibliotheca Oxoniensis), Oxford: Clarendon, 1958.
Ashworth, E.J. (1976) ' "I promise you a horse": A Second Problem of Meaning and Reference in Late Fifteenth- and Early Sixteenth-Century Logic', *Vivarium* 14: 62–79, 139–55.
—— (1978) 'Theories of the Proposition: Some Early Sixteenth Century Discussions', *Franciscan Studies* 38: 81–121.
—— (1981) 'The Problems of Relevance and Order in Obligational Disputations: Some Late Fourteenth Century Views', *Medioevo* 7: 175–93.
—— (1985) 'English *Obligationes* Texts after Roger Swyneshed; the Tracts Beginning "Obligatio est quaedam ars" ' in O. Lewry (ed.) *The Rise of British Logic*, Toronto: Pontifical Institute of Mediaeval Studies, 309–33.
Asztalos, M. (ed.) (1986) *The Editing of Theological and Philosophical Texts from the Middle Ages* (Acta Universitatis Stockholmiensis, Studia Latina Stockholmiensia 30), Stockholm: Almqvist & Wiksell.
Augustine, *Confessionum libri XIII*, ed. P. Knöll (CSEL 33), Vienna: F. Tempsky, and Leipzig: G. Freytag, 1896.
—— *Contra duas epistulas pelagianorum*, ed. C.F. Urba and J. Zycha (CSEL 60), Vienna: F. Tempsky, and Leipzig: G. Freytag, 1913.
—— *Contra Faustum*, ed. J. Zycha (CSEL 25), Vienna: F. Tempsky, and Leipzig: G. Freytag, 1891.
—— *Contra Gaudentium*, ed. M. Petschenig (CSEL 53), Vienna: F. Tempsky, and Leipzig: G. Freytag, 1890.
—— *De civitate Dei*, ed. B. Dombart and A. Kalb (CCSL 47–8), Turnholt: Brebols, 1955.
—— *De diversis quaestionibus LXXXIII*, ed. A. Mutzenbecher (CCSL 44A), Turnholt: Brebols, 1975.
—— *De natura et gratia*, ed. C.F. Urba and J. Zycha (CSEL 60), Vienna: F. Tempsky, and Leipzig: G. Freytag, 1913.
—— *De spiritu et littera*, ed. C.F. Urba and J. Zycha (CSEL 60), Vienna: F. Tempsky, and Leipzig: G. Freytag, 1913.
—— *Enchiridion*, ed. E. Evans (CCSL 46), Turnholt: Brebols, 1969.
—— *Epistulae*, pars IV, ed. A. Goldbacher (CSEL 57), Vienna: F. Tempsky, and Leipzig: G. Freytag, 1911.

Averroes (Ibn Rushd), *Aristotelis Opera cum Averrois Commentariis*, Venice, 1562–74 (reprinted, Frankfurt am Main: Minerva, 1962).
—— *Averroes' Questions in Physics*, ed. and translated by H.T. Goldstein (The New Synthese Historical Library 39), Dordrecht: Kluwer, 1991.
Avicenna (Ibn Sīnā), *Remarks and Admonitions*, Part One, *Logic*, translated by S.C. Inati, Toronto: Pontifical Institute of Mediaeval Studies, 1984.
Bacon, Roger, *Summulae dialectices: I. De termino, II. De enuntiatione*, ed. A. de Libera (1986), *Archives d'histoire doctrinale et littéraire du moyen âge* 53: 139–289.
Balme, D.M. (1987) 'Teleology and Necessity', in A. Gotthelf and J.G. Lennox (eds) *Philosophical Issues in Aristotle's Biology*, Cambridge: Cambridge University Press, 275–85.
Baudry, L. (1950) *La querelle des futurs contingents (Louvain 1465–1475). Textes inédits* (Etudes de philosophie médiévale 38), Paris: Vrin. Translated by R. Guerlac (1989) *The Quarrel over Future Contingents (Louvain 1465–1475)* (Synthese Historical Library 36), Dordrecht: Kluwer.
Becker, A. (1968) *Die aristotelische Theorie der Möglichkeitsschlüsse*, Darmstadt: Wissenschaftliche Buchgesellschaft (1st edn, 1933).
Becker, O. (1952) *Untersuchungen über den Modalkalkül*, Meisenheim am Glan: Anton Hain.
Becker-Freyseng, A. (1938) *Die Vorgeschichte des philosophischen Terminus 'contingens': Die Bedeutungen von 'contingere' bei Boethius und ihr Verhältnis zu den Aristotelischen Möglichkeitsbegriffen* (Quellen und Studien zur Geschichte und Kultur des Altertums und des Mittelalters D 7) Heidelberg: Bilabel.
Beonio-Brocchieri Fumagalli, M.T. (1969) *The Logic of Abelard* (Synthese Historical Library 1), Dordrecht: Reidel.
Berengar of Tours, *Rescriptum contra Lanfrannum*, ed. R.B.C. Huygens (CCCM 84), Turnholt: Brebols, 1988.
Bernard of Clairvaux, *Apologia ad Guillelmum*, PL 182, 895–918.
Billingham, Richard, *Speculum puerorum*, ed. A. Maierù, in 'Lo *Speculum puerorum sive Terminus est in quem* di Riccardo Billingham', *Studi Medievali*, 3a serie 10.3 (1969), 297–397.
Bobzien, S. (1986) *Die stoische Modallogik* (Epistemata. Würzburger wissenschaftliche Schriften, Reihe Philosophie 32), Würzburg: Königshausen & Neumann.
Bocheński, I.M. (1956) *Formale Logik* (Orbis Academicus III, 2), Freiburg, Munich: Karl Alber.
Boehner, Ph. (1958) *Collected Articles on Ockham*, ed. E.M. Buytaert, St Bonaventure: The Franciscan Institute.
Boethius, Anicius Manlius Severinus, *Commentarii in librum Aristotelis Perihermeneias*, vols I and II, ed. C. Meiser, Leipzig: Teubner, 1877–80.
—— *De hypotheticis syllogismis*, ed. with translation and commentary by L. Obertello, Brescia: Paideia Editrice, 1969.
—— *De syllogismis categoricis*, PL 64, 793–832.
—— *De topicis differentiis*, PL 64, 1174–1216.
—— *In Categorias Aristotelis*, PL 64, 159–294.
—— *In Ciceronis Topica*, PL 64, 1039–1169.
—— *Philosophiae consolatio*, ed. L. Bieler (CCSL 94), Turnholt: Brebols, 1957.

Boethius of Dacia, *De aeternitate mundi*, ed. N.J. Green-Pedersen (Corpus Philosophorum Danicorum Medii Aevi VI, 2) Copenhagen: Gad, 1976.
—— *Quaestiones super librum Topicorum*, ed. N.J. Green-Pedersen and J. Pinborg (Corpus Philosophorum Danicorum Medii Aevi VI, 1), Copenhagen: Gad, 1976.
Boh, I. (1982) 'Consequences', in N. Kretzmann, A. Kenny and J. Pinborg (eds) *The Cambridge History of Later Medieval Philosophy*, Cambridge: Cambridge University Press, 300–14.
—— (1985) 'Divine Omnipotence in the Early Sentences', in T. Rudavsky (ed.) *Divine Omniscience and Omnipotence in Medieval Philosophy* (Synthese Historical Library 25), Dordrecht: Reidel, 185–211.
—— (1986a) 'Belief, Justification, and Knowledge – Some Late Medieval Epistemic Concerns', *Journal of the Rocky Mountain Medieval and Renaissance Association* 6: 87–103.
—— (1986b) 'Elements of Epistemic Logic in Later Middle Ages', in C. Wenin (ed.) *L'homme et son univers au moyen âge II* (Philosophes médiévaux 27), Louvain-la-Nouve: Editions de l'Institut Supérieur de Philosophie, 530–43.
—— (1990) 'On Medieval Rules of Obligation and Rules of Consequence', in I. Angelelli and A. d'Ors (eds) *Estudios de Historia de la Lógica*, Pamplona: Ediciones Eunate, 39–102.
Bonaventure, *Opera omnia*, Quaracchi: Collegium S. Bonaventurae, 1882–1902.
Bos, E.P. (ed.) (1985) *Medieval Semantics and Metaphysics. Studies Dedicated to L.M. de Rijk* (Artistarium Supplementa 2), Nijmegen: Ingenium Publishers.
Bosley, R. (1978) 'In Support of an Interpretation of *On Int.* 9', *Ajatus* 37: 29–40.
Braakhuis, H.A.G. (1979) *De 13de Eeuwse Tractaten over syncategorematische Termen*, Meppel: Krips Repro.
Broadie, A. (1987) *Introduction to Medieval Logic*, Oxford: Clarendon.
—— (1989) *Notion and Object. Aspects of Late Medieval Epistemology*, Oxford: Clarendon.
de Bruyne, E. (1969) *The Esthetics of the Middle Ages*, translated by E. Hennessy, New York: Ungar.
Buchner, H. (1970) *Plotins Möglichkeitslehre* (Epimeleia 16), Munich, Salzburg: Anton Pustet.
Buridan, John, *In Metaphysicen Aristotelis quaestiones*, Paris, 1518 (reprinted Frankfurt am Main: Minerva, 1964).
—— *Quaestiones in duos libros Analyticorum priorum Aristotelis*, ed. H. Hubien (forthcoming).
—— *Quaestiones longe super librum Perihermeneas*, edited with an introduction by R. van der Lecq (Artistarium 4), Nijmegen: Ingenium Publishers, 1983.
—— *Quaestiones super decem libros Ethicorum Aristotelis*, Paris, 1513 (reprinted Frankfurt am Main: Minerva, 1964).
—— *Quaestiones super libris quattuor De caelo et mundo*, ed. E.A. Moody, Cambridge, MA: The Medieval Academy of America, 1942.
—— *Quaestiones super octo Physicorum libros Aristotelis*, Paris, 1509 (reprinted Frankfurt am Main: Minerva, 1964).

—— *Sophismata*, ed. T.K. Scott, Stuttgart-Bad Canstatt: Frommann-Holzboog, 1977.
—— *Sophisms on Meaning and Truth*, translated by T.K. Scott, New York: Appleton-Century-Crofts, 1966.
—— *Tractatus de consequentiis*, ed. H. Hubien, (Philosophes médiévaux 16), Louvain: Publications Universitaires, 1976.
Burley, Walter, *De puritate artis logicae tractatus longior with a Revised Edition of the Tractatus brevior*, ed. Ph. Boehner (Franciscan Institute Publications, Text Series 9), St Bonaventure, NY: The Franciscan Institute, 1955.
—— *Expositio super decem libros Ethicorum Aristotelis*, Venice, 1521.
Byrne, E.F. (1968) *Probability and Opinion. A Study in the Medieval Presuppositions of Post-medieval Theories of Probability*, The Hague: Martinus Nijhoff.
Calcidius, *Timaeus a Calcidio translatus commentarioque instructus*, ed. J.H. Waszink (Plato Latinus IV), Leiden: Brill, 1962.
Chadwick, H. (1981) *Boethius: The Consolations of Music, Logic, Theology, and Philosophy*, Oxford: Clarendon.
Chenu, M.-D. (1935–6) 'Grammaire et théologie aux XIIe et XIIIe siècles', *Archives d'histoire doctrinale et littéraire du moyen âge* 10: 5–28.
Chisholm, R. (1963) 'Contrary-to-duty Imperatives and Deontic Logic', *Analysis* 24: 33–6.
Cicero, *De fato*, with an English translation by H. Rackham (Loeb Classical Library), London: Heinemann and Cambridge, MA: Harvard University Press, 1968.
*Commentarius Cantabrigiensis in Epistolas Pauli e Schola Petri Abaelardi*, vols I–IV, ed. A. Landgraf (Publications in Mediaeval Studies 2), Notre Dame, IN: Notre Dame University Press, 1937–45.
Coombs, J.S. (1990) 'The Truth and Falsity of Modal Propositions in Renaissance Nominalism', Ph.D. dissertation, University of Texas at Austin.
Cooper, J.M. (1987) 'Hypothetical Necessity and Natural Teleology', in A. Gotthelf and J.G. Lennox (eds) *Philosophical Issues in Aristotle's Biology*, Cambridge: Cambridge University Press, 243–74.
Copleston, F.C. (1972) *A History of Medieval Philosophy*, London: Methuen.
Corcoran, J. (1974) 'Aristotle's Natural Deduction System', in J. Corcoran (ed.) *Ancient Logic and Its Modern Interpretations* (Synthese Historical Library 9), Dordrecht: Reidel, 85–132.
Corsi, G., Mangione, C. and Mugnai, M. (eds) (1989) *Atti del Convegno Internazionale di Storia della Logica. Le Teorie delle Modalità*, Bologna: CLUEB.
Courtenay, W.J. (1973) 'John of Mirecourt and Gregory of Rimini on Whether God can Undo the Past', *Recherches de théologie ancienne et médiévale* 40: 147–74.
—— (1978) *Adam Wodeham: An Introduction to His Life and Writings* (Studies in Medieval and Reformation Thought 21), Leiden: Brill.
—— (1984) Nature and the Natural in Twelfth-Century Thought', in W.J. Courtenay, *Covenant and Causality in Medieval Thought*, London: Variorum Reprints, III.
—— (1985) 'The Dialectic of Omnipotence in the High and Late Middle

Ages', in T. Rudavsky (ed.) *Divine Omniscience and Omnipotence in Medieval Philosophy* (Synthese Historical Library 25), Dordrecht: Reidel, 243–69.

Craig, W.L. (1988) *The Problem of Divine Foreknowledge and Future Contingents from Aristotle to Suarez*, Leiden: Brill.

Damian, Peter, *Lettre sur la Toute-Puissance Divine (De divina omnipotentia)*, introduction, critical text, translation and notes by A. Cantin (Sources Chrétiennes 191), Paris: Cerf, 1972.

Dancy, R. (1981) 'Aristotle and the Priority of Actuality', in S. Knuuttila (ed.) *Reforging the Great Chain of Being: Studies of the History of Modal Theories* (Synthese Historical Library 20), Dordrecht: Reidel, 73–115.

—— (1986) 'Aristotle and Existence', in S. Knuuttila and J. Hintikka (eds) *The Logic of Being: Historical Studies* (Synthese Historical Library 28), Dordrecht: Reidel, 49–80.

Danto, A.C. (1973) *Analytical Philosophy of Action*, Cambridge: Cambridge University Press.

Dazeley, H.L. and Gombocz, W.L. (1979) 'Interpreting Anselm as Logician', *Synthese* 40: 71–96.

Dekker, E. (1989) 'Non ita manifesta: Een onderzoek naar de synchrone contingentietheorie van Duns Scotus en haar receptie bij Ockham, Molina en Suarez', unpublished thesis, University of Utrecht.

Deman, T. (1936) 'Probabilisme', *Dictionnaire de théologie catholique 13*, Paris, 417–619.

Denyer, N. (1981) 'Time and Modality in Diodorus Cronus', *Theoria* 47: 31–53.

Descartes, R., *Oeuvres de Descartes*, ed. C. Adam and P. Tannery, Paris: Cerf, 1887–1913.

—— *Philosophical Letters*, ed. and translated by A. Kenny, Oxford: Clarendon, 1981.

Diogenes Laertius, *Lives of Eminent Philosophers*, with an English translation by R.D. Hicks (Loeb Classical Library), London: Heinemann, and Cambridge, MA: Harvard University Press, 1925.

Donagan, A. (1977) *The Theory of Morality*, Chicago, IL: University of Chicago Press.

Döring, K. (1972) *Die Megariker: Kommentierte Sammlung der Testimonien*, Amsterdam: Grüner.

Doucet, V. (1953) 'Le studium franciscain de Norwich en 1337', *Archivum franciscanum historicum* 46: 89–93.

Dronke, P. (1988a) 'Thierry of Chartres', in P. Dronke (ed.) *A History of Twelfth-century Western Philosophy*, Cambridge: Cambridge University Press, 358–85.

—— (ed.) (1988b) *A History of Twelfth-century Western Philosophy*, Cambridge: Cambridge University Press.

Duin, J.J. (1954) *La doctrine de la providence les écrits de Siger de Brabant* (Philosophes médiévaux 3), Louvain: Editions de l'Institut Supérieur de Philosophie.

Dunlop, D.M. (1962) 'Averroes on the Modality of Propositions', *Islamic Studies* 1: 23–34.

Duns Scotus, John, *Abhandlung über das Erste Prinzip (De primo principio)*, ed. and translated by W. Kluxen, Darmstadt: Wissenschaftliche

Buchgesellschaft, 1974.
—— *Opera omnia*, ed. L. Wadding, Lyon, 1639.
—— *Opera omnia*, studio et cura Commissionis Scotisticae, Vatican City: Vatican Press, 1950.
Ebbesen, S. (1981) *Commentators and Commentaries on Aristotle's Sophistici elenchi*, vols I–III (Corpus Latinum Commentariorum in Aristotelem Graecorum 7.1–3, Leiden: Brill.
—— (1982) 'Ancient Scholastic Logic as the Source of Medieval Scholastic Logic', in N. Kretzmann, A. Kenny and J. Pinborg (eds) *The Cambridge History of Later Medieval Philosophy*, Cambridge: Cambridge University Press, 101–27.
—— (1986) 'The Chimera's Diary', in S. Knuuttila and J. Hintikka (eds) *The Logic of Being: Historical Studies* (Synthese Historical Library 28), Dordrecht: Reidel, 115–43.
—— (1987) 'Boethius as an Aristotelian Scholar', in J. Wiesner (ed.) *Aristoteles, Werk und Wirkung II*, Berlin: Walter de Gruyter, 286–311.
Ebbesen, S., Fredborg, K.M. and Nielsen, L. (eds) (1983) 'Compendium Logicae Porretanum ex codice Oxoniensi Collegii Corporis Christi 250: A Manual of Porretan Doctrine by a Pupil of Gilbert's', *Cahiers de l'Institut du Moyen-âge grec et latin, Université de Copenhague* 46.
Einarson, B. (1936) 'On Certain Mathematical Terms in Aristotle's Logic', *American Journal of Philology* 57: 34–54, 151–72.
Eliot, T.S. (1943) *Four Quartets*, New York: Harcourt.
van Elswijk, H.C. (1966) *Gilbert Porreta, sa vie, son oeuvre, sa pensée*, Louvain: Spicilegium Sacrum Lovaniense.
Endres, J.A. (1910) *Petrus Damiani und die weltliche Wissenschaft* (Beiträge zur Geschichte der Philosophie des Mittelalters 8.3), Münster: Verlag der aschendorffschen Verlagsbuchhandlung.
Engberg-Pedersen, T. (1990) *The Stoic Theory of Oikeiosis* (Studies in Hellenistic Civilization 2), Aarhus: Aarhus University Press.
Engel, P. (1988) 'Plenitude and Contingency: Modal Concepts in Nineteenth Century French Philosophy', in S. Knuuttila (ed.) *Modern Modalities. Studies of the History of Modal Theories from Medieval Nominalism to Logical Positivism* (Synthese Historical Library 33), Dordrecht: Kluwer, 179–237.
Epictetus, *Dissertationes*, ed. by H. Schenkl, Leipzig: Teubner, 1916.
van Ess, J. (1985) 'Wrongdoing and Divine Omnipotence in the Theology of Abū Ishāq an-Nazzām', in T. Rudavsky (ed.) *Divine Omniscience and Omnipotence in Medieval Philosophy* (Synthese Historical Library 25), Dordrecht: Reidel, 53–67.
Estermann, J. (1990) *Individualität und Kontingenz: Studie zur Individualitätsproblematik bei Gottfried Wilhelm Leibniz*, Bern: Peter Lang.
al-Fārābī, *Commentary and Short Treatise on Aristotle's De interpretatione*, translation with introduction and notes by F.W. Zimmermann (The British Academy Classical and Medieval Logic Texts 3), Oxford: Oxford University Press, 1981.
Faust, A. (1931–2) *Der Möglichkeitsgedanke. Systemgeschichtliche Untersuchungen*, vols I and II, Heidelberg: Carl Winter.
Federici Vescovini, G. (1983) *'Arti' e Filosofia nel Secolo XIV*, Florence: Nuovedizioni Enrico Vallecchi.

## Bibliography 205

Frank, R. (1985) 'Can God Do What is Wrong', in T. Rudavsky (ed.) *Divine Omniscience and Omnipotence in Medieval Philosophy* (Synthese Historical Library 33), Dordrecht: Reidel, 69–79.

Freddoso, A.J. (1980) 'Ockham's Theory of Truth Conditions', in A.J. Freddoso and H. Schuurman (transl.), *Ockham's Theory of Propositions: Part II of the Summa Logicae*, Notre Dame, IN: Notre Dame University Press, 1–76.

—— (1988) *Luis de Molina: On Divine Foreknowledge, Part IV of the Concordia* (translation with introduction and notes), Ithaca, NY: Cornell University Press.

Frede, D. (1970) *Aristoteles und die 'Seeschlacht'. Das Problem der Contingentia Futura in De interpretatione 9* (Hypomnemata 27), Göttingen: Vandenhoeck & Ruprecht.

—— (1985) 'The Sea-Battle Reconsidered: A Defence of the Traditional Interpretation', *Oxford Studies in Ancient Philosophy* 3: 31–87.

Frede, M. (1967) *Prädikation und Existenzaussage: Platons Gebrauch von '. . . ist . . .' und '. . . ist nicht . . .' im Sophistes* (Hypomnemata 18), Göttingen: Vandenhoeck & Ruprecht.

—— (1974a) *Die stoische Logik* (Abhandlungen der Akademie der Wissenschaften in Göttingen, Phil. hist. Klasse, 3. Folge 88), Göttingen: Vandenhoeck & Ruprecht.

—— (1974b) 'Stoic vs. Aristotelian Syllogistic', *Archiv für Geschichte der Philosophie* 56: 1–32.

Frede, M. and Patzig, G. (1988) *Aristoteles 'Metaphysik Z'* (text, translation and commentary), 2 Vols, Munich: Beck.

Freppert, L. (1988) *The Basis of Morality According to William Ockham*, Chicago, IL: Franciscan Herald Press.

Funkenstein, A. (1986) *Theology and the Scientific Imagination from the Middle Ages to the Seventeenth Century*, Princeton, NJ: Princeton University Press.

Furley, D. (1967) *Two Studies in the Greek Atomists*, Princeton, NJ: Princeton University Press.

Gadamer, H.-G. (1965) *Wahrheit und Methode*, Tübingen: Mohr.

Garland the Computist, *Dialectica* (Wijsgerige teksten en studies 3), ed. L.M. de Rijk, Assen: Van Gorcum, 1959.

Gelber, H.G. (1974) 'Logic and Trinity: A Clash of Values in Scholastic Thought 1300–1335', Ph.D. dissertation, University of Wisconsin.

Gibson, M. (1981a) 'The *Opuscula Sacra* in the Middle Ages', in M. Gibson (ed.) *Boethius: His Life, Thought and Influence*, Oxford: Basil Blackwell, 214–34.

—— (ed.) (1981b) *Boethius: His Life, Thought and Influence*, Oxford: Basil Blackwell.

Gilbert of Poitiers, *The Commentaries on Boethius*, ed. N.M. Häring, Toronto: Pontifical Institute of Mediaeval Studies, 1966.

Goddu, A. (1984) *The Physics of William of Ockham* (Studien und Texte zur Geistesgeschichte des Mittelalters 16), Köln: Brill.

—— (1989) 'The Dialectic of Certitude and Demonstrability according to William of Ockham and the Conceptual Relation of His Account to Later Developments', in S. Caroti (ed.) *Studies in Medieval Natural Philosophy* (Biblioteca di Nuncius. Studi e Testi 1), Florence: Leo S. Olschki, 95–131.

Gotthelf, A. (1987) 'Aristotle's Conception of Final Causality', in A. Gotthelf and J.G. Lennox (eds) *Philosophical Issues in Aristotle's Biology*, Cambridge: Cambridge University Press, 204–42.
Gotthelf, A. and Lennox, J.G. (eds) (1987) *Philosophical Issues in Aristotle's Biology*, Cambridge: Cambridge University Press.
Gracia, J.J.E. (1984) *Introduction to the Problem of Individuation in the Early Middle Ages*, Munich: Philosophia-Verlag.
Graeser, A. (ed. with commentary) (1973) *Die logischen Fragmente des Theophrast* (Kleine Texte für Vorlesungen und Übungen 191), Berlin: Walter de Gruyter.
Grant, E. (1979) 'The Condemnation of 1277, God's Absolute Power, and Physical Thought in the Late Middle Ages', *Viator* 10: 211–44.
—— (1986) 'Science and Theology in the Middle Ages', in D.C. Lindberg and R.L. Numbers (eds) *God and Nature: Historical Essays on the Encounter between Christianity and Science*, Berkeley, CA: University of California Press, 49–75.
Grant, R.M. (1952) *Miracle and Natural Law in Graeco-Roman and Early Christian Thought*, Amsterdam: North-Holland.
Green, R. (forthcoming) *The Logical Treatise 'De obligationibus': An Introduction with Critical Texts of William of Sherwood (?) and Walter Burley*, St Bonaventure: The Franciscan Institute.
Green-Pedersen, N.J. (1984) *The Tradition of the Topics in the Middle Ages*, Munich: Philosophia-Verlag.
Gregory, T. (1988) 'The Platonic Inheritance', in P. Dronke (ed.) *A History of Twelfth-century Western Philosophy*, Cambridge: Cambridge University Press, 54–80.
Gregory of Rimini, *Lectura super primum et secundum Sententiarum*, vol. VI, *Super secundum, dist. 24–44*, ed. V. Marcolino, W. Simon and V. Wendland (Spätmittelalter und Reformation. Texte und Untersuchungen 11) Berlin: Walter de Gruyter, 1980.
Grosseteste, Robert, *De libero arbitrio*, in *Die philosophischen Werke des Robert Grosseteste*, ed. L. Baur (Beiträge zur Geschichte der Philosophie des Mittelalters 9), Münster: Verlag der aschendorffschen Verlagsbuchhandlung, 1912.
Haaparanta, L. (1988) 'Frege and his German Contemporaries on Alethic Modalities', in S. Knuuttila (ed.) *Modern Modalities. Studies of the History of Modal Theories from Medieval Nominalism to Logical Positivism* (Synthese Historical Library 33), Dordrecht: Kluwer, 239–74.
Hacking, I. (1975) *The Emergence of Probability. A Philosophical Study of Early Ideas about Probability, Induction, and Statistical Inference*, Cambridge: Cambridge University Press.
Hartmann, N. (1938) *Möglichkeit und Wirklichkeit*, Berlin: Walter de Gruyter.
—— (1957) 'Der Megarische und der Aristotelische Möglichkeitsbegriff', in N. Hartmann, *Kleinere Schriften II*, Berlin: Walter de Gruyter, 85–100.
Haskins, C.H. (1927) *The Renaissance of the Twelfth Century*, Cambridge, MA: Harvard University Press.
Henry, D.P. (1967) *The Logic of Saint Anselm*, Oxford: Oxford University Press.
—— (1974) *Commentary on De Grammatico: The Historical-Logical*

*Dimension of a Dialogue of St Anselm's* (Synthese Historical Library 8), Dordrecht: Reidel.
—— (1985) 'Abelard's Mereological Terminology' in E.P. Bos (ed.) *Medieval Semantics and Metaphysics. Studies Dedicated to L.M. de Rijk* (Artistarium Supplementa 2), Nijmegen, Ingenium Publishers, 65–92.
Henry of Ghent, *Quodlibeta*, Paris, 1518 (reprinted, Louvain: Bibliothèque S.J., 1961).
Hintikka, J. (1957) 'Necessity, Universality and Time in Aristotle', *Ajatus* 20: 65–90.
—— (1962) *Knowledge and Belief: An Introduction to the Logic of the Two Notions*, Ithaca, NY: Cornell University Press.
—— (1964) 'The Once and Future Sea Fight', *Philosophical Review* 73: 461–92.
—— (1969) *Models for Modalities* (Synthese Library 23), Dordrecht: Reidel.
—— (1972) 'Leibniz on Plenitude, Relations, and "the Reign of Law" ' in H.G. Frankfurt (ed.) *Leibniz: A Collection of Critical Essays*, Garden City, NY: Doubleday, 155–190. Reprinted in S. Knuuttila (ed.) (1981) *Reforging the Great Chain of Being: Studies of the History of Modal Theories* (Synthese Historical Library 20) Dordrecht: Reidel, 259–86.
—— (1973) *Time and Necessity: Studies in Aristotle's Theory of Modality*, Oxford: Oxford University Press.
—— (1978) 'Aristotle's Incontinent Logician', *Ajatus* 37: 48–65.
—— (1981) 'Gaps in the Great Chain of Being', in S. Knuuttila (ed.) *Reforging the Great Chain of Being: Studies of the History of Modal Theories* (Synthese Historical Library 20) Dordrecht: Reidel, 1–17.
—— (1986) 'The Varieties of Being in Aristotle', in S. Knuuttila and J. Hintikka (eds) *The Logic of Being: Historical Studies* (Synthese Historical Library 28), Dordrecht: Reidel, 81–114.
Hintikka, J. with Remes, U. and Knuuttila, S. (1977) *Aristotle on Modality and Determinism* (Acta Philosophica Fennica 29, 1), Amsterdam: North-Holland.
Hissette, R. (1977) *Enquête sur les 219 articles condamnés à Paris le 7 Mars 1277* (Philosophes médiévaux 22), Louvain: Publications Universitaires.
Hoenen, M.J.F.M. (1989) *Marsilius van Inghen over het goddelijke weten*, Nijmegen: Ingenium Publishers.
Holcot, Robert, *Exploring the Boundaries of Reason: Three Questions on the Nature of God by Robert Holcot*, ed. H.G. Gelber (Studies and Texts 62), Toronto: Pontifical Institute of Medieval Studies, 1983.
—— *In quatuor libros Sententiarum quaestiones . . . Determinationes item quarundam aliarum quaestionum*, Lyon, 1518 (reprinted Frankfurt am Main: Minerva, 1967).
—— *Quodlibeta*, Ms. London, British Library, Royal 10, C VI, f. 141vb–173vb.
Holmström-Hintikka, G. (1991) *Action, Purpose and Will. A Formal Theory* (Acta Philosophica Fennica 50), Helsinki: Societas Philosophica Fennica.
Holopainen, T. (forthcoming) *Faith and Reason in the Eleventh Century*.
Holopainen, T.M. (1991) *William Ockham's Theory of the Foundation of Ethics* (Publications of Luther-Agricola-Society B 20), Helsinki: Luther-Agricola-Society.

Honnefelder, L. (1972) 'Die Lehre von der doppelten *ratitudo entis* und ihre Bedeutung für die Metaphysik des Johannes Duns Scotus', in *Deus et Homo ad mentem I. Duns Scoti: Acta Tertii Congressus Scotistici Internationalis 1970* (Studia Scholastico-scotistica 5), Rome: Commissio Scotistica, 661–71.

—— (1979) *Ens inquantum ens: Der Begriff des Seienden als solchen als Gegestand der Metaphysik nach der Lehre des Johannes Duns Scotus* (Beiträge zur Geschichte der Philosophie und Theologie des Mittelalters, NF 16), Münster: Aschendorff.

Hopkins, J. (1972) *A Companion to the Study of St Anselm*, Minneapolis, MN: University of Minnesota Press.

Hourani, G. (1972) 'Ibn Sina on Necessary and Possible Existence', *The Philosophical Forum* 4: 74–86.

Hugh of Saint-Victor, *De sacramentis christianae fidei*, PL 176, 173–618.

Hughes, G.E. (1989) 'The Modal Logic of John Buridan', in G. Corsi, C. Mangione and M. Mugnai (eds) *Atti del Convegno Internazionale di Storia della Logica. Le Teorie delle Modalità*, Bologna: CLUEB, 93–111.

Irwin, T. (1988) *Aristotle's First Principles*, Oxford: Clarendon.

Isaac, J. (1953) *Le Peri Hermeneias en Occident de Boèce à Saint Thomas* (Bibliothèque Thomiste 29), Paris: Vrin.

Ivry, A.L. (1982) 'Maimonides on Possibility' in J. Reinharz and D. Swetschinski (eds) *Mystics, Philosophers, and Politicians: Essays in Jewish Intellectual History in Honor of Alexander Altmann*, Durham, NC: Duke University Press, 67–84.

—— (1985) 'Providence, Divine Omniscience and Possibility: The Case of Maimonides', in T. Rudavsky (ed.) *Divine Omniscience and Omnipotence in Medieval Philosophy* (Synthese Historical Library 25), Dordrecht: Reidel, 143–59.

Jacobi, K. (1977) 'Kontingente Naturgeschehnisse', *Studia Mediewistyczne* 18: 3–70.

—— (1980) *Die Modalbegriffe in den logischen Schriften des Wilhelm von Shyreswood und in anderen Kompendien des 12. und 13. Jahrhunderts: Funktionsbestimmung und Gebrauch in der logischen Analyse*, Cologne: Brill.

—— (1983) 'Statements about Events: Modal and Tense Analysis in Medieval Logic', *Vivarium* 12: 85–107.

—— (1985) 'Diskussionen über unpersönliche Aussagen in Peter Abaelards Kommentar zu *Peri hermeneias*', in E.P. Bos (ed.) *Medieval Semantics and Metaphysics. Studies Dedicated to L.M. de Rijk* (Artistarium Supplementa 2), Nijmegen: Ingenium Publishers, 1–63.

—— (1986) 'Peter Abelard's Investigations into the Meaning and Functions of the Speech Sign "est" ' in S. Knuuttila and J. Hintikka (eds) *The Logic of Being: Historical Studies* (Synthese Historical Library 28), Dordrecht: Reidel, 145–80.

—— (1988) 'Logic: The Later Twelfth Century', in P. Dronke (ed.) *A History of Twelfth-century Western Philosophy*, Cambridge: Cambridge University Press, 227–51.

Jalbert, G. (1961) *Nécessité et contingence chez Saint Thomas d'Aquin et chez ses prédécesseurs*, Ottawa: Editions de l'Université d'Ottawa.

Jerome, *Epistulae*, ed. I. Hilberg (CSEL 54), Vienna: F. Tempsky, 1910.

John of Salisbury, *Metalogicon*, ed. C.C.J. Webb, Oxford: Clarendon, 1929.
Jolivet, J. (1966) 'Eléments du concept de nature chez Abélard', in *La filosofia della natura nel medioevo. Atti del terzo congresso internazionale di filosofia medioevale*, Milan: Società editrice Vita e pensiero, 297–304.
—— (1982) *Arts du langage et théologie chez Abélard*, Paris: Vrin.
Jolivet, J. and de Libera, A. (eds) (1987) *Gilbert de Poitiers et ses contemporains: Aux origines de la logica modernorum* (History of Logic 5), Naples: Bibliopolis.
Judson, L. (1983) 'Eternity and Necessity in *De Caelo* I.12: A Discussion of Sarah Waterlow, *Passage and Possibility: A Study of Aristotle's Modal Concepts*', *Oxford Studies in Ancient Philosophy* 1: 217–55.
Kahn, C. (1973) *The Verb 'Be' in Ancient Greek* (Foundations of Language, Supplementary Series 16), Dordrecht: Reidel.
—— (1986) 'Retrospect on the Verb "to be" and the Concept of Being', in S. Knuuttila and J. Hintikka (eds) *The Logic of Being: Historical Studies* (Synthese Historical Library 28), Dordrecht: Reidel, 1–28.
Kane, W.H. (1957) 'The Extent of Natural Philosophy', *New Scholasticism* 31: 85–97.
Kant, I. (1983) *Grundlegung zur Metaphysik der Sitten*, in *Werke*, vol. 6, ed. W. Weischedel, Darmstadt: Wissenschaftliche Buchgesellschaft.
Kantola, I. (forthcoming) *Probability and Moral Uncertainty in Late Medieval and Early Modern Thought*.
Kapp, E. (1931) 'Syllogistik', in Pauly-Wissowa, *Real-Encyclopädie der classischen Altertumswissenschaft*, vol. IV A, Stuttgart: Metzlersche Verlagsbuchhandlung, 1046–67. A partial English translation is in J. Barnes, M. Schofield and R. Sorabji (eds) (1975) *Articles on Aristotle 1: Science*, London: Duckworth, 35–49.
—— (1943) *Greek Foundations of Traditional Logic*, New York: Columbia University Press.
Karger, E. (1980) 'Would Ockham Have Shaved Wyman's Beard', *Franciscan Studies* 40: 244–64.
Kenny, A. (1969) *The Five Ways* (Studies in Ethics and the Philosophy of Religion), New York: Schocken Books.
—— (1979) *The God of the Philosophers*, Oxford: Clarendon.
Kilvington, Richard, *Sophismata*, ed. N. Kretzmann and B. Kretzmann (Auctores Britannici Medii Aevi 12), Oxford: Oxford University Press, 1990.
King, P. (1985) *Jean Buridan's Logic. The Treatise on Supposition. The Treatise on Consequences* (translation with introduction and notes) (Synthese Historical Library 27), Dordrecht: Reidel.
Kirwan, C. (1971) *Aristotle's Metaphysics, Books IV, V, and VI* (translation with notes) (Clarendon Aristotle Series), Oxford: Clarendon.
—— (1986) 'Aristotle on the Necessity of the Present', *Oxford Studies in Ancient Philosophy* 4: 167–87.
—— (1989) *Augustine*, London: Routledge.
Kneale, W. and Kneale, M. (1962) *The Development of Logic*, Oxford: Clarendon.
Knuuttila, S. (1981a) 'Time and Modality in Scholasticism', in S. Knuuttila (ed.) *Reforging the Great Chain of Being: Studies of the History of Modal Theories* (Synthese Historical Library 20), Dordrecht: Reidel, 163–257.

—— (ed.) (1981b) *Reforging the Great Chain of Being: Studies of the History of Modal Theories* (Synthese Historical Library 20), Dordrecht: Reidel.
—— (1982) 'Modal Logic', in N. Kretzmann, A. Kenny and J. Pinborg (eds) *The Cambridge History of Later Medieval Philosophy*, Cambridge: Cambridge University Press, 342–57.
—— (1986a) 'Being qua Being in Thomas Aquinas and John Duns Scotus', in S. Knuuttila and J. Hintikka (eds) *The Logic of Being: Historical Studies* (Synthese Historical Library 28), Dordrecht: Reidel, 201–22.
—— (1986b) 'Remarks on the Background of the Fourteenth Century Limit Decision Controversies', in M. Asztalos (ed.) *The Editing of Theological and Philosophical Texts from the Middle Ages* (Acta Universitatis Stockholmiensis, Studia Latina Stockholmiensia 30), Stockholm: Almqvist & Wiksell, 245–66.
—— (ed.) (1988) *Modern Modalities. Studies of the History of Modal Theories from Medieval Nominalism to Logical Positivism* (Synthese Historical Library 33), Dordrecht: Kluwer.
—— (1989) 'Natural Necessity in Buridan', in S. Caroti (ed.) *Studies in Medieval Natural Philosophy* (Biblioteca di Nuncius. Studi e Testi 1), Florence: Leo S. Olschki, 155–76.
—— (forthcoming) 'Trinitarian Sophisms in Robert Holcot's Theology', in S. Read (ed.) *Sophisms in Medieval Logic and Grammar*, Dordrecht: Kluwer.
Knuuttila, S. and Hintikka, J. (eds) (1986) *The Logic of Being: Historical Studies* (Synthese Historical Library 28), Dordrecht: Reidel.
Knuuttila, S. and Lehtinen, A.I. (1979) 'Change and Contradiction: A Fourteenth-century Controversy', *Synthese* 40: 189–207.
Knuuttila, S. and Yrjönsuuri, M. (1988) 'Norms and Action in Obligational Disputations', in O. Pluta (ed.) *Die Philosophie im 14. und 15. Jahrhundert* (Bochumer Studien zur Philosophie 10), Amsterdam: Grüner, 191–202.
Knuuttila, S., Ebbesen, S. and Työrinoja, R. (eds) (1990) *Knowledge and the Sciences in Medieval Philosophy. Proceedings of the Eighth International Congress of Medieval Philosophy II*, Helsinki: Luther-Agricola Society.
Köpf, U. (1974) *Die Anfänge der theologischen Wissenschaftstheorie im 13. Jahrhundert* (Beiträge zur historischen Theologie 49), Tübingen: J.C.B. Mohr.
Kretzmann, N. (1976) 'Incipit/desinit', in P.K. Machamer and R.G. Turnbull (eds) *Motion and Time, Space and Matter*, Columbus, OH: Ohio State University Press, 101–36.
—— (1982a) 'Continuity, Contrariety, Contradiction, and Change', in N. Kretzmann (ed.) *Infinity and Continuity in Ancient and Medieval Thought*, Ithaca, NY: Cornell University Press, 270–84.
Kretzmann, N. (ed.) (1982b) *Infinity and Continuity in Ancient and Medieval Thought*, Ithaca, NY: Cornell University Press.
—— (1985) ' "*Nos ipsi principia sumus*": Boethius and the Basis of Contingency', in T. Rudavsky (ed.) *Divine Omniscience and Omnipotence in Medieval Philosophy* (Synthese Historical Library 25), Dordrecht: Reidel, 23–50.
—— (1987) 'Boethius and the Truth about Tomorrow's Sea Battle', in L.M. de Rijk and H.A.G. Braakhuis (eds) *Logos and Pragma. Essays on the*

*Philosophy of Language in Honour of Professor Gabriel Nuchelmans* (Artistarium Supplementa 3), Nijmegen: Ingenium Publishers, 63–97.
—— (1988a) 'Tu scis hoc esse omne quod est hoc: Richard Kilvington and the Logic of Knowledge', in N. Kretzmann (ed.) *Meaning and Inference in Medieval Philosophy. Studies in Memory of Jan Pinborg* (Synthese Historical Library 32), Dordrecht: Kluwer, 225–45.
Kretzmann, N. (ed.) (1988b) *Meaning and Inference in Medieval Philosophy. Studies in Memory of Jan Pinborg* (Synthese Historical Library 32), Dordrecht: Kluwer.
Kretzmann, N. and Kretzmann, B. (1990) *The Sophismata of Richard Kilvington* (translation with introduction and commentary), Cambridge: Cambridge University Press.
Kretzmann, N. and Stump, E. (eds) (1988) *The Cambridge Translations of Medieval Philosophical Texts I: Logic and the Philosophy of Language*, Cambridge: Cambridge University Press.
Kretzmann, N., Kenny, A. and Pinborg, J. (eds) (1982) *The Cambridge History of Later Medieval Philosophy*, Cambridge: Cambridge University Press.
Kusch, M. (1989) *Language as a Calculus vs. Language as Universal Medium. A Study in Husserl, Heidegger and Gadamer* (Synthese Library 207), Dordrecht: Kluwer.
—— (1990) 'Natural Necessity in William of Ockham' in S. Knuuttila, S. Ebbesen and R. Työrinoja (eds) *Knowledge and the Sciences in Medieval Philosophy. Proceedings of the Eighth International Congress of Medieval Philosophy II*, Helsinki: Luther-Agricola Society, 231–9.
Lambert of Auxerre, *Logica (Summa Lamberti)*, ed. F. Alessio, Florence: La Nuova Italia Editrice, 1971.
Langston, D. (1986) *God's Willing Knowledge: The Influence of Scotus' Analysis of Omniscience*, University Park, PA: Pennsylvania University Press.
—— (1990) 'Scotus and Possible Worlds', in S. Knuuttila, S. Ebbesen and R. Työrinoja (eds) *Knowledge and the Sciences in Medieval Philosophy. Proceedings of the Eighth International Congress of Medieval Philosophy II*, Helsinki: Luther-Agricola Society, 240–7.
Leaman, O. (1988) *Averroes and the Philosophy*, Oxford: Clarendon.
Lear, J. (1980) *Aristotle and Logical Theory*, Cambridge: Cambridge University Press.
van der Lecq, R. (1981) 'Buridan on Modal Propositions', in H.A.G. Braakhuis, C.H. Kneepkens and L.M. de Rijk (eds) *English Logic and Semantics from the End of the Twelfth Century to the Time of Ockham and Burleigh* (Artistarium Supplementa 1), Nijmegen: Ingenium Publishers, 427–42.
—— (1987) 'The Sententiae secundum magistrum Petrum', in J. Jolivet and A. de Libera (eds) *Gilbert de Poitiers et ses contemporains. Aux origines de la logica modernorum* (History of Logic 5), Naples: Bibliopolis, 43–56.
Leibniz, G.W., *Die philosophischen Schriften I–VII*, ed. C.I. Gerhardt, Berlin, 1875–90 (reprinted Hildesheim, Olms 1965) (*Discours de Métaphysique* in vol. IV, 427–63).
—— *Philosophical Papers and Letters*, translated and edited with introduction and notes by L.E. Loemker, 2nd edn (Synthese Historical Library 2),

Dordrecht: Reidel, 1976.
Lenzen, W. (1978) *Recent Work in Epistemic Logic* (Acta Philosophica Fennica 30, 1), Amsterdam: North-Holland.
Lewis, D. (1986) *On the Plurality of Worlds*, Oxford: Basil Blackwell.
Lewis, N.T. (1987) 'Determinate Truth in Abelard', *Vivarium* 25: 81-109.
Lewry, O. (1981) 'Boethian Logic in the Medieval West', in M. Gibson (ed.) *Boethius: His Life, Thought and Influence*, Oxford: Basil Blackwell, 90-134.
de Libera, A. (1982) 'The Oxford and Paris Traditions in Logic', in N. Kretzmann, A. Kenny and J. Pinborg (eds) *The Cambridge History of Later Medieval Philosophy*, Cambridge: Cambridge University Press, 174-87.
Locke, J., *An Essay Concerning Human Understanding*, ed. P.H. Nidditch, Oxford: Clarendon, 1975.
Lombard, Peter, *Sententiae in IV libris distinctae*, vols I and II (Spicilegium Bonaventurianum 4), Grottaferrata: Editiones Collegii S. Bonaventurae ad Claras Aquas, 1971.
Long, A.A. (1970) 'Stoic Determinism and Alexander of Aphrodisias *De fato* (i-xiv)', *Archiv für Geschichte der Philosophie* 52: 247-68.
Lovejoy, A. (1936) *The Great Chain of Being: A Study of the History of an Idea*, Cambridge, MA: Harvard University Press.
Łucasiewicz, J. (1951) *Aristotle's Syllogistic from the Standpoint of Modern Logic*, Oxford: Clarendon.
Luscombe, D.E. (1970) *The School of Peter Abelard*, Cambridge: Cambridge University Press.
—— (1988) 'Peter Abelard', in P. Dronke (ed.) *A History of Twelfth-century Western Philosophy*, Cambridge: Cambridge University Press, 279-307.
McCall, S. (1963) *Aristotle's Modal Logic*, Amsterdam: North-Holland.
—— (1969) 'Time and the Physical Modalities', *Monist* 53: 426-46.
McDermott, A.C.S. (1972) 'Notes on the Assertoric and Modal Propositional Logic of the Pseudo-Scotus', *Journal of the History of Philosophy* 10: 273-306.
McGrade, A.S. (1985) 'Plenty of Nothing: Ockham's Commitment to Real Possibles', *Franciscan Studies* 45: 145-56.
Maier, A. (1949) *Die Vorläufer Galileis im 14. Jahrhundert*, Rome: Edizioni di Storia e Letteratura.
—— (1967) *Ausgehendes Mittelalter. Gesammelte Aufsätze zur Geistesgeschichte des 14. Jahrhunderts II*, Rome: Edizioni di Storia e Letteratura.
Maierù, A. (1972) *Terminologia logica della tarda scolastica* (Lessico Intellettuale Europeo 8), Rome: Edizioni dell' Ateneo.
—— (1986) 'Logique et théologie trinitaire dans le moyen-agê tardif', in M. Asztalos (ed.) *The Editing of Theological and Philosophical Texts from the Middle Ages* (Acta Universitatis Stockholmiensis, Studia Latina Stockholmiensia 30), Stockholm: Almquist & Wiksell, 186-212.
—— (1988) 'Logic and Trinitarian Theology: De modo predicandi ac sylogizandi in divinis' in N. Kretzmann (ed.) *Meaning and Inference in Medieval Philosophy. Studies in Memory of Jan Pinborg* (Synthese Historical Library 32), Dordrecht: Kluwer, 247-95.
Maimonides, Moses, *The Guide of the Perplexed*, vols I and II, translated

with introduction and notes by Sh. Pines, Chicago, IL: University of Chicago Press, 1974.
Manekin, C.H. (1988) 'Problems of "Plenitude" in Maimonides and Gersonides', in R. Link-Salinger, R. Long and C.H. Manekin (eds) *A Straight Path: Studies in Medieval Philosophy and Culture: Essays in Honor of Arthur Hyman*, Washington, DC: Catholic University of America Press, 183–94.
—— (1992) *The Logic of Gersonides*, a translation of *Sefer ha-Heggesh ha-Yashar (The Book of the Correct Syllogism)* of Rabbi Levi ben Gershom with introduction, commentary and analytical glossary (The New Synthese Historical Library 40), Dordrecht: Kluwer.
Marenbon, J. (1981) *From the Circle of Alcuin to the School of Auxerre*, Cambridge: Cambridge University Press.
—— (1983) *Early Medieval Philosophy (480–1150): An Introduction*, London: Routledge & Kegan Paul.
—— (1988a) 'Gilbert of Poitiers', in P. Dronke (ed.) *A History of Twelfth-century Western Philosophy*, Cambridge: Cambridge University Press, 328–52.
—— (1988b) 'A Note on the Porretani', in P. Dronke (ed.) *A History of Twelfth-century Western Philosophy*, Cambridge: Cambridge University Press, 353–7.
—— (1991) 'Abelard's Concept of Possibility', in B. Mojsisch and O. Pluta (eds) *Historia philosophiae medii aevi: Studien zur Geschichte der Philosophie des Mittelalters*, Festschrift für Kurt Flasch, Grüner: Amsterdam.
Marmura, M.E. (1984) 'The Metaphysics of Efficient Causality in Avicenna', in M.E. Marmura (ed.) *Islamic Theology and Philosophy: Studies in Honor of G.F. Hourani*, New York: State University of New York Press, 172–87.
—— (1990) 'The Fortuna of the *Posterior Analytics* in the Arabic Middle Ages', in M. Asztalos, J.E. Murdoch and I. Niiniluoto (eds) *Knowledge and the Sciences in Medieval Philosophy. Proceedings of the Eighth International Congress of Medieval Philosophy I* (Acta Philosophica Fennica 48), Helsinki: Philosophical Society of Finland, 85–103.
Martin, C.J. (1987) 'Embarrassing Arguments and Surprising Conclusions in the Development of Theories of the Conditional in the Twelfth Century', in J. Jolivet and A. de Libera (eds) *Gilbert de Poitiers et ses contemporains: Aux origines de la logica modernorum* (History of Logic 5), Naples: Bibliopolis, 377–400.
Mates, B. (1968) 'Leibniz on Possible Worlds', in B. van Rootselaar and J.F. Staal (eds) *Logic, Methodology, and Philosophy of Science III: Proceedings of the Third International Congress* (Studies in Logic and the Foundations of Mathematics), Amsterdam: North-Holland, 507–29.
—— (1986) 'Identity and Predication in Plato', in S. Knuuttila and J. Hintikka (eds) *The Logic of Being: Historical Studies* (Synthese Historical Library 28), Dordrecht: Reidel, 29–47.
Meyerhoff, H. (1968) *Time in Literature*, Berkeley, CA: University of California Press.
Michael, F.S. (1976) 'What is the Master Argument of Diodorus Cronus?', *American Philosophical Quarterly* 13: 229–35.

Mignucci, M. (1969) 'Albert the Great's Approach to Aristotelian Modal Syllogistic', in *Arts libéraux et philosophie au moyen âge: Actes du IVe Congrès international de philosophie médiévale*, Montréal: Institut d'Études Médiévales, and Paris: Vrin, 901-11.
—— (1978) 'Sur la logique modale des stoiciens', in J. Brunschwig (ed.) *Les Stoiciens et leur logique*, Paris: Vrin, 317-46.
—— (1989) 'Truth and Modality in Late Antiquity: Boethius on Future Contingent Propositions', in G. Corsi, C. Mangione and M. Mugnai (eds) *Atti del Convegno Internazionale di Storia della Logica. Le Teorie delle Modalità*, Bologna: CLUEB, 47-78.
Miller, F.D. (1974) 'Aristotle on the Reality of Time', *Archiv für Geschichte der Philosophie* 56: 132-55.
—— (1982) 'Aristotle against the Atomists', in N. Kretzmann (ed.) *Infinity and Continuity in Ancient and Medieval Thought*, Ithaca, NY: Cornell University Press, 87-111.
Minio-Paluello, L. (ed.) (1958) *Twelfth Century Logic: Texts and Studies II*, Rome: Edizioni di Storia e Letteratura.
Moody, E.A. (1953) *Truth and Consequence in Medieval Logic* (Studies in Logic and the Foundations of Mathematics), Amsterdam: North-Holland.
—— (1975) *Studies in Medieval Philosophy, Science, and Logic: Collected Papers 1933-1969*, Berkeley, CA: University of California Press.
Moonan, L. (1980) 'Impossibility and Peter Damian', *Archiv für Geschichte der Philosophie* 62: 146-63.
Morgan, C.G. (1979) 'Modality, Analogy, and Ideal Experiments according to C.S. Peirce', *Synthese* 41: 65-83.
Morrow, G.R. (1966) 'Qualitative Change in Aristotle's Physics', in I. Düring (ed.) *Naturphilosophie bei Aristoteles*, Heidelberg: Carl Winter Universitätsverlag, 154-67.
de Muralt, A. (1986) 'La toute-puissance divine, le possible et la non-contradiction. Le principe de l'intelligibilité chez Occam', *Revue philosophique de Louvain* 84: 345-61.
Murdoch, J.E. (1974) 'Philosophy and the Enterprise of Science in the Later Middle Ages', in Y. Elkana (ed.) *The Interaction between Science and Philosophy*, New York: Humanities Press, 51-74.
—— (1975) 'From Social into Intellectual Factors: An Aspect of the Unitary Character of Medieval Learning', in J.E. Murdoch and E.D. Sylla (eds) *The Cultural Context of Medieval Learning* (Synthese Library 76), Dordrecht: Reidel, 271-339.
Newell, J.H. (1990) 'Grammaticus et Ethicus: William of Conches' Search for Order', in S. Knuuttila, S. Ebbesen and R. Työrinoja (eds) *Knowledge and the Sciences in Medieval Philosophy. Proceedings of the Eighth International Congress of Medieval Philosophy II*, Helsinki: Luther-Agricola Society, 275-84.
Nicholas of Cusa, *Trialogus de Possest*, ed. R. Steiger (*Opera omnia iussu et auctoritate Academiae Litterarum Heidelbergensis* XI, 2), Hamburg: Meiner, 1973.
Nielsen, L. (1982a) *Theology and Philosophy in the Twelfth Century: A Study of Gilbert Porreta's Thinking and the Theological Expositions of the Doctrine of the Incarnation during the Period 1130-1180* (Acta Theologica Danica XV), Leiden: Brill.

—— (1982b) 'Thomas Bradwardine's Treatise on "incipit" and "desinit". Edition and Introduction', *Cahiers de l'Institut du Moyen-âge grec et latin*, Université de Copenhague 42.
Niiniluoto, I. (1986) 'Hypothetical Imperatives and Conditional Obligations', *Synthese* 66: 111-34.
—— (1988) 'From Possibility to Probability: British Discussions on Modality in the Nineteenth Century', in S. Knuuttila (ed.) *Modern Modalities. Studies of the History of Modal Theories from Medieval Nominalism to Logical Positivism* (Synthese Historical Library 33), Dordrecht: Kluwer.
Normore, C. (1975) 'The Logic of Time and Modality in the Later Middle Ages: The Contribution of William of Ockham', Ph.D. dissertation, University of Toronto.
—— (1982) 'Future Contingents', in N. Kretzmann, A. Kenny and J. Pinborg (eds) *The Cambridge History of Later Medieval Philosophy*, Cambridge: Cambridge University Press, 358-81.
—— (1985) 'Divine Omniscience, Omnipotence, and Future Contingents: An Overview', in T. Rudavsky (ed.) *Divine Omniscience and Omnipotence in Medieval Philosophy* (Synthese Historical Library 25), Dordrecht: Reidel.
—— (1986) 'Meaning and Objective Being: Descartes and His Sources', in A. Rorty (ed.) *Essays in Descartes' Meditations*, Berkeley, CA: University of California Press, 223-241.
—— (1987) 'The Tradition of Mediaeval Nominalism', in J.F. Wippel (ed.) *Studies in Medieval Philosophy* (Studies in Philosophy and the History of Philosophy 17), Washington, DC: Catholic University of America Press, 201-17.
Nuchelmans, G. (1973) *Theories of the Proposition: Ancient and Medieval Conceptions of the Bearers of Truth and Falsity* (North-Holland Linguistic Series 8), Amsterdam: North-Holland.
—— (1982) 'The Semantics of Propositions', in N. Kretzmann, A. Kenny and J. Pinborg (eds) *The Cambridge History of Later Medieval Philosophy*, Cambridge: Cambridge University Press, 197-210.
Oakley, F. (1984) *Omnipotence, Covenant, and Order. An Excursion in the History of Ideas from Abelard to Leibniz*, Ithaca, NY: Cornell University Press.
Obertello, L. (ed.) (1981) *Atti del congresso internazionale di studi Boeziani*, Rome: Editrice Herder.
Origen, *In Matthaeum commentariorum series*, in *Opera*, PG 13.
Owens, J. (1963) *The Doctrine of Being in the Aristotelian Metaphysics*, 2nd edn, Toronto: Pontifical Institute of Mediaeval Studies.
Panaccio, C. (1990) 'La logique comme science pratique selon Occam', in S. Knuuttila, S. Ebbesen and R. Työrinoja (eds) *Knowledge and the Sciences in Medieval Philosophy. Proceedings of the Eighth International Congress of Medieval Philosophy II*, Helsinki: Luther-Agricola Society, 618-25.
Patch, H.R. (1935) 'Necessity in Boethius and the Neoplatonists', *Speculum* 10: 393-404.
Patterson, R. (1989) 'The Case of the Two Barbaras: Basic Approaches to Aristotle's Modal Logic', *Oxford Studies in Ancient Philosophy* 7: 1-40.
Patzig, G. (1969) *Die aristotelische Syllogistik*, 3rd edn, Göttingen: Vandenhoeck & Ruprecht. In English in *Aristotle's Theory of the*

*Syllogism* (Synthese Library 16), Dordrecht: Reidel, 1968.
Peirce, C.S. (1901) 'Modality', in J.M. Baldwin (ed.) *Dictionary of Philosophy and Psychology*, Cloucester, MA: Smith.
Peter of Ailly, *Questiones super libros Sententiarum*, Paris, 1500.
Peter of Poitiers, *Sententiae*, vols I and II, ed. P.S. Moore and M. Dulong (Publications in Medieval Studies 7, 11), Notre Dame, IN: Notre Dame University Press, 1961.
Peter of Spain, *Tractatus called afterwards Summule logicales*, ed. L.M. de Rijk (Wijsgerige teksten en studies 22), Assen: Van Gorcum, 1972.
Philoponus, *In Aristotelis Analytica priora commentaria*, ed. M. Wallies (Commentaria in Aristotelem Graeca 13.2), Berlin: Reimer, 1905.
Pinborg, J. (1972) *Logik und Semantik im Mittelalter. Ein Überblick*, Stuttgart-Bad Canstatt: Frommann-Holzboog.
—— (1979) 'The English Contribution to Logic before Ockham', *Synthese* 40: 19–42.
Plato, *Opera*, ed. J. Burnet (Scriptorum Classicorum Bibliotheca Oxoniensis), Oxford: Oxford University Press, 1900–7.
Plotinus, *Opera*, vols I and II, ed. P. Henry and H. R. Schwyzer (Museum Lessianum, Series philosophica 33–34), Paris: Desclée de Brouwer, 1951–9.
Plutarch, *De stoicorum repugnantiis*, in *Plutarch's Moralia*, vol. 13.2 (Loeb Classical Library), ed. with notes by H. Cherniss, London: Heinemann, and Cambridge, MA: Harvard University Press, 1976.
Poser, H. (1969) *Zur Theorie der Modalbegriffe bei G.W. Leibniz* (Studia Leibnitiana Supplementa 6), Wiesbaden: Franz Steiner.
—— (1988) 'The Failure of Logical Positivism to Cope with Problems of Modal Theory', in S. Knuuttila (ed.) *Modern Modalities. Studies of the History of Modal Theories from Medieval Nominalism to Logical Positivism* (Synthese Historical Library 33), Dordrecht: Kluwer, 311–27.
Prior, A.N. (1955) 'Diodoran Modalities', *Philosophical Quarterly* 5: 205–13.
—— (1957) *Time and Modality*, Oxford: Clarendon.
—— (1967) *Past, Present and Future*, Oxford: Clarendon.
—— (1968) *Papers on Time and Tense*, Oxford: Clarendon.
Purtill, R. (1973) 'The Master Argument', *Apeiron* 7: 31–6.
Randi, E. (1986) '*Lex est in potestate agentis*: Note per una storia della idea scotista di *potentia absoluta*', in A. Vettese (ed.) *Sopra la volta del mundo*, Bergamo: Pierluigi Lubrina Editore.
Raoul of Longchamps (Radulphus de Longo Campo), *In Anticlaudianum Alani commentum*, ed. J. Sulowski, Wrocław: Ossolineum, 1972.
Reesor, M.E. (1965) 'Fate and Possibility in Early Stoic Philosophy', *Phoenix* 19: 285–97.
Rescher, N. (1963) *Studies in the History of Arabic Logic*, Pittsburgh, PA: University of Pittsburgh Press.
—— (1964) 'Aristotle's Theory of Modal Syllogisms and Its Interpretation', in M. Bunge (ed.) *The Critical Approach to Science and Philosophy. In Honor of Carl Popper*, Glencoe, IL: The Free Press, 152–77.
—— (1966a) *Temporal Modalities in Arabic Logic* (Foundations of Language, Supplementary Series 2) Dordrecht: Reidel.
—— (1966b) 'A Version of the "Master Argument" of Diodorus Cronus', *Journal of Philosophy* 63: 438–55.

—— (1968) 'Truth and Necessity in Temporal Perspective', in R. Gale (ed.) *The Philosophy of Time: A Collection of Essays*, New York: Humanities Press, 183–220.
Rescher, N. and Urquhart, A. (1971) *Temporal Logic*, Vienna: Springer.
Richard of Campsall, *The Works of Richard of Campsall I: Quaestiones super librum Priorum Analeticorum*, ed. E.A. Synan, Toronto: Pontifical Institute of Mediaeval Studies, 1968.
van Rijen, J. (1989) *Aspects of Aristotle's Logic of Modalities* (Synthese Historical Library 35), Dordrecht: Kluwer.
de Rijk, L.M. (1962, 1967) *Logica Modernorum. A Contribution to the History of Early Terminist Logic:* vol. I; *On the Twelfth Century Theories of Fallacy*; vol. II, 1–2, *The Origin and Early Development of the Theory of Supposition* (Wijsgerige teksten en studies 6, 16), Assen: Van Gorcum.
—— (1973) 'The Development of Suppositio Naturalis in Medieval Logic II: Fourteenth Century Natural Supposition as Atemporal (Omnitemporal) Supposition', *Vivarium* 11: 43–79.
—— (1974) 'Some Thirteenth Century Tracts on the Game of Obligation', *Vivarium* 12: 94–123.
—— (1975a) 'Some Thirteenth Century Tracts on the Game of Obligation', *Vivarium* 13: 22–54.
—— (1975b) 'Another "Speculum puerorum" attributed to Richard Billingham. Introduction and text', *Medioevo* 1: 203–35.
—— (1976) 'Some Thirteenth Century Tracts on the Game of Obligation', *Vivarium* 14: 26–49.
—— (1982) 'The Origins of the Theory of the Properties of Terms', in N. Kretzmann, A. Kenny and J. Pinborg (eds) *The Cambridge History of Later Medieval Philosophy*, Cambridge: Cambridge University Press, 161–73.
—— (1988) 'On Boethius's Notion of Being: A Chapter of Boethian Semantics', in N. Kretzmann (ed.) *Meaning and Inference in Medieval Philosophy. Studies in Memory of Jan Pinborg* (Synthese Historical Library 32), Dordrecht: Kluwer, 1–29.
de Rijk, L.M. and Braakhuis, H.A.G. (eds) (1987) *Logos and Pragma. Essays on the Philosophy of Language in Honour of Professor Gabriel Nuchelmans* (Artistarium Supplementa 3), Nijmegen: Ingenium Publishers.
Rist, J.M. (1967) *Plotinus: The Road to Reality*, Cambridge: Cambridge University Press.
—— (1969) *Stoic Philosophy*, Cambridge: Cambridge University Press.
Robert of Melun, *Oeuvres II*, ed. R.M. Martin (Spicilegium Sacrum Lovaniense 18), Louvain, 1938.
Rohr, M.D. (1981) 'Empty Forms in Plato', in S. Knuuttila (ed.) *Reforging the Great Chain of Being: Studies of the History of Modal Theories* (Synthese Historical Library 20), Dordrecht: Reidel, 19–56.
Roseth, Roger, *Lectura super Sententias*, Ms. Oxford, Oriel College 15, *f.* 235r–279v.
Roure, M.-L. (1970) 'La problématique des propositions insolubles au XIIIe siècle et au début du XIVe, suivie de l'édition des traités de W. Shyreswood, W. Burleigh et Th. Bradwardine', *Archives d'histoire doctrinale et littéraire du moyen âge* 37: 205–326.

Rudavsky, T. (ed.) (1985) *Divine Omniscience and Omnipotence in Medieval Philosophy* (Synthese Historical Library 25), Dordrecht: Reidel.
Russell, B. (1956) *Logic and Knowledge. Essays 1901–1950*, ed. R.C. Marsh, London: Allen & Unwin.
Ryan, C.J. (1983) 'Man's Free Will in the Works of Siger of Brabant', *Mediaeval Studies* 45, 155–99.
Saarinen, R. (forthcoming) *Weakness of Will in Medieval Christian Thought*.
Sambursky, S. (1971) *Physics of the Stoics*, London: Hutchinson (1st edn, London: Routledge & Kegan Paul, 1959).
Schepers, H. (1965) 'Zum Problem der Kontingenz bei Leibniz. Die beste der möglichen Welten', in *Collegium Philosophicum. Studien Joachim Ritter zum 60. Geburtstag*, Basel: Schwabe, 326–50.
Schmidt, K.J. (1989; 'Eine modal prädikatenlogische Interpretation der modalen Syllogistik des Aristoteles', *Phronesis* 34: 80–106.
Schmidt, M.A. (1956) *Gottheit und Trinität nach dem Kommentar des Gilbert Porreta zu Boethius, De Trinitate*, Basel: Verlag für Recht und Gesellschaft.
Schuhl, P.-M. (1960) *Le dominateur et les possibles*, Paris: Presses Universitaires de France.
Schwamm, H. (1934) *Das göttliche Vorherwissen bei Duns Scotus und seinen ersten Anhängern* (Philosophie und Grenzwissenschaften V, 1–4), Innsbruck: Rauch.
Scott, T.K. (1965) 'John Buridan on the Objects of Demonstrative Science', *Speculum* 40: 654–73.
Sedley, D. (1977) 'Diodorus Cronus and Hellenistic Philosophy', *Proceedings of the Cambridge Philological Society, New Series* 23: 74–120.
Seel, G. (1982) *Die Aristotelische Modaltheorie* (Quellen und Studien zur Philosophie 16), Berlin: Walter de Gruyter.
Segerberg, K. (1989) 'Getting Started: Beginnings in the Logic of Action', in G. Corsi, C. Mangione and M. Mugnai (eds) *Atti del Convegno Internazionale di Storia della Logica. Le Teorie delle Modalità*, Bologna: CLUEB, 221–50.
*Sententiae Petri Abaelardi (Sententiae Hermanni)*, ed. S. Buzzetti, Firenze: La Nuova Italia Editrice, 1983.
Serene, E. (1981) 'Anselm's Modal Conceptions', in S. Knuuttila (ed.) *Reforging the Great Chain of Being: Studies of the History of Modal Theories* (Synthese Historical Library 20), Dordrecht: Reidel, 117–62.
Shank, M.H. (1988) *'Unless You Believe, You Shall Not Understand': Logic, University, and Society in Late Medieval Vienna*, Princeton, NJ: Princeton University Press.
Sharples, R.W. (1975) 'Aristotelian and Stoic Conceptions of Necessity in the *De fato* of Alexander of Aphrodisias', *Phronesis* 20: 247–74.
—— (1978) 'Alexander of Aphrodisias *De fato*: Some Parallels', *Classical Quarterly* 28: 243–66.
—— (1982) 'An Ancient Dialogue on Possibility: Alexander of Aphrodisias, *Quaestio* I.4', *Archiv für Geschichte der Philosophie* 64: 23–38.
—— (1983) *Alexander of Aphrodisias on Fate*, text, translation and commentary, London: Duckworth.
Shiel, J. (1958) 'Boethius's Commentaries on Aristotle', *Mediaeval and Renaissance Studies* 4: 217–44.

Siger of Brabant, *Quaestiones in Metaphysicam: Edition revue de la Reportation de Munich, texte inédit de la Reportation de Vienne*, ed. W. Dunphy (Philosophes médiévaux 24), Louvain-la-Neuve: Editions de l'Institut Supérieur de Philosophie, 1981.
—— *Quaestiones in Physicam*, in *Ecrits de logique, de morale et de physique*, ed. B. Bazán and A. Zimmermann (Philosophes médiévaux 14), Louvain: Publications Universitaires, 1974.
Simon of Tournai, *Disputationes*, ed. J. Warichez (Spicilegium Sacrum Lovaniense 12), Louvain, 1932.
—— *Expositio super simbolum*, ed. N.M. Häring (1974) *Archives d'histoire doctrinale et littéraire du moyen âge* 41: 39–112.
Simplicius, *In Aristotelis Categorias commentarium*, ed. C. Kalbfleisch (Commentaria in Aristotelem Graeca 8), Berlin: Reimer, 1907.
Smith, R. (1989) *Aristotle's Prior Analytics*, translated with introduction, notes and commentary, Indianapolis, IN: Hackett.
Sorabji, R. (1976) 'Aristotle on the Instant of Change', *Proceedings of the Aristotelian Society*, supplement 50: 69–89.
—— (1980) *Necessity, Cause, and Blame: Perspectives on Aristotle's Theory*, Ithaca, NY: Cornell University Press.
—— (1983) *Time, Creation and the Continuum: Theories in Antiquity and the Early Middle Ages*, London: Duckworth.
Spade, P.V. (1980) *Peter of Ailly: Concepts and Insolubles* (translation with notes) (Synthese Historical Library 19), Dordrecht: Reidel.
—— (1982a) 'Obligations: Developments in the Fourteenth Century', in N. Kretzmann, A. Kenny and J. Pinborg (eds) *The Cambridge History of Later Medieval Philosophy*, Cambridge: Cambridge University Press, 335–41.
—— (1982b) 'Quasi-Aristotelianism', in N. Kretzmann (ed.) *Infinity and Continuity in Ancient and Medieval Thought*, Ithaca, NY: Cornell University Press, 297–307.
—— (1982c) 'Three Theories of *Obligationes*: Burley, Kilvington and Swyneshed on Counterfactual Reasoning', *History and Philosophy of Logic* 3: 1–32.
—— (1982d) 'Insolubilia', in N. Kretzmann, A. Kenny and J. Pinborg (eds) *The Cambridge History of Later Medieval Philosophy*, Cambridge: Cambridge University Press, 246–53.
Spade, P.V. and Stump, E. (1983) 'Walter Burley and the *Obligationes* Attributed to William of Sherwood', *History and Philosophy of Logic* 4: 9–26.
Stanislaus of Znaim, *De vero et falso*, ed. V. Herold, Prague: Czechoslovak Academy of Sciences, 1971.
Stump, E. (1978) *Boethius's De topicis differentiis*, translated with notes and essays on the texts, Ithaca, NY: Cornell University Press.
—— (1982) 'Obligations: From the Beginnings to the Early Fourteenth Century', in N. Kretzmann, A. Kenny and J. Pinborg (eds) *The Cambridge History of Later Medieval Philosophy*, Cambridge: Cambridge University Press, 315–34.
—— (1988) *Boethius's In Ciceronis Topica*, translated with notes, Ithaca, NY: Cornell University Press.
—— (1989) *Dialectic and Its Place in the Development of Medieval Logic*,

Ithaca, NY: Cornell University Press.
Stump, E. and Kretzmann, N. (1981) 'Eternity', *Journal of Philosophy* 78: 429–58.
Sullivan, M.W. (1967) *Apuleian Logic* (Studies in Logic and the Foundations of Mathematics), Amsterdam: North-Holland.
Swyneshed, Roger *Obligationes*, ed. with commentary by P.V. Spade (1977), *Archives d'histoire doctrinale et littéraire du moyen âge* 44: 243–85.
Tabarroni, A. (1989) ' "Incipit" and "desinit" ', *Cahiers de l'Institut du Moyen-âge grec et latin, Université de Copenhague* 59: 61–111.
Tachau, K. (1987) 'Wodeham, Crathorn and Holcot: The Development of the Complexe significabile', in L.M. de Rijk and H.A.G. Braakhuis (eds) *Logos and Pragma. Essays on the Philosophy of Language in Honour of Professor Gabriel Nuchelmans* (Artistarium Supplementa 3), Nijmegen: Ingenium Publishers, 161–87.
—— (1988) *Vision and Certitude in the Age of Ockham. Optics, Epistemology and the Foundations of Semantics 1250–1345* (Studien und Texte zur Geistesgeschichte des Mittelalters 22), Leiden: Brill.
Talanga, J. (1986) *Zukunftsurteile und Fatum. Eine Untersuchung über Aristoteles'* De interpretatione 9 *und Ciceros* De fato *mit einem Überblick über die spätantiken Heimarmene-Lehren*, Bonn: Rudolf Habelt.
Tertullian, *De cultu feminarum*, ed. A. Kroymann (CSEL 70), Vienna: Hoelder-Pichler-Tempsky, and Leipzig: Becker & Erler, 1942.
Thierry of Chartres, *Commentaries on Boethius by Thierry of Chartres and his School*, ed. N.M. Häring, Toronto: Pontifical Institute of Mediaeval Studies, 1971.
de la Torre, B.R. (1987) *Thomas Buckingham and the Contingency of Futures: The Possibility of Human Freedom. A Study and Edition of Thomas Buckingham, 'De contingentia futurorum et arbitrii libertate'* (Publications in Medieval Studies 25), Notre Dame, IN: Notre Dame University Press.
Trifogli, C. (forthcoming) 'Giles of Rome on the Instant of Time', *Synthese*.
Tweedale, M. (1976) *Abailard on Universals*, Amsterdam: North-Holland.
—— (1988) 'Logic from the Late Eleventh Century to the Time of Abelard', in P. Dronke (ed.) *A History of Twelfth-century Western Philosophy*, Cambridge: Cambridge University Press, 196–226.
Uthred of Boldon, *Quaestiones seu determinationes*, q. 5, a. 1–2, Ms. Fribourg, Convent des Cordeliers 26, *f.* 112vb–117va.
Vitruvius, *De architectura*, ed. F. Granger (Loeb Classical Library), London: Heinemann, and Cambridge, MA: Harvard University Press, 1955.
Vos, A. (1985) 'On the Philosophy of the Young Duns Scotus: Some Semantical and Logical Aspects', in E.P. Bos (ed.) *Medieval Semantics and Metaphysics: Studies Dedicated to L.M. de Rijk* (Artistarium Supplementa 2), Nijmegen: Ingenium Publishers, 195–220.
Vuillemin, J. (1979) 'L'argument dominateur', *Revue de métaphysique et de morale*: 225–57.
—— (1983) 'Le carré chrysippéen des modalités', *Dialectica* 37: 235–47.
—— (1984) *Nécessité ou contingence: l'aporie de Diodore et les systèmes philosophiques*, Paris: Les Editions de Minuit.
Wallace, W.A. (1972) *Causality and Scientific Explanation I*, Ann Arbor, MI: University of Michigan Press.

—— (1981) *Prelude to Galileo: Essays on Medieval and Sixteenth-Century Sources of Galileo's Thought* (Boston Studies in the Philosophy of Science 62), Dordrecht: Reidel.
Walton, D. (1976) 'Logical Form and Agency', *Philosophical Studies* 29: 75–89.
Waterlow, S. (1982a) *Passage and Possibility: A Study of Aristotle's Modal Concepts*, Oxford: Clarendon.
—— (1982b) *Nature, Change, and Agency in Aristotle's Physics*, Oxford: Clarendon.
Weidemann, H. (1980) 'Ansätze zu einer Logik des Wissens bei Walter Burley', *Archiv für Geschichte der Philosophie* 62: 32–45.
—— (1981) 'Zur Semantik der Modalbegriffe bei Peter Abaelard', *Medioevo* 7: 1–40.
—— (1986a) 'Aristoteles und das Problem des kausalen Determinismus (*Met*. E 3)', *Phronesis* 31: 27–50.
—— (1986b) 'Die Aristotelische Modaltheorie: Eine Auseinandersetzung mit dem gleichnamigen Buch von Gerhard Seel', *Zeitschrift für philosophische Forschung* 40: 104–20.
Welsch, W. (1987) *Aisthesis: Grundzüge und Perspektiven der aristotelischen Sinneslehre*, Stuttgart: Klett-Cotta.
Wetherbee, W. (1988) 'Philosophy, Cosmology, and the Twelfth-Century Renaissance', in P. Dronke (ed.) *A History of Twelfth-century Western Philosophy*, Cambridge: Cambridge University Press, 21–53.
White, M.J. (1985) *Agency and Integrality. Philosophical Themes in the Ancient Discussions of Determinism and Responsibility* (Philosophical Studies Series in Philosophy 32), Dordrecht: Reidel.
Wieland, W. (1966) 'Die aristotelische Theorie der Notwendigkeitsschlüsse', *Phronesis* 11: 35–50.
—— (1972) 'Die aristotelische Theorie der Möglichkeitsschlüsse', *Phronesis* 17: 124–52.
—— (1975) 'Die aristotelische Theorie der Syllogismen mit modal gemischten Prämissen', *Phronesis* 20: 77–92.
Wiles, M.F. (1965) 'Miracles in the Early Church', in C.F.D. Moule (ed.) *Miracles*, London: Mowbray, 221–34.
William of Auxerre, *Summa aurea*, ed. J. Ribaillier, Paris: Editions du CNRS, and Rome: Editiones Collegii S. Bonaventurae ad Claras Aquas, 1980–6.
William of Conches, *Dragmaticon*, ed. G. Gratarolus, Strasbourg, 1567 (reprinted, Frankfurt am Main: Minerva, 1967).
—— *Philosophia*, ed. G. Maurach, Pretoria: University of South Africa, 1980.
William of Ockham, *Opera philosophica et theologica*, St Bonaventure: Franciscan Institute of St Bonaventure University, 1967–84 (OP, Opera philosophica; OT, Opera theologica).
—— *Scriptum in librum primum Sententiarum. Ordinatio, prol. and dist. 1*, ed. G. Gál and S. Brown (OT 1), St Bonaventure: Franciscan Institute of St Bonaventure University, 1967.
—— *Scriptum in librum primum Sententiarum. Ordinatio, dist. 2–3*, ed. S. Brown and G. Gál (OT 2), St Bonaventure: Franciscan Institute of St Bonaventure University, 1970.

—— *Scriptum in librum primum Sententiarum. Ordinatio, dist. 4–18*, ed. G. I. Etzkorn (OT 3), St Bonaventure: Franciscan Institute of St Bonaventure University, 1977.

—— *Scriptum in librum primum Sententiarum. Ordinatio, dist. 19–48*, ed. G.I. Etzkorn and F.E. Kelley (OT 4), St Bonaventure: Franciscan Institute of St Bonaventure University, 1979.

—— *Quaestiones in librum tertium Sententarium. Reportatio*, ed. F.E. Kelley and G.I. Etzkorn (OT 6), St Bonaventure: Franciscan Institute of St Bonaventure University, 1982.

—— *Quaestiones variae*, ed. G.I. Etzkorn, F.E. Kelley and J.C. Wey (OT 8), St Bonaventure: Franciscan Institute of St Bonaventure University, 1984.

—— *Quodlibeta septem*, ed. J.C. Wey (OT 9), St Bonaventure: Franciscan Institute of St Bonaventure University, 1980.

—— *Summa logicae*, ed. Ph. Boehner, G. Gál and S. Brown (OP 1), St Bonaventure: Franciscan Institute of St Bonaventure University, 1974.

—— *Expositio in librum Perihermeneias Aristotelis*, ed. A. Gambatese and S. Brown (OP 2), St Bonaventure: Franciscan Institute of St Bonaventure University, 1978.

—— *Expositio super libros Elenchorum*, ed. F. del Punta (OP 3), St Bonaventure: Franciscan Institute of St Bonaventure University, 1979.

—— *Expositio in libros Physicorum Aristotelis, prol. et libri I–III*, ed. V. Richter and G. Leipold (OP 4), St Bonaventure: Franciscan Institute of St Bonaventure University, 1985.

—— *Expositio in libros Physicorum Aristotelis, libri IV–VIII*, ed. R. Wood, R. Green, G. Gál, J. Giermek, F. Kelley, G. Leipold and G. Etzkorn (OP 5), St Bonaventure: Franciscan Institute of St Bonaventure University, 1985.

—— *Brevis summa libri Physicorum, Summula philosophiae naturalis, Quaestiones in libros Physicorum Aristotelis*, ed. S. Brown (OP 6), St Bonaventure: Franciscan Institute of St Bonaventure University, 1984.

William of Sherwood, *Introductiones in logicam*, ed. M. Grabmann (Sitzungsberichte der Bayerischen Akademie der Wissenschaften, Phil. hist. Abteilung 1937, 10), Munich: Verlag der Bayerischen Akademie der Wissenschaften, 1937.

—— *Syncategoremata*, ed. J.R. O'Donnell (1941) *Mediaeval Studies* 3: 46–93.

—— *William of Sherwood's Introduction to Logic*, translated with an introduction and notes by N. Kretzmann, Minneapolis, MN: University of Minnesota Press, 1966.

—— *William of Sherwood's Treatise on Syncategorematic Words*, translated with an introduction and notes by N. Kretzmann, Minneapolis, MN: University of Minnesota Press, 1968.

Williams, C.J.F. (1965) 'Aristotle and Corruptibility', *Religious Studies* 1: 95–107, 203–15.

—— (1982) *Aristotle's De generatione et corruptione* (translation with notes) (Clarendon Aristotle Series), Oxford: Clarendon.

Wippel, J.F. (1977) 'The Condemnations of 1270 and 1277 at Paris', *Journal of Medieval and Renaissance Studies* 7: 169–201.

—— (1981) 'The Reality of Nonexisting Possibles According to Thomas

Aquinas, Henry of Ghent and Godfrey of Fontaines', *Review of Metaphysics* 34: 729–58.
—— (1985) 'Divine Knowledge, Divine Power and Human Freedom in Thomas Aquinas and Henry of Ghent', in T. Rudavsky (ed.) *Divine Omniscience and Omnipotence in Medieval Philosophy* (Synthese Historical Library 25), Dordrecht: Reidel, 213–41.
Wodeham, Adam, *Lectura secunda in librum primum Sententiarum*, ed. R. Wood and G. Gál, St Bonaventure, NY: St Bonaventure University Press, 1990.
Wolf U. (1979) *Möglichkeit und Notwendigkeit bei Aristoteles und heute*, Munich: W. Fink.
Wolfson, H.A. (1956) *The Philosophy of the Church Fathers I*, Cambridge, MA: Harvard University Press.
—— (1961) *Religious Philosophy*, Cambridge, MA: Harvard University Press.
—— (1976) *The Philosophy of the Kalam*, Cambridge, MA: Harvard University Press.
Wolter, A.B. (1947) *The Transcendentals and Their Function in the Metaphysics of Duns Scotus*, St Bonaventure: The Franciscan Institute.
—— (1950) 'Ockham and the Textbooks: On the Origin of Possibility', *Franziskanische Studien* 32: 70–96. Reprinted in J.F. Ross (ed.) (1971) *Inquiries into Medieval Philosophy. A Collection in Honour of Francis P. Clarke*, Westport, CN: Greenwood.
von Wright, G.H. (1971) 'Deontic Logic and the Theory of Conditions', in R. Hilpinen (ed.) *Deontic Logic: Introductory and Systematic Readings*, Dordrecht: Reidel.
—— (1979a) 'Diachronic and Synchronic Modalities', *Teorema* 9: 231–45.
—— (1979b) 'The Master Argument of Diodorus', in E. Saarinen, R. Hilpinen, I. Niiniluoto and M. Provence Hintikka (eds) *Essays in Honour of Jaakko Hintikka* (Synthese Library 124), Dordrecht: Reidel, 297–307.
—— (1979c) 'Time, Truth, and Necessity', in C. Diamond and J. Teichman (eds) *Intention and Intentionality. Essays in Honour of G.E.M. Anscombe*, Brighton: Harvester, 237–50.
—— (1984) *Truth, Knowledge, and Modality*, Oxford: Basil Blackwell.
Yrjönsuuri, M. (forthcoming) 'Aristotle's Topics and Medieval Obligational Disputations', *Synthese*.
Zimmermann, A. (ed.) (1968) *Ein Kommentar zur Physik des Aristoteles aus der Pariser Artistenfakultät um 1273* (Quellen und Studien zur Geschichte der Philosophie 11), Berlin: Walter de Gruyter.

# Index of names

Abbo of Fleury 62
Abelard, Peter 45, 62, 70–2, 75, 80–96, 107, 110–11, 118, 122, 128, 182–3, 188, 197
Adam, C. 203
Adam of Balsham (Parvipontanus) 96
Adams, M. 147, 168, 197
Aertsen, J. 131, 197
Alan of Lille 78, 101–2, 197
Alanen, L. viii, 7, 147, 149, 197–8
Albert the Great 99, 107, 110–14, 119–20, 198
Albert of Saxony 181, 198
Alessio, F. 211
Alexander of Aphrodisias 18, 30–4, 38, 42, 51, 118, 198
Allan, D.J. 199
Ammonius 198
Angelelli, I. 201
Anselm of Canterbury 45, 70–5, 95, 198
Anthony of Frachantian 177
Apuleius 115, 198
Aquinas, Thomas 13, 50, 60, 99, 100, 102–7, 110, 120–1, 128–36, 141, 145, 147, 155–8, 179, 187, 194, 198
Aristotle vii, 1–16, 19–48, 50–3, 55, 62, 81, 83–8, 91, 99, 101, 105–11, 114–15, 118, 120, 124–5, 130, 136, 141, 158–63, 165–8, 174–5, 177, 179, 186, 198–9
Ashworth, E.J. 123, 150, 196, 199
Asztalos, M. 199, 210, 212–13
Augustine vii, 21, 45, 49, 66–70, 77, 86, 94, 100, 154, 161, 186, 199
Averroes (Ibn Rushd) 99, 112–14, 133, 200
Avicenna (Ibn Sīnā) 99, 114, 133, 200

Bacon, Roger 106–7, 115, 200
Baconthorpe, John 160–1
Baldwin, J.M. 216
Balme, D.M. 35, 200
Bandinelli, Roland 122
Barnes, J. 39, 209
Baudry, L. 145, 200
Baur, L. 206
Bazán, B.C. 219
Bazzi, P. 198
Becker, A. 42, 200
Becker, O. 6, 200
Becker-Freyseng, A. 107, 200
Beonio-Brocchieri Fumagalli, M.T. 83, 200
Berengar of Tours 63, 71, 200
Bernard of Chartres 96
Bernard of Clairvaux 102, 200
Bieler, L. 200
Billingham, Richard 181, 200
Bobzien, S. 16–18, 30, 200
Bocheński, I.M. 42, 198, 200
Boehner, Ph. 162, 200, 202, 222
Boethius, Anicius Manlius Severinus 13, 15–18, 29–31, 44–66, 77–83, 91–2, 95–8, 100–1, 106–7, 116, 128, 135, 145, 165, 200
Boethius of Dacia 124, 136, 179, 201

# Index of names

Boh, I. 96, 122, 168, 177–8, 201
Bonaventure 77, 100, 103–4, 128, 147, 201
Borgnet, A. 198
Bos, E.P. 201, 207–8, 220
Bosley, R. 59, 201
Bossuat, R. 197
Braakhuis, H.A.G. 109, 201, 210–11, 217, 220
Broadie, A. 167, 178–9, 201
Brown, S. 221–2
Brunschwig, J. 214
de Bruyne, E. 102, 201
Buchner, H. 37, 201
Bunge, M. 216
Buridan, John 138–9, 156–60, 162–3, 166–75, 180, 201–2
Burley, Walter 124, 128, 147, 166, 180–1, 188, 190, 196, 202
Burnet, J. 216
Busse, A. 198
Buytaert, E.M. 197, 200
Buzzetti, S. 218
Byrne, E.F. 180, 202
Bywater, I. 199

Calcaterra, M. 198
Calcidius 62, 98, 202
Cantin, A. 63, 203
Caraccioli, Landulph 160–2
Caramello, P. 198
Caroti, S. 205, 210
Cathala, M.R. 198
Centi, T.S. 198
Chadwick, H. 46, 202
Chenu, M.-D. 202
Cherniss, H. 216
Chisholm, R. 193, 202
Chrysippus 18, 31
Cicero 18, 31, 45, 61–3, 94, 96, 202
Clarembald of Arras 96
Cleanthes 18
Comte, A. 6
Coombs, J.S. 147, 172, 202
Cooper, J.M. 35, 202
Copleston, F.C. 65, 202
Corcoran, J. 41, 202
Corsi, G. 202, 208, 214, 218
Cournot, A.A. 50

Courtenay, W.J. 69, 75, 78, 100, 183, 185, 202–3
Craig, W.L. 59–60, 69, 134, 203

Damian, Peter 63–8, 70–1, 75, 78–9, 203
Dancy, R. 9, 23, 32, 203
Danto, A.C. 72, 203
Dazeley, H.L. 72, 203
Dekker, E. 147, 203
Deman, T. 179, 203
Democritus 34–5
Denyer, N. 6, 15, 203
Descartes, R. 147–9, 203
Diamond, C. 223
Diodorus Cronus 14–16, 18, 29–30, 37, 44, 48, 56, 65, 86, 112, 119, 130
Diogenes Laertius 16–17, 203
Dombart, B. 199
Donagan, A. 186, 203
Döring, K. 15, 203
Doucet, V. 183, 203
Dronke, P. 97, 203, 206, 208, 212–13, 220–1
Duin, J.J. 120, 133–5, 203
Dulong, M. 216
Dunlop, D.M. 113, 203
Dunphy, W. 219
Duns Scotus, John vii, 70, 138–50, 155–7, 160, 162, 184–5, 203–4
Düring, I. 214

Ebbesen, S. 46, 63, 82, 111, 119, 136, 204, 210–11, 214–15
Einarson, B. 40, 204
Eliot, T.S. 1, 204
Elkana, Y. 214
van Elswijk, H.C. 78, 204
Endres, J.A. 65, 204
Engberg-Pedersen, T. 31, 204
Engel, P. 6, 50, 204
Epictetus 14, 18, 204
Epicurus 36
van Ess, J. 104, 204
Estermann, J. 144, 204
Etzkorn, G.I. 222
Eudemus 42
Evans, E. 199

al-Fārābī 114, 204
Faust, A. 31, 86, 204
Federici Vescovini, G. 158, 204
Francis of Marchia 160
Francis of Meyronnes 160
Frank, R. 104, 205
Frankfurt, H.G. 207
Fredborg, K.M. 204
Freddoso, A.J. 145, 162, 205
Frede, D. 59, 205
Frede, M. 16–17, 23, 31, 36, 41, 118, 205
Frege, G. 23
Freppert, L. 185, 205
Funkenstein, A. 69, 100, 105, 205
Furley, D. 20, 205

Gadamer, H.-G. 1, 205
Gál, G. 197, 221–3
Gale, R. 217
Gambatese, A. 222
Garland the Computist 62, 116, 205
Gelber, H.G. 153, 205, 207
Gerbert of Aurillac 62
Gerhardt, C.I. 211
Gersonides 114, 213
Geyer, B. 82, 197
al-Ghazālī 104
Gibson, M. 46, 63, 205, 212
Giermek, J. 222
Gilbert of Poitiers 45, 70–1, 75–82, 86, 95, 101, 144, 205
Goddu, A. 156, 180, 205
Goldbacher, A. 199
Goldstein, H.T. 200
Gombocz, W.L. 72, 203
Gotthelf, A. 26, 35, 200, 202, 206
Grabmann, M. 222
Gracia, J.J.E. 81, 206
Graeser, A. 42, 206
Granger, F. 220
Grant, E. 136, 206
Grant, R.M. 67, 206
Gratarolus, G. 221
Green. R. 124–9, 181, 190, 196, 206, 222
Green-Pedersen, N.J. 61, 201, 206
Gregory, T. 206
Gregory of Rimini 183, 206
Grosseteste, Robert 122–3, 127, 206

Guerlac, R. 200

Haaparanta, L. 6, 206
Hacking, I. 179, 206
Häring, N.M. 96–7, 197, 205, 219–20
Hartmann, N. 6, 206
Haskins, C.H. 75, 206
Helias, Peter 96
Hennessy, E. 201
Henry, D.P. 60, 72, 95, 206–7
Henry, P. 216
Henry of Ghent 100, 103–4, 139–40, 147, 149, 185, 207
Hermann of Carinthia 96
Herold, V. 219
Hicks, R.D. 203
Hilberg, I. 209
Hilpinen, R. viii, 223
Hintikka, J. viii, 1, 3, 5, 7, 9, 12, 14–16, 23, 25, 28, 32, 42–3, 53, 81, 106, 144, 177, 203–4, 207–10, 213
Hissette, R. 136, 207
Hoenen, M.J.F.M. 145, 207
Holcot, Robert 151–4, 162, 178–9, 183, 188, 207
Holmström-Hintikka, G. 70, 207
Holopainen, T. 67, 207
Holopainen, T.M. 149, 184–5, 207
Honnefelder, L. 141, 208
Hopkins, J. 74, 208
Hourani, G. 114, 208
Hubien, H. 159, 162, 201–2
Hugh of Newcastle 160
Hugh of St Cher 100
Hugh of St Victor 122, 208
Hughes, G.E. 162, 169, 171, 175, 208
Huygens, R.B.C. 200

Inati, S.C. 200
Irwin, T. 23, 208
Isaac, J. 65, 208
Ivry, A.L. 104–5, 208

Jacobi, K. 72, 87–8, 106, 109–10, 112–13, 121, 131, 208
Jalbert, G. 114, 208
Jenkins, D. viii

Jerome 65, 67, 208
Joachim, H.H. 199
John the Canon 160
John of Cornwall 162
John of Jandun 160
John of Salisbury 82, 96, 107, 209
Jolivet, J. viii, 83, 91, 209, 211, 213
Judson, L. 9, 11, 209

Kahn, C. 23, 209
Kalb, A. 199
Kalbfleisch, C. 219
Kane, W.H. 103, 209
Kant, I. 6, 185–6, 209
Kantola, I. 179, 209
Kapp, E. 39, 209
Karger, E. 147, 209
Kelley, F.E. 222
Kenny, A. 67, 103, 201, 203–4, 209–12, 215, 217, 219
Kilvington, Richard 150, 209
King, P. 159, 162, 168, 173–4, 209
Kirwan, C. 29, 49, 70, 209
Klima, G. viii
Kluxen, W. 203
Kneale, M. 15–17, 42, 44, 209
Kneale, W. 209
Kneepkens, C.H. 211
Knöll, P. 199
Knuuttila, S. 6–7, 23, 56, 93, 119, 124, 140–1, 143, 147, 149–50, 153, 157, 160, 198, 203–4, 206–11, 213–18
Köpf, U. 154, 210
Kretzmann, B. 150, 209, 211
Kretzmann, N. 22, 47, 50–1, 59–60, 109–10, 115, 118, 124, 150, 160, 180–1, 201, 204, 209–15, 217, 219–20, 222
Kripke, S. 171
Kroymann, A. 220
Kusch, M. 152–3, 156, 211

Lambert of Auxerre 106, 110–13, 119, 211
Landgraf, A. 202
Lanfranc 63, 71
Langston, D. viii, 144–5, 211
Leaman, O. 114, 211
Lear, J. 41, 211

van der Lecq, R. 80, 201, 211
Lehtinen, A.I. 160, 210
Leibniz, G.W. 81, 134, 144, 147, 211
Leipold, G. 222
Lennox, J.G. 35, 200, 202, 206
Lenzen, W. 177, 212
Lewis, C.I. 6
Lewis, D. 152, 212
Lewis, N.T. 128, 212
Lewry, O. 62, 199, 212
de Libera, A. viii, 106, 200, 209, 211–13
Lindberg, D.C. 206
Link-Salinger, R. 213
Locke, J. 19, 212
Loemker, L.E. 144, 211
Lombard, Peter 94, 122, 212
Long, A.A. 31, 212
Long, R. 213
Lovejoy, A. 4, 36, 68, 212
Łucasiewicz, J. 41, 212
Lucretius 36
Luscombe, D.E. 83, 197, 212

McCall, S. 11, 42, 212
McDermott, A.C.S. 162, 212
McGrade, A.S. 147, 212
Machamer, P.K. 210
Macrobius 62
Maggiòlo, M. 198
Maier, A. 133–4, 157, 162, 212
Maierù, A. 109, 153, 200, 212
Maimonides, Moses 99, 102, 104–5, 212
Mandonnet, P. 198
Manekin, C.H. 105, 114, 213
Mangione, C. 202, 208, 214, 218
Marc, P. 198
Marcolino, V. 206
Marenbon, J. viii, 63, 67, 79–80, 82, 94, 213
Marius Victorinus 106
Marmura, M.E. 104, 114, 213
Marsh, R.C. 218
Martin, C.J. 96, 213
Martin, R.M. 217
Mates, B. 23, 144, 213
Maurach, G. 221
Meiser, C. 200

## 228  Modalities in Medieval Philosophy

Mersenne, M. 148
Mews, C.J. 197
Meyerhoff, H. 1, 213
Michael, F.S. 15, 213
Michael of Massa 160
Migne, J.P. 197
Mignucci, M. 16, 56, 58–60, 113, 214
Miller, F.D. 20, 214
Minio-Paluello, L. 80, 83, 197–8, 214
Mojsisch, B. viii, 213
de Molina, L. 145, 205
Moody, E.A. 157–8, 180, 201, 214
Moonan, L. 67, 214
Moore, P.S. 216
Moos, M.F. 198
Morgan, C.G. 7, 214
Morrow, G.R. 20, 214
Moule, C.F.D. 221
Mugnai, M. 202, 208, 214, 218
de Muralt, A. 142, 214
Murdoch, J.E. 136, 190, 213–14
Mutzenbecher, A. 199

Newell, J.H. 79, 214
Nicholas of Cusa 97, 214
Nidditch, P.H. 212
Nielsen, L. 76, 78–9, 91, 160, 204, 214–15
Niiniluoto, I. 6, 186, 213, 215, 223
Normore, C. 13, 122–3, 142–3, 145, 162, 167, 215
Nuchelmans, G. 89, 116, 122, 215
Numbers, R.L. 206

Oakley, F. 65, 100, 215
Obertello, L. 46, 200, 215
Odetto, E. 198
O'Donnell, J.R. 109, 118, 222
Oesterle, J.T. 130, 134, 198
Origen 69, 86, 215
d'Ors, A. 201
Owens, J. 23, 215

Panaccio, C. 185, 215
Pardo, J. 172
Patch, H.R. 60, 215
Patterson, R. 42, 215
Patzig, G. 23, 36, 39, 205, 215

Paul of Pergula 177
Paul of Venice 177
Peck, A.L. 199
Peirce, C.S. 7, 216
Pera, C. 198
Pession, P.M. 198
Peter of Ailly 179, 216
Peter of Mantua 177–8
Peter of Poitiers 101, 122, 177, 187–9, 216
Peter of Spain 106–8, 110, 112, 117–19, 216
Petrus Rogerii (Clement the Sixth) 162
Petschenig, M. 199
Philo 29–30, 38, 44, 48
Philoponus 30, 216
Pinborg, J. 63, 106, 201, 204, 210–12, 215–17, 219
Pines, Sh. 213
Plato 4, 21, 23, 35–6, 45, 62, 67–8, 98, 161, 216
Plotinus 21, 36–7, 216
Pluta, O. viii, 210, 213
Plutarch 18, 216
Porphyry 45, 62, 82
Poser, H. 6, 144, 216
dal Pra, M. 82, 197
Prior, A. 6, 14–15, 134, 216
Provence, M. 223
Pseudo-Scotus 139, 162, 166–72, 175–6
del Punta, F. 222
Purtill, R. 15, 216

Quine, W.V. 6

Rackham, H. 202
Randi, E. 185, 216
Raoul of Longchamps (Radulphus de Longo Campo) 115, 216
Read, S. 210
Reesor, M.E. 18, 216
Reinharz, J. 208
Remes, U. 207
Rescher, N. 15, 42, 59, 113–14, 216–17
Ribaillier, J. 221
Richard of Campsall 111, 154, 163–6, 217

Richter, V. 222
van Rijen, J. 10–11, 13, 41–3, 217
de Rijk, L.M. 81, 83, 106–8,
　110–11, 115–18, 121, 124, 126–9,
　159, 176, 197, 205, 210–11,
　216–17, 220
Rist, J.M. 18, 217
Robert of Melun 101, 217
Rohr, M.D. 36, 217
Roncaglia, G. viii
van Rootselaar, B. 213
Rorty, A. 215
Roseth, Roger 183–4, 188–96, 217
Ross, J.F. 223
Ross, W.D. 25, 40, 198–9
Roure, M.-L. 196, 217
Rudavsky, T. 201, 203–5, 208, 210,
　215, 218, 223
Russell, B. 6, 23, 218
Ryan, C.J. 135, 218

Saarinen, E. 223
Saarinen, R. 186, 218
Sambursky, S. 31, 218
Samuel ibn Tibbon 105
Schenkl, H. 204
Schepers, H. 144, 218
Schmidt, K.J. 42, 218
Schmidt, M.A. 78, 218
Schmitt, F.S. 198
Schofield, M. 209
Schuhl, P.-M. 15, 218
Schuurman, H. 205
Schwamm, H. 145, 218
Schwyzer, H.R. 216
Scott, T.K. 159, 180, 202, 218
Sedley, D. 15, 218
Seel, G. 5–6, 9, 33, 41, 218
Segerberg, K. 72, 218
Serene, E. 71–3, 218
Sextus Empiricus 44
Shank, M.H. 153, 218
Sharples, R.W. 18, 31–4, 59, 198,
　218
Shiel, J. 49, 218
Siger of Brabant 99, 120, 129,
　133–6, 219
Simon, W. 206
Simon of Tournai 101, 219
Simplicius 30, 219

Index of names　229

Smith, R. 42, 219
Sorabji, R. 5, 9, 13, 15, 21–2, 29,
　32, 59–60, 104, 209, 219
Southern, R.W. 198
Spade, P.V. 124, 150–1, 160, 196,
　219–20
Spiazzi, R.M. 198
Staal, J.F. 213
Stanislaus of Znaim 154, 219
Steiger, R. 214
Strode, Ralph 177
Stump, E. 46, 50, 60–1, 109, 124,
　150–1, 168, 180–1, 211, 219–20
Suárez, F. 148
Sullivan, M.W. 115, 220
Sulowski, J. 216
Swetschinski, D. 208
Swyneshed, Roger 150–1, 153–4,
　220
Sylla, E.D. 214
Synan, E.A. 163, 217

Tabarroni, A. 160, 220
Tachau, K. 111, 178–9, 220
Talanga, J. 31, 220
Tannery, P. 203
Teichman, J. 223
Tempier, E. 136
Tertullian 69, 220
Theophrastus 42
Thierry of Chartres 75, 96–8, 220
Thomas, P. 198
de la Torre, B.R. 77, 120, 145, 220
Trifogli, C. 160, 220
Turnbull, R.G. 210
Tweedale, M. 83, 87, 106, 220
Työrinoja, R. 210–11, 214–15

Urba, C.F. 199
Urquhart, A. 15, 217
Uthred of Boldon 192, 196, 220

Venn, J. 6
Vettese, A. 216
Vitruvius 102, 220
Vos, A. 143, 220
Vuillemin, J. 15–16, 33, 220

Wadding, L. 204
Wallace, W.A. 157–8, 220

Wallies, M. 198, 216
Walton, D. 72, 221
Warichez, J. 219
Waszink, J.H. 202
Waterlow, S. 10–11, 25–6, 33, 221
Webb, C.C.J. 209
Weidemann, H. 32–3, 92–4, 181, 221
Weischedel, W. 209
Welsch, W. 29, 221
Wendland, V. 206
Wenin, C. 201
Wetherbee, W. 75, 221
Wey, J.C. 222
White, M.J. 5, 14–15, 18, 30–1, 34, 36, 221
Wieland, W. 42, 221
Wiesner, J. 204
Wiles, M.F. 67, 221
William of Auxerre 187–9, 221
William of Champeaux 87
William of Conches 70, 79, 221
William of Heytesbury 180–1
William of Ockham vii, 138, 145–9, 151–3, 155–7, 160, 162, 166–73, 175, 177–8, 182, 184–6, 188, 193, 221–2
William of Sherwood 106–10, 114–19, 124, 127, 222
Williams, C.J.F. 5, 9–10, 29, 222
Wippel, J.F. 103, 136, 139, 215, 222–3
Wodeham, Adam 178, 223
Wolf, U. 5, 9, 223
Wolfson, H.A. 49, 67, 104, 223
Wolter, A.B. 139, 142, 144, 149, 223
Wood, R. 197, 222–3
von Wright, G.H. 6, 15, 31–2, 58, 195, 223

Yrjönsuuri, M. 124, 128, 150, 210, 223

Zeno 29
Zimmermann, A. 136, 219, 223
Zimmermann, F.W. 204
Zycha, J. 199

# Index of subjects

abstraction 36, 91, 102, 158
accidental attributes 8, 13, 23, 51, 156, 161
ampliation 111–12, 121, 127, 166–7, 174–5
applied modal logic 176–96
apprehensive act 177–8
assent 156, 177–9
atomism 15, 35–6
axioms: Stoic 16–17

being: Thomas Aquinas 141; Aristotle 23–4; John Duns Scotus 141; Parmenides 35; Plotinus 36
beings: contingent 1–3, 35, 52, 132; eternal 1–3, 5, 7–10, 13, 37; impossible 102; merely possible 68–9, 77, 86, 95, 103, 121, 142, 144, 147, 159, 167, 169–72; necessary 2–3, 46, 52, 172
belief 176–9
book of nature 154

capacity 2–3, 24–7, 31, 38, 48, 51, 72–3, 91, 100 *see also* potency
categorematic terms 109, 118
categorical vs. hypothetical imperative 185–6
categories 19–20, 22–4, 81, 141
causality 30–4, 38, 47–51, 56, 60, 62, 71, 98, 101–2, 104, 131–6, 155, 158, 179
chance 7, 31–2, 35, 47, 49–51, 56, 135, 158
change 2–4, 16, 19–24, 26, 28, 32–3, 37–8, 52, 63–4, 90, 92, 95, 116, 127, 160–1
chimera 102, 142
class-inclusion 23, 40–1
complexly signifiable 179
compossibility 138, 140, 142–3, 148, 168
compound vs. divided sense *see* modal sentence
conditional: Peter Abelard 96; Boethius 61–2; Diodorus 44; Richard Kilvington 150; Philo 44; school of Petit Pont (parvipontani) 96; Stoics 18, 44
conditional norms 189–90, 193–6
conjunction 151, 154, 181, 188
consequence: 'as of now' 183; consequence of nature 61, 96; simple 151, 183
contingency: Albert the Great 110, 112–13, 119–20; Thomas Aquinas 110, 120, 130, 133–4; Aristotle 2, 5, 12–14, 31, 39–43, 51; Averroes 113–14; Boethius 51, 55–62; John Buridan 167–8, 170, 173–4; Comte 6; *contingens ad utrumlibet* 51, 57, 65, 112; *contingens infinitum* 112; *contingens natum* 112; *contingens* vs. *possibile* 107; John Duns Scotus 143–4; *Excerpta Norimbergensia* 110; Lambert of Auxerre 112–13; obligations treatises 127–8; Pseudo-Scotus 167–8, 170; Richard of Campsall 163–5; Siger of Brabant 135;

statistical 56, 110, 129–30, 134, 143, 179; Stoics 17; synchronic 143–4, 149; William of Ockham 167–8, 170–2, 175; William of Sherwood 118
continuity 20–2, 161
contradiction in nature 138, 160–2
contradictory terms 19–21, 160–1
contrary terms 19–22
contrary-to-duty imperative 193
conversion rules 39–40, 42–3, 84, 87, 99, 111–14, 163–7, 169–71
creation 63–4, 66, 69, 72, 75, 77, 86, 104, 132, 141–2, 145–6, 156

*de dicto* vs. *de re see* modal sentence
Demiurge 4
demonstration: *ex suppositione* 157–8; *propter quid* 158; scientific 104
deontic logic 182–3, 186, 188, 190–6
determinism 14–16, 18, 28, 30–3, 37, 47–50, 53, 56, 58, 62, 69, 134–5
dictative practical knowledge 185
*dictum* 87, 109, 116–18, 121, 167, 181
*dictum de omni et nullo* 173
disjunction 151, 154
disjunctive norms 186
disputations: Aristotle's rules 124–5 *see also* obligations logic
divine law 184, 191, 193, 196
domain of discourse 151, 154
double effect doctrine 187

*ecthesis* 39
efficient cause 25–6, 33–4, 47–8, 51, 62, 72, 101, 104, 131–6, 143, 155, 158
emanation 36
empirical generalizations 155
epistemic capacity 60, 101–3, 128, 134, 136
epistemic logic 176–82
epistemic sentence: *de dicto* vs. *de re* 180–1; intermediate reading 180
*esse essentiae* 139

*esse intelligibile* 140–3, 145
*esse possibile* 140
essence 22, 100, 102–3, 132, 139, 141, 147, 152, 164
essential attributes 13, 16, 23, 47, 103–4, 164
eternity: omnitemporal 1–3, 5, 7–9, 30, 37, 48, 52, 174; timeless 60, 66–7, 133–4, 145, 147
ethics 182–5
ethics of disputation 125, 150, 189
existence 1–2, 6, 23, 36–7, 48, 52, 65, 73, 78, 85, 87, 94–5, 97, 102–4, 110, 114, 116, 138–9, 141, 144–7, 155, 157, 166
existential generalization 180
falsity *see* truth and falsity
fate 18, 30, 48–9, 97–8
fictitious beings 102
form: Thomas Aquinas 102, 132; Aristotle 2, 20, 23, 36; Augustine 68; Gilbert of Poitiers 80; Moses Maimonides 104; Plato 36
freedom of the will (free choice) 47–51, 56, 62, 69–70, 74–5, 98, 143–5, 159, 184
future contingents 10, 12–15, 55–60, 74–5, 94, 128, 130, 145, 159

generation and corruption 1–2, 19–22, 27, 161
God: acting by choice vii, 67, 69–70, 77–8, 81–2; essence imitated by finite beings 100, 139, 147; freedom 45, 70, 94, 100, 143; intellect 141, 145–6, 148, 154; knowledge 60–1, 69, 74, 94, 121–2, 133–5, 141–2, 145, 148, 154; omnipotence 62–70, 73, 77–8, 81, 100–5, 120, 132, 136, 142–3, 145, 155–7; *potentia absoluta* 79, 100, 184, 191–2, 196; *potentia ordinata* 79, 100, 184, 191–2; providence 49–50, 62, 66–70, 76–7, 81, 98, 100–1, 133; will 64, 68–70, 74, 76–8, 81–2, 105, 134, 140, 143, 145–6, 148–9, 156

ideas (Platonic) 36, 67

identity 23, 80
imagination 103–5
implication 44
impossibility: Peter Abelard 87, 90–1, 182; Alan of Lille 101–2; Anselm of Canterbury 72–7; Thomas Aquinas 130; Aristotle 2–5, 7, 11, 16, 27, 43–4, 106; Augustine 68–9; Boethius 51–2, 54, 57; Peter Damian 65–7; Diodorus Cronus 14–16; John Duns Scotus 140–2; *ex impossibili quodlibet* 96, 129; Gilbert of Poitiers 76–7; Henry of Ghent 139, 149; Moses Maimonides 105; Peter of Spain 117–18; *per se* vs. *per accidens* 99, 114–18, 120, 128; Philo 29; *positio impossibilis* 129, 150–2; Russell 6; Stoics 16–18, 30; William of Ockham 151–2; William of Sherwood 114–15
indeterminism 33–4, 48–9, 50–1, 54, 60, 135
individual: Peter Abelard 90, 95; Boethius 18; John Duns Scotus 144–5; Gilbert of Poitiers 79–82
inference rules: assertoric 41; deontic 182–3, 192–3; epistemic 177; modal 10, 43, 87, 168, 176, 193
infinity 69, 134
instant of nature 139–40, 145–6, 161
instant of time 20–2, 27, 127–8, 144, 160–1
intellect 36, 102–4, 114, 141–2, 145–6, 148, 154
intelligibility 35–7, 100, 102–4, 138, 147–8
is: copula 23, 72, 108–9, 166, 168; Frege-Russell thesis 23; multiplicity of uses (Aristotle) 23

judicative act 177–8

knowledge 11, 25–6, 55, 58, 60–1, 69, 74–5, 91, 94, 103, 120–1, 133–4, 145, 155, 158, 176–81, 185

language as the medium of understanding 153

*Index of subjects* 233

law of contradiction 65, 67, 161–2
law of excluded middle 13, 21, 59, 162
law of identity 162
laws of nature 64, 77, 155, 157–9
limit decision 19–22, 27, 160, 196
logic and theology 63–5, 70, 120–2, 151–3, 162

Master argument 14–16, 18, 65, 86
matter 2, 35, 47, 97–8
matter of sentence 110, 113, 129–30, 167
Megarians 27–8
miracle 64–8, 101, 104, 132, 158
modal logic 6, 38–44, 53–61, 84–96, 107–23, 138–9, 144, 149–51, 162–96
modal sentence: affirmative vs. negative 108; compound vs. divided (*in sensu composito, in sensu diviso*) 10, 27, 84–6, 88, 94, 109, 111, 118–19, 163–5, 167–75; *de dicto* vs. *de re* 42, 84–90, 94, 99, 107–12, 118–19, 121, 139, 163, 167–8, 172, 176–7; equipollent 84, 87–8, 99, 107, 114, 138, 163, 168–9; impersonal 84–7, 95; *per conjunctionem* 85–6, 89–90; personal 84; proper 83, 88; with adverbial modes 83–4, 108; with iterated modes 174; with nominal modes 83–4, 108–9
modal syllogistic 38–43, 99, 107, 110–11, 113–14, 139, 165–6, 168–9, 173–5
modality: diachronic vii, 12, 30–4, 38, 50, 54, 56–8, 65, 69, 92, 95, 99, 119–20, 127, 144, 159; divine 45, 65, 67–9, 73, 76–8, 86, 99–106, 132, 135–6, 139; extensional interpretation 143; logical vii, 11, 17, 31, 35, 47, 135, 138, 142–3, 145–8, 157; multiplicity of reference vii, 70, 82, 121, 138, 147; natural 11, 14, 17, 26, 31, 34–5, 37, 47, 49, 63–6, 68, 70, 76–7, 99–106, 132, 135–8, 155–60, 172; *per se* vs. *per accidens* 114–18, 120–1, 128;

proper vs. improper 72, 74, 83; psychological interpretation 6; 'scholastic' (according to Peirce) 6; synchronic vii, 9–10, 31–3, 38, 45, 54, 57, 70–1, 82, 92, 94–5, 99, 120–2, 127, 138, 143–7, 149, 171; temporal frequency (statistical) interpretation vii, 5–16, 33, 37, 44, 51–4, 58–9, 65, 68, 91, 99, 101–3, 113–14, 117, 119, 121, 130, 133, 135, 158–9
motion: 3, 8–9, 15, 19–28, 32–3, 35, 53, 76, 127, 132

natural moral law 189
nature 26, 29, 34–7, 46–52, 55, 57, 61–8, 76, 80, 87, 90–1, 95, 101–5, 130–4, 138–9, 146, 154–61, 182
necessity: Peter Abelard 83–4, 87, 91–2, 96, 182; Albert the Great 112–13, 120; Alexander of Aphrodisias 33; Anselm of Canterbury 72, 74–5; antecedent 32; Thomas Aquinas 120–1, 130–4; Aristotle 2–14, 25–6, 32–5, 37, 39–44, 46; Augustine 68; Averroes 113–14; Avicenna 114; Roger Bacon 115; Boethius 46–61; John Buridan 156–60, 167–75; causal 31–4, 47–51, 63, 104–5, 133–5; compulsory 34, 49, 72, 74; Comte 6; conditional 14, 34, 50–4, 60–1, 155, 172; customary 64, 75–6, 101, 104–6; Peter Damian 63–4; Democritus 34–5; determinate 91–2; *Dialectica Monacensis* 117; Diodorus Cronus 6, 14–15; John Duns Scotus 143, 155; al-Ghazālī 104; Gilbert of Poitiers 75–7, 79, 82, 101; hypothetical 34, 132, 157, 159; improper vs. proper 72, 74; intrinsic vs. extrinsic 132; Lambert of Auxerre 111; *Logica 'Ut dicit'* 116–18; Moses Maimonides 105–6; metaphysical 95, 132, 156, 158–9; natural (physical) 11, 14, 26, 31, 34–5, 37, 49, 63–4, 70, 76, 101–4, 132, 136, 155–60; natural vs. logical 31, 138, 155–7, 159, 172; *necessarium ex quolibet* 96; *necessitas antecedens (praecedens)* vs. *necessitas subsequens (sequens)* 74–5; *necessitas consequentiae* vs. *necessitas consequentis* 60, 120–1; nomic 138, 155, 157, 160, 185; *per se* vs. *per accidens* 114–18, 128; Philo 29; Plato 35; Pseudo-Scotus 167–72; Raoul of Longchamps 115; Richard of Campsall 111, 163–5; Russell 6; Siger of Brabant 120, 133–5; simple vs. qualified 12, 17, 32, 35, 51–4, 56, 61, 91, 97, 172; statistical 4, 54, 101, 130, 133, 135; Stoics 16–18, 30–1, 34; strong vs. weak 32; teleological 34–5; temporal 53, 61, 64, 91–2, 95, 135, 165, 172; Thierry of Chartres 97; William of Ockham 155–6, 167–73, 175; William of Sherwood 114–15; 118; with beginning vs. without beginning 123
necessity of the past 14–15, 57, 64–5, 74, 79
necessity of the present 12, 32–3, 53–5, 57–8, 64–5, 74, 79, 111–12, 121, 127, 134, 138, 143, 158, 164–5
negation 99, 108, 142, 163, 168–9
non-necessary: Diodorus Cronus 15; Philo 29; Stoics 16–17
nothingness 66, 141

obligations logic 99, 123–9, 138, 144, 149–54, 180–1, 189–90; *petitio* 190; *positio* 123, 125–8, 189–90; *positio dependens* 190, 195–6
occasionalism 104
omnipotence *see* God
ostensive practical knowledge 185–6

Parisian condemnations 100, 136–7, 139
possibility: Peter Abelard 83–95, 182; absolute 97, 100, 103, 131, 136; Alan of Lille 101–2; Albert

# Index of subjects

the Great 112; Anselm of Canterbury 72–5; Thomas Aquinas 130–4; Aristotle 2–13, 16, 19, 26–9, 31–3, 36–40, 43–4; Augustine 67–70; Averroes 113; Avicenna 114; Boethius 46–58; Boethius of Dacia 136; John Buridan 158–9, 169–71, 173–4; Comte 6; constitutionally conditional 38; Peter Damian 65–7; Descartes 148–9; determinate 97; diachronic (antecedent, prospective) 12, 31–4, 38, 50, 54, 56–8, 65, 69, 92, 119–20, 127, 144, 159; *Dialectica Monacensis* 117; Diodorus Cronus 6, 14–15, 48, 112; divine 65, 67–9, 73, 76–8, 86, 99–105, 132, 135–6, 139; John Duns Scotus 140–8; epistemic interpretation 31, 38, 134–5; Eudemus 42; al-Fārābī 114; Gilbert of Poitiers 76–82, 101; Robert Grosseteste 122–3; Henry of Ghent 139–40, 149; Lambert of Auxerre 111–12, 119; Leibniz 81, 134, 144; *Logica 'Ut dicit'* 116–17; logical (conceptual) vii, 138, 142–3, 145–8, 157; Moses Maimonides 103–5; natural (physical) 26, 47, 51, 65, 68, 91; natural vs. divine 65–6, 68, 76–7, 99–106, 136–7; natural vs. logical 11, 17, 31, 47, 135; objective 143; ontological foundation in God's essence 103–4, 132; partial vs. total (full) 26, 29–31, 48, 73, 159; Peter of Poitiers 101, 122; Peter of Spain 112, 119; Philo 29–30, 38, 48; Plato 36; Plotinus 36; as a potency vii, 12, 19, 26–9, 37, 46–8, 51, 73, 158; proper 40, 42–4, 72, 106–7, 163; Pseudo-Scotus 169–71; relative temporalized 11–12, 33; Robert of Melun 101; Russell 6; *secundum inferiorem causam* 101–2, 122; *secundum superiorem causam* 101–2, 122, 155; Siger of Brabant 133, 136; Simon of Tournai 101; statistical 58, 68, 91, 101–2, 119; Stoics 16–18, 30–1, 34, 38, 48, 51; synchronic alternative 9–10, 31–3, 38, 45, 54, 57, 70–1, 82, 92, 94, 120–1, 127, 138, 143–4; Theophrastus 42; Thierry of Chartres 97; two-edged 39, 106–7; Venn 6; William of Ockham 145–9, 167–8, 170–3, 175; William of Sherwood 118–19; without ontological foundation 140, 148

possible worlds 81, 143–4, 149–50, 152–3, 171–2

possible worlds semantics 138, 143, 171

potency 2, 9, 19, 24–30, 34–8, 46–8, 63, 73, 87, 97, 184–5; active 24–6, 29–30, 34, 37–8, 47–8, 63, 87, 131; first order 25–6, 29–30, 37; logical 142, 145; non-rational 24–6; partial 25–6, 38, 48, 73–4, 158; passive 2, 24–6, 29–30, 34, 37–8, 47–8, 63, 87, 97, 131; *potentia oboedientialis* 132, 155; rational 24–6; second order 25, 29–30, 37; total (full) 26–7, 48, 74 *see also* God: omnipotence

potentiality vs. actuality 2, 9, 19, 22–4, 26–9, 37–8, 48, 70, 73, 131, 142, 144, 158

*potuit sed noluit* 69, 77, 100, 120

predication: Anselm's theory 71–2

prima facie duty 126, 189

principle of bivalence 13, 59, 128

principle of continuity 4

principle of plenitude 4–5, 9–10, 33, 36, 68, 102, 104–5

principle of unilinear gradation 4

probabiliorism 179

probabilism 179

probability 6, 35, 50, 70, 157; epistemic 134, 179–80; objective 179

providence *see* God

rationality of a system of norms 191, 193

rest 21–2

scepticism 36
semantic paradox 166, 196
semantic relation: inaccessible 153, inexhaustive 153
sentence: future tense 12–13, 17, 116–17, 130, 163, 166; past tense 14–15, 17, 57, 117, 163, 166; temporally definite 12–13, 15, 53, 55–6, 58–9, 91, 122, 130; temporally indefinite 3–4, 8, 12, 16, 52–3, 55–6, 59, 89–90, 92, 116, 127–9, 165 *see also* modal sentence, truth and falsity, truth value
species of beings 4, 8, 13, 35–7, 47, 62, 69, 72, 89–91, 102–3, 105, 159, 174
square of opposition 88, 99, 107–8, 115, 163, 168
Stoics 16–18, 29–31, 33, 38, 47–51, 56, 118, 135
substance 1, 7–8, 10, 19–23, 27, 36, 47, 76, 85, 90, 141, 144
substitutivity of identity 180–1
supererogative act 192
supposition theory 122, 159, 166
syncategorematic terms 109–110, 118, 160

technical norm 125, 185
teleology 34–5, 67, 75–6
tense logic 166–7
theology and philosophy 45–6, 62–5, 67, 70–1, 75–6, 96, 99–106, 120–1, 132, 136, 151–4, 162
time (temporal) 1–22, 28, 30–4, 37–8, 46, 49–61, 64–7, 69, 74, 76–9, 82, 88–94, 111–23, 127–30, 143–5, 149, 155, 158–61, 163–7, 174, 196
Trinity 75, 81, 151–3
truth and falsity 3–4, 6–7, 11–18, 29, 31–2, 52–6, 58–60, 75, 89–90, 92, 94, 96, 110, 113–23, 127–30, 148–9, 156–9, 164–6, 171, 178, 195–6
truth value: absent 14, 55, 59, 161; changing 3–4, 12, 15, 52–3, 55–6, 59, 89, 116–17, 127–8; determinate 128; indeterminate 13, 55–8, 120, 128

will 47–51, 56, 62, 64, 68–70, 73–8, 81, 98, 105, 134, 143–6, 149, 159, 179, 184–9, 191, 194

For Product Safety Concerns and Information please contact our EU representative GPSR@taylorandfrancis.com
Taylor & Francis Verlag GmbH, Kaufingerstraße 24, 80331 München, Germany

Engaging with the Philosophy of Dismas A. Masolo

*Quest: An African Journal of Philosophy /
Revue de Philosophie Africaine*, XXV, nos. 1-2

# EDITORIAL

Determined to bring *Quest: An African Journal of Philosophy / Revue Africaine de Philosophie*, up to date again, this is the third annual volume we publish within half a year. Two more are lined up for imminent publication, which should put the record straight once more. The present volume marks *Quest*'s 25$^{th}$ anniversary, and we wish to thank all authors, readers, members of the Editorial Board and the advisory Editorial Board, subscribers (their patience and trust have been severely taxed in recent years), and readers, for helping us attain this milestone. We are particularly indebted to the two founding editors, Roni M. Khul Bwalya (†) and Pieter Boele van Hensbroek, who launched this journal as a daring undertaking from the Department of Philosophy, University of Zambia. We are also immensely grateful for the institutional support which *Quest* has received over the years, initially from the University of Zambia and from Groningen University, and in the last decade from the African Studies Centre, Leiden, the Netherlands. For the present annual volume 25, we have been fortunate to draw on the intellectual efforts of a guest editor, Professor Thaddeus Metz, Professor (Research Focus) and Head, Philosophy Department, University of Johannesburg, South Africa. This special issue *Engaging with the Philosophy of Dismas A. Masolo* reflects an important and critical exchange between one of the leading figures in African philosophy, and a group of prominent South African philosophers clustering on the Johannesburg Department. The debate has been heated, and initially the positions were so far apart that constructive dialogue took long to materialise; also due to a series of serious medical problems, the collection for a long time risked to be left without Professor Masolo's incisive and illuminating 'Reply to critics'. However, when that text was yet written under very trying circumstances, the road was clear for another one of the memorable discussions for which *Quest* has been famous over the years. We thank all contributors, and particulars Professors Masolo and Metz, for their hard work towards this special issue.

Wim van Binsbergen, Editor

ISSN 1011-226X

# QUEST

An African Journal of Philosophy / Revue Africaine de Philosophie

*vol. 25, nos 1-2*

## Engaging with the Philosophy of Dismas A. Masolo

Guest editor: Thaddeus Metz

in collaboration with Wim van Binsbergen

ISSN 1011-226X

ISBN: 978-90-78382-23-2

© 2014 this collection: *Quest: An African Journal of Philosophy / Revue de Philosophie Africaine (please, send your submissions, subscription request, orders, reprint requests, and all other correspondence to:* shikandapress@gmail.com )

the copyright of the individual contributions is retained by the authors; however, submission of their contributions automatically implies that the copyright holders tacitly grant *Quest: An African Journal of Philosophy / Revue de Philosophie Africaine* such use rights as needed to publish and republish their texts in printed form and online.

*Quest: An African Journal of Philosophy / Revue de Philosophie Africaine* is published by the non-profit Shikanda Press, Haarlem, the Netherlands (http://shikanda.net/PRESS/index.htm ; shikandapress@gmail.com)

Volumes of *Quest: An African Journal of Philosophy / Revue de Philosophie Africaine* enjoy free-access availability at http://quest-journal.net

# CONTENTS

0. Editorial
   by Wim M.J. van Binsbergen
   p. 2

1. Introduction: Engaging with the Philosophy of D.A. Masolo
   by T. Metz
   p. 7

2. The Concept of Identity in Masolo
   by M.B. Ramose
   p. 17

3. Therapeutic African Philosophy
   by P.A. Tabensky
   p. 31

4. Some Doubts about "Indigenous Knowledge", and the Argument from Epistemic Injustice
   by K. Horsthemke
   p. 49

5. On Being an African
   by A. Olivier
   p. 77

6. Two "Normative" Conceptions of Personhood
   by K. Behrens
   p. 103

7. Personhood: Social Approval or a Unique Identity?
   by M. Tshivhase
   p. 119

8. Two Conceptions of African Ethics
   by T. Metz
   p. 141

9. Exorcising the Communitarian Ghost: D.A. Masolo's Contribution
   by B. Matolino
   p. 163

10. The Case for Communitarianism: A Reply to Critics
    by Dismas A. Masolo
    p. 185

11. Notes on Contributors
    p. 231

    Colophon, and Directions for Contributors
    p. 235

# Engaging with the Philosophy of D.A. Masolo

## by Thaddeus Metz

*Abstract: Engaging with the Philosophy of D. A. Masolo.* This is an introduction to the special issue of *Quest* devoted to D. A. Masolo's latest book, *Self and Community in a Changing World.* It situates this book in relation to not only Masolo's earlier research on African philosophy but also the field more generally, sketches the central positions of the contributions to the journal issue, and in light of them makes some critical recommendations for future reflection.

*Résumé: S'engager avec la Philosophie de D. A. Masolo.* Ceci est une au numéro spécial de *Quest* consacré au dernier livre de D.A. Masolo, *Self and Community in a Changing World.* Il situe ce livre par rapport non seulement aux recherches antérieures de Masolo sur la philosophie africaine mais aussi au champ plus générale; il esquisse les positions centrales des contributions au numéro de la revue, et fait quelques recommandations essentielles à leur lumières pour une réflexion future.

*Key words:* D. A. Masolo, African philosophy, identity, method, knowledge, sub-Saharan morality, personhood

*Mots-clés:* D. A. Masolo, philosophie africaine, identité, méthodes, connaissance, moralité subsaharienne, personnalité

## 1. Overview

Professor Dismas Masolo is an elder in the African philosophical community, a well-known contributor to the field from Kenya alongside the likes of John Mbiti and Henry Odera Oruka. Masolo's most significant contribution, at least up to now, has been his *African Philosophy in Search of Identity*, published in 1994 and still in print 20 years later. As most scholars of African philosophy know, it is a critical, wide-ranging discussion of a variety of the metaphysical, epistemological and methodo-

7

logical themes that largely dominated the field in the post-war era.

*Self and Community in a Changing World*, published in 2010, is Masolo's major sole-authored follow up.[1] It, too, is in the first instance a work of the history of African philosophy, albeit peppered with independent judgment, and it also discusses important authors and ideas from Francophone, Anglophone and, often enough, indigenous language literatures.

*Self and Community in a Changing World* differs from the earlier book mainly with regard to the topics on which it focuses, namely, philosophical anthropology, ethics and politics. Whereas major themes in *African Philosophy in Search of Identity* are Tempels' ethnophilosophy, Mbiti's conception of time, and Kagame's categories of being, in the new book salient topics are the nature of mind and personhood in Kwasi Wiredu's oeuvre, the analysis of immorality to be found in work by the poet and anthropologist Okot p'Bitek, and communitarianism and socialism in Leopold Senghor's writings.

As it is fairly rare for substantial, single-authored monographs to be published in the field of African philosophy, at least by such a well-regarded thinker, a number of us based in South Africa decided to come together for a two-day workshop at the University of Johannesburg in March 2012 in order to critically analyze various facets of *Self and Community in a Changing World*, and to do so in the presence of the author himself. Those of us who gathered came from a variety of backgrounds in terms of nationality, ethnicity, age and philosophical orientation. The present volume of *Quest* consists of selected proceedings from our conversations with Professor Masolo.

---

[1] Notable papers since *African Philosophy in Search of Identity* and leading up to *Self and Community in a Changing World* include Masolo (1997, 2001, 2004a, 2004b, 2005). Also worth mentioning is *African Philosophy as Cultural Inquiry*, a collection of essays edited by Masolo and Ivan Karp (2000).

## 2. Methodology and epistemology

Although the main thrust of Masolo's latest book discusses human nature, its communal orientation, and how best to live in light of it, when doing any sort of African philosophy methodological issues are hard to avoid. Masolo takes up a variety of them, as do contributors to this volume.

In his article, Mogobe Ramose addresses the questions of which language(s) to use when doing African philosophy and what the ethical import is of this choice. Masolo by and large recommends that philosophers write in their indigenous tongues, but makes what Ramose calls a 'concession' that these languages are not well suited for 'practical professional' purposes (Masolo 2010: 44). Ramose disagrees, contending that it is best to do African philosophy in an African language, and unethical not to do so for tending to lead to distortion, even suppression, of other peoples' cultures.

Ramose does not argue that one should *never* do African philosophy in a non-African language. After all, he has written his own article in English, while advancing a moral perspective that is presumably grounded on an African worldview. One might wonder, however, whether the fact that Ramose has expressed himself in English suggests that there are indeed 'practical professional' reasons that often recommend discussing African philosophical issues with a non-African vocabulary. Is there a tension here or not?

Another contributor who explores mainly methodological issues is Pedro Tabensky. Whereas Ramose discusses which linguistic means to use when doing African philosophy, Tabensky reflects on the proper final ends of doing it. Most of those doing African philosophy are interested in obtaining knowledge, or at least justified belief or the truth, but Tabensky finds in Masolo's work the suggestion that there are also non-epistemic reasons to do it, namely, to overcome 'dependency' on others, especially intellectuals who come from a Western culture that spawned colonialism. Tabensky maintains that there are additional non-epistemic reasons that do and should drive people to engage with sub-Saharan philosophy and worldviews, namely, interests in promoting self-esteem, the ability to cope with stressors, and other forms of psychological health.

Tabensky's essay explores the subtle tensions that exist when one does philosophy for competing aims; although it is rare that self-esteem will be enhanced by believing in a perspective recognized to be false, there are probably many times when it can be improved by believing in a view that is false but not recognized to be, perhaps because of a self-deceptive neglect of evidence. How to balance cognitive interests in knowledge or justification with non-cognitive concerns to be self-confident or otherwise motivated is a tough matter of judgment.

That is true not merely in the first-person case, but also when interacting with others. Suppose that by deceiving others one would be likely to foster their self-esteem to an important degree. What should one do? Or, setting deception aside, one might sensibly ask whether it was right for Tabensky to present the findings of his article, or for Masolo to discuss them publicly with Tabensky, or for me to suggest that they be published in this journal. Is it so clear that *informing* people about their competing interests in the epistemic and the non-epistemic will foster the right balance between them? Does so informing favour the epistemic, perhaps to the detriment of the non-epistemic? If Tabensky is correct that interests in 'discovering the world' need to balanced with those in 'creative worldmaking', should he perhaps have kept his mouth shut, and not shared that very discovery?

Kai Horsthemke can be read as having little patience for non-cognitive values in his critical discussion of Masolo's sympathy toward something he believes is fairly called 'indigenous knowledge'. One motivation for the comparative dimension of Masolo's work, e.g., where he contrasts Kant's conception of human nature with Wiredu's, is that there are different perspectives on knowledge that vary depending on their cultural origins and that can be judged in terms of their similarities and differences. Horsthemke is interested in whether one can sensibly do more than just compare. It appears that two perspectives can conflict about a common subject matter, and, if so, which is to be believed, and for what reasons? Merely because beliefs have been long-standing and widely held in a particular locale does not mean they are justified, so Horsthemke maintains, which, for him, means that automatically labelling such beliefs 'indigenous *knowledge*' is inappropriate. Whether they are constitutive of knowledge is something that has to be ascertained over time.

One sympathetic to Tabensky or Masolo might suggest some non-cognitive reasons for bestowing the dignity of the title of 'knowledge' on African beliefs. Or it might be that the word 'knowledge' tends not to be used so literally by advocates of so-called 'indigenous knowledge', and is meant merely to indicate a system of beliefs, abstracting from whether they are justified or not. Note that if African beliefs have not yet been determined to count as knowledge, Masolo's comparative project still seems worth undertaking. However, Horsthemke's question about which beliefs to hold consequent to the comparison does beg for an answer.

Horsthemke is interested in what might be called 'objective' knowledge claims, those about the nature of reality as it truly is. In contrast, in his contribution Abraham Olivier takes up 'subjective' knowledge about what it is like for an individual to experience the world in a particular way. More specifically, Olivier primarily aims to answer the phenomenological question of what it is like to be an African (which differs from the ontological question of what it is to be an African). In general, Masolo conceives of a variety of issues relating to the self in communal terms. Running with that general perspective and extending it to experiential issues, Olivier constructs a way by which to grasp—in relational or social terms—the content of a characteristically sub-Saharan way of perceiving the world.

Olivier does not suggest that he is an African, and even suggests that he is not one, and so one might wonder whether he is suitably qualified to speak about what it is like to be an African. Doesn't it take one to know one? In reply, Olivier would likely claim that his article is not intended to provide a detailed account of what it is like to be an African, but instead an analysis of the general social structure that would necessarily inform such an account. If that is correct, then another paper waits to be written that would fill in the details.

## 3. Morality: Status, virtue, rightness, justice

The remaining four contributions to this special issue focus on four distinct aspects of morality. First off, Kevin Behrens notes that the word 'personhood' is central to debates in both African ethics and Western bioethics and that in both discourses personhood is distinguished from mere biological species. These facts give one *prima facie* reason to doubt that personhood is 'the pinnacle of an African difference in philosophical theory' (Masolo 2010: 135), a view that Masolo attributes to Kwasi Wiredu with apparent approval. However, Behrens ends up contending that, upon reflection, one sees that the same word is used differently in the two discourses.

In a sub-Saharan context, 'personhood' most often indicates virtue or human excellence, a quality that varies from individual to individual based on her attitudes and decisions. In contrast, Anglo-American bioethicists use the same term to pick out moral status or standing, a feature that is often thought to be invariant among individuals (or at most to vary based on differential capacities, rather than actualizations of them). Basically, in the West, a person is one owed moral treatment, whereas below the Sahara, a person is one who has given others moral treatment they are owed.

The title of Behrens' article speaks of 'two normative conceptions of personhood', but it is worth noting a third, descriptive understanding of personhood, one that is arguably shared by both traditions. This third sense of the word 'person' is roughly the idea of an individual aware of itself over time and able to act consequent to deliberation, such that human babies are not yet persons and God is always already a person (on some conceptions). This concept of personhood is ontological, and does not include any moral ideas about values or norms. I submit that the Menkiti-Gyekye debate on personhood should be revisited while keeping an eye on these three distinct senses of 'person'.

In her article titled 'Personhood: Social Approval or a Unique Identity?', Mpho Tshivhase is clearly addressing the sense of personhood as human excellence or good character. She finds in Masolo's lengthy discussion of this characteristically African concept two logically distinct respects in which relationship with community might make one virtuous, but she questions both, and for the same basic reason. At bottom, Tshivhase doubts that human excellence is entirely a function of other-regard or relationality. She argues that at least some of what constitutes a genuinely human way of life is individualistic, involving ideals of autonomy and authenticity that communal considerations fail to capture.

One way of putting Tshivhase's point is to say that 'a person is a person through other persons', but not *merely* through other persons. No doubt many African philosophers, including Masolo, will want to contest her position, and it would be of interest to see how they might do so. Note that it will not suffice for critics merely to point out that sub-Saharan philosophy has its own, social or relational ideals of autonomy and authenticity, according to which one is governing one's true self just insofar as one is a communal being. For Tshivhase's point is that there are non-communal, irreducibly individualist elements to the best understanding of these values.

In my contribution, I focus not on good character but rather right action. I argue that Masolo's discussion of the nature of sub-Saharan morality indicates two conceptions of what fundamentally makes actions permissible that he, along with the field more generally, does not adequately differentiate. On the one hand, there is the idea that an act is right insofar as it promotes the welfare of those in the community, while, on the other hand, there is the view that an act is right insofar as it fosters (or honours) communal relationships, some of which include welfare promotion. I work to clarify the differences between these approaches, and to argue that the latter is preferable to the former.

Of course some in the field might welcome a pluralist basis to morality, and contend that both approaches are not only typically African, but also philosophically attractive. Perhaps permissible behaviour from a sub-Saharan perspective is that which either promotes well-being or enters into community. However, I work to show that there are cases in which one cannot do both and must choose between them, requiring an answer to the question of which is to be preferred to the other. In addition, I maintain that moral concerns about the well-being of others are adequately captured by a prescription to prize communal relationships.

In the final contribution, Bernard Matolino raises serious concerns about a tendency to 'essentialize' African thought in communal terms. Although he is content to grant that communitarian views have been very influential in sub-Saharan philosophy, he firmly rejects the idea that a philosophy counts as sub-Saharan only to the extent that it is communitarian. In addition, Matolino believes that an overriding interest when theorizing about justice and related matters in social and political philosophy should be to establish and hold positions that are plausible for accepting kernels of truth in modernity, regardless of whether they are African or not. On both counts, Matolino finds Masolo's approach to communitarianism welcome, more welcome than both the 'extreme' form of communitarianism associated with Ifeanyi Menkiti (1979) and the 'moderate' form that Kwame Gyekye famously advances (1997: 38-70).

Defenders of Menkiti or Gyekye will of course want to consider whether Matolino has succeeded in providing reason to transcend the duality between them that has dominated the field for about 20 years. In addition, it is worth considering whether, even if one should reject both Menkiti and Gyekye, one should accept Masolo. Another sensible project to undertake at this point is to consider whether there are problems with Masolo's version of communitarianism that should lead us to search for still another version.

## 4. How to learn from elders

While some contributors agree with the views that Professor Masolo supports in *Self and Community in a Changing World* and develop them further, and while others disagree with them and point us in a different direction, all have found his new book to provide the occasion for serious philosophical reflection. A good book is not the last word, but is instead one that prompts many more words.

## References

Gyekye, K. (1997). *Tradition and Modernity: Philosophical Reflections on the African Experience.* New York: Oxford University Press.
Masolo, D. A. (1997). African Philosophy and the Postcolonial: Some Misleading Abstractions about 'Identity'. In *Postcolonial African Philosophy: A Critical Reader.* Edited by Eze, E. C. London: Blackwell Publishers, pp. 283-300.
Masolo, D. A. (2001). Critical Rationalism and Cultural Traditions in African Philosophy. Reprinted in *Explorations in African Political Thought: Identity, Community, Ethics.* Edited by Kiros, T. New York: Routledge, 2001, pp. 81-95.
Masolo, D. A. (2004a). Western and African Communitarianism: A Comparison. In *A Companion to African Philosophy.* Edited by Wiredu, K. Malden, MA: Blackwell Publishing Ltd.
Masolo, D. A. (2004b). The Concept of the Person in Luo Modes of Thought. In *African Philosophy: New and Traditional Perspectives.* Edited by Brown, L. New York: Oxford University Press, pp. 105-130.
Masolo, D. A. (2005). The Making of a Tradition: African Philosophy in the New Millenium. Polylog, 6, available at: http://them.polylog.org/6/amd-en.htm.
Masolo, D. A. & Karp, Ivan (Eds.) (2000). *African Philosophy as Cultural Inquiry.* Bloomington: Indiana University Press.
Menkiti, I. 1979. Person and Community in African Traditional Thought. Repr. in *African Philosophy: An Introduction*, 3$^{rd}$ edition. Edited by Wright, R. A. New York: University Press of America, 1984, pp. 171-181.

# The Concept of Identity in Masolo

## by M. B. Ramose

*Abstract: The Concept of Identity in Masolo.* In this article, I use D A Masolo's *Self and Community in a Changing World* as a springboard for critical discussion of the appropriateness of doing African philosophy in languages other than indigenous ones.

*Résumé*: Le Concept d'Identité chez Masolo. Dans cet article, je me sers de *Self and Community in a Changing World* de D A Masolo comme un tremplin pour une discussion critique de la convenance de faire de la philosophie africaine dans d'autres langues que les langues indigènes.

*Keywords*: identity, African philosophy, self, community, indigenous knowledge

*Mots-clés:* l'identité, philosophie africaine, individu, la communauté, la connaissance indigène

### Introduction

One of the famous works of Masolo is: *African Philosophy in Search of Identity*. This title suggests that African philosophy and identity are the major topics for discussion. Furthermore, the suggestion appears to be that the topics will be discussed from the perspective of searching, "in search". The importance of this suggestion is that the debate over what is African philosophy continues. Philosophers like Hume and Berkeley deliberated extensively on the question of "identity", in particular, "personal identity" as a philosophical problem. Neither solved the problem definitively and so, the debate over the meaning of "identity" continues.

Masolo's *African Philosophy in Search of Identity* may be considered as part of this debate except that he does not discuss the concept itself in the manner of either Hume or Berkeley. Instead, he simply uses the concept in its ordinary meaning. He argues for this usage in these terms: "The meaning of a specific word in ordinary language, ...must be sought in 'what it stands for' for the majority of its speakers, who never have to qualify first as metaphysicians before they qualify as speakers of their own language, whether it is their native language or a new one" (Masolo 1994: 102). Having thus set aside the need to adopt the philosopher's, the linguist's or the "expert's" use the concept of identity, Masolo then turns to a discussion of some of the specific phases and faces of African philosophy. The text itself reveals and revolves around the many faces and phases of the identity of African philosophy. This is a better rendition of "identity" in general and the identity of African philosophy in particular.

It is necessary to emphasise that the question 'what is African philosophy' is distinct and different from the question, 'does African philosophy exist?' The latter is not the primary focus of Masolo in the text mentioned nor shall I devote special attention to it despite its persistence among some scholars and lay sceptics. I take the view that African philosophy exists and from this I propose to inquire into its identity in the preferred sense of the faces and phases of African philosophy. Does it follow from this that a study of Masolo's text will provide the identity of African philosophy according to him? What Masolo does in the text referred to is what he continues to do in the new text, *Self and Community in a Changing World*. He gives a critical philosophical analysis of the faces and phases of African philosophy. By so doing, he maintains consistency with regard to his approach to the meaning of identity. Also, Masolo retains focus on the regulative concept of "identity" in his thought by recourse to "Self" and "Community" as neither can exist with absolutely no "identity". Thus the answer to the question whether or not Masolo gives a specific identity to African philosophy is that for Masolo African philosophy does have many identities. It does not have an immutable and permanent identity.

Furthermore, Masolo preserves the idea of "search", found in the previous text, through the use of the term "changing" in the title of the second text. The temptation is almost irresistible to aver that the second text is the continuation of the first in terms of its content and method. With regard to the former, new emphases are laid and, certain arguments are refined. Concerning the latter, there is no change either insofar as the procedure is first to adopt the ordinary meaning of the key words, especially "identity", "self" and "community" and then present the different phases and faces of African philosophy. These two submissions will receive further elaboration below.

The third step will be the consideration of the question whether or not the title of my essay is justified. The point of discussion in this context will be the question why "in" and not "according to Masolo". The discussion is important, as it is a focus upon the method of Masolo as distinct from his approach to the question of "identity" or the "self" of African philosophy in both texts. This will be followed by 'methodological considerations'. The meaning of identity and the self will also be discussed separately.

Following upon the discussion of the method, I will discuss, 'philosophy and indigenous knowledge' from Masolo's *Self and Community in a Changing World*. Instead, of a broad focus on this I will select in particular the section entitled 'the language of the indigenous'. My proposal in this context is to engage in critical dialogue with Masolo. In this connection Masolo presents contending arguments on the problem of the translatability of African languages. By and large, his commentary on this problem is fair and balanced. The commentary deserves special admiration in the light of his conclusion that despite the practical question about the intellectual benefits of writing in African vernacular languages and the challenge related to such an enterprise, the writing "must be attempted for two reasons: to encourage local debate about the understanding and interpretation of indigenous concepts and theories and to preserve these thought expressions in their original rendition". (Masolo 2010: 44) This conclusion is vitiated by Masolo's concession, in the same paragraph, that the beauty of our African languages is "less attractive for practical professional reasons". My argument is against this concession. It is that beneath the pragmatism inspired "practical" is to be found the surreptitious borrowing and transportation of an epistemological paradigm that is conceptually and practically not necessarily consonant or harmonious with the indigenous African vernacular to which it refers. Such borrowing is philosophically problematical especially if it ultimately results in the distortion and subordination of the indigenous vernacular epistemological paradigm. If the latter is the result then the borrowing is also unethical. Accordingly, there is an ethical dimension to translatability and this must be taken into account at all times to prevent suppression and oppression.

## Masolo's approach to African philosophy

The first of Masolo's texts mentioned in the preceding discussion leaves no doubt that African philosophy is the subject matter. The same cannot be said about the recent text prior to actually reading it. This is because it leaves open the question of whose "self" is precisely under discussion. This question is answered at page 1 of the *"introduction"*, namely, that African philosophy is the subject matter of *Self and Community in a Changing World*. This answer is reaffirmed in the statement of the two aims of the book (Masolo 2010:14-15). Like its predecessor, the recent text is about African philosophy.

I have already suggested that both texts share a common approach to the study of African philosophy. What is this approach? Masolo selects specific themes such as ethnophilosophy. He discusses the evolution of the selected theme and in the process delivers critical commentary on the positions adopted and defended by the proponents of the position. The number and variety of the themes selected appear to be the object of the implicit message that: all these phases and faces described and discussed in their complexity constitute individually or collectively the identity of African philosophy.

Masolo's approach to the question of the identity of African philosophy in the manner described above is neither isolated nor peculiar. It is, for example, similar to the one adopted in Organ's *The Self in Indian Philosophy* and Taylor's *Sources of the Self: The Making of the Modern*

*Identity*. The terms "self" and "identity" in Taylor's title are an interesting coincidence appearing in the separate titles of the two books of Masolo. Like Masolo, Taylor does not devote special attention to the conceptual discussion of these terms. Organ does the same with regard to the term "self". Taylor discusses the "self" through the articulation of the "history of the modern identity" of the West (Taylor 1989: ix). With regard to Taylor's idea of "history" we do find yet another coincidence with Masolo. One of his aims in the writing of *Self and Community in a Changing World* is to provide the reader with "a handle on the *historical origins and broader contexts*" of African philosophy (Masolo 2010: 14). The concept of "history" refers to the evolution of the "identity" of African philosophy in the case of Masolo and, in the case of Taylor the "self" refers to the "history" of modernity in the West. In these two cases as well as in the case of Organ, the evolution is described and explained in terms of specific themes. It is then left to the reader to infer the "identity" or the "self" of the subject from the description and explication of the themes. There is merit in this approach to the extent that it leaves the reader to decide on the meaning of "identity". The decision of the reader is likely to deepen and widen one of the themes. By so doing, it would contribute to the ongoing debate precisely because identity is subject to the frequentative "in search", that is, "a changing world" which by implication may result in a changed identity.

## *Justification of the essay title*

It may be objected though that the merit of Masolo's approach is not sufficient reason to neglect the conceptual clarification of the "*self*". The question remains despite the identification of African philosophy as the "self". As already stated, the question what is African philosophy is different from does African philosophy exist. The desideratum for conceptual clarification might be construed as an expression of the contested claim that the function of philosophy is the clarification of concepts. One of the reasons for questioning this claim is that it sidesteps substantive problems of philosophy and concentrates instead on its methods. My suggestion that a conceptual clarification of the "self" is required does not rest on this contested claim about the function of philosophy. Nor does it rely on its opposite namely, an over concentration on the substantive problem at the expense of the method (Organ 1964: 12). Instead, it is the point that the "self", as a concept, need not be restricted to African, Indian, Chinese or Western philosophy. For this reason, a separate elaborate discussion of this concept is important so that the reader can relate the themes to it and understand why they constitute its "identity".

In expressing the need for a conceptual clarification of the "self", I am aware, for example, of the argument that:

> "what is" questions are never fruitful, although they have been much discussed by philosophers. They are connected with the idea of *essences* – "what is the self essentially?" – and so with the very influential philosophy which I have called 'essentialism' and which I regard as mistaken. "What is" questions are liable to degenerate into verbalism – into a discussion of the meaning of words or concepts, or into a discussion of definitions. But, contrary to what is still widely believed, such discussions and definitions are useless (Popper and Eccles 1977: 100).

Suffice it to state, by way of response, that contrary to the declared futility of conceptual questions, the authors proceed for the next nineteen immediately following pages to engage in a conceptual discussion of the "self". Surely, such a discussion is unwarranted in terms of their own argument. Their disregard of their own argument affirms the utility of discussing conceptual questions. I take their criticism that 'what is' questions are likely to be grounded in "essentialism". But this is merely a likelihood and not an inevitability. For my purposes, the 'what is' question is crucial since it will assist me to stay clear of attributing to Masolo ideas or concepts that he does not espouse explicitly. I now turn to methodological considerations.

## Methodological considerations

Masolo's method, as distinct from his approach, is to give an exposition of a particular theme and in the process of doing so, provide a critical commentary. As such it is an invitation to the reader to consider: (i) the reliability of his exposition; (ii) tenability of his criticism and, (iii) depending on the outcome of the deliberation on his criticism, to decide on whether or not to construct Masolo's concept of the issue discussed under a specific theme.

### Identity and self

Identity as a concept presupposes a specific bearer of qualities. The bearer may be understood as the "self". This is consistent with the standard meaning of the word offered, for example, in the 1980 edition of Webster's New Collegiate Dictionary. Identity can also mean that one thing is the same as another if and, only if the two coincide in every feature. This meaning is not particularly relevant to my discussion. Identity can also mean that one reference can be understood in two senses, that is, the denotative and the connotative. This meaning is relevant to my discussion especially in view of the approach to African philosophy adopted by Masolo. "In another sense, one speaks of the identity of a single object maintaining itself through the passage of various outside influences; ... Closely related to this is the notion of PERSONAL IDENTITY, which remains the same throughout one's lifetime...." (Vesey and Foulkes 1990: 147). This latter is the meaning of the "self". I accept this meaning on the proviso that it is not associated with essentialism. Against this background I turn to Masolo's discussion on '*the language of the indigenous*'.

### The language of the indigenous

One of the commonplace assumptions about philosophy is that it is born of experience. A common experience of humankind is the possession and use of an own language. Often language is considered as one of the elements constituting one's identity. The language in which one is born and which one learns initially to the exclusion of all other languages is one's vernacular: it is one's indigenous language. Human contact has revealed the existence of a multiplicity and diversity of languages which form the vernacular of one or more groups of human beings.

An extended story on language according to Heidegger or Wittgenstein, for example, is not called for here. Suffice it to state that language is the medium through which meaning is conveyed in the course of communication; oral, written or even body language. Rootedness in experience means that all experience is not necessarily the same. Thus words, concepts and their meaning may differ according to the existential experience in which they are rooted. Communication in the course of interaction between different linguistic groups gives rise to the problem of the translatability of words, expressions and concepts. The critical issue here is the question whether or not translation transports and conveys the same meaning in the original language into another different language. This is one of the problems discussed by Masolo rather obliquely in chapter four, Language and Reality of *African Philosophy in search of Identity*. In this chapter the rubric, "Ordinary Language, or Philosophy?" is particularly important because it is here that Masolo declares,

Human languages have great importance for the inter-subjective function that they perform. Although it is the means by which we convey our ideas about the world, language cannot be reduced to a subordinate or secondary position in relation to thought. Experience shows that there are many ideas for which we have no words, as well as words that do not correspond exactly with our perceptions of reality in their general grammatical structure and classifications (Masolo 1994: 96).

It is noteworthy that Masolo refers to "languages" in plural. The import of this point is that "inter-subjectivity" in the context of interaction among languages is meaningful only if the idea of translatability or, even stronger, translation is presupposed. This is then the first hint at translation. Next Masolo distinguishes between "language" and "thought". In the next sentence he appears to use "ideas" as synonym of "thought" in the previous sentence. He uses the distinction as an anchor for the thesis that whatever is thought is not always translatable into language and that language does not always hand itself over as a complete translation of what we perceive. He continues this discussion on the problem of translation further in these terms,

It is true that language is a good store of people's ideas about their own environment and that by learning another people's language we are better able to understand that people's worldview. But the question one raises quickly here is: How much is the language of a people a denoter of the *a priori* and not only of the referent which is the object of communication?....while it is true that language is built upon our perception of reality in its diversity, and that therefore one is able to arrive at the structure of reality of a particular people beginning from their language, language is not made dependent upon the reality of experience on the basis of an analytical knowledge of the world" (Masolo 1994: 101).

Here again Masolo reaffirms the problem of translation without actually having used the word in the two citations referred to. "Indigenous language" is the new element introduced by the second citation with the words: "the structure of reality of a particular people beginning from their language".

The above is the prefiguration of Chapter one, Philosophy and Indigenous Knowledge, of *Self and Community in a Changing World*. It is particularly under the rubric, "Ethnophilosophy and the Controversy over Indigenous Knowledge" of chapter one that Masolo uses the terms "translate" and "translation" expressly at page 30 in his discussion predicated on Kagame and flowing into the views of Quine and Wiredu. There is little doubt that this discussion is in substance, an echo of the earlier one under the rubric, "Ordinary Language, or Philosophy?" contained in *African Philosophy in Search of Identity*. Support for this observation is that in his discussion from Kagame flowing into Quine and Wiredu, Masolo quite explicitly refers to the "ordinary language philosophy" to which the latter are "partially intellectually descended" (Masolo 2010:

31). In this instance, Masolo included the reference to Quine and Wiredu as an addition. Furthermore, both the comma and the disjunctive "or" in the interrogatively constructed early rubric already referred to are dropped in favour of simply "ordinary language philosophy". Masolo's option is by no means alien to the well-known "philosophy of language" – note the omission of the implicit "ordinary" – discourse. Against this background, I now turn to an extended discussion of the problem of translation.

*The problem of translation*

From the immediately preceding discussion, it may be inferred that the problem of translation revolves around the recognition that language does not always re-present either what is thought or perceived on a one-to-one and thus complete and comprehensive basis. In the conveyance through language of what is thought or perceived something is lost. This is the case within the same linguistic community and, even outside of it. For this reason, the problem of translation does not arise only when thought or perception is conveyed from one indigenous vernacular language to another. In the light of this it is possible to understand Masolo's question: "Do we lose anything, or put another way, can we preserve the conceptual and theoretical integrity of indigenous African thought when we use other languages to express it" (Masolo 2010: 40)? One answer is that "reasonable conceptual translation" is possible. Proponents of this reply do acknowledge that some aspect of the original meaning in the original vernacular may actually be lost. The loss is, however, something one can live with. Hence the term "reasonable".

In some cases, vernacular languages borrow some words or technical terms from other languages. Such borrowing is simply not the insertion of a new word into the language. In my view, it is the importation of a foreign cultural epistemological paradigm into another different paradigm of knowledge. The question is not only whether or not the two cultural epistemological paradigms can or speak to each other. It is also necessary to ascertain and measure the impact of the borrowing on the overall indigenous cultural epistemological paradigm. By this I mean that for example, even if it may be "reasonable" to translate the concept "university" into one's vernacular as *unibesithi*, the translation becomes the importation of the cultural epistemological paradigm that goes along with this. The importation does not necessarily carry over simultaneously the contemporary criticism of this concept as reducing diversity and plurality to one, *unius*, and; consequently perpetuating suppression and oppression of other ways of knowing and doing with particular reference – in this case – to education. It seems the necessary paradigm shift and change implied by this criticism will be postponed indefinitely for as long as the concept of "university" is not replaced by *pluriversity*. This is just an illustration of the problem connected to the concession that "reasonable" translation is possible. It is indeed possible but its consequences remain unpredictable and ethically problematical. The ethical problem arises precisely with the recognition that the suppression and oppression of other ways of knowing and doing constitute the denial and deprivation of the freedom of the other. Whenever this violation of the principle of equality of human beings is perpetrated then justification – as a question of ethics – is imperative. I turn to an elaboration of this point.

The concession to the reasonableness of translation is that the practical consequences often turn out to be the suppression and oppression of the other. One need reflect only about the translation of the Christian bible and the problems that arose and continue to afflict the indigenous African peoples who have only the translated version as their source of the knowledge of Christianity. Similarly, knowledge of philosophy as a "professional enterprise" means to date primarily the relegation of indigenous African languages to the periphery. Such marginalisation is itself ethically and academically questionable. With regard to the former we find a theoretical construct with the potential to open the gates to the subordination of the epistemological paradigm of the indigenous African peoples, or indeed, any other peoples at the theoretical level. The potentiality may translate itself into the practical subordination, suppression and oppression of indigenous African peoples. Their ways of knowing and doing are discarded and this compels them to assimilate, adopt and even adapt to other ways of knowing and doing at the expense of their own. The result is that they become imitators. Their status as imitators is a far cry from communication and conversation proper. "Objective" scientific knowledge cannot arise out of the condition of the deliberate suppression and oppression of other ways of knowing and doing. The deficit of representativity here speaks for itself. What we have under this condition is unrepresentative "scientific" knowledge masquerading as "objective" and, without sustainable ethical justification. Such a claim to knowledge cannot pass the test of professionalism. Nor can it validly justify its academic credentials. It is for these reasons that I propose to substitute ethical for Masolo's "practical". On the basis of this substitution – note my change in the citation that follows – I agree with Masolo that:

> the *ethical* question about the intellectual benefits of writing in vernacular remains challenging but must be attempted for two reasons: to encourage local debate about the understanding and interpretation of indigenous concepts and theories and to preserve these thought expressions in their original renditions (Masolo 2010: 44).

The wretched of the Earth have naturalised the centuries' long coercion to learn foreign languages. Such learning has turned insidiously into knowledge of these languages by consent. This goes against the ethical principle of human equality. The imperative remedy to this is readiness to learn other languages in order to respect, defend and promote human equality. It is the democratisation of learning and education (Kimmerle 1997: 43-56). This is the route to intercultural philosophy, a human engagement that is long overdue.

### *Conclusion*

In his discussion of "The Language of the Indigenous" Masolo has brought to light the basic problem of translation. He has shown that this problem is rooted in the attempt to convey whatever is thought or perceived through the medium of language. With particular reference to African philosophy in relation to other world philosophies (Van Rappard and Leezenberg 2010), Masolo identified "the practical question about the intellectual benefits of writing in vernacular" and advanced solid reasons why this challenge must be pursued. I accept Masolo's reasons for accepting and pursuing the challenge on the proviso that "practical" is substituted with *ethical*. In this way, the equality principle shall be protected and this is an important basis in the pursuit and construction of intercultural philosophy.

## *References*

Kimmerle, H. (1997). The Philosophical Text in the African Oral Tradition: The Opposition of Oral and Literate and the Politics of Difference. In *Philosophy and Democracy in Intercultural Perspective*. Edited by Kimmerle, H. and Wimmer, F. Amsterdam: Rodopi.

Masolo, D.A. (1994). *African Philosophy in Search of Identity*. Bloomington and Indianapolis: Indiana University Press.

Masolo, D.A. (2010). *Self and Community in a Changing World*. Bloomington and Indianapolis: Indiana University Press.

Popper, K.R. and Eccles, J.C. (1977). *The Self and Its Brain*. London: Routledge and Kegan Paul.

Taylor, C. (1989). *Sources of the Self: The Making of the Modern Identity*. Cambridge, Massachusetts: Harvard University Press.

Van Rappard, H. and Leezenberg, M. (Eds.). (2010). *Wereld Filosofie*. Amsterdam: Bert Bakker.

Vesey, G. and Foulkes, P. (1990). *Collins Dictionary of Philosophy*. London and Glasgow: Collins.

# Therapeutic African Philosophy[2]

## by Pedro A. Tabensky

*Abstract*: Therapeutic African Philosophy. Taking D. A. Masolo's survey of African philosophy in his Self and Community in a Changing World (2010) as my starting point, I will argue that epistemic and non-epistemic goods can conflict with one another and at times it may be better to privilege non-epistemic goods over epistemic ones. I will argue that the value of true belief, knowledge or understanding is tied up with the roles these play in, among other things, promoting the non-epistemic values of autonomy and self-esteem, such that, if they posed a threat to these, they shouldn't be pursued. Some general conclusions about the aims of philosophy and, more generally, intellectual work, will drawn from this discussion.

*Résumé*: Philosophie Africaine Thérapeutique. Prenant l'enquête de D.A. Masolo sur la philosophie africaine dans son Self and Community in a Changing World (2010) comme point de départ, je vais démontrer que les biens épistémique et non-épistémique peuvent entrer en conflit et que, parfois, il peut être préférable de privilégier des biens non-épistémique aux biens épistémique. Je montrerai que la valeur de la croyance vraie, la connaissance ou la compréhension est lié avec le rôle qu'elles jouent dans, entre autres, la promotion des valeurs non-épistémiques de l'autonomie et de l'estime de soi, de sorte que, si elles constituent une menace grave pour ceux-ci, ils ne devraient pas être poursuivit. Certaines conclusions générales sur les objectifs de la philosophie et, plus généralement, sur le travail intellectuel, seront tirées de cette discussion.

*Key words*: epistemic value, ethnophilosophy, fantasy, health, post-colonialism, self-deception, self-esteem, truth

*Mots-clés*: valeur épistémique, ethnophilosophie, fantaisie, santé, le post-colonialisme, l'aveuglement, l'estime de soi, la vérité.

---

[2] I would like to thank Thaddeus Metz and Dylan Futter for their insightful comments on previous drafts of this piece.

# 1

My focus text here will be D. A. Masolo's recent and rich critical survey of African philosophy in his *Self and Community in a Changing World* (2010), particularly the first two chapters which, among other things, deal in detail with Paulin Hountondji's "unrelenting anti-ethnophilosophy crusade" (2010: 18). In Masolo's words, Hountondji seeks to undermine "a culture of passivity or conformism" (2010: 18), which is expressed in ethnophilosohical discourse.

My aim here will not so much be to engage with the details of Masolo's discussion as much as to deal with an issue which is not sufficiently explored by Masolo or by the tradition which he describes and which I think is of central importance to it (and to intellectual work as a whole). Using the rich gamut of cases from the African philosophy tradition, most of which are highlighted by Masolo, I will defend the idea that at times there are good non-epistemic reasons for believing falsehoods. But the reasons in question are not justificatory. They are good insofar as they show why a subject should, for pragmatic reasons, hold a given falsehood even though it is the case that, if she were to discover that she was under the spell of illusion, she would be compelled to abandon it. By showing this, I will be taking up Masolo's invitation to his reader "to develop a reflection on the issues for himself or herself" (2010: 15). I will show, contra Masolo and Hountondji, that the reason ethnophilosophy is problematic has less to do with the fact that it is largely a false body of belief as it does with the fact that it is an unhealthy one. I agree with these authors that ethnophilosophy is problematic and I agree with them that this is largely because it perpetuates a "culture of passivity and conformism" insofar as it perpetuates the damage to self-esteem and autonomy brought about by colonial violence. But, contrary to them, I show to what extent epistemic and non-epistemic value can work against each other such that there could be good reasons for holding falsehoods.[3] These reasons do not

---

[3] For a thought-provoking analysis of how epistemic and non-epistemic values can

justify holding falsehoods, but they explain why a given subject could and even should, for pragmatic reasons, hold them (despite the fact that she could not endorse them were she to find out that they are false). So, the mere fact that ethnophilosophy is largely a false body of belief does not necessarily mean that it is of little or no value. What is ultimately wrong with ethnophilosophy is that it is an unhealthy doctrine, so there are good non-epistemic reasons for leaving the movement behind, in addition to the standard epistemic ones. Nothing of epistemic or non-epistemic value is gained by advocating ethnophilosophy.

## 2

Franz Fanon concludes his postcolonial masterpiece, *Black Skin, White Masks*, with a prayer:

O my body, make of me always a man who questions![4]

This claim powerfully expresses a key prejudice of philosophy and intellectual work in general that in intellectual work epistemic goods should always take precedence over other goods—I will be focusing on therapeutic goods here—if they conflict with the epistemic aims of inquiry. At the heart of this widespread category of prejudice is the even more extreme view that all epistemic and non-epistemic goods ought necessarily to be in harmony with one another, making it the case that conflict is always a sign—measured against what I think is the implausible ideal of perfect unity of goods—of defect. Fanon's prayer is Platonic at heart. His psycho-existential explorations aim fundamentally at the therapeutic aim of decolonizing the mind. But his decolonizing efforts are guided by the vision that only perfect fidelity to the truth will cure the colonized subject

---

conflict with one another and why at times non-epistemic value should privileged over epistemic value see Glasgow (2009: 133-154).

[4] Fanon (2008: 220).

of psycho-existential woes. Only truth can cure, Fanon implicitly thinks. That is why he so strongly believes that postcolonial subjects must always question in the sense of always aiming to get at the truth, even if it is unbearably painful. My aim is to substantiate the claim that Fanon ought to replace his prayer with the following one:

O my body, make of me a healthy person!

And the ideal of health mandates that at times we engage in practices of deception (self-deception and caring other-deception). Deception can of course be very damaging to the self, but so can too much exposure to the painful truths. The position I wish to put forward here is broadly Nietzschean, but this is not the place to show that this is the case. For Nietzsche, as I understand him, the aim of life is health. And knowledge is only one aspect of mental life, which is valuable only insofar as it is ultimately at the service of health.[5] So knowledge, for Nietzsche, ultimately serves non-epistemic aims. And, if this is correct, it would be wrong of a subject to pursue truth if it is damaging of health. A healthy subject is for Nietzsche one who lacks *resentiment*. For our purposes, a subject who lacks this has acceptable levels of self-esteem and autonomy. Such a subject is not prone to unwarranted self-admonition and dependency as a consequence of being dominated by a party believed to be stronger (Masolo, 2010: 75-76). She, for instance, does not think of herself as inferior and has not succumbed to "herd mentality" or his or her character is not largely defined from without by, or in relation to, a dominating group. Avoiding *resentiment* may involve self-deception, often, for instance, relating to rationally unwarranted confidence in the self and one's people or, more generally, in the abilities of mortals living, as they do, in challenging circumstances.

What I am particularly concerned to show here is that there are good reasons for philosophers and intellectuals generally to hold falsehoods for therapeutic reasons. But this can only be done at the cost of self-

---

[5] See, for instance, Carlisle (2003: 1-7).

deception, for one cannot hold that something is the case knowing explicitly that it is not. And it is also arguable, although I will spend little time exploring this possibility, that there is a case for the deliberate deception of others. It is arguable that there are good epistemic reasons for advancing falsehoods at times, but these are not the sorts of reasons that are relevant to our present concerns. Often, for instance, schematic approximations are more epistemically useful than cumbersome truths. Elegance—an aesthetic value—can arguably also in some circumstances be of epistemic value. But elegant falsehood can also be held for good non-epistemic reasons. Consider the case of an elegant noble lie and the role that such a lie may play in instilling positive social cohesion and hope. More generally, often we are warranted in believing for reasons that relate to protection from too much exposure to painful truths that threaten autonomy and self-esteem. It is cases of this last sort that I will be exploring, paying particular attention to the case of African philosophy. African philosophy is awash with non-epistemic value precisely insofar as it has core therapeutic aims that are less easy to detect in the Western cannon, which is not to say that they are not there.

## 3

Masolo's critical survey defends the idea that philosophy is always "part of a wider sociological process" (2010: 60) by which he means, following Hountondji in particular, who was influenced by Louis Althusser's version of Marxism, that the meaning and purpose of philosophy flows from the socio-historical space within which it is produced, and its aims should accord with the social ideal of justice, which is ultimately concerned with the betterment of the conditions of life (Hountondji 1996). And, Hountondji argues and Masolo agrees, one of the first steps required for reaching this ideal is the "termination of the dependency syndrome" (Masolo 2010: 60), which damages self-esteem and stops people from exercising genuine responsible agency (Masolo 2010: 60). But what if the termination of the syndrome requires self-deception?

Jean-Paul Sartre entertains this possibility indirectly when claiming that the Negritude movement was a "minor term" in a dialectic leading to liberation.⁶ But neither Sartre, Hountondji, nor Masolo seem fully aware that understanding intellectual work as ultimately therapeutic challenges the dominant paradigm of intellectual work as aiming ultimately at knowledge (truth or understanding). They implicitly hold the old Platonic prejudice that both therapeutic and epistemic aims can always ideally be made to complement each other. Or, put more strongly, that intellectual truth seeking is never necessarily incompatible with therapeutic aims. I grant that intellectual truth may be ideally therapeutic and that epistemic and non-epistemic concerns should, in some very ideal sense, always be complementary, but these may not be realizable in the concrete circumstances in which intellectuals actually operate. We could speculate that this means that there is something wrong with the circumstances. And to this I reply that one must cautiously avoid utopian thinking. Much of what we value in life requires that we live in circumstances where the best alternative available to us may be self-deception.⁷

I should further add that my qualified defense of self-deception does not amount to a defense of alienation.⁸ Alienation, as I see it, is a form of negative self-deception, that is, for our purposes, self-deception that negatively affects autonomy and self-esteem. So alienation requires more than merely self-deception. The self-deception in question must be damaging to health. Masolo implicitly acknowledges this when discussing the Luo proverb:

> When an intruder you consider stronger than yourself steps on and breaks your mother's pipe, you turn to your mother and rebuke her thus: "Why don't you learn to keep your things tidily so they don't sit in the path of those who are walking?" (2010: 75).

---

⁶ See Fanon (2008: 101).

⁷ For an explicit defense see Tabensky (2009: 37-53).

⁸ See Masolo (2010: 75-76).

The problem here, as Masolo comes close to admitting, is not so much that the person who rebukes his mother is self-deceived, but that the self-deception in question is damaging of health. The person is expressing his lack of self-esteem and independence from the person (or group) considered to be the stronger.

African philosophy as an academic discipline emerged at a very particular time in the history of the Continent. This was the transition between the violent humiliation of the African subject by centuries of colonial rule and the relative freedom of the postcolonial period. It emerged with a sense of urgency, not so much because of a kind of detached curiosity but because of a deep—one could even say desperate—yearning to assert something that was significantly lost: autonomy and self-esteem. This comes out very clearly in Masolo's book. And there are many dangers with this project, for one cannot simply decide to recover autonomy and self-esteem by an act of will. This is not a matter of choice in the first instance. It is, rather, a complex matter requiring, among other things, recognition from those who have for centuries seen in the African subject nothing but a caricature of the human that they have been terribly mistaken (something that can probably only occur with substantial changes in structural conditions). And it also requires acquiring a sense that what remains of the ways of being that were significantly destroyed by colonialism is worthy of being valued, especially in light of the fact that the colonial subject has largely internalized the oppressor's value system, which explicitly denigrates the African pre-colonial experience. This fundamental contradiction at the heart of the African postcolonial experience is, I speculate, what accounts for the desperate tone of much of African philosophy. This is expressed in the rarefied air of much of ethnophilosophy, from Temples to Senghor, which artificially attempts to impose identity on those who are not in a position to receive it. One cannot kick-start a new way of being by an act of will. But one cannot simply sit back and wait and do nothing about the matter. It is in difficult situations of this sort where illusion serves as a kind of escape valve aimed at relieving the tension caused by an impossible situation. In cases of this sort, where contradictions are at the very emotive heart of our beings, a fantasy may be the only way of protecting ourselves from high level of existential pain. Since epistemic aims are part of the web of life one cannot expect that the sole aim of intellectual activities is to offer us a crystal clear window to the world (or something analogous to this naïve picture).

Those with Darwinian sensitivities should observe that this picture implies that we should aim to have sufficient knowledge of the world, where sufficiently is measured against the fundamental requirement of coping with the difficulties of life. That is why a perfectly transparent relationship to the world, assuming this was possible, may be undesirable.

If we think that philosophy and other intellectual disciplines are forms of inquiry then—assuming that to inquire is to track truth—it would be true by definition that philosophy aims first and foremost to track truth and to increase understanding or knowledge. But, what I am doing here is challenging the view that intellectual pursuits just are modes of inquiry. In my view, the aim of intellectual disciplines is to represent or to picture. Representations and pictures needn't be realistic and, in the cases that interest us, they needn't be entirely realistic. The standards of goodness that define good from bad pictures or representations are different from those that define successful inquiry, although there is considerable overlap. Good pictures or representations—at least those that are relevant here—do things such as evoke, inspire and uplift, in addition to enlightening. Good pictures or representations enlighten and make our lives better and, in this sense, promote health and hence are therapeutic. And good pictures or representations don't just better our lives by enlightening, although they do this as well. Too much light can at times be blinding and thus stunting. One of the principal problems with mainstream epistemology is that it does not fully recognize that the epistemic faculty is only one aspect of the complex web of life, and it is only good if it is not destructive of the web.

**4**

And philosophy itself has played a role in the West's high levels of confidence in itself. Many other things have as well, but one cannot ignore the power of the intellectual narrative that extends back to Pythagoras' baptismal act. And evidence of the power of having philosophy on one's side is the eagerness with which Henry Odera Oruka (1990), for instance, defends the idea that philosophy existed in Africa long before colonialism, or the essentialist eagerness with which Leopold Senghor defensively defends the idea that, although Africans are not so good in the philosophical domain, they have other aptitudes which actually make them better than philosophical Caucasians. "Emotion", Senghor tells us, "is completely Negro as reason is Greek".[9] The field of philosophy is often thought of as exploring the most fundamental of all truths. Cultures find pride in seeing themselves as possessors of great truths, so the therapeutic function of philosophy is largely related to the confidence that comes with the belief in the possession of the truth, or at least that one is on its path.

What I am discussing here is what could be described as the non-epistemic dimension of truth tracking. We are motivated to search for it in part because our self-esteem depends on its possession. And we are motivated to think of ourselves as possessing it, even if at times we do not. The gap that may exist between actually holding something that is the case and believing that one does may at times only be filled in by illusion. This is especially the case in times of desperate need, where deep-seated lack of confidence—in one's epistemic abilities in the case that interests us, due to colonial violence—puts pressure on the African intellectual to seek consolation by feigning epistemic confidence (The more nationalistic varieties of African philosophy, including Negritude, Sage Philosophy, and *Ujamaa*, are cases in point). Epistemic self-esteem depends on epistemic confidence.

---

[9] Quoted and fruitfully discussed in Fanon (2008: 96).

So there is a very real relationship, it seems, between belief in one's ability to have true beliefs, particularly those associated with key features of nature and of the human condition—as opposed to boring home truths—and self-esteem. The scar that colonialism left is to a large extent related to the role that it played in breaking down the conviction that Africa has something to offer by way of truth. And one of the central necessary ingredients for seeing one's people as failed is to have lost a sense that one's culture embodies a worldview that is at least largely correct. The myth of the African as primitive is inseparable from the myth that his culture has nothing to offer by way of truth. This perhaps explains why the early W.E.B. DuBois (1897: 5-17) and, much later, Senghor, found it necessary to state that all peoples have a unique message to convey to the world. "If we were missing", Senghor tells us, "civilization would lack the rhythm section of its orchestra, the bass voices of the choir" (2001: 438-447).

Conversely, the seemingly inexpugnable pride of the prototypical Western subject—male in particular, for reasons relating to domination—is also largely blind conviction of partaking of a culture informed by the light of truth. That accounts for the blind conviction—expressed in innumerable ways, as discussed by thinkers with a postcolonial sensitivity—that the West is the norm, the measure of the good. Too much confidence can lead to blinding arrogance. And it can also lead to complacency and blind acceptance. Indeed, arrogance in this case, is an illusion of superiority and it is an illusion that—through domination—can lead the psychic damage of the oppressed. And it can also lead to damage of the oppressor group, which is something I have defended more fully elsewhere (2010).

Low self-esteem can have its advantages. It encourages questioning and search whereas there is a tendency among the arrogant to be complacent and conservative about their beliefs. So, there is a very fine balance to be had between the therapeutic benefits and pitfalls of confidence. And achieving such a balance may at times require self-deception.

# 5

One of Masolo's central concerns is to show to what extent African philosophers are warranted in engaging intimately with everyday cultural practices in Africa. Following Hountondji in the first instance, he argues that objective knowledge is always grounded everyday practices and that African philosophy shows this explicitly. This move has two non-epistemic functions: it helps the African intellectual move away from epistemic "dependency syndrome" (Masolo 2010: 60) on the colonizers' science and, relatedly, it contributes to the growth of human knowledge from the vantage point of the local. According to Masolo, Hountondji's is a "call for the return of the African subject, but a responsible subject who will chart out and take up responsibility for and control of her own intellectual, social, political, scientific, and economic destiny" (2010: 61). So, for Hountondji and Masolo responsibility and autonomy are key values that must be promoted by African philosophy. Self-esteem is at the heart of their concerns, for the "dependency syndrome" is an expression of the colonial view that all belief-systems originating in Africa are primitive and pseudo-scientific, and this gets in the way of responsibility and autonomy. The "dependency syndrome", as Masolo stresses, is manifested in the nationalistic nostalgia of ethnophilosophy, which reacts to the internal mental trace of the colonial enemy by erecting static, essentialist and nostalgic fantasies which do quite the opposite to promoting responsible and independent subjecthood. Such a subject would be one who is properly able to respond to the actual conditions of life in postcolonial Africa.

One of my principal concerns with Hountdondji and Masolo is analogous to my concern with Fanon (and much of philosophy for that matter). They do not seem to recognize the positive role that illusion can and does play in our intellectual representations. I think Hountondji—and Masolo largely agrees with him—is right to critique ethnophilosophy, but I do not think he fully recognizes what follows from his own critique. What follows, I think, is that what is wrong in the first instance with ethnophilosophy is that it does not promote health. Rather, it perpetuates the "dependency syndrome" and hence undermines autonomy and self-esteem. It is not so much because it is false that it does this, but because it is poison that perpetuates unhealthy dependency (*resentiment*, to use Nietzchean vocabulary). Ethnophilosophy is stifling insofar as it is essentialising of the African experience, aiming to force the African experience into a prefabricated mould. This is incompatible with the responsible agency that both Hountondji and Masolo defend.

What Masolo focuses on somewhat less than on his "standpoint" account of knowledge is on why this concern with the African standpoint should emerge in the first place and why, by contrast, Western philosophy typically does not dwell anywhere nearly as much on Western everyday practices, except, typically, to arrogantly boast about its grandiosity. And my tentative response is that culture is a problem for African philosophy, something in need of defense, something that does not sit easily with those attempting to defend it, something that the African subject has to struggle to be proud of, not for reasons pertaining to content but for reasons relating to the African subject's relationship to his or her own culture. Colonial violence drew a wedge between Africa's (largely) internally motivated pre-colonial historical unfolding and the African subject. The defense of African philosophy is not solely in the first instance for the sake of the advancement of knowledge or understanding. Instead it substantially aims at the recuperation of lost self-esteem on account of centuries of humiliating colonialism. The ultimate aim of Hountondji's "unrelenting anti-ethnophilosophy crusade", Masolo claims, is not so much to get at the truth but, rather, to undermine "a culture of passive conformism" (2010: 18). But both Hountondji and, following him, Masolo, believe that this can only be achieved by avoiding a "retreat into subjectivity" (Hountondji 2002: 28).[10] Both authors believe that passive conformism and dependency can only be cured if one rids oneself of all illusion.

---

[10] Quoted in Masolo (2010: 67).

One of Masolo's central aims is to show that all knowledge is localized and that there is no fact of the matter regarding which locale is better in an absolute sense from the epistemic point of view. This sort of move needs to be understood as a reaction against the deep-seated conviction imported into the African continent by force that Africa is the home of the primitive. The aim here is not so much to show that this view is not true—a strictly epistemic aim—but to find a path to health. Masolo argues that the African intellectual is not at best "the native informant", as Spivak would say (1990: 59-60), or "the junior collaborator" (Masolo 2010: 24), as Hountondji's would put it.[11] Following Spivak general line of thinking, it seems to me that one of Masolo's central aims is to show that African philosophy should be "taken seriously" (almost, one could be tempted to claim, a plea that it be taken seriously). He approvingly quotes Spivak:

> For me, the question "Who should speak?" is less crucial than "Who will listen?" . . . The real demand is that, when I speak from that position, I should be listened to seriously (Masolo 2010: 25).[12]

One could say that one of Masolo's primary aims in his book is to make a further case for African philosophy to be taken seriously, but he does not explicitly discuss the fact that this is not an epistemic aim. Its aim is largely therapeutic.

Indeed, Masolo endorses Hountondji's view that the aim of knowledge creation in Africa is development (Masolo 2010: 27). Hountondji, in Masolo's words, "was concerned with Africa's performance on the global stage" (2010: 53). And Hountondji was not only concerned with the fact that ethnophilosophy was a largely false body of beliefs. He was also and primarily concerned that the texts were "directed at appeasing a Western audience" (Masolo 2010: 55). Generally, much of African philosophy is concerned to defend African philosophy as a legitimate mode of philoso-

---

[11] See Hountondji (1995).

[12] Originally in Spivak (1990: 59-60).

phy, as a deserving member of "the global stage".

Despite the fact that Masolo acknowledges that African philosophy no longer needs justification, one must wonder why this claim needs to be made in the first place. It would be odd if a representative of Western philosophy made an analogous claim about her tradition. Masolo still feels—rightly so in my view—that it is necessary to write a book explaining and defending it. And his sustained engagement with Hountondji about the idea of orality and the possibility of systematic inquiry points to the need to justify the tradition, to shows that it is a tradition worthy of respect (a non-epistemic value). He also endorses Hountondji's view that Africa needs to work to terminate its "dependency syndrome", as the place where "raw data" is collected and left to be processed by the allegedly more able minds found in the West (Masolo 2010: 60). Following Hountondji, Masolo defends the idea that the ultimate function of African philosophy is liberation, that is, of freeing the African subject of a demeaning dependency on the West while at the same time existing side to side on the global stage with philosophies originating in the West. But he shares Fanon's prejudice that liberation and enlightenment will necessarily go together.

African philosophy is not solely fueled by a dispassionate desire to understand. This is acknowledged by some African philosophers—particularly those having postcolonial sensitivities and who typically take their lead from Fanon. But those, including Fanon, who recognize this, believe that this is always a consequence of distortion. And I disagree. The picture that I have of mind is one of competing values—epistemic, pragmatic and perhaps even aesthetic—fighting over the same territory: the mind. And it is not at all clear to me that the values associated with understanding should always take precedence over the values associated with coping. And while an inquiring subject may never be able to justify to herself that a given belief is held for non-epistemic reasons, it is nevertheless the case that it could be good non-justificatory reasons not available to the believer. There may be good reasons for delusion. The epistemic faculty is what one could refer to as the window to the world, but too much external vision can be a hindrance to organic life, so protective psychological mechanisms are required for sheltering ourselves from the risks that come when the window shows us more than we can deal with.

Academic African philosophy is largely a postcolonial response to centuries of damnation where the narratives that gave sustenance to hundreds of distinct peoples was replaced by the demeaning narratives of the colonizer. The colonizers' beliefs were imposed by force, which is a very effective way of entrenching beliefs. The colonial narrative that replaced what was there before is the narrative of humiliation. I think it is reasonable to suppose that all cultural narratives born from an unconquered people are of pride and self-respect. Conquest and oppression are the sole sources of cultural humiliation. Almost all civilizations have humiliated subjects and proud ones and the humiliated ones are always those who have been conquered by a dominating type (conceivably, the dominating type could be nature). Humiliation of a people always involves conquest of one sort or another, and the narrative of humiliation always finds its source in conquest. What a humiliated people lose is a sense of their own agency. They become patients of change where once they were agents.

Peoples whose lives have been taken from them, who have been made captives by others, and who later regain freedom (even if only partially), must start again. They must attempt to remember all that has been lost and take this as their starting point for a future that has yet to be built. This is a fraught process, plagued with danger, especially if the period of captivity stretches back several generations. So what I should stress here is that the explicit engagement with tradition which informs much of African philosophy is not merely localized for epistemic reasons. It is also localized for psycho-social reasons. And the energy—hope, passion and at times rage—with which academic African philosophers tend to engage with tradition is significantly motivated by the struggle to come to terms with humiliation. When Cheikh Anta Diop tells us that philosophy originates in Africa (in ancient Egypt), when Leopold Senghor tells us that the African is "richer in gifts than in works",[13] when Kwame Nkrumah, Julius Nyerere and Senghor tell the world that socialism was invented in Africa, when Henry Odera Oruka spends his intellectual energy defending orality against the imputation that in this medium philosophy proper cannot take place, they are doing quite a lot more than merely defending certain views against the charge that they may be false. They are fighting to redeem something that has been destroyed, something at the very heart of Africa's autonomy and self-esteem. And the fact that a large percentage of African philosophers were involved in political activity is more grist for the mill that their thought to a large extent aims at liberation, which is at bottom a social-therapeutic process.

If I am right to follow Nietzsche and think of health as the aim of human living, then we should see the space of mind as a kind of battlefield of competing values, epistemic and non-epistemic. And health—contra Fanon, Hountondji, Masolo and many others—makes it the case that epistemic value may be trumped by, say, the values of autonomy and self esteem. But the balance is, of course, extremely precarious. Autonomy and self-esteem can come at the cost of wishful thinking and too much of this is one of the central features of madness or complacency. But, on the other hand, an unwavering commitment to understanding can lead to immense self-destructive suffering. And an unwavering confident commitment to what is believed to be the case can also lead to a stifling of creativity. We are makers of worlds, and the ability to do this lies somewhere in between knowledge and fantasy. This is as true of intellectual endeavors as it is of life in general. And the ultimate criterion for successful world creation is whether such creation promotes health. The features of health that we have explored are autonomy and self-esteem.

---

[13] See Fanon (2008: 96).

6

Intellectuals create representation of the world with the ultimate aim of coping as best we can. The criterion for differentiating healthy from unhealthy self-deception is what role the self-deception plays in promoting a life that is not stifled by the exigencies of life but which is also not entirely alienated from the world. An alienated subject can hardly be said to be an agent precisely insofar as he or she is the victim of radical delusion. But to be stifled is to become a slave of circumstances, unable to move beyond what is strictly given and imagine new—at times even deeply unlikely, but not necessarily impossible—ways of being in the world. We are makers of worlds as much as we are discoverers. And the ideals of discovery and creative world-making often pull us in opposite directions. Discovery speaks to a large extent to our epistemic interests and world-making is significantly a response to pragmatic and aesthetic needs. So, Fanon should have said (but does not):

O my body, make of me a *healthy* person!

## References

Carlisle, C. (2003). Nietzsche's *Beyond Good and Evil*: "Why Insist on the Truth?" *Richmond Journal of Philosophy* 4: 1-7.
Du Bois, W.E.B. (1897). The Conservation of Races. *The American Negro Academy Occasional Papers* 2: 5-17.
Fanon, F. (2008). *Black Skin, White Masks*. Translated by Markmann, C.L. London: Pluto Press. (Original work published 1952.)
Glasgow, J. (2009). *A Theory of Race*. New York: Routledge.
Hountondji, P.J. (1995). Producing Knowledge in Africa Today. *African Studies Review*, 38(3): 1-10.
Hountondji, P.J. (1996). *African Philosophy: Myth and Reality*. 2nd edition. Bloomington: Indiana University Press.
Hountondji, P.J. (2002). *The Struggle for Meaning: Reflections on Philosophy, Culture, and Democracy in Africa*. Translated by Conteh-Morgan, J. Athens: Center for International Studies, Ohio University Press.
Masolo, D.A. (2010). *Self and Community in a Changing World*. Bloomington: Indi-

ana University Press.
Oruka, H.O. (1990). *Sage Philosophy: Indigenous Thinkers and Modern Debate on African Philosophy.* Leiden: J. Brill.
Senghor, L.S. (2001). Negritude and African Socialism. In *The African Philosophy Reader.* Edited by Coetzee, P.H. and Roux, A.P.J. London: Routledge, pp. 438-447.
Spivak, G.C. (1990). Questions of Multiculturalism. In *The Post-Colonial Critic: Interviews, Strategies, Dialogues.* Edited by Harasym, S. New York: Routledge, pp. 59-60.
Tabensky, P.A. (2009). Tragic Joyfulness. In *Philosophy and Happiness.* Edited by Bortolotti, L. London: Palgrave, pp. 37-53.
Tabensky, P.A. (2010). The Oppressor's Pathology. *Theoria: A Journal of Social and Political Theory*, 125: 77-98.

# Some Doubts about 'Indigenous Knowledge', and the Argument from Epistemic Injustice

## by Kai Horsthemke

*Abstract*: Some Doubts about 'Indigenous Knowledge', and the Argument from Epistemic Injustice. In his book Self and Community in a Changing World, Dismas Masolo writes that 'there appears to be little disagreement that there is knowledge that is indigenous to Africa – that is, knowledge that is unique, traditional or local knowledge that exists within and develops around the specific conditions of the experiences of African peoples'. While I agree that there are beliefs and that there may be skills that are unique and indigenous to Africa, I doubt whether the same can be said about propositional knowledge, or 'knowledge that'. More importantly, I think that the case for indigenous knowledge is helped neither by the Yoruba definition of knowledge presented by Barry Hallen and J.O. Sodipo nor by Kwasi Wiredu's epistemological theory of 'truth as opinion', sources on which Masolo draws extensively in his book. Consequently, I consider the preoccupation with indigenous knowledge as 'a viable tool for transforming the world' to be misguided. After discussing the political dimension of the debate, with special reference to the idea of epistemic injustice, I close with some thoughts about 'truth and reconciliation'.

*Résumé*: Quelques Doubtes sur 'La Connaisance Indigène', et l'Argument de l'Injustice Épistémique. Dans son livre Self and Community in a Changing World, Dismas Masolo écrit que 'il semble y avoir peut de désaccord qu'il y a une connaissance qui soit indigène à l'Afrique – c'est-à-dire, une connaissance qui soit unique, traditionnel ou local et qui existe au sein et se développe autour des conditions spécifiques des expériences des peuples africains.' Bien que je convienne qu'il y a des croyances et qu'il peut y avoir des compétences qui lui sont propres et indigènes à l'Afrique, je doute que la même chose peut être dit á propos de la connaissance propositionnelle, ou du 'savoir que'. Plus important encore, je pense que le cas de la connaissance indigène est aidé ni par la définition de connaissance Yuraba présenté par Barry Hallen et J.O. Sodipo, ni par la théorie épistémologique de Kwasi Wiredu de la 'vérité comme opinion', les sources sur lesquelles Masolo s'inspirent largement dans son livre. Par conséquent, je considère la préoccupation de la connaissance indigène comme 'un outil viable pour transformer le monde' d'être sans support et même erronée. Après avoir discuté de la dimension politique du débat, avec une référence particulière à l'idée d'injustice épistémique, je terminerai par quelques réflexions sur la 'vérité et réconciliation'.

*Key words*: epistemic injustice, gbàgbó (belief), indigenous knowledge, mò (knowledge), reconciliation, truth (as opinion)

*Mots-clés:* injustice épistémique, gbàgbó (croyance), connaissance indigène, mò (connaissance), réconciliation, vérité (comme opinion)

## *Introduction*

I came across the following story some time ago. Although it is contrived (understandably – it is in the nature of jokes that they tend to be contrived), I repeat it here, because it arguably resonates with some of the central ideas this paper is concerned with. The aborigines in a remote part of northern Australia asked their new elder whether the coming winter was going to be cold or mild. Since he was an elder in a modern community he had never been taught the old secrets. When he looked at the sky he couldn't tell what the winter was going to be like. Nevertheless, to be on the safe side, he told his tribe that the winter was indeed going to be cold and that the members of the tribe should collect firewood to be prepared. But, being a practical leader, he called the Bureau of Meteorology and asked whether the coming winter in the northern area was going to be cold or mild. The meteorologist responded, 'It looks like this winter is going to be cold.' So the elder went back to his people and told them to collect even more wood in order to be prepared. A week later he called the Bureau of Meteorology again. 'Does it still look like it is going to be a cold winter?' The meteorologist again replied, 'Yes, it's actually going to be a very cold winter.' The elder again went back to his community and instructed them to collect every scrap of firewood they could find. Two weeks later the elder called the Bureau again. 'Are you absolutely sure that the winter is going to be very cold?' he asked. 'Absolutely,' the man replied. 'It's looking more and more like it is going to be one of the coldest winters ever.' 'How can you be so sure?' the elder asked. The weatherman replied, 'Our satellites have reported that the aborigines in the north are collecting firewood like crazy, and that's always a sure sign.'

I have not been able to determine the original source of this story. Nor have I been able to verify whether an elder who has not been educated in or initiated into the 'old ways' or traditions can be designated or elected leader of an aboriginal community. (This *does* seem rather unlikely.) What is noteworthy about this story is that the traditional, rural community (i.e. the elder speaking for the indigenous people) and the scientific establishment (i.e. the meteorologist speaking for the weather bureau) appear to rely on each other, with regard to their epistemic justification. Each takes the assumed 'knowledge' of the other as the basis for their own predictions: which not only raises something like the 'chicken-or-the-egg' question but also causes one to doubt whether or not we are actually dealing with *knowledge* here. The joke is derived from the implication that, at least in this instance, it is *both* aboriginal knowledge *and* scientific knowledge that constitute myths.

I want to argue the following: science (e.g. meteorology) can – with some degree of accuracy, on the basis of available evidence – make predictions (e.g. about the impending seasons). Similarly, non-scientists (i.e. people not formally schooled or trained in science) can – with some degree of accuracy, on the basis of their own and others' experiences – make certain predictions (e.g. about the weather). But can one really, and meaningfully, distinguish between 'mainstream' and 'indigenous' knowledge? I do not think so – and I will attempt to show in this paper why not.

A further set of questions arises with the definition of, say, 'coldness' – not to mention individual and communal experiences of coldness. These questions do not seem to be immediately relevant to the present concerns – but it may still be illustrative how one might try to address them. While it is clear that experiences of coldness, warmth and heat vary, it can nonetheless be stated that temperature is objectively measurable. Not only that, but one might also say that (as far as weather is concerned) anything below 0° Celsius is cold, while anything above 40° Celsius is hot. Of course, what is 'cold' to members of a San community is not what is so to members of an Inuit community, and the same thing can be said about experiences and perceptions of what is 'hot'. In fact, our individual perceptions change all the time. Does this mean that everything is relative, that there are only subjective 'truths'? No, because our personal and communal perceptions and experiences relate in some way or other to the way the world is, to how things are. For example, it is possible for me to perceive (at the same time) the same body of lukewarm water as 'cold' and as 'hot' – depending on where I have previously had my hands. If I place one of my hands in hot water, the other hand in cold water, and then place both in a bucket filled with lukewarm water, the water will feel cold to one hand and very warm (if not hot) to the other. Yet, I *know* the water is lukewarm. It just *seems* cold or hot.

There is much I agree with in Dismas Masolo's admirably engaging and wide-ranging work. But, because this paper constitutes part of a philosophy colloquium and because philosophers tend to prize healthy misgivings and critical engagement above sycophantic agreement, I have made it my task in this paper to target phrases and ideas that on occasion suggest more extreme views in Masolo. I will argue that neither the Yoruba nor the Akan conceptions of knowledge advance the case for 'indigenous knowledge', a concept about which I remain rather sceptical. After also discussing the political dimension of the debate, with special reference to the idea of epistemic injustice, I close with some thoughts about 'truth and reconciliation'.

### The idea of 'indigenous knowledge'

In his book *Self and Community in a Changing World*, Masolo writes that 'there appears to be little disagreement that there is knowledge that is indigenous to Africa – that is, knowledge that is unique, traditional or local knowledge that exists within and develops around the specific conditions of the experiences of African peoples' (Masolo 2010: 51-52).

Well, my voice has been, and will be in this paper, one of dissent. While I agree that there are beliefs and that there may be skills that are unique and indigenous to Africa, I doubt whether the same can be said about propositional knowledge, or 'knowledge that'. More importantly, I think that the case for indigenous knowledge is helped neither by the Yoruba definition of knowledge presented by Barry Hallen and J.O. Sodipo nor by Kwasi Wiredu's epistemological theory of 'truth as opinion', sources on which Masolo draws extensively in his book. Consequently, I consider the preoccupation with indigenous knowledge as 'a viable tool for transforming the world' (Masolo 2010: 18) to be misguided.

One of 'the themes that stand out in the recent history of Africans' philosophical reflections' is 'the question of reworking and integrating indigenous knowledge into the new philosophical order'. The 'issue of the status of indigenous knowledge in contemporary Africa runs through all the matters discussed' in Masolo's book (Masolo 2010: 7):

Philosophy is always about the familiar and the indigenous, whatever its form or epistemic status; it interrogates, deconstructs, analyses, interprets and tries to explain it. Philosophy is related to indigenous knowledge as the written is to the oral (Masolo 2010: 28).

Isn't this a false analogy? At least we can be sure that 'the oral' exists. And when Masolo goes on to consider 'examples that illustrate philosophy's ties with the ordinary and with everyday language' (Masolo 2010: 28), the rejoinder might be that 'the ordinary and everyday language' is not the same as 'indigenous knowledge'.

But what then *is* 'indigenous knowledge'? What accounts for its relatively recent emergence[1], and what is its advocacy meant to achieve? I

---

[1] Although the manifestation of what is taken to be indigenous knowledge could presumably be traced back roughly to the origins of humankind, the idea of indigenous knowledge is a relatively recent phenomenon. It has arguably gained conceptual and discursive currency only during the last 30-40 years. Especially in recent years it has been the subject of congresses, conferences, meetings, as well as countless papers,

will deal with the first of these questions a little later. Masolo lists several reasons for the '*re*emergence of interest in indigenous knowledge in recent years' (emphasis mine). First, the effects of industrialisation 'in the Western sphere or the global North', namely '[o]zone depletion and environmental poisoning, ... have made once-scorned simpler ways of life and controlled scales of industrialisation more attractive for their stances towards biodiversity and their general friendliness to the environment, at least at the intellectual level' (Masolo 2010: 25-26). Clearly (and here I concur with Masolo), Western industrialisation has led to, or have had as a significant goal, the subjugation of nature, and so far has been devastatingly efficient. The pursuit of nuclear energy, wholesale deforestation and destruction of flora and fauna, factory farming of nonhuman animals for human consumption, vivisection and genetic engineering are deplorable and – indeed – *ir*rational (see Horsthemke 2010, ch. 3), as is the relentless preoccupation with and pursuit of 'growth'. Second, with the end of the Cold War,

the politics of numbers in the scramble for alliances and geopolitical spheres of influence is a thing of the past, thus making the sustenance of the dependency of distant nations and peoples a far less attractive policy and a sacrifice for regimes and taxpayers in developed nations. There is neither political nor economic gain for such sacrifice. Consequently, the current focus of aid agencies ... is on helping the disadvantaged governments of economically and technologically disadvantaged nations establish self-reliant and internally sustainable programs (Masolo 2010: 26).

I am not altogether clear about the intended force of this argument: after all, aid provision has a substantial downside that is well-documented (see Kabou 1991, Seitz 2009). Nonetheless, there are additional factors that account for the (re?)emergence of interest in indigenous knowledge systems. With the rise of multiculturalism, the inferiorisation of indigenous peoples' practices, skills and insights has, to a large extent, been unmasked as arrogant and of dubious 'rationality'. There has also developed

---

articles and reports.

a strong tendency to view current attempts by industrial and high-tech nations to (re)colonise or appropriate for commercial gain these practices, skills and insights as exploitative and contemptible.

With regard to the question what the focus on indigenous knowledge is hoped to achieve, there are several related ideas that appear again and again (see Semali & Kincheloe, eds. 1999 *passim*; Odora Hoppers, ed. 2002 *passim*; and De Sousa Santos, ed. 2007 *passim*): reclamation of cultural or traditional heritage; decolonisation of mind and thought; recognition and acknowledgement of self-determining development; protection against further colonisation, exploitation, appropriation and/ or commercialisation; legitimation or validation of indigenous practices and worldviews; and condemnation of, or at least caution against, the subjugation of nature and general oppressiveness of non-indigenous rationality, science and technology.

To return to the initial question: what actually *is* 'indigenous knowledge'? 'Inspired by the claim that knowledge takes place in and reflects the social worlds of its creators in expression and use,' according to Masolo, 'formerly suppressed systems liberated themselves from foundationalist claims and monolithic canons and called for different, more rigourous, and comparative approaches to the epistemological enterprise in the latter part of the twentieth century' (Masolo 2010: 18).

Like its cognates (local, native, original, old, or insider) and its antonyms or counterparts (migrant, alien, new, settler, or outsider) the term "indigenous" is used to define the origin of an item or person in relation to how their belonging to a place is to be temporally characterised, especially in comparison to other contenders in claiming belonging. ... The term "indigenous" has not always had positive connotations for those to whom it was intended to introduce and create awareness of distant worlds. ... Implications of diversity persist even as the idea of indigeneity acquires more positive connotations. As pluralism takes centre stage in contemporary thought and practical orientations in both the public and private realms, indigenous systems are not only encouraged to remain and show more autonomy, they are also thought to have the capacity to sustain themselves (Masolo 2010: 21).

'Indigenous knowledge', then, is generally taken to cover local, traditional, non-Western beliefs, practices, customs and worldviews, and frequently also to refer to alternative, informal forms of knowledge. Rather perplexingly, while a lot has been said and continues to be said about the idea of indigeneity (again, see Semali & Kincheloe, eds. 1999 *passim*; Odora Hoppers, ed. 2002 *passim*; and De Sousa Santos, ed. 2007 *passim*), there have been very few writers or authors willing to furnish an explanation of their understanding or concept of 'knowledge'. Although (or because?) the terms 'knowledge' and 'epistemology'/ 'epistemological' are used in liberal abundance, no account is given of the actual meaning/s of the terms. Thus, there is a general failure among theorists to appreciate and engage with the ramifications of these concepts. Instead, 'indigenous knowledge' is unquestioningly employed as an umbrella concept to cover practices, skills, customs, worldviews, perceptions, as well as theoretical and factual understandings. Happily, Masolo does not shy away from this philosophical challenge. In fact, he draws on two sources, the Yoruba definition of knowledge presented by Hallen and Sodipo, as well as Wiredu's epistemological theory of 'truth as opinion'. In what follows, however, I will attempt to show not only that neither account helps to render the idea of 'indigenous knowledge' plausible, but also that Masolo fails to bring these two conceptions into conversation with one another.

### *Mò and gbàgbó: The Yoruba definition of knowledge*

In their book *Knowledge, Belief, and Witchcraft: Analytical Experiments in African Philosophy* Hallen and Sodipo explore the contrast between 'knowledge as justified true belief'[2] and the Yoruba concept of knowl-

---

[2] The traditional understanding of propositional knowledge can be traced back to Socrates and Plato, whose dialogues *Meno* (99c-100a) and *Theaetetus* (200e-202d)

edge. Masolo provides the following sketch of Hallen and Sodipo's account:

When an ordinary Yoruba speaker – one who is not an *onisegun* [an indigenous cultural expert] – says that she can "*gbàgbó*" (believe) rather than "*mò*" (know) that [*p*, on the basis of a well-placed source's testimony], it is probable (and indeed is often the case) that she says so only because that is how any Yoruba speaker would be expected to correctly deliver that kind of judgement. ... [I]f pressed on why she only "believes" that [*p*, despite the well-positioned source asserting so] the Yoruba speaker may, upon the demands of the Yoruba language alone, correctly respond that she has no firsthand knowledge of the situation herself and so can only believe but not claim to "know" the state of the matter (Masolo 2010: 30).

This appears to be perfectly in keeping with the traditional (Platonic) definition of knowledge: the source's testimony offers some degree of justification for the speaker's belief, but it does not guarantee 'knowledge'. But there is more to Hallen and Sodipo's distinction:

According to the analysis, the Yoruba concept of *mò* (knowledge) exacts stringent conditions under which belief (*gbàgbó*) can qualify as or become knowledge (*mò*). It is not enough, as appears in the Anglo-American rendition of this epistemological problem, that one be justified in believing, for example, that *p* for one to know that *p*, even if *p* were to be true (Masolo 2010: 45).

Hallen and Sodipo observe that in Yoruba

> *Gbàgbó* that may be verified is *gbàgbó* that may become *mò*. *Gbàgbó* that is not open to verification and must therefore be

---

contain the essence of this definition. Traditionally, 'knowledge' has been defined as comprising three individually necessary and jointly sufficient components: belief (or opinion; this is its subjective component), truth (its objective component) and appropriate or suitable justification (which serves a bridging function between the subjective and objective).

evaluated on the basis of justification alone (*àláyé, papò*, etc.) cannot become *mò* and consequently its *òótó* [truth] must remain indeterminate. The point of difference between the two systems that we find of greatest significance is the relative role of testimony or second-hand information. In the Yoruba system any information conveyed on the basis of testimony is, until verified, *ìgbàgbó*. In the English system [by contrast] a vast amount of information conveyed on the basis of testimony is, *without verification*, classified as "knowledge that" (Hallen and Sodipo 1997: 81; quoted in Masolo 2010: 45; emphasis added).

Reliance on testimony and second-hand information arguably renders possible progress in the natural and social sciences.[3] Yet usually, unverified claims are not classified as propositional knowledge. Take the Nonqawuse case: historians entertain certain hypotheses, but they claim knowledge only of certain aspects of the story. Thus, it is taken to be a historical fact that her account of having been spoken to by her ancestors, and in the process receiving pertinent instructions as to how to free her people from the colonial yoke, led to the cattle-killing and crop-burning among the Gcaleka Xhosa in the middle of the 19th century. Yet, there is

---

[3] There are two common types of testimony, oral and written. We normally assume that the oral testimony of others is true, unless we have some reason to believe that it is not. Believing others and accepting their claims, unless there is a reason not to, is an enormously time-saving strategy. Trying to find out everything for oneself would not only be a huge waste of time but would be irrational. With written testimony (e.g. newspapers, magazines, encyclopaedias, relevant books), similarly, we tend to accept claims as true, unless we find some reason not to, if a claim conflicts with something else we know. Most of the time, when we accept written testimony, we can learn countless truths we would have neither the time nor the leisure to observe or simply could not observe because the event is historically or geographically remote. Again, accepting written testimony is, generally, the rational thing to do. The medium of both oral and written testimony is language. This also relates to education. Both the teaching and the learning of a language depend for their success crucially on truthfulness and trust. If young children did or could not believe that certain words uttered by their parents and educators referred or corresponded to objects in the world they would be unable to acquire linguistic skills. Perhaps one could go so far as to say that truthfulness and trust are essential for making basic sense of the world.

insufficient evidence that she was on the pay-roll of the Eastern Cape settlers at the time, that the Eastern Cape government deliberately deceived her, that she suffered from delusions and hallucinations, that she was waging a personal vendetta against her people, etc.

Furthermore, the 'English system' is mindful of the problems surrounding verification. Either way, it is as yet unclear in what way/s the distinction between *gbàgbó* and *mò* is meant to contribute to establishing the plausibility of *indigenous* knowledge. Indeed, when Masolo lauds the Yoruba understanding of knowledge for requiring 'first-person experiential (verifiable) testimony and not *mere justification*' (Masolo 2010: 46; emphasis mine), 'direct, first-hand experience' (Masolo 2010: 47, 48), and when he acknowledges that the '*mò-gbàgbó* distinction does not privilege tradition or any other form of received information' (Masolo 2010: 48), the same question arises: Where does this leave 'indigenous knowledge'? 'In fact', he contends,

> it is so sceptical of untested claims that it even robs science of its predictive strength. Above all, it makes a mockery of the English-language (analytical) definition of knowledge based on *mere justification of belief* (Masolo 2010: 48; emphasis added).

This is surely a red herring: I am not aware of any card-carrying representative of the analytical tradition subscribing to this 'definition' (see previous footnote).[4] More seriously, because the 'Yoruba system draws a much smaller map for knowledge-claims' (Masolo 2010: 46), the possibility of indigenous knowledge would be thereby reduced to (truthful reports of) direct, first-hand experience. In addition, such experience would have to be immediate, not remembered – since memory can and often does fail us, and falsify or exaggerate events. Finally, even direct, first-hand expe-

---

[4] It might be contended that Masolo's reference to 'mere justification of belief' is just shorthand for the 'justified true belief' account, especially in the light of his awareness of the truth condition (Masolo 2010: 30, 45). Yet, the inclusion of the word 'mere' certainly gives the impression that he is setting up a straw person here for easy demolition.

riential knowledge-claims are potentially problematic. A problem that pertains to observation, albeit not to sensation, is that of fallibility. Yes, I can be mistaken about the actual *object* of my sense experience, but I cannot be mistaken about my sensation *as such*. It *just is* the way it appears to me. Unlike events of sensation, however, observations are frequently unreliable or deceptive (as in illusions or hallucinations), and also partial and subject to perceptual relativism. In other words, there is also the possibility of different interpretations of, or our vantage points affecting, what we observe. Indeed, we may focus on different aspects of a given observed event – which explains why the accounts of several eye-witnesses often diverge, if not contradict each other.

There are two additional points that need to be made about observations. First, we do claim to have knowledge about things that we might not be able to observe. The inside of a molecule cannot be seen with the naked eye, and yet we claim to know what is going on in there. Then there are places like the bottom of the ocean, deep toward to centre of the earth, or deep space, which we cannot observe directly because we cannot go there. We do, however, build instruments like microscopes, telescopes, and cameras to do the work for us and, on this basis we claim to have 'seen' places we normally are incapable of seeing. Second, much of what we observe occurs against the backdrop of some or other theory we have about what it is we are looking at. A geologist who goes underground to examine a vein of gold would not be able to distinguish the vein were it not for his prior training. His learned theory enables him to see much better than if he did not have theory at all. Similarly, an educator's observations of her learners depend partly on her theories of, for example, learning and development.

Finally, the Yoruba rejection of received information as a source of knowledge (second-person testimony) may not only be mistaken but also in conflict with a cherished African traditional principle in education. I think John Hardwig is correct when he says:

Modern knowers cannot be independent and self-reliant, not even in their own fields of specialisation. In most disciplines, those who do not trust cannot know; those who do not trust cannot have the best evidence for their beliefs (Hardwig 1991: 693-694).

The role of trust in knowledge, on this account, indicates a noteworthy communalist orientation. To denigrate the epistemic significance of trust, and of epistemological division of labour through reliance on other people's testimony, may well be in contradiction of African communalism.

I suggest, then, that a reduction of 'indigenous knowledge' to first-hand, direct, experiential knowledge-claims – that may, indeed, be mistaken! – strips the case for indigenous *knowledge* of much of its intended force. This leaves Masolo's claim (echoing Thomas Kuhn, Sandra Harding, Bruno Latour, and Paulus Gerdes[5]; Masolo 2010, 22, 23, 60) that *all* knowledge is local. On the subject of scientific knowledge in particular,

> according to Sandra Harding, all sciences are local knowledge systems. ... Because all sciences are locally grounded, they are ethnosciences. ... all knowledge claims are only points of view, some at the individual level (such as those who profess relativist[6] stands) and others (such as those that incorporate stern and open modes of inquiry) more embedded in culture[7] (Masolo 2010: 22, 23).

Again with Harding, Masolo argues that, 'despite the fact that good science is characterised by strong objectivity, inclusive rationality, and universal validity, the corpus of scientific knowledge remains an aspect of local knowledge' (Masolo 2010: 60). *If* that is so – which is very doubtful – then why insist on retaining the descriptor 'local' (or 'indigenous')?

---

[5] Doubts about the credibility of these sources have been expressed in Horsthemke 2004a, Benson and Stangroom 2006: 50-55 and 55-59, and Horsthemke and Schäfer 2007, respectively.

[6] The preferable and more accurate term here would be 'subjectivist', rather than 'relativist'.

[7] *This* would be a (cultural) relativist stand.

This is as uninformative as to refer to the *Catholic* pope, or to *human* philosophers. Where does all this leave the notion of 'indigenous knowledge'? I want to claim the following: If the important term here is 'indigenous', then it refers either to indigenous practices or skills ('knowledge how'), or to indigenous belief(s). On the other hand, if it actually is meant to refer to 'knowledge' in the factual or propositional sense, then the idea of 'indigenous' knowledge simply fails to make sense. The term 'indigenous' then becomes redundant[8]: what we are dealing with here is knowledge as such. My assumption (shared by the Yoruba definition, it would appear) is that truth (*òótó*) is 'a significant component of knowledge' (Masolo 2010: 47). It acts as the objective anchor of our more or less adequately justified beliefs. Or does it?

### *'Truth as opinion'*

In his book *Philosophy and an African Culture*, Wiredu notes that the correspondence theory of truth[9] cannot without circularity be expressed in

---

[8] One might point out, of course, that 'indigenous' ought to be understood as referring to geographical origin, or source, rather than the scope of validity. Thus, knowledge about the thirst- and appetite-suppressing properties of the *!khoba* cactus (*Hoodia gordinii*) originated with the San, before it became global (and commercially exploited) knowledge. This is uncontroversial and, indeed, plausible. My problem arises with the demarcation of 'indigenous' knowledge as 'unique' and 'distinct' (see Masolo 2010: 51) and with its purported viability as a 'tool for transforming the world' (Masolo 2010: 18).

[9] Without being able to elaborate on the matter, or to critique rival conceptions of truth (coherence, consensus, pragmatism, redundancy, etc.), I am suggesting here that the commonsense account of truth assumes that there is *at least some* correspondence between the statements I utter and the world as it exists, i.e. independently of me. The central element of correspondence theories of truth is that, other things being equal, the truth/ falsity of what is said has something to do with a reality that is *independent* of the statements made about it. I might legitimately for different purposes describe the world in many different ways. But for those descriptions and distinctions to stick, there must be features of the world that enable them to be made. One cannot get away

the Akan language. He

suggests that truth is an unattainable ideal both in the sense that it is something worth aiming for and in the sense that it is something we are ultimately incapable of realising. He argues that the solipsistic approach to the problem of truth as suggested in the significantly dominant aspect of the Western tradition, such as is encountered in the correspondence theory, makes it fundamentally indistinguishable from opinion. Truth, he asserts "is opinion[10] or point of view", for someone always knows something from some point of view, regardless of the number of people who might find themselves sharing one point of view (Masolo 2010: 140).

It is difficult to see how Wiredu wants to avoid logical inconsistency when he advances these claims as having truth content. Masolo continues:

Every individual person has this special relationship to the world as an individual, on the one hand, and an essential relationship to others as the source of meaning-making, on the other. What we "know" of the world does not and cannot emerge from only one of these sides of our relation to the world. Rather, what we "know" of the world is a constant striving to reconcile both sides of our relation to the world, namely, reconciling what we (empirically) experience as a stream of physical stimuli with what we have learned these stimuli to be or to mean. This ... is the philosophical-anthropological condition of personhood that grounds the epistemological theory of "truth as opinion" (Masolo 2010: 160; see also 175ff.).

No – I would argue: what this indicates, rather, is that the vast majority of

---

from reality – and from the truth/ falsity of statements that give an account of it.

[10] This is a point Wiredu made on more than one occasion during the ISAPS (International Society of African Philosophy and Studies) 15th Annual Conference was hosted in April 2007 by the Rhodes University Philosophy Department in Grahamstown, South Africa.

our beliefs arises from our situation as related, relational beings in communities of inquiry, as well the complexity of justification and the interaction of different sources or kinds of justification: sense-experience and observation, on the one hand, and memory, testimony, and deductive and non-deductive reasoning, on the other. Truth is not a convention, a matter of meaning-making between consenting adults. So, if Wiredu's 'position favours a dialogical sense of truth over the objectivist one' (Masolo 2010: 161), I suspect he may be quite wrong.[11]

Wiredu explicitly rejects relativism, which in his opinion is 'an absurd doctrine'. He says:

> It is the insistence on the need for belief to be in accordance with the canons of rational investigation which distinguish my view from relativism. Truth is not relative to point of view. It is, in one sense, a point of view ... born out of rational inquiry, and the canons of rational inquiry have a universal application (Wiredu 1980: 176-177; quoted in Masolo 2010: 177).

Yet, I am not sure how Wiredu's position – equating, as it does, truth and belief – *can* avoid relativism, however much he rejects the doctrine's tendency to make 'truth arbitrary, whimsical, and ungrounded in serious gnostic endeavour' (Masolo 2010: 177).[12] 'Truth is a point of view'. Is this truth (if it is that) also a point of view? If so, why should it impress others with a different point of view? If not, then there exists at least one

---

[11] Didier Kaphagawani commits a related error. When he explains that, in his home language Chewa, '(w)hat is true is what is seen ... or perceived by either an individual or a collection of individuals' (Kaphagawani 1998: 241), he clearly confuses truth and justification. As I have indicated above, observation and perception are sources of justification and knowledge. Given the possibility of observational error and perceptual relativity, they are not identical with truth as such. Even consensus among all individuals about what they perceive does not amount to truth, the way things really are.

[12] I am suggesting here that this is a problem for Wiredu more than it is for Masolo, who explicitly disavows relativism.

truth that is not a point of view. 'It may be true for you, but it is not true for me'. Is this my truth? Or is it also your truth? If the former, why should it impress those who are of a different opinion? If the latter, this indicates that reconciliation is possible – yet, again at the expense of a doxastic basis of truth and in favour of universalism. Either way, the 'truth-is-opinion' theorist will be caught up in paradox, in a logical conundrum. At some point, he will want to claim that his statements about the doxastic nature of truth are, in fact, non-doxastically, universally true (that is, independently of belief or opinion or point of view) – which he cannot do consistently, given his perspectivalism. Wiredu's position is all the more puzzling in that, elsewhere, he does appear to subscribe to an understanding of truth that avoids any reference to belief or opinion: *nea ete saa*, which is an Akan phrase for 'that which is so' (Wiredu 1998: 235). Either way, it remains doubtful whether Wiredu's theory can do the requisite work for a defence of 'indigenous knowledge'. Moreover, the Yoruba definition of knowledge and Wiredu's relational position are not brought into conversation with one another, at least not explicitly, by Masolo.

Sometimes, 'happily', the author says,

> when we have the opportunity to know the characteristics of other knowledge communities, we may venture to compare them with our own, meaning that there is little (if anything) that impenetrably closes one knowledge system from another. At the minimum, and barring any unwarranted contempt for or dismissal of the unfamiliar, they can be compared (Masolo 2010: 11-12).

The question might now be posed whether scepticism about the notion of 'indigenous knowledge systems' does not amount to 'epistemic injustice', is not a matter of inflicting epistemic harm. Or could this be seen as a form of '*warranted* dismissal'?

## The idea of epistemic injustice

Having observed that 'the really crucial problem for Third World intellectuals is that of being taken seriously' (Masolo 2010: 25), Gayatri Spivak writes:

> For me, the question "Who should speak?" is less crucial than "Who will listen?" ... The real demand is that, when I speak from that position, I should be listened to seriously (Spivak 1990: 59-60; quoted in Masolo 2010: 25).

One might argue that what Spivak is driving at here is the demand for epistemic justice.

'Epistemic injustice', argues Miranda Fricker, is a distinct kind of injustice. She distinguishes between two kinds, 'testimonial injustice' and 'hermeneutical injustice', each of which consists, 'most fundamentally, in a wrong done to someone specifically in their capacity as a knower' (Fricker 2007: 1; see also 21).

Testimonial injustice occurs when prejudice causes a hearer to give a deflated level of credibility to a speaker's word; hermeneutical injustice occurs at a prior stage, when a gap in collective interpretive resources puts someone at an unfair disadvantage when it comes to making sense of their social experiences (Fricker 2007: 1).

Central to her analysis is the notion of (social) 'power', which Fricker defines as 'a socially situated capacity to control others' actions' (Fricker 2007: 4; see also p. 13). Power works 'to create or preserve a given social order', and is displayed in various forms of enablement, on the one hand, and disbelief, misinterpretation and silencing, on the other. It involves the conferral on certain individuals or groups, qua persons of that kind, 'a credibility excess' or 'a credibility deficit' (Fricker 2007: 21). The primary characterisation of testimonial injustice, according to Fricker, 'remains such that it is a matter of credibility deficit and not credibility excess' (Fricker 2007: 21). This is certainly plausible, although we can think of instances where credibility excess is disadvantageous: an overburdened teacher or lecturer being asked questions by his students that call for a more specialist training. Similarly, promoting someone to a position (e.g. through affirmative action) for which they are not equipped, simply to rectify past wrongs, may be argued to involve epistemic harm.

Fricker's interest resides specifically with 'identity power' and the harms it produces through the manifestation of 'identity prejudices'. The latter are responsible for denying credibility to, or withholding it from, certain persons on the basis of their being members of a certain 'social type' (Fricker 2007: 21). Thus, testimonial injustice involves rejecting the credibility of their knowledge claims, while hermeneutical injustice involves a general failure of marshalling the conceptual resources necessary for understanding and interpreting these knowledge claims. The result is that these people are hindered in their self-development and in their attainment of full human worth: they are 'prevented from becoming who they are' (Fricker 2007: 5). In white patriarchal societies, these 'epistemic humiliations' (Fricker 2007: 51)[13] carry the power to destroy a would-be (black or female) knower's confidence to engage in the trustful conversations (Fricker 2007: 52-3) that characterise well-functioning epistemic communities. As Fricker suggests, they can 'inhibit the very formation of self' (Fricker 2007: 55). Although they are experienced (and may be performed) individually, testimonial and hermeneutical injustice constitute not only individual harms: they originate within a social fabric of which the biases and prejudices that enliven and perpetuate them are a characteristic part. Contesting such injustices and harms, according to Fricker, requires 'collective social political change' (Fricker 2007: 8).

In order to bring about such change, what is required[14] at a testimonial

---

[13] Fricker borrows the notion of epistemic humiliation from Simone de Beauvoir.

[14] A link might be forged here with Masolo's reference to 'a viable tool for transform-

level is 'reflexive awareness of the likely presence of prejudice', and this 'anti-prejudicial virtue is the virtue of testimonial justice' (Fricker 2007: 91-2). Testimonial justice, says Fricker, is 'both ethical and intellectual in character, at once a virtue of truth and a virtue of justice' (Fricker 2007: 124). Thus, apart from being able to rely on the competence and sincerity of speakers (Fricker 2007: 72), and apart from sensitivity (Fricker 2007: 72) and empathy (Fricker 2007: 79), 'hearers need dispositions that lead them reliably to accept truths and to reject falsehoods' (Fricker 2007: 115). However,

> there is no guarantee that epistemic and ethical ends will harmonize. If some down-trodden schoolteacher is told in no uncertain terms by the unscrupulous head teacher that when the school inspector visits the classroom, he must ask the pupils a question and make sure that he picks from among the sea of raised hands someone who will come out with the right answer. This epistemic aim might be best served by a policy that is not remotely just. It might be best served, for instance by picking a pupil who, notoriously, always gets her big brother to text her the answers on her mobile (Fricker 2007: 126).

'Hermeneutical justice, like testimonial justice, is a hybrid virtue' (Fricker 2007: 174), says Fricker. What it is meant to counteract is hermeneutical injustice – which occurs when (members of certain) groups or communities lack the hermeneutical tools to make sense of their own social experience (Fricker 2007: 146). 'For something to be an injustice, it must be harmful but also wrongful, whether because discriminatory or because otherwise unfair' (Fricker 2007: 151). When there is unequal 'hermeneutical participation with respect to some significant areas(s) of social experience, members of the disadvantaged group are hermeneutically marginalised' (Fricker 2007: 153). Fricker's account, of course, raises the question whether there could be hermeneutical *self*-marginalisation. I am thinking in particular of Axelle Kabou's own 'in-

ing the world'.

side' understanding in referring to ordinary African women and men as having refused development and modernisation (Kabou 1991; see especially Part 2).[15] Fricker appears to deny this:

Hermeneutical marginalisation is always socially coerced. If you simply opt out of full participation in hermeneutical processes as a matter of choice ..., then you do not count as hermeneutically marginalised – you've opted out, but you could have opted in. Hermeneutical marginalisation is always a form of powerlessness,

---

[15] Kabou, in her much-maligned pamphlet 'Et si l'Afrique refusait le développement?' ('And if Africa refused development?'; Kabou 1991), blames not only power-crazy heads of state and the corrupt elites for the plight of the continent, but also ordinary people, each and every individual. According to Kabou, Africans still believe that the world owes them salvation of the continent, as belated compensation for past injustices, their victim- and beggar mentality being strengthened by the sentimental humanitarianism of naïve white aid workers. Africans should look in the mirror, in order to realise their own part in this misery. Yet, writes Kabou, they refuse to do this. It is invariably the others who are to blame, foreign companies, the unjust global system of trade, the World Bank, the debt and poverty trap -- not to mention the inherited burdens of colonialism. The black elites and the white helpers are united in their dogma that there exists a century-old plot by the white man against the black man, while they refuse to contemplate the more complex causes of this perpetual crisis. Many consider Kabou's claim, that 'Africa-this-wonderful-continent-that-was-in-perfect-harmony-before-the-invasion-of-the-colonisers' is an anti-colonialist myth and has nothing to do with reality, downright blasphemous. Certainly, her pamphlet is not without stereotyping, of 'the Africans' as such. She tends to neglect the external factors of this chronic crisis, like the deprivation syndrome that white rule has left behind in the collective psyche. She also forgets that Africa lacks the springboard for the huge leap from agrarian society to industrial society. Modernisation was forced onto a continent that was unable to support it, socio-structurally and culturally, while the existing entrepreneurship and infrastructure were systematically undermined and destroyed by the colonial 'masters' (Grill 2003: 115). There is no room for such historical subtleties in Kabou's general account. Nonetheless, no serious debate about the problems facing Africa can afford to ignore her fundamental thesis. She refers not only to the *failed* modernisation of postcolonial Africa but to modernisation that was also *refused*, Africans being the only people on earth who still think that others must take care of their development. Kabou does not simply intend to condemn her African contemporaries. She wants to rouse them into shaking off their 'unbearable mediocrity'. Indeed, the demand for self-criticism makes her argument compelling.

whether structural or one-off (Fricker 2009: 153).

Yes, one might respond, but one can be responsible for one's powerlessness, as in the case of Kabou's 'ordinary Africans'. It would seem to follow that hermeneutical injustice and hermeneutical marginalisation are not identical, insofar as the latter can be seen to include self-marginalisation.

Given how prejudice affects various levels of credibility, and given that the critical interrogation of 'indigenous knowledge' has sometimes been part of a hegemonic discourse and constituted epistemic injustice, the question might now be raised whether my critique of this notion is not part of this discourse. Louise Antony suggests the adoption of 'epistemic affirmative action' by men as a 'working hypothesis that when a woman, or any member of a stereotyped group, says something anomalous, they should assume that it's they who do not understand, not that it is the woman that is nuts' (Antony 1995: 89; quoted in Fricker 2007: 171). By contrast, Fricker does not believe a policy of epistemic affirmative action across all subject matters to be justified: 'the best way to honour the compensatory idea is in the form of a capacity for indefinitely context-sensitive judgement – in the form … of a virtue' (Fricker 2007: 171). At what point, then, can a white man judge a woman, or any member of a stereotyped group, to be 'nuts' – if ever? Does epistemic justice require me, as a matter of course, to reserve judgement, to keep 'an open mind as to credibility' (Fricker 2007: 172)? As I have indicated above, if 'credibility deficit' is a matter of epistemic injustice, then why should 'credibility excess' (giving previously 'epistemologically humiliated' people or groups lots of credibility) not also constitute epistemic harm? More fundamentally, surely there is a difference between criticising someone's view on the mere grounds that she is black, or a woman, and criticising the views held or expressed by someone, who happens to be black or a woman, on the grounds of faulty or fallacious reasoning. Nonsense is not culturally, racially or sexually specific. Indeed, although she gestures in the direction of a basic 'do no harm' principle (Fricker 2007: 85), Fricker herself insists that a '"vulgar" relativist' resistance to passing moral judgment on other cultures 'is incoherent' (Fricker 2007: 106).

According to Fricker,

> any epistemic subject will have a reason to get at the truth. This is not to underestimate the complex and often troubled nature of our relationship with truth. Human beings are obviously subject to all sorts of powerful motivations, and indeed reasons, for shielding themselves from painful truths through mechanisms of denial or repression. On the whole, however, one must see such mechanisms against a background of a more general *motivation to truth* ... (Fricker 2007: 102-3; emphasis added).

Bernard Williams identifies three collective epistemic needs: first, the need to possess sufficient truths (and not too many falsehoods) to facilitate survival; second, the need to participate in the practice of an epistemic community, where there exists a division of epistemological labour, i.e. where information is shared or pooled; and third, the need to promote dispositions in individuals that will stabilise relations of trust. The practical virtue of competence and the epistemic virtues of accuracy and sincerity spring directly from these fundamental epistemic needs. Williams expresses the hope that his 'genealogical story' will assist in making 'sense of our most basic *commitments to truth and truthfulness*' (Williams 2002: 19; emphasis added).

## *'Truth and reconciliation'*

According to Masolo,

> Wiredu's theory of truth gives the phrase "truth and reconciliation", now central as a strategy and process for healing broken trusts and healing from public conflicts, an important epistemological grounding. Reconciling our different and often conflicting aims and aspirations is the path to a collectively acceptable and worka-

ble world (Masolo 2010: 181).

The Truth and Reconciliation Commission (TRC) was set up after the first democratic election in South Africa in order to bring to light and address the injustices and moral wrongs committed under apartheid – and indeed to 'heal the divisions of the past' and contribute towards establishing 'a society based on democratic values, social justice and fundamental rights' (see Horsthemke November 2004a). One of the principal contributions of the TRC was to turn *knowledge* – in other words, that which so many people already knew – into public *acknowledgement*, allowing the nation to acknowledge atrocity for what it is (*cf.* Villa-Vicencio 2003: 15). Asked to name the most significant achievements of the TRC in a national survey, the vast majority of South Africans, irrespective of race, referred to the disclosure of the *truth* about the past.

Let us pause to think about the present use of the terms 'knowledge' and 'truth'. There is arguably a reason why the TRC was not called '*Belief* and Reconciliation Commission' or '*Consensus* and Reconciliation Commission'. There is a premium here not on personal perceptions (although these are also important), but on historical truth – on what actually took place/ happened/ occurred, independently of what people sincerely believed and perhaps even agreed on. I want to suggest that the use of the terms 'knowledge' and 'truth' in the particular enterprise referred to here cannot be matters of personal opinion, that knowledge and truth are not dependent on a particular set of cultural relationships or social context. If it did not involve an understanding of truth as transcultural or universal (and as objectively anchoring knowledge), as reflecting what actually happened, that is, facts about South Africa's past, setting up a commission like this would be pointless.

What, then, constitutes 'a viable tool for transforming the world' (Masolo 2010: 18)? Recognition, protection against exploitation, appropriation, counteracting wholesale subjugation of everything that is deemed subjugatable is best achieved not on the basis of appeals to the validity of 'local knowledge' or 'indigenous knowledge systems'[16], but by locating the pleas for recognition, etc. in a rights-based framework (Horsthemke 2005; Horsthemke 2010). The latter has potential for the necessary educational, ethical and political clout to effect lasting changes. Insofar as human rights are anchored in as well as responsive to human agency, rights are essential for the protection of human differences. In essence, taking rights seriously implies taking individual, social and cultural identity seriously. Perhaps a first set of steps towards transformation (or what Fricker calls 'collective social political change'; Fricker 2007: 8) is constituted by a process or project that has rights as its backbone – and reconciliation as its heart.

## Postscript

The following is a pertinent excerpt from a play by Bertolt Brecht. Although this parable is ostensibly about reality, and our perception of it, it also serves as a fitting epitaph to the discussion of the problem of knowledge with which I began this paper.[17]

*The teacher*: Si Fu, name the central questions of philosophy!

*Si Fu:* Are things outside of us, for themselves, also without us, or are the

---

[16] Without being able to go into detail (for more elaborate argument and illustration, see Horsthemke 2004b and Horsthemke 2006), I suggest here that, apart from its frequent proximity to questionable customs and traditions, and to relative lack of agency and autonomy, the idea of 'indigenous' or 'local' knowledge tends to have a (self-)marginalising effect. Despite its ostensible contribution to 'independence from colonialism', it is less empowering and has less transformative potential than is commonly assumed.

[17] In other words, the parable can also be taken to pose questions around the nature of knowledge, realism versus constructivism, and objectivity-versus-subjectivity of truth and truth-claims. The very reason why an answer has not been furnished actually constitutes the answer – and directs us away from subjectivism, relativism and constructivism.

things within us, for ourselves, not without us?

*The teacher:* Which opinion is the correct one?

*Si Fu:* No verdict has been reached yet.

*The teacher:* What was the latest tendency among the majority of our philosophers?

*Si Fu:* The things are outside of us, for themselves, also without us.

*The teacher*: Why did the question remain unsolved?

*Si Fu:* The conference that was supposed to yield the final verdict took place, as it has done for the past two hundred years, in the monastery Mi Sang, on the banks of the Yellow River. The question was: Is the Yellow River real, or does it exist only in people's heads? During the conference, however, there was a melting of snow in the mountains, and the Yellow River rose above its banks and swept away the monastery Mi Sang and all conference participants. The proof that the things are outside of us, for themselves, also without us, therefore, has not been furnished.[18] (Bertolt Brecht, *Turandot or The Conference of Whitewashers*; my translation.)[19]

---

[18] *Der Lehrer:* Si Fu, nenne uns die Hauptfragen der Philosophie!
*Si Fu:* Sind die Dinge außer uns, für sich, auch ohne uns, oder sind die Dinge in uns, für uns, nicht ohne uns?
*Der Lehrer:* Welche Meinung ist die richtige?
*Si Fu:* Es ist keine Entscheidung gefallen.
*Der Lehrer:* Zu welcher Meinung neigte zuletzt die Mehrheit unserer Philosophen?
*Si Fu:* Die Dinge sind außer uns, für sich, auch ohne uns.
*Der Lehrer:* Warum blieb die Frage ungelöst?
*Si Fu:* Der Kongress, der die Entscheidung bringen sollte, fand, wie seit zweihundert Jahren, im Kloster Mi Sang statt, welches am Ufer des Gelben Flusses liegt. Die Frage hieß: Ist der Gelbe Fluss wirklich, oder existiert er nur in den Köpfen? Während des Kongresses aber gab es eine Schneeschmelze im Gebirge, und der Gelbe Fluss stieg über seine Ufer und schwemmte das Kloster Mi Sang mit allen Kongressteilnehmern weg. So ist der Beweis, dass die Dinge außer uns, für sich, auch ohne uns sind, noch nicht erbracht worden. (Bertolt Brecht, *Turandot oder Der Kongress der Weißwäscher*, Stücke, Band 14: 36)

[19] I am grateful to all participants of the colloquium on the Philosophy of D.A. Masolo at which this piece was initially presented and especially to Thaddeus Metz for his incisive comments on earlier drafts of the present paper.

## References

Antony, L. (1995). Sisters, Please, I'd Rather do it Myself: A Defense of Individualism in Feminist Epistemology. *Philosophical Topics*, 23(2): 59-94.
Benson, O. and Stangroom, J. (2006). *Why Truth Matters*. London: Continuum.
De Sousa Santos, B. (Ed.). (2007). *Another Knowledge is Possible: Beyond Northern Epistemologies*. London: Verso.
Fricker, M. (2007). *Epistemic Injustice: Power and the Ethics of Knowing*. Oxford: Oxford University Press.
Grill, B. (2003). *Ach, Afrika: Berichte aus dem Inneren eines Kontinents*. Berlin: Siedler.
Hallen, B. and Sodipo, J.O. (1997). *Knowledge, Belief, and Witchcraft: Analytical Experiments in African Philosophy*. 2nd edition. Stanford: Stanford University Press.
Hardwig, J. (1991). The Role of Trust in Knowledge. *The Journal of Philosophy*, 88(12): 693-709.
Hoppers, C.O. (Ed.) (2002). *Indigenous Knowledge and the Integration of Knowledge Systems: Towards a Philosophy of Articulation*. Claremont: New Africa Books.
Horsthemke, K. (2004a). Knowledge, Education and the Limits of Africanisation. *Journal of Philosophy of Education*, 38(4): 571-587.
Horsthemke, K. (2004b). 'Indigenous Knowledge', Truth and Reconciliation in South African Higher Education. *South African Journal of Higher Education*, 18(3): 65-81.
Horsthemke, K. (2005). Redress and Reconciliation in South African Education: The Case for a Rights-based Approach. *Journal of Education*, 37: 169-187.
Horsthemke, K. (2006). The Idea of the African University in the Twenty-First Century: Some Reflections on Afrocentrism and Afroscepticism. *South African Journal of Higher Education*, 20(4): 449-465.
Horsthemke, K. (2010). *The Moral Status and Rights of Animals*. Johannesburg: Porcupine Press.
Horsthemke, K. and Schäfer, M. (2007). Does 'African' Mathematics Facilitate Access to Mathematics? *Pythagoras*, 65: 2-9.
Kabou, A. (1991). *Et si l'Afrique Refusait le Développement?* Paris: L'Harmattan.
Kaphagawani, D.N. (1998). Themes in a Chewa Epistemology. In *Philosophy from Africa*. Edited by Coetzee, P.H. and Roux, A.P.J. Cape Town: Oxford University Press Southern Africa, pp. 240-244.
Masolo, D.A. (2010). *Self and Community in a Changing World*. Bloomington: Indiana University Press.
Seitz, V. (2009). *Afrika wird armregiert oder Wie man Afrika wirklich helfen kann*. München: Deutscher Taschenbuch Verlag.
Semali, L.M. and Kincheloe, J.L. (Eds.). (1999). *What is Indigenous Knowledge?: Voices from the Academy*. New York: Falmer Press.
Spivak, G.C. (1990). Questions of Multiculturalism. In *The Post-colonial Critic: In-*

*terviews, Strategies, Dialogues*. Edited by Harasym, S. New York: Routledge.
Villa-Vicencio, C. (2003). No Way around the Past. *Sowetan*, June 23:15.
Williams, B. (2002). *Truth and Truthfulness: An Essay in Genealogy*. Princeton: Princeton University Press.
Wiredu, K. (1980). *Philosophy and an African Culture*. Cambridge: Cambridge University Press.
Wiredu, K. (1998). The Concept of Truth in the African Language. In *Philosophy from Africa*. Edited by Coetzee, P.H. and Roux, A.P.J. Cape Town: Oxford University Press Southern Africa, pp. 234-239.

# On Being an African[33]

## by Abraham Olivier

*Abstract*: On Being an African. What is it like to be an African? This paper is an attempt to answer this question by taking Masolo's challenge to demonstrate the relational basis of subjectivity. I do not intend to develop a definition of "Africanity" as such. Rather I confine myself to a phenomenological description of the way sociality shapes subjectivity and my reflection on "Africanity" will mainly serve as a case in point. African philosophers concentrate on moral conceptions of personhood and have not articulated and defended with any thoroughness a social conception of selfhood as is done in this paper. I develop two major arguments. Firstly, I argue for the social basis of subjectivity in the sense of subjective experience. Accordingly, I show that and how far there is something like an African experience. Secondly, I argue for the social basis of subjectivity in the sense of selfhood. As a result I develop an answer to the question as to what it is like to be an African.

*Résumé*: Être un Africain. Qu'est-ce que c'est que d'être un Africain? Cet article est une tentative de répondre à cette question en prenant le défi de Masolo pour démontrer le fondement relationnel de la subjectivité. Je n'ai pas l'intention de développer une définition de 'l'Africanité' en tant que tel. Je me borne plutôt à une description phénoménologique de la façon dont la socialité forme la subjectivité et ma réflexion sur 'l'Africanité' servira principalement comme exemple. Les philosophes africains se concentrent sur des conceptions morales de la personnalité et n'ont pas formulé et défendue avec rigueur une conception sociale de l'ipséité comme je le fait dans cet article. Je développe deux arguments principaux. Tout d'abord, je défends l'idée de la base sociale de la subjectivité dans le sens de l'expérience subjective. En conséquence, je montre que et dans qu'elle mesure il y a quelque chose comme une expérience africaine. Deuxièmement, je défends l'idée de la base sociale de la subjectivité dans le sens de l'ipséité. En conséquence, je développe une réponse à la question de savoir ce que c'est que d'être un Africain.

*Keywords*: subjectivity, selfhood, sociality, African identity

---

[33] I am indebted to Thaddeus Metz for very helpful detailed critical comments on drafts of this paper, some of which express discussions of the paper at the recent Masolo workshop.

*Mots-clés:* subjectivité, ipséité, socialité, identité africaine

## Introduction

"How do African people think differently from other people and what are those differences? What do they stem from? Or do we differ at all?" As the title of his recent book indicates, these are some, if not the most central, of questions Masolo asks in *Self and Community in a Changing World*. His questions are challenging, not merely because they provoke politically, but because of the way they open up some "hard" philosophical problems. What is it like to be an African? Is there at all anything that it is like to be an African? If there is, must I go to the "forest" to become an African? Can I become an African at all? How does social experience affect our sense of selfhood and personhood? Do African minds differ from other minds?

Masolo's book addresses some topics in African philosophy and aims to engage readers in various contemporary debates. I shall concentrate on what I take to be the most central of these topics: the enquiry into the relationship between subjectivity and sociality. Subjectivity, so I shall explain, refers both to "subjective experience" and "selfhood". The challenging thesis of the book is that subjectivity has a relational basis, in other words, that the "self" is based on the changing contexts of the "community".[34]

My aim is to explore this thesis from a phenomenological perspective. I

---

[34] This thesis is reflected in various chapters. Chapter 1 revisits the ethnophilosophical debate on the way ethnicity shapes the "lenses of our thinking" (9). Chapter 2 compares Husserl's and Hountondji's views on the question as to how socio-ethnic contexts relate to the concept of subjectivity. Chapter 3 and 4 discuss Masolo's adoption of Wiredu's concept of the relational basis of subjectivity in the sense of personhood, which Chapter 5, on "juok", expands on concretely. Chapter 6 finally compares this view of relational subjectivity to African and Western brands of communalism.

shall bring to the fore what I take to be Masolo's challenge, which is to demonstrate the relational basis of subjectivity. As an example I explore how far an "African" world of living shapes subjectivity. So I do not intend to develop a definition of "Africanity" as such. Rather I confine myself to a phenomenological description of the way sociality shapes subjectivity and my reflection on "Africanity" will mainly serve as case in point. To the best of my knowledge this has not been done before, at least not thoroughly, and I would like to try to fill the gap. Sections I and II start with a brief discussion of terms and methods, in particular, I introduce Hountondji's adoption of Husserl's phenomenological question concerning the sociality of subjectivity. Sections III to V address Masolo's challenge and argue for the social basis of subjectivity in the sense of subjective experience; in short, I shall show that there is something like an African experience. Sections VI to VII subsequently argue for the social basis of subjectivity in the sense of selfhood; I shall address the question as to what it is like to be an African, before concluding by addressing some objections in Section VIII.

# 1

The question as to how African people differ from other people pierces into the heart of problems, or after Chalmers, the "hard problem".[35] Is there anything that it is like to be an African? This question opens up a number of questions. The question is, first and foremost, in Nagel's classical terms, what does it mean to say, "there is something it is like to be African"?[36] Do Africans "experience" things differently? What should an "African experience" be like? Is there anything like "African subjectiv-

---

[35] Chalmers (1996: 24ff). To recall, "easy problems" of consciousness refer to those concerning the explanation of various cognitive functions (discriminatory abilities, reportability of mental states, the focus of attention, the control of behavior) whilst the hard problem refers to phenomenal or subjective consciousness.

[36] Of course, I am referring to Nagel's (1997) essay, "What is it like to be a bat?".

ity"? How is what we experience related to *where* we experience it? What does this tell about consciousness or selfhood?

Before we dig into Masolo's text it might be helpful to give a preliminary outline of some standard distinctions made between terms such as "consciousness", "experience", "subjectivity", "intentionality", "selfhood", "personhood", and "human nature" – although we immediately encounter the difficulty that it is part of the hard problem to deal with these distinctions.

"Human nature in particular is accorded great attention in African thought", writes Masolo (2010: 151). There is a kind of minimum agreement among philosophers of all traditions that the hard problem of "human nature" is the explanation of the human mind. Scientific research seems to confirm our common-sense experience that, unlike our observable physical properties, we seem to have mental properties that evade empirical observation and explanation.[37] You won't simply get what Africans or Chinese or Italians are like by watching their bodily appearances or even behavior. You have to, as it were, study their minds. What are minds? Most philosophers think that the hard problem of the human mind is the explanation of consciousness.[38] Typically, philosophers of mind distinguish between subjective and intentional consciousness. Subjective consciousness is usually referred to as first personal experience, phenomenal consciousness, or qualia (the quality of experience). Subjective consciousness is often described in terms of what consciousness is like.[39] Intentional consciousness is generally defined in terms of what consciousness is about or directed toward.[40] We can also refer to subjective and intentional consciousness as subjectivity and intentionality. Typically

---

[37] See Olivier 2011: 184.

[38] See the instructive essay of Güzeldere (1997: 1-67) entitled "The Many Faces of Consciousness: A Field Guide".

[39] See Güzeldere (1997: 2, 22-23, 30) with reference to Chalmers (1996).

[40] Güzeldere (1997: 22-23), Gallagher and Zahavi (2008: 109ff.).

subjectivity is associated with an internal domain of consciousness and intentionality with the external world to which consciousness is directed. The real hard problem is thought to be the explanation of the evasive inner sphere of subjectivity. Furthermore, some take "subjectivity" to be a broader term than "subjective consciousness" as far as it also pertains to "selfhood" or "personal identity".[41] "Selfhood" is usually employed to refer to that which gives us a sense of the "self" or "mineness" or "identity" of our experience. "Selfhood" is mostly applied in connection with "personhood". As Thaddeus Metz puts it in personal comments on this paper: "It is one thing to ask what essentially makes me who I am and another thing to ask how I (whatever I essentially might be) can develop into a *real* person or an individual..." The former is a metaphysical question of selfhood, the latter a moral or at least evaluative one of personhood. As indicated, I shall concentrate on selfhood rather than personhood.[42]

On the basis of this preliminary outline, we can say "subjectivity" refers to first person "subjective consciousness or experience" as well as "self" or "selfhood". Although Masolo does not state this explicitly, he does seem to use the term "self" in terms of subjectivity in its twofold sense of subjective experience and selfhood. We can take this preliminary outline of the terms as a point of departure in exploring the meanings of these terms in more detail. The question thus is how our particular social settings, such as African communities, affect our subjective experience or sense of selfhood.

---

[41] Güzeldere 1997: 36. This is also what the title of Zahavi's (2005) book, "Subjectivity and Selfhood", indicates.

[42] As I said, African philosophers concentrate on concepts of personhood rather than selfhood. See, for instance, Gbadegesin (2002); Gyekye (2002); Kaphagawani (2004); Menkiti (2004).

## 2

Masolo takes as his point of departure Hountondji's adoption of Husserl's view of phenomenology. The focus is on phenomenology qua study of the social origin of subjectivity. Husserl and Hountondji are both classics but in opposite senses and contexts – so it appears. Husserl is a Western classic for making strong the "life world" as the basis of consciousness and for that matter, all knowledge. The other, Hountondji, an African classic, is particularly a classic for calling a view such as Husserl's myth – so it seems. Hountondji (1983: 55ff) states in his book *African Philosophy: Myth and Reality*, that the myth of African philosophy is that its philosophy is founded in myth, that is, in life world experiences expressed in mythical forms (Hountondji 1983: 55ff.). Hountondji has indeed become a classic for challenging the views that advocate the ethnic underpinnings of philosophy.

Masolo thinks Hountondji is a classic, yet not for rejecting but rather for advocating the philosophical significance of ethnicity. My purpose is not to discuss his detailed defence of Hountondji. Suffices to say that Masolo argues that Hountondji is no adversary but rather an advocate of the "reconciliation of indigenous African orders of experience with the orders of philosophical knowledge", and in this regard "he is one of the most insistent and the most recognized of contemporary African philosophers" (Masolo 2010: 52). In fact, so Masolo puts it, "Hountondji's writings strongly call for the return of the African subject" (61).

This is a strong claim. What is meant by the call for the return of the African subject? On his "path toward the definition of African subjectivity" (61), Hountondji explicitly takes Husserl to be an ally and not a rival. This brings us to a closer look at Husserl's approach to phenomenology.

In its technical sense Husserl views phenomenology as a method that consists in the (a) suspension of the myth of the given, i.e., the natural attitude that things are given and that we have to match our experience with what is given, (b) reduction (leading back or returning) to how things are given to experience, and (c) intersubjective corroboration of the essential features (eidetic variation) of shared experience.[43] Because of its methodological focus on subjective experience, phenomenology is often wrongly confused with a subjective account of experience – also called introspectionism or phenomenalism. Phenomenology, rather, attempts to maintain objectivity in its account of subjective experience. Typically, however, phenomenology emphasises a first or second personal approach to experience, which means it takes as a point of departure our first and second personal access to experience. Nevertheless, the aim is to arrive at objectivity and to do this by means of the intersubjective corroboration of the essential features of shared experience.

Hountondji clearly follows Husserl's "pathway" into phenomenology. As Masolo quotes him: "This return to the subject does not however imply a retreat into subjectivity—on the contrary! The investigation of experience seeks to confirm the objectivity of essences, by identifying in experience itself an internal element of transcendence that obliges it to recognize its objective correlate." The point is thus to "return" to the pre-reflective first person experiences and intuitions of the "life world", if you want to, the everyday context and community we inhabit, and objectively identify structures common to various subjects.

Hence, if Hountondji calls for "the return of the African subject", its phenomenological sense is a return to the particular, prereflective, social roots of African subjects as the starting point of a philosophical or scientific assessment of their subjectivity. Hountondji follows Husserl's aim to "reduce", that is, return our focus to the prereflective, social roots of subjectivity. For Husserl it is our life world experience, for Hountondji it is the indigenous community, in short African subjectivity.

However, so Hountondji warns in his The Struggle for Meaning, one cannot simply take a collective set of prereflective intuitions to be as such

---

[43] See also Olivier (2011: 185). For this explanation I rely on Gallagher and Zahavi succinct definition of phenomenology in Gallagher and Zahavi (2008: 23ff.)

a complete reflection of the roots of subjectivity. He accuses ethnophilosophy of such uncritical generalisation, of uncritically taking the chorus of an anonymous crowd for the voice of any individual. As a result you are, for instance, black due to your "ensemble of characteris-tics, of manners of thinking, of feeling, proper to the black race; belong-ing to the black race." (Masolo 2010: 83). Conversely, if you are black, you think like all blacks – you are, to put it in Heidegger's terms, like Masolo does, reduced to "being-black-in-the-world".

But how exactly should we then understand the call for the return of the African subject? How should we, for that matter, understand adjacent ideas such as "black consciousness", or "black is beautiful"? In short, what does the claim for the social basis of subjectivity exactly mean if the subject is not to be reduced to the chorus of the crowd?

Masolo deals with these questions in more depth in the following chapters of the book. The next four sections (III-V) bring to the fore what I take to be Masolo's challenge to demonstrate the relational basis of subjectivity, in particular, subjective experience.

## 3

The return of the African subject – so there must be something that it is like to be an African. Africa should not simply be the cradle of mankind, but rather, Africa seems to be the birthplace of a subject of its own kind. But, how could one call for the return of the African subject without, as Hountondji warns, reducing subjectivity to the anonymous chorus of a crowd?

Masolo consults Wiredu's view of human nature for an answer (142ff.), and I would like to discuss his answer from a phenomenological perspective. Here is a brief summary of Wiredu's view. We can understand human nature fairly well by explaining the properties specific to the biological type to which humans belong. The human body has the ability to respond in different ways to a variety of stimuli. Our major ability consists of our capacity to respond to each other by means of communication. "The capacity to process and respond to communicative stimuli is what is called mind" (140). This means: the mind is not entirely physical, it is only "partly" or "kind of" or "quasi" physical, and "borne into action by the communicative stimuli of others". Masolo concludes that the physical constitution of humans is a necessary but *not sufficient* basis for explaining subjectivity. The meaning of experience, and of self, arises from within a social environment.

"Meanings just ain't in the head". And neither are minds. Masolo would agree with Putnam's and McDowell's witty précis of the externalist view of mind.[44] *Prima facie* I think also phenomenologists would concur. Externalism, so Gallagher and Zahavi (2008:122) point out, basically means to say: "...our experience depends upon factors that are external to the subject possessing the mental states in question." Internalism states the opposite: the meaning of a subject's experience is constituted by what is going on in its mind, or brain, rather than its environment (121).

Phenomenologists, however, work on dissolving the division rather than adopting either internalism or externalism. The quest to dissolve the division between "internal" and "external" goes back to Heidegger's view that human being is "*Dasein*", being here and now in the world. Hence, Heidegger's well-known phrasing of human being as "being-in-the-world". Heidegger characterizes human being (*Dasein*) as being primarily overt or open toward the world. For Heidegger, to our most basic state of mind belongs a tuning in to, understanding of and discourse with our environment. As such *Dasein* naturally belongs to the world. Heidegger famously states, in directing itself toward and in grasping something, *Dasein* does not first go outside of the inner sphere in which it is initially encapsulated, but rather, it is always already outside together with some being encountered in the world (Heidegger 1986: 62). Merleau-Ponty

---

[44] See Gallagher and Zahavi 2008: 123.

(1962: 430) rounds it off: the world is inseparable from the subject, but from a subject that is nothing but a project of the world, and the subject is inseparable from the world, but from a world which the subject itself projects. To summarise, the phenomenological verdict is that as bodily subjects we are anchored in contexts which give meaning to our subjectivity. We are bodily subjects, and as bodily beings we are anchored in contexts, which on the rebound shape our subjectivity. To be means to be in a particular space which gives meaning to our being.

It is significant that Masolo points outs that Wiredu defends the view that "there is no equivalent, in Akan, of the existential 'to be' or 'is' of English, and that there is no way of pretending in that medium to be speaking of the existence of something which is not in space." (Masolo 2010: 156) According to Wiredu, "in the Akan language to exist is to *wo ho,* which, in literal translation, means 'to be at some place.'" In the Akan understanding, existence is always locative, in relation to something else. Consequently, the notion of the transcendental self in the philosophies of Descartes and Kant as an autonomous instance that bestows meaning upon experience regardless of the space they occur in, is hard for the Akan to comprehend and to express in their language.

"Wo ho" – to be is to be at some place. This is the place where meanings are. The idea of *"wo ho"* shows strong resemblance with the notion of *Dasein* – being here and now in the world. The way our experience is imbedded in our *Dasein* is beautifully explained by Merleau-Ponty's view of the embodiment of experience. According to him, sensed qualities (colours, sounds, smells, tastes, tactile qualities) "radiate" around them a certain mode of existence, that is, the qualities shape the way I am in the world. As I contemplate the blue of the sky, I am not set against it as an acosmic subject; I do not possess it as an objective reality spread out in front of me. Instead, I abandon myself to it, my gaze resides in it, it becomes my world, it determines my mode of being (Merleau-Ponty 1945: 249). Merleau-Ponty phrases this intentional structure as follows:

"The sensible gives back to me what I lent to it, but this is only what I took from it in the first place" (248).[45]

My contention is, however, that one can take Masolo's view further than Merleau-Ponty's view, or for that matter than the mainstream of phenomenology and philosophy of mind allows going, *viz.*, one can claim that subjective experience is socially and in this sense externally based.

## 4

Consider the Capgrass syndrome. Capgrass experiences a colour qualia inversion: his emotional response to colours has changed, his preference for red over green has been reversed as have all his other colour preferences. He finds the world disgusting this way.[46] Imagine that you wake up one morning and see a yellow ocean, red trees, a green sky. You make an espresso to pull you out of this nightmare, but the espresso is pink. On the top of it, the espresso has a soapy smell and seems to be thick like shampoo. Your children run upstairs to embrace you but they have the colour of green Martians and they don't speak but squeak.

What goes wrong with Capgrass in this exaggerated depiction shows what goes right in all normal cases of sensory experience. In all normal cases, sensations – colours like sounds and smells – come with particular effects. Their effects depend on the objects they belong to and the context within which I have these sensations. Sensations affect me by drawing my attention to positions, situations, and objects, thereby filling in my experiences in different ways. The devastating effect of an inversion of

---

[45] Note that the idea of embodied or situated experience has become a popular topic of research recently also among analytical philosophers and psychologists. To mention but three books: Fuchs, Sattel, Henningsen (2010), Robbins and Aydede (2009), Thompson (2007).

[46] See Dennett 2006: 95-96.

sensations demonstrates this clearly. This means that every sensation is characteristically intentional for it directs and ties me to objects and contexts in particular ways. I am not aware of a colour or a smell or taste without it occupying me in a certain way. I can imagine a patch of green or the taste of sweetness detached from an object or situation in an *ad hoc* sort of way, say in a thought experiment, but I cannot imagine returning from my experiment into a world of "flying qualia" detached from objects or situations. Otherwise Capgrass' inversion of sensations would not have been such a nightmare. My claim thus is, in all normal cases, a sensation is always in some way identified with and characterized by its intentional effect.

The same applies, for instance, to pain experience. Masolo (2010: 154) states that "the sensations that we associate with the idea of pain or of pleasure belong to the body". I venture to differ. A pain in my leg is not, as Masolo puts it, an idea that I learn to associate with a sensation in my leg, or as Michael Tye argues, a representation of a disturbance in my leg.[47] Rather, as the pain is intentionally bound to my leg, the pain is defined in terms of the leg that disturbs me, and therefore, the intentional effect of the pain is what the pain is all about. I don't have a senseless pain sensation and then learn to make sense of it by perceiving it as a kind of pain. Rather the pain will have some kind of meaning also even when it is indefinite and if I do not yet know how to describe it.

Thus, I define subjective experience in terms of *intentional effects*.[48] I think that hereby I take a step into where "ways into phenomenology" (to use Heidegger's phrase), and I daresay analytical philosophy of mind as well, typically bring to a halt.[49] Usually we speak of intentional con-

---

[47] Tye 1996: 113.

[48] The term "effect" qua "affectedness" originates from Hume and Kant. See Olivier (2011: 189). "Effect" has an intentional and no causal meaning.

[49] Analytical philosophers of mind generally accept as a received view that qualia and intentionality can be viewed separately (Güzeldere 1997: 22). This view is criticized by philosophers such as John Searle, Richard Rorty, Michael Tye and Fred Dretske,

sciousness in terms of, to use Searle's phrase, a direction of fit: a subject is directed towards the world and the world is what his or her consciousness is about.[50] If we say that consciousness is defined by intentional effects, the direction of fit is inversed and it is the world that primarily directs consciousness. Then consciousness is essentially a result of our intentional alignment to our environment. This means that the world is seen as having a continuously formative and in this sense directive effect on our consciousness. I call this "conditional" (contextual) formation of consciousness *inversed intentionality*. This radicalises, or rather, inverses Merleau-Ponty's claim: the subject is the project of a world that the subject does not itself primordially project.[51] Whereas phenomenology typically takes subjectivity to be inherently intentional, the direction of fit is still subject-world oriented. The subject is still presupposed as the condition of experience. I turn this relation around by stating that experience is the effect and not condition of our alignment with the world.

This conception of inversed intentionality offers a way to explain why and how sociality can be seen as the basis of subjectivity. This brings me to the question whether there is something like an "African experience".

## 5

Masolo (2010: 241) recounts that, typically, in traditional African villages, before their initiation, children are trained to carry messages across villages to kin and friends of the family. Although it might appear simple,

---

but in a different way than I am doing. My view draws on but also differs from the connection phenomenologists see between qualia and intentionality. For an overview of their views, see Gallagher and Zahavi (2008: 107).

[50] Note Searle (2004: 167ff.) understands "direction of fit" on some point in another way.

[51] Again, Merleau-Ponty contends that the subject is a project of the world that the subject itself projects.

the act of sending children as messengers across villages has a very central meaning for their social development. Apart from training them to sharpen their ability to carefully listen, understand, remember, and precisely transmit verbal messages it gives them mental training by practicing remembering and delivering verbal messages. Also the children learn the virtues of obedience and service to others and to fit into the larger social system of the extended family and beyond. Later so he writes, children go through all kinds of processes before they get the rite of passage. One of them is initiation. Such rituals, are an important aspect of the rites of passage, they "'create' a person out of the untamed and unmolded body of a child" (242). To demonstrate the point, Masolo cites an Ogiek elder's preparatory address to a young initiation candidate: "At the end of it (initiation) you will be transformed from somebody's child who has become a person" (242).

Of course not all Africans undergo initiation or pass the "forest". The practices are still widely sustained, also among modern Africans. But the point here is not to identity forms of what we might call typical African experiences. Rather, these accounts demonstrate the way "inversed intentionality" works, that is, the way our experiences are directed by the social conditions (positions and situations) we have in our "life world". This means that different conditions of living create different forms of experience. My Xhosa students usually prefer Dwight Juda Ward's African version of the last supper to Leonardo da Vinci's original. Our experiences are accordingly shaped by our conditions of living in a manifold of ways.

But you might still like to ask: What does "Africa" or "African" mean exactly? In other words, what does "place" exactly mean for the "Africanity" of experience. To be sure, I take "place" to mean our "world of living", that is, positions and situations in which we are socially involved. Of course, communities in Africa, like in the rest of the world, are not confined to local areas but are linked by language and culture. You can foster the Akan culture while living in Berlin. My purpose is not at all to delineate the exact boundaries of a place called Africa. I do not want to offer any statutory or metaphysical or mystical account of what Africa might be. Rather I confine myself to a phenomenological description of the way place shapes our subjective experience – and identity – and Africa serves as an example like Europe or Asia or America could have. In fact, to refer to Africa as a "place" would be nonsensical, for there is too huge a hybrid of African "life worlds" to refer to such a place meaningfully.

I argued that as experience is conditioned by our life world, an African world of living will produce a particular African way to experience things. We can *know* what an African experience is like by studying the conditions of living which are affecting people. But this answers one part of the question as to what an African experience could be like. It is one thing to *know* what an African experience is like, it is yet another to *be* an African, for *"wo ho"* – to be is to be at some place. To be at some place means to be affected and formed by that place. It is, for instance, one thing to know that to some African cultures the forest is a rite of passage, and another to have gone through that forest. You might know that the period of seclusion in the forest "gives society the space and time to cultivate and groom the person in the etiquette that gives the person a rite of passage", but if you were not there, you will not really understand Masolo's contention that this etiquette "embodies the fundamentally altruistic impulse underlying social being" (Masolo 2010: 243). To be is, to put it in Heidegger's terms, to open up to the world. This definition has a conversed side. A world can be closed to you. This happens naturally if you are not there, if you are not in that world. To be there means to be someone with a different experience. Finally, to be there means to be someone different. This brings me to the next section – to the relation between subjectivity in the sense of subjective experience and in the sense of selfhood.

# 6

If my experience is African, does this also make me become an African? What is the relationship between subjective experience and selfhood? In the following section I want to explore in more detail my contention that subjectivity, also in the sense of selfhood, is constituted by sociality.

Let me start with a very brief overview of some conceptions of selfhood. There is no widespread consensus about what it means to be a self.[52] There is, in fact, a lot of scepticism about the legitimacy of notions of the self. I shall defend the thesis that there is something that it is like to be a self. The most widespread classic view that there is a self is based on the classic conception of the self as identity pole. Kant is a major proponent of this view of the self as the subject to which any episode of experience refers back (200). The self is as such not experiential, but rather the unifying principle of our manifold experiences. There are two major current models, which offer alternative notions to the identity-pole model of the self – they are the following.

The first is the self as narrative construction. A very popular version of narrative notions of the self is offered by Charles Taylor (1989) in *Sources of the Self*. Basically, Taylor's idea is that the self is an achievement. It is not a given, not a living organism, but rather realised through a person's projects and actions. Eventually the self is constructed through a narrative of self-interpretations of these projects and actions. This view finds resemblance in Paul Ricoeur's phenomenological idea of the self as *leitmotiv* of our lives. As Ricoeur's book title, *Time and Narrative*, shows, the *leitmotiv* has a temporal order. Who am I is told by my life story, which links the beginning by birth with the end by death. In his version of the narrative self in *After Virtue*, Alisdair MacIntyre (1985), puts emphasise on its social order. Our narrative is embedded in larger

---

[52] See Gallagher and Zahavi (2008: 197ff.). I rely partly on their book for a helpful discussion of debates on the self.

historical and communal meaning-giving structures. This means, we are not the only authors of our lives. My story is caught up in the stories of others. This implies yet another dimension, that is, our belonging to cultural-linguistic settings whose aims and ideals to a great extent write the stories of our lives. The notion of narrative self can of course turn into a notion of a fictive self (202). In *Sweat Dreams*, among others, Daniel Dennett argues that we cannot prevent inventing ourselves; we are hardwired to become language users, and once we are caught up in the web of language and begin spinning our own stories, we are not totally in control, but rather our tales tend to spin us.

In short, the narrative self is seen as an abstract centre of narrative gravity; it is where all the stories (of fiction or biography) of an individual meet up.

The second model is the self as experiential dimension. This notion of selfhood is supported by all major phenomenologists – Husserl, Heidegger, Sartre and Merleau-Ponty. Ironically, in their earlier works, both Husserl and Sartre supported self-scepticism, but later, both distanced themselves from it. For Husserl, in the *Ideas*, the ego of self is not given as material entity, but rather it is constituted in the process of experience as the subject of that experience. The self is the one that carries ownership of a particular experience as the "I" of the experience, but it is also the one that synthesises the flow of many different experiences into a history of experiences. So, there is no "second self", but rather the "self in abstraction", or rather synthesises in the process of experience. Heidegger's view in *Being and Time* is that every experience is characterised by the fact that I am always somehow acquainted with myself. Being-in-the-world means a prereflective awareness of *my*-being-in-the world, of the mine-ness (*Jemeinigkeit*) of the world. Thus every form of consciousness is also self-consciousness (46). Sartre, in *Being and Nothingness*, contends that subjective experience or consciousness is at bottom characterised by self-appearance or self-reality, which he terms ipseity: selfhood (from the Latin "ipse"). The "self" coincides with phenomenal or first-person consciousness – there is always a sense of mineness to any experience (203). Merleau-Ponty in his *Phenomenology of Perception*, understands ipseity in terms of embodiment – as he famously states, "I am my body, I am a body-subject". In other words, to experience means to be some-body that experiences and is in some way always aware of his or her being that body experiencing. In fact, the way objects affect us always also goes along with self-experience, of a self affecting itself by tuning itself into these objects.

Contrary to the narrative versions of the self, the experiential version, in particular phenomenology, does not take selfhood as precondition or product of consciousness, but as an integral part of it. One is prereflectively aware of one's own experience, and this makes experience subjective in the first place. The self is not the same as experience, but the mineness that accompanies all experiences. A sense of self always goes along with one's experience, one's subjective consciousness coincides with one's self-consciousness. Thus there is the assumption of a core self, some minimal form of self-*experience*, i.e., experience as subjective or first-person experience, to be essential for self-hood.

African philosophers, to my view, introduces a third kind of view – the notion of a communalist self. This view is not worked out in terms of selfhood, but personhood, that is, in moral terms. As I said, Masolo indicates a socially based concept of selfhood that I would like to bring to the fore. My own view differs and agrees with both the narrative and experiential view. Let me explain my own view and then compare it to the above views of selfhood.

# 7

We are in a position now to tackle the question as to how far the "Africanity" of my experience makes me become an African. In the following section I try to answer this question by showing why also subjectivity in the sense of selfhood is constituted by sociality.

My view takes George Herbert Mead's *Mind, Self, and Society* as a point of departure. But much as I appreciate Mead's view and views adjacent to Mead's position, I think we should go somewhat further.[53] In Mead's view, the precondition for human interaction is that one "I" acts upon another "I" by taking its position, consequently they interact with each other from each others' positions. Thus, a minimum conception of an "I" acting is presupposed. I do not presuppose any "I" as a precondition for but rather view the "I" as the product of interaction. What I am, I become first and foremost by virtue of societal positions, for instance, by inheriting the perspective of an African infant on the back of my parent, later carrying messages from one village to another, undergoing initiation, and going to the forest before I obtain the rite of passage to society. Furthermore, I gain experience from situations by being a village African infant, or messenger, undergoing initiation, bearing the forest, such that my experience is, ever so unwittingly, continuously formed and informed by the positions I take in such situations. I don't first decide to take and learn these positions, but rather, these positions demand to be taken and I learn to take them in terms of their demands. Finally, these positions and situations have different effects on me; they change me continuously, they form my experience such that I can eventually claim that experience to be my experience.

Subsequently, we can argue that positions subject me to forms of experience that I identify with and therefore make me become the *subject* of my experience. The positions that I occupy make me what I am; they originally give me a sense of *selfhood*, of the self or mineness or identity of my experience. One could thus say that subjectivity, both in the sense of "inner" first-person or subjective experience and selfhood, is based on "external" positions.

The ontological implication of this view is that my social experience con-

---

[53] Note that Mead's theory of the interaction of I and Me is a radicalization of William James' theory of this relation (1890: 291ff.). See also Backtin's (1981) and Herman's (2003) versions of James' position.

tinually constitutes what I am. If my social world of living, call it life world, is an African context, then this life world will make me an African. If it is not, I can be no African. No matter how much I learn to love the African way of life, being a foreigner, I shall never be affected by the African life world in the way of inhabitants who have lived it. In Nagel's terms, if I live as a bat, I shall have different experiences, consequently I shall be a different being. Nagel's ascribes this difference to the physiognomy of the bat. I agree. Only, Africans are not bats but humans like all humans are, and physiognomic differences are not that decisive, as is rightly stressed by Hountondji and Masolo. But Africans differ from Chinese and Chinese from Americans by virtue of sociality. This means, if I would have been reared in an African community, I would have had different experiences, and by virtue of the intentional effects of these experiences, I would have developed another sense of selfhood. Conversely, if I have not been reared in an African community, I shall not become an African, no matter how hard I try.

A question that was raised whilst presenting this paper is to which extent one's African identity would change upon moving to another place. Again, I take "place" to mean our "world of living", that is, positions and situations in which we are socially involved. Two factors seem to determine the effect of changing places on identity most decisively. The first is education, the other integration. Consider, for instance, Turkish women who will not speak German after 30 years of living in Germany because they are not taking part in German society on any level. Their children will be bilingual soon, and will most likely prefer to speak German because it is the language of their school or tertiary education and later occupation. There is a difference in the effect of changing places in the case of the person that is not educated or integrated in her new place and her children who are. Many Turkish families have been forced to moving back to Germany. Their children often have a nightmare to cope because they will call Germany home and themselves German. Where we are educated and integrated shapes what we are, and if we change places any re-education or re-integration will radically change our identity. A Xhosa child adopted and reared in Germany will be much less an "African" than a Bavarian child raised in a local community in an African country. You learn to become an "African" by virtue of the specific place in a local African community that you take, that is, by virtue of the positions or situations that you learn to adopt in such a community. In this sense there is no single Africa or African identity but a huge hybrid of the same.

Take the black German referred to above again. To refer to a black person walking the streets of Berlin as an African reduces Africanity to a phenotype, to the anonymous crowd, as Hounjondji calls it, and misses the phenomenology of the way a specific place, a local German community and the culture it is linked to, has constituted the person's identity. Africa like Europe, or for that matter, South Africa like Germany, consist of numerous places. To refer to someone coming from the African continent as African *simpliciter* is nonsensical, because it gives a too general reference to his or her identity to make sense. Metaphysically posed political or ethical appeals to "African unity" should not be confused with a phenomenological description of African identity in its particularity. In sum, to refer to African identity refers to one's belonging to a particular place in Africa and not to a detached metaphysical idea of Africa.

What about losing your "African" identity? Wiredu (2004) contends that Amo never completely lost his Akan identity even after decades of living in a German household and that his reading of Descartes clearly shows traces of Akan thinking. Not every African is an Amo. Who leaves home for long enough will go through another forest and might not quite return as the same person. Fanon commented on this with much wit in *Black Skin, White Masks*. It seems to be easier to lose than to learn, but the point remains the same: the way sociality shapes identity is particularly clear in the case of changing places. African identity – like any other social identity – cannot be based on detached unitary metaphysics, but rather is bound to the physics of place, of local social positions and situations, and a chance of place does have an effect on identity.

We can thus also say that selfhood is not in the first place an issue of the self-ascription of characteristics of a culture. I am borne in and educated into a particular African culture or not, and if I do not directly resist such a culture, I will naturally assume the roles this culture will ascribe to myself. But I am free to fill the roles in my own way, I am free to, in Biko's words, "write what I like". In this sense, selfhood does allow the freedom of self-ascription. But self-ascription only follows on the positions a society has already ascribed to my-self. "Other-ascription" precedes "self-ascription".

This freedom of self-ascription does make it possible to adopt a foreign culture to some extent. If I did not go to the forest, I shall not be an African. I shall never pass the question, "Why do you act (or reason) like you never went to the forest?" But I can move to Africa, and try to go through the rites of passage – learn the language, assume social positions and engage in a local society. I can even try to go to the forest. My tongue will forever betray my self-ascription. But I am free to choose to see my-self as an African and try to live as an African.

## 8

I would like to draw to a close by considering two possible objections, which one can anticipate from proponents of narrative and experiential accounts of selfhood.

1. Take the narrative account first. You might object that Alisdair MacIntyre makes a similar point in *After Virtue* (cited by Masolo 227):

> We enter human society, that is, with one or more imputed characters—roles into which we have been drafted—and we have to learn what they are in order to be able to understand how others respond to us and how our responses to them are apt to be construed. I am someone's son or daughter, someone else's cousin or uncle; I am a citizen of this or that city, a member of this or that guild or profession; I belong to this or that clan, that tribe, this nation.

There is, however, a slight but decisive difference between MacIntyre's and my own view. MacIntyre like Mead still presupposes a "we", that is, an "I" that enters human society and needs to learn to manage its roles", whilst I take the "we" or "I" to be a product rather than precondition of society. I become what I am due to the intentional effect of the positions and situations which I inherit. Of course, narrative versions also take the self as the eventual product of life-stories, but only after assuming it as the beginning of these stories as well. Thus a minimal form of self is presupposed.

2. Consider another possible objection from the side of experiential notions of the self. If it is my contention that my social experience shapes the way I am, is this not simply another version of the experiential notion of the self, i.e., of the self as part of processes of experience? If the experiential notions take the self as owner of experiences, they presuppose a minimal concept of the self to take that ownership. This kind of assumed ownership is ever so subtly apparent in Husserl's "ego", Sartre's "ipseity", Heidegger's "Jemeinigkeit", as well as Merleau-Ponty's "body-subject". The same goes for recent phenomenologists such as Gallagher and Zahavi (205)[54], who consider more complex forms of self development in social contexts. Despite their refined and insightful reflections, which I cannot discuss here, both assume what they call a *core self*, a sense of experiential mineness, as the necessary condition for the social development of selfhood. The decisive difference with my view is – similar to the difference with narrative versions – that I do not presuppose any minimal conception of self, but view the self as the product, or more exactly, intentional effect of social experience.

I take this conception of selfhood to be an answer to Masolo's challenge to demonstrate the social basis of selfhood. Again, African philosophers have not, to the best of my knowledge, articulated and defended with any thoroughness a social conception of selfhood as I have tried to do. In-

---

[54] See also, for instance, Zahavi in Fuchs, T., Sattel, H., Henningsen, P (Eds.). 2010: 6-7, 19.

stead, as far as I can see the literature confines itself to the development of moral reflections on communitarian views of *personhood*. My attempt has been to fill this gap.

*****

So, are Africans different? Yes they are. There is something that it is like to be an African. Africans are different like Chinese, Americans, Germans and Arabians are different. They are different, because to be human means to be socially conditioned. In short, subjectivity is constituted by sociality. I agree with Masolo's thesis of the social basis of subjectivity and accepted what I take to be Masolo's challenge to render the social basis of subjectivity stronger than it is typically done in phenomenology or philosophy of mind. I did not go to the forest, thus I cannot be an African. To be an African human being, I need to be socially conditioned in the kind of local and cultural setting that we typically call "African". To be human means inevitably to belong to a particular community and culture. How I experience and what I become because of my experience will be directed by my context and culture. "Wo ho" – to be is to be at some place. It does not matter whether I am bilingual or bicultural, or a cosmopolitan trotter of the global village, I shall always inhabit and be affected by a local community and cultural context. I can go to Africa and live with as well as adopt the life style of a particular African community. But my tongue will forever betray me, and even if not, if I think I am completely African, the community will ever so subtly convey to me the contrary. They might not exclude me, but they will never completely include me – I have not been in their forest. Of course I cannot, as it were, be an African "human", but I can choose to see "myself" as an African. I am indeed free to choose to live as an African. This freedom of self-ascription sets me free to go through any forest and become any person I want to be. There is something that it is like to be an African that I cannot be. But there is something it is like to choose to be an African. That I can be.

## References

Bakhtin, M.M. (1981). *The Dialogical Imagination. Four Essays.* Austin: University of Texas Press.
Bennet, M.R. and Hacker, P.M.S. (2003). *Philosophical Foundations of Neuroscience.* London: Blackwell Publishing.
Chalmers, D. (1996). *The Conscious Mind.* Oxford: Oxford University Press.
Dennett, D. (2006). *Sweet Dreams.* Cambridge, MA: MIT Press.
Fanon, F. (1986). *Black Skin, White Masks.* London: Pluto Press.
Fuchs, T., Sattel, H. and Henningsen, P. (Eds). (2010). *The Embodied Self. Dimensions, Coherence and Disorders.* Stuttgart: Shattauer.
Gbadegesin, S. (2002). Enìyàn: The Yoruba Concept of a Person. In *The African Philosophy Reader.* 2nd edition. Edited by Coetzee, P.H. and Roux, A.P.J. New York: Routledge, pp. 175-192.
Güzeldere, G. (1997). The Many Faces of Consciousness: A Field Guide. In *The Nature of Consciousness. Philosophical Debates.* Edited by Block, N., Flanagan, O. and Güzeldere, G. Cambridge, MA: MIT Press, pp. 1-67.
Gyekye, K. (2002). Person and Community in African Thought. In *The African Philosophy Reader.* 2nd edition. Edited by Coetzee, P. H. and Roux, A.P.J. New York: Routledge, pp. 297-313.
Heidegger, M. (1986). *Sein und Zeit.* Tübingen: Max Niemeyer.
Hermans, H.J.M. (2003). The Construction and Reconstruction of a Dialogical Self. *Journal of Constructivist Psychology,* 16: 89-130.
Hountondji, P. (1983). *African Philosophy: Myth and Reality.* London: Hutchinson.
James, W. (1890). *The Principles of Psychology* (Vol. 1). London: Macmillan.
Kaphagawani, D. (2004). African Conceptions of a Person: A Critical Survey. In *A Companion to African Philosophy.* Edited by Wiredu, K. Malden, MA: Blackwell, pp. 332-342.
Kendel, R., Schwartz, J.H. and Jessell, T.M. (1995). *Essentials of Neural Science and Behaviour.* Stamford, CT: Appleton and Lange.
Masolo, D.A. (2004). Western and African Communitarianism: A Comparison. In *A Companion to African Philosophy.* Edited by Wiredu, K. Malden, MA: Blackwell, pp. 483-498.
Masolo, D.A. (2010). *Self and Community in a Changing World.* Bloomington and Indianapolis: Indiana University Press.
Mead, G.H. (1934). *Mind, Self, and Society.* Edited by Morris, C. Chicago: The University of Chicago Press.
Menkiti, I. (2004). On the Normative Conception of a Person. In *A Companion to African Philosophy.* Edited by Wiredu, K. Malden, MA: Blackwell, pp. 324-331.
Merleau-Ponty, M. (1962). *Phenomenology of Perception.* Translated by Smith, C. New York: Routledge.
Nagel, T. (1997). What is it Like to be a Bat? In *The Nature of Consciousness. Phi-*

*losophical Debates*. Edited by Block, N., Flanagan, O. and Güzeldere, G. Cambridge, MA: MIT Press, pp. 519-529.

Olivier, A. (2011). Phenomenology of the Human Condition. *South African Journal of Philosophy*, 30(2): 94-106.

Olivier, A. (2012). How Ethical is Leadership? *Leadership* 8(1): 67-84.

Robbins, P. and Aydede, M. (2009). *The Cambridge Handbook of Situated Cognition*. Cambridge: Cambridge University Press.

Searle, J.F. (2004). *Mind*. Oxford: Oxford University Press.

Thompson, E. (2007). *Mind in Life*. Cambridge, MA: Harvard University Press.

Tye, M. (1996). *Ten Problems of Consciousness*. Cambridge, MA: MIT Press.

Wiredu, K. (2004). Amo's Critique of Descartes' Philosophy of Mind. In *A Companion to African Philosophy*. Edited by Wiredu, K. Malden, MA: Blackwell, pp. 343–351.

Zahavi, D. (2005). *Subjectivity and Selfhood*. Cambridge, MA: MIT Press.

# Two 'Normative' Conceptions of Personhood

## by Kevin Gary Behrens

*Abstract:* Two 'Normative' Conceptions of Personhood. The account of an African notion of personhood given by Dismas Masolo initially appears to share similar characteristics with the Western normative notion of personhood typically appealed to in bioethics. I argue that these two notions are in fact very distinct, and show how they differ. I consider whether either of these two conceptions of personhood is more valid than the other, concluding that neither is, and that retaining both, whilst clearly distinguishing between them, can only enrich our moral philosophical reasoning and ethical discourse.

*Résumé:* Deux Conceptions 'Normatives' de la Personnalité. Le compte d'une notion africaine de la personnalité donnée par Dismas Masolo apparait d'abord de partager des caractéristiques similaires à la notion normative occidentale de la personnalité á laquelle la bioéthique fait appel. Je démontre que ces deux notions sont en effet très distinctes, et montre en quoi elles diffèrent. Je considère si l'une des deux conceptions de la personnalité est plus valable que l'autre, et concluent qu'aucune n'est, et que les retenir, tout en distinguant clairement entre eux, ne peut qu'enrichir notre raisonnement philosophique morale et discours éthique.

*Key words:* personhood, bioethics, African conception of personhood, moral status, normative ethics, abortion.

*Mots-clés*: personnalité, bioéthique, conception africaine de la personnalité, statut moral, éthique normative, l'avortement

## Introduction

Making a distinction between biological membership of the human species and personhood is not unique to African thought, at least not in ethical (and particularly, bioethical) discourse. The question of what exactly constitutes personhood as something distinct from merely being a member of the species *homo sapiens* has been central to many important philosophical debates in the fields of bioethics, animal ethics and environmental ethics, for instance. Thus the claim that '...[b]eing a person and being a human being are not the same thing' (Masolo 2010: 154) ought not to sound that strange or unfamiliar to philosophers. Even the idea that we are '...born humans but become persons' (Masolo 2010: 13) has a familiar ring. As far back as 1972, Joseph Fletcher argued for a number of necessary criteria to establish personhood: criteria that excluded not just fetuses, but even infants – arguably for the first few years of their lives – from personhood (Macklin 1983: 38). Peter Singer has also denied that new-born human babies are persons: 'Human babies are not born self-aware, or capable of grasping that they exist over time. They are not persons' (Singer 1979: 122). For these theorists, the capabilities or characteristics that they claim are necessary to establish personhood, are not possessed by human infants. They too suggest that babies are not persons, and will only become persons at a later point in their development: they may be born as humans, but they will need to develop into personhood.

If both Western bioethicists and some African philosophers make a distinction between being a mere human biologically and 'personhood' as something that is attained by humans after some process of maturation, why should we think that there is anything particularly distinctive about the notion of personhood in African thought? Yet, D.A. Masolo apparently agrees with Kwasi Wiredu that an African notion of personhood '...makes it the pinnacle of an African difference in philosophical theory' (Masolo 2010: 135). Two full chapters of *Self and Community in a Changing World* are dedicated to characterising this African notion, which is indicative of the central place personhood is taken to fill in African philosophy. Masolo asserts that there is an African conception of personhood that is not only distinct from Western notions, but is also foundational and characteristic of African philosophical thought. He and Wiredu are not alone in making such claims. Similar assertions are made by other African theorists, such as Godfrey Tangwa (2000), Panteleon Iroegbu (n.d.) and Ifeanyi Menkiti (1984).

Thus, despite the apparent parallels between the African and the Western bioethical notions of personhood, African theorists insist that they are distinct from each other in very important ways. In this article, I seek to clarify this distinction. I argue that, despite the fact that both African philosophers and Western theorists make a distinction between merely being human and being persons, the respective conceptions of personhood itself are very different from each other. What personhood is taken to mean in African thought is nothing like what it is understood to be by Western bioethicists. A failure to recognise the fundamental distinction between these two conceptions of personhood could lead to serious and even dangerous confusion, and result in Africans and Westerners talking past one another.

In seeking to clarify this distinction, in the following section, I firstly distinguish both of these normative conceptions of personhood from some of the other ways in which the notion of personhood is used in everyday language and philosophy. In section 3, I give an account of the Western normative notion of personhood, as employed primarily by bioethicists. In section 4, I characterise an African normative conception of personhood, and distinguish it from the bioethical notion. Finally, in section 5, I consider whether either of these two normative conceptions of personhood is more valid than the other, ultimately arguing that they are both important and make a valuable contribution to our ethical discourse and moral reasoning.

## Two 'normative' conceptions of personhood

The term 'personhood' is used in many different ways, both in our everyday use of language and in philosophy. In ordinary conversation, personhood is often taken to mean something akin to individual identity: one might say that a strong attack on one's character is perceived as an affront to one's very personhood. Employed in this way, one's 'personhood' is synonymous with one's 'person', and is related to one's sense of oneself as a unique individual. By contrast, personhood is also often taken as an attribute that distinguishes human persons from other beings, such as animals. Here the focus is on a class of beings (persons) who share a set of characteristics that distinguish them from other classes of beings.

A similar distinction is found in how personhood is used philosophically in the West. Sometimes it denotes the development of the self or individual identity, and in other cases it is also employed to distinguish a class of persons from other beings. These two notions can also be conflated: for instance, it can be argued that what distinguishes persons from other beings is that they are capable of conceiving themselves as having a unique self or personal identity. Personhood has variously been treated as a metaphysical, ontological or normative notion in Western philosophy.

Turning to African notions of personhood, in everyday African thought a basic distinction is made between persons and animals and other beings. Yet, there is little in African accounts of personhood that correlates with the Western notion of individual personal identity or selfhood. Given the strong emphasis on communitarian thinking in Africa, this is perhaps unsurprising. Personhood is nonetheless also used in different senses by African theorists, too. Polycarp Ikuenobe distinguishes between what he calls a 'descriptive metaphysical' and a 'normative' philosophical conception of personhood:

A metaphysical account of personhood may seek to analyse the essential ontological make-up of a person, examining, for instance, whether he or she is essentially material or immaterial, or whether he or she has one or two essential natures. Analyses of the nature of the mind and body, and the relationship between them, are efforts to give metaphysical accounts of personhood… However, it is the normative and not the metaphysical idea of personhood that is germane to African communal traditions, as personhood is a status earned by meeting certain community standards, including the ability to take on prescribed responsibilities that are believed to define personhood. (Ikuenobe 2006: n.p.).

Ikuenobe's analysis is insightful. He characterises what he regards as the more 'germane' conception of personhood in African thought as being normative in nature. The Western conception of personhood that I am interested in this article might similarly be described as normative. Both are essentially moral philosophical notions. My project in this paper is limited to a comparison of two normative notions of personhood: the Western conception commonly appealed to in bioethical discourse, and the African notion described by Ikuenobe as being '…germane to African communal traditions' and by Masolo as being '…the pinnacle of an African difference in philosophical theory' (Masolo 2010: 135).

I have already pointed out some similarities between these two normative conceptions of personhood, but, what essentially distinguishes both from other notions is that they are normative in nature, and are employed as moral philosophical constructs. In both cases the term 'personhood' is used to denote some morally relevant status attributed to those who might be identified as persons. What I will show in what follows is these two normative conceptions of personhood are completely distinct, and that they should not be conflated or confused with each other.

## *The Western bioethical normative conception of personhood*

I begin by giving an account of the Western notion of personhood in order to be able to distinguish it from the African view. The conception of personhood prevalent in the Western bioethics literature, in particular, is related to the notion of moral status or standing. Persons are thought to have a special moral status that entails that we ought to treat them differently from non-persons. Tristram Engelhardt explains that on this approach to personhood, *special* status belongs to persons, not to mere humans. 'Morally competent humans have a central moral standing not possessed by human fetuses or even young children… It is persons who are the constituents of the secular moral community' (Engelhardt 1996: 135). Ruth Maklin, in a survey of the bioethics literature, claims:

> Almost all writings in this vein are set within a particular context in

bioethics in which a determination of personhood is perceived as necessary for resolving vexing moral problems... The main contexts are those surrounding the beginning and end of life; abortion and withholding or terminating life support in a range of cases involving neurological damage, dementing illness and comatose states (Macklin 1983: 36-7).

This Western bioethical notion of personhood thus conceives of entities as being either persons or non-persons. Persons are those who possess the necessary capabilities or properties to be identified as such; and moral agents have a different set of obligations towards persons. Typically, for instance, taking the life of a person is regarded as a more serious wrong than taking the life of a non-person.[55]

What exactly the defining differences are between persons and non-persons is, of course, what the debate centres around. Some theorists set the bar for personhood very high, requiring self-consciousness (Tooley 1976), consciousness, sentience, reasoning, self-directed activity, communication and / or self-awareness (Warren 1975). Joseph Fletcher, one of the first bioethicists to argue for a distinction between biological humanity and personhood, identifies a large number of distinguishing criteria for personhood, including a sense of time and of a past and future, relationality, curiosity, concern for others and noecortical functioning (Macklin 1983:47). Others set a far lower standard, with John Noonan claiming that being conceived by human parents is all that is required for

---

[55] This is not to suggest that that some Western theorists do not conceive of personhood as something that admits of degrees. So, for instance, it might be claimed that a fetus is less of a person than a two year old baby, who in turn is less of a person than a normal adult, who might be said to be a full person. Even where this is the case, though, a distinction is still drawn between the moral duties owed to 'full persons' and those owed to 'lesser persons'. Full persons have more moral claims on us than lesser persons. Here the significant moral distinction is between 'full persons' and 'lesser persons', rather than 'persons' and 'non-persons', but the distinction still works to grant a different kind of moral status to those clearly in the one category rather than the other.

a being to be a person (Macklin 1983:41). On this end of the spectrum, it is even argued that there is no need to make any distinction between being biologically human and being a person. It is not necessary for me to cover the full range of diverse views on what constitutes personhood in this literature, nor to examine their ethical implications. What is important is to highlight that this Western bioethical conception of personhood is meant to do the work of differentiating between two kinds of moral patients, towards whom our moral duties are different: persons and non-persons, or alternatively, 'full persons' and 'lesser persons'. It is a notion related to the moral standing of other entities and to what we owe them morally.

## *The African normative conception of personhood*

The African normative conception of personhood described by Masolo is an entirely different thing. It also distinguishes between persons and mere biological human beings, but on completely different grounds. It is significant that the Masolo/Wiredu account not only represents a distinct conception of personhood, it also identifies this notion as being so fundamental to African philosophical thought that it could be said to be the key to what is different about African philosophy: one great distinguishing feature of African thought (Masolo 210: 138). This is a strong claim and, as such, it warrants careful attention. It is not as though we are dealing here just with some conception one will find in African philosophy, this is a conception that is said to play a fundamental, defining role in African thought. On the basis of this strong claim, it is clearly important to identify how this notion of personhood differs from that of Western bioethics. I now turn to trying to delineate this difference.

The key to this distinction, as I understand it, lies in the claim that 'the project of becoming a person is always incomplete' (Masolo 2010: 13). So, herein lies the rub: whatever an African notion of personhood entails, it is not an attribute something either has or does not have. This notion does not seek to draw a distinguishing line between persons and non-persons. If no-one ever fully attains personhood, as those who hold this position seem to suggest, then personhood is not something an entity either possesses or does not, and full personhood is an ideal towards which one strives rather than a status that can be obtained. It is not simply a matter of distinguishing persons from non-persons; it is a matter of how much of a person one is.

Another important clue as to the meaning of personhood in African thought is provided by Masolo, when he describes the process of becoming a person in terms of a developing competency acquired through associating with others with whom we share a mutual dependency:

This process of depending on others for the tools that enable us to associate with them on a growing scale of competence is the process that makes us into persons. In other words, we become persons through acquiring and participating in the socially generated knowledge of norms and actions we learn to live by in order to impose humaneness on our humanness (Masolo 2010: 155).

Thus, the process of becoming a person is one in which the quality of humaneness is added to our basic humanity, as we gradually acquire competency as moral agents. Since humaneness is commonly understood as exhibiting kindness, mercifulness and compassion, Masolo's account suggests that personhood, in African thought, is probably best understood in terms of acquiring virtue. This is supported by Ifeanyi Menkiti who also describes acquiring personhood in African thought as a process (Menkiti 1984: 173). He claims that personhood is an attribute each individual should strive to develop maximally; something more like a goal we should seek to attain than a status we either possess or do not possess:

> ...the African view reaches ... for what might be described as a maximal definition of the person. As far as African societies are concerned, personhood is something at which individuals could fail, at which they could be competent or ineffective, better or worse. Hence, the African emphasized the rituals of incorporation

and the overarching necessity of learning the social rules by which the community lives, so that what was initially biologically given can come to attain social self-hood, i.e., become a person with all the inbuilt excellencies implied by the term (Menkiti 1984: 173).

Menkiti's association of the term 'excellencies' with personhood also implies that the becoming a person is essentially related to developing virtue. Thus, the African conception of personhood could be thought to propose a theory of ethics that brings to mind what Western philosophy calls 'perfectionism': Persons should seek to develop a good or virtuous nature in order to become true or fully moral persons. Thaddeus Metz explains this conception of a person by likening it to the Yiddisch notion of a 'mensch', a person of high moral character, basically, a good person (Metz 2007).

By now it ought to be clear that the Western bioethical normative conception of personhood and the African notion are completely distinct. Another way of expressing this distinction is to consider the object of the focus of the term 'personhood'. In Western thought, personhood is concerned with the status of moral *patients*, whereas the African approach focuses on the character of a person as a moral *agent*. Tangwa rejects the Western emphasis on '…criteria for personhood that would clearly segregate those entities worthy of moral consideration from those without or with less moral worth' (Tangwa 2000: 40) in favour of a view of personhood that establishes

> …human persons as moral agents; carrying the whole weight of moral obligations, responsibilities and duties on their shoulders… [T]he morality of an action or procedure is to be determined from the standpoint of the agent rather than that of the patient (the recipient of action)… What the attributes of self-consciousness, rationality, and freedom of choice do… is load the heavy burden of moral liability, culpability, and responsibility on the shoulders of their possessor. Human persons are not morally *special*, they are morally *liable*. (Tangwa 2000: 40).

Menkiti makes a similar distinction when he describes the Western view of the person as a 'minimal definition' that focuses on establishing the status of persons as moral patients, to be contrasted with a 'maximal definition' of the person according to which personhood is essentially a measure of the virtue of the moral agent (Menkiti 1984: 73).

Clarifying this distinction is important in order to ensure that Western and African philosophers do not end up talking at cross-purposes. An African claim that an individual's personhood is diminished should not be taken to imply that such an individual has diminished status as a moral patient, and can be treated with less moral consideration. That a new-born human baby is thought not to have developed much by way of personhood would not, on the African definition, provide any grounds for attributing it less moral worth as an object of our moral concern. Tangwa expresses this clearly:

> ...the difference between, say, a mentally retarded individual or an infant and a fully self-conscious, mature, rational, and free individual do not entail, in the African perception, that such a being falls outside the 'inner sanctum of secular morality' and can or should be treated with less moral consideration. (Tangwa 2000: 42).

The important distinction between these two normative notions of personhood is that in the Western tradition it is essentially understood in terms of the moral status of patients, whereas it relates to the degree of virtue of moral agents in the African tradition.

## *Is either of these notions of personhood more valid than the other?*

Having made the distinction between these two normative notions of personhood clear, I now consider whether there are reasons for thinking that either notion is more valid than the other, and whether either should be rejected in favour of the other. I begin by considering whether the African notion of personhood should be preferred over the Western bioethical notion. At least one African philosopher, Tangwa, asserts that the Western bioethical notion of personhood is erroneous, at least in terms of the conclusions it comes to in ascribing different moral status to some humans than to others. He claims that the African conception of personhood, which focusses on the person as moral agent, rather than moral patient '...seems to accord better with our ordinary moral intuitions and sensibilities and is thus more appropriate for non-discriminatory morality in general' (Tangwa 2000: 43). He expresses his main thesis thus:

The central thought I want to advance is that the Western conception of a human person, as a category or subset of human being, is appropriate only for the ascription of moral responsibility, liability, and culpability rather than for the ascription of moral worth, desert, eligibility, or acceptability into the moral community made up, as it necessarily is, of both moral agents and patients (2000: 42-3).

This represents no less than an outright rejection of the Western bioethical conception of personhood, certainly as it has hitherto been put to use in moral philosophy. This is a strong challenge which is surely deserving of a hearing and a response.

Tangwa's proposal that it is only appropriate to identify a sub-set of human beings as persons, when persons are understood as those capable of moral agency, and personhood is not at the same time taken to confer different moral standing on those who qualify as persons, would have the effect of making the bioethical conception of personhood far less contentious. Indeed, he rejects it exactly because he finds some its conclusions and implications morally objectionable. He clearly disapproves of non-therapeutic abortion and organ transplantation (Tangwa 200: 41) and claims:

Intuitively, from the point of view of the common sensibilities and practices of human beings in most societies the world over, it would appear that a human infant or a mentally or physically handicapped human being deserves if anything greater moral consideration than a paradigmatic *per-*

*son* as [defined by Western bioethicists] (Tangwa 2000: 40).

I am unconvinced that such a broad intuitive consensus, in fact, exists. Perhaps Tangwa means to appeal to a moral intuition that the especially vulnerable or powerless ought to be given special protection. This should not so much be understood as their being deserving of greater moral consideration, as their being deserving of different moral consideration, the kind of moral consideration that recognises the special needs of the vulnerable as morally significant. But, to support the idea that we should give special consideration to the needs of the vulnerable does not, by way of example, depend on a claim that a severely mentally handicapped vulnerable human being has the same moral status as a human being who is capable or rational thought, moral agency, and self-consciousness. Indeed, the argument that we ought to treat such a handicapped human being differently, perhaps with greater compassion, could be strengthened by the recognition that such a being's moral status is different.

It is possible that the use of phrases such as 'lesser moral status' and 'full personhood' by some bioethicists has damaged the credibility of this position: such phrases suggest a quantitative hierarchical ordering of moral status, presumably with persons at the apex. This might be taken to suggest that persons are morally more important than other beings. I think it is unfortunate that some bioethicists have used language suggesting that moral status is a quantitative rather than a qualitative notion. If all that a distinction between persons or 'full persons' and other beings is meant to do is explain why our moral obligations towards such categories of beings is qualitatively different, then the distinction is less problematic. It seems obvious to me that there are good reasons for thinking that a human fetus of 4 weeks has a different moral status to that of a normally functioning human adult. This does not, on its own, justify non-therapeutic abortion, but it does explain why we ordinarily regard the deliberate killing of an adult human as murder, while we are less inclined to describe abortion as murder.

Be that as it may, there are compelling grounds for retaining the bioethical notion of personhood. It is a useful theoretical construct that supports some of our basic moral intuitions without having to rely on obviously speciesist considerations. We do ordinarily think that autonomous, rational, self-conscious beings, capable of moral agency (roughly what bioethicists often denote as persons) require different moral treatment than beings without these attributes. That is why most of us would think we ought to save the life of an adult human being before that, of say, a dog, presuming we could only save one or the other. It is morally more attractive to justify this on the grounds of the specific attributes of persons, than on the speciest grounds that those with human DNA require special treatment merely because they belong to the human species. Furthermore, where we are placed in the difficult position of having to decide whether to continue with a pregnancy, knowing that the child to be born will never have any of the attributes of personhood, or of whether to remove a person in a persistent vegetative state from life-support, this distinction is exceptionally significant and helpful. The Western bioethical notion of personhood enriches out ethical discourse, helps clarify some difficult ethical issues, is preferable to speciesist conceptions, and should therefore be retained.

I am unaware of any theorist who has directly challenged the validity of the African normative notion of personhood, per se. This might be attributable to the fact that this conception is not widely known outside of African philosophical circles. It is nonetheless reasonable to consider whether or not this notion has merit. Certainly, this notion of personhood does not lead to highly contentious moral conclusions in quite the same way that the bioethical notion does. If it is to be challenged, then it is likely that it would be questioned mainly because of its unfamiliarity or strangeness, at least to Western thinkers. However, suitably explained, there does not seem to be anything intrinsically unsound about conceiving of personhood as a measure of the moral virtue of the agent. Clearly, this use of the term 'personhood' is distinct from the Western bioethical notion, as I have already argued. But, this should not be taken as grounds for rejecting it. Indeed, this notion of personhood is theoretically attractive in its own right. In turning the focus from the status of moral patients to the moral stature of the agent, it draws attention to our moral obligations and responsibilities, especially with regard to our relationships with others.

I think that both of these notions of personhood have their merits, and retaining both can only enrich and deepen our ethical discourse. Neither is better or more valuable than other. Clearly, there is the danger that unless the distinctions between these two notions are clearly understood, confusion would be inevitable. But, it is possible to clarify the distinction, as I have attempted to do in this article. And, on the basis of such clarification, Western and African ethicists ought to be able to engage with one another in a way which can only be of benefit to moral philosophy.

### References

Engelhardt, T. (2000). *The Foundations of Bioethics*. New York: Oxford University Press.
Ikuenobe, P. (2006). The Idea of Personhood in Chinua Achebe's *Things Fall Apart*. *Philosophia Africana*, 9: 117-131.
Iroegbu, P. (n.d.). The Human Person in the Western and African Traditions: A Comparative Analysis. Available from: http://people.stfx.ca/wsweet/00-PCT/Vol.%201%202002%20Iroegbu.pdf. (Accessed 23 March 2012).
Macklin, R. (1983). Personhood in the Bioethics Literature. *The Milbank Memorial Fund Quarterly Health and Society*, 61: 35-47.
Masolo, D.A. (2010). *Self and Community in a Changing World*. Bloomington: Indiana University Press.
Menkiti, I. (1984). Person and Community in African Traditional Thought. In *African Philosophy, An Introduction*. Edited by Wright, R. Lanham, MD: University Press of America.
Metz, T. (2007). Toward an African Moral Theory. *Journal of Political Philosophy*, 15: 321-341.
Singer, P. (1979). *Practical Ethics*. Cambridge: Cambridge University Press.
Tangwa, G. (2000). The Traditional African Perception of a Person. Some Implications for Bioethics. *Hastings Center Report*, 30: 39-43.
Tooley, M. (1976). Abortion and Infanticide. In *Moral Problems in Medicine*. Edited by Beauchamp, T. and Walters, L. Encino: Dickenson.

Warren, M. (1973). On the Moral and Legal Status of Abortion. *The Monist*, 57: 43-61.

# Personhood: Social Approval or a Unique Identity?

## by Mpho Tshivhase

*Abstract*: Personhood: Social Approval or a Unique Identity? In this article, I assess the African view of personhood and hence am interested in evaluating the role that moral norms and social expectations play in the process of cultivating personhood. I draw the conclusion about the African view of personhood that it is too focused on the other and thus not compatible with human excellences associated with individual uniqueness. I illustrate my claim by critically engaging with the way D.A. Masolo articulates and defends the African view of personhood.

*Résumé*: Personnalité: Approbation Social ou Identité Unique? Dans cet article, j'évalue la perspective africaine de la personnalité. Je suis donc intéressé à évaluer le rôle que les normes morales et les attentes sociales jouent dans le processus de cultiver la personnalité. La conclusion que je tire à propos de la perspective africaine de la personnalité est qu'elle est trop centré sur l'autrui et qu'elle n'est donc pas compatible avec les excellences humaines associées à l'unicité individuelle. J'illustre mon argument en engageant de manière critique la façon dont D.A. Masolo articule et défend la perspective africaine de la personnalité.

*Keywords*: Personhood, human excellence, self, community, autonomy, authenticity, uniqueness

*Mots-clés:* Personnalité, excellence humaine, le soi, communauté, autonomie, authenticité, unicité

## Introduction

A popular understanding of personhood appeals to five criteria to delineate what a person is. A person is, first and foremost, distinct from a thing. Heidegger's notion of Dasein's Being-in-the-world is viewed as one way of distinguishing persons from mere objects (Hall 1992: 88). Another way of outlining the distinction involves characterizing a person as an individual whose existence is not limited to her biological make-up. In other words, a person is not just a human being (Masolo 2010). Persons are also, in the Kantian sense, valuable as ends in themselves and not simply means to an end. Another feature of personhood involves a person's claim to legal rights and duties. Finally, persons are embedded in societies within which they have functions and roles to play (Hall 1992: 88). The African view of personhood is not directly related to most of the criteria mentioned above, at least not in the view as championed by Kwasi Wiredu (1992: 199-200), whose views are also articulated and defended by Masolo in his book *Self and Community in a Changing World* (2010). Masolo, being a proponent of the African view of personhood, endorses personhood that is communalistic and morally loaded. Viewed in this way, personhood is realized when one conducts her life in a way that is morally virtuous and, so, humanly excellent.

In this article, I am mostly concerned to assess the African view of personhood and hence am also interested in evaluating the role morality plays in the process of cultivating personhood. I want to use this article to draw a conclusion about the African view of personhood, namely, that it is too focused on the other and thus not compatible with values associated with individual uniqueness. I will illustrate my claim by looking at the way that Masolo articulates and defends the African view.

I will proceed as follows: in the first section I will contextualize Masolo's view on personhood. I will use the second section to discuss what I understand to be one major way that Masolo conceives of personhood, the 'morality model', and illustrate my objection by appealing to the value of authenticity. In the third section, I will explain another model of personhood that Masolo discusses, which I have dubbed 'the expectations model', and will criticise it for limiting one's autonomy. In the final section, I will recommend uniqueness as a model of personhood that avoids and explains the problems faced by Masolo's morality and expectations models. The conception of uniqueness I have in mind is grounded in the values of authenticity and autonomy. I want to show that a theory of personhood that prioritizes personal interests while also encouraging moral discipline is more worthy of pursuit than the African view, which prioritizes only a community's interests. In short, I will argue against the African view of personhood, at least as articulated by Masolo, and will advocate uniqueness as an alternative model of human excellence that redresses the imbalance between community's interests and personal interests.

## An African view of personhood

Masolo approaches personhood by analysing some African languages or certain words in them. In doing so, he hopes, in part, to make better sense of the relation between personhood and society in characteristic African cultures. His opinion is that people have an awareness of their status as human beings, but for them to cultivate their awareness into that of personhood they must be part of a community, as personhood is a socially developed way of being. This point of view relies on the perspective that we are born humans who can develop to become persons, where that process of becoming a person is always incomplete and includes the possibility of one failing at it (Masolo 2010; Menkiti 2004: 326). As I will show in this section, Masolo's African view of personhood stands in direct distinction from the Western view, which singles out one particular feature of an individual, such as the capacity for intelligence, to use as the defining feature of personhood (Menkiti 1984: 171).

There is a notable distinction that should be kept in mind when thinking about Masolo's discussion on personhood. This distinction is between the nature of personhood itself and the means to acquiring it. Masolo does not make this distinction clear. However, I think the models used to address personhood as an end in itself and the means to personhood are different, even though they might overlap in some respects. In order to make my point with clarity, I have separated the two questions regarding personhood, i.e., 'what is personhood?' and 'how does one acquire personhood?'. Defining personhood itself, according to Masolo, is a matter of adhering to moral principles which are dominated by a concern for the well-being of others or conforming to community's expectations, while acquiring personhood involves being part of a community and participating in socializing processes. Masolo often weaves the meaning of personhood and the means to personhood together, but I think that they each have an independent logic and so I will discuss them separately. It is the question of what personhood is that interests me in this paper, and so I will pay attention only to the plausible characterizations of it.

With regard to the nature of personhood, Masolo supports a typically African view instead of the Western view as characterized by Kant. Kant's view, as Masolo interprets it, defines personhood by appealing to an individual's rationality and perceives persons as atomistic entities with mechanistic minds (Masolo 2010: 139; Menkiti 2004: 326). Furthermore, Kant depicts the relation of a person to the world as autonomous and disinterested (Masolo 2010: 158). In short, a person is a rational subject of understanding. Masolo supports Wiredu's African view because

> [w]hile Kant starts with human nature as phenomenologically complete in its (metaphysical) constitution at least in the domain of understanding, Wiredu seeks to establish the view that such defining characteristics of being human are not endowed in humans by a force that exists outside an already existing environment of the deliberate actions of other humans, namely the socializing processes out of which the actualization of human capacities emerges (Masolo 2010: 138).

In other words, Kant thinks what makes humans genuinely human lies in their rational psychology, while Wiredu and many other sub-Saharan thinkers maintain that it lies in the activities that take place within a community; "...personhood is a conception of an individual who through mature reflection and steady motivation is able to carve out a reasonably ample livelihood for self, 'family' and a potentially wide group of kin dependants, besides making substantial contributions to the well-being of society at large" (Wiredu 1992: 200). In African thought, personhood is a communal process.

African conceptions of personhood cite group solidarity as a central feature of a traditional society (Menkiti 2004: 324). Ifeanyi Menkiti and Kwame Gyekye, central figures in the African debate on personhood, argue differently about the extent of the community's power in the definition of a person. Menkiti argues that the community wholly defines personhood (Menkiti 1984: 171). Menkiti's view is characterized by John Mbiti's "I am because we; and since we are, therefore I am", which Menkiti accepts as the "cardinal point in understanding the African view of man (Mbiti 1969: 108-109). Gyekye criticizes Menkiti for giving in to the "…temptation of exaggerating the normative status and power of the cultural community in relation to those of the person and thus obfuscating our understanding of the real nature of the person" (Gyekye 1992: 106). With the aim to collapse the tension between the self and community, Gyekye develops a more flexible view, the moderate or restricted communitarian view, which accommodates communal and autonomous individual values and practices (Gyekye 1992: 106-113, 115-116, 120-121). African thought presents different conceptions of personhood, but most theorists are in agreement that personhood is largely if not exclusively a communal matter (Kaphagawani 2006: 332, 337-338).

The implications that arise from the African view defy, according to Masolo, the boundaries of metaphysics and epistemology and, to a large extent, ethics in the restrictive Kantian sense which illustrates the autonomous status of a person as the measure of an individual's grasp of reality grounded in her rational capacity to deliberate on moral and political ends (Masolo 2010: 13, 141, 158-159). This defiance is, more specifically, indicative of a normative approach to understanding persons that is favoured by Masolo. The African view of personhood characterizes persons as products of their community where their personhood comes through learning and participating in certain societal norms, roughly either adhering to the communally beneficial moral guiding principles or conforming to the society's expectations (Masolo 2010: 155). It is this communally oriented definition of personhood that Masolo finds attractive and revealing.

I am going to argue against this African view of personhood, which is descriptive and evaluative; it describes the criteria central to what personhood is and it evaluates the acceptable moral attitude and conduct that an individual should display in the interest of the community's welfare. I will start my discussion of the African view of what personhood is by looking at what I call the 'morality model', one of two major ways that Masolo can be read as conceiving of personhood from a sub-Saharan perspective. I will discuss Masolo's characterization of morality which, when coupled with a demonstration of compassion, he believes to be the fundamental element of human excellence that is characteristic of a desirable personhood. I will illustrate that such human excellence does not sufficiently include the realization of a personal self and neglects an individual's inner being. My view is that moral virtues are not always personally fulfilling, especially when they move an individual to supress his own interests.

### *The Morality model of personhood*

The moral principle that should ideally guide an individual is aimed at improving and maintaining the welfare of her community, in Masolo's view. Herein an individual's conduct should not only avoid harming others, but should also help others to advance their wellbeing. Masolo's moral guiding principle states that "at all times in our conduct we ought to manifest concern for the interests of others" (Masolo 2010: 172). That is to say, when one makes decisions or behaves in a certain way, she must always do so in a way that improves the welfare of others instead of hindering it. One must never act to ensure merely individual interests, as this would be selfish in a way that does not reflect a desirable condition of the moral relationship between a person and a community. Personhood, then, involves a kind of human excellence that is characterized by the morally virtuous conduct that one displays within her community when interacting with other people. Masolo promotes the morality model of personhood in order to reveal appropriate principles that should ideally govern the way that individuals treat others.

The appropriate moral principle for personhood is usefully illustrated by the kind of attitude one should avoid. The attitude that Masolo finds unattractive for personhood is called 'juok' in the Luo language of Eastern Africa. Juok is the antisocial attitude which can be demonstrated by behaviour that is intentionally aimed at harming others. Juok is also a quality that invokes moral blame (Masolo 2010: 200). "Juok is the darkening and unrestrained capacity to commit evil" so that anyone who is charged of juok is regarded a well-reasoning but evil agent who acts with an immoral motive (Masolo 2010: 202-204). Juok is a deviation from desirable social standing as it does not build proper relations with others (Masolo 2010: 205). Such a deviant individual is called a *'jajuok'* (*ibid*).

A *jajuok* is someone who practices *juok* or has *juok* qualities. A *jajuok* is a loner who does not care much about moral integrity (Masolo 2010: 207). The character of a *jajuok* is secretive and opposes the virtues of mutual sympathy. As such, a *jajuok* is rejected and often shamed by society. To become a person, humans must refrain from practicing *juok*; to cultivate human excellence they must adopt an attitude that encourages mutual dependency and sharing with others, as this is the moral means to creating, reproducing and holding the community together (Masolo 2010: 217). Morality is presented here as standards of humanly excellent conduct that make up criteria for the survival and wellbeing of others (Masolo 2010: 172). Moral principles are said to develop when people comprehend the needs of others as equal to their own (*ibid*). Moral principles are meant to guide us "from a false sense of autonomy and a fixation on the self to the realization of mutual dependency on others" (*ibid*). Such a fixation on the self is deemed undesirable and is aligned with the behaviour of a 'jajuok'. So, in order to cultivate human excellence, or personhood, in the African tradition, individuals must set aside their personal interests and a sense of self-governance, and replace these with mutual dependency and sharing. In this way, they avoid the immoral behaviour of a jajuok and thus not only refrain from harming others, but also go out of their way to help them.

Masolo is right to assert that individuals should focus on improving their moral character. It is generally accepted that morality involves at least not doing harm to others. I have no issue with the moral prevention of harm to others. What I have an issue with is the idea that, to be real persons, we must place the concern for the well-being of others *at all times* before our own. Masolo's idea of morality is exclusively focused on the other, and so it presents a tension between personal and communal interests. Morality, here, is dominated by the concern for the interests of others and, in so doing, it neglects the personal self – as I will argue below. I, like Susan Wolf (1982: 424), think there is something undesirable about the pursuit of moral excellence when it dominates a person in a manner that requires a lack of or denial of the existence of an identifiable personal self.

We often understand the personal self to have some passions or interests and an appreciation for certain talents and skills and other activities that may lack moral motivations (Wolf 1982: 422). One could pursue a doctoral degree in Linguistics, or have a keen passion for collecting rare and expensive artworks, and derive fulfilment from pursuing such interests. Such interests are not immoral and they do not harm anyone, but they also do not necessarily add anything to another's life. Nonetheless, entertaining these personal interests can invoke guilt in an individual whose life is dominated by the concern for others. Such an individual would opt to suppress these personal interests in order to cultivate moral virtues necessary for Masolo's conception of personhood. Masolo's view does not concern itself with the kind of life that is led in an individual's interest but with the interests that would be desirable for an individual to adopt for the good of society. Personhood, then, is a matter of living a life that is good for others, the underlying assumption being that only people who are committed to the welfare of others live fulfilled lives that are admirable.

On the contrary, I think that often a life exclusively committed to improving the welfare of others with a lack of personal interests can be unusually empty and thus unattractive (Wolf 1982: 421). Consider the case of Mother Teresa. She lived a life of the kind of moral saint discussed by Susan Wolf. Mother Teresa lived a morally virtuous life but professed to feel agony and loneliness even though she lived and did good for the community (Van Biema 2007). She lived a life that resembled Wolf's 'rational moral saint' (1982: 424) who knowingly sacrifices her own interests for possible fear of damnation or at least guilt. Mother Teresa probably paid less attention to herself and her own welfare to avoid the risk of overriding her concerns for moral virtues. She was loyal to her moral duties towards others, yet she felt that her life was empty. The emptiness of her life makes a case for the view that what we admire about an individual is not merely her moral virtuosity and how we benefit from it; in addition, we admire an individual's personal excellences which resonate with her personal goals in addition to her sense of self. We often deem real people to include those who are less than morally perfect but have managed to achieve personal excellence, like the art connoisseur and the Linguistics major, with an acceptable level of morality (Wolf 1982: 423). My point is we should, sometimes, aim for personal excellence regardless of whether it improves other people's welfare or not.

A second but related objection to moral perfection as exhaustive of the best human life is that moral conduct and an agent's attitude are not always aligned, so that if we promote conduct over attitude we create inauthentic moralists, like Mother Teresa. Masolo asserts that morality is a matter of our virtuous conduct and it necessarily regulates our self-interested nature (Masolo 2010: 172). It is only when we act in a manner that illustrates evidence of our moral virtuosity that we can be regarded as having achieved human excellence. However, at times our actions and attitudes can clash. One could have developed an attitude disinclined to helping others. This person may have difficulty mastering compassion in the way Masolo asserts we should. For instance, such an individual may find it difficult to sacrifice his time to do charity work but hides this disinterest by doing charity work anyway – perhaps to maintain a good reputation. In so doing, he does his bit to advance the lives of others, which, in Masolo's view, is good, although it could be bad in another, say, for driving people to develop socially approved public personas that are appropriate and private jajuok personas that are inappropriate. Although it is more harmful to herself than others, the clash between Mother Teresa's public and private personas is evident in her confession regarding her smile being "a mask…a cloak that covers everything" (Van Biema 2007: 2). A development and maintenance of personas is a clear indicator of inauthentic human excellence – something which Masolo's personhood seems not to take into consideration as it champions moral conduct that improves the welfare of others as, alone, that which matters.

In response, Masolo may say that Mother Teresa misunderstood the proper purpose and application of relational interdependency and the right way to cultivate moral personhood. When he speaks of prioritizing the welfare of community, perhaps he does not mean that one should, in literally every action, sacrifice one's wellbeing in order to ensure that of others. If anything, he may encourage Mother Teresa to find meaning in her life first before helping others, as an empty person cannot be maximally helpful to the society in the long run. He could reasonably argue that she could have done more for others over the long haul if she had led a personally meaningful life. If she had found meaning in her life before helping others, there would have been no development of a persona. A meaningful life seems to resolve both issues of neglect of personal excellence and of inauthenticity when invariably acting with moral aims. In sum, Masolo can argue that, in misunderstanding the workings of relational interdependency, Mother Teresa could not have developed her personhood all that well. In essence, we are better equipped to treat others morally and do more to help improve their lives when we first take care of ourselves, as we do when we find ourselves in a crashing plane; we first put an oxygen mask on ourselves in order to save the next person, such as our child.

Is a meaningful life, then, a precondition for helping others? I doubt that this is true. Extended loyalty to communal interests is detrimental to and limits personal interests and the potential to pursue personal goods. It is implausible to think that Mother Teresa could have done more for others, if she had done more for herself first, since she had already gone beyond the call of duty in her compassionate deeds for others. The point I am making is that Mother Teresa seems to lack some personal goods and that these goods probably would not benefit the community.

Furthermore, to encourage people to pursue personal goals, but only for the sake of improving the lives of others, still points to the primacy of the community. I maintain that there are personal goods that are worthy of pursuit in themselves and not for others as I illustrated earlier with the Linguistics degree student and the art connoisseur. The solution to Mother Teresa's case does not lie in what she has to do for herself before she serves the community; it is a matter of what Mother Teresa should do in order to become whom she should be. Her becoming necessarily involves her ability to cultivate personal excellences that merit pursuit for their own sake. An ability to do this would minimize her need to develop personas to appear a saint in public while she is in turmoil. This process would not be about taking care of oneself so as to care for others; it would be about taking care of oneself for the good of oneself. What matters most would be her wellbeing in and of itself, and not for the community. The point is that meaning in life is not merely a means to helping others, but it is part of what it means to be conscious of the things that matter to oneself in the process of cultivating human excellence.

I believe that one should not always sacrifice one's personal self in the process of pursuing moral excellence. When moral virtues do little for an individual's well-being to an extent where an individual sacrifices her personal interests and starts to look more like a slave to society than an independent individual among other individuals, we have to concede that morality is not always of benefit to the inner self. Morality would be better suited for personhood if it was restructured to form only part of an individual's self-understanding instead of being a rite of passage to personhood wherein the individual could be mistaken for a mere means to society's welfare.

What I have done above is argue that morality is more beneficial to the community than it necessarily is to the person, and that a life lived in service of the interests of others is not as admirable as Masolo conceives of it. Part of this involved showing that human excellence is not always grounded in moral perfection. I referred to the two cases of Mother Teresa and the inauthentic moralist to illustrate my point. What is similar about these cases is that they are all motivated by moral intentions and perform moral actions, at least as Masolo construes them, yet they lack an identifiable personal self and integrity, constituents of being a genuine person.

## The eExpectations model of personhood

So far I have explained Masolo's view of personhood, and have singled out morality as one of the models that he uses to articulate its nature. He views personhood as human excellence that is comprised of commitment to the welfare of others. I criticised the morality model for being unconcerned with interests good for the person and exclusively concerned with interests that are good for others. I illustrated that morality on its own is probably the wrong model for personhood, as it does not permit individuals to pursue personal forms of excellence, except insofar as they conduce to benefiting other people. I referred to Mother Teresa's case to dismiss the assumption that only morally virtuous people live admirable lives. I also argued that a life that is primarily concerned with the interests of others is not always authentic. In this section, I will turn my attention to the expectations model of personhood that I also find in Masolo's discussion of what personhood essentially is.[56] This model endorses conformity to society's expectations when cultivating personhood.

Fundamentally, I think that morality and abiding by expectations are not

---

[56]When I discussed the 'expectations model' in conversation with Prof Masolo, he rejected it, but I find that it nonetheless is a natural way to read his text.

necessarily compatible, and, hence, I make the distinction between the two models. Although Masolo does not make this distinction, the logic of abiding by expectations and that of adopting moral excellence are not the same. One can be moral without conforming to expectations, like a homosexual human rights activist in a conservative society, and one can conform to expectations without being moral, like a funeral respected parlour owner who illegally sells body parts on a very willing black market. The two models are not necessarily consistent with each other, and even when put together I maintain that they do not really illustrate what a person is. The morality model encourages a life of service to the interests of others to an extent that threatens one's authenticity. The expectations model, in contrast, when followed hinders one's autonomy, and I will use this section to illustrate this point.

The expectations model of personhood is the view that personhood is constituted by fulfilling society's expectations of whom one should become. The society has norms regarding the kinds of persons humans should become and these involve a display of a positive public image that one may identify or be identified with. A positive public image is one that abides by the community's expectations. The person that the society expects one to be is determined by qualities, roles and capacities that the society can endow one with. The qualities, roles and capacities are meant to "enable a person to be known to be...the person he is supposed to be" (Masolo 2010:207). Becoming the person that the society expects one to be involves "adjusting one's conduct in accordance with known or assumed expectations of other members within any relational circuit" (Masolo 2010: 206). The expectations model is based on a framework where one's conduct is judged according to the evaluations by other members of the community to which one belongs. Masolo believes that the key to a society requires "people to recognize their place in the social network and to abide by the expectations that hold the network together" (Masolo 2010: 217). The person whom one is supposed to be is one who abides by the community's expectations, which typically function to keep the community united (Masolo 2010: 217). What the community often expects from its members is moral behaviour, but, as noted above, not all expectations need have moral content. Communal unity grounded in moral or otherwise expected behaviour is the fundamental value of a community which is apparently, for Masolo, meant to justify the expectations that people should abide by.

The objections raised to the morality model are also relevant to the expectations model, i.e., the problems of neglect and inauthenticity. The model neglects the personal self and one's personal goals because people should abide by the expectations of others. The problem of inauthenticity comes up in situations where one has to abide by the society's expectations even if one does not necessarily agree with or endorse the rules and norms that one is expected to adhere to. Viewed in this way, the expectations model encourages people to live, not according to one's chosen mode of existence, but in accordance with the way other people believe you should conduct your life.

There is an additional problem that applies to the expectations model, which is the problem of autonomy. I think that adhering to the expectations model would tend to encourage individuals to suspend their autonomous judgement. People lend their subjectivity to collective beliefs and activities when they conform to the norms of the society. I find that the idea of conformity is an unattractive view of how to live, as one aspires to live a life that is not based on autonomous consideration of what is good for one's life, but rather fulfilling roles that are expected by one's community, in order to fulfill the principle of social unity. When a person lives according to a community's expectations, his subjectivity or first-personal concern and autonomy become limited. In abiding by the community's expectations, one restricts oneself and does not develop one's own autonomy since one simply does what others expect. A person lacking in autonomy is much like an emotionally abused woman who knows she is in a bad relationship but is still afraid to leave her partner, so much so that she constantly challenges herself to become the woman he expects her to be irrespective of the fact that he does not appreciate or respect her. Such an individual has no sense of self-governance. She is an example of what people should not aspire to become.

Masolo could, in response, argue that autonomy is a false sense of freedom that is not conducive to the principle of mutual dependency. Autonomy cannot be part of the structure of communal life which is governed by the norms of society that organise individuals in positions that are good for members of the society or keep the society united. Masolo could further argue that people who abide by expectations do not see themselves separate from the society within which their lives are embedded, which is a desirable trait. He could even invoke John Mbiti's well-known dictum – "I am because we are; and since we are, therefore I am" (Mbiti 1969: 108-109) to argue that unity cannot stem solely from autonomous conduct and that conforming to society's norms is part of what it really means to belong to a society. When one abides by society's expectations, one gains acceptance and so becomes part of something more meaningful than individual self-governance. Social unity could be seen as a value, and the ability to enhance as a value that enhances the meaning of an individual's life. Masolo could also argue that brutish behaviour, of the abusive sort, is a result of prizing individual autonomy. The kind of liberty that Masolo would endorse is the kind that is consistent only with creating a community, i.e., by uniting the people. His view of autonomy could be understood in terms of a freedom to act for the sake of social togetherness. This, as Robert Birt puts it, is a communal or social freedom, not a property that individuals possess on their own (Birt 2002: 87-88, 94-95).

However, I maintain that understanding freedom as the ability to act for others is not enough. The battered woman case cannot be solved by saying that freedom is an 'other' focused ethic, a mere ability to do what others would like us to do. We can hope that her husband, at some later point, will understand and exercise his freedom as Masolo conceives of it, but this does little to help the woman out of her situation. The woman has internalized the abuse and to point out that her freedom is externally derived – that someone else has to be free enough to act for her sake does not help her, nor does it truly unite her with her community, especially if she lives in a patriarchal community that expects her to be a good woman and to look only to her husband for love and protection. My point is that the African view of freedom is not enough; there are other desirable forms of autonomy that would be neglected by the expectations model.

Furthermore, I think that self-governance does not presuppose isolation, and that an attractive kind of social unity is possible among autonomous individuals. A person is inescapably embedded in a community and can even join another community, say, through marriage, or even one that is entered into by choice. I think it is the capacity to choose for oneself that is limited by abiding to expectations. Autonomy affords one the space to choose what matters to one and such a choice can be made without necessarily exhibiting disregard for societal norms. A society whose norms and expectations are designed to be exempt from scrutiny does not encourage people to make sense of the world in their own way. A person should be able to exercise her self-governance in questioning the legitimacy and authority of societal expectations. People should understand cultivation of autonomy as a project that is not to be undertaken at the expense of the individual's sociability or with a disregard for the value of one's community, but as a project that should be undertaken in constant interrogation of the norms that are supposed to govern one's life, while nonetheless adhering to certain moral constraints. I think an individual can live autonomously with others.

In the next section I will present the uniqueness model of personhood and show how it avoids the pitfalls of the morality and expectations models. I will illustrate that where Masolo's models hinder authenticity and autonomy to benefit the society or to keep it united, the uniqueness model uses authenticity and autonomy to ground a kind of personhood that does not neglect an identifiable personal self and at the same time restrains individuals from treating others with harmful intent.

### The uniqueness model of personhood

To this point I have discussed what personhood is by means of analysing Masolo's morality and expectations models, both of which place great emphasis on the interests of the other. The main criticism I raised was that they both neglect the personal self by championing a life lived in servitude of the community and thus both models fail to recognise a person as an end in himself. I have indicated my dissatisfaction with Masolo's communitarian view of personhood and so I now use this section to suggest an agent-centred view of personhood. I think that Masolo's personhood theory has neglected this inner self by assuming that it will benefit from treating others well and by charging merely personal interests as immoral. I am interested in rescuing the inner self from obscurity in Masolo's campaign to do what is good for the society, and I think a uniqueness model of personhood is a good alternative to Masolo's morally loaded conception of personhood.

In my view, Masolo's models do a better job of explaining elements that ensure the wellbeing of a community as opposed to the wellbeing of a person. The society's wellbeing does not presuppose the person's wellbeing, at least not in its entirety. In the African view, personhood is a means by which a society secures the welfare of others. This means that a person is not viewed as an agent with intrinsic value. To be classified as an agent means that there are things that matter to you as a person; there are things in this world that have significance for an agent (Taylor 1985: 99) and a community's wellbeing need not be one of those things, at least not primarily so. A reading of Masolo gives one the impression that personal concern is undesirable as it neglects the community's well-being, and that the admirable life is solely one that is dominated by a concern for the interests of others, whether moral rules or social norms. I have argued above that such a life lacks autonomy and authenticity and that if we shift the primary focus from community to person we will find that a person's interests can have personal as well as social benefits. Uniqueness as a model of personhood does a better job of capturing the excellence of the self and community as it makes it possible for an individual to recognize and be recognized as an end and not a mere means to an end. I think such recognition is possible when one adopts a unique lifestyle, namely, one that is both authentic and autonomous.

A life is usually deemed authentic when it is led from the inside (Kymlicka 1988: 183). An authentic person is true to herself and accounts for her existence internally (Baugh 1988: 478-479; Cohen 1993: 114-115; Tshivhase 2010: 29-34). In other words, authenticity involves the self-understanding of the self in question. Authenticity implies discovering, developing and being faithful to one's true self, with a refusal to live according to an externally prescribed life plan to ensure that one achieves happiness and fulfillment (Reisert 2000: 307). In contrast with Masolo, an authentic life would not be dominated by the prescribed ideal of moral perfection or social conformity as a precondition for fostering personhood. Uniqueness, as I conceive it, is partly a matter of authentic self-awareness. It is this kind of self-awareness that is conducive to the exploration and realization of an identifiable personal self.

However, an authentic personal self is not good enough for oneself, if one lacks autonomous conduct. It is possible for one to be authentic in a way that lacks autonomy. One could rightfully claim to be an authentic member of a thieving gang wherein membership is terminated only by death. This could be genuinely chosen from one's inner self, but it would display an undesirable mode of life lacking autonomy since the gang member would be trapped unless he is willing to lose his life. One can surely not claim that such a life is good, for needs to be able to make alternative choices. I think autonomy is necessary for one to be in a position to choose well to ensure that one's authentic values are realized.

Autonomy, understood as a capacity to govern oneself, is one's ability to rule oneself free of dictation (Taylor 2005: 602). When understood as partially constituted by autonomy, uniqueness prevents that which is external to the self from becoming its source. In this way a person is able to see himself as an entity that is both socially embedded and independent from the society. One lives amongst others but can and should understand oneself apart from others. The point is that autonomy enables the individual seeking uniqueness to conduct one's authentic vision free of dictation from social circumstances.

My intuition is that authenticity and autonomy actively enable an attractive kind of uniqueness as they could allow each person to be the kind of person who is true to, and governs himself with an acceptable level of accountability for one's conduct. One apparent problem is that authenticity and autonomy do not ensure that we always live in accordance with moral integrity. We can perhaps grant a serial killer some human excellence by virtue of being unique, but he would surely be missing some substantial degree of personhood, as murder is an unjust act that impairs the wellbeing of others. Uniqueness of this kind would be very immoral and thus undesirable on the whole. It appears that, in this case, uniqueness does not give a complete account of personhood. What it does, however, is present an element that the African view does not have. For an individual to be appropriately identified as a person of human excellence, a balanced combination of authenticity, autonomy and something like Masolo's conception of morality is necessary. In other words, a well-rounded personhood involves personal and communal consideration.

A society that allows each individual a space to experiment with her self-understanding need not risk losing the communitarian side of human excellence. If anything, such a community produces persons who understand what it means to be an individual among other individuals who deserve to be treated with respect and kindness and are equally responsible for treating others with the same considerations. Doing virtuous deeds for others authentically and autonomously, or at the very least alongside such behaviour, seems more conducive to the development of a social network as opposed to people doing only morally good deeds and merely out of obligation and the hope of obtaining personhood. I am championing a life dominated by a well-rounded concern for one's welfare in a sense that is neither selfish nor selfless.

My main point is personal uniqueness is worth pursuing as a principle that, although internally constructed and constituted by authenticity and autonomy, does not and should not isolate a person from her community; nor should it prevent cognitive and moral development. Personhood should not be defined solely by what a person should do for others. Personhood is a phenomenon of living a genuinely human way of life and should not be a mere matter of unifying a community. Unifying a community is a duty that one can choose to perform but it should not come before, or at the great expense of, developing one's self-understanding and one's interests. A community cannot be united, at least not in the right way, by people who do not know who they are. I think a community benefits fairly when its people are aware of who they are and what it is they can and should do to improve the very social network they depend on for their own development and self-interpretations. However, such a social good, as I have explained, would not exhaust the rationale for uniqueness. Interaction between individual and community should exist, where the community does not pressure individuals to conform to expectations that deny a person a well-rounded life.

## *Conclusion*

In this article, I have dealt with the question of what personhood essentially is. I articulated Masolo's African view of personhood, which is communalistic and morally loaded. According to Masolo and sub-Saharan ethicists in general such as Kwasi Wiredu and Ifeanyi Menkiti, personhood involves adopting moral virtues or abiding by society's expectations. Masolo endorses human excellence as leading a life dominated by the interests of others. I criticised his view for neglecting one's inner self and argued that such a life is often empty and not admirable. I illustrated that such a life is not personally beneficial and can create a community that is 'united' by people who do not know or like themselves. In the end I have recommended the uniqueness model as an alternative that, although agent-centred, need not isolate one from community or promote immorality, but can endorse the idea of social and personal development. The main point is this: personhood is not merely what we can do to improve the lives of others, but a self-understanding that should ideally be authentic, autonomous and moral, all of which, as African philosophers such as Masolo rightly emphasize, cannot be successfully realized outside a community.

## References

Baugh, B. (1988). Authenticity Revisited. *The Journal of Aesthetics and Art Criticism*, 46(4): 477-487.
Birt, R. (2002). Of the Quest for Freedom as Community. In *The Quest for Community and Identity: Critical Essays in Africana Social Philosophy*. Edited by Birt, R. New York: Rowan & Littlefield Publishers, pp. 87-104.
Cohen, R.A. (1993). Authentic Self-hood in Heidegger and Rozenzweig. *Human Studies*, 16(1/2): 111-128.
Gyekye, K. (1992). Person and Community in Akan Thought. In *Person and Community: Ghanaian Philosophical Studies, I*. Edited by Wiredu, K. and Gyekye, K. Washington DC: The Council for Research in Values and Philosophy, pp. 101-122.
Hall, R. (1992). Plato and Personhood. *The Personalist Forum*, 8(2): 88-100.
Kaphagawani, D.N. (2006). African Conceptions of a Person: A Critical Survey. In *A Companion to African Philosophy*. Edited by Wiredu, K. Oxford: Blackwell Publishing, pp. 332-342.
Kymlicka, W. (1988). Liberalism and Communitarianism. *Canadian Journal of Philosophy*, 18: 181-203.
Masolo, D.A. (2010). *Self and Community in a Changing World*. Indianapolis: Indiana University Press.
Mbiti, J. (1969). *African Religions and Philosophy*. London: Heinemann Educational Books Ltd.
Menkiti, I.A. (1984). Person and Community in African Traditional Thought. In *African Philosophy: An Introduction*. Edited by Wright, R.A. New York: University Press of America, pp. 171-181.
Menkiti, I.A. (2004). On the Normative Conception of a Person. In *A Companion to African Philosophy*. Edited by Wiredu, K. Oxford: Blackwell Publishing, pp. 324-331.
Reisert, J.R. (2000). Authenticity, Justice and Virtue in Taylor and Rousseau. *Polity*, 33(2): 305-330.
Slurink, P. (1994). Paradox and Tragedy in Human Morality. *International Political Science Review*, 15(4): 347-378.
Taylor, C. (1985). *Philosophy and the Human Sciences: Philosophical Papers Volume 2*. Cambridge: Cambridge University Press.
Taylor, S.R. (2005). Kantian Personal Autonomy. *Political Theory*, 33: 602-628.
Tshivhase, M.T. (2010). *Realizing an Authentic and Unique Personal Identity*. Unpublished Master's Dissertation. Johannesburg: University of Johannesburg.
Van Biema, D. (2007). *Mother Teresa's Crisis of Faith*. Available from:

http://www.time.com/time/printout/0,8816,1655415,00.html (Accessed 1 March 2012).

Wiredu, K. (1992). Moral Foundations of an African Culture. In *Person and Community: Ghanaian Philosophical Studies, I.* Edited by Wiredu, K. and Gyekye, K. Washington DC: The Council for Research in Values and Philosophy, pp. 193-206.

Wolf, S. (1982). Moral Saints. *Journal of Philosophy,* 79(8): 419-439.

# Two Conceptions of African Ethics

## by Thaddeus Metz

*Abstract*: Two Conceptions of African Ethics. I focus on D. A. Masolo's discussion of morality as characteristically understood by African philosophers. My goals are both historical and substantive. First, with regard to history, I argue that Masolo's analysis of sub-Saharan morality suggests two major ways that the field has construed it, depending on which value is taken to be basic. According to one view, the ultimate aim of a moral agent should be to improve people's quality of life, which she can reliably do by entering into community with other persons, while the other view is that community should instead be valued for its own sake, with the enhancement of welfare being morally relevant only insofar as it is part of that. I claim that Masolo does not indicate a clear awareness of how these two perspectives differ and is not explicit about how they relate to one another. After pointing out that Masolo is not alone in these respects, I, second, draw what is meant to be a definitive, clear distinction between the two ethical philosophies, and then provide strong reason to prefer the community-based conception of sub-Saharan ethics to the welfare-based one.

*Résumé*: Deux Notions d'Éthiques Africaine. Je me concentre sur la discussion de la morale de D A Masolo comme elle est typiquement comprise par les philosophes Africains. Mes objectifs sont à la fois historiques et substantiels. Tout d'abord, en ce qui concerne l'histoire, je démontre que l'analyse de la morale subsaharienne de Masolo suggère deux manières principales dont le champ d'étude l'a interprété, en fonction de la valeur qui est considérée comme fondamental. Selon une vue, le but ultime d'un agent moral devrait être d'améliorer la qualité de vie des gens, ce qu'elle peut faire de manière fiable en entrant en communauté avec d'autres personnes, alors que l'autre point de vue est que la communauté devrait plutôt être appréciée pour elle-même, avec l'amélioration du bien-être étant moralement pertinente que dans la mesure où elle fait partie de cela. Je démontre que Masolo n'indique pas la façon dont ces deux points de vue diffèrent et ne dis pas explicitement comment ils se rapportent l'un à l'autre. Après avoir rappelé que Masolo n'est pas le seul à ces égards, j'établis ensuite ce qui est censé être une distinction claire et définitive entre les deux philosophies éthiques, et donne de fortes raisons de préférer la conception communautaire de l'éthique subsahariennes á celle du bien-être.

*Key words*: African ethics, communitarianism, moral theory, partiality, sub-Saharan morality, welfare

*Mots-clés:* éthique Africaine, communautarisme, théorie morale, partialité, moralité

## 1. Introduction

D.A. Masolo is an elder in the African philosophical community, a wise historian of the field who has provided vital guidance to it. His latest book, *Self and Community in a Changing World* (2010),[57] discusses a wide array of topics and authors, ranging from Paulin Hountondji on indigenous knowledge to Kwasi Wiredu on the nature of mind to Leopold Senghor on socialism. It can be read not merely as providing an overview of major contemporary philosophies grounded in sub-Saharan traditional worldviews, as the author intends, but also, where Masolo is sympathetic to those he is expounding, as a communitarian philosophical anthropology, an account of what it means to be a human being with essential reference to her as part of a community.

In this article, I focus on Masolo's discussion of morality as characteristically understood by African philosophers. My goals are both historical and substantive, meaning that I use reflection on Masolo's book as an occasion to shed light not only on the nature of recent debates about African ethics, but also on African ethics itself.

With regard to history, I argue that Masolo's discussion of sub-Saharan morality suggests at least two major ways that the field has construed it, depending on which value is taken to be basic and which ones are deemed derivative. According to one perspective, the ultimate aim of a moral agent should be to improve people's quality of life, which she can reliably do by supporting community in certain ways, while the other view is that community should instead be valued for its own sake, with the enhancement of welfare being morally relevant only insofar as it is part of that. I claim that Masolo does not indicate a clear awareness of

---

[57] All page references in the text refer to this book.

how these two perspectives differ and is not explicit about how they relate to one another. After pointing out that Masolo is not alone in these respects, as others in the field also appear to advance conflicting accounts of the values fundamental to African morality, I draw what is meant to be a definitive, clear distinction between the two major ethical philosophies.

Next, I provide what I deem to be conclusive reason to prefer the community-based conception of sub-Saharan ethics to the welfare-based one. I argue principally on grounds of philosophical plausibility, but also suggest that the community-based theory is more characteristically African than is the welfare-based one, despite the fact that some of the most influential African moral theorists, including Kwame Gyekye and John Bewaji, have expressed adherence to the latter.

I begin by providing an overview of the way Masolo approaches moral issues in *Self and Community in a Changing World*, namely, by articulating ways that African thinkers have construed the nature of personhood in search of a non-relativist ethic (sec. 2). After that, I demonstrate that Masolo's discussion points to two competing theoretical ways to understand morality in light of sub-Saharan values, one that takes community to be the basic value and the other that takes welfare to be (sec. 3). I investigate the logic of each approach, and also critically respond to the suggestion that both goods, and not merely one of them, should be deemed fundamental. Next, I argue in favour of a theory based solely on the value of communal relationships, contending that it captures uncontroversial elements of morality that not merely Africans, but also people more globally, tend to hold (sec. 4). I conclude by indicating some additional philosophical approaches to sub-Saharan morality that Masolo does not take up in depth but that would need to be in order to provide something like the final word on the most defensible conception of African ethics (sec. 5).

## 2. Morality à la Masolo

Personhood is of course the conceptual category through which it is natural to enter into discussion of African thought about ethics. As is well-known, personhood, as understood among many black traditional peoples below the Sahara, is a value-laden concept, and one that admits of degrees. That is, one can be more or less of a person, where the more one is a person, the better. More specifically, to have personhood, or to exhibit *ubuntu* (humanness) as it is famously known among Nguni speakers in southern Africa, is to be virtuous, to be an excellent human being.

*2.1. Ends v. means*

Supposing one wants to develop one's personhood, so construed, it is natural to pose the question of how to acquire it. Notice, though, that this question is vague, admitting of two senses that it is important to distinguish. On the one hand, one might be asking about what one or one's society could do in order to make personhood likely to be realized. This is a question about the *means* by which one could become a person, i.e., what would enable it or cause it. Here, Masolo discusses the views of Kwasi Wiredu, among others, who point out that, in order to become virtuous, human beings must be socialized in certain ways, and above all must engage in communication with one another, particularly about in/appropriate behaviour (e.g., 2010: 173). Such claims, I submit, are not controversial; who would, or reasonably could, deny that an infant left to his own devices on a deserted island would, after any number of years, be more animal and selfish than genuinely human or morally upright?

The truly contested issue occasioned by asking how to acquire personhood is what the essential nature of personhood is. What constitutes a genuinely human way of life? Which attitudes and actions are virtuous and why? What should be one's final end? These questions, which I take to be more or less equivalent for the field, are the ones philosophers are most interested in answering.

Before analyzing the answers that Masolo addresses, I first point out that too often the language in his text blurs the distinction between the means by which one can obtain personhood and the nature of personhood itself. He, with a large thrust of the field, clearly believes there is a close relationship between being part of a certain kind of society and being a person, but the nature of the relationship too often is not characterized precisely. Sometimes Masolo uses *logical* distinctions to express the sort of relationship involved, which unfortunately gloss whether it is one of means or ends. For example, he says that 'if a person were to be isolated from society and be deprived of communication with other humans from birth they would be confined to a "solitary, poor, nasty, and brutish" and no doubt also very short life' (2010: 265). Pointing out that isolation is a sufficient condition for a bad life does not tell the reader whether social interaction is a means by which to live well or whether it is to live well in itself, our proper end.

Other times Masolo uses *modal* language to express the relationship between society and personhood, which is equally vague. Consider the claims: 'The intervention of society is, in this sense, a necessary requirement for our growth and development' (2010: 163) and '(A) world where everyone is left to their own fate cannot be a world of happy people' (2010: 246). Again, noting that self-realization would be impossible without social interaction does not indicate in what respect, viz., whether the latter is a necessary tool to bring self-realization about or is the content of self-realization as such.

Still other phrases, which are well understood as expressing a relationship of *supervenience* of personhood on society, are also ambiguous. Consider the claims that 'interdependence is what breeds the ideal human condition' (2010: 246), that 'attainment of human needs and interests is best served in union with others' (2010: 245), and that 'humans who are deprived....of the ability to communicate are deprived of something fundamental to their nature, namely, full participation in the world of persons' (2010: 165). Again, these statements beg the question of whether interdependence, union and communication are instrumental for bringing about human flourishing or whether they constitute it.

Masolo is not alone in speaking in ways that seem to me to be ambiguous between a relationship of means and one of ends; recall the phrases ubiquitous among African philosophers that the community is 'prior to' the individual (see Senghor quoted in Masolo 2010: 231) or that the individual 'depends on' the community for her development (Masolo 2010: 174, 218, 226). My current purpose is to use Masolo's text as an occasion to urge the field to be careful when discussing the precise nature of the relationship between social interaction and personhood.

*2.2. Relativism v universalism*

Despite the vague turns of phrase, Masolo is of course aware of the conceptual distinction between means and ends that I am drawing, and he provides revealing discussions about the latter. What I find of particular importance in Masolo's analysis of the nature of personhood is that he draws on African thought about it, while denying that such thought is applicable only to Africans. Masolo is emphatic about eschewing relativism (2010: 24, 106, 121, 130, 174, 180), which implies that he is in search of an ethic that applies to human beings generally, regardless of where they live or the culture in which they have been reared. In focusing on, and indeed favouring, sub-Saharan thought about ethics, he believes that African thinkers tend to have some insight into objective moral matters that others, particularly those from Western cultures such as Immanuel Kant, do not. That is a bold and intriguing perspective, one that differs from the much more dominant tendency of those who explore indigenous worldviews to suggest that the local is apt for locals and the foreign is apt for foreigners.

There are some phrases in Masolo's book that readers might think are indicative of moral relativism, but I suggest they are best read otherwise. For example, Masolo often contends that personhood is closely related to: incorporating 'the values deemed by society to be worth pursuing as goals' (2010: 96); functioning 'in the service of socioculturally imposed ends' (2010: 154); adjusting 'one's conduct in accordance with known or assumed expectations of other members within any relational circuit' (2010: 206); and protecting 'the customary ways through adherence to them' (2010: 243). Since norms and customs differ from society to society, it appears from these quotations that Masolo is committed to a relativistic view of personhood.

There are two reasons to think, in fact, that these phrases are consistent with Masolo's rejection of moral relativism. First, at several points, he is speaking about means, and not ends, pointing out that the way one develops virtue is through a socialization process that involves, among other things, learning how one's society functions and adapting to that society (probably 2010: 154-155, 205-206, 241). The basic idea is that children must become members of society *in the first place*, before they can take the next step and learn how to become *good* members. For instance, at one point Masolo is explicit about the '(communitarian) system of mutual dependence that adherence to custom produces' (2010: 263); conformity, here, is apparently deemed to be a means by which (in combination with other things, no doubt) community as a final end will be produced.

However, there are other places where it appears that Masolo is not making a point about means, but rather about ends, to the effect that a person is one who fulfils society's expectations (see esp. 2010: 96, 218-219, 243). I submit that, second, on a number of these occasions Masolo is presuming that what the community values will be what is of value to the community. Speaking of conformity to a community's norms, then, is often shorthand for reference to living in ways that that would benefit society, which is ultimately what matters (see esp. 2010: 96-97). And one does find, on occasion, Masolo qualifying which social expectations count, for instance, 'reasonable' ones (2010: 244).

Having established, then, that Masolo is seeking a universally applicable ethic that is informed largely by sub-Saharan values, I now turn to his characterizations of it. Sometimes he construes the nature of personhood in piecemeal terms, providing lists of specific virtues that a real person exhibits (2010: 171, 208, 218, 239-240, 251). Among other excellences, Masolo mentions being wise, being polite, exhibiting generosity, being loving, being a leader, working hard, and considering oneself to be bound up with one's fellows.

Of more interest to me are those occasions when Masolo goes beyond giving the reader a grab-bag of human goods, and instead discusses them from a theoretical perspective. At times Masolo aims to sum up what all virtues have in common, to provide a unified account of what makes something a human excellence. The claim that I will make in the next section is that Masolo discusses two theories of personhood that are not clearly distinguished, but should be.

## 3. Welfare v. community

There are passages in Masolo's book indicating that personhood is constituted by, and not merely caused by, certain relationships with other human beings. The relevant relationships for Masolo and the African tradition more generally are communal ones, which he sometimes sums up as 'cohesion' (2010: 240). According to what I call a 'community-based' conception of personhood, one lives a genuinely human way of life just insofar as one enters into or prizes community with others. This theory 'posits the existence of others as an essential part of the very structure of the self' (2010: 249), such that realizing one's true nature is nothing over and above living communally.

Strong evidence that Masolo discusses such a view, if not also adheres to it, comes in a passage where he is looking for the fundamental moral value that would best explain interests in conditions such as promoting socialism, engaging in palaver, reconciling after conflict and living in a society in which people are routinely and deeply concerned about one another's well-being. Speaking in particular of the latter, Masolo says that

> its value lies in the general or common conditions of relations that

results from it, not just in this specific example but in all other cases and examples of good neighborliness....sociomoral states that every child is taught and that every right-thinking person is called upon to consider implementing as the objective of his or everyday conduct.....A life of cohesion, or positive integration with others, becomes a goal, one that people design modalities for achieving. Let us call this goal communalism, or, as other people have called it, communitarianism. In light of this goal, the virtues listed above also become desirable (2010: 240).

This is the clearest passage in Masolo's book expressing the theoretical view that communal relationship is what should be valued as an *end*, i.e., as constitutive of personhood, and not merely as a means to it (see also 2010: 194, 218, 263).[58] Cohesion is the apparent 'master value' that unites the particular excellences of generosity, a sense of belonging, hard work and the like; these traits make one a better person just insofar as they are expressive of, or conducive to, community. Vices, in contrast, are traits that tend to divide people, and particularly to promote conflict or discord between them.

As clear as the passage is, there are others in Masolo's book that suggest a different theory about fundamental moral value. For example, at one point, Masolo says that 'no aspect of culture, however noble, is an end unto itself', such that a way of life should be given up if it fails to improve people's quality of life (2010: 122). And at other points, Masolo suggests that the value of cohesion is derivative and instrumental, lying in the effectiveness by which it makes people feel safe. Here, he says that

---

[58] For another clear adherent to a community-based perspective, see the work of Desmond Tutu, who at one point says of African views of ethics, 'Harmony, friendliness, community are great goods. Social harmony is for us the *summum bonum* – the greatest good. Anything that subverts or undermines this sought-after good is to be avoided like the plague' (1999: 35). Consider as well Peter Kasenene's remark that 'in African societies, immorality is the word or deed which undermines fellowship' (1998: 21). See, too, the moral anthropological work of Silberbauer (1991: 20) and Verhoef and Michel (1997: 397).

'individual and group security is fostered through a network of social relations ruled by a strong sense of unity and caring' (2010: 216), and that 'well-being is complete when (apart from material prosperity) people feel that they are in an atmosphere of positive relations with other members of society or neighborhood' (2010: 250). These passages strongly suggest what I call a 'welfare-based' conception of personhood, according to which one is more of a person, the more one acts to improve others' quality of life--something one can often do by *means* of entering into community.

Such a theoretical perspective is particularly salient in Masolo's book when he approvingly discusses Kwasi Wiredu's account of morality (2010: 172-174, 206, 265-266).[59] For Wiredu, good character and right acts are a function of sympathetic impartiality, in which one gives the well-being others equal consideration consequent to imagining what it would be like to be them. Although this smacks of utilitarianism, Wiredu is well-known for maintaining that such a morality is instead best captured by the Golden Rule, the principle according to which you ought to treat others as you would like to be treated if you were in their position. Masolo does not indicate a clear preference for the Golden Rule, but does suggest that moral principles are nothing other than 'criteria for survival and well-being' (2010: 172), and can be summed up by the prescription to create 'humane conditions that, at least, enhance the community's ability to reduce unhappiness and suffering' (2010: 250; see also 124, 155, 210, 244). By this welfare-based account of personhood, what makes a behaviour or character trait a virtue is that it reliably improves people's quality of life, where a vice in contrast is an action or attitude that tends to fail to do so or, indeed, makes others worse off.

The ideals of welfare and community are not completely unrelated; for Masolo, as for most African theorists of communitarianism, communal

---

[59] Other influential African moral theorists who take well-being to be the basic value include Kwame Gyekye (1997: 50; 2010) and John Bewaji (2004).

relationships include ones of mutual aid.[60] However, there are at least three crucial respects in which community is not reducible to a relationship in which people are 'always concerned about the well-being of other people around them' (2010: 238).

First, the theories ground different fundamental explanations of why one ought to help others and would enhance one's personhood by doing so. The welfare-based theory says that one should share one's wealth, time, labour and so on at bottom because doing so is likely to make others' lives go better. In contrast, the community-based theory prescribes helping others ultimately because doing so would be part of what it is to enter into community with them, or perhaps to foster communal relationships among them.

Second, a natural understanding of the moral value of community is partial, at least to some degree. That is, prizing community implies caring for the well-being of one's own family and society more than that of others ('family first', 'charity begins at home'), which contrasts notably with Wiredu's morality of sympathetic impartiality. There is nothing in the Golden Rule indicating that one should provide greater weight to those related to oneself, when it comes to fellow-feeling and beneficent action consequent to it.

Third, and most starkly, community as understood by Masolo, and by the sub-Saharan tradition more broadly, includes relationships that have no essential reference to beneficence, mutual aid, etc. For instance, Masolo discusses relationships in which people identify with, or share a way of life with, one another, which are a matter of, on the one hand, experiencing a sense of togetherness (2010: 232, 240), and, on the other, having common customs, traditions, culture and the like (2010: 225, 226, 234, 244). Although such relationships *might* have the effect of improving people's well-being, they do not essentially include it.

---

[60] For an analysis of the concept of community as it functions in African moral thinking, see Metz (2007).

Masolo is not the only one analyzing African thought about morality whom I have found to be unclear about which values are fundamental and which are not. For example, I believe that Wiredu's corpus includes such ambiguity. On the one hand, as we have seen, Wiredu believes that, from a sub-Saharan perspective, morality is captured by the principle of sympathetic impartiality, particularly as expressed in the Golden Rule. However, when Wiredu famously defends a consensus-based form of democracy, he does so in large part by appeal to the idea that such a polity would produce harmony and reduce divisiveness in society (1996: 172-190).[61] Here, then, are two values: well-being and harmony; which one is fundamental? Similarly, Polycarp Ikuenobe in a fairly recent book-length treatment of African morality is vagueabout whether welfare or community is ultimately what matters from a sub-Saharan standpoint. One finds some passages indicating that African ethics essentially prescribes engaging in caring relationships or maintaining harmonious ones (2006: 6, 65, 114, 128, 138), and other ones saying that the promotion of human well-being is key (2006: 80, 103-104, 111, 119, 123, 127).

Now, I have been supposing that it makes most sense to presume that only one value, either community or welfare, is fundamental to morality, but what about the possibility that both are?[62] Perhaps cohesion and well-being should be pursued as separate ends that are to be prized for their own sake, and maybe they are often mutually supportive means with regard to one another. On this reading of Masolo's text, there is no contradiction as to which value is fundamental; rather they belong together side by side, as aims that are often compatible.

---

[61] In other parts of his work, Wiredu points out that his people, the Akan, believe that human beings have a dignity in virtue of being children of God, a superlative worth that demands respect (1992). That is a third, apparently distinct, value, something that I address briefly in the conclusion.

[62] Something that Masolo has suggested at a workshop on The Philosophy of D. A. Masolo sponsored by the Philosophy Department at the University of Johannesburg 24-25 March 2012.

Such a pluralist reading of the foundations of African morality might well be the most charitable way to read Masolo's text. However, I am in the first instance interested in pursuing a monistic interpretation of sub-Saharan ethics, mainly since one can know that more than one basic end must be posited only upon first having posited a single one and having found it inadequate. The project of systematically differentiating basic ends and considering which one, if any, would suffice to ground an attractive sub-Saharan moral philosophy is still in its infancy and is something toward which I aim to contribute. Therefore, in the rest of this article, I suppose not only that community and welfare are distinct ends, but also that it is worth enquiring as to whether one of them, on its own, is more plausible than the other and is a reasonable contender for grounding morality generally.

Another reason for being careful about the differences between welfare and community as fundamental aims is that, as I discuss in the next section, sometimes they prescribe divergent decisions. In this section I have sought to demonstrate that Masolo's discussion of sub-Saharan moral thought includes two logically distinct conceptions that he, along with others in the field, does not differentiate. The differences between the two accounts of personhood should become all the more clear in what follows, where I argue that a community-based account of personhood is able to account for widely held moral judgments that a welfare-based one cannot. I will demonstrate that the logics of the two views have different implications for how to behave, some of which are more philosophically plausible than others.

## 4. For a communitarian conception of personhood

In this section I advance two general considerations that to my mind provide adequate reason to reject the welfare-based conception of personhood, as characterized in Masolo's work, in comparison to the community-based one. The arguments are not intended to demonstrate that the latter is most justified relative to all competitors, only in relation to a morality that takes human well-being to be the sole basic value.[63]

## 4.1. The Relevance of Past Decisions

The first major argument for the community-based conception of personhood is that it, unlike the welfare-based one, can account for the moral relevance of decisions people have taken. Many of us, whether working in the African tradition or otherwise, have intuitions that sometimes the way we should treat someone in the present is to a large degree a function of how that person voluntarily acted in the past. Here are three examples, relating to punishment, self-defence and rationing.

Nearly all of us believe that it is grave injustice to punish someone known to be innocent of any wrongdoing. As is common to point out in the literature critical of utilitarianism, there can be situations in which meting out a penalty to an innocent person would be most conducive to the greater good, but in which doing so would be impermissible. The best explanation of why it would be immoral to punish an innocent includes the fact that the person is innocent, i.e., did not do anything wrong in the past.

A welfarist morality has difficulty accounting for that judgment. Utilitarianism famously implies that past actions are morally irrelevant in themselves; all that in principle matters, from this perspective, is whether what one does now will maximally benefit society in the future. Suppose one is a sheriff in a position to frame an innocent person, where such an action would alone prevent a marginally greater degree of harm to society. According to the principle of sympathetic impartiality, one should give everyone's interests equal weight, which would, like utilitarianism, appear to

---

[63] I acknowledge that a more rights-oriented ethic, according to which the innocent have an equal claim to well-being, promises to avoid some of the objections I raise below. For an instance of such a view in the Anglo-American literature, see the work of Richard Arneson (e.g., 1989).

entail that one ought to punish the innocent person, since doing so, *ex hypothesi*, would satisfy the most interests. Or if one elects to apply the Golden Rule in this case, notice that the outcome is indeterminate: when placing oneself in the shoes of the innocent individual, one sees that one would not want to be punished, and when placing oneself in the shoes of those who would be harmed in the absence of such punishment, one see that one would want punishment to be inflicted so as to prevent the harm. The Golden Rule therefore provides no guidance about which course of action to take.

Turn, now, to issues of self- and other-defence, which are widely accepted among African societies in response to colonialism and perceived witchcraft, to mention just two salient examples. It is uncontroversial to hold that if someone is unjustly attacking an innocent person, that innocent (or a third party) may rightly use force for the purpose of warding off the threat. The rough principle operative in such cases is that burdens may be imposed on aggressors in order to prevent aggression toward those who are not aggressing.

However, a welfare-based conception of personhood cannot easily account for such a principle. Suppose a group of four men are trying to kill one innocent woman, merely because she belongs to a different ethnic group. It is incontrovertible that the woman (or, say, a police officer) may shoot the men, if necessary and sufficient to save her life. But that intuition cannot be accommodated by the Golden Rule, which would require her to put herself in the shoes of her aggressors and ask herself whether she would want to be shot. Since she would not, she would be wrong to shoot them. Similar remarks go for a more consequentialist interpretation of sympathetic impartiality; weighing up all the equal interests in living well, the lives of four outweigh the life of one.

For a third and final example, consider the fact that nearly all of us believe that, in cases of scarcity, where one cannot distribute life-saving resources to all those who need them, it would be proper to save those who are not responsible for the fact of needing to be saved. For instance, suppose that a wife has become HIV positive because her husband cheated on her behind her back and did not use protection when doing so. And suppose that you, who have a single regimen of antiretroviral treatment, must choose which of them to save. You have strong reason to give the treatment to the wife and not the husband, and to do so because he is responsible for the fact that she needs the treatment and she is not.

But, again, a welfare-based ethic cannot accommodate that judgment. If you employ the Golden Rule, you discover that you cannot decide whom to save, since you would like to receive the treatment if you were in the position of the wife or in that of the husband. And a broader orientation toward well-being also appears to be indeterminate, supposing the consequences of saving one or the other would be the same. However, I submit that the past actions of the husband provide some, very weighty consideration to save his wife, and not him, in the case where you cannot save both.

A community-based ethic, at least when interpreted in a certain way, can account for the relevance of past actions in determining how one ought to treat people in the present.[64] Suppose one holds the view that one ought to treat people with respect in virtue of their capacity for community, or that one is more of a person, the more one honours (not maximizes) communal relationships. It follows from this sort of principle that one may act in an anti-social way toward those who are being anti-social, if necessary to stop or compensate for their anti-social behaviour. It need not be degrading of a person's capacity for community to treat him in an anti-social manner, when doing so is necessary to prevent or correct for a comparable anti-sociality on his part, for respecting another's capacity for community can require basing one's interaction with him on the way he has exercised it. Or, alternately put, it does not fail to honour the value of community to act in a divisive manner when doing so is necessary to prevent or make up for divisiveness.

---

[64] The present analysis is drawn from Metz (2011, 2012a).

Such an analysis can account for the above intuitions about why it is unjust to punish the innocent but need not be unjust to punish the guilty, why it can be right to use force against aggressors, and why it would be suitable not to save those who are responsible for needing to be saved, when doing so would come at the expense of those who are not so responsible. It would be unjust to punish the innocent, since they have not behaved in an anti-social manner and punishing them would therefore fail to honour (their capacity for) communal relationships. It can be right to use force against aggressors in order to protect the innocent, since being divisive toward those being divisive does not disrespect the value of community. And, finally, it would be right to ration life-saving treatment away from those whose anti-sociality is the cause of their need for it, when doing so would prevent the victims of their anti-sociality from dying.

*4.2. Non-harmful wrongdoing*

So far, I have argued that viewing personhood entirely as a matter of doing what one can to improve others' quality of life, can hardly account for the moral relevance of past actions at a principled level; in contrast, as I have also argued, a community-based conception of virtue can do so with relative ease. Now I argue that there is a second class of actions that the welfare-based view cannot easily accommodate, namely, those in which one agent does something to another, albeit without her knowledge that anything has changed. In many of these kinds of cases, it is plausible to maintain that the other's well-being is not reduced, but that the action is wrong or a vice nonetheless.

For a first example, consider the case of a spouse who systematically cheats on you behind your back, and is so careful and conniving that you have virtually no chance of finding out. Or think about a team of medical researchers who observe intimate behaviour of yours, such as bathing, without telling you they are doing so and for what purpose. Or imagine a situation in which people insult you behind your back—perhaps literally in the form of deftly pinning a derogatory sign on the back of your shirt and then removing it before you have a chance to discover it. Or suppose that I break into your house in order to sleep in your bed, listen to your stereo and bathe in your tub while you are away at work, taking care to ensure that things are organized so that you can never know I was there. I presume that readers, whether working in African or Western traditions, believe that these actions are wrong, at least to some substantial degree.

In all four cases, there is no apparent reduction of well-being on the part of the one acted upon, and not even the realistic threat of such, given the way the hypothetical scenarios are framed. When one applies the Golden Rule, the actions appear permissible. After all, if I put myself in your shoes and imagine what it would be like to be you, I do not come away feeling bad. Masolo or Wiredu might reply that I would feel bad upon sympathizing with you in the situation in which you were aware of what I propose to do. However, the damning response to them, I think, is that what I am proposing to do to you includes *not* making you so aware.

Similar remarks apply, I submit, to any other interpretation of sympathetic impartiality. To sympathize with someone is roughly to experience a negative emotion such as sorrow toward another's unhappiness consequent to empathizing with it, where empathy is a matter of imagining what it is like to be the other person. When I imagine what it is like to be you upon breaking into your house and using your things while you are away and unaware of what I am up to, there is no unhappiness on your part with which to sympathize. It follows, then, that I do no wrong and exhibit no vice, on a welfare-based conception of morality.[65] However, in this case, and the others above, there would in fact be action incompatible with personhood.

---

[65] One might propose a different conception of well-being, according to which one is objectively worse off if treated in these ways, something that Pedro Tabensky has suggested to me in conversation. However, such a conception does not square with a principle of sympathetic impartiality, to which Wiredu adheres, and it strikes me mushing together distinctions that are better kept apart, namely, the disvalue of harm done to an individual, on the one hand, and, say, that of disrespectful treatment of a person, on the other.

The community-based conception of personhood can do much better on this score. As discussed above, part of what is involved in a communal relationship is engaging in mutual aid, acting so as to improve others' quality of life, but another part is sharing a way of life, where this includes experiencing a sense of togetherness and participating in common activities. It is these latter values that would be flouted by the present actions. To genuinely *share* a way of life with others requires transparency about the way one is interacting with them. To relate to others without their informed consent is to treat the value of community, or those individuals capable of it, with disrespect and hence is incompatible with developing one's personhood.

In this section, I have provided two major arguments against a welfare-based conception of personhood and in favour of a community-based one. With Masolo, I am interested in articulating a conception of ethics that is both African and plausible. I submit that, on both grounds, community is to be favoured over welfare, supposing one is interested in formulating and evaluating a moral theory grounded on a single basic value.

## 5. Conclusion

D.A. Masolo's *Self and Community in a Changing World* is a magisterial, sympathetic overview of themes in contemporary African philosophy, occasioning reflection on several key facets of characteristic sub-Saharan thought about morality. I have argued that a close reading of the text indicates two different conceptions of human excellence that neither Masolo nor many in the field have adequately recognized are distinct, or at least are worth analyzing as having separate logics. According to one theory, an individual develops personhood or lives a genuinely human way of life solely to the extent that his attitudes and actions improve others' quality of life, while according to the other, he does so just insofar as he honours communal relationships, which include mutual aid but are not exhausted by it and also include sharing a way of life with others. I have worked to show that these two perspectives have different implications about how we ought to live. Finally, I have argued that the implications of the community-based account are more plausible, and hence that it is more worthy of belief than the welfare-based one.

I conclude by noting that welfare and community do not exhaust either Masolo's discussion of African ethics, or the literature on it more generally. There are additional categories that appear to be good candidates for basic values that merit exploration in other work. For example, at one point Masolo mentions the idea that human beings have a dignity (2010: 124; see also 119, 237-238). To have a dignity is roughly for an individual to have a superlative final value that is independent of usefulness to others or social recognition. Human dignity is a moral concept that is apparently not reducible to well-being and that might well be distinct from community, too, and it is one that is well known for being believed by many traditional African cultures (e.g., Gyekye 1997: 63-64; Deng 2004). For another example, Masolo touches only briefly on the vitalist tradition in African ethics, according to which attitudes and actions ought to promote life-force, either in oneself or among one's fellows (2010: 13, 234-235). Here is another a promising candidate for a fundamental good, apparently distinct from welfare and community, that has its own logic and has been explored and developed by theorists such as N. K. Dzobo (1992), Bénézet Bujo (1997), Laurenti Magesa (1997) and myself (Metz 2012a, 2012b). In defending a community-based conception of personhood relative to the welfare-based one discussed in Masolo's book, I have not shown that the former is the most African and the most plausible; that would require engaging with additional major strands of ethical thought that one finds below the Sahara.

## *References*

Arneson, R. (1989). Equality and Equal Opportunity for Welfare. *Philosophical Studies*, 55: 77-93.
Bewaji, J. (2004). Ethics and Morality in Yoruba Culture. In *A Companion to African*

*Philosophy*. Edited by Wiredu, K. Oxford: Blackwell Publishing Ltd, pp. 396-403.

Bujo, B. (1997). *The Ethical Dimension of Community: The African Model and the Dialogue between North and South*. Translated by Nganda, C.N. Nairobi: Paulines Publications Africa.

Deng, F. (2004). Human Rights in the African Context. In *A Companion to African Philosophy*. Edited by Wiredu, K. Oxford: Blackwell Publishing Ltd, pp. 499–508.

Dzobo, N.K. (1992). Values in a Changing Society: Man, Ancestors, and God. In *Person and Community; Ghanaian Philosophical Studies, Volume I*. Edited by Wiredu, K. and Gyekye, K. Washington, D.C.: Council for Research in Values and Philosophy, pp. 223-240.

Gyekye, K. (1997). *Tradition and Modernity: Philosophical Reflections on the African Experience*. New York: Oxford University Press.

Gyekye, K. (2010). African Ethics. In *Stanford Encyclopedia of Ethics*. Edited by Zalta, E. Available from: http://plato.stanford.edu/archives/fall2010/entries/african-ethics/.

Ikuenobe, P. (2006). *Philosophical Perspectives on Communalism and Morality in African Traditions*. Lanham, MD: Rowman & Littlefield Publishers.

Kasenene, P. (1998). *Religious Ethics in Africa*. Kampala: Fountain Publishers.

Magesa, L. (1997). *African Religion: The Moral Traditions of Abundant Life*. Maryknoll, NY: Orbis Books.

Masolo, D.A. (2010). *Self and Community in a Changing World*. Bloomington: Indiana University Press.

Metz, T. (2007). Toward an African Moral Theory. *Journal of Political Philosophy*, 15: 321-341.

Metz, T. (2011). *Ubuntu* as a Moral Theory and Human Rights in South Africa. *African Human Rights Law Journal*, 11: 532-559.

Metz, T. (2012a). African Conceptions of Human Dignity: Vitality and Community as the Ground of Human Rights. *Human Rights Review*, 13: 19-37.

Metz, T. (2012b). Developing African Political Philosophy: Moral-Theoretic Strategies. *Philosophia Africana*, 14: 61-83.

Silberbauer, G. (1991). Ethics in Small-scale Societies. In *A Companion to Ethics*. Edited by Singer, P. Oxford: Basil Blackwell, pp. 14-28.

Tutu, Desmond, 1999, *No Future without Forgiveness*, New York: Random House.

Verhoef, H. and Michel, C. (1997). Studying Morality within the African Context. *Journal of Moral Education*, 26: 389-407.

Wiredu, K. (1992). The Moral Foundations of an African Culture. In *Person and Community; Ghanaian Philosophical Studies, Volume I*. Edited by Wiredu, K. and Gyekye, K. Washington, D.C.: Council for Research in Values and Philosophy, pp. 193-206.

Wiredu, K. (1996). *Cultural Universals and Particulars: An African Perspective*. Bloomington: Indiana University Press.

# Exorcising the Communitarian Ghost: D.A. Masolo's Contribution

## by Bernard Matolino

*Abstract*: Exorcising the Communitarian Ghost: D.A. Masolo's Contribution. It is not an exaggeration to claim that traditional and modern African philosophy's bedrock is communitarian in make. The evidence for this is to be found in the frequent use of communitarianism either as support for a particular philosophical thesis or its frequent defence as an authentic mode of African thought and existence. In its assorted forms it has been adumbrated and defended in varied philosophical genres ranging from ethics to metaphysics and political philosophy to identity. However, there has been substantial disagreement on both its nature, in pristine traditional African society, and how it ought to be understood and applied in modern African societies. Firstly, what is the authentic representation of communitarianism and how is its dominance to be interpreted in African thought? Secondly, the issue will revolve around finding an appropriately sensitive communitarian mode of expression that takes modernity into account. In this paper I seek to offer some reasons as to why D.A. Masolo's interpretation of communitarianism is more defensible, in respect of these two considerations, than any other classical communitarian approach.

*Résumé*: Exorciser le Fantôme Communautaire : La Contribution de D.A. Masolo. Ce n'est pas une exagération de dire que la philosophie africaine traditionnelle et moderne est, dans sa constitution, communautaire. La preuve de cela se trouve dans l'utilisation fréquente du communautarisme en tant que support pour une thèse philosophique particulière ou dans sa défense fréquente comme un mode authentique de la pensée et de l'existence africaine. Elle a été esquissée dans des formes variées et défendue dans des genres multiples philosophique allant de l'éthique à la métaphysique et de la philosophie politique à l'identité. Cependant, il y a eu un désaccord substantiel à la fois sur sa nature dans la société traditionnelle africaine primitive et sur la façon dont elle doit être comprise et appliquée dans les sociétés africaines modernes. Tout d'abord, qu'elle est la représentation authentique du communautarisme et comment doit être interprétée sa position dominante dans la pensée africaine ? Deuxièmement, la question se posera S'il est possible de trouver un mode d'expression communautaire qui soit sensible de façon appropriée et qui prend en compte la modernité. Dans cet article, je cherche à offrir quelques raisons pour lesquelles l'interprétation du communautarisme de D.A. Masolo est plus défendable à l'égard de ces deux considérations que toute autre approche communautaire classique.

*Key words*: Masolo, communitarianism, social and political philosophy, African metaphysics

*Mots-clés*: Masolo, communautarise, philosophie sociale et politique, métaphysique africaine

## *Introduction*

Communitarianism has been punted widely as the basis of African ontology or African reality. Expressed in different modes and for different purposes; it has been used as justification for the adoption of certain polities, it has been claimed as the authentic ethic, and it has been claimed to be the ultimate basis of personhood in African thought. Although the articulation of communitarianism in its respective manifestations has not been universal, this lack of universality has been explained as necessitated by the local condition. However, there have been serious contestations about the core interpretation of communitarianism; particularly the ontological priority of the community vis-a-vis individual rights. What this debate has largely shown are the unwavering allegiances between what Kwame Gyekye has identified as radical and moderate communitarianism. In essence, lines have been drawn between those who advocate a moderate interpretation of communitarianism and those who support its radical form.

While such a debate has merit, its major drawback is that it fails to take the communitarian debate to a level where it can be said that African communitarianism is responsive to the modern realities that are now chiefly characteristic of African societies. But more seriously, on the philosophical level, this debate seems unable to extricate African philosophy and consequently communitarianism from the essentialist rendering of African thought. It is primarily for this reason that the first part of my title is conceived. It indicates my own impatience with the continued ontologising of communitarianism in African philosophy. My own philosophical commitment seeks to exorcise the ghost of essentialising communitarianism from African philosophy.

As for the second part of the essay, I read Masolo to be involved in the project of exorcising the ghost of essentialism. It could be the case that Masolo does not conceive his work in the same manner as I do, and it could be the case that he could possibly not agree with my proposed project. However, my interpretation of his work leads me to think that he is at least involved in an attempt to re-state communitarianism in ways that do not seek to essentialise it as the sole ontological basis of African thought. He also appears to be engaged in attempts to cast communitarianism in ways that are sensitive to either Africa's quest to modernise or to the fact of modernisation. The significance of the modernising element, in the communitarian discourse, is borne out of the ever constant background tensions between tradition and modernity. At times, modernity has been blamed for the decadence that attends to many facets of African societies and, at times, tradition has been blamed for some backward views and practices that plague the continent. Finding a balance between these two competing influences has presented a daunting challenge to the project of developing African philosophy. While some thinkers are content with articulating positions that seek to glorify Africa's past and may even seek to find ways of returning Africa to that glorious past, other thinkers have sought to deal with the reality of present day Africa albeit with a reference to the influences of the past. In the latter camp, the most striking attempt comes from Kwame Nkrumah's development of his theory of consciencism (1964: 95). These varied attempts have enjoyed limited success. Part of the main reason why these attempts have registered modest success has to do mainly with the manner in which they base all their philosophical discourse on the claimed fundamental nature and influence of communitarianism in African thought. Where such an assumption is made it would then entail arguments that seek to defend communitarianism or at least seek to align with the core tenets of communitarianism.

On my conception, this proclivity is to be identified as the problem of essentialism. In this paper I seek to argue that Masolo's interpretation of communitarianism avoids the philosophical problem of essentialism. I should caution at this early stage of my paper that my intention is not to dismiss the entire project of communitarianism. My real worry and attempt to exorcise the communitarian ghost has to do with its ready acceptance as the ontology of African thought. I am persuaded that such an acceptance has impoverished both African thought in itself and how it is perceived.

At the outset I wish to state a proviso of the limits of my consideration and the motivation for it. The communitarianism I wish to consider in this paper is mainly one that has been divided by Gyekye into two camps which he has identified as radical and moderate communitarianism. Following Gyekye, if we take radical communitarianism to be chiefly supported by Placide Tempels (1959: 66-67), John Mbiti (1970: 141) and Ifeanyi Menkiti (1984: 171-173) – we could call it a classical account of communitarianism. If we take Gyekye's (1997: 49) critique of Menkiti as a pointer to philosophical errors in the classical account as well as his argument for moderate communitarianism as an attempt at improving the classical account, then we could identify this entire debate as a classical debate on communitarianism. We could even call the philosophical commitments gleaned from these positions as classical African communitarianism. The term classical African communitarianism is simply taken to refer to those works by figures that are considered to be pioneers in the field of African philosophy/communitarianism. Hence this paper does not seek to be a tour de force on the whole scope of African communitarianism. My motivation for this limit is twofold; firstly, the classical account of communitarianism has so much to offer in terms of its potential to be developed into a viable philosophy and ethic that is of Sub-Saharan indigenes. Gyekye admits as much when he points that while Menkiti's position is riddled with errors and incoherencies it nevertheless adumbrates an interesting notion of personhood that is couched in moral reference. Secondly, I am of the view that the classical account is still in need of further philosophical investigation to either eliminate or minimise the philosophical incoherencies that bedevil it. It is for this reason that I consider

D.A. Masolo's work to be a continuation of ongoing attempts to re-adumbrate the classical account in ways that are not so patently incoherent. My proclivity to compare Masolo's work to Gyekye's, and subsequently argue in favour of Masolo is based on the fact that both are among the most influential and pioneering figures of modern day African philosophy. They also both offer extensive arguments for communitarianism albeit with subtle but important differences. It is for the importance of the implications of these differences that I seek to argue that Masolo's account is preferable to all accounts in the classical camp – the camp of influential pioneers.

This paper is divided into three sections. In the first section I sketch out the problem of communitarian essentialism as a philosophical concern. I also outline other debates around the nature of communitarianism. In particular I seek to show how the debate on the distinction between moderate and radical communitarianism is somewhat stagnant. In the second section I seek to present Masolo's construal of communitarianism. In the third and final section I offer some arguments in support of Masolo's version of communitarianism.

## *The problems of essentialism*

The problem of essentialism as I conceive it here refers to the philosophical position that views communitarianism as the determinant of African ontology. This is typically exemplified in the works of Placide Tempels, John Mbiti and Ifeanyi Menkiti. These thinkers, though relying on different terminology and strategies, invariably ascribe all African ontology or 'essence' to communitarianism. This philosophical commitment, in turn, buttresses the economic and socio-politico theories and practices of African socialism popularised by Leopold Sedar Senghor, Juluis Nyerere and Kwame Nkrumah.

Although Masolo claims that Nkrumah, Nyerere and Senghor were not philosophers but doubled as political leaders and theorists – it is interesting to note how their ideas on the communitarian basis of their socialism, is given ample credence by some African philosophers. If we briefly and crudely state the main claims of the nationalists to be an argument for socialism based on the idea of communitarianism, which in turn informs the African personality – the nature of persons; how they are conceived as a metaphysical category and how they are expected to conduct themselves as a result of that ontology, we might be tempted to review these three thinkers' non-philosophical status. The reason for this is to be found in the existence of a considerable body of work that has been developed by philosophers who offer a communitarian notion of being that easily supports the socialist interpretation developed by the nationalists.

Gail Presbey (2002: 58) argues that the proponents of this position were mainly driven by the need to be seen as defenders of an authentic African view. However, this position has not gone without detractors. For example, Didier Njirayamanda Kaphagawani argues that this view conflates ontological issues with epistemological issues. On the other hand, Kwame Gyekye has argued against this extreme interpretation of the core meaning of communitarianism.

The real problem of the communitarian thesis is that it extends itself in ways that appear harmless and true yet its subtle implication is quite significant. In its appearance as a harmless and true explanation of African life, it appears to be a mere explanation of the ways that Africans live, or an account of how Africans perceive reality. Its dominance all over the continent and the fact that many ethnic groups identify and share in its major claims makes it the ultimate truth of African life. Such a harmless and truthful exposition of a people's way of life, must as a matter of necessity, give a full picture of who these people are and what their experience of reality is. Or better, what these people are and what factors shape their experience of reality. In this manner it becomes the authoritative point of reference in not only defining the African but also defining the things that shape the African. If this brief description is true, it is easy to see how the community is either ontologised or referred to approvingly by various thinkers. Either way, it is seen as such a fundamental category in African thought. While this may appear to be harmless and true I suggest that the case is far from being this simple.

For a start, the main claims of classical communitarianism are of an ethnophilosophical nature. The major problem is that these claims do not only affirm a traditionalistic outlook of life but actually affirm the uncritical part of African philosophy. Ranging from rehashes of communitarianism, to developing theories inspired by communitarianism or seeking to return to communitarianism, or seeking to show its authentic nature, or essentialising it to the African condition appears to be serving witches brew as Wiredu (1980: 46) calls it.

But at a philosophical level classical communitarianism, like ethnophilosophy, its major proponent and exponent, reduces African thinking to a group activity that is both static and unanalytical. This charge proceeds from what I see to be classical communitarianism's main concern – finding the African difference and seeking to retrieve its core claims to guide present African ontology. To essentialise African reality as communitarian ignores two crucial albeit basic facts namely: one; social life and other reality attached to the communal experiences of the individuals and the subsequent interactions arising thereof are conventions of the time, and, two; the reality of Africans both philosophical and communal are in a constant state of transformation.

In response to this claim the friend of classical communitarianism could marshal two possible rejoinders: In the first he could argue that not only is change possible but actual. Hence, he could argue, though change has occurred it has done so within the broader essentialist communitarian framework. Or, alternatively, the essentialist could argue that any change that has not been communitarian in nature is not truly African – but inspired by external forces such as Islam, Christianity or the Western influence.

My response to the first claim is that the essentialist is being disingenuous. If he claims that change happens within a broader communitarian framework – then her communitarian account must also change to reflect the reality of that change. But since she fails to adjust her essentialism to this broad communitarianism, it means she does not accept the authenticity of that broad communitarianism. Further, it could be argued against the essentialist that there are changes that have occurred in Africa that are not consistent with the essentialist or classical communitarian view. The example I have in mind has to do with the basic organisation of communal structures and the resultant notion of self. I suggest that if we look at the way in which some African communities have come to be structured – those structures are no longer consistent with the essentialist view of 'community'. While essentialists view the African notion of community as essentially constituted by individuals who share a deep connection and commitment to the same good, such that individuated interests are seen as concomitant to communal interests, it is doubtful that all (or even most) African communities are constituted in this manner. The essentialist view is that the individual's fate is not restricted to the individual but is constitutively extended to affect the entire community hence automatically soliciting shared sympathy or joy from other members of the society (depending on what the individual's station is). This effectively means that the individual sees himself as essentially constituted by the community. As Menkiti argues, the community is a perduring and stubborn reality of the individual's own conception of self. This view of the self is informed by the communal structure that is said to make no distinction between individual reality and communal reality. And yet essentialists take it to be the case that the communitarian view is the authentic African metaphysics of the self.

I simply wish to point that certain changes in some African communities have rendered this view obsolete. For some communities it is no longer the case that they are constituted by individuals who share a common communal good or who conceive their own notion of self as seriously constituted by the community. The reason for this is to be found in the fact that most parts of Africa are fairly modernised and are governed by rules and structures that do not retain the strictures of classical communitarianism. Take any large African city such as Johannesburg, Dakar, Nairobi, Accra or Abuja, and many others like them; the many Africans who live and work in these cities do have a sense of community – but it is hardly a revelation to state that their sense of community is much weaker than the classical and essentialist account. Yet all these Africans who live in suburbia and exude sophistication, wealth, education and social prestige – all attained through individual merit and thrift – cannot be said to be less African than any other African.

To this, the essentialist, may predictably object by pointing out that modernity is responsible either for the erosion of the African spirit (read community having priority over the individual or the individual's sense of self being constituted by the community) or has completely destroyed the natural habitat of many Africans by Westernising many through force or persuasion. Put in other words the objection is that these large cities are becoming more like Western European cities or North American cities – thus creating individualistic tendencies among Africans.

I do not think that this suggestion is entirely true. While there has been a degree of Westernisation among many Africans two crucial factors count against the essentialist's latest point. First, though African cities are said to be modern and probably modelled on Western cities – they still retain a certain inimitable African flavour – so to say. There is just something African about Johannesburg, Dakar, Nairobi, Accra and Abuja. Something about these cities makes them African – it could be the many Africans who live in these cities or the African cultures that permeate the whole function and nature of these cities. There is something about these cities that, despite their modernity, do not quite make them the equivalents of Helsinki, London, Paris, Berlin, New York and Lisbon. One can still talk of the existence of an African culture and even community when referring to large African cities without fear of contradiction. As Masolo's book title suggests the African self and his community are indeed in a changing world.

With regard to the second essentialist objection that change that has occurred that is not communitarian is not African, the essentialist could, predictably again, argue that since all reality is communally embedded, any change that does not affirm the metaphysical reality of the community in any or all matters is against the basic philosophical notion of being African. My response to this objection will be limited to pointing out the disingenuous nature of the objection itself or the disingenuous manner in which the essentialists present African reality as monolithic. I just wish to point out one example of this disingenuousness. Classical communitarians mostly claim that the only concept of person on the continent is communitarian. Yet according to Kaphagawani (1998: 167) there are three (shadow, communitarian, force) and according to Polycarp Ikuenobe (2006: 51) there are two (descriptivist and communalist). While it is true that there is such a concept as a communitarian concept of personhood – one needs to keep in mind that it is not the only authentic African concept of persons and secondly, that the communitarian concept itself is not universally agreed on. To my mind, the most pressing philosophical problem pertains to how classical communitarianism, having been marshalled as ontology or the key African system, is actually conflated with other philosophical categories. If we look carefully at the work that communitarianism is supposed to cover, we find that it is an ethic, ontology, theory of personhood, political philosophy, social philosophy, interpersonal relational account, a determinant of personal achievement and failure as well as a psychology. By any account this is stretching the function of a theory and this can only make the theory thin or overused. My argument does not seek to deny that communitarianism has a role to play in African philosophy. I am willing to acknowledge that if communitarianism is conceived as a social or ethical theory, or both, and strictly limited to these considerations – then communitarianism might be able to show its authentic value. What I am strictly opposed to are attempts at essentialising it as if it were the beginning and end of the determinant of African philosophy.

### *Masolo's communitarianism*

In this section I seek to present Masolo's position on communitarianism.

Masolo approaches his discussion of communitarianism by comparing two forms of communitarianism – the Western mode and the African mode. He traces the seeds of Western communitarianism to Germany's rediscovery which was propelled by Hegel. This rediscovery was aimed at resisting French influence through a retrieval of a mystical sense of being German, which in turn led to the awakening of German history and a desire to penetrate and understand its past (Masolo 2010: 223). Masolo's articulation of the German development of Heidelberg Romantik is very similar to the development of the communitarian school in African scholarship. The most striking similarity is that both schools are manifested immediately after a period seen as having been responsible for the destruction of the essential spirit of the nation. In Germany it was a reaction against French dominance, and in Africa it was a reaction against erstwhile colonial dominance. The second similarity has to do with how the restoration of the spirit is seen as a necessary and sufficient operative condition for the successful and smooth functioning of society. If that spirit is restored all other things fall into their respective categories with natural ease. If that is not the case then legislation must be moulded in such a manner that it seeks to give effect to the retrieved spirit.

According to Masolo, Hegel conceives of the state in three senses as the legislative, the civil (characterised as the mass arrangements that individuals make with one another), and, as the sum of all ethical values. It is in the last category that Hegel claims the individual to be able to flourish. Hence he considers that category to be the most important of all senses of the state. Masolo reads Hegel to be an advocate of subjective freedom as he condemns oppressive states that do not allow the individual to flourish. According to Masolo, since Hegel's time a thin layer of communitarianism has survived, in the West, up to this day. Masolo claims that Charles Taylor has directly continued with this Hegelian thought that the individual attains her freedom within a larger whole. In Germany itself, Jurgen Habermas argues for the importance of communication as leading to consensus which leads to the acceptance of values and subsequently the formation of culture. Other important communitarians are Michael Sandel, Michael Walzer, Alasdair MacIntyre and John Kekes – who are all united in their rejection of individualism (ibid: 225). Thus, in Masolo's view, the German notion of the individual is conceived as an anti-thesis to the French view which is dissolutionist and atomistic. The German view sees the self-fulfillment of the individual as happening within society.

Turning to the second type of communitarianism, Masolo identifies pioneers of African communitarian thought as Nkrumah, Nyerere and Senghor. He argues that unlike their Western counterparts these leaders were not philosophers. In support of their communitarianism they could cite specific traditional African societies that existed at a certain time. Inspired by the need to develop a system that was both in opposition to Western colonial doctrines as well socialist doctrines; these leaders developed African socialism. Allowance for both the terminology and the direction that the particular brand of socialism was going to take was determined by the local conditions of each nation.

I endorse Masolo's rejection of Nyerere and Senghor's view that African socialism as an attitude of the mind. Masolo does not see this attitude as wired in African minds. Rather, he argues, instinct drives people to act in ways that pursue self-interest. But they recognise that such actions do not augur well for survival as interests are likely to conflict. Masolo argues that in the view of this it is not enough to just tell people to act good, he makes the example of a colony of ants that all work together and to the benefit of all. Their acts are, however, not seen as good. What then makes an act good, Masolo asks? According to Masolo, for Nyerere what made the act good was the rational choice meaning "a separate value made the principle good and that 'acting with regard to others' welfare' depended upon the realisation of the worth of this other value. In other words, there must be something else that, being greater in value, would be brought about or preserved when we act as required by the principle he called 'African Socialism'" (ibid: 236). Masolo argues that the real question is what would it benefit people if all acted in ways that sought to beneficiate the other. "In another sense, we may also ask whether there is anything to be gained by establishing a social atmosphere where people are at peace with each other because of actions of actual mutual dependence but also, and more importantly, as a matter of principle" (ibid: 238). I take Masolo's point to be that it is not good to be communitarian in itself but there is a need to go beyond communitarianism to secure a good in which communitarianism could be said to be in service of. Thus he claims that:

Communitarianism is the political view or ethic that developmental and participatory rather than liberal democracy is the most effective means for checking and containing aberrant policy and polity. It is developmental because its major concern is to forge avenues for the recognition of new rights, and it is participatory because in order to win such recognition, it depends not only on rational argumentation but also on collective political action as an inseparable means of pressing for these new rights, which, in turn, are collectively shared with others. Communitarianism, then, is the collectivist vision then of a polity in its struggle for moral and other group goals (ibid: 245).

From this Masolo argues that the obligations, imposed on the individual, including economic obligations to help others, proceed from the consideration that one is connected to others by belonging to a community. This sense of belonging informs the individual's moral outlook. Such a communitarian moral outlook does not proceed from some metaphysical force as envisaged by nationalists, theologians and other philosophers who support the extreme version of communitarianism. He succinctly puts the matter as follows:

The recognition of common belonging should draw anyone toward the ethical principles that everyone is expected to take part in making it possible to realise the basic ideals of life. These aspirations do not flow out of Africans with a natural or metaphysical force. They are taught, and on different occasions people are reminded about the higher values of relational living (ibid: 249).

Further, Masolo argues that unlike the early versions of communitarianism, that did not see any place for individual rights in their political schemes, his version differs significantly in this respect as it takes individual rights as inalienable within the communitarian scheme. He writes:

I believe differently. I believe that communitarianism has its value yet places burdens on individuals and that these burdens, if properly defined, do not oppress the individual as much as is often believed. But the values and expectations of the communitarian ethic can be misunderstood or even abused, just as the liberties of the individual under liberalism have been. I believe that because it calls for everyone to honour mutual and reciprocal responsibilities toward others, communitarianism is based on an inevitable fact of human life: that to exist within a social space--to occupy a point or to be an individual within a social space--is to differ, to be different (ibid: 249-250).

I find the foregoing assessment sober and refreshing as the manner in which it interprets the nature of communitarianism frees African philosophy from the ghostly grip of the former. In the section below I seek to give reasons why Masolo's account is the most persuasive rendition of communitarianism.

### *Reasons for accepting Masolo's version*

In this concluding section, I wish to offer some reasons why I think Masolo's interpretation of communitarianism is the version that must be accepted as most persuasive. There are many versions of communitarianism that differ on certain fine detail such as whether individual rights are recognised or not, the weight given to those rights if they are recognised, the role of the community in the individual's identity, the political and social organisation therefrom and the metaphysical status of communitarianism in African thought. While some of these differences can be dismissed as enthusiastic articulations of nationalists and theologians, as Masolo does, it must not be taken to mean that there are no philosophers who are sympathetic to this extreme interpretation of communitarianism.

Keeping in line with this philosophical debate I seek to provide reasons that I consider to be of a philosophical nature – or at least reasons that have currency in philosophical debates – showing why Masolo's version is correct. There are two levels at which we could consider an interpretation of communitarianism being correct. On the first level we could refer to any instance of communitarian interpretation and presentation as either correct or wrong depending on how it either closely or distantly resembles the facts of social life in traditional communities. The second level occurs when we look at whether a particular communitarian account's claims follow. In other words, an account is made true by its coherence, non-contradictoriness and how it remains faithful to other philosophical requirements that make an argument valid and convincing. This does not mean that my support of Masolo is based on a desire to eliminate differences; my aim is to show which account makes more sense compared to other accounts. The sense I look for here is good old philosophical sense. I suggest that there are at least three reasons to accept Masolo's account.

The first reason is that Masolo's account is true. While philosophers may not always have the benefit of engaging in either anthropological or historical investigations to verify which communitarian claim is correct, certain arguments made in support of either this or that interpretation can easily be shown to be false. Philosophers make propositions, and a proposition can either be true or false. It is possible that the true or false state of a proposition can be made intentionally or unwittingly. In either respect, it does not count for much since the motive of the philosopher is not at stake. What is at stake is the content and claim of the proposition. In our case of communitarianism, we can look at two propositions that are in contrast made by, I believe, two decent philosophers. Menkiti claims that in traditional society there was no room for the recognition of individual rights. Gyekye, on the other hand, claims that traditional societies did recognise individual rights. Masolo shares the latter view. What we have are two contrasting statements, and they cannot both be correct. One is wrong and the other is right. How then do we work out which one is most likely to be correct?

I suggest that the matter may be solved by looking at two crucial issues. Firstly we look at the nature of humanity and secondly we look at the nature of societies that do not allow for individual rights to be recognised.

Regarding our first consideration, I think Masolo's view on humanity is correct. As shown above, Masolo argues that to be human means to be different, every instance of being human means being different. This view is correct and where humans co-exist that difference will come to the fore and each human, or at least most humans, will seek to live out a life that bears testimony to that difference. In order to live out that difference the individual's right to be – who she conceives herself to be – has to either exist or be brought into existence. Put in other terms no society can ignore the regime of individual rights because the nature of being human and being an individual demands that such rights be created and be respected. Hence we can conclude in this regard that all communities including traditional communitarian African societies have to reckon with the issue of rights.

The second issue will have to do with an investigation into the nature (i.e. social and political organisation) of societies that do not recognise individual rights – or in Menkiti's terminology give individual rights secondary importance. In my view, such societies are essentially characterised by a tendency to openly agitate against such individual rights. It is their official programme to persecute those who are seen as either advocates or practitioners of a different doctrine – individual rights. The persecution is of such a serious nature that it leads to the loss of life of those who are seen as opposed to the regime of disregarding rights. Such a regime will essentially be conceived as dictatorial and oppressive. Any cursory investigation reveals that this is not the case with the structures and organisation of traditional societies. The investigation I have in mind to prove that traditional societies were free and not against individual rights is not an anthropological or historical investigation. I have in mind philosophical texts that adumbrate on the philosophical analysis of the structures of traditional societies. Advocates of consensual democracy, who are philosophers such as Kwasi Wiredu, Joe Teffo and Edward Wamala, argue for the adoption of this political programme by analysing the social and political organisation of the same societies that extreme communitarians analyse. In this respect it is important to note that Wiredu (1996: 187) distances his project from one party state advocacy of the nationalists that was claimed to be based on traditional political outlook. Although consensual politics aimed at arriving at a consensual position that would be shared and recognised by everyone – it did not do so by suppressing dissent and hounding difference. Rather it sought to arrive at that consensus, according to Wiredu, through logical persuasion. This shows that the analysis and the reality of traditional society must tip towards an interpretation of communitarianism that respects individual rights unequivocally as Masolo's account does.

It might be objected that descriptions of what societies were do not translate into what they valued; in other words statements of how societies were organised and what they claimed to value does not mean that they lived up to these values. My response to this worry is that all societies have ideals and values that they aspire to. A combination of factors may work to militate against the attainment or translation of those values into practice. But, philosophically, it is important to note that, according to this account, the African polity was committed to these values as opposed to the proclamations of socialists and extreme communitarians.

The second reason why we should accept Masolo's version as correct is that it is simple, clear and it avoids unnecessary confusion. We could here refer to Gilbert Ryle's (1973: 18) notion of the category mistake. I do not intend going into details arguing what the category mistake could be and how it obtains with other versions of communitarianism except perhaps to point out that the essentialising of communitarianism has stretched communitarianism to categories that can only be seen as erroneous. This is where Masolo's account enjoys significant advantage over other communitarian interpretations. In the first instance he uses philosophical categories in the ordinary manner in which they are ordinarily understood by philosophers. In other words he desists from the temptation of finding the African difference to include a different usage of categories such as metaphysics and ontology. Secondly he correctly identifies what counts as social and political philosophy to be disparate, for example, from issues of personhood. Such a move makes his interpretation not only simple but it also becomes an interpretation that is unencumbered by incoherencies. The other accounts of communitarianism are unnecessarily thickened by the burden of having to be everything that is African philosophy, and subsequently, having to account for everything that passes as African philosophy. This should not be taken to mean that Masolo's account is reductionist. On the contrary, Masolo's account is simple and clear. Its simple articulation and clarity is found in his succinct statement that communitarianism is a social and political philosophy that interprets social and political life differently from liberalism. This makes his articulation correct as it simply seeks to articulate what communitarianism is and what it amounts to when conceived as a social and political theory.

The third and final reason is that Masolo's account is presented in a persuasive manner. In other words it does not rely on the authoritative traditional interpretations of reality. Neither does it seek to present itself as a specifically African decree that is metaphysically bound to the reality of African people. In his tracing of the development of Western communitarianism, Masolo succeeds in showing that there are certain crucial similarities in the development of Western communitarian thought and the development of African communitarianism. Both are conceived as an affirmation of a spirit and history of a formerly disenfranchised people. Both reject the spirit imposed through foreign influence. The merit of this comparison is that it begins to show that there is nothing either unique or essential about the African communitarian position, except what Masolo points out – that the nationalists could point out their traditional societies as having practised the communitarian lifestyle they were relying on to reinvigorate African socialism. The importance of this move is that it shows that Africans have theoretical counterparts in the West. Whereas it had been the ordinary belief, among nationalists and their supporting scholars, that all Western thought was individualistic and liberal, Masolo now shows that this is not the case. There are other Westerners, philosophers for that, who are also drawn to the communitarian interpretation of political and social life. This removal, of the ontological nature of communal reality from the socio-politico philosophical articulation of communitarianism, makes Masolo's position one that is refreshingly argued for. His communitarian politics is no longer presented, as its predecessors had done, as a matter of constitutive reality – but a rational choice that seeks to affirm something more than merely acting communitarian. Masolo's account is no longer one that seeks to claim that the ancestors lived as communitarians or African reality has to be restored. On the contrary it advocates communitarianism as a social and political philosophy. For these reasons I am persuaded that Masolo's communitarianism is the most acceptable version thus far.

It could be argued that my presentation of Masolo's position does not do better than Gyekye's moderate communitarianism or, alternatively, that I have presented a caricature of communitarianism that must not be taken seriously. I wish to start by addressing the second concern. If the objection is to be understood charitably, it will be developed along these lines: The sort of communitarianism as advocated by Tempels, Mbiti and Menkiti no longer retains the kind of dominance that it had in years gone by. There are other recent interpretations of African communitarianism that are fairly less radical or more progressive or even moderate in comparison to what I have termed classical communitarianism. It may then be argued that I should engage Masolo's argument in the light of these latest developments. To this objection I wish to point out that the radical interpretation as articulated by Menkiti is still supported by certain highly respected philosophers of our time. In particular, I have in mind Kwasi Wiredu's approval of Menkiti's articulation of the radical interpretation of the communitarian concept of person as the correct African view (Wiredu 1996: 221). In an endnote, numbered 37, Wiredu notes that there have been various debates in African philosophy on the interpretation of the normative account of personhood. Among the persons he cites is Menkiti and he points the reader to the critique that Gyekye has made against Menkiti's radical position. However he writes: "My own exposition is in basic agreement with Menkiti's" (ibid). It could be easy to dismiss Wiredu's agreement with Menkiti as his own philosophical position, an unenlightened one at that, but I am afraid we cannot do that. This is particularly so if we take into account that Wiredu is fully aware of Gyekye's devastating critique of Menkiti and his restatement of the communitarian notion of person based on the Akan – which both Wiredu and Gyekye are. What this means is that Wiredu and Gyekye both have a different understanding of the Akan communitarian notion of personhood. Wiredu interprets it as radical and Gyekye interprets it as moderate. This means that, effectively, the things said against Menkiti by Gyekye, for Wiredu are also true for the Akans. For that reason the classical radical/essentialist view is very much alive. That this account is very much alive is also amply shown by Menkiti's (2004) article, wherein he not only seeks to defend his account as the correct interpretation of African communitarianism but also seeks to develop its normative basis in his explication of the use of "it" as a moral source of personhood. In that article he gives a far much detailed explanation of how "it" operates in order to amplify the suggestion he had made 20 years earlier[66]. So I suggest the classical account has to be seen in that light and has to be addressed in accord with these developments.

As to the first concern that Masolo's account and my support of him do not do better than Gyekye's communitarianism, I wish to point out that there are certain arguments made by Gyekye in the process of explaining his moderate communitarianism that make his account not different from Menkiti's. For my extensive discussion of this point refer to my previous work (Matolino 2009: 168-169) where I argue that Gyekye's account of rights is equivalent to Menkiti's own views of the secondary status of individual rights.

Further, Gyekye's claim that acts such as homosexuality is permissible if done in private is most disingenuous. If we take whatever he is referring to by homosexual acts to refer to the actual sexual act or encounter – the actual copulation – of two or more people of the same sex, then his account is open to serious questions. We must note here that Gyekye limits the acceptability of homosexuality if it is kept away from the public eye. In other words, such people must refrain from making their orientation

---

[66] In my earlier work I have offered an extensive criticism against Menkiti's usage of 'it' to an 'it' as a signifier of the best communitarian interpretation of personhood, see (Matolino 2011: 23-37).

public just in case they offend societal values of peace, stability and harmony. But this is where Gyekye's problem lies: his communitarian account does not allow homosexual people to be open and free about their orientation for doing so is violating the social code. He calls on them to hide that orientation in their private spaces and become homosexual in those private spaces – read copulation – and once they are done they must be what society expects them to be. But this position is hypocritical; to call homosexuals to do their thing in private is akin to calling on heterosexuals to do their thing in private. The vast majority of people of any sexual orientation go to a great effort to have sex in private. Heterosexuals do not exploit the fact that heterosexual copulation is approved, to engage in wild or meek public engagements in sexual acts. Most heterosexual people, except perverts, do not enjoy being watched having sex and do not appreciate being confronted with public sex by other heterosexuals. Yet public displays of affection between heterosexuals, open and known relationships, marriage and the protection of their union under law are guaranteed. Why? Because heterosexual relations are not taken to be a threat to social peace, stability and harmony. They are not offensive to the public's sense of morality and Gyekye's communitarianism is prepared to abridge that which is offensive to the public's sense of right. The irony of all this is that homosexuals are persecuted in Africa and Gyekye helpfully proposes that they should keep their orientation behind closed and locked doors. Is that a right at all when so much is at stake about the rights and equality of same sex couples?

This difficulty (of balancing social and individual rights) could perhaps explain Menkiti and Wiredu's advocacy for radical communitarianism. But I suggest that this need not be the advocacy we should accept as Masolo has succeeded in not only stating communitarianism as a non-essential feature of being African but has most importantly given an erudite treatment of what the notion of self entails, and what the regime of rights in African thought is vis-a-vis the reality of the community in a changing world. Effectively, Masolo, unlike Menkiti, Wiredu and Gyekye, is free from the haunting presence of the communitarian ghost.

## References

Gyekye, K. (1997). *Tradition and Modernity: Philosophical Reflections on the African Experience*. New York: Oxford University Press.

Ikuenobe, P. (2006). *Philosophical Perspectives on Communalism and Morality in African Traditions*. Lanham, MD: Lexington Books.

Kaphagawani, D.N. (1998). *African Conceptions of Personhood and Intellectual Identities. In Philosophy from Africa: A Text with Readings*. Edited by Coetzee, P.H. and Roux, A.P.J. Johannesburg: International Thomson Publishing Southern Africa (Pty) Ltd, pp. 169-176.

Masolo, D.A. (2010). *Self and Community in a Changing World*. Bloomington: Indiana University Press.

Matolino, B. (2009). Radicals versus Moderates: A Critique of Gyekye's Moderate Communitarianism. *South African Journal of Philosophy*, 28(2): 160-170.

Matolino, B. (2011). The (Mal) Function of "it" in Ifeanyi Menkiti's Normative Account of Person. *African Studies Quarterly*, 12(4): 23-37.

Mbiti, J.S. (1970). *African Religions and Philosophies*. New York: Anchor Books.

Menkiti, I.A. (1984). Person and Community in African Traditional Thought. In *African Philosophy: An Introduction*. Edited by Wright, R.A. Lanham, MD: University Press of America, pp. 171-181.

Menkiti, I.A. (2004). On the Normative Conception of a Person. In *A Companion to African Philosophy*. Edited by Wiredu, K. Malden, MA: Blackwell Publishers, pp. 324-331.

Nkrumah, K. (1964). *Consciencism: Philosophy and Ideology for Decolonization and Development with Particular Reference to the African Revolution*. London: Heinemann.

Presbey, M.G. (2002). Maasai Concepts of Personhood: The Roles of Recognition, Community, and Individuality. *International Studies in Philosophy*, 34(2): 57-82.

Ryle, G. (1973). *The Concept of Mind*. Middlesex: Penguin Books.

Tempels, P. (1959). *Bantu Philosophy*. Paris: Presence Africaine.

Wiredu, K. (1980). *Philosophy and an African Culture*. Cambridge: Cambridge University Press.

Wiredu, K. (1996). *Cultural Universals and Particulars: An African Perspective*. Bloomington: Indiana University Press.

# The Case for Communitarianism: A Reply to Critics

## by Dismas A. Masolo[67]

*Abstract.* This essay originated from a workshop organized and hosted by the Department of Philosophy at the University of Johannesburg, South Africa, in March 2012. The focus of the workshop was to provide a platform for critical philosophical discussions of my book, *Self and Community in a Changing World*. The forum provided me with an invaluable opportunity to listen to different readings of the book. I gained greatly from the Johannesburg discussions, and I am immensely grateful to the philosophy department at the University of Johannesburg, especially gratitude to Professor Thaddeus Metz, the department chair and convener, for his generosity in hosting the workshop. I am indebted to all the participants at the workshop for sharing their thoughts. Seeking to respond to the incisive criticism levelled at my work during the Johannesburg meeting and in the present collection, I will re-iterate my position by stating the case for communitarianism, under the following headings: Cheerleading for the individual; The communitarian view; The self as local and universal: The management of knowledge; Self and moral values; Personhood and agency; Of ends and means; and finally: Mind, self, and society

*Key words:* agency, communitarian, individual, knowledge, local, Metz (Thaddeus), mind, moral values;, personhood, self, *Self and Community in a Changing World* (Masolo), society, universal

This essay originated from a workshop organized and hosted by the Department of Philosophy at the University of Johannesburg, South Africa, in March 2012. The focus of the workshop was to provide a platform for

---

[67] I gratefully acknowledge the insistent intercession of Wim van Binsbergen, thanks to whose efforts the present 'reply to critics' could be produced at all, and be appended to this special issue in time.

critical philosophical discussions of my book, *Self and Community in a Changing World*[68]. The forum provided me with an invaluable opportunity to listen to different readings of the book. As I say in the book itself, besides an author's self reading, there is perhaps no one reading of a text by others, as literary critics reminded us in years past when they coined the expression "death of the author". Hans-Georg Gadamer, the German hermeneutician, argued that human understanding was subject to what he called "the historically effected consciousness", claiming by this that humans interpret texts based upon what the specific cultures they are embedded in give them as the lens through which they look at the world around them. Without necessarily implying that every readership of any text is always somehow skewed, the differences that emerge between a reader's rendering and the author's own "object" engender critical debates that can do at least two things: they can expand the author's scope or they can elicit greater clarity in the author's articulation of her/his project. I gained from the Johannesburg discussions in both ways, and I am immensely grateful to the philosophy department at the University of Johannesburg, especially gratitude to Professor Thaddeus Metz, the department chair and convener, for his generosity in hosting the workshop. I am indebted to all the participants at the workshop for sharing their thoughts.

I have not tried in this essay to respond to all the issues raised in the critical essays in this issue. Nor have I undertaken to give detailed replies to them. Both undertakings will come at another and more appropriate time. The chief purpose now is to acknowledge the counterpoints to the positions I hold in *Self and Community* and to state briefly what I consider obvious enough misreadings of *Self and Community* to warrant some response at this time. While I leave to the convener the statement about the gathering and of its intended impact on the rapid demographic and curricular transformations in South African academia, I believe that aca-

---

[68] Published by Indiana University Press, 2010. From here onwards in this essay, it is frequently referred to simply as *Self and Community*

demic and scholarly gatherings such as the one from which these essays emerged are the crucial beginnings of a greater and desirable integration of the practice of philosophy in the country. This integration is needed because South African universities have become the training ground for young and emerging philosophers from around the continent, especially from the non-Arab parts of Africa. The universities have become the destination of choice for the graduate work of such scholars because of South Africa's command of professional and financial resources. This was a major factor in making the workshop on *Self and Community* possible. However, much appears to await greater mental transformation if African philosophy is to be integrated into the regular philosophy curriculum at all South African institutions that offer that discipline.

## *1. Cheerleading for the individual*

It is pretty straightforward that I think of human selves as communitarian rather than as atomic individuals. A major misconception of a communitarian conception of human selves is that it erases their individuality. Among the essays in this special issue of *Quest*, the piece by Mpho Tschivhaze is notably emphatic that the communitarian view of self such as I espouse in Self and Community denies the individual of her/his unique identity. Nothing could be farther from the truth. No-one needs any theorization to notice that we are born, live, and function pretty much as individuals. Biology affirms that each one of us humans bears a unique genetic coding that not even identical twins are, contrary to the conventional usage of the term, really "identical". Denying this sense of individuality would therefore dwindle into triviality. To be sure, communitarians uphold this individuality as pivotal to some of the core positions it holds such as democracy as a socio-political process, and human fallibilism in the quest for epistemological truth. But Ms. Tschivhaze makes other claims against communitarianism which may require a longer reply that we will save for another time. For now, let me say that she casts her own understanding of the self as unique not only in her/his individuality, a position which we share, but also as the object of moral endeavors. Her argument, hardly new, is that social values which direct both moral and political ideals ought to be directed at the cultivation or promotion of the interests of the individual. As individuals, then, our primary focus is the promotion of self-interests, and the broader social realms should be evaluated in respect of whether or not they provide the conditions that enhance and protect individual interests. Based on this position she lambasts communitarianism for allegedly holding the view that individuals have obligation to their communities rather than to themselves. On account of this alleged communitarian position, she claims that community therefore would appear to hold the key to whether or not its individual members attain personhood which, also in her view, is measured by the degree of every individual's allegiance to community. It therefore would follow, she disapprovingly contends, that personhood is the gift of approval by communities to their individual members.

First, let us say something about individuality and how it is experienced sometimes. As I sit here at my desk and strive to make sense of the many ideas that run through my mind, I experience no doubt that I am alone. I look through the window and wonder what a beautiful late summer day it is. I am thinking about whether the many goals I have for the day have any scale of priority or whether they should matter to me at all. At some point in the day, I will feel the urge to eat or drink something because my body will feel a certain way that will indicate that I am hungry or thirsty, or that I simply desire a little bit of good alcoholic drink. I have received several requests to contribute to efforts to help people who either have been struck by a disaster or who face difficulties in trying to solve one or more problems in their lives, and I wonder whether and why their problems should matter to me. As I sift through these and numerous other matters of my experience, I am alone, just like many other individuals might be, if they are like me, and the ideas and thoughts I produce appear to come solely from me alone. Everything I do ought to arise only from how I evaluate its worth to me. My obligation, I frequently think, ought to be directed toward attaining or improving my interests. This is not only how the human condition *can* be perceived, it is indeed how people tend to think of themselves; how they think they are constituted based on the activities I have described above. Some people go farther than these constitutive descriptions of self. They claim that the mental activities listed above are evidence of the centrality of "the individual" and hence of its unity and reality, of body and psychology (things of the mind generally), and have an autonomy that no other good can surpass. In this view, no social or political system can have goals that supersede the interests of the individual, and hence the worth of the actions of everyone, and indeed of a political system, should be measured only in terms of whether or not they promote those interests. Stating the value of the individual such that everything else can have value only to the extent of its recognition of the primacy of the individual and her/his interests is called *individualism*.

As I discuss in *Self and Community*, the history of the term "individualism" in the sense I have just described can be traced to the general history of Western thought and to the social and political transformations on the European continent as people sought a feasible and desirable social order. In these traditions, individualist tendencies in general and individualist thought specifically permeate different layers of society and people's interests. For example, current debates in the United States over gun control or over the new universal health insurance law that will require universal healthcare protection and will protect people with existing conditions from discrimination by health insurance companies have produced polarized opinions about the extent to which the government can legitimately impose policies that curtail constitutionally-protected individual freedoms. In the sharply contrasting positions around these issues, even some poor people whose lives would become far better by having subsidized health insurance have voiced strong opposition to the introduction of universal health insurance because of what they perceive to be an infringement on the freedoms of the individual. In their eyes, every individual has the right to own a gun and to decide how her/his healthcare should be managed. At the same time, some people in these same groups vehemently oppose the right of a woman to choose, as an individual, whether or not to have abortion.

In the two examples of American public debate on individual rights one can identity three forms of individualism, namely epistemological individualism, ethical individualism, and political individualism. The individual is sovereign over what is true or false, just as she is sovereign over what is the right thing to do, and over determining who makes decisions about how people should live their lives. But the examples also show that individuals do not necessarily hold all three views. Consider, for example, how the proponents of political individualism would read Jean-Paul Sartre's radical existentialist individualism, or Friedrich Nietzsche's anti-Christ; both strongly oppose the imposition of group beliefs, values, and myths on individuals. In these expressions individualism is viewed primarily as the antonym of "socialism", "collectivism", "communalism" or "communitarianism", the "masses", or what may be indicated by such terms (usually in pejoratively, by Nietzsche, for example) as the "herd", the "crowd," and so on. The question, however, is the extent to which, short of anarchistic position, both Sartre's and Nietzsche's respective brands of individualism explain the psychological constitution of the individual and the basis of individuals' pursuit of values, including the very idea of individuality as a value.

In some traditions, then, communitarianism is regarded and studied predominantly as a sociopolitical idea. It was once regarded as the driving idea in some parts of western Europe such as France, for example, before it lost its influence in the wake of the Enlightenment and the French Revolution. It flourished in France under the theocratic system in which the papacy of the Catholic Church had authority over whole societies under the direction of Church leadership on behalf of God. As I explained briefly in *Self and Community* (Chapter 6), there are varieties of communitarianism. What is apparently unclear to some people is whether the espousal of communitarianism is or is not compatible with upholding of the value of the individual. In what follows, I hope to dispel the impression that communitarianism is incompatible with upholding the view that the individual has irrevocable importance and undeniable degrees of autonomy based on her/his natural capacities , especially in the present time of heightened awareness of the rights of the individual. I hope to clarify further that naturalism, which recognizes all the capacities and endowments of the individual for moral and cognitive functional autonomy, leads directly to communitarisnism rather than to individualism, as those who subscribe to the uncompromising trends of liberalism claim.

Individualism, writes Rosalind Shaw[69], stands "in contrast to the 'collectivist' ideas of the individual...[as] a more 'atomist' strand of thought, derived from philosophers such as Hume and Hobbes, developed into nineteenth-century liberal and utilitarian ideas. This strand, in which human beings are defined as self-interested, 'rational' calculators of individual advantage, has.. The strongest claim to be the precursor of modern individualism..., long dominant in [such places as] the United States, where 'individualism' primarily came to celebrate capitalism and liberal democracy', and 'became a symbolic catchword of immense ideological significance.'"[70] In these two countries, in both dominant social theory and strong political organizations, the individual became the preeminent agent from whose actions the nation-state depends and whose interests become the defining factor that separates good and desirable sociopolitical conditions from bad ones. Concluding, Shaw writes that "The rhetoric of 'the individual' thus proceeds based on the use of implicit contrasts with relational systems of personhood in which such formulations as 'the shackles of tradition', 'unchanging social custom,' 'tribalism,' 'determinism,' 'fatalism,' etc., construct negative, mirror-image descriptions of the kinds of societies in which both individuality and personal agency are supposedly erased."[71]

There cannot be enough condemnation of bad practices in the name of community, such as the denial of freedom to individuals in the course of practicing culture, regardless of how crucial a customary practice may be deemed to be as a marker of individuals' group membership. *Self and*

---

[69] Shaw 2000: 28.

[70] Shaw quotes from Lukes 1973: 26.

[71] Shaw 2000: 29.

*Community in a Changing World* bears testimony to my own condemnation of the persistent yet unwarranted denial to millions of individuals each year of their basic right to make personal choices, especially on matters of denying education to the girl-child, forcing girls into the universally condemned practice of female circumcision, subjecting girls to child labor, and dragging girls into prearranged child marriage. As I have argued there against these malpractices that contravene the female child's right to self-preservation (with references to Pièrre Bourdieu[72], Corinne Kratz[73], Kwame Anthony Appiah[74], and Ngũgĩ wa Thiong'o and Ngũgĩ wa Mĩriĩ [75], among others), these constraints on the individual are usually perpetrated by persons – either parents or guardians – who view themselves as custodians of their traditions. Note that the authors I have just mentioned display concern with how overzealous protection of the ways of traditional institutions of society generates conflict between the values of the individual and those of the community. But while they depict these values in sharp contrasts, they also affirm the relative autonomy of the individual as stemming from the constant and dialectical engagement with other consciousnesses in public space. I hold the view that the relational reality in which the individual lives is the only factor that shapes her/his rationality. Through training in social environments the individual learns about the nature and importance of truth, and about a host of ethical and social values like truthfulness, trust, right, wrong, good, bad, kindness, honesty, friendship, and others alongside their regulative applications to deliberation and action. Similarly, we learn from society the principles of artistic and aesthetic judgment. The view that people learn these values from society rather than intuitively on the strength of some

---

[72] Bourdieu 1977.

[73] Kratz 1994. Note that Kratz does not trace the effects of tradition and custom on the individual like Bourdieu and Appiah do, hence it is not easy to say whether she shares or disagrees with their views about the matter.

[74] Appiah 1992.

[75] wa Thiong'o& Ngũgĩ wa Mĩriĩ 1982.

ontological constitution is based on what I term philosophical anthropology which, again in my view, asks questions about how we become who we believe we are in both our thoughts and conduct. Is there an inner "I" that intuitively discovers itself as "me" without the mediation of experience or exposure to the outside world? Our integral (somatic, cognitive, moral, and emotional) development prepares us to become effective participants in or active members of the communities we live in. I use the term "learn" not in a passive sense, but to indicate the interactive experience that enables individuals to grow and develop into agents. To fully attain this participatory role in our lives, we often have to resist the dominating powers of the institutions of society because they disable our capacity for full development and effective participation. The question, then, of whether good communities make good individual persons, or good individual persons make good communities appears to be a perennial one as it has been asked by thinkers of almost every millennium, albeit for different motivations, and it lies in the heart of contemporary debates in all disciplines that study different aspects of the human condition.

The often-asked question "What's in it for me?" summarizes popular attitudes about the interests of the individual. Concepts of the dignity and freedom of the individual are powerful and appealing reminders of what every individual should be accorded. Dissidents against different types of twentieth-century authoritarian governments in both colonial and post-independence Africa were empowered by the ideals and appeals of individual freedoms. Long before the collapse of the Cold War, these same ideals empowered dissidents in the Soviet Union against the mighty Communist Party. More recently, we have seen a similar campaign for individual freedoms in the confidence and resolve of Chinese students in the famous Tiananmen Square standoff. The good (bonum) driving these instances of resolve, as it drove the global student uprisings of 1968 or uprisings in South Africa for over two hundred years, especially in the struggles against the racist and unilaterally legalized segregation policy there between 1948 and 1994, was the quest for greater freedoms of speech, association, and of personal choice. The ideal of autonomy and the freedoms affiliated with autonomy appeal to anyone who values the ability to make decisions for her or himself. The goal of opposition to colonial rule, both peaceful and armed, was to win back and reestablish these freedoms for citizens of occupied territories, countries, or nations.

That we are individuals is quite obvious for everyone to see. At birth, we are ushered into the world as single individuals. Even in multiple births, the arrival of one infant after another is what is regarded as normal. Conjoined twins are an anomaly, and advancements in medical technology have made it possible in some cases to separate the pair – to give each sibling his or her own individuality. Fair enough, and really no-one would deny the need for this kind of autonomy; it is necessary for both basic biological functioning and the exercise of the capacities that give individuals personal autonomy, such as performing and expressing thoughts and making decisions. A well-developed brain demonstrates the ability of its different compartments to execute functions that which are regarded to be the basis of every individual's autonomy – such as motor functions, sensory functions, cognitive functions, moral functions, and emotional functions. In this sense, and without any slight implied, the makeup of every individual human is comparable to, say, the composite makeup of a bicycle or any other composite and complex machine whose various parts must be "well" or "healthy" in both their makeup and functional roles in order for the composite entity – in this case the bicycle – to be and to function as it is intended to do. That said, we should now turn to see how an organistically healthy individual becomes a person.

## 2. The communitarian view

Thaddeus Metz has raised questions regarding the relation of individuals to community, and how this relationship plays out in respect to the concept of personhood. Besides making some sweeping, unwarranted, and admonishing remarks directed at what can only be understood as "the field" of African philosophy. That charge is about the now almost rhetorical claims that "in African thought, 'community comes before the individual', or, as in some idioms, 'I am because we are'", and so on. The background provided by the literature in which these idioms have been prominent have certainly influenced Metz in his remarks.

The view that I hold is not a function of my identity, nor is it an essentialist claim about how some assumed "African personhood" ought to be understood. It is simply how, to my understanding, the human condition is. I will start by stating that the idea of communitarianism is neither inimical to nor incompatible with some aspects of liberalism, at least not in the strong sense like communism is. Yet, in contrast to liberalism, it does not espouse a picture of social reality as made up of atomistic individuals whose relations with others are purely but informally contractual. Communitarianism is committed to the view that for human beings the world starts with the individual. This is why the freedom of the individual plays a central role in understanding, according to this philosophy, how the individual arrives at his/her self-awareness., of why epistemological objectivity is inherently problematic. Elements of communitarianism differ from those that accompany the idea of "public" or "socialist"states in which society tends to be thought of as comprised of empty and depersonalized institutions. Communitarianism, by contrast, sees community, or society, if you wish, as a valuable reality within which, besides becoming able to grasp the sense of "I" through the interactive mediation of (the presence of) others, the individual acquires also other forms of language and the conceptual realm it relates to, whether it is descriptive or normative. The individual acquires these abilities only in community or harmony with the interests and goals of others. These special characteristics of communitarianism are universal, and so do not describe biological characteristics special to Africans. What is astonishing, as revealed by Metz, is how it escapes the unwarranted and obviously misplaced arrogance of individualists. Descartes showed them the way.

Liberalism thrives in the recognition and celebration of the individual as an autonomous and therefore a complete cognitive and moral agent. By contrast, communitarianism sees the self as part of a biosocial context in which her/his organistic capacities such as the ability to imitate others and to form ideas and concepts are not only dependent on behavior for active appearance ("showing up"), but are also oriented toward behavior. Babies are spoken to so they can imitate, and they are propped to take that first step in walking when the mother takes the lead in slow motion, and so on, just like people, adults or not, are taught to hit the right note in singing when the conductor leads them to repeat several times in *practice*. In other words, what we come to know as mind, for example, would not even be known to be if a human being were not immersed in a communicative system, any system of rational communicants. It is the case, for example, that one of the early signs of autism, a condition widely considered in medical circles an obstacle to human socialization, is a baby's or child's inability to respond to behavioral props. Subsequently, the so-enabled active capacity becomes a necessary tool for abiding within that particular and any other system of rational communication by learning both the language of the group and the norms of conduct that define good citizenship in the group.[76]

Among several implications of the indeterminate concept of mind is the fact that it is not just the as-yet-to-be-enabled mental capacity of an infant that can be adapted to any given cultural system, the minds of adults can adapt too. I consider the former case to be unproblematically obvious. A

---

[76] Extreme cases of developmental anomalies are the subject of stories, both fictional and real, about what is generally referred to as the "feral child" or the "wild child". Imagined or known to have been isolated from human contact from a very young age and therefore lacking human care, the "feral child" is usually depicted as lacking in the idea or showing of love, social behavior, and most importantly, human language. "Feral children" may be the result of accidental separation from parents or other family members, or they may be victims of deliberate seclusion due to a condition that other family members do not wish to associate with or expose to the outside world. In the latter case, the child is usually locked up in a secrete part of the family residence and is given food without any other form of contact. If not inflicted by malformations, the "feral child" may operate on the basis of instinctive drive in his/her encounter with the world around him/her, but cannot function as a person unless trained to immerse into a human community.

child born, say, in Louisville, Kentucky, of biological ancestry of white-skinned parents can be made to grow to become a member of the Luo community if, from birth or soon thereafter, the child were taken to grow up with Dholuo (the language of the Luo) as its primary mode of communication and the culture of the Luo was the primary source of concepts for making sense of the world and the norms of conduct. Since being a Luo is a cultural rather than a biological attribute, this lad would grow up as a Luo person no less than, say, my own or my brother's children who are brought up under the same system. Contrary to the biases our upbringings tend to tell us, we can never tell for sure what it means biologically to be Polish, Swede, Tonga, Shona, or anything else. What we do is to identify with any one of the groups in the world as the cultural system by which we organize our conduct.[77]

I define personhood as a socially generated category, or one that is conferred by society in a variety of ways depending on the context in ques-

---

[77] Politics of culture, and subjection to cultural domination of Africa have left many Africans not only unable to recognize their indigenous languages as respectable modes of communication, but much less as sources of concepts of the nature of the world and of normative principles for moral conduct and for socio-political organization. This collection of essays contains many examples of such disdain for use of concepts from African languages. Human reality reveals, however, that we think in words, and words belong to specific languages, which are the products of specific cultures. Sometimes I wish there was a language better than the one I grew up speaking, but I have found none, just as I believe anyone who has grown up with her/his own believes about her/his own like I do about mine. If you have been privileged with learning and speaking more languages than just your own, like most formerly colonized peoples do, tracing a concept and the subtle variations it acquires when expressed in different languages should not be considered a futile exercise. As regards the role of language in the construction of the self, it has been observed, and it is easily observable in children's growth, that the gradual process of acquiring linguistic capacity unveils the fact that we are fallible, a trait which comes from our embodiment, a condition that 'conditions' us to learn from lived experiences of intersubjective relations with other embodied selves, mainly through language which spurs an internal language in the child or any learner of a new form of linguistic structure of "the world".This picture reveals a social self, not a hidden Cartesian self that wakes up only to find that it is contemplating itself.

tion, invariantly depicting society's expectations of an individual, usually based on society's awareness of the degree of an individual's development. Thus, for example, to say that " a person X is morally rotten" is not synonymous with saying that "X is not person", or that "X lacks personhood". Living and acting in society not only makes us become aware of regulation of conduct such as the moral implications of some of our actions, it is also the place where we improve our moral character. Moral awareness and character are derived from and are improved in society. Society sets standards in different domains of life which it expects its able members to try to attain. And while it generally blames violators, the average member goes almost unnoticed, and praise is generally reserved for those who exceed the average expectations in any circumstance. Regarding the latter, for example, the lad who helps the elderly lady down the street by pushing her trash can back to her garage earns praise in a world where folks don't easily give such help any more. Or the man who maintains calm and peace when he is pushed out of his path by a rogue lad is praised for his composure and rejection of a retaliatory action where such would have been a general expectation.

The cattle thief from across the river is no less a person than the disciplined and virtuous army captain whose life is a model of a good member of society. They are both persons, and maybe they are siblings, but the cattle thief is a bad one. While he is averagely normal in most senses of good health, he developed bad habits that cause him continuously to makes bad choices. On this basis, he may be reported to the village chief for arrest and prosecution. His captain brother, on the other hand, habitually makes choices that reflect what he was taught was the proper way for people to conduct themselves: one does not take other people's property without their permission. But if it were to be determined that the brother who takes people's cattle or other property was in fact not acting out of free will but by a compulsive push to do so, then his family might be asked to restrain him by means other than having him arrested and prosecuted. Instead, they might want him to be admitted to a specialized health facility for treatment. Likewise, if his brother was not a soldier but only dressed like one and marched around the village like the army captain that he was before he was discharged from the military because of mental illness, people in the village would pity rather than adore or praise him, even if they had fond memories of him dressing in a similar way when he was a real soldier. In both of these latter cases, the respective personhoods of the two brothers are diminished. They would not be assigned duties in the village that require proper judgment because their capacities for this expectation of all healthy persons are compromised.

The idea of personhood as conferred calls for the need to understand personhood in terms of a balance that gives equal weight to culturally objectified, and subjectively apprehended aspects of social life. In their discussions of what persons are, philosophers often focus on transcendental categories that fail to capture the impact of the lived experiences of individuals who, besides having a pretty good idea of who/what they believe they are, confront the expectations that society imposes on them every day of what it means to be *someone*. They do this by behaving as they presume or project that society expects them to behave. This observation is not new, as it is what all humans experience everyday.

Perhaps a bit of consideration of what the social sciences teach us to observe would help. The German phenomenologist Edmund Husserl developed what he called transcendental phenomenology in order to develop an approach that avoided (by suspending or, as he preferred to call it, bracketing) the details and variations of the natural stance, by which he meant everyday lived experiences. This approach drew a sharp critique from Jean-Paul Sartre, who insisted that understanding the existential condition of humans cannot suspend any aspect of experience, including the contradictions of everyday experience that characterize precisely our strivings in the quest for freedom. The thesis behind Sartre's radical existentialism can be summarized as claiming that the very conditions of our existence have placed us in the position of striving to escape the strictures of everyday life; we cannot ignore or wish them away. The term "strictures" should be understood to describe all kinds of conditions of limitation imposed on individuals by other individuals, groups of individuals, institutions, as well as by collective beliefs, customs and traditions. These limitations "herd" individuals toward already chosen beliefs and practices, thus giving individuals no freedom to make their own choices. For example, discrimination against black people based on their race, or against women based on their gender, against other categories of people based on their ethnicity, or against yet another category of people based on their sexual orientation have all long been opposed as wrongly assuming that people in those categories were inferior and therefore undeserving of treatment equal to that of people who were unlike them – namely white, male, straight, and of Anglo-Saxon descent. It was Sartre's view that besides these politically and socially more pronounced conditions, even in ordinary existential conditions the "I" is always in oppositional relation to another "Is" and the circumstances created by the fact of their "being- there". In this sense, Sartre says, "what I am can be revealed as the term of a relation... It implies as such a comprehension of what I am as being-there. But at the same time it is very necessary to define what I am from the standpoint of the being-there of other 'thises.'"[78]

Earlier, Marcel Mauss had indicated this concept of self in lived experience by separating that aspect of personhood that he referred to as *moi*, the awareness of self, from *la personne morale*, the ideological definition of self in terms of rules and roles[79], although he thought of the latter in terms that focused on the experiences of the self that are deep, interior, and idiosyncratic, as opposed to wearing a mask that is meant for people we want to judge us in a particular way. Understanding personhood as competence to exercise agency in a social world does not, therefore, use the idea of "competence" in terms of virtuous perfection; it uses this word in Mauss's sense of *personne morale*, or the public aspect of human life. In this conceptualization, the active participation of humans is defined by the correlativity of stimulus and response; people act as agents because they exhibit their cognitive, emotional, and moral ability to live in society. This understanding of personhood recognizes but also differs from

---

[78] Sartre 1956: 632.
[79] See Mauss 1939.

the substantialist view that one finds, for example, in Aristotle, Descartes, and Locke. It claims that reason, conceived as ability to engage in both reflective and nonreflective experience, occurs as a natural attribute of mind. This attribute is affected by society in the sense that it is the result of specifically human responses to the stimulations of the conduct of people in our social environment. In this sense, the mind "erupts" as a responsive impulse of the human organism (we are not free to choose to have or not have mind), and its functional order is gradually shaped through informal and formal guidance by those who surround us. The experiential aspect of mind is "wired" appropriately for its "ignition" by virtue of its presence in the natural conditions of social experience.

The primary tool of social engagement is language. A combination of words and ostensive behavior introduces all children to "the world" they are located in. For many children, this world starts with relating certain types of sounds with ingestible objects and with words and tones of voice that indicate reassurance, such as "Okay, everything is okay., here we go", which the parent or any other caregiver follows with specific actions such as feeding. Alongside these primary forms of socialization, children are introduced to concepts of the social world around them, usually relational concepts with "Mother" or Daddy" leading the list. Later, other concepts about the specific social world of the baby are formed that follow and reflect the expanding world of the child. Opinions differ about when exactly in its growth and development the child begins to sense and react to the social events happening around it, thus signaling when the mind comes into function. Regardless of where and with whom, every child's life begins with exposure of the biological individual – the child – to a minimal society whose communicative conduct transforms the child into a minded individual.

### 3. The self as local and universal: The management of knowledge

In his essay, Kai Horsthemke raises a fundamental question about the very idea of indigenous knowledge. He argues that there is no use of promoting the idea of indigenous knowledge if the belief that make up such an idea were false. The joke he tells at the beginning of his essay is about the physical world; it is about members of an Australian tribe that relies on their chief to predict how severe the impending winter is likely to be so they can prepare for it effectively. The point of the story is that there is nothing indigenous about knowledge. If the tribesfolk in the anecdote had used the appropriate methods, not only would they have attained the desired answers to their worries, but, also, the answers could have been attained by anyone applying the same methods - in this case, the methods of predicting the weather.- correctly.

The assumption Horsthemke works with is not new. Here is a brief statement as a start: while the world of physical objects, of their laws, and just of natural events generally precede us, and probably will go on with or without us, our discourses about it do not. The reader probably will remember my use in *Self and Community* of the opening statement of Wittgenstein's well known *Tractatus*: "The world is all that is the case."[80] The significance of this statement for me in relation to what I say about indigenous knowledge is what is required to fully describe "the world". As Russell says in his introduction to Tractatus, "The world is fully described if all atomic facts are known, together with the fact that these are all of them."[81] *The difficulty unveiled by Russell's comment does not lie in the logical sense or possibility of "fully describing the world." It lies in the view of Wittgenstein that such descriptions would have to be empirical, leaving no doubt that for the Wittgenstein of this stage, there was one universal language whose propositions had this special picture-relation*

---

[80] Wittgenstein 1961: 5.

[81] Russell 1961.

to reality, as every proposition is a truth function of all atomic facts of which it is constituted. The idea that we can fully describe the world by taking into consideration only the totality of facts about that world gives the false impression that there must be a limited number of facts about the world which must be experienced by all people in identical ways as only this can lead to a universal language whose claims are assessable by anybody. Not only would this deny the possibility of private language at the personal level, but would, by sort of a poor extension, also deny the possibility of language restricted to groups of people. The argument, usually associated with Wittgenstein's other work, Philosophical Investigations, claims that if a person assigns signs to the sensations that only he/she experiences, hence are private, he/she would never be able to assign the same sign to any subsequent sensation because he/she would never know that they are identical sensations; hence it would be impossible to assess whether his/her subsequent signage is correct or incorrect, as this would assume some sort of publicly accessible process and criteria. We cannot make sense of of the notion of correctly (or incorrectly) reapplying a signage to a private sensation, and we cannot make sense of the notion of a private language. In addition, a language with terms for publicly accessible objects, or natural conditions like in Horsthemke's argument, would, if regarded to be private or indigenous to its users, still be claimed to lack criteria for the correct reapplication of such terms. Hence, he argues, the claims about indigenous knowledge, which he takes to be a broadened notion of private language, is equally incoherent.

Two things: one, Horsthemke's argument overextends the idea and problems related to "private language" which, in its historical origins dating back to Hume and taken up more recently by the proponents of positivism, addresses only mental occurrences as opposed to "what it is like to live through an exceptionally cold winter". Assessment of the latter may include memory of known folks who have either perished or suffered in some other ways because they were not as prepared for an exceptionally severe winter. The idea of "experience" that informs concerns with a season is not identical to that of "direct experience" in sensation. Two, Horsthemke appears unduly to think that knowledge is only about empirical claims. The world of humans is made of far more than preoccupation with just empirical claims about "the world", or only with the truth value of such claims. Objects may be the same to a group of people who populate a particular region, but it does not follow that everyone in that region thinks only of the same atomic facts out of such objects even if it would make sense to them when made. Horsthemke's argument rests implausibly on a reductionist definition of "experience" as pure somatic movements of nerves, muscles, lenses, and so on. In other words, the meaning of "experiencing objects" would have to be restricted to what occurs when we encounter one in empirical senses alone; but is it?

To borrow from Appiah[82] *on a matter that has long been debated in a variety of ways, knowledge that a few words with hands extended over a cup of wine does not turn the wine into blood does not bar the Christians who sip the wine from believing that it has been "converted" into blood, or, likewise, that the wafer they eat during communion is suddenly the body of a man who asked them to do so. The conversions are definitely questionable from the standpoint of science, but it has not prevented sound scientists of repute from engaging in these rituals. Appiah narrates how when European travellers, some of whom were missionaries who had come to Africa to tell the Ashanti that engaging in the rituals I just described were acts of salvation, observed Ashanti offerings of gold to their god, they were quick to remark that the Ashanti falsely assumed that God would "actually" take the gold dust offered to him. Christians, not the Ashanti, believe that prayer and extension of the consecrated hands of the priest effect a transubstantiation that warrants the belief that drinking the wine and eating the wafer following the consecration is indeed drinking the blood and eating the body of Christ. Fillipo Selvaggi, who taught me metaphysics and the philosophy of science in college, was as good a physicist and a member of the Italian Council of Nuclear Physics as he was a devout Jesuit priest. The view, therefore, that the world of science eliminates the idea of indigenous knowledges is as unreflective as the*

---

[82] Appiah 1992: Chapter Six.

*belief that because womanhood is biologically the same everywhere, there is nothing that warrants differences in the idea of motherhood. The language of Christianity or of Ashanti rituals may not have made it into Wittgenstein's notion of atomic facts or the totality of complex propositions that have been built out of those facts, but knowledge of the Ashanti experience of the world would not be complete without considering how they regard gifts, favors, respect, and matters of that kind, both in the terrestrial sense, and in their relations with their gods. Today, however, some people reject religious beliefs or arguments for such beliefs on scientific or agnostic grounds. The idea of indigenous knowledge is far broader than how people express concerns or make claims about empirical reality. It is also about people's creative transformation of the physical world around them in response to their needs; and it is also about* how people design norms of conduct to regulate their relations as well as access to and distribution of resources.

The joke that Kai Horsthemke shares at the beginning of his article is bad, to put it very mildly. If people collect wood to feed their furnaces when it is cold, preparing for the condition, if true, by collecting wood will always be the rational action to take. People who have been through a similar condition would be well served by their memory in order to make the appropriate judgement about what to do. In the narrative, in fact, people seek any sign (prediction) from their elders that the precedent (an exceptionally cold winter) is indeed going to be the case. The elder, for whatever reason, tells the people that the precedent has been predicted to be true (severe cold winter ahead). The people's reaction by deciding to do what they believe any reasonable person or reasonable people should do when the winter is cold, namely collect wood to feed their furnaces, is both reasonable (seek warmth in cold conditions) and rational (concluding, appropriately, the rational course of action in such circumstances). I see this kind of behavior all the time where I live when the city readies salt trucks "because" the weatherwoman has predicted that a snowstorm is headed our way. Just remember that weather predictions are independent of people's reactions to the news. They are not materially related as there is no causal relation between them. Not everyone prepares for the storms that are coming when the forecast announces their imminent arrival. Because they fear the severity of the consequences of storms and winters generally, people seek preparedness by consulting predictive sources that have proven reliable in the past. Sometimes these predictions err, intentionally or not, so people "reasonably" prepare for what does not come to pass.

In another example, the aborigine chief who chooses to intentionally cheat his people does not consult as they probably expected him to do. His capacity to consult is why they believe his advice is credible. Because they trust him to give a reliable prediction, like his predecessors have probably done, the people gather wood. Surely the gathering of wood does not predict the weather, even when a neighbor might retort that "it appears that winter will be cold" simply because they have seen their neighbor gathering wood. The remark "it appears that winter will be cold" neither claims nor even remotely implies that gathering wood proves that winter will be cold. It only states that "this neighbor of mine might have heard it from somewhere." The trust is not in what the neighbor is doing as proof. Rather, it is in the assumed reliability of the source the neighbor is assumed to base his action on. For other examples, we might think of people who die because their physicians misdiagnosed their condition or people who died because their nurse knowingly gave them a lethal drug. In both of these cases, people perished because they trusted what the titles of these caregivers stood for.

Thus, trust is always part of knowledge-creation, especially when and where the field of envisaged consumer(s) is broader than that of the creator her/him-self. If a weather siren sounds, we become worried about of what might be about to happen because we trust the person who operates the siren switch. We take a quick glance at the sky and say, "The weatherwoman is telling us that something bad is about to happen and that we should heed what she is telling us to do by sounding the siren. We trust her competence, her ability to detect and retain information about the kind of event or fact in question. Secondly, we also believe that the weatherwoman is using the tools of her trade as she is turning the siren on. She is in the weather room as opposed to being in a hospital bed where she is being treated for cerebral malaria. Thirdly, we believe that she is being sincere or honest about what she is telling us and not playing a prank. Now, what would happen if instead of the weatherwoman sounding the siren herself, or us believing that that is indeed what is happening, someone else comes up and says we should run to a safe place because she heard the siren and believes the weatherwoman is telling us something and that she trusts her? How do we deal with the second-hand reporter? And what if there were a third-hand reporter?

Since chiefship is not directly related to expertise in weather detection expertise (this would be the case only if only expert weathermen were appointed chiefs), we would need additional evidence as the basis for trusting the chief on matters of weather reporting. There ought to have been an additional narrative to explain why the people of the tribe resorted to their chief on these matters. In the end, of course, he abused the trust by degrading himself to the rank of a con man, just as would be the case if an expert weatherwoman reported a weather-related event from her hospital bed while stricken with cerebral malaria.

Finally, it should be pointed out that the term "indigenous" is not a synonym for "non-Western" or for "non-modern," although it was given these connotations in colonial language and literature. Its variant, "native", is equally common. Horsthemke refers to Hallen and Sodipo's discussion of the distinction in Yoruba language between belief and knowledge, one hich, perhaps inappropriately, I brought into affinity with Wiredu's concept of truth as opinion in *Self and Community*. Hallen and Sodipo's distinction between belief and knowledge relates, as I understand it, to an important point about the role of testimony in considering whether or not to accept as true statements that are delivered by a second-hand or third-hand reporter. Layers of reportage, as Alvin Goldman called them, are often present in the treatment of knowledge in social contexts.[83] *The idea*

---

[83] Goldman 1999: 103 - 130.

*that there is "a reduction of 'indigenous knowledge' to first-hand, direct, experiential knowledge-claims that may, indeed, be mistaken!"*[84] *is a false reading of Self and Community.* My discussion of Hallen and Sodipo's comparative analysis of the concept of truth in English and Yoruba was not offered as an illustration of "indigenous knowledge." The concept of "indigenous knowledge" is not exclusively about truth-claims, much less about the inference that all indigenous knowledge is true. The idea that a perfect translation is difficult to attain when moving between different languages has its own merit as a philosophical problem, and Hallen and Sodipo used the fascinating Yoruba example to illustrate the point. On the other hand, assuming that it is indeed a form of indigenous knowledge, then what would exempt the definition of knowledge as "justified true belief" from being an example of indigenous Western knowledge?

## 4. Self and moral values

Communitarianism does not imply that we are all limited to our specific experiences in groups such as our families or ethnic communities, even if the experience of self as socially embedded is best exemplified in them. The family in particular functions as the primary location of social experience for many people. It is where socialization starts for most children, however it (the family) is defined. It is because experience has a social dimension, because the self or the human organism is always located in a field with others, that we feel ourselves to be anthropologically situated to start the human journey with the social act of communication and to ground the development of personhood on a complex system of social interactions. On this topic, I quoted Meyer Fortes in *Self and Community*:

---

[84] Horsthemke, this volume, p. 7 of the draft.

"Thus, from whichever way we approach oue enquiry we see how important it it to keep in mind the two aspects of personhood. Looking at it from the objective side, the distinctive qualities, capacities and roles with which a society endows a person enable the person to be known to be, and also to show himself to be the person he is supposed to be. Looked at from the subjective side, it is a question of how the individual, as actor, knows himself to be – or not to be – the person he is expected to be in a given situation and status. The individual is not a passive bearer of personhood; he must appropriate the qualities and capacities, and the norms governing its expression to himself."[85]

I have decided to go back to this quote for a reason: that read carefully, and reflectively about the multiple ways of expressing senses of a person, some folks may desist from arrogantly claiming that they know "the precise [ assuming there was only one] meaning of the relationship between social interaction and personhood" (Metz, p. 4 of draft).

My account of the self claims that self-awareness is derived rather than direct or intuitive, and that it develops from birth as a function of the communicative conduct of those who make up the primary social environment of the child. Social distinctions, the pivotal point of which is the onset of the idea of "I" as distinct from others, are followed by the development of agency, namely that bodily interactions with objects cause them to change. For example, a child's furious throwing of arms can cause her dinner plate to fall on the floor and break, thereby making her food no longer available. Because these actions are regularly followed by comments of the parent or any other caregiver; ("See, you don't throw things to the floor; now you don't have dinner, it is all gone!"), the child learns agency, that their actions can cause undesirable situations. On other occasions, the child is warned not to pull the cat's tail because the cat could bite her, but she does so anyway. Then the cat turns around fast with a hiss of disapproval and lurches at her hand and gives her a bite, to which the observing mother retorts: "See? I told you". From this the child will learn several things: first, that she can be wrong, be a source of error; second, that other people's testimony can correctly describe the world out

---

[85] Fortes 1973: 273.

there, which they know and she does not; and third, that some mistakes can have painful consequences. Gradually, as the child develops a way to make sense of the world around her, learning through trial and error as in the case of the cat, she develops a sense of who she is, not only in relation to the world of objects but also in relation to other people, who she comes to learn to be the other "Is". She comes to regard and trust other people as possible sources of reliable beliefs and knowledge. Like herself, they too make mistakes sometimes. She realizes that everyone is fallible.

Although it is biologically true that as an individual each person has a unique identity defined by their DNA that through the wonders of biology he or she has inherited from their ancestors, the same cannot be said of what makes us into cultural subjects. What we learn when we become self-aware is our relationship to the world, including and driven by the social environment of our growth and development. As biosocial beings, we are at the same time the products and the vehicles of this process.

To term this understanding of personhood as uniquely African, or that understanding African ethics is based on the idea of personhood, is a misunderstanding of what communitarianism is all about. Communitarianism is a general theory that claims that the distinctive qualities and capacities that define us as persons are socially generated, and that the constitution of the self as a cognitive and moral agent comes not from a special cognitive faculty of intuition but from our interactions with others and our conduct in the world. Born with utter deficiency except for her or his biological capacity and readiness for the social world, the self is totally dependent on the social world and thus can be understood only by external and public criteria (as all observations of human growth attest), not by criteria that are internal and private. This position reverses the order of priority for the Cartesian who holds that thought is grounded in self-consciousness. From the brief outline above of a child's communicative encounter with the world through the gradual leads of parents or other acquaintances, the child learns basic principles that anchor her or his sense of self and the basic attributes of self.

Hence, the child, and all humans for that matter, do not develop their sense of the world, including their sense of themselves, from an innate faculty that grasps not only the sense of self but also, as presented by Descartes, the application of the inferential principle (ergo)from which it grounds its primacy. This sounds like "I am because I am" of the biblical Yahweh's proclamation of his primacy. The Cartesian tradition may probably lead there, and Descartes might have wittingly made the analogy, but that is not our preoccupation here. Mine is a naturalist view that stands up against the perception, central to Descartes' "thinking substance" and Kant's "transcendental ego", that there is an innate order of cognitive and moral reason that works for humans as a transcendental law of the atemporal substantive self.

Does the "acquisition of personhood" have a time line? The problem lies in the misunderstanding of the term "acquisition", which some read as "coming into the position of having or possessing something", usually by doing something else. Applied to personhood, "acquiring" seems, in this sense, to suggest that one has to work hard in order to "achieve" personhood, which quickly (mis)leads into thinking of personhood as an additional quality that society bestows on its members as just pay after their successful performance of a duty or task, hence conferred upon them as recognition of their excellence. That is not the case.

In common usage, persons are human beings, and human beings are persons. In common, we use the term "person" to apply to all members of the species *homo sapiens*. This is why, I think, some readers appear to be confounded by the idea that certain conditions, such as the moral agency of a human being, transforms one into more than just a human being. However, it is a mistake to conclude that ascriptions of personhood function only in a purely descriptive manner. The term "person" is often used in declarative utterances and statements that are meant to emphasize an individual's normative standing. "But she/he too is a person (*En be en mana dhano*)" is a common form of declarations that are usually used to protest inappropriate treatment of an individual as if she/he was a thing. The term "human being" is frequently used in similar senses.

The normative sense conveyed by the term "person" when used in the manner that specifically conveys claims of rights – for example, expectations of treatment by others – may indeed apply to individuals or groups of individuals merely by virtue of their membership in the species *homo sapiens*, as can be exhibited by the physical type expected of all members of the species as a minimum requirement. The difference between human beings and other animals is their dependency on each other for much longer time than most animals need. Humans need each other virtually all their lives, as they move from being totally dependent to the state of relative autonomy in adulthood, which corresponds to stages of learning that lead later to role playing, acting on one's own, or coming out of the mask that was society, or, more specifically, the family acting on our behalf. Marcel Mauss has written a beautiful, albeit brief, historical trace of the concept *persona* through the "eyes" of different cultures (Classical Greece, Rome, Africa, China, India, and Australia), all of which, in his reckoning, point to an interestingly common notion of "that which sounds behind the mask", *per/sonare*, as the Romans put it.[86] In Mauss's cultural history of the term is the legal sense it acquired among the Romans is significant. Since then, in law, legal experts say, there are only personae, res, and actiones. But "person" has come to mean more than it does in its classical juridical sense. Declarations of the form "She/he too is a person (*En be en mana dhano*)" inject a moral sense into the idea of a "person". When the appeal to the normativity of personhood is dropped (which is done by dropping the comparative "too" in English and the word "be" in Dholuo), the resultant declaration, "She is just a human being (*En en mana dhano*)"[87] appeals to the fallibility of persons. Persons, or human beings, are fallible, a realization that is imprinted into our self-awareness

---

[86] Mauss, *o.c.* Someone should clarify to youth under their care that the approach of clarifying concepts by tracing their uses in different contexts, or distinguishing them from their cognates is not the same thing as "analyzing words".

[87] Variants are: "*Aparo kaka dhano* (that is just my human reason), usually used by a speaker to indicate their modesty by indicating that despite trying their best, human reason always has room for error.

early in life, when we are children.

Many African cultures may not reveal a separation between the juridical and moral senses of the term "person" in their different popular or "traditional" expressions, at least to my knowledge. That is not what cultures do in their traditional forms. Because custom and tradition tend to produce maxims of conduct rather than analytical distinctions of meanings in their respective language traditions, they tend to focus overwhelmingly, but not exclusively, on the moral senses of the term "person.". The point Mojalefa Koenane has made is therefore quite a valid one. Analytical distinctions at the traditional level do occur in the context of conflict resolution, sometimes very intensely, especially where there is an interpretative disagreement about a path of action. Disputes on such occasions can produce interesting and complex nuances of meaning buried within apparently trouble-free uses of terms. What might be absent in this context is the analyticasl distinctions that produce and preserve meanings under different disciplinary categories or formalized institutional usages. The practice of conceptual analysis of meanings for its own sake – that is, to produce knowledge that is believed to be useful to proper understanding as an end in itself – is often left to someone else in society – namely you and I and all our cohorts and colleagues in their respective fields.

Yet this division of labor does not imply that such a distinction could not be easily made on proper occasions. Here is an example I ran into one time. In a particular village I was visiting, there was a young man who was severely autistic. Although he could not speak at all, he could on occasion respond to restraining tones of voice, especially if the voice was accompanied by some gestures. He had to be kept within sight so he could be stopped from causing mischief. One day, however, he slipped out of the otherwise careful watch of his brothers and parents who took turns watching over him. He walked over to where a neighbor had tethered his goats so they could browse and clubbed one of them to death. In the ensuing debate *over* what had happened, it was quickly and unanimously resolved that the young man could not be blamed as "he was not a 'person' who could bear blame (*Ok en dhano ma inyalo kaw richo*)." So, while the normative declaration given earlier emphasized rights for the individual by conferring upon her/him a normative status of "personhood (*dhano*)", in the latter case "personhood" is exempted from blame because the person in this case is said to lack the capacity that would form the basis for imputing culpability on him. Hence he was totally exonerated. His parents could replace the neighbor's dead goat on the grounds of sympathy alone. As the quote from Meyer Fortes indicated, community places expectations on persons based on the qualities, capacities, and roles it bestows upon them. The quality and capacities of this young man's personhood did not come up to the level where they would be subject to society's codes of public conduct.

Every person or human being of reasonable age is usually fairly aware of things they believe they deserve, either by virtue of specific contracts or by the mere fact that they are human beings. Children are aware that they deserve to be fed by their parents or treated fairly in relation to their siblings. Most people believe they deserve a certain amount of freedom from harassment, whether it is by the state or by other persons, and to be treated justly and fairly by the law. These types of rights, which lie at the base of the declaration form we mentioned earlier, are believed to belong to all, irrespective of their position on religion, age, gender, sexual orientation, education, or skin color. Because they proclaim the normative status of personhood at the passive or receptive level, they are usually considered basic human rights. No one should ever have to beg or fight for them. In other words, their basis is the demand that circumstances exist that allow everyone's humanity to flourish to the fullest degree their faculties allow. The declaration of the form "she/he too is a person (*en be en mana dhano*)" says that the individual cannot be treated as if he or she has descended below the category of "human being". Implying that there may be instances where this might not be the case, the declaration urges that the individual be treated like they deserve to be, namely like all human beings ought to be treated. In the case of the autistic young man, however, the observation addresses a different aspect of "personhood", and that aspect is not different from what we would have in mind when we claim, for example, that a five-year old child cannot be held legally or morally liable when they pick up a gun and shoot a sibling or a friend. We commonly argue that at that age a child does not yet have the judgment capacity to fully understand the nature of their actions, even if they show a partial grasp of what "hurt" means (like physical hurt that is associated with pinching or the hurt that occurs when another child takes their icecream). In this latter example, the child is a person, just like the autistic youth, or like a mentally ill person of any age, but not in the sense that society expects of a grown and all-around healthy individual.

## 5. Personhood and agency

The all-around healthy individual deserves to receive other things besides their fair share of goods given out to, say, all members of a family. If membership in the family is the sole criterion for distribution, then it should not matter that one or more members are not all-around healthy. Their rights in this regard are protected by the fact that they too are members of the family no less and no more than all the other members of the family group. These rights are protected by our first principle, which emphasizes on the moral status of a "human being or "person". In a slightly different wording, but bearing the same moral weight, the Luo say *"En be en mana nyodo* (she/he too is an offspring like everyone else)", which literally means "she/he too is the result of sperm and egg," like all other offspring.

But let us go back to our autistic youth. When his community evaluated his action, it recognized that although the act itself was wrong, he was to be exonerated from blame. Why? While the receptive sense of his personhood remained intact, he was not regarded as an agent of his actions. If he were to cause physical harm to another person, that act ould be seen as wrong, both legally and morally, but he would hardly face punishment by law, nor would he be scorned as a moral outcast. If he came from the community I come from, he would be subjected to a ritual cleansing, as any normal person would , because the act is regarded as a breach of the integrity of another human being. In other words, the act, not necessarily the actor, treats another human being as if they were just a thing. Hence, anyone who sheds another person's blood, accidentally or at war or in any form of self-defense, must still go through the cleansing ritual for the act. One more thing should be explained about the autistic youth. The decision to not blame him is informed by the assumption of his society that full-fledged persons not only have rights, they also have duties. This belief implies that a full-fledged person has awareness not only of self, which they develop – gradually from childhood – by recognizing and having an understanding of how the external world responds to their actions (what can happen when they fail to heed the counsel of other people, for example), but also of the expectations of others, which she/he may have learned from the reactions of others over time. Our understanding of self (Mauss's *moi*) comes not as a function of a special faculty of intuition that makes the appearance of such awareness to occur as a sort of epiphany, but from our interactions with others and our conduct in the world. That is the order of nature. The autistic child remains trapped within the realm of Mauss's *moi*, living a life that unfolds on a track that runs parallel to that of a *personne morale*[88]. For the *personne morale*, self-awareness rises out of the circumstances in which she/he interactively participates, by judging and being judged, erring and being cor-

---

[88] Mauss's use of this expression should not be misunderstood as implying that anyone who is socially aware is moral in the sense of being virtuous or morally right, like the opposite of "immoral". The expression *"personne morale"* means simply she/he who can be held responsible, or can be judged, as in the opposite of "amoral", like most people with mental impairment, such as the severely autistic youth of our example, are regarded to be. Similarly, contrary to the misunderstanding shown by some readers of my use of the adverb "successfully" to describe the accomplished or ideal personhood as implying a sort of perfection in the acquisition of personhood, a successfully acculturated person is she/he who, by virtue of being averagely all-round healthy, becomes one who learns the behavioral ways of her/his society as a "normal person" who, among other things, is also fallible as they may have learned just too well in the course of their growth and development. Nor does being a behaviorally successful member of society imply that such a person is greeted with approval at every turn.

rected, and so forth. According to the indicators of human development, sociality is regarded as indicative of successful development while unperturbed fixation on the self, the "I" that expresses itself in spontaneous actions that lack variation and sometimes in unpredictable spontaneity that ignores "norms", is considered to be both medically and socially problematic.[89] "Successful" in the previous sentence is intended to mean possessing all the qualities, capacities, and abilities that enable an individual to live an average human life that entails, among other things, averagely well functioning organs (including the brain, of course). In addition to the uniqueness encoded in the genes inherited from one's mother and father, this body has the capacity to perform all the activities expected of a human body, including the capacity for sensory experience and a brain life from which mental life springs.

Because the body is susceptible to as many different types of malaise that may result from its encounter with its surroundings, it is also furnished with responsive abilities to thwart illness or injury on its own or to overcome or to compensate for other negative conditions by its own endowments of resistance and adaptation. The brain discharges the function of commanding and co-ordinating the various functions of the body. The same brain also produces mental functions and experiences that include emotional reactions such as sadness and happiness, liking and disliking, different levels of loving, feelings of pain and pleasure, and, ultimately, the use of reason. The performance of the latter function, like all the other functions, takes place under very specific conditions that apply to it. From changing skin color to deal with the abundance or deficiency of the vital Vitamin D to developing habits of body postures to deal with irritations in its nervous system, the human body is a complex organistic system that organizes and adjusts itself to the kind of environmental stimuli it has to deal with.

---

[89] Among the early signs of autism is lack of variation in a child's reaction to its surroundings, and avoiding to look people in the eye. Even as the child grows, it tends to cling to single objects, or performs repetitive actions that appear not to have much sense.

Both consciousness and thought are part of the same organism, are products of the same process of the need to adapt to the environment in which humans live. Again, this is not a description of the "human being" as a perfect organism, for humans are hardly perfect, but these elements are the physio-psycho-social elements that make us who we are. They are in the hero just as much as they are in the horrific, which is why we check the organistic system each time someone does an unthinkable thing in an attempt to determine if the action was intentional or was the result of a faulty organistic makeup. Intentional actions are regarded as having a causal agent, in contrast to actions of our autistic youth or of anyone else whose actions may be the result of a break in the human hardwiring, or the result of some dominating compulsive disorder.

The regularity and character of the habits of human agency are "molded" by factors in the environment in which humans live and develop in their infancy. Most people who have brought up children with some care will remember their struggle to create regularity in the infants' primary environment, the home. Children learn quickly which parent gives in more easily to their demands; sometimes this difference in parenting creates unnecessary confusion about directions for the child, and conflict between the parents themselves. To resolve such a situation, parents learn quickly that the regularity of children's habitual activity parallels the regularity of their environment, in this case the parents' establishment of clear and regular paths of conduct in relation to specific needs of habit formation. If one parent tells the child that it is okay. to go play on a Saturday morning before cleaning their room and the other parent denies permission until the condition is met, not only does the child get confused, but she/he quickly learns to play the parents against each other. If on the other hand, the environment provides regular forms of answers, activities, or responses to certain requests, the child will develop regular habits. In addition, the child will also learn to trust the value of shared opinions, especially if the consequent of the conditional statement is delivered as promised. Thus the Kiswahili saying that *"Umleavyo mtoto ndivyo akuavyo*(A child grows into what they are brought up to become)" sounds apt, and, when placed in relation to accounts of the emergence of human agency from the natural circumstances of community, speaks to the interactive character of experience and human nature. Another Kiswahili saying proclaims that "*Asiyefundishwa na wazazi hufundishwa na ulimwengu* (the child who does not take in parental counsel quickly runs into the unforgiving teachings of the outside world)." Together, these two sayings appear to confirm as true the thesis that the self is a product of social interaction, so one had better take the sympathetic and cuddly counsel of the family rather than wait to face the unbending ways of the (indifferent) world.

For readers who experience confusion because, in their reading (of *Self and Community*), sometimes I appear to prioritize community and other times to prioritize the individual, the above should give them a less obscure answer. The individual is never a passive subject, as we saw from Meyer Fortes. If she/he were, then she/he would never become an agent. Her/his agency grows out of her/his constant interactive encounters with the environment in the form of different stages of community (family, school, sport, workplace, etc.). But each human person is already a unique product of the inherited and complex genetic makeup that can only be her/him, and exercising this uniqueness in the encounter with the given environment stamps further characteristics on this uniqueness. Emphasis is on the concept of experience which, in these terms, is not limited to sensing. Rather, in the interactive encounters, the give-and-take that happens when, for example, a child enters a room full of many other children he has never met before who are gathered to celebrate a birthday, and an interesting dynamic unfold. The already gathered group, both as a group and each one individually, takes a pose to look at the newcomer, and he too looks at them, scanning each one rapidly before turning around to give the escorting grandfather or parent a look as if to say: "Kwara, I'll be okay., I can handle this..." As each child wants to stamp their way on how the play should go, the dynamic progresses toward a kind of truce based sometimes on consensus and sometimes on dictatorship and conflict. Experiences are the interactive dynamics defined by perceptions and counterperceptions that create a path toward group activity. Look at how this encounter makes it possible for each child to come to self-awareness as he looks into the eyes of the other child when both of them grab the same toy. Cries such as "I want it!,.It is mine!," or "I touched it first!" are characteristic of this scenario. While an observer may never know what exactly goes on in each child's mind at that moment, the observable behavior usually includes exchanges of slaps or punches, and more cries. Conflict! In this type of situation, the winner often does not exactly celebrate her or his victory. Sometimes, the winner might abandon the booty altogether, perhaps even showing some sense of shame.

In this example, conflict defines both protagonists as having similar desires that, because of limited supply at the specific time, cannot both be satisfied. But while it places added value on the object, it also teaches the participants that actions have consequences, some of which may be unpleasant. The shame the winner finally feels is an indication of how our public actions generate reflexivity for participants, especially if the unpleasant nature of those actions are immediately made known to the protagonist in question. Our sense of self is predominantly "thrown" into us by our active presence in the public space. To be sure, we often find ourselves mulling, alone and in the privacy of our conscience, over our past actions and the consequences they have had on other people. On further thought, however, one realizes that there is not much that is private on these occasions. The replay in our private mind places the action in its original public space, only now represented in our memory. Conscience becomes the privately (in the mind) recreated public stage on which our individualism is put to test by making the "I", or *moi* of Marcel Mauss, question if its action made it worthy in the public eye.

### 6. Of ends and means

Some critics have stated that I do not make a distinction between interaction as a means to an end or as an end in itself. I mulled over whether to address this critique many times, because in fact I do distinguish between these two ideas.[90] I finally decided to give it a brief reply for the benefit of the undergraduate student who may be given *Self and Community* as a reading assignment. So here is my attempt at a reply.

Think of the millions of folks who wake up in the morning to go to their farms, let's say to plant at the peak of the season. When a farmer buries the millet seeds in the ground, what is her purpose with the seeds? I still do this beside my mother whenever opportunity allows me to be in my "Tall-grass" neighborhood. Last time I was there, my mother had a different breed of millet seeds, which prompted me to ask her: "Nyar Oloo, why this kind of seed this time?" What she proceeded to describe to me was not the seeds we had in our baskets, ready to throw into the ground. She said: "Are you remembering our old indigenous breed of millet? That one has become rare, and not many people like its *kuon* [bread made from its flour]..This one yields a bigger head [meaning more grain], and its stalk is shorter and more stout, so birds don't fell it so much. Finally, it withstands drought far better, and ripens in about three months as opposed to the five months the indigenous breed used to take."

My mother told me something about what she *expects* of the seeds, what, subject to the climatic conditions they need, they should become, namely the stout cereal grass with long blade-like leaves that, in maturity, bears a ball-like cluster of tiny grain seeds that are ground into flour for making a variety of staple foods in many tropical lands. All things whose nature involve motion of sorts or change have ends, what they become when mature, before further change starts to result in their degradation. For my mother's millet, the growing process, her tending of the plants during weeding, and generally all of the tasks that ensure that the process has no hindrance, are, together, the means. If you go to buy seeds from a supplier, they usually will be in packets that show a picture of what will result from the seeds. That picture depicts the "end result", a tautology of sorts. Hence the idea of ends is present in every vocabulary and is always

---

[90] *Self and Community*, p. 237-9. For the convenience of a critique, Metz cites different pages but skirts around these specific ones.

a consideration, not only of things that change by their very nature, but also of the many things that humans do. So if the end of my mother's millet seeds is the grass stalk with a ball of grain seeds on its top, and then the end at the next le3vel is the type of bread thhat results from its flour, and then the satisfaction of the grower and consumer, what is the end of human life? It seems a truism, some would say, that given the means, we ought to realize our ends, and given the ends, we ought to take the means that best promote them. This truism applies to my mother's farming just as well as it does to the realm of ethics.

In the history of ideas, different thinkers, particularly philosophers, have weighed in on this question. The concepts of Buddha and Brahman have explained what humans ought to strive for, and that they could attain this end if they followed specific prescriptions of ideal conduct, generally known as the Eight-fold path. Shaaban (bin) Robert gave us the concept of *Utu bora*, ideal human life that is characterized by hard work, humility, and love and practice of justice among other virtues; and Plato and Aristotle, the noted fathers of the idea of ends in Western philosophy, used a term in their vernacular called *eudaimonia*, usually translated into English as "happiness", a term coined from the adjective *eudaimon*, happy. Commentators have pointed out that the Greek term does not mean happy as in having pleasure, or being blissful. In view of the multitude of human capacities and desires, in all segments of life (such as intellectual, moral, social, biological, emotional, etc.), it is hard to imagine a single human being who can attain perfection in all these areas, let alone, as Socrates suggested, knowing (and knowing that one knows) what is meant by perfection in any one of those areas. Because humans are differentiated from other animals by their capacity for rational thought, any sense of "happiness" ought to start with this function, which humans would have to put to use with excellence. Hence, exercising rationality with excellence in all domains of life would be a significant constituent of *eudaimonia*, and this would have to be done throughout life, and this would have to include having pleasure. In these terms, even Shaaban Robert thought that *Utu bora* is a life-long pursuit, not a specific achievement of excellence in one area of life. Hence, in these senses, happiness can be identified only with a life-long performance. If communitarianism (interactive living) is a relational state that describes how human life is lived in a manner that is fundamental to human flourishing, then it is an end. Yet because it is not a passive state but rather one in which active human experiences are accomplished, *Utu bora* is an active state, an end, like *eudaimonism*, or states as suggested by such terms as liberalism, socialism, communism, individualism, Confucianism, or Buddhism. With the exception of the last two, these terms signify types of society characterized or defined by practices of specific modes of economic production and distribution, political structures, regulation of property ownership and other amenities, and so on. In these senses, each one of these sociopolitical visions stands, in the eyes of their proponents, for the best of all possible worlds. And who says that modal language cannot describe a vision of the best of all possible worlds from an ideological standpoint?

My use of the term "interaction" goes beyond the everyday encounters between individuals as happen between neighbors, colleagues at work, family members, and so on, namely meeting with people during the several excursions we make out of our homes on a daily basis. It is true that while these interactions are part of the broader idea of human intersubjectivity as its specific instances, they become possible only on the strength of the social orientation that guides our growth and development from infancy. The intersubjective nature of early infant-mother interactions, a fundamental and important aspect of "proper" human development[91], leads children toward the development of a sense of self that is significantly social and mindful of others. Play time with other children later in life reinforces this discovery and affirmation of self as located in the midst of other selves. From these interactions the self learns limitations and the virtues of social living such as those Shaaban lists in *Koja la*

---

[91] We take into consideration the millions of children without their biological mothers with whom to have these bonds, but that undesirable circumstance does not eliminate or even lessen the necessity of the socializing function of the interactions. Foster mothers or other care-givers can still stand in to provide the functions.

*Lugha*. These include the virtues of moderation, kindness, justice, knowledge, respect, peacefulness, courage, humility, and reasonableness.[92] There is no hidden self in us that primarily contemplates itself or that makes inferences about its own existence from its own self-consciousness.

The idea of being mindful of the welfare of others comes directly from the "seed" of other-regarding that we get in infancy. And while this idea may fit with an institutionalized sense of "social welfare" as practiced in some countries around the world (for example most Scandinavian countries, and Qatar in the Middle East, or the United States), it is not how I use the idea in *Self and Community*. In these countries welfare is legally protected for the fulfillment of the basic needs of those who cannot, unaided, fulfill those needs on their own. Usually examples of this public assistance includes food stamps or an unemployment income and shelter. Together, when these protections against economic deprivation are ingrained into a country's laws as rights, we have a welfare state. Some countries levy taxes for this public care-taking of needy citizens, but leave the actual disbursement to nonprofit or charity organizations such as Churches. Germany and Switzerland are two examples of this brand of organized or institutionalized public welfare practice. Hence I have been totally surprised to see this idea used to try to discredit my idea that communitarian regard for the welfare of others as making a false statement. Nowhere in *Self and Community* do I make any claim that African governments practice welfare systems. is absent in Africa. I know no African country, other than Botswana in some limited or selected ways, that practices this social policy, but if there were to be, they would be institutionalizing what I call for, but which, for now, I described only in the form of the informal, culturally-based, or morally-driven way of minding needy folks' interests. The word "welfare" is frequently used, in philosophy and ordinary English alike, interchangeably with the term "interests". For the most part, in many African societies, minding the welfare of those

---

[92] Robert 1945: 17-19. These virtues are discussed in *Self and Community*, pp. 260- 2.

in need is practiced as an informal but culturally embedded practice.

The drive behind institutionalized welfare is noble, because helping those in need addresses a dimension of human character that should be promoted, namely that minimizing the degree of suffering for deprived members of society adds a humane dimension to how happiness can be distributed on utilitarian grounds as a start. Some historically significant Western philosophers like John Locke[93], for example, argued that once born, every human being has a right to self-preservation, especially by having such natural needs for subsistence as food and water, or other needs as nature may call for. In the United States, the proposed universal healthcare policy (in)famously or pejoratively called Obamacare, by the objecting Republicans, could be understood as fitting this bill as its postulation is that everyone should have a right to healthcare.

Prior to its recent overwhelming proportions, culturally-supported welfare was ingrained into society for noble reasons, which was the reduction of levels of inequality between the worst-off and the best-off in lineages or clans. The practice was deemed to be ethically necessary to curb the possibility of crime or labor-related abuses such as minor forms of enslavement of the poor by the economically more able members of a community. It was driven by the principle that is stated by John Locke. Every human being has a right to self-preservation. In many African communities, this basic human principle was translated into a duty for mambers of communities to not let one of their own fall below the levels of human dignity for want of basic necessities of life. It is said in the language of the Luo people that a man is only as good as his kin are. Nobody should take pride in his achievements if there are several destitute people or families in his lineage. To ward off this shame, members of a lineage would come together to provide their needy relatives with start-up investment (either in the form of land or of other economic asset) from which the needy person or family would gradually gain economic inde-

---

[93] Locke 1980 [1690], § 25, p. 18.

pendence. The idea is seen to be grounded on the view that there are certain basic requirements that every human being, subject to their health condition, should have as their natural right. For example, while the autistic child or adult would not gain from being given start-up capital on which to gradually build her/his economic independence, they nonetheless have the right to food, drink, shelter, clothing, and, as Locke says, "other provisions that nature may endow upon [her/him under their specific health conditions]." On the same principle, orphans were quickly taken in by the extended family, while no son of a lineage was allowed to stay unmarried for lack of assets for a dowry. But the relatively healthy neighbor or kin whose lacking is limited to the economic deprivation they are suffering was deemed as deserving the start-up capital, and the counsel that goes with it, to ensure that he made the right decisions that would enable him to profitably engaged in economically rewarding activities.

## 7. Mind, self, and society

Let us reconsider the personal experiences I described as I was sitting at my desk. There is no doubt that most people like you and I can have the kind of experiences I described there. What is not clear, but what the supporters of individualism are particularly prone to wrongly inferring to be the case, is whether mental experiences sufficiently justify the view that we are individuals in the strong atomistic sense. There is no doubt that the exercise of physical and mental capacities emanates from and solidifies each of us as individuals who, in the practice of these capacities, appear to be cut off from others. Everyday, we perform activities that reflect this autonomy. The liberal understanding of the priority of rights stems from the belief that the unhindered amelioration and defense of these capacities is necessary for the attainment of our individual well-being as our human end.

A major question, then, is how one arrives at the experience of oneself as an integral subject, designated in most human languages as the equivalent of the English "I" (German "Ich"; French "moi"; Italian "Io"; Dholuo "An"; Kiswahili "Mimi"). These indicators announce or identify a speaker or actor as the subject of their action; they are forms of identifying oneself as the performer of an action. Hence, through them, self-identity springs from every locutor as the anchor or originator of their own actions. Although such expressions as "I do" and "I think" indicate a sense of the integrity of the self as the source of its own actions, something that I presume to be normal, the point is that they do not tell us much, or anything at all, about the origin of the self's own awareness.

We ordinarily tend to think that there is some commonality between a human being, a person, and a self. Yet we often equate only the "human being" with "person", even when we make important distinctions between the different moral senses in which "personhood" is given different qualities and capacities. We rarely substitute either "human being" or "person" for "self" in those locutionary habits or even in situations bounded by moral concerns. Yet "self", in terms of its connotations of the unity of subjectivity underlies "human being" and "person" as well. When we talk of "the many chambers of selfhood" as a description of the many and conflicting capacities that we exhibit (love, hate, calm, rage, reason, impulse, strength, weakness, kindness, cruelty, generosity, selfishness, etc.), we attribute them to "self", not to "person" or "human being". (Dholuo has only one term, *dhano,* for all three, except in relational descriptions, when "ng'ato" is used.)

Communitarians admit this *descriptive* rendition of the functional capacities of the individual. Among the implications of communitarianism with regard to those functional capacities is the view that the relative autonomy of the individual plays itself out – emerges and stays – within the interactive conditions that both community and the external circumstances, which I sometimes refer to merely as "environment", generally provide. It is not only the biological aspect of humans that belongs to natural origins. Her/his psychological and sociological aspects belong to those origins too. The body, which is the perceptive and organizational tool for interacting with the external world, is the *sine qua non* organ for shaping human experience in a broader sense. Here I am using "Okham's razor" to separate a naturalist approach to understanding the human condition from otherworldliness and mythical accounts of what are truly psychological (cognitive and emotive) and sociological (moral and other normative) domains in the understanding of human nature. I am in sympathy with the position held by Kwasi Wiredu, one that I have referred to as communitarian[94] because it locates the origin of mind and intelligence in conduct, and suggests that the moral domain should be understood only by reformulatig concepts of human goods in terms of attitudes toward and results of the socially determinable concerns and their relation to value. For him, then, mind, by which he means the full-fledged, reflective, creative, responsible, self-conscious mind, appears within the natural conditions of conduct. Wiredu answers the question of how the human mind and self arise in the process of conduct in biosocial terms. The individual act is seen within the social act.

To call this view communitarian does not imply that all individuals are obligated or are tied to their respective ethnic groups or family.[95] *It is an account of how humans (in the very* general sense of the term as members of the species) acquire the capacities of self-consciousness, thinking, abstract reasoning, purposive behavior, and moral devotion. It presupposes

---

[94] This does not imply his agreement.

[95] The origin of the related misperception – that communitarianism is only another term for "group interests", or that it cherishes "tribalism" – is that in attempts to rid reference to groups who share cultural values and practices such as language and custom of the colonial lexicon of "tribe", an alternative term, "ethnic communities", has in recent years been preferred and increasingly more used in scholarly and general vocabulary over "tribe". With this misperception, some people have expressed fear that "communitarianism" would encourage a return to the idea that one needs to stick with her/his ethnic group. The fear is legitimate, especially in the context of fresh memories of the Rwandan, Burundian and other instances of ethnic cleansing. Communitarianism has nothing to do with the object of such fear except in describing the family, whose members would normally claim to be related, as the primary "environment" of human socialization. But the concept of family no longer refers exclusively to people related by blood other than for the two or more principal heads.

that such a biological organism would acquire these defining capacities irrespective of where they are born, where they live, or with whom they interact in the course of being exposed to the social circumstances out of which these capacities are generated. Its emphasis is solely and generally on the biosocial characteristic of humans as rational animals.

Communitarianism is only now emerging as a framework for reconsidering what has not worked in the long history of side-stepping the basic foundations of human experience. The challenges it faces are not uncommon to similar perspectives whose impact is often viewed as a disruptive challenge to the old and familiar view that has long enjoyed the embrace of many who, often by unquestioned intellectual habits of inherited culture, may continue to regard it as the "obvious" view. This is the challenge that communitarianism faces from individualism, not because the latter is a better principle but mostly because it is the axiomatic assumption of a culture whose domination across the globe has gone largely unquestioned in its supply of theories of experience – of thought and practice – and the orders of reality.

## *References*

Appiah, Kwame A., 1992, *In My Father's House: Africa in the Philosophy of Culture*, London and New York, Oxford University Press.
Bourdieu, Pierre F., 1977, *Outline of A Theory of Practice* (English transl. Richard Nice), Cambridge (UK) and New York, Cambridge University Press.
Fortes, Meyer, 1973, "On the Concept of the person among the Tallensi", in G. Dieterlen, ed., *La Notion de Personne en Afrique Noire*, Paris, Editions de Centre National de la Recherche Scientifique.
Goldman, Alvin, I., 1999, *Knowledge in a Social World*, Oxford (UK), Oxford University Press. .
Horsthemke, Kai, contribution to the present collection
Kratz, Corinne A., 1994, *Affecting Performance: Meaning, Movement, and Experience in Okiek Women's Initiation*, Washington, DC, Smithsonian Institution Press.
Locke, John, 1980 [1690], *The Second Treatise of Government* (Edited with an Introduction by C. B. Macpherson), Indianapolis, Hackett Publishing,.
Lukes, Steven, 1973, *Individualism*, Basil Blackwell, Oxford.

Masolo, D.A., 2010, *Self and Community*, Indiana University Press

Mauss, Marcel, 1939, "Une categorie de l'esprit humaine: La notion de la personne, celle du moi", *Journal of the Royal Anthropological Institute*, Vol. 68: 263-282; a translation of this work (by W. D. Halls) exists as "A Category of the human mind: the notion of person; the notion of self", in Carruthers, Michael, S. Collins, & S. Lukes, eds., *The Category of the Person: Anthropology, Philosophy, History*, Cambridge, UK, Cambridge University Press, 1985, pp. 1 - 25.

Robert, Shaaban bin, 1945, *Koja la Lugha*, Nairobi.

Russell, Bertrand, 1961, "Introduction", in Ludwig Wittgenstein, *Tractatus Logico-Philosophicus*, London: Routledge and Kegan Paul, Ltd.

Sartre, Jean-Paul, 1956, *Being and Nothingness* (English Transl. with an introduction, Hazel E. Barnes), Washington Square Press, New York.

Shaw, Rosalind, 2000, " 'Tok Af, Lef Af': A Political Economy of Temne Techniques of Secrecy and Self", in Karp, Ivan, and D.A. Masolo, eds., *African Philosophy as Cultural Inquiry*, Indiana University Press, Bloomington.

wa Thiong'o, Ngũgĩ and Ngũgĩ wa Mĩriĩ, 1982, *I Will Marry When I Want* (translated by the authors from the Gikuyu original, *Ngaahika Ndeenda*), Nairobi, Heinemann Educational Books.

Wittgenstein, Ludwig, 1961, *Tractatus Logico-Philosophicus*, London, Routledge and Kegan Paul.

# Notes on Contributors

## (in order of appearance in this volume)

THADDEUS METZ is Research Professor of Philosophy at the University of Johannesburg, where he writes on four major topics: resolving practical controversies by appealing to the value of human dignity; developing and evaluating theories of the meaning of life; addressing normative issues in higher education; and interpreting sub-Saharan morality analytically and applying it to contemporary problems. With regard to the latter, Metz has had dozens of journal articles and book chapters published and even more accepted for publication, including: 'An African Theory of Moral Status' *Ethical Theory and Moral Practice* (2012); 'Developing African Political Philosophy' *Philosophia Africana* (2012); and 'African Conceptions of Human Dignity' *Human Rights Review* (2012). His book, *Meaning in Life: An Analytic Study*, is appearing in 2013 with Oxford University Press.

    Philosophy Department B605
    University of Johannesburg
    PO Box 524
    Auckland Park 2006
    South Africa
    Email: tmetz@uj.ac.za

MOGOBE B. RAMOSE is Professor Extraordinarius in Philosophy at the University of South Africa, in the Department of Philosophy. His many publications include "I Doubt, Therefore African Philosophy Exists", and his recent publications include "Reconciliation and Reconfiliation in South Africa" and "The Death of Democracy and the Resurrection of Timocracy". He is also the author of *African Philosophy through Ubuntu* and *A Century is a Short Time: New Perspectives on the Anglo-Boer War*. He is deeply interested in the fields of Theoretical and Applied Ethics, Social and Political Philosophy, Philosophy of Liberation, African Philosophy, Philosophy of International Relations.

    Department of Philosophy
    P. O. Box 392
    University of South Africa
    Pretoria 0001
    South Africa
    Email: ramosmb@unisa.ac.za

PEDRO A. TABENSKY is the director of the newly formed Allan Gray Centre for Leadership Ethics (AGCLE), nested in the Department of Philosophy, Rhodes University (South Africa). He is the author of *Happiness: Personhood, Community, Purpose* (London: Ashgate, 2003) and of several articles and book chapters. Tabensky is also the editor of and contributor to *Judging and Understanding: Essays on Free Will, Narrative, Meaning and the Ethical Limits of Condemnation* (London: Ashgate, 2006) and of *The Positive Function of Evil* (London: Palgrave, 2009). A recent writing project has been his solo authored book on the roots of evil, *Grounding Goodness*. And he is the editor of the forthcoming collection of essays in institutional culture in the context of higher education (Durban: UKZN Press, 2014). Tabensky runs yearly roundtable series on critical issue in higher education and on issues pertaining to ethical agency and leadership. He is a regular commentator in the written media both nationally and internationally.

>Allan Gray Centre for Leadership Ethics
>Department of Philosophy
>Rhodes University
>P.O. Box 94
>Grahamstown
>Eastern Cape 6140
>South Africa
>E-mail: p.tabensky@ru.ac.za

KAI HORSTHEMKE. Educated both in Germany and in South Africa, Kai Horsthemke was awarded his PhD in Applied Ethics in the Department of Philosophy, University of the Witwatersrand / South Africa. A professional musician for several decades, he has been involved in stage, studio, television and cruise-ship work in South Africa, Namibia, Mozambique, Germany, Luxembourg, England, Indian Ocean islands, Japan, Hawai'i and Colombia). He joined the Wits School of Education in a full-time capacity in 2002. He is an Associate Professor, teaching philosophy of education – ethics, social and political philosophy, epistemology, philosophy of science, logic and critical thinking, all with a strongly educational focus. He has published extensively since 2004; most recently a book entitled *The Moral Status and Rights of Animals* (Porcupine Press, 2010). Apart from animal rights, his research interests include African philosophy (of education), indigenous knowledge (indigenous science, ethnomathematics, ethnomusicology), as well as humane and environmental education. He is currently working on a book provisionally entitled *The Myth of 'Indigenous Knowledge'*.

>Wits School of Education
>University of the Witwatersrand
>Private Bag 3
>Wits 2050
>South Africa
>E-mail: Kai.Horsthemke@wits.ac.za

ABRAHAM OLIVIER is Professor and Head of the Department of Philosophy at the University of Fort Hare. He is Co-Founder and Co-Chair of the South African Centre for Phenomenology. In addition to this he is Editor of the South African Journal of Philosophy and member of the Executive Committee of the Southern African Philosophical Society (PSSA). Olivier obtained his PhD from the University of Tübingen and has held lecturing and research posts at the Universities of Tübingen, Stellenbosch, Hamburg and Padua. He is the author of *Being in Pain* as well as numerous international peer-reviewed articles on issues of mind, time, space, language, ethics, society and nature.

>Department of Philosophy
>University of Fort Hare
>P.O. Box 7426
>50 Church Street
>East London 5201
>South Africa
>Email: aolivier@ufh.ac.za

KEVIN GARY BEHRENS, D Litt et Phil, is a lecturer at the Steve Biko Centre for Bioethics, School of Clinical Medicine, University of the Witwtersrand, Johannesburg. He obtained his doctorate in Public Philosophy and Ethics from the University of Johannesburg under the supervision of Thaddeus Metz. He holds an MA in Applied Ethics from the University of the Witwatersrand, a BTh Hons in Theological Ethics from the University of South Africa and a BA from the then University of Natal. His main research interest is in African ethics, and in particular, its application to bio-ethical and environmental ethical issues.

>3 Ambush Street
>Kensington
>2094
>South Africa
>E-mail: kevin.behrens@wits.ac.za

MPHO TSHIVHASE is currently a lecturer in the Department of Philosophy at the University of Pretoria. She was born in Limpopo, South Africa. She is completing her doctoral degree at the University of Johannesburg. This article forms part of her doctoral degree. She was recently awarded an Andrew Mellon Scholarship from the University of Pretoria, and in the past was awarded a New Generation Scholarship from the University of Johannesburg, where she was also a lecturer.

>P.O. Box 79
>Melville
>Johannesburg 2109
>South Africa
>E-mail: Mpho.tshivhase@up.ac.za

BERNARD MATOLINO is a lecturer in philosophy at the University of KwaZulu-Natal,

Pietermaritzburg campus. His work has been published in Theoria (SA), South African Journal of Philosophy, African Studies, African Studies Quarterly and Philosophia Africana.

    University of KwaZulu-Natal
    Philosophy – NAB 309
    Private Bag X01
    Scottsville 3201
    South Africa
    Email: matolinob@ukzn.ac.za

DISMAS A. MASOLO is professor of philosophy at the University of Louisville, Louisville KY, United States of America; e-mail address: dismas.masolo@louisville.edu. The present volume is dedicated to his work, and provides ample information on his writings and person.

WIM VAN BINSBERGEN is emeritus professor of the foundations of intercultural philosophy, Erasmus University Rotterdam, the Netherlands, and life Honorary Fellow of the African Studies Centre, Leiden, the Netherlands. He is also a published poet, a certified and practising *sangoma*, a Zambian prince, a percussion student in Indian *dhrupad* classical music, husband of the singer and breathing therapist Patricia Saegerman, and father of five. He has been Editor of *Quest: An African Journal of Philosophy / Revue Africaine de Philosophie* since 2002. Among his recent books may be mentioned *Researching power and identity in African state formation* (UNISA Press, in press, with M.R. Doornbos); *Before the Presocratics: Cyclicity, transformation, and element cosmology: The case of transcontinental pre- or protohistoric cosmological substrates linking Africa, Eurasia and North America* (2012); and the edited collections *Lines and rhizomes: The transcontinental element in African philosophies* (2008) and *Truth in Politics: Rhetorical approaches to democratic deliberation in Africa and beyond* (2004, with P.-J. Salazar, and S. Osha). For contact details, see next page.

*QUEST: An African Journal of Philosophy / Revue Africaine de Philosophie*
## Colophon, and Directions for Contributors

Editor: **WIM VAN BINSBERGEN** (African Studies Centre. Leiden / Erasmus University Rotterdam)
Editorial Team: **SANYA OSHA** (University of South Africa); **KIRSTEN SEIFIKAR** (Erasmus University Rotterdam; terminated office 1-1-2014); **WIM VAN BINSBERGEN**
Advisory Editorial Board: **PAULIN HOUNTONDJI** (University of Cotonou, Benin); **KWASI WIREDU** (University of Ghana, Legon / University of South Florida, USA); **LANSANA KEITA** (Fourah Bay College, Sierra Leone / University of Arizona, USA); **PIETER BOELE VAN HENSBROEK** (University of Groningen. the Netherlands); **VALENTIN Y. MUDIMBE** (Duke University, North Carolina, USA)

*QUEST:* **An African Journal of Philosophy** seeks to act as a channel of expression for thinkers in Africa, and to stimulate philosophical discussion on problems that arise out of the radical transformations attending Africa and Africans. *QUEST* includes materials both on current subjects relating to Africa, and on subjects of general philosophical interest. *QUEST* serves an international public of professional philosophers, as well philosophically-interested intellectuals in other disciplines. Subject to peer review, original articles written in either English or French are eligible for publication. *QUEST* (ISSN 1011-226X) appears in principle twice a year, in June and December; however, both issues tend to be combined into one volume.

Directions for contributors (the numbered items constitute a checklist): Preferably, articles do not exceed 40.000 chars, in length. When submitting a contribution, the author's name and e-mail address must be included in the heading. Any submission should be accompanied by an abstract in both (1) English and (2) French, max. 1,000 chars, each; and by max. 8 key words both in (3) English and in (4) French. Manuscripts should contain minimum formatting but *italics* (no **bold**, no underline) are allowed, and footnotes should be of the standard MSWord hyperlinked type. Manuscripts should follow the journal's citation format (consult a recent issue). Include full author details also for co-authors, as well as place, publisher, year of edition used (identify original title when using a translation), and sub-title of publications cited; give first and last pages of articles cited; however, in your bibliography, do not specify the number of pages when listing entire books; refer to specific pages rather than to entire publications; end all bibliographical items and all footnotes on a period; no period after headings; of proper names, only capitalise the first letter; if a footnote mark occurs near punctuation, a bracket, etc. it should **always** come last; **always** insert one single space in order to separate words, numbers, etc. even if they are already separated by punctuation, footnote mark, bracket, etc. Contributors are to present themselves in (5) a short bio-bibliographical note. max. 1,000 chars., in the article's language. Moreover, contributors are to provide (6) their full postal address (just to send the author's copies to), and to cite (7) an e-mail address that can be printed with the article in case of acceptance. Manuscripts (8) are to be submitted in electronic form *i.e.* MSWord recent version: preferably by e-mail (see below) but if online facilities are totally lacking locally, a Windows CD-ROM or USB-stick may be sent (3.5" discs being obsolete). Regrettably, submissions not complying with these directions cannot be considered.

Authors retain the copyright to their contribution, but submission automatically implies that, in case of acceptance, the author tacitly cedes to *QUEST* such use rights as enable *QUEST* to publish the contribution both in hard copy and online. Authors used to receive two hard copies of the volume in which their contribution appears; this arrangement is currently under review.

Subscriptions terminated: Due to the excessive costs and efforts of handling, package and postage, and alternatively the easy and free availability of Quest on the Internet anyway, and also in view of the progressive penetration of the Internet in African contexts today, *QUEST* has decided to follow the example of many more affluent and centrally-placed journals, and to discontinue its subscription routine. Individual copies of each new volume will still be made available by the publisher (see *QUEST* website) and through well-known international channels for book distribution; standard price Euro € 40 (postage not included), regardless of the individual or institutional status of the buyer, or of the latter's country of residence.

*QUEST* is **online** at: http://quest-journal.net. Here current and back volumes may be consulted free of charge, and detailed information is offered (including electronic reply forms) concerning subscriptions (to the printed version only), ordering of back copies, submission of manuscripts, reprint permissions, *QUEST*-related activities, etc. **You may contact *QUEST* by e-mail** at shikandapress@gmail.com, or at the editor's personal mail address: wimvanbinsbergen@gmail.com. *QUEST's* ordinary postal address is:
  *QUEST:* **An African Review of Philosophy**
  c / o Prof. Wim van Binsbergen, Honorary Fellow
  African Studies Centre,
  P.O. Box 9555,
  2300 RB Leiden,
  **the Netherlands**
  fax 00-31-71-5273344

www.ingramcontent.com/pod-product-compliance
Lightning Source LLC
Chambersburg PA
CBHW070603300426
44113CB00010B/1381